RELIGIOUS TRADITIONS AT VIJAYANAGARA
AS REVEALED THROUGH ITS MONUMENTS

VIJAYANAGARA RESEARCH PROJECT MONOGRAPH SERIES

GENERAL EDITORS

John M. Fritz
George Michell
D.V. Devaraj

Vol. 1. *Pots and Palaces* by Carla M. Sinopoli

Vol. 2. *The Ramachandra Temple at Vijayanagara* by Anna L. Dallapiccola, John M. Fritz, George Michell and S. Rajasekhara

Vol. 3. *The Vijayanagara Courtly Style* by George Michell

Vol. 4. *Religious Traditions at Vijayanagara as Revealed through its Monuments* by Anila Verghese

Vol. 5. *The Irrigation and Water Supply Systems of the City of Vijayanagara* by Dominic J. Davison-Jenkins

The General Editors of the Vijayanagara Research Project Monograph Series would like to acknowledge a generous grant from Mrs. Eleanor Schwartz which has made possible the publication of Dr. Anila Verghese's monograph. A contribution from the travel company, "Our Personal Guest", has also been most helpful.

The American Institute of Indian Studies, especially its President-Elect, Professor Frederick Asher, and Director-General, Dr. Pradeep Mehendiratta, has continued to promote this Series.

We also extend our thanks to Mr. Ajay Jain and the staff of Mahohar Publishers & Distributors for maintaining high standards and overseeing this monograph through the press.

RELIGIOUS TRADITIONS AT VIJAYANAGARA
AS REVEALED THROUGH ITS MONUMENTS

Anila Verghese

Manohar
AMERICAN INSTITUTE OF INDIAN STUDIES
NEW DELHI
1995

Cover: Yantrōddhāraka Āñjanēya, Vijayanagara
(from *Annual Report of South Indian Epigraphy* of 1919, opposite p. 7)

ISBN 81-7304-086-9

First Published 1995

Published by Ajay Kumar Jain
Manohar Publishers & Distributors
2/6 Ansari Road, Daryaganj, New Delhi - 110 002 for
American Institute of Indian Studies
D-31, Defence Colony, New Delhi - 110 024

Photoset by AJ Software Publishing Co. Pvt. Ltd.
305, Durga Chambers, 1333, D.B. Gupta Road,
Karol Bagh, New Delhi - 110 005
and printed at Rajkamal Electric Press
B 35/9 G.T. Karnal Road, Delhi 110 033

Contents

Preface			vii
Acknowledgements			ix
List of Illustrations			xi
List of Abbreviations			xiii
Chapter 1	:	Introduction: Historical, Religious and Archaeological Background	1
Chapter 2	:	Śaivite Traditions	16
Chapter 3	:	The Narasiṁha Cult	34
Chapter 4	:	The *Rāmāyaṇa* Tradition	43
Chapter 5	:	Kṛishṇa and Viṭhala Cults	54
Chapter 6	:	Śrī-Vaishṇava Traditions from the Tamil Country	69
Chapter 7	:	Minor Cults and Popular Religion	85
Chapter 8	:	Temples and Festivals	99
Chapter 9	:	Ascetics, Maṭhas and Agrahāras	111
Chapter 10	:	Non-Hindu Religions	121
Chapter 11	:	Conclusion	132
Appendix A	:	Grants, Gifts, etc., made in Vijayanagara city in the presence of Virūpāksha, Viṭhala and other Deities	141
Appendix B	:	Preliminary Inventory of Monuments in the "Sacred Centre" and the "Irrigated Valley"	155
Bibliography			161
Index			175
Figures			183
Plates			219
Map Series			259

Preface

This monograph deals with the religious traditions and cults prevalent in the city of Vijayanagara (the capital of the great medieval Hindu Vijayanagara empire) prior to its destruction in A.D 1565. Although the political and socio-economic history of Vijayanagara has been studied in depth by several scholars, little work has been done on religion in the city. The monograph is an attempt to fill this lacuna.

It is based primarily on the archaeological sources, i.e., the monuments (structures and sculptures) extant at the site of Vijayanagara city (namely, modern Hampi and its environs) and the numerous inscriptions to be found on them. Epigraphs from elsewhere in the empire that throw light on religious traditions in the capital have also been cited. Literary works, whether contemporary or later writings in Sanskrit, Kannada, Telugu, etc., or the accounts of foreign visitors to the city, have been used only to support or corroborate the evidence available from the monuments and to give some additional information.

The reasons for relying primarily on the archaeological data are many. Most of the earlier writings on Vijayanagara history have relied heavily on literary sources. But, little work has been done using the wealth of data supplied by the actual remains of the city of Vijayanagara. It is true that in the last ten years the Directorate of Archaeology and Museums, Government of Karnataka, and the Vijayanagara Research Project have undertaken publications using the monumental data. However, they have not focused on the religion in the city.

Apart from this, many of the literary sources of Vijayanagara history (e.g., *Prapannāmṛitam, Keḷadinṛipavijaya, Vidyāraṇya-Kālajñāna, Narasiṁhapurāṇam,* etc., to cite just a few) are post-1565 writings. Hence the historical accuracy of their narrations of pre-1565 events is questionable.

There are, of course, pre-1565 literary works. But, some of these (e.g., *Śrī Vyāsayōgicharitam* by Sōmanātha) are hagiographical works and due to their sectarian bias cannot be relied on to give an objective or fully accurate picture of religious life in Vijayanagara. Still others (e.g. *Madhurāvijayam* by Gaṅgādēvī and *Varadāṁbikāpariṇaya* of Tirumalāmba) are Sanskrit *kāvyas* and, therefore, contain literary embellishments and exaggerations typical of this genre of literature.

Many of the modern historians on Vijayanagara have referred extensively to the accounts of the foreign visitors to the city and the empire, such as Nicolo Conti, 'Abdur Razzāk, Domingo Paes, Fernão Nuniz, etc. Although these accounts are valuable, they have their own limitations. Foreigners when meeting with an entirely alien culture naturally tended to emphasise the bizarre and the exotic in their travelogues. Besides, since they had little knowledge of Indian customs, their observations on religious rituals and practices may have been distorted or exaggerated.

The monuments, on the other hand, provide evidence that is not coloured by prejudice, sectarian bias, distortions and inaccuracies. Even the inscriptions, although they might resort to some hyperbole when listing the titles of kings or the achievements of donors, are more or less factual statements of grants, benefactions etc. Of course, the monumental sources, too, have some drawbacks. Firstly, only some of the structures of the Vijayanagara period are extant at the site; the vast majority of them, especially the dwellings, have vanished, leaving little trace behind. Secondly, the monuments, though providing accurate evidence, cannot give a complete picture of the vigour and vitality of religious life in the city, the diversity of rites, ceremonies and religious activities. However, in spite of these limitations, by relying primarily on the archaeological sources, a fairly comprehensive picture can be traced of cults and religious traditions, their spread, popularity and patronage.

It is to be noted that the monuments are used in this monograph only as sources of information. Hence detailed descriptions of temples, sculptures, iconography and inscriptions have not been given.

In order to gather the monumental data for this research work, I have undertaken since 1985 a number of field trips to the site, spending in all about four months at Hampi exclusively for this purpose. The study of the epigraphs has been almost entirely from published epigraphical works.

A series of maps of the site is included in the monograph. These are from the Map Series prepared by the Vijayanagara Research Project, and for convenience the system of identification used in the Map Series has been followed. The first map in the series includes the entire region around Vijayanagara, from Gangawati in the north-east to Hospet in the south-west. This area is divided into twenty-five equal squares. Each square is designated by a capital letter, from A to Z (omitting I). Thus, square N is the area of the city proper, including the so-called "sacred centre", the "agricultural zone" (or "irrigated valley") and the "urban core". This square has again been divided into twenty-five squares and a second capital letter is used to designate each of these such as NA, NB, NC, etc. Each of these has in turn been divided into twenty-five squares and assigned a small letter NH a, NH b, and so on. Within this smaller square the individual structures are numbered (1, 2, 3, 4, etc.). Thus, NH a/1 is the reference for the Viṭhala temple, NM h/1 of the Tiruveṅgaḷanātha (or Achyutarāya) temple, NR p/3 of the Islamic style "Elephant Stables", and so on. Gateways have been usually designated only according to the square in which they fall, e.g., NJ s is the Areśaṅkara Bāgilu (known nowadays as the Talarighat gate). This reference code provides a unique designation to each monument and an easy and quick system of identification.

For the purposes of this research a fairly exhaustive survey has been made of all the extant monuments within square N, an area of approximately twenty-five square kilometres. Important monuments in the suburban centres of the city, from Anegondi in the north-east to Hospet in the south-west, have also been studied.

In Appendix B a list of the extant monuments within the so-called "sacred centre" and "irrigated valley" has been made, since hitherto no inventory of all the monuments in this part of the city had been undertaken. The structures within the "urban core" have not been included in this inventory because these, excluding those within the "royal centre," have been listed and described in detail, along with drawings, and photographs, in the book by Dr G. Michell, *Vijayanagara: Architectural Inventory of the Urban Core. The Royal Centre at Vijayanagara—Preliminary Report,* by Drs J.M. Fritz, G. Michell and M.S. Nagaraja Rao, has covered in depth all the structures within the "royal centre".

Acknowledgements

I should like to express my deep gratitude to all the persons and institutions without whose help and support this work would not have been possible:

The Management and the Principal, Dr (Sr.) L. Rodrigues, of Sophia College, Bombay, for their unfailing co-operation and for granting me study leave from 20th June 1987 to 19th June 1989.

The Indian Council of Historical Research, for sanctioning me the Pay-Protection Fellowship, with Contingent Grant, from 20th June 1987 to 19th June 1989, thus making it possible for me to devote my full time to research during this period.

I am also grateful to the University of Bombay, for the Research Grant given to me in 1986-87, which covered the travel and photographic expenses of the field trips undertaken that year to Dharwar, Hampi, Gadag and Hyderabad.

I extend my sincere thanks also to Dr (Fr.) John Correia-Afonso S.J. of the Heras Institute and Heras Society (St. Xavier's College, Bombay), for the Heras Society Scholarship for 1986-87 and the grant from the Khilachand Research Award in the same year for the field trip to important temple sites in Tamil Nadu.

The Librarian, Professor A.C. Tikekar, and the staff of the University of Bombay library, provided me with all the facilities for my research.

I am also grateful to the library staff of other libraries that I have frequented or visited, including that of the Asiatic Society (Bombay), Deccan College Post-graduate and Research Institute (Pune), Karnatak University (Dharwar), Osmania University (Hyderabad), the Directorate of Archaeology and Museums, Karnataka (Mysore) and the University of Mysore.

The Directors of the Vijayanagara Research Project and Joint-Editors of the Vijayanagara Research Project Monograph Series, Dr J.M. Fritz (Associate Professor, Dept. of Anthropology, University of New Mexico, Albuquerque) and Dr G. Michell (Architectural Historian, London), gave me their unfailing encouragement and help; the temple plans, the maps and some of the photographs given in this monograph are theirs.

I wish to acknowledge the assistance received from other scholars associated with the Vijayanagara Research Project, especially of Dr Anna L. Dallapiccola (Professor of Indian History of Art, South Asia Institute, Heidelberg University), who helped me with inconographical identifications and Dr A.A. Shapiro (Sanskritist, Vrindaban), for providing the synopsis in English of the *Hemakutakhanda of the Skanda Purana* and the notes on the car festival at Hampi, also for helping with photography.

To the Director and the Staff of the Directorate of Archaeology and Museums, Government of Karnataka, my thanks for the very kind permission to stay at their camp at Hampi and for the assistance rendered to me on all my field trips to the site. I am also grateful to the Director for granting me permission to go through, before it was published, the epigraphical section of *Vijayanagara: Progress of Research 1984-1987*, which I have often cited in this monograph.

Dr S. Nagaraju (Professor of History, Central University Hyderabad) suggested the topic of this research work. My thanks are due to Dr B.R. Gopal (Professor of History, Sri Krishnadevaraya University, Anantapur), Dr M.S. Mate (retired Professor of Ancient Indian History and Culture, Deccan College, Pune), Dr S. Rajasekhara (Reader, Department of History, Karnatak University, Dharwar), Dr A Sundara (Professor of Ancient Indian History, Karnatak University, Dharwar), Dr K.K.A. Venkatachari (Director, Anantacharya Indological Research Institute, Bombay), Dr S.U. Kamath (Chief Editor, Karnataka State Gazetteer) and Shri C.T.M. Kotraiah for information regarding Vijayanagara art and architecture, iconography, religion and epigraphy.

Mrs. Vidyulata Sasnur (Kannada novelist), taught me the basics of the Kannada script and language and helped with the translation of some of the inscriptions and texts.

Last, but not least, my grateful thanks to Dr A. Cherian, retired Head of the Department of History, Wilson College, Bombay, for his constant encouragement, scholarly guidance, wise counsel and affectionate interest in all the matters concerning this research work.

Anila Verghese

List of Illustrations

Figures

1. Vijayanagara City
2. Śaivite tradition
3. Narasiṁha cult
4. Rāmāyaṇa tradition
5. Śrī-Vaishṇava traditions
6. Minor cults
7. Goddess cults
8. Popular cults
9. Jainism
10. Islam
11. Ascetics, maṭhas, āśramas and agrahāras
12. Plan, Virūpāksha temple complex (NF w/1)
13. Plan, Virūpāksha temple, main shrine area
14. Plan, Prasanna Virūpāksha temple complex (NQ y/1)
15. Plan, Rāmachandra temple complex (NR w/1)
16. Plan, Mālyavanta Raghunātha temple complex (NT d/1)
17. Plan, Kṛishṇa temple complex (NL m/4)
18. Plan, Viṭhala temple complex (NH a/1)
19. Plan, Tiruveṅgaḷnātha temple complex (NM h/1)
20. Plans; above, Kunthu Jinanātha (Gāṇigitti) temple (NX n/1); below Pārśvanātha temple (NS q/1)
21. Musical Instruments

Plates

1. View of Virūpāksha temple complex (NF w/1)
2. Virūpāksha temple complex
3. Virūpāksha temple on Hēmakūṭa hill (NL b/19)
4. Bhairava (NM z/2)
5. Vīrabhadra (NQ u/1)
6. Sāsivekāḷu Gaṇēśa monolith (NL g/2)
7. Kōṭī-liṅga
8. Narasiṁha temple (NG t/4)
9. Mahānavamī platform (NW d/1)
10. Mahānavamī platform, south steps
11. Mahānavamī platform, Cheñchū-Lakshmī and Narasiṁha
12. Cheñchū-Lakshmī and Narasiṁha (temple NF w/5)
13. Narasiṁha (Virūpāksha temple complex)
14. Lakshmī-Narasiṁha (near NG n/3)
15. Lakshmī-Narasiṁha monolith (NL m/1)
16. Rāmachandra temple (NR w/1)
17. Rāmāyaṇa Panels (Rāmachandra temple, enclosure wall)
18. Paṭṭābhirāma temple complex
19. Seated Rāma (Kṛishṇa temple complex NL m/4)
20. Seated royal figure (Rāmachandra temple, enclosure wall)
21. Kṛishṇa temple complex (NL m/4)
22. Bālakṛishṇa (Kṛishṇa temple complex), now Government Museum, Madras
23. Royal devotee adoring Bālakṛishṇa (Kṛishṇa temple complex)
24. Royal devotee adoring liṅga (Kṛishṇa temple complex)
25. Prāta-Viṭhala temple (NG w/5)
26. Viṭhala (Rāmachandra temple, south entrance)
27. Viṭhala temple complex (NH a/1)
28. Viṭhala temple complex
29. Viṭhala temple complex
30. Pārāṅkuśa mandapa (NJ g/1)
31. View of Tiruveṅgaḷanātha temple complex (NM h/1)
32. Raṅganātha (NG s/2)
33. Tiruveṅgaḷanātha (behind NG w/3)
34. Varadarāja episodes (temple NC w/3)
35. Rāmānuja and Nammāḷvār (temple NG s/2)
36. Tirumaṅgai-āḷvār temple (NC v/3)
37. Teṅgalai nāmam (Viṭhala temple complex, hundred-pillared hall)
38. Vaḍagalai nāmam (Viṭhala temple complex, hundred-pillared hall)
39. Vishvaksēna (temple NG s/2)

40. Harihara (Tiruveṅgaḷanātha temple complex, pillared hall)
41. Vīra-Āñjanēya
42. One of the Chaturviṁśatimūrtis (Rāmachandra temple)
43. Dēvīs with Gaṇēśa and Bhairava (NM x/2)
44. Lajjā-Gaurī (Rāmachandra temple, east gateway)
45. Chaturbhuja Hanumān (NG n/1)
46. Yantrōddhāraka Āñjaṇēya (NG w/3)
47. Nāga-stones (Yantrōddhāraka Āñjaṇēya temple, NG w/3)
48. Satī-stone (NP q/1)
49. Satī-stone (NG o/3)
50. Memorial-stone (near NN z/2)
51. Mahānavamī procession (Rāmachandra temple, enclosure wall)
52. Vasantōtsava, Kāma and retinue (Viṭhala temple complex, north-east pavilion)
53. Matsyēndranātha (temple NF w/5)
54. Ascetic (Viṭhala temple complex, hundred-pillared hall)
55. Bṛindāvana of Raghunandana (NG n/1)
56. Chaityālaya of Kunthu Jinanātha (temple NX n/1)
57. Jina, chaityālaya of Kunthu Jinanātha
58. Ahmad Khān's mosque and tomb (NO q/1 and 2)
59. Portuguese horse-traders (Viṭhala temple complex)

List of Abbreviations

ARIE	*Annual Report of Indian Epigraphy*
ARSIE	*Annual Report of South Indian Epigraphy*
ASI	*Archaeological Survey of India*
EC	*Epigraphia Carnatica*
EI	*Epigraphia Indica*
FE	*A Forgotten Empire*, by R. Sewell
Further Sources	*Further Sources of Vijayanagara History*, edited by K.A. Nilakanta Sastri and N. Venkataramanayya.
Hemakutakhanda	*Hemakutakhanda of the Skanda Purana*, synopsis by A.A. Shapiro in English of the Sanskrit manuscript.
IA	*Indian Antiquary*
IHQ	*Indian Historical Quarterly*
JAHRS	*Journal of the Andhra Historical Research Society*
JBBRAS	*Journal of the Bombay Branch of the Royal Asiatic Society*
JIH	*Journal of the Indian History*
JOR	*Journal of Oriental Research, Madras*
JRAS	*Journal of the Royal Asiatic Society of Great Britain and Ireland*
MAR	*Annual Report of the Mysore Archaeological Department*
Nel. Ins.	*A Collection of the Inscriptions on Copper-plates and Stones in the Nellore District*, edited by A. Butterworth and V.Venugopal Chetty.
Pampamahatmya	*Sri Pampa Mahatme or The Holy Eminence of the Pampa*, by Guru Omsiddhalingeshvara Swamiji, Translated into English by G.S. Kalburgi.
PIHC	*Proceedings of the Indian History Congress*
QJMS	*Quarterly Journal of the Mythic Society*
SII	*South Indian Inscriptions*
SITI	*South Indian Temple Inscriptions*, edited by T.N. Subramaniam.
Soc. & Pol.	*Social and Political Life in the Vijayanagara Empire*, by B.A. Saletore
Sources	*Sources of Vijayanagar History*, edited by S. Krishnaswami Aiyangar.
Top. List	*A Topographical List of the Inscriptions of the Madras Presidency*, edited by V. Rangacharya.
TTDES	*Tirumalai-Tirupati Devasthanam Epigraphical Series*, edited by Sadhu Subramanya Sastry, V. Vijayaraghavacharya and G.A. Narayan.
Vij. City & Emp.	*Vijayanagara City & Empire: New Currents of Research*, edited by A.L. Dallapiccola.
VPR '79-83	*Vijayanagara : Progress of Research 1979-1983*, edited by M.S. Nagaraja Rao.
VPR '83-84	*Vijayanagara : Progress of Research 1983-1984*, edited by M.S. Nagaraja Rao.
VPR '84-87	*Vijayanagara : Progress of Research 1984-1987*, edited D.V. Devaraj and C.S. Patil.
VPR '87-88	*Vijayanagara : Progress of Research 1987-1988*, edited D.V. Devaraj and C.S. Patil.
VSCV	*Vijayanagara Sexcentenary Commemoration Volume*

CHAPTER 1

Introduction: Historical, Religious and Archaeological Background

1. Historical Context

Four dynasties, which arose from the ruins of the Chōḷa and later Chālukyan empires, that is, the Yādavas of Dēvagiri, the Kākaṭīyas of Warangal, the Hoysaḷas of Dvārasamudra and the Pāṇḍyas of Madurai dominated the political scene south of the Vindhyas in the thirteenth century. These kingdoms were swept away by the irresistible might of the invading Islamic forces in the early fourteenth century. By A.D. 1328 the whole of south India was brought under the control of Delhi.

Soon however revolts broke out against the rule of Delhi. In the far south the independent sultanate of Ma'bar was set up in Madurai; it lasted from A.D. 1335 to 1378.[1] Shortly after this the empire of Vijayanagara was born and in A.D. 1347 the Bahmanī sultanate came into existence. Thus, the political vacuum in south India, caused by the destruction of the earlier Hindu kingdoms, resulted in the emergence of the Vijayanagara empire.

There is some difference of opinion among historians regarding the date of the founding of this empire. Although A.D. 1336 has been traditionally described as the foundational year, the year A.D. 1346 has also been suggested. It is likely that the emergence of Vijayanagara's statehood was a gradual process. The Saṅgama brothers, who may have risen to prominence sometime around or after A.D. 1336, slowly consolidated their authority and were firmly in power by A.D. 1346, when they celebrated the famous "festival of victory" at Śriṅgēri.[2]

The Vijayanagara empire, up to A.D. 1565, was ruled by three dynasties–the Saṅgama (A.D. 1336-1485), the Sāḷuva (A.D. 1485-1505) and the Tuḷuva (A.D. 1505-1570) dynasties. The first king, Harihara I (A.D. 1336-1356), the eldest of the five sons of Saṅgama, ably assisted by his brother Bukka, built up within a few years a kingdom stretching from coast to coast. During the latter part of his reign the Bahmanī kingdom was established beyond the Kṛishṇā river and with this commenced an era of constant warfare, the *doāb* between the Tuṅgabhadrā and the Kṛishṇā being a bone of contention between the Vijayanagara and Bahmanī states.

A great achievement of the reign of Bukka I (A.D. 1356-1377) was the destruction of the Ma'bar sultanate by Kumāra Kampaṇa, Bukka's son. This is described in the Sanskṛit poem *Madhurāvijayam* by princess Gaṅgādēvī.

Harihara II (A.D. 1377-1404) was the first ruler of the dynasty to assume the imperial title of *Mahārājādhirāja*. His reign saw the expansion of the Vijayanagara empire over the whole of south India to the south of the river Kṛishṇā. The *Vēdabhāsya*, begun under Bukka I, was completed now and earned for Harihara II the epithet of *Vaidikamārga-sthāpanāchārya.*

On the death of Harihara II there was a dispute over the succession among his three sons, Virūpāksha I, Bukka II and Dēvarāya I. Ultimately Dēvarāya I secured the throne and ruled from A.D. 1406 to 1422. He was followed by his sons Rāmachandra and Vīra Vijaya both of whom ruled for brief periods. Vīra Vijaya was succeeded by his son Dēvarāya II (A.D 1424-1446), the greatest of the Saṅgama rulers. Following his reverses in wars against the Bahmanīs, Dēvarāya II introduced reforms in his army and employed Muslims, especially in the archery and cavalry. He was a scholar and author, and a liberal patron of the arts and literature.

The glorious rule of Dēvarāya II was followed by a period of decline and disruption during the reigns of Mallikārjuna (A.D. 1446-1465) and Virūpāksha II (A.D. 1466-1485). The weak rule of these two kings facilitated the rise to power of Sāḷuva Narasiṁha, governor of Chandragiri, who usurped the throne in A.D. 1485.

Sāḷuva Narasiṁha (A.D. 1485-1491) was an able ruler who set himself to restore the might and the prestige of the empire. He was succeeded by his minor sons Timma (1491) and Immaḍi Narasiṁha (A.D. 1491-1505), who had, as their regent, the Tuḷuva minister Narasa Nāyaka and later his son Vīra Narasiṁha. The latter assassinated the Sāḷuva emperor and assumed power. With this second usurpation the Tuḷuvas attained the imperial throne. Vīra Narasiṁha (A.D. 1505-1509), after a short reign, was succeeded by his half brother Kṛishṇadēvarāya.

Kṛishṇadēvarāya (A.D. 1509-1529) was not only the greatest king in Vijayanagara history, but also one of the most brilliant monarchs in medieval India. His armies were successful everywhere—against the Bahmanī sultān, 'Ādil Shāh of Bijāpur and the Gajapati ruler of Orissa. Kṛishṇadēvarāya maintained friendly diplomatic relations with the Portuguese on the west coast. An accomplished scholar and poet in Sanskṛit and Telugu, Kṛishṇadēvarāya wrote the Telugu work *Āmuktamālyada*. The noted Telugu poet Allasāni Peddaṇṇa was his poet laureate and at his court were the eight poets known as the *ashṭa-diggajas*. Kṛishṇadēvarāya renovated dilapidated temples throughout his empire, built new ones and gave munificent gifts and grants to temples.

Achyutarāya succeeded his half brother Kṛishṇadēvarāya on the throne. Achyutarāya (A.D. 1529-1542) was a capable ruler and a liberal patron of arts and letters.

In the power struggle following Achyutarāya's death, the faction led by Kṛishṇadēvarāya's son-in-law, Rāmarāya, triumphed and Sadāśiva, nephew of the previous ruler, was placed on the throne, although Rāmarāya remained the de facto ruler as the regent.

Rāmarāya became entangled in the interstate rivalries of the Deccan Sultanates that had been formed after the disintegration of the Bahmanī kingdom. As a result of alliances and wars, Vijayanagara regained the territory lost after Kṛishṇadēvarāya and even extended its limits beyond the Kṛishṇā. But, in the long run, Rāmarāya's policy proved disastrous. The Deccan Sultanates, alarmed at the growing power of Vijayanagara, buried their differences and in a joint action defeated Rāmarāya in the decisive battle of Rakkasa-Taṅgaḍi—also known as the battle of Tāḷikōṭa—in January A.D. 1565. The capital city Vijayanagara was temporarily occupied and sacked by the allied Muslim armies. The Vijayanagara state never fully recovered from the catastrophe of Rakkasa-Taṅgaḍi; the northern parts of Karṇāṭaka came under Muslim rule and Vijayanagara ceased being the imperial capital. The truncated empire lingered on in the south, under the Āravīḍu dynasty (A.D. 1570-1646), while its feudatories became independent one after the other. Rāmarāya had died in the battle, his brother Tirumala, the founder of the Āravīḍu dynasty, moved to Penugoṇḍa in the Anantapur district taking with him the puppet ruler Sadāśiva. Later, in A.D. 1592, the capital was shifted further south to Chandragiri in North Arcot district[3] and in A.D. 1606 to Vellore.[4]

Most historians writing about the nature of the Vijayanagara polity emphasize that it was a Hindu empire, acting as a bulwark against the southward expansion of Islam. It is assumed that the empire "came into existence for (1) the purpose of saving South India from being completely conquered by Muhammadans, (2) to save Hindu religion and give it a chance for its natural development, at least in this corner of India without molestation from outside agencies, and (3) to save for India as much of its culture and learning as it was possible."[5] "The empire was founded for the protection of *Dharma*.... In the whole range of South Indian history an instance of an empire founded with the purpose of giving protection to a religion irrespective of different sects, has yet to be discovered.... Religion did not mean ... Śaivism alone or Vaiṣṇavism alone, but it embraced all the systems of religious thought."[6] "In matters spiritual the policy was the protection of *Dharma* understood in its widest sense; in matters social, it was the protection of the various *varṇāśrama dharmas*...i.e., the peaceful observation of the rules of conduct as enjoined by the castes to which one belonged."[7] The Vijayanagara rulers claimed to be followers of *Pūrvada maryāda* (ancient constitutional usage).[8]

This traditional notion regarding the essence of the Vijayanagara state has been challenged by others. According to Stein, "this kind of interpretation stems from a modern nationalist sentiment and an only slightly older indologism."[9] Earlier writers have interpreted titles such as "supporters of dharma" or "upholders of the ancient constitutional usage" too literally. Such titles constitute an important part of the traditional pedigree of the kings of ancient India and "protection of dharma" formed part of the coronation oath of the Hindu kings.[10] It is true that wars against the Bahmanī sultāns were frequent. But their cause was more political and economic rather than religious. It was but a revival of the ancient feud that had existed between the Deccan and south India under the earlier Hindu sovereigns, e.g., between the Chālukyas of Bādāmi and the Pallavas, the Chālukyas of Kalyāṇi and the Chōḷas, the Yādavas and the Hoysaḷas.[11] Besides, the major victims of the Vijayanagara arms were not always the Muslims. The expansion and maintenance of the Vijayanagara empire also necessitated military expeditions against less powerful Hindu rulers, such as the Śaṁbuvarāyas, the Reḍḍis of Koṇḍavīḍu, the Vēlamas and the Gajapatis. Also, Muslim soldiers played an important part in the successes of the Vijayanagara army.

Therefore, the Hindu nature of the Vijayanagara state should not be overstressed. However, it must be accepted that the empire did create conditions for the defense of Hindu culture and institutions and it succeeded in limiting the expansion of Muslim power in the Deccan for over two centuries. During this period the outlook of the Hindus of the south developed into an orthodoxy in social and religious matters.[12] The encouragement of religion by the Vijayanagara monarchs, as revealed by the numerous inscriptions, included promotion of Vēdic and other studies, support of brāhmaṇas, generous patronage extended to *maṭhas* and temples, pilgrimages to religious places and celebration of public rituals.

Under the patronage of the early Vijayanagara sovereigns, notably Bukka I, a syndicate of scholars, headed by Sāyaṇa, undertook the prodigious task of commenting upon the *Saṁhitās* of all the four *Vēdas* and many of the *Brāhmaṇas* and *Āraṇyakas.*[13] A codification of the philosophical systems was effected in the *Sarvadarśana-saṅgraha.* Lands in villages and sometimes entire villages were granted to individual scholars[14] or to groups of brāhmaṇas.[15] Achyutarāya's *dāna* (gift) of *Ānandanidhi* by which he made "Kubēras of the brāhmaṇas" is recorded in different temples within the capital[16] and elsewhere in the empire.[17] Among the *dānas,* the gift of the weight of a man in gold or pearls, the *tulāpurusha-dāna,* was considered especially meritorious. Dēvarāya I performed the *tulāpurusha* in gold in the capital city[18] and Achyutarāya that of pearls in Kāñchi at the Varadarāja-svāmi temple.[19] Kṛishṇadēvarāya in the course of the Orissan campaign performed this ceremony at the Amarēśvara temple at Amarāvati.[20]

Gifts to ascetics and sectarian leaders by the monarchs was common. Thus, Kṛishṇadēvarāya granted a number of villages to the Mādhva sage Vyāsarāya.[21] Endowments to *maṭhas* encouraged religious learning and activities. The Advaita *maṭha* at Śṛiṅgēri was the recipient of many royal grants; an inscription of Harihara II lists the benefactions to the *maṭha* made by him and his predecessors.[22]

The Vijayanagara rulers encouraged pilgrimages within their own empire, possibly to integrate the different language zones within the realm. Besides, visits to the northern sacred sites had become increasingly difficult due to the occupation of north India by the Muslims. The important pilgrimage centres were: Chidambaram, Virūpāksham, Kāḷahasti, Tirupati, Kāñchi, Śrīśailam, Tiruvaṇṇamalai, Harihara, Ahōbalam, Sangamēśvara, Śrīraṅgam, Jaṁbukēśvaram, Kuṁbhakōṇam, Mahānadi, Gokarṇam, Ramēśvaram and Anantaśayanam. Several of these were considered to be substitutes for the northern pilgrim sites, for instance, a visit to Ēkāmranātha in Kāñchi was equivalent to a visit to Vārāṇasī. The Vijayanagara rulers themselves often undertook pilgrimages.[23]

Inscriptions are scattered throughout south India which record the benefactions to temples by the Vijayanagara rulers. The emperors and their subordinates built hundreds of new temples, repaired or made extensive additions to several old ones, settled disputes among temple servants and endowed the temples richly with lands (known as *dēvadāna* lands), money, taxes due to the state and jewels for the daily worship or for new festivals that were instituted. Such favours extended to Śaivite, Vaishṇavite and Jaina institutions. Besides state support, temples also enjoyed wide patronage from private donors such as rich individuals, sectarian leaders, professional guilds and communal groups.

The celebration of public rituals was an important royal function. For it was believed that flourishing festivals would strengthen *dharma*, establish the presence of divine powers in the kingdom and stimulate the cosmic flow of gifts and fertility.[24] During this period the most important of these rituals preserving cosmic order was, undoubtedly, the annual nine-day *Mahānavamī* festival. Paes has left a vivid account of this festival,[25] a careful perusal of which makes clear that the festival, although basically religious in character, had political, economic, social and military significance. The focus of the ceremonies was upon the reigning king and the revitalization of his kingdom and his realm.[26] The various rites of this festival reveal that the king and the deity (being worshipped) were at least homologous, if not equal.[27]

The patronage of religion, especially the royal celebration of public rituals such as the *Mahānavamī*, highlights the fact that in the Vijayanagara system the relationship between kings and gods was one of partnership. "Sovereignty is conceived as shared between powerful humans (Rājas) and powerful divinities (Devas); the sovereignty of neither is complete; the sovereignty of both, together, is perfect."[28] Although the king himself was not seen as divine, kingship frequently was and the great royal rituals were attempts to bring into being this divine analogy.[29] The transactions between kings, temple deities, priests and sectarian leaders point to a relationship of mutual interdependence. There was a triangular relationship linking them.[30] The priests made offerings to and performed services for the gods, the gods preserved the king, his kingdom and his subjects and the king protected and awarded material rewards to the temples, the priests or sectarian leaders. Thus, while the temples and sectarian leaders bestowed honours and blessings on the king, the ruler in turn conferred on them protection and riches. Even though the kings were not conceived to be gods, kings manifested divinity and maintained divine order in the world. Prosperity, fertility, success in war, the right relationships between the castes and other groups—all resulted, ultimately, from royal activity.[31]

2. Religious Situation in South India

The centuries just prior to the foundation of the Vijayanagara empire and the period of this study were marked by intense religious activity in south India. In order to understand the history of the religious traditions in the city of Vijayanagara, a survey of the important sects and revivalist movements during this age and the religious affiliations and attitudes of the Vijayanagara kings is essential.

A. *Religious Developments*

A towering figure in the Hindu renaissance of the early medieval era was the great Śaṅkarāchāryā (A.D. 781-820). Relying on the *Upanishads*, the *Vēdānta Sūtras* and the *Gītā*, Śaṅkara gave a definite shape to the monistic or non-dualistic school of Vedānta philosophy known as the Advaita system. The entire philosophy of this school was summed up by Śaṅkara in half a verse, "Brahman is real : the world is an illusory appearance; the individual soul (*jīva*) is Brahman alone, not other." The non-duality of Brahman, the non-reality of the world, and the non-difference of the soul from Brahman—these constitute the essence of the teaching of Advaita.[32] The Smārtas are the followers of the Advaita philosophy of Śrī Śaṅkarāchārya. They worship five gods, Śiva, Vishṇu, Dēvī, Sūrya and Gaṇēśa, together known as *Pañchāyatana*, but they give preference mostly to Śiva.[33] The two important Advaita *maṭhas* at Śṛiṅgēri and Kāñchipuram, besides a number of others, propagated the Smārta religious system and the Advaita philosophy. Inscriptions from A.D. 1346 onwards reveal the close links between the Vijayanagara rulers and the former *maṭha*. Two copper plate grants record the gift of villages to the latter by Kṛishṇadēvarāya.[34]

The Pāśupata sect of Śaivism and its offshoots, the Kāpāḷika and the Kāḷāmukha, were important Śaivite sects. The Pāśupata sect is anterior to the Christian era, but in the second century A.D. it was reorganized by Lakulīśa.[35] One great difference between the Advaitins and the Pāśupatas appears to have consisted in the fact that while the former laid great stress on the *Vēdas*, the latter did so to the Śaiva *Āgamas*. The Kāpāḷikas worshipped mainly the Kāpāḷin form of Śiva and also Chāmuṇḍa.[36] This sect was present in south India from the seventh century onwards but by the fourteenth century it seems to have virtually died out.[37] The sect was perhaps absorbed by the Śaivite tāntric orders such as the Kānphaṭas and the Aghorīs.[38] By the time of the origin of the Vijayanagara empire the Pāśupatas and the Kāpāḷikas appear to have lost their influence.[39]

The Kāḷāmukhas were very popular all over south India between the ninth and fourteenth centuries. They were so called because of a black streak worn across the forehead.[40] They worshipped Śiva as Mahākāla (the great destroyer) or as Bhairava[41] and also the goddess Kāḷī.[42] The Kāḷāmukhas have been misrepresented by many. The great philosopher, Rāmānuja, wrongly identified them with the Kāpāḷikas and this was accepted by R.G. Bhandarkar.[43] The Kāḷāmukhas have made a great contribution, especially in the field of education. Baḷḷigāve and Kuppatūr, both in the Shimoga district of Karṇāṭaka, and Śrīśailam in the Kurnool district in Āndhra were the most influential centres of the Kāḷāmukhas. The Koḍiya-maṭha of the Kedārēśvara temple in Baḷḷigāve was a very important and famous educational institution during the eleventh and twelfth centuries A.D. Some of the Kāḷāmukha priests also acted as *rāja-gurus.* Among them were Sarvēśvaraśakti and Rudraśakti, both of Kuppatūr, and Vāmaśakti of Baḷḷigāve.[44] The names of the Kāḷāmukha ascetics mostly end in śakti, rāśi, ābhāraṇa or Śiva. While the last three endings may be found in the names of persons of other Śaivite sects as well, that of śakti is particular to the Kāḷāmukha sect.[45]

After the early fifteenth century we do not hear anymore of the Kāḷāmukhas. "It is possible that the democratic Liṅgāyat sect (and the enlightened Advaita religion?) absorbed the Kāḷāmukhas and they practically disappear from history."[46] That the Kāḷāmukha sect was absorbed by the reformist Vīraśaiva religion is indicated by the fact that many of the former Kāḷāmukha temples and *maṭhas,* including the Kedārēśvara temple at Baḷḷigāve, the Trikuṭēśvara temple at Gadag and the *maṭha* at Śrīśailam, are now controlled by the Vīraśaivas. Even more significant, perhaps, is the fact that few Vīraśaivas are found in areas not formerly dominated by the Kāḷāmukhas.[47]

Another school of medieval Hindu mysticism which flourished in the Deccan was the Nātha *saṁpradāya,* founded by Matsyēndranātha and Gorakhnātha. The followers of this school are known as the *nāthas, yogīs* or *kānphaṭas.*[48] They are votaries of Śiva and Śaktī with a strong bias towards the Śākta tradition. They also worship the nine saints known as the *navanāthas* and the eighty-four *siddhas.* The fifteenth century Telugu work, *Navanāthacharitramu* by Gauranna, mentions members of this sect in Āndhra. Śrīśailam was an important centre of this cult and it was also popular in coastal Karṇāṭaka during this period. Pietro della Valle, who passed through Mangalore in A.D. 1623, gives a detailed account of the Nātha monastery at Kadire.[49]

Another important Śaivite school was that of the Tamil Śaiva-Siddānta. It is based on the *Vēdas,* the twenty-eight *Śaivāgamas* and their *Upāgamas* and the mystical poems of the Śaiva saints of south India, the sixty-three *nayanārs.* Tamil Śaivism is neither pure Advaita, nor is it Dvaita or Viśishṭādvaita. It is a doctrine by itself.[50]

The Śivādvaita school was spearheaded by Śrīkanta in twelfth century A.D. His work, the *Śrīkanta Bhāshya,* was commented upon by that versatile sixteenth century scholar Apayya Dīkshita. Except in minor details the Sivādvaita is not very different from the Śaiva-Siddhānta.

The Vīraśaiva reform of the twelfth century A.D. spread rapidly from Karṇāṭaka to Āndhra and Tamil Nāḍu. The Vīraśaivas are also called the Liṅgāyats on account of the *liṅga* that the followers of this sect wear on their person. Besides the *Vēdas,* the *Āgamas* and the *Purāṇas,* the Vīraśaivas accept the authority of the sixty-three Tamil Śaiva saints whom they refer to as the *purātanas* (ancients) and the 770 later Vīraśaiva saints. Tradition avers that this sect is very old that it was founded by five *āchāryas,* Ēkōrāma, Paṇḍitāradhya, Rēṇuka, Daruka and Viśvārādhya. But the real founder was Basava, the minister of Bijjaḷa (A.D. 1162-1167), the Kalachūri king. The Vīraśaivas consider Basava to be the incarnation of Nandi.

This new faith is a departure from the ritualism of the Vēdic traditions. The goal of human life is the union of the individual soul with the Supreme. This can be achieved by following the rules of the *ashṭāvaraṇa,* the eight-fold spiritual aids, the *pañchāchara* or the five-fold conduct and the *shaṭsthaḷa,* the six-fold stages which lead one on the path of spiritual progress and perfection. Among the *ashṭāvaraṇa,* the triad, the *guru* (the spiritual guide), the *liṅga* (the mystic emblem of the Supreme) and the *jaṅgama* (the itinerant teacher) are the most important.

The Vīraśaiva reform differed in many essentials from the Vaidika social practices. Thus, the Vīraśaivas allow widow remarriage and the burial of the dead; they do not follow sex and caste distinctions and neither do they wear the sacred thread. Basava emphasised the importance of labour, vegetarianism and the abstention from all intoxicants.

Vaishṇavism received a great impetus in south India because of the work of the two great *āchāryas*, Rāmānuja and Madhva.[51]

Rāmānuja (A.D. 1017-1137), the great philosopher of Viśishṭādvaita, or qualified monism, followed a long line of Vaishṇava thinkers in Tamil Nāḍu. Twelve poet saints, the *āḷvārs* (third to ninth centuries A.D.) had poured out their devotion in the form of songs. These were collected into what is called the *Nāḷayira-Prabandham*. These songs constitute the basis of Viśishṭādvaita, together with the *Upanishads* and the *Bhāgavata*. The *āḷvārs* were followed by a succession of *āchāryas* (teachers), the greatest of whom was Rāmānuja. According to his system, Vishṇu is the Supreme deity, accompanied by Śrī or Lakshmī who represents divine grace. That is why the religion is called Śrī-Vaishṇavism. In the place of the abstract, impersonal God or *Nirguṇa Brahman* of the Advaita school, Rāmānuja justified the need for a personal God, possessed of all good qualities (*Saguṇa Brahman*). He repudiated the doctrine of illusoriness of the material world and the finite self and postulated that Ultimate Reality is one, in which the material world and the finite self find a necessary place. He stressed the importance of *bhakti* (devotion) and *prapatti* (self-surrender) as means to receive the Lord's favour. Śrī-Vaishṇavism won many followers in Tamil Nāḍu. It also spread to parts of Karṇāṭaka following the conversion of the Hoysaḷa king Vishṇuvardhana by Rāmānuja.

In the early fourteenth century the Śrī-Vaishṇava sect split into two groups—the Vaḍagalai, the northern or Sanskṛit (Bhāshyic) school and the Teṅgalai, the southern or Tamil school. Vēdānta Dēśika was the *āchārya* of the former, while the latter was headed by Piḷḷai Lōkāchārya and Maṇavāla Mahāmuni.

The Vaḍagalais favour the Sanskṛit philosophical literature while the Teṅgalais give more importance to the Tamil *Prabandham*. For the attainment of salvation individual effort is the first step according to the Vaḍagalais (*Markaṭanyāya* or the monkey analogy), while for the Teṅgalais only surrender to the Lord is necessary (*Mārjāranyāya* or the cat analogy). The Teṅgalais believe that, since God's grace was spontaneous, sins could be committed without any reference to punishment; the Vaḍagalai reject this view. For the Vaḍagalais, Śrī is infinite and is a part and parcel of the Lord, but, the Teṅgalais relegate her to a lower position. The Vaḍagalais adhere strictly to the caste system, while the Teṅgalais contend that *prapatti* transcends all caste and creed barriers. Vaḍagalais consider that prostration should be made only to deserving persons like a *guru*, a brāhmaṇa, or the wife of the *guru*, etc., while the Teṅgalais perform the *namaskāra* to every Vaishṇava of their school. There are some other minor differences: the Vaḍagalais enjoin the tonsure of widows while the Teṅgalais do not, the Teṅgalais are opposed to animal sacrifices, they do not ring the bell during *pūjā* while the Vaḍagalais do.[52] With regard to the *nāmam*, or the sacred mark worn by Śrī-Vaishṇavas on their foreheads, the Vaḍagalai wear a U-like mark with a prominent curvature and the Teṅgalais have a different type with a distinct *pāda* projection at the bottom.[53] Śrīraṅgam became the stronghold of the Teṅgalais and Kāñchipuram the centre of the Vaḍagalais.[54]

Madhvāchārya (A.D. 1238-1317) preached the philosophy of Dvaita or dualism in Karṇāṭaka. The Dvaita system, while admitting two ultimate principles constituting Reality as a whole, regards only one of them (God) as *Svatantra* or Independent, the other, that is the world and souls, is *Paratantra* or Dependent. He stressed five types of differences or *pañchabhedas*: those between God and the soul, between God and matter, between matter and soul, between one soul and another soul, and between matter and matter. Madhva is supposed to have set up eight *maṭhas* in Uḍipi. It is, however, the three other *maṭhas* represented by a group of four disciples of Madhva—Padmanābha, Ṅarahari, Mādhava and Akshobhya Tīrtha and continued by their successors—which have made the most solid contribution to the propagation of Mādhvaism. Vyāsarāya was a great Mādhva saint of the fifteenth-sixteenth centuries. Following the Dvaita philosophy of Madhvāchārya a movement was started in Karṇāṭaka in the fifteenth century, known as the Haridāsa movement, which greatly spread the cult of Vishṇu.

Besides the Śaivite and Vaishṇavite sects, there was also the Śākta cult. The Śāktas worship the Supreme Deity exclusively as a female principle. Its followers are of two schools, the Dakshiṇāchārī (Walkers of the Right Way) and Vāmāchārī (Walkers in the Left Way).

Side by side with the "greater" or Sanskṛitic sects of Śaivism, Vaishṇavism and Śāktism, there existed the "lesser" or non-Sanskṛitic cults of the popular or folk deities. Most of the *grāma-dēvatas* are conceived of not as supreme cosmic powers, but only as local deities with jurisdiction limited to the village.[55] Most of these deities are female.[56] The fertility cult and the predominant role of women in an agrarian economy perhaps were the reasons for this. Yellammā, Irukulammā, Poḷaladēvī, Mūkāṁbikadēvī were some of the village deities worshipped during the period under review.[57] The worship of snakes, represented by *nāga-kals*, of sacred trees and of men and women who had died under heroic circumstances were also a part of popular religiosity.

For about fifteen centuries Jainism had been the dominant religion in this region. Its advent into Karṇāṭaka is traditionally attributed to the migration of Bhadrabāhu and Chandragupta Maurya in the third century B.C.[58] Jainism appears to have spread from the north, via Kaliṅga, to the Āndhra region in the sixth century B.C.[59] Throughout south India, for centuries, Jainism played a very significant role. But, the Hindu renaissance in Tamil Nāḍu led by the *āḻvārs* and the *nayanārs* and the Śaiva revival in Āndhra struck a death blow to Jainism and it had virtually disappeared from these regions before the fourteenth century A.D. Its last stronghold in the south was in Karṇāṭaka, where it had enjoyed much royal patronage under the Kadaṁbas, the early western Chālukyas, the Rāshṭrakūṭas and the Hoysaḷas. Even though the Vīraśaiva movement resulted in the decline of Jainism, it continued to be fairly influential in Karṇāṭaka during the period under review and it received patronage from the Vijayanagara rulers. However, by the sixteenth century the decline was irreversible and Jainism came to be mainly restricted to certain areas, such as the Tuḷuva country. Jainism in south India was dominated by the Digambara order. The Yāpanīya sect was exclusive to Karṇāṭaka.

Islam reached south India via the Arab traders who visited and settled along the west coast. With the Muslim invasions, the presence of Islam was felt for the first time throughout south India. During the Vijayanagara period, the employment of Muslim soldiers in the army resulted in the wider spread of Islam.

Although there were Christians in Malabār long before the period under survey, it was only with the coming of the Portuguese that Christianity spread to other areas. However, Christianity was restricted to a few pockets and its impact, therefore, was minimal.

B. *Religious Affiliations of the Vijayanagara Rulers*

Historians differ about the affiliations of the Vijayanagara sovereigns. Were the early Saṅgamas the disciples of Vidyāraṇya and the Śṛiṅgēri *maṭha* or of Kāḷāmukha *gurus*? To what sect did the later Saṅgamas belong? When did the shift from Śaivism to Vaishṇavism take place? Were the Sāḷuvas and early Tuḷuvas Mādhvas or Śrī-Vaishṇavas? When did Śrī-Vaishṇavism gain predominance?

A careful study of the epigraphical and literary sources reveal that the *rāja-gurus* of the early Saṅgamas were Kāḷāmukhas. In this they were following the traditions of the Karṇāṭaka monarchs, who from the middle of the eleventh century A.D had set the precedent of selecting their *rāja-gurus* from one or other of the famous Kāḷāmukha centres—Baḷḷigāve, Kuppatūr or Śrīśailam.[60] At the same time the kings showed great devotion to the Śṛiṅgēri Advaita *maṭha* and to its pontiffs Vidyātīrtha, Bhāratitīrtha and Vidyāraṇya, the last of whom came into contact with Vijayanagara only twenty years after its founding.[61]

There are epigraphical and literary references to the Kāḷāmukha Kriyāśakti *gurus* from A.D. 1347 to 1442. At least three different Kriyāśaktis are mentioned—Kāśīvilāsa, Vāṇīvilāsa and Chandrabhūshana. It is evident that the first name in the full title is the personal designation of the *guru* and the second that of his office. Two inscriptions of A.D. 1347 refer to Kriyāśakti as the *guru* of the famous minister Mādhavamantrin.[62] A stone inscription of Bukka I's reign dated A.D. 1368 speaks of Kāśīvilāsa Kriyāśakti as the preceptor of this minister.[63] During this same reign, in *Madhurāvijayam* Gaṅgādēvī pays obeisance to guru Kriyāśakti.[64] A copper-plate grant of Harihara II dated A.D. 1378 mentions Kriyāśakti as the *kula-guru* (family preceptor of the king).[65] Another record of A.D. 1379 refers to the *rāja-guru* Vāṇīvilāsa Kriyāśakti.[66] Two other copper-plate grants of 1398 and A.D. 1399 praise Harihara II as the worshipper of the feet of *rāja-rāja-guru-pitāmaha* Kriyāśaktidēva.[67] An inscription of A.D. 1410 refers to Dēvarāya I as having received supreme knowledge by the favour of *rāja-guru* Kriyāśakti.[68] In the same year in a grant of his son Vijaya-Bhūpati, Kriyāśakti is referred to as the *guru.*[69] A grant was made by Dēvarāya II in A.D. 1429 to certain brāhmaṇas with Kriyāśakti at their head.[70] Another record of the same reign, dated A.D. 1431, mentions Kriyāśaktidēva.[71] The record of A.D. 1442[72] referring to *rāja-guru* Kriyāśakti-Oḍeya is the last epigraphical reference to these preceptors. Śrīnātha, the Telugu poet, relates of the presence of Chandrabhūshana Kriyāśakti in the court of Dēvarāya II.[73] After his reign no more is heard of the Kāḷāmukhas.

The close relationship between the Śṛiṅgēri monks and Vijayanagara is evident from A.D. 1346 onwards. Harihara I and his relatives in A.D. 1346[74] and Bukka I in A.D. 1356[75] paid homage to Vidyātīrtha and made land grants to Bhāratitīrtha. Harihara II was zealous in his devotion towards this *maṭha* and to Vidyāraṇya. In 1380 he confirmed all the previous grants.[76] In A.D. 1384 he made a donation to two disciples of sage Vidyāraṇya.[77] In 1386-87, after Vidyāraṇya's death, the same ruler made a generous land grant near Śṛiṅgēri in honour of the *guru.*[78] Bukka II in A.D. 1406 gave an endowment for the renovation and proper maintenance of a library belonging to the *maṭha.*[79] The gifts of land made by Dēvarāya II in A.D. 1431[80] and by Mallikārjuna in A.D. 1451[81] show that the later Saṅgama rulers continued to patronise the Śṛiṅgēri *maṭha.* Such a relationship of the Vijayanagara rulers with the Śṛiṅgēri *gurus* is not at variance with their having Kāḷāmukhas as their family preceptors, for no exclusiveness existed at the time in the matter of paying respects to more than one venerable teacher.[82]

Vīraśaivism was influential in the later Saṅgama period. According to one school of thought Dēvarāya II and his immediate successors were Vīraśaivas,[83] but there is no conclusive evidence to support this contention. Yet it is undoubtedly true that this sect enjoyed favour. The *Chennabasava Purāṇa* by Virūpāksha Paṇḍita (A.D. 1584) informs us that Dēvarāya II revered and patronised the Liṅgāyat *gurus* Kerasthaḷada Vīraṇṇa and Basavēśa and he even gave his daughter in marriage to the former.[84] It is believed that 101 *viraktas* ("the passionless ones") propagated the religion in the empire. Among them were General Lakkaṇṇa, the author of *Śivatattva Chintāmaṇi* and Chamarasa, who wrote *Prabhuliṅgalīlē.*[85]

According to some historians the last Saṅgama monarch, Virūpāksha II, was converted to Śrī-Vaishṇavism. This is based on the account in *Prapannāmṛitam* by Anantāchārya.[86] It is not supported by epigraphical, archaeological or other literary evidences. Besides, the *Prapannāmṛitam* is a Śrī-Vaishṇava hagiographical work of the seventeenth century. The historical accuracy of such a source is questionable. Hence, it is most likely that Virūpāksha was a Śaiva like his predecessors.

The shift to Vaishṇavism occurred with the change in dynasty. Sāḷuva Narasiṁha was a devotee of Veṅkaṭēśvara of Tirupati and Narasiṁha of Ahōbalam. His guru was Kandāḍai Rāmānujaiyangār, a prominent spiritual leader at Tirumalai and Tirupati.[87]

According to *Śrī Vyāsayōgicharitam* by Sōmanātha, the Mādhva sage Vyāsarāya was the *rāja-guru* of Sāḷuva Narasiṁha, Tuḷuva Vīra Narasiṁha, Kṛishṇarāya and Achyutarāya. Going by this account, it is claimed that these rulers favoured the Mādhva sect.[88] But, without other corroborating evidences the assertion of *Śrī Vyāsayōgicharitam* cannot be accepted. For, although Somanātha was a contemporary of the sage, he was also his devout disciple. Besides, his work, a *chaṁpū-kāvya,* is replete with embellishments typical of this literary genre. No inscriptions refer to Vyāsarāya's influence over Sāḷuva Narasiṁha,[89] or over Vīra Narasiṁha. Many epigraphs point to the great reverence of Kṛishṇadēvarāya for this *guru*.[90] Still from this it cannot be definitely stated that the king was a Mādhva. His relationship with the sage might have been more personal than sectarian. Inscriptions also refer to Śrī-Vaishṇava ascetics whom he venerated, such as Govindarāja, who is called his *guru*,[91] and Veṅkaṭa Tātāchārya.[92] The king's favourite deity was Veṅkaṭēśvara of Tirupati and his strong leaning towards Śrī-Vaishṇavism is revealed in the *Āmuktamālyada*.[93] Under the last Tuḷuva emperor, Sadāśiva and his regent Rāmarāya, Śrī-Vaishṇavism won an undisputed ascendancy; Pañchamatabhañjanam Tātāchārya was the *guru* of Rāmarāya.[94]

Harihara I and his successors had placed the realm under the protection of Śrī Virūpāksha and had adopted this name as their "sign-manual". Despite the change in the sectarian affiliation there was no alteration in this till the Āravīḍu king, Veṅkaṭa II, replaced "Śrī Virūpāksha" by "Śrī Veṅkaṭēśa" as the official signature.

The conscious effort at religious conciliation seen in the Jaina-Vaishṇava accord of Bukka I in A.D. 1368[95] was continued by the later rulers. For, despite their sectarian preferences, the Vijayanagara rulers, on the whole, adopted the deliberate policy of tolerance towards all sects, so as to incorporate them all within the polity. Thus, Dēvarāya II endowed the Śrī-Vaishṇava temples at Śrīraṅgam[96] and Tirumalai,[97] favoured Jaina institutions in the capital[98] and elsewhere,[99] employed Muslims in his army[100] and allowed them to practise their religion freely.[101] The Vaishṇava Kṛishṇadēvarāya bestowed lavish grants and gifts on Śaiva temples[102] and Achyutarāya, on the occasion of his coronation, gave an equal number of villages to the temples of Ēkāmbaranātha and Varadarāja at Kāñchi.[103] Under Sadāśiva and Rāmarāya, however, although there was no persecution of Śaiva institutions, the official patronage was primarily extended towards Śrī-Vaishṇava ones. This departure from the traditional policy had unhappy consequences.

3. The City of Vijayanagara

"The City of Bidjanagar is such that the pupil of the eye has never seen a place like it, and the ear of intelligence has never been informed that there existed anything to equal it in the world",[104] remarked 'Abdur Razzāk, the Persian ambassador to the court of Dēvarāya II. The city is situated in magnificent surroundings, the most striking element of which is the river Tuṅgabhadrā that flows here in a north-easterly direction through rugged, rocky terrain, particularly inhospitable on the northern bank. The pinkish-grey granite boulders form fantastic shapes as though piled up by some mysterious spirit. To the south of the river are two ridges, separated by a valley, and low hills such as Hēmakūṭa and Mataṅga. Immediately south of these the landscape changes, there are open valleys with isolated rocky outcrops, including Mālyavanta. Gradually the hills disappear and the land becomes increasingly flat and open. The larger valleys are irrigated; the contrast between the stark rocks and the green, fertile valleys adds to the picturesqueness of the site.

The remains of the imperial city of Vijayanagara, popularly known as "the Hampi ruins", are spread over an extensive area of about twenty-five square kilometres, from the village of Hampi in the north to Kāmalāpuram in the south (see Fig. 1). The outer lines of its fortifications and the suburban areas, however, include a much larger area,[105] from Ānegoṅdi in the north to the modern town of Hospēṭ in the south.

The city was called Hosapaṭṭaṇa, the "New City", for some time. Later it came to be known as Vijayanagara the "City of Victory" and in the sixteenth century, it also came to be called Vidyānagara. Hampe, Pampā-kshētra, Bhāskara-kshētra, Pampā-pura, Virūpāksha-kshētra, these are some of the other names by which the site is identified in inscriptions,[106] though, perhaps, these refer more particularly to the sacred area on the south bank of the river and not to the entire metropolis. Besides 'Abdur Razzāk, other visitors have left glowing accounts of the splendour of Vijayanagara. These include the Italian Nicolo Conti in the early fifteenth century, his compatriot Varthema in the beginning of the sixteenth and the Portuguese Duarte Barbosa, Domingo Paes and Fernão Nuniz.

The Saṅgamas did not build the capital in an uninhabited desert land. The discovery of neoliths and handmade pottery at the site proves that the history of the Hampi region dates back to the neolithic/chalcolithic times.[107] Buddhist occupation here approximately between the first and the third/fourth centuries A.D. is indicated by an inscription in Brāhmī characters found during excavations near the "King's Audience Hall"[108] and the more recent find in A.D. 1985 of five limestone slabs with elaborate reliefs. Epigraphical evidences show that this area was under the control of the various dynasties that ruled Karṇāṭaka successively, including the early western Chālukyas,[109] the Chālukyas of Kalyāṇi,[110] the Hoysaḷas[111] and the Kampili chiefs.[112] Liṅgāyat poets, such as Harīśvara and Rāghavāṅka, were active here in the twelfth century A.D.[113] This site, from pre-Vijayanagara times, has an unbroken tradition of sanctity. It is a place of pilgrimage hallowed by goddess Pampā and her consort Virūpāksha. Kishkindhā of the Rāmāyaṇa is also believed to be close to Hampi.

Although the popular tradition of the "hare and the hounds"[114] and some spurious inscriptions ascribe the foundation of the city to Harihara I and Vidyāraṇya, Vijayanagara became the imperial capital only during the reign of Bukka I.[115] Harihara I ruled from Ānegoṅdi on the north bank of the Tuṅgabhadrā.[116] An inscription dated A.D. 1349 of Harihara found in Ānegoṅdi[117] and the absence of all epigraphical or archaeological remains of his reign in Vijayanagara gives weight to this supposition. Paes refers to Ānegoṅdi as the "old capital".[118]

A record of A.D. 1368 states that Bukkarāya was "on the throne of the new Vijayanagara"[119] and another of A.D. 1378 asserts that Bukka "built a splendid city, called the city of victory."[120] The "royal centre" was built during this reign; inscriptions from the site refer to two gates, the Siṅghārada Hebbāgilu (NS g) and the Sōmavārada Bāgilu (NS s), in the fortification wall around this centre, as being "east of the city of Vijayanagara of Śrī Vīra Bukkarāya".[121]

Under Harihara II the capital was already a well-developed city extending from the present Hampi to Kāmalāpuram. Near the former was built in A.D. 1386 a Śiva temple,[122] while close to the latter, in A.D. 1385, General Irugappa constructed the *chaityālaya* of Kunthu Jinanātha ("Gāṇigitti" temple).[123] In the sixteenth century Kṛishṇadēvarāya shifted the royal residence

to the newly built suburban area to the south of the main city.[124] He returned, however, to the city proper, for the celebration of public rituals.[125]

To facilitate documentation at the site, the entire area has been divided into four functional zones—the "sacred centre", the "intermediate irrigated valley", the "urban core" and the "sub-urban centres".[126] The "sacred centre" is to the south of the Tuṅgabhadrā. Here, in the confined areas of flat land or at the summits of rocky outcrops, are located the largest temple complexes of the city, numerous smaller temples and shrines, sculptures and inscriptions. To the south of this is an "irrigated valley"; the paucity of buildings and potsherds here indicate that this was an agricultural zone. The "urban core" occupies a series of hills, ridges and valleys to the south of the agricultural zone. The greatest concentration of population was located here, as is revealed by the traces of residences, tanks, wells, roads, stairways, pottery and also of the remains of many small shrines and larger temples. This zone is surrounded by a complete circuit of fortification walls, broken only by well-defended gateways. In the southwest end of the "urban core" is the "royal centre" (also referred to as the "palace zone" or "citadel"), which had its own enclosure wall, only parts of which have survived. To the north, the "urban core" is bounded by the north ridge. In the east end of the north ridge and the northeast valley was the Muslim quarter. Beyond this zone, further south and west, as far as modern Hospēṭ, were laid out the great residential suburbs. A few isolated temples in these are all that remain of the once populous "sub-urban centres".

The validity of such a division of the site into four parts have been questioned and it has been suggested that the site should be viewed as a whole.[127] However, it must be noted that the authors themselves do not consider this designation as definitive.[128] For the sake of convenience, and for want of a better terminology to differentiate between areas in this vast city, these terms have been used in this monograph.

What were the city's limits? In the time of Bukka I, as already seen, the "royal centre" within its own fortifications appears to constitute the city of Vijayanagara. In a later period the "urban core" was viewed as the furthest extent of the city. Thus, Paes differentiates between 'Crisnapor', the area around the Kṛishṇa temple, from 'Bisnaga' (Vijayanagara).[129] From another point of view the city may be considered to embrace the whole site—"sacred centre", "urban core", and "sub-urban centres".[130] In this monograph, the city proper is assumed to comprise only the "sacred centre", the "irrigated valley" and the "urban core", where extensive field work has been carried out. In the "sub-urban centres" to the south and Ānegoṅdi to the north, which are included in the metropolitan area of the city, the field research has been restricted to the important monuments and remains.

Inscriptions and literary sources supply information about some of the quarters, suburbs, canals, markets, gates, etc., many of which date from the sixteenth century. The area around the Virūpāksha temple (NF w/1) was variously known as Virūpākshapura or Haṁpe, Paṁpa-kshētra,[131] Paṁpā-pura[132] or Bhāskara-kshētra.[133] The Viṭhala temple (NH a/1) was located in Viṭhalāpura.[134] On his return from the victorious Udayagiri campaign Kṛishṇadēvarāya installed the *mūrti* of Bālakṛishṇa in the Kṛishṇa temple (NL m/4) in Kṛishṇāpura,[135] an *agrahāra.*[136] The area in which at present the A.S.I. office and the Traveller's Bungalow are situated in Kāmalāpuram was called Koṇḍamarasayana-Pāḷya.[137] Kāmalāpuram was known by that name at least from A.D. 1531 onwards.[138] An inscription of A.D. 1541 mentions Kāmalāpuram and the big tank there.[139] Gōri-keḷagana-grāma (village downwards of the the tombs)[140] was, probably, the "Moorish quarter" of Paes;[141] Hiriya Tirumalarāja, the brother-in-law of Achyutarāya built the Tiruveṅgaḷanātha temple (NM h/1) in Achyutarāyapura.[142]

Achutarāya-pēṭe was in Achyutarāyapura.[143] Other markets included the Kṛishṇāpura-pēṭe,[144] the Peḍḍa-aṅgaḍi-vīdhi (big bāzaar street) near the Mādhava temple (NR t/2)[145] and the Kramuka-parnāpaṇa-vīdhi (pān-supāri bāzaar) in which the *chaityālaya* of Pārśvanātha (NS q/1) is situated.[146]

The so-called Turutta canal was originally known as the Hiriya Kāluve (big canal).[147] The small canal, on either side of which there are stone plates (NW m), was called the Ūṭada kāluve (canal for eating).[148] Along the river, besides Paṁpā-tīrtha, other sacred spots were Chakra-tīrtha (NG r)[149] and Kōṭi-tīrtha (NG m).[150]

During the reign of Kṛishṇadēvarāya the *agrahāra* township of Nāgaladēvīpura was called after the king's mother (modern Nāgēnahaḷḷi).[151] Sāle-Tirumale-Mahārāya-pura[152] (modern Anantaśāyanaguḍi) was built in A.D. 1524 in honour of the heir apparent. Tirumaladēvī-ammana-paṭṭana, named after the principal queen, forms the nucleus around which the town of Hospēṭ has grown.[153] During Achyutarāya's reign the new suburbs of Varadadēvī-ammana-paṭṭana extended from the Paṭṭābhirāma (or Raghunātha) temple towards the Penugoṇḍa gate.[154]

The monuments within the city consist mainly of religious, civil and military buildings. The religious structures, such as the small shrines, large temple complexes and sculptures, provide the main source of information for this monograph.

While the bulk of the temples belong to the Vijayanagara period, a small proportion may be assigned to the pre-Vijayanagara times. These are mostly located in the original pilgrimage centre at the site, i.e., on the Hēmakūṭa hill and in and around the Virūpāksha temple complex. These early temples are built in the styles typical of the Deccan architecture—the Rāshṭrakūṭa, Kadaṁba and the late Chālukya/Hoysaḷa styles.[155] The earliest temples, dating from the ninth to tenth centuries A.D., are in the Rāshṭrakūṭa idiom. There are at least two of these, the best example being the Durgā-dēvī temple near the Manmatha tank (NF w/25). There are many "Kadaṁba-style" temples on the Hēmakūṭa. These are characterised by the stepped, pyramidal stone super-structures, the open porches with overhanging eaves and the plain outer walls with a horizontal band of geometric designs in the middle.[156] Some of these have triple shrines. The Bhuvanēśvari shrine within the Virūpāksha complex, with its fine lathe-turned chlorite columns and elaborate door-frame and ceilings, is in the later-Chālukya-Hoysaḷa idiom.

There are hundreds of small shrines and some large temple complexes within the city dating from the Vijayanagara period. The former, comprising only a *cella* or a *cella* and porch or a *cella*, small *maṇḍapa* and porch are found all over the site, while the latter are mainly restricted to the "sacred centre".

Two distinct strains are to be seen in the Vijayanagara style of temple art and architecture—the Karṇāṭaka tradition (of the Rāshṭrakūṭas-later Chālukyas-Hoysalas) and the Tamil traditions (of the Pallavas-Chōḷas-Pāṇḍyas). The temple style of the Tamil region satisfied the increasingly elaborate ritualistic needs better than the Karṇāṭaka type of temple with fewer components and smaller dimensions. Thus, in the developed style of Vijayanagara temple architecture the material used (granite, with brick and mortar for the super-structures), the general plan and the various auxiliary structures are mainly from the Tamil tradition, but the sculptural themes and the decorative motifs come from the Karṇāṭaka traditions.[157]

A medium-sized temple in the city has a *garbha-gṛiha*, a *śukanāsi* (antechamber), an *antarāla* (second antechamber) and a *raṅga-maṇḍapa*, all arranged axially.[158] Larger ones have in addition a closed *pradakshiṇā* (circumambulatory) passage around the sanctum and an open *mahā-maṇḍapa* or *mukha-maṇḍapa* in front. Such temples stand within one or more *prākāras* (courtyards). The auxiliary structures within the temple courtyard include the separate shrine for the goddess, the *kalyāṇa-maṇḍapa* with the raised platform in the centre for the reception of the deity and his consort at the annual celebration of their marriage, the temple kitchen and store-rooms, the hundred-pillared hall for music and dance, shrines of the subsidiary deities or saints, the *pushkaraṇi* or temple tank, the towering *gōpuras* and the *ratha-vīdhi* or chariot street. The temple pillars are decorative. In the fourteenth and early fifteenth centuries the Kalyāṇi-Chālukyan pillar-type remained popular.[159] The most characteristic type of pillar is one in which the shaft is cut into three square blocks, usually with reliefs on each side, separated by sixteen and octagonal sections. The composite pillars are a sixteenth century feature. In these the central shaft has either a rearing *yāli*/horse with the rider in front or a cluster of columnettes attached to it. In the *chitra-khaṇḍa* variety of pillars the shaft is composed of a series of miniature shrines, one over the other. The typical Vijayanagara corbel is of the *pushpa-pōdigai* variety. The wide roll cornice with a double flexure is an important decorative element in these temples.

The fourteenth century temples, such as the Prasanna Virūpāksha ("Underground") temple (NQ y/1) and the Jaina temple of Kunthu Jinanātha are in the Deccan style. The early fifteenth century Rāmachandra temple (NR w/1) is the first major construction in the city in the imported southern style. During the fifteenth century there was gradually a total absorption of the southern influence into the characteristic Vijayanagara style as can be seen from the Mādhava (NR t/2), Tiruveṅgaḷanātha (NX f/1) and Chandraśēkhara (NX l/1) temples within the "royal centre". In the sixteenth century many additions were made to existing temples and new temples complexes were constructed. The most important of these are the Virūpāksha (NF w/1), Kṛishṇa (NL m/4), Tiruveṅgaḷanātha (NM h/1), Viṭhala (NH a/1), Mālyavanta Raghunātha (NT d/1) and Paṭṭābhirāma.[160]

A large number of non-religious themes—soldiers on horseback, clowns, acrobats, wrestlers, folk dancers, animals, and birds—are incorporated into the temple sculptures. The variety of deities depicted, often not according to the canonic texts, and the large number of non-religious themes represented indicate innovations in and new interpretations of the iconographical rules that guided artists in the early periods.[161] Besides the sculptures in the temples, there are also a vast number of reliefs carved on free-standing boulders and also a few monolithic statues.

Besides the Hindu and Jaina temples and sculptures there are also remains of a number of Muslim tombs, gravestones and at least two mosques.

Contemporary with the religious monuments are secular structures of different types. Among these are some that employ easily recognisable Islamic elements such as arches, domes, stucco decoration and parapets. The most important of these are the so-called "Lotus Mahal" (NR t/3) and the three watch towers in the "Zenāna Enclosure", the "Queen's Bath" (NW p/1), the Octagonal Fountain (NW g/3), the "Guards'

Quarters" NR o/3) and the "Elephant Stables" (NR p/3). A careful study shows that these buildings demonstrate an effective synthesis of different architectural styles. Despite using Islamic elements they are neither Islamic nor Hindu, but are typically Vijayanagara. This was an imperial style reserved for buildings connected with the king, court and army.[162]

Although no palace structure has survived intact, the recent excavations conducted at the site by the Archaeological Survey of India and the Directorate of Archaeology and Museums, Government of Karṇāṭaka, have exposed the basements of a number of courtly residences. These follow an almost uniform pattern.[163] Associated with the court life were other platforms such as the "King's Audience Hall" (NW c/1) and the "Māhanavamī Dibba" (NW d/1), also called the "House of Victory" or the "Throne Platform".

The city was fortified by circuits of defensive walls. According to 'Abdur Razzāk[164] there were seven circles of fortifications, while Nikitin[165] and Varthema[166] describe only three. The only more or less intact circuit wall is the one around the "urban core". The names of some of the strongly defended gateways that controlled movement in and out of the city are provided by epigraphs, such as the Areśaṅkara Bāgilu (NJ s), Udayagiri Bāgilu, (NU d) and Penugoṇḍa Bāgilu,[167] the Koṭiśaṅkaradēvara Bāgilu (NQ s & x)[168] and the Bēṭekārara Hebbāgilu (NYe).[169]

The destruction of this rich and splendid city was sudden and dramatic. Following the climacteric of Rakkasa-Taṅgaḍi, Vijayanagara was first looted by bands of robbers and then systematically plundered by the victorious Deccan armies. The large quantities of charcoal found during the archaeological excavations prove that parts of the city were burnt, while the mutilated sculptures render mute testimony to the iconoclastic zeal of the invaders. However, as Caesar Frederick relates, the city was not fully destroyed in A.D. 1565 and Tirumalarāya even attempted, though unsuccessfully, to restore it as the capital.[170] No longer the setting of an imperial dynasty, the city soon fell into decay. Later treasure seekers[171] and vandals added to the despoliation of the city and the forces of nature completed the destruction begun by man.

Notes

[1]S. Krishnaswami Aiyangar, *South India and her Muhammadan Invaders*, p. 170.

[2]*EC* VI, Sg. 1.

[3]Manjula Sinnur, "The Capitals of the Vijayanagara Empire," in *The Vijayanagara Urbanity*, ed. K.R. Basavaraja, p. 48.

[4]Ibid.

[5]S. Krishnaswami Aiyangar, "The Character and Significance of the Empire of Vijayanagara in Indian History," in *Vijayanagara Sexcentenary Commemoration Volume* (henceforth cited as *VSCV*), p. 16.

[6]H. Heras and V.K. Bhandarker, "Vijayanagara Empire—A Synthesis of South Indian Culture," in *VSCV*, p. 33.

[7]Ibid., p. 35.

[8]A.V. Venkata Ratnam, *Local Government in the Vijayanagara Empire*, p. 3.

[9]Burton Stein, "Vijayanagara and the Transition to Patrimonial System," in *Vijayanagara—City & Empire: New Currents of Research*, ed. A.L. Dallapiccola (henceforth cited as *Vij. City & Emp.*), vol.1, p. 73.

[10]B.S.L. Hanumantha Rao, "Inspiration for the Foundations of Vijayanagara and other Hindu Kingdoms," in *Dr. N. Venkataramanayya Commemoration Volume*, p. 162.

[11]Gurty Venket Rao, "The Bahamani-Vijayanagara Relations," *PIHC*, 2, 1938, p. 264.

[12]K.A. Nilakanta Sastri, *A. History of South India: From Prehistoric Times to the Fall of Vijayanagara*, p.10.

[13]Ibid., p. 331.

[14]*MAR* of 1925, no. 20; *EC* III, Nj. 179; *EC* IX, Dv. 81; *EC* XII, Tm. 11; *EC* IV, Gu. 67; *JAHRS* 10, pp. 121-142; *ARIE* of 1963-64, A. 22.

[15]*EC* V, Cn. 265; *EC* V, B1. 148; *ARIE* of 1965-66, A. 1; *EI* III, pp. 35-41; *EC* X, Gd. 77; *EI* XVIII, pp. 165-166; *EC* XI, Hk. 132.

[16]*ARSIE* of 1889, nos. 27, 28, 39 and 40; *ARSIE* of 1904, nos.1, 17 and 20; *ARSIE* of 1922, nos. 684 and 685.

[17]*ARSIE* of 1926-27, B.K. 7 and 14; *ARSIE* of 1928-29, B.K. 186; *EC* XI, Dg. 24.

[18]*MAR* of 1925, no. 34.

[19]*ARSIE* of 1919, nos. 541 and 549; *SII* IX, pt. II, nos. 547 and 548.

[20]*EI* VII, pp. 17-22.

[21]*MAR* of 1941, no. 28; *EC* XIV, Tn. 161 and 162; *ARSIE* of 1919, no. 370.

[22]*MAR* of 1933, no. 33.

[23]Job Thomas, "Cultural Developments in Tamil Nadu During the Vijayanagara Period," in *Vij. City & Emp.*, vol. 1, pp. 24-25.

[24]D.D. Hudson, "Two Citrā Festivals in Madurai", in *Religious Festivals in India and Sri Lanka*, ed. G.R. Welbon and G.E. Yocum, p. 138.

[25]R. Sewell, *A Forgotten Empire* (henceforth cited as *FE*), pp. 269-274.

[26]Burton Stein, "Mahānavamī : Medieval and Modern Kingly Ritual in South India," in *All the Kings Mana: Papers on Medieval South Indian History*, p. 312.

[27]Ibid., p. 319.

[28]Ibid., p. 320

[29]A. Good, "Divine Coronation in a South Indian Temple," in *Religion and Society in South India*, ed. V. Sudarsan et al., p. 40.

[30]Ibid.; see also A. Appadurai, "Kings, Sects and Temples in South India," in *South Indian Temples*, ed. Burton Stein, pp. 47-55.

[31]J.M. Fritz, "Chaco Canyon and Vijayanagara", in *Mirror and Metaphor*, ed. D. Ingersoll and G. Bronitsky, p. 331.

[32]T.M.P. Mahadevan, *Outlines of Hinduism*, p 141.

[33]D.A. Pai, *Monograph on the Religious Sects in India among the Hindus*, p. 70.

[34]*EI* XIII, pp. 122-132; *EI* XIV, pp. 168-175.

[35]D.A. Pai, op. cit., pp. 61-62.

[36]P. Jash, 'The Kapalikas: An Obscure Saiva Sub-Sect," *PIHC*, 34, pp. 152-153.

[37]D.N. Lorenzen, *The Kāpālikas and Kāḷāmukhas: Two Lost Śaivite Sects*, p. 53.

[38]Ibid.

[39]B.S.L. Hanumantha Rao, op. cit., p. 151.

[40]G.W. Briggs, *Gorakhnāth and the Kānphaṭa Yogis*, p. 223.

[41]Ibid., p. 224.

[42]Ibid., p. 166.

[43]R.G. Bhandarkar, *Vaiṣṇavism, Śaivism and Minor Religious Systems*, pp. 127-128.

[44]Sadyojata Swamiji, "Śaiva and Vīraśaiva Maṭhas in Karṇāṭaka", (Ph.D. diss.), p. 64.

[45]A. Venkata Subbiah, "A 12th Century University in Mysore", *QJMS*, VII, p. 178.

[46]R. Rama Rao, "Hinduism under Vijayanagara Kings", in *VSCV*, p. 44.

[47]D.N. Lorenzen, op. cit., p. 170.

[48]G.W. Briggs, op. cit., p. 1.

[49]Pietro della Valle, *Travels in India*, vol. II, pp. 345-352.

[50]A.P. Karmarkar, *The Religions of India, Vol. I: The Vrātya on the Dravidian System*, p. 285.

[51]To distinguish the Mādhvas from the Śrī-Vaishṇavas, in Karṇāṭaka (and possibly elsewhere in south India), the former are often referred to as Vaishṇavas. In this monograph, however, the word Vaishṇava is used in its more common connotation as that pertaining to Vishṇu and his followers in general. To avoid any confusion, the followers of Rāmānuja are always referred to as Śrī-Vaishṇavas and their system as Śrī-Vaishṇavism, while the followers of Madhvāchārya are called Mādhvas and their system as Mādhvaism.

[52]T.V. Mahalingam, *Administration and Social Life Under Vijayanagara* pt. II, pp. 196-198.

[53]K.V. Raman, *Srī Varadarājaswāmi Temple-Kāñchi*, pp. 86-87.

[54]A. Govindacharya, "Tengalai & Vadagalai," *JRAS*, 1912, p. 714.

[55]H. Whitehead, *The Village Gods of South India*, p. 17.

[56]Ibid.

[57]K. Sarojini Devi, "Religion in Vijayanagara", (Ph.D. diss.), p. 368.

[58]M.S. Ramaswami Ayyangar & B. Seshagiri Rao, *Studies in South Indian Jainism*, pt. I, pp. 23-24.

[59]P.B. Desai, *Jainism in South India and Some Jaina Epigraphs*, Preface, p. ix.

[60]B.A. Saletore, "The Raja-Guru of the founders of Vijayanagara and the pontiffs of the Śṛiṅgēri Matha," *JAHRS*, 9, p. 42.

[61]P.B. Desai, op. cit., p. 191.

[62]*EC* VIII, Sb. 375; *MAR* of 1929, no. 90.

[63]*EC* VII, Sk. 281.

[64]Gaṅgādēvī, *Madhurāvijayam*, Canto I, verse 4.

[65]*EC* V, Cn. 256.

[66]*ARSIE* of 1924-25, A. 15.

[67]*MAR* of 1912, p. 47.

[68]*EC* XI, Dg. 23.

[69]*EI* XIV, pp. 68-83.

[70]*MAR* of 1941, no. 20.

[71]*ARSIE* of 1930-31, no. 344.

[72]*ARSIE* of 1928-29, no. 467.

[73]S. Krishnaswami Aiyangar, *Sources of Vijayanagara History* (hereafter cited as *Sources*), p. 61.

[74]*EC* VI, Sg. 1.

[75]*MAR* of 1933, p. 117ff.; *ARIE* 1961-62, no. 500.

[76]*MAR* of 1933, no. 33.

[77]Ibid., no. 23.

[78]Ibid., no. 24.

[79]*ARSIE* of 1936-37, no. 283.

[80]Ibid., no. 284.

[81]*MAR* of 1934, no. 31.

[82]P.B. Desai, op. cit., p. 192.

[83]B.V. Sreenivasa Rao, "The Religious Policy of Saṅgama Rulers," *JAHRS*, 29, pp. 35-36.

[84]R. Rama Rao, op. cit., p. 45.

[85]S. Rajasekhara, "Saṅgamas and Vīraśaivism", in *Early Vijayanagara : Studies in its History and Culture*, ed. G.S. Dikshit, pp. 85-93.

[86]*Sources*, pp. 71-73.

[87]*TTDES* VI, pt. II, p. 224.

[88]R. Rama Rao, op.cit., p. 50.

[89]S. Krishnaswami Aiyangar, *A History of Tirupati*, vol. II, p. 81.

[90]*ARSIE* of 1919, no. 370; *MAR* of 1941, no. 28; *EC* XIV, Tn. 161 & 162; *EC* IX, Cp. 153; *EI* XXXI, pp. 139-162; *TTDES*, vol. III, nos. 157, 158 and 159: *EC* VII, Sh. 85; *SII*, vol. IV, no. 277.

[91]*EC* XIV, Md. 115.

[92]*MAR* of 1918, p. 52.

[93]K. Sarojini Devi, op.cit., p. 149.

[94]*EI* XII, p. 347.

[95]*EC* II, SB. 344; for details see M. Chidananda Murthy, "Fresh Light on Bukka's Inscription at Shravanabelgola," in *Early Vijayanagara: Studies in its History and Culture*, ed G.S. Dikshit, pp. 95-100.

[96]*EI* XVIII, pp. 110-111.

[97]*TTDES* I, no. 192.

[98]*SII* I, no. 153.

[99]*ARSIE* of 1901, no. 33; *ARSIE* of 1928-29, A. 12.

[100]*EC* III, Sr. 15.

[101]*FE*, p. 72.

[102] e.g. *EI* I, pp. 361-171; *EI* VII, pp. 17-22; *SII* VIII, no. 165; *ARSIE* of 1913, no. 371.

[103]*SITI* I, no. 406.

[104]'Abdur Razzāk, in *India in the Fifteenth Century*, ed.

R.H. Major, p. 23.

[105]D. Devakunjari, *Hampi*, pp. 1-2.

[106]C.T.M. Kotraiah, "The Metropolis of the Vijayanagara Empire," in *The Vijayanagara Urbanity*, ed. K.R. Basava Raja, p. 15.

[107]D. Devakunjari, op. cit., p. 4.

[108]*Indian Archaeology: A Review*, 1975-76, p. 20; also *ARIE* of 1975-76, B. 94.

[109]IA VI, pp. 85-88; also *JBBRAS*, XII, p. 337 (late 7th century A.D.).

[110]*QJMS* VII, 4, p. 286 (late 10th century A.D.); *SII* IX, pt. I, no. 80 (A.D. 1018); *ARIE* of 1975-'76, B. 95. (A.D. 1077); H. Krishna Sastri, *Munirabad Stone Inscription of 13th year of Tribhuvanamalla* (A.D. 1088).

[111]*Annual Report of the ASI of 1925-'26*, p. 140. (A.D. 1237).

[112]*ARSIE* of 1935-36, no. 353 (early 14th century A.D.)

[113]R. Narasimhacharya, *Karnataka Kavi Charite*, pt. I, pp. 257-277.

[114]*FE*, p. 299.

[115]B.A. Saletore, *Social and Political Life in the Vijayanagara Empire (A.D. 1346-A.D. 1646)* (henceforth cited as *Soc. & Pol. Life*), vol. I, pp. 102-106.

[116]Sugandha, "History and Archeology of Anegondi" (Ph.D. diss.), p. 49.

[117]M.S. Nagaraja Rao, (ed.), *Vijayanagara : Progress of Research 1983-'84* (hereafter cited as *VPR '83-84*), no. 74, p. 50.

[118]*FE*, p. 259.

[119]*EC* VII, Sk. 281.

[120]*EC* V, Cn. 256.

[121]*VPR '83-84*, no. 2, p. 21 & Ibid., no. 3, p. 23.

[122]Ibid., no. 11, p. 29.

[123]*SII* I, no. 152.

[124]*FE*, p. 246 and p. 252.

[125]Ibid., p. 262.

[126]J.M. Fritz, G. Michell and M.S. Nagaraja Rao, *The Royal Centre at Vijayanagara: Preliminary Report*, pp. 9-13.

[127]Burton Stein, "The Problematical 'Kingdom of Vijayanagara'," in *Vij. City & Emp.*, vol. 1, p. 2.

[128]Fritz, Michell and Nagaraja Rao, op. cit., p. 8.

[129]*FE*, p. 290.

[130]J.M. Fritz and G. Michell, "Interpreting the Plan of a Medieval Hindu Capital," *World Archaeology*, 19, no. 1, p. 122.

[131]*VPR '83-84*, no. 11, p. 29.

[132]*SII* IV, no. 267.

[133]*VPR '83-84*, no. 12, p. 29.

[134]*SII* IV, no. 272.

[135]*SII* IV, no. 254.

[136]*ARSIE* of 1935-36, no. 337.

[137]*SII* IX, pt. II, no. 533.

[138]Ibid.

[139]*SII* IV, no. 245.

[140]Ibid., nos. 272, 273, 278.

[141]*FE*, p. 256.

[142]*SII* IX, pt. II, no. 564.

[143]Ibid.

[144]*SII* IV, nos. 265 & 266.

[145]Ibid., no. 248.

[146]*SII* I, no. 153.

[147]*SII* IV, nos. 265 and 266.

[148]Ibid., no. 245.

[149]*SII* XVI, no. 217.

[150]*Pampamahatmya*, an English translation by G.S. Kalburgi (not yet published) of *Srī Pampa Mahatme or the Holy Eminence of the Pampa* (Kannada) by Guru Omsiddhalingeshvara Swami, 1983; the latter is based on the Sanskṛit text, in Telugu characters, entitled *Srī Pampa Mahatme*, ed. Koratamaddi Venkataramasastri, 1933 (henceforth cited as *Pampamahatmya*. It is the English translation that is referred to throughout this monograph and since it is not yet published chapters, instead of pages, are cited) pt. I, chapter 75.

[151]*SII* IX, pt. II. no. 504.

[152]*ARSIE* of 1922, no. 683.

[153]*SII* IX, pt. II, nos. 539 and 573.

[154]Ibid., nos. 573 and 595.

[155]G. Michell, "Architectural Traditions at Vijayanagara : Temple Styles," in *Vij. City & Emp.*, vol. 1, p. 274.

[156]G.M. Moraes, *The Kadamba Kula*, pp. 310-312.

[157]K.V. Raman, "Hoysaḷa Influence on the Vijayanagara Art," in *Śrīkaṇṭhikā: Dr. Srīkantha Sastri Felicitation Volume*, pp. 55-58.

[158]*SII* IV, no. 280.

[159]See *Vijayanagara : Progress of Research 1979-'83, (VPR '79-83)*, p. 63.

[160]G. Michell, op.cit., pp. 275-276.

[161]Dr. A.L. Dallapiccola, personal communication.

[162]G. Michell, "Architectural Traditions at Vijayanagara : Islamic Styles," in *Vij. City & Emp.*, vol. 1, pp. 282-286.

[163]C.S. Patil, "Palace Architecture at Vijayanagara : New Excavations," in *Vij. City & Emp.*, vol. 1, pp. 229-239.

[164]'Abdur Razzāk, *loc. cit.*

[165]A. Nikitin, in *India in the 15th Century*, ed. R.H. Major, p. 29.

[166]Varthema, *The Itinerary of Ludovico di Varthema*, trans. J.W. Jones, p. 51.

[167]M.S. Nagaraja Rao and C.S. Patil, "Epigraphical References to City Gates and Watch Towers of Vijayanagara," in *VPR '83-84*, pp. 96-100.

[168]*VPR '84-87*, nos. 83 and 84.

[169]Ibid., no. 105.

[170]Caesar Frederick, in *Purchas His Pilgrims*, by Samuel Purchas, pp. 93-98.

[171]*Annual Reports of the ASI* of 1903-04, p. 63 and of 1916-17, pp. 28-29.

A number of examples can also be given of the damage wrought by treasure seekers or vandals at the site even during the past few years. One very recent example will prove that the destruction at Vijayanagara was not exclusively the work of the looters of A.D. 1565. In temple (NG m/2) by the river there are three magnificent groups of portrait sculptures, with labels mentioning the names of the figures (see *VPR '83-84*, pp. 140-141 and plates XCI a and b and XCII a). These are the finest portrait sculptures at the site. Early in 1988, one of these groups (Ibid., Plates XCI b) was severely mutilated by some unknown persons. This was, indeed, a senseless and vicious act of vandalism.

CHAPTER 2

Śaivite Traditions

Even before the founding of the Vijayanagara empire the site was a significant Śaivite pilgrimage area. Pre-Vijayanagara period Śaivite shrines, such as those on Hēmakūṭa hill and the south bank, some even dating back to the ninth and tenth centuries A.D., along with epigraphical and literary data, prove the antiquity of the place as a Śaivite *kshētra.* The most ancient religious tradition within the city is that of Paṁpā-dēvī, the local goddess of Haṁpe-tīrtha, who in course of time came to be absorbed into the Śaivite pantheon by marriage to Virūpāksha, a form of Śiva. Virūpāksha was, undoubtedly, the most important deity of the city in pre-Vijayanagara, Vijayanagara and post-Vijayanagara times. He was the guardian deity of the Vijayanagara kings and empire. Bhairava, Vīrabhadra, Gaṇēśa and a number of other Śaivite deities were also popular, especially in the Vijayanagara period.

1. Paṁpā

The eponymous goddess Paṁpā is the local goddess and the most ancient deity of the Haṁpe (Haṁpi) area. This is evident from the fact that the place, the pilgrimage area, the river and a lake are named after her and even the principal male deity of the city is often referred to as Paṁpāpati (i.e., the lord or husband of Paṁpā).

This word Haṁpe (Haṁpi) is derived from Paṁpā (or Paṁpē). The letter 'P' in old Kannaḍa is often replaced by 'H' in more modern Kannaḍa. Indeed, the goddess herself is at times referred to as Haṁpā-dēvī[1] and the city as Paṁpā. For example, according to the *Pampamahatmya,* "the great city of Paṁpā is situated on the south bank of the river Paṁpā."[2] 'Haṁpe', probably the oldest name of the city, has been in continuous usage till modern times. The pilgrimage area was generally referred to as Paṁpā-kshētra, although it was also known as Paṁpā-pura, Bhāskara-kshētra, Virūpāksha-kshētra, etc.[3] The popular usage of "Paṁpā' as a name of the Tuṅgabhadrā at the site is not only attested to by the *Pampamahatmya,* but also by a few Vijayanagara inscriptions that record grants made on "the banks of the Paṁpā."[4] The Paṁpā lake is mentioned in the *Pampamahatmya*[5] as well as in epigraphs.[6]

It is difficult to determine the antiquity of this local goddess. Possibly, her cult goes back to very early times, for the "worship of the goddess probably has deep roots in prehistoric Indian religion, predating the introduction of Aryan forms of worship."[7] It is certainly anterior to the seventh century A.D. when an epigraph of the Chālukyan king Vināyaditya refers to a royal camp "on the banks of the Paṁpā."[8] There are also two later Chālukyan records of the late tenth[9] and early eleventh century[10] that mention "by Paṁpe" and the "tīrtha of Paṁpāpura," respectively.

There is not sufficient evidence for us to determine the exact nature and origin of the this local goddess. According to one opinion Paṁpā was "originally the goddess of the tribal food gatherers who was entrusted with the function of ensuring equitable distribution of the tribal catch."[11] However, there is little literary or archaeological data to back this viewpoint. It is significant that the earliest references to the word "Paṁpā" (i.e., in the above-mentioned seventh and tenth century inscriptions) is either to the river or the lake. This hints at the possibility of the genesis of Paṁpā as an aquatic deity, who, in the course of time, came to be personified as the local goddess of the site. The fact that the Tuṅgabhadrā is considered very holy lends credence to this. It is referred to as the "Ganges of the South" in an eleventh century inscription[12] and in a Vijayanagara record[13] and this view prevails even today.[14]

This local or folk goddess came to be "Sanskṛitized" in the pre-Vijayanagara period by marriage to Virūpāksha, a form of Śiva. Marriage with Śiva or one of his incarnations was the almost universal and favourite method in south

India of absorbing local goddesses into the brahmanical pantheon.[15] As a result Paṁpā came to be considered an incarnation of the goddess Pārvatī and is, therefore, often referred to as Paṁpāṁbikā,[16] Aṁbikā being another name of Pārvatī . The story of Paṁpā and Virūpāksha follows the typical pattern of the southern *sthaḷa-purāṇas* (texts that recount the mythic origin and traditions of temples), the central element in which is the myth of the *dēvī*'s marriage to the god.[17] Most of these *sthaḷa-purāṇas* adhere to the classical Śaiva mythology of the goddess using *tapas* as a means to win Śiva for her husband, the gods sending Kāma to wound Śiva with the arrows of passion, with the important exception that the goddess is made to perform her austerities in a particular local spot, instead of in the Himālayas, her usual place of penance.[18] Thus, the *Pampamahatmya*, the local *sthaḷa-purāṇa*, describes Paṁpā as the "mind-born" daughter of Brahmā, who performed her severe *tapas* at Paṁpā-saras[19] and as a result was married to Virūpāksha.[20] Later, she was reborn as Dakshayānī, daughter of Daksha[21] and again as Pārvatī, daughter of the Himālaya mountain.[22] As a result Virūpāksha came to be known as Paṁpā-Virūpāksha, or more commonly, as Paṁpāpati. Among the ceiling frescoes in the *mahā-raṅga-maṇḍapa* of the Virūpāksha temple are the scenes of Kāma-dēva shooting his arrow of flowers at Virūpāksha (Śiva), who is seated in meditation, and the divine marriage of Paṁpā and Virūpāksha (Pārvatī and Śiva). The most important annual festivals in the Virūpāksha temple to this day are the *Phalapūjā* (betrothal) and the *Kalyāṇōtsava* (marriage festival).

As a result of this process of Sanskṛitization the goddess became less important and from her former position as the senior most and preeminent deity of the place she was gradually reduced to the position of a minor deity. This is proved by the fact that there is only one shrine dedicated to Paṁpā in the entire city, the small and rather insignificant one in the Virūpāksha temple complex (see Fig. 13:21). This is a pre-Vijayanagara, structure that, as a result of the sixteenth century expansion of the Virūpāksha temple, got absorbed into the temple complex.

In the Vijayanagara iconography, too, Paṁpā-dēvī does not figure prominently. The present *mūrti* in the Paṁpā-dēvī shrine is of a goddess standing in *dvibhaṅga*, with a lotus in her right hand and the left hand hanging down. There is nothing exceptional in its iconography, since this is the traditional way in which many goddesses (Pārvatī, Lakshmī, etc.) are depicted. Probably this is not the original *mūrti*.[23] Many sculptures of goddesses are to be found in the city (see chapter 7, 3) but none that can be identified definitively as Paṁpā-dēvī.

Epigraphical references to this goddess are also few. In the A.D. 1199 inscription from the Durgā temple she is mentioned along with other divinities of Haṁpā-tīrtha.[24] From the Vijayanagara period, the only example of a royal grant referring to her is one of Harihara II, of A.D. 1385, which records a grant made in the presence of "Tuṅga, Paṁpā and Virūpāksha".[25] There is an undated inscription in the city in which a small gate (NQ h) is named "the gate of Haṁpā-dēvī." evidently after the goddess.[26] The most important reference to her is in the inscription from the Rāmachandra temple (NR w/1) invoking Paṁpā's blessing on king Dēvarāya.[27]

Thus, Paṁpā is the most ancient and originally the most important deity of the site. However, her adoption into the Śaivite pantheon resulted in her virtual relegation to the background.

2. Virūpāksha

Haṁpi is the centre of the Virūpāksha cult. This god had emerged as the principal deity of the site before the founding of the empire. He continued to enjoy this position of preeminence throughout the empire period (except briefly during the later Tuḷuva times, when the Viṭhala cult temporarily eclipsed the cult of Virūpāksha in the city) and in the post-1565 times also. The great Virūpāksha or Paṁpāpati temple complex (NF w/1) remains an important pilgrimage centre even today. Due to the importance of this deity in the city and the empire, during the Vijayanagara period two more temples were dedicated to him in the capital and many Virūpāksha temples were built throughout the empire.

The name Virūpāksha literally means "he with oblique eyes"[28] or "of misformed eyes."[29] The Virūpāksha-liṅga on Hēmakūṭa is included among the sixty-eight *svayaṁbhū* (i.e., "self manifest", not fashioned by man but naturally manifest in nature) *liṅgas*.[30] In inscriptions[31] and in literary works[32] the deity is often referred to as 'Virūpāksha- liṅga'. Paes, the Portuguese visitor, has described the principal idol in the Virūpāksha temple as "a round stone without any shape."[33] Thus Śiva as Virūpāksha is not portrayed in the iconic form. Indeed, the iconic *utsava-mūrtis* (processional images) of the Virūpāksha temple are known as Śiva and Pārvatī , rather than Virūpāksha and Paṁpa-dēvī, names which seem to be reserved for the *liṅga* within the sanctum and the image of the goddess within her shrine.[34] The *svayaṁbhū* Virūpāksha-liṅga is usually covered with a mask. That this was the practice even in the Vijayanagara times is evident from a panel of the ceiling frescoes[35] of the *mahā-raṅga-maṇḍapa* in which the Virūpāksha-liṅga, with Nandi in attendance before him, is shown.[36]

Virūpāksha is called "the lord of Hēmakūṭa."[37] In inscriptions there seems to be some disagreement as to the location of the Virūpāksha temple vis-à-vis Hēmakūṭa, for Virūpāksha is said to be "in Hēmakūṭa" (Appendix A : no. 35), "in the region of Hēmakūṭa" (no. 38), "at the foot of Hēmakūṭa" (nos. 48 and 49) and "near Hēmakūṭa" (no. 68); while, according to the *Jāṁbavatīkalyāṇam*, the drama by Krishṇadēvarāya, Virūpāksha resides "on the top of the mountain Hēmakūṭa."[38] The temple itself is not on the hillock, but at the foot of it. In fact however, there is no contradiction, because 'Hēmakūṭa' is seen in two ways. Firstly, is refers to the sacred hill situated on the south bank of the river (Fig.1:B), "Hēmakūṭa mountain is like the heart of the sacred region of the Paṁpā."[39] Secondly, it also means the entire pilgrimage area, comprising not only the city and its suburbs but also the surrounding region, for it is claimed that "Hēmakūṭa has a circumference of nearly ten to twelve miles. There are four main gateways and four subsidiary ones."[40] Thus , it is equated with Paṁpā-kshētra, which is also described as having the four main and the four subsidiary gates.[41]

Virūpāksha-liṅga is considered to be at the centre of the *kshētra*. He is the ruler or the presiding deity of Paṁpā- kshētra.[42] The four main gates of Hēmakūṭa/Paṁpā-kshētra are Kinnarēśvara to the east, Jambavatēśvara to the south, Sōmagiri to the west and Māṇibhadrēśvara to the north.[43] If in a wider sense 'Paṁpā-kshētra' includes the entire pilgrimage area, in a more limited sense it refers only to the sacred area on the south bank of the river. For while Virūpāksha (Appendix A: nos. 2, 5, 8, 24, etc.)—and in one inscription even Viṭhalēśvara (Appendix A: no.114)—are said to be in Paṁpā-kshētra, inscriptions at the site do not include the temples in the "urban core" or the "suburban centres" within Paṁpā-kshētra. Indeed, according to a record of 1410-11 A.D., the Mālyavanta hill (Figure 1: C), within the "urban core", is to the "east of Paṁpā-kshētra."[44]

Already by the twelfth century A.D. Haṁpi was a reputed religious centre, with Virūpāksha as its presiding deity. This is evident from the writings of the twelfth century Vīraśaiva poets Harihara and his nephew Rāghavāṅka. Harihara lived for many years and produced some of his greatest works under the shadow of the Virūpāksha temple. Among his writings is the *mahā-kāvya, Girijā-kalyāṇa*, about the marriage of Śiva and Pārvatī (Paṁpā) which celebrates the *sthaḷa-purāṇa* of the place. This work begins and ends with salutations to Paṁpā-Virūpāksha. This proves that the conflation of the Paṁpā and Virūpāksha cults was already an established fact by the twelfth century A.D. His *Paṁpāśataka* is a centum of verses in praise of Virūpāksha. Each of the hundred and one stanzas of the *Rakshakavacha* ends with "let god Virūpāksha, the lord of Paṁpā-pura protect me." Rāghavāṅka was also a native of Haṁpi. In his *Hariśchandra-kāvya*, he begins with the praise of Paṁpā-Virūpāksha and Paṁpāṁbikā. At the end he again invokes the Virūpāksha-liṅga and gives his name as Haṁpeya Rāghavāṅka.[45]

Epigraphical data supports the literary evidence of the existence of the Virūpāksha temple in pre-Vijayanagara times. The A.D. 1199 inscription on a stone slab in the Durgā temple (Fig.12:28) records a grant to god Virūpāksha and other deities of Haṁpā-tīrtha.[46] Another of A.D. 1237 on a slab in the northern *gōpura* of the Virūpāksha temple, mentions the gift of the revenue of a village by the Hoysaḷa king Sōmēśvara for the worship of Virūpāksha at Paṁpā-kshētra and for the feeding of brāhmaṇas in the *chattra* attached to it.[47]

There is also corroborating monumental data on this. The temple complex is a collection of buildings, erected at different periods, some dating back to the pre-Vijayanagara times. For example, large parts of the Paṁpā and Bhuvanēśvarī shrines (Fig. 13: 21 & 22) appear to be of the later Chālukyan period, of about the eleventh or twelfth century A.D. The pillars are of the lathe-turned type. The Bhuvanēśvarī shrine has an elaborately carved ceiling, highly decorative door-frames and delicately carved and pierced cut-work screens. The shrines to the north of the complex are mostly pre-Vijayanagara, among the earliest being the Durgā temple in the Rashṭrakūṭa idiom of the ninth to tenth centuries A.D.[48] The original pre-Vijayanagara shrine of Virūpāksha can hardly be seen since it is totally enveloped by the empire-period additions. Probably, it was a small structure, like the pre-Vijayanagara Durgā temple or the small temples on Hēmakūṭa, comprising only a *cella*, an antechamber and, possibly, a *maṇḍapa*. In other words, the original Virūpāksha temple included only the sanctum and one or two chambers in front of it. There would have been no enclosure wall around it. A north-south pathway would have linked it with the shrines to its south atop Hēmakūṭa and those to its north, up to the river. The existence of such a pathway is proved by the presence of the double storeyed south (NL b/21) and north (NF w/3) gateways on Hēmakūṭa. The latter no longer serves any purpose since it now fronts the enclosure wall of the Virūpāksha complex, built during the empire period expansion of the temple.

The Virūpāksha cult gained greatly in importance with the founding of the Vijayanagara empire, with its capital built in the proximity of this temple. The founders accepted Virūpāksha as their patronal deity, a practice continued by the later Saṅgamas and also the Sāḷuva and Tuḷuva rulers (whose *Ishṭadēvatas*, or personal deities, were Vaishṇava gods such as Veṅkaṭēśvara, Viṭhala or Narasiṁha). Thus of Harihara II it is written that along with the city he inherited "Virūpāksha himself as the supreme deity of his family."[49] This king is described as a "royal bee at the lotus feet of (the god) Virūpāksha."[50] He and his successors, up to Dēvarāya II, are described in epigraphs as ruling in Vijayanagara "in the presence of the god Virūpāksha."[51]

The name of the guardian deity was adopted as the "sign-manual" by the emperors of Vijayanagara (the Śaivite Saṅgamas and the Vaishṇava Sāḷuvas and Tuḷuvas). Their inscriptions usually end with "Śrī Virūpāksha," which took the place of the signature of the emperor. Even after A.D. 1565 and the shift of the capital from Vijayanagara, the early Āraviḍu rulers, up to Śrīraṅga I, continued to sign their grants with "Śrī Virūpāksha." Veṅkaṭa II A.D. 1586-1614 broke this tradition forever by replacing "Śrī Virūpāksha" by "Śrī Veṅkaṭēśa" at the end of all grants. [52]

Such was the importance of this divinity that from the reign of Bukka I onwards, grants made in the capital by kings and others in the presence of a deity were usually made in the presence of Virūpāksha (see Appendix A). During the Saṅgama period, except for a few grants made in the presence of god Chandramauḷi and one in the presence of Viṭhalēśvara, the rest are all registered in the presence of the guardian deity. An inscription of Dēvarāya II even refers to the special "*dāna maṇḍapa*" in the presence of Virūpāksha.[53] From the Sāḷuva period onwards some grants also began to be issued in the presence of Viṭhala and in the last twenty years before the destruction of the city in A.D. 1565 practically all the grants were made in the presence of the latter.

The Vijayanagara period saw the tremendous expansion of the temple complex (Plates 1&2). We have only one inscription mentioning constructional activity in the temple, that of Kṛishṇadēvarāya, dated A.D. 1509-10, made on the occasion of his coronation.[54] It mentions the construction of the *mahā-raṅga-maṇḍapa* (Fig. 12: I), the inner *gōpura* (E) and the repair of the outer *gōpura* (A) by the king. The approximate dating of the other additions to the complex have to be done either on stylistic grounds or with reference to these dated structures.

By early fifteenth century, the original pre Vijayanagara temple must have already been enclosed by the addition of a closed *pradakshiṇā-patha* (circumambulatory passage) and the *raṅga-maṇḍapa*, one or more antechambers, and the open, pillared passage on the three sides of the *vimāna*. The granite portion of the northern *gōpura* is also of the fifteenth century (its brick and mortar superstructure is a post-1565 development), for the flat pilasters on it are typical of the pre-sixteenth century *gōpuras*. The large eastern *gōpura* must also have been constructed in the fifteenth century. According to the *Narasiṁhapurāṇam* it was built by Prōluganṭi Tippa, during the reign of Dēvarāya II.[55] Since this is a late sixteenth century text, its reliability could be questioned. But the fact that this *gōpura* needed to be repaired in the early sixteenth century gives weight to the surmise that it was constructed in the fifteenth, probably the early fifteenth, century.[56] The *Virūpāksha-sthāna-varaṇanam*, written during Dēvarāya II's reign by Chandrakavi, a Vīraśaiva poet, describes the audience hall or the "court' of Paṁpeya-Virūpāksha.[57] Evidently, by this time the temple was already a fairly large and elaborate complex.

The open *mahā-raṅga-maṇḍapa* built by Kṛishṇadēvarāya, with its composite pillars, is a typical sixteenth century construction. Besides this and the inner east (*rāya*) *gōpura*, other sixteenth century additions include the pillared gallery around the inner courtyard and the pillared hall (D), locally known as the old '*Phalapūjā-maṇḍapa*,' which have composite pillars. The long *ratha-vīdhi* with *maṇḍapas* on either side, 732 metres long and about 10.6 metres wide, which extends from the east *gōpura* to the *Nandi-maṇḍapa* (NM b/1), was in existence in the sixteenth century. Paes describes it as "a very beautiful street of very beautiful houses with balconies and arcades, in which are sheltered the pilgrims that come to it..."[58]

Therefore, by the Tuḷuva period the temple was a large complex (see Figs. 12&13), comprising an outer and inner courtyard, three *gōpuras*, pillared halls, a kitchen, galleries, a temple tank, the principal shrine and a number of sub-shrines.

At present many subsidiary deities are placed in shrines or niches in the complex, not all of them are ncessarily from the pre-1565 period, but some of them must be. By the time the *sthaḷa-purāṇas* were composed many of these were extant, for they provide elaborate stories relating to some of the deities or mention some of the shrines.[59] These texts refer to Vighnēśvara and Kumārasvāmi at the entrance and to Narasiṁha,[60] Tarakēśvara, Pātalēśvara, Bhasmēśvara, Vyomēśvara, Rudrakēśvara and Kumbhēśvara (*liṅgas*), Navadurgā and Bhuvanēśvari,[61] Paṁpā-dēvī to the north of Virūpāksha,[62] the sacred tank known as the Brahma-kuṇḍa or the Manmukha or the Manmatha tank,[63] various *liṅgas* around the temple[64] and also the Lokapāvana tank (NF v/1) to the west of the complex.[65]

Vijayanagara period inscriptions from within the temple and elsewhere referring to the Virūpāksha temple highlight its importance. Within the temple, in the northern *gōpura* is a second slab on which is engraved the gift of land made to the temple at the command of Harihara II, in A.D. 1379.[66] The inscription of Kṛishṇadēvarāya of A.D 1509-10 apart from referring to constructional activity, also records the gift of a village to Virūpāksha "who abides on the Hēmakūṭa" and a number of golden and silver objects. It is significant that the Virūpāksha temple was singled out for generous benefactions on the occasion of Kṛishṇadēvarāya's coronation. A record of A.D. 1510 refers to the gift of some land by Bukkājī-amma, the king's grandmother.[67] On both sides of the southern entrance of the *raṅga-maṇḍapa* is an inscription of Kṛishṇadēvarāya, dated A.D. 1513 donating a number of villages and some golden and silver articles on the occasion of a solar eclipse.[68] This is the last royal grant inscribed in the temple. According to local tradition, a gem-studded gold *repoussé* mask that adorns the *liṅga* on major festival days was the gift of Kṛishṇadēvarāya. Although no record of such a gift is available, this fabulous ornament could well be the donation of this ruler. The latest inscription in the temple is the one engraved on the inner *prākāra* wall, to the south of the *rāya gōpura*. It records a private donation of land to the temple in A.D. 1529.[69] A badly flaked copy of the same grant is located elsewhere in the city.[70]

Epigraphs from elsewhere in the city and the empire reveal the popularity of the Virūpāksha temple. One from Shimoga district of A.D. 1366 records the gift of a village to god Virūpāksha at Haṁpe by Virupaṇṇa, son of Bukka I.[71] An inscription of the same year from the city notes a land grant by a minister.[72] One, engraved to the south of the Virūpāksha temple, refers to a private gift made in A.D. 1406.[73] A damaged record of the same year, from Hēmakūṭa hill, refers to god Virūpāksha.[74] A copper-plate grant of A.D. 1435 of Dēvarāya II, mentions the donation of an *agrahāra* to brāhmaṇas in which three shares are assigned to "Virūpāksha of Hēmakūṭa"[75] An inscription from Achyutarāya's reign on a pillar in a temple to the west-south-west of Haṁpi, dated A.D. 1536, records a land grant to the temple by Virupaṇṇa of Penugoṇḍa.[76] One of A.D. 1543 from outside the city is of the re-grant of a village that had reverted to the government treasury, due to the extinction of the family of the original donee, to the temple by Sadāśiva.[77] An epigraph from Chitradurga district refers to a grant of a village to the *sthānadhipati* of Virūpāksha of Haṁpe, for service in the temple, by a chieftain in A.D. 1559.[78] Some undatable inscriptions, such as one on Hēmakūṭa hill,[79] and two others[80] from elsewhere at the site, also mention gifts of land to the deity.

Some brief, undated inscriptions from Mataṅga hill note the obeisances of some private individuals to god Virūpāksha.[81] On Hēmakūta is an inscription of A.D 1494-95 invoking the blessing of Paṁpā-Virūpāksha.[82] A brief record on a boulder in the river (NF r) north of the temple, engraved around a carved pair of feet, describes it as the feet of Virūpāksha and records a curse to those who came there and did not worship.[83]

Despite the large number of records, there is no inscription within the temple complex from after the reign of Kṛishṇadēvarāya and the last royal grant is dated A.D. 1513. It is interesting that the first record within the Viṭhala temple is of A.D. 1513[84], of the royal grant made on the occasion of solar eclipse (when the king also made grants to the Prasanna Virūpāksha and Rāmachandra temples, besides the temples of Virūpāksha and Vithala). From A.D. 1513 onwards there are numerous inscriptions in the Viṭhala temple of grants and other gifts of kings and others, engraved within that temple complex. There appears to be a direct co-relation between the rising importance of the Viṭhala cult in the city and the decline in the patronage of the Virūpāksha cult. The study of grants registered in the capital in the presence of deities (see Appendix A) corroborates this. Of the period prior to Kṛishṇadēvarāya there are only three grants made in the presence of Viṭhala (nos. 25, 53 and 54). In the first few years of Kṛishṇadēvarāya reign all the grants were made in Virūpāksha's presence. But from A.D. 1516 onwards, a few were also made in the presence of Viṭhalēśvara; more that half the grants of Achyutarāya's rule were issued in the presence of Viṭhala and under Sadāśiva almost all the grants were made in the presence of the Vaishṇava deity. Thus, the Tuḷuva period saw the gradual shift in court patronage from Virūpāksha to Viṭhala, whose cult in the last years before the destruction of the city overshadowed that of Virūpāksha. There is a superstition that the decline of the Vijayanagara empire was due to the denial of his rightful place to Virūpāksha, the guardian deity.[85]

The catastrophe of A.D. 1565 did not result in the destruction of the Virūpāksha temple. Although there are no post-1565 epigraphical references to the temple, there are literary mentions of it. For example, the *Chennabasava Purāṇa*, by the Vīraśaiva Virūpāksha Paṇḍita, written in A.D. 1584 begins with salutations to Paṁpā-Virūpāksha.[86] According to the *Rāmarājiyamu*, by Venkayya, the Āravīḍu prince Tirumala, a nephew of Śrīraṅga III built the lofty eastern *gōpura* of the Virūpāksha temple and maintained the worship of Virūpāksha.[87] Since the *gōpura* is a pre-1565 monument, this may refer to some major repair or renovation of it.

Many Vīraśaivas (e.g., Harihara in the twelfth, Chandrakavi in the fifteenth and Virūpāksha Paṇḍita in the sixteenth centuries) had a special devotion to Paṁpā-Virūpāksha. But according to tradition, the great Vidyāraṇya was also closely associated with this temple.[88] It is likely that, at least from Vijayanagara times onwards, the temple was under the supervision of the head of Vidyāraṇya-svāmi *maṭha,* which is just behind the temple and has direct access to it, and that it was served by Smārta brāhmaṇas. This is the situation at present.

Due to the great veneration of Virūpāksha by the Vijayanagara rulers, the temple of Prasanna Virūpāksha (NQ y/1) was constructed within the "royal centre". This deserted monument is known nowadays as the 'Underground Temple'. Built in a number of successive phases spanning the whole Vijayanagara period, the temple consists of a "confusing cluster of shrines, columned halls, colonnades, porches, altars, and gateways"[89] (see Fig.14). At the nucleus of this is a small temple comprising only a sanctuary, antechamber and an open-columned porch, which is probably the earliest intact structure in the "royal centre".[90] The location of the temple and the numerous additions made to it indicate its importance. There is only one inscription[91] inside this temple. Dated A.D. 1513, it records the grant by Kṛishṇadēvarāya of villages, gardens, etc. to Prasanna Virūpāksha. Another record of the same date on a boulder near Kaḍirāṁpuram[92] specifically mentions one of the villages granted by the king.

The construction of a third temple to this deity is revealed by two inscriptions of A.D. 1398 on Hēmakūṭa, one intact and the other damaged.[93] These state that god Virūpāksha manifested himself in Hēmakūṭa and that Virūpāksha-Paṇḍita and Vināyaka-Paṇḍita constructed a shrine for the deity together with a *śukanāsa* and excavated a tank to the left of the temple. The undamaged inscription is found on the vertical face of a tank near temple NL b/19. It is likely that the latter is the temple mentioned in this record. This east-facing temple in the early Vijayanagara style consists of a shrine (*garbha-gṛiha*), an antechamber (*śukanāsa*) and a *maṇḍapa* (Plate 3). The tank is to the left of the temple.

At present a pre-Vijayanagara temple on Hēmakūṭa, NL b/13, is locally known as the Mūla ("root" or original) Virūpāksha temple. The fairly large *liṅga* here is not a *svayaṁbhū* one. Nowadays the Vīraśaivas, who generally do not enter the great Virūpāksha temple, worship here. However, there appears to be no evidence to indicate whether or not this was a Virūpāksha temple in Vijayanagara times.

So great was the popularity of the Virūpāksha cult that shrines to this deity were constructed during the Vijayanagara period in different parts of the empire. Epigraphs recording the construction of or grants to Virūpāksha temples are available from the districts of Anantapur,[94] North Arcot,[95] Kolar,[96] South Kanara,[97] Chikmagalur,[98] and Bellary.[99]

3. Bhairava

Bhairava, an embodiment or manifestation of the terrible aspect of Śiva, was one of the more popular Śaivite deities in the city. The word 'Bhairava' literally means terrible, frightful, horrible or formidable. Bhairava is so called because he both protects the universe (*bharaṇa*) and because he is terrifying (*bhīshaṇa*).[100] He is also known as Kālabhairava, for even Kāla (the god of death) trembles before him.[101] Bhairava has many forms; according to the various *āgamas* there are sixty-four Bhairavas, divided into groups of eight.

Iconographically, Bhairava is depicted with round eyes, side-tusks and a flabby belly. He wears a garland of skulls and is adorned with snakes as ornaments. He has several arms, holding various weapons.[102] Bhairava is accompanied by a dog. This emphasises his unorthodox character, because the dog is considered unclean among the quadrupeds.[103] In the Vijayanagara sculptures, the usual attributes of Bhairava are the *khaḍga* (sword) and *kapāla* (skull-bowl) in the lower hands, the *triśūla* (trident) and *ḍamaru* (small hour-glass shaped drum) in the upper ones. At times, a skull is shown attached to the hand holding the *kapāla*. This is the skull of Brahmā. For although in the classical myth of Śiva cutting off the head of Brahmā, Śiva is himself burdened with Brahmā's skull and forced to wander about to atone for the sin of brāhmaṇicide, in another version the sin is transferred to Bhairava, an aspect of Śiva.[104] Occasionally, Bhairavī, the consort of Bhairava, is shown alongside the deity. She holds the same attributes as the god.

Bhairava was especially venerated by the Pāśupatas, Kāḷāmukhas, Kāpāḷikas and Nāthas.[105] Of these sects, the Kāḷāmukhas were active in the city till the early fifteenth century and the Nāthas were probably also present.[106] When the Kāḷāmukhas were absorbed into the Vīraśaiva fold, the veneration of Bhairava was continued by the latter.[107]

Bhairava is rarely found as the principal deity in the sanctum of a shrine or temple. More commonly, he is one of the *parivāradēvatas* in the Śiva temples.[108] Bhairava also acts as a guardian deity and is, therefore, often found in gateways.[109] According to the *Pampamahatmya*, each of the eight gates of Paṁpā-kshētra is connected with a guardian or Bhairava, besides the principal *liṅga*, a goddess and a Gaṇēśa.[110]

The few Vijayanagara period shrines of Bhairava extant in the city, namely, NL h/6, NM r/3 and NR h/2, are small and inconspicuous structures enshrining roughly carved *mūrtis* of the deity. To the north of the north *gōpura* of the Virūpāksha temple, east of the passageway, is the sub-shrine of Bhairava; but whether or not this was originally a Bhairava shrine cannot be determined. Sculptures of this deity are found all over the city[111] and there are also some images and a shrine of Bhairava in Ānegoṅdi.[112] These, along with the large number of Bhairava sculptures to be seen in the Haṁpi Museum[113] attest to the prevalence of Bhairava worship at the site. Pillar reliefs of Bhairava occur not only in Śaivite temples but also in some Vaishṇava ones, for example in the Rāmachandra temple, the hundred-pillared hall in the Viṭhala temple, and the pillared hall in the Tiruveṅgaḷanātha or Achyutarāya temple.

Epigraphical references to Bhairava in Vijayanagara are few; these are not from the city proper but from the metropolitan area. Two are from Ānegoṅdi, both of the reign of Dēvarāya II. The first records a land grant by the king to god Bhairava of Ānegoṅdi.[114] The second mentions the construction of the temple of Bhairavadēva.[115] Another inscription is located on a rock to the east of the Kaḷasāpura-Āñjanēya temple on the Kāmalāpuram-Kaṁpili road (about 1 1/2 kilometres beyond the limits of the map of the city proper). It records a gift of land made in A.D. 1556 to the temple of Ānanda-Bhairava near Kaḷasāpura by the Āravīḍu chief *Mahāmaṇḍalēśvara* Raghunātharājadēva-Mahārāja.[116]

Bhairava was thus a popular deity in the city. We have no evidence of the existence of this cult in the city in pre-Vijayanagara times, except for the mention of Bhairavadēva among the gods of Haṁpā-tīrtha in the A.D.1199 inscription from the Durgā temple.[117] This is not surprising, because although images of this deity were common from the ninth century onwards, prior to the Vijayanagara period the erection of temples exclusively for Bhairava is hardly known.[118] Sculptures and inscriptions prove that Bhairava worship was prevalent from the Saṅgama to the Tuḷuva periods. However, the absence of any large temple dedicated to the deity and the limited number of the Bhairava shrines and of inscriptions referring to him indicate that, despite his popularity, Bhairava was a minor god and not one of the principal deities at the site. Even though Bhairava worship received some court patronage (as seen in the grants of Dēvarāya II and of the Āravīḍu chief), on the whole, the greater support and patronage of the cult seem to have come from the people.

4. Vīrabhadra

Vīrabhadra was another of the *saṁhara* (destructive) aspects of Śiva that was highly popular in Vijayanagara . Vīrabhadra is a form Śiva assumed at the time of the destruction of the *yajña* (sacrifice) of Daksha.[119] Bhadrakāḷī is his consort.[120]

There is no evidence of the cult of Vīrabhadra in the city prior to the empire period, for the same reason as in the case of Bhairava, namely, that temples dedicated to Vīrabhadra hardly existed before Vijayanagara times.[121] It is probable that of these two *saṁhara-mūrtis* Bhairava gained popularity here before Vīrabhadra. For in the early structures, such as the early fifteenth century parts of the Rāmachandra temple complex (NR w/1) and the so-called 'Āñjanēya temple' (NV o/1) of the reign of the Mallikārjuna, while reliefs of Bhairava are present there are none of Vīrabhadra. However once the Vīrabhadra cult gained ground, it outdid the Bhairava cult in popularity. There are many more shrines and temples dedicated to Vīrabhadra than to Bhairava.

The Vīrabhadra cult owed its popularity to a great extent to the Vīraśaivas.[122] In the invocatory verses in Vīraśaiva texts and inscriptions Vīrabhadra is often mentioned. It may seem surprising that the Vīraśaivas worshipped Vīrabhadra, who is represented in an iconic form, for the Vīraśaiva reform strongly disapproved of image worship. According to the Vīraśaiva doctrine, Śiva must be worshipped only in the form of the *Ishṭaliṅga*, i.e. the personal *liṅga* obtained from the *guru* at the time of initiation. The veneration of Vīrabhadra is, therefore, a later growth in Vīraśaivism. Changes in fundamental principles and practices occurred in the course of time within this sect, as happened with earlier religions like Buddhism, which had also strongly opposed image-worship. Possibly, one reason for the adoption of the cult of Vīrabhadra and the worship of his *mūrtis* was to counteract the influence of Jainism and Vaishṇavism.[123] Another reason was the absorption into Vīraśaivism of the Kāḷāmukhas who were worshippers of *saṁhara-mūrtis*. Through their influence the worship of Vīrabhadra, not found in the early phase of Vīraśaivism, became popular among the Vīraśaivas in general.[124]

However the question may be asked as to why Vīraśaivas preferred the worship of this particular *saṁhara-mūrti*. The myth of the origin of Vīrabhadra provides a clue to this. This deity was specifically created by Śiva, together with Bhadrakāḷī formed by Pārvatī, to destroy the *yajña* of Daksha and wreck havoc on the sacrificial place. Therefore, the Vīraśaivas, who reject Vēdic traditions, sacrifices and rituals, have a special affinity to this divinity. Moreover, the militant nature of the Vīraśaiva creed is reflected in the destructive aspect of Vīrabhadra.[125]

The Vīrabhadra icons in Vijayanagara generally are four-armed, holding the weapons prescribed in the *Kāranāgama*, that is the *khaḍga* (sword), *khētaka* (shield), *dhanus* (bow) and *bāṇa* (arrow)[126] (Plate 5). Regarding the *khaḍga* held by Vīrabhadra (an attribute of many gods in their destructive aspect), it has been suggested that "it symbolised the warring spirit of the Vīraśaivas against the non-Vīraśaivas, like Jainas and Vaishṇavas".[127] Usually Vīrabhadra is attended by Daksha, who has a goat's head, with hands joined in *añjali*. At times, he is also accompanied by Bhadrakāḷī.

The most famous Vīrabhadra temple in the Vijayanagara empire was the temple at Lēpākshi (in Anantapur district, Āndhra Pradesh) built by the brothers Virupaṇṇa and Vīraṇṇa, important chieftains during the reign of Achyutarāya. The king also made grants to this temple.[128]

Within the capital there were a number of Vīrabhadra shrines and temples. The most important of these is the one (NM g/1) on the summit of Mataṅga hill, the highest point in the city. The temple itself is of little architectural significance. There is no foundational inscription to help date its construction. On stylistic grounds it could, possibly, be assigned to the early Vijayanagara period; but it has undergone changes. Besides its strategic location, the importance of the temple is also revealed by a number of inscriptions found on the hill, in which the deity is referred to as Vīrabhadra, Vīrēśvara and Mataṅgēśvara. Among these is a partially defaced inscription referring to Vīrabhadra,[129] some epigraphs mentioning visits of private individuals to the shrine[130] and others specifying donations to the deity. Of this last category one is of Achyutarāya's reign[131] and another, though not clearly dated, is probably of Sadāśiva's period since it is a record of the Āravīdu chief Koṇḍarāja.[132] There is a *mūrti* in this temple that is currently worshipped. However, that there was a break in the conduct of rituals here is indicated by *Chennabasava Purāṇa*, composed a few years after the catastrophe of A.D. 1565 where it is mentioned that the unshakeable Vīrēśa on Mataṅga had been taken away.[133]

The Mudu Vīraṇṇa temple (NL w/3), known nowadays as the Uddhāna Vīrabhadra temple, was consecrated in A.D. 1545 by a Vīraśaiva general, Jaṅgamaya, the agent of Yera-Timmarāja, the younger brother of Aḷiya Rāmarāya, in Kṛishṇāpura, near the Hiriya Chattra (NL w/4).[134] This Vīrabhadra temple must have been attached to the Vīraśaiva *maṭha* known as the Hiriya-maṭha or Hiriya Chattra, for in many a Vīraśaiva *maṭha* there is a temple to Vīrabhadra.[135] Even today, the worship in this temple is conducted by Vīraśaiva ritualists. Although from the architectural point of the view this temple is of little importance, the enormous, 3.6 metres high, *mūrti* of Vīrabhadra is interesting.[136] The Mudu Vīraṇṇa temple is of significance as being one of the few Śaiva structures to be constructed during the Tuḷuva period, the only extant one, of which we have evidence, that was built during Sadāśiva's reign.

Besides these two important temples, there are also a number of small, undated and unpretentious Vīrabhadra shrines in the city.[137] The Vīrabhadra cult evidently enjoyed wide popular support and patronage.

Apart from the Vīrabhadra images in the temples and shrines there are also many independent sculptures of this deity at the site.[138] However, some of the largest and finest Vīrabhadra sculptures are found in the site Museum.[139] There is a lot of variety in the Vīrabhadra icons. In some the god is standing in *samabhaṅga,* in others he is in *tribhaṅga,* or in a striding pose or even kneeling. Although most of the images are four-armed, two-armed and even multi-armed *mūrti*s also exist. There is variation in the manner in which the attributes are held and in the ornaments and apparel of the deity[140] Vīrabhadra reliefs are also found on pillars, especially in Śaivite temples.

The numerous shrines and sculptures of Vīrabhadra reveal the extensive popularity enjoyed by this deity in Vijayanagara. This cult has not disappeared from the site, since in two temples the deity is worshipped to this day.

5. Gaṇēśa and Kārtikēya

Gaṇēśa, the eldest son of Śiva and Pārvatī , is a very prominent deity in the Hindu pantheon and also one of the most popular. Gaṇēśa or Gaṇapati is "the lord and leader of the hosts of Śiva." He is also Vighnēśvara, "the lord and master of obstacles." He is invoked by all Hindus, excepting the Śrī-Vaishṇavas, at the commencement of every religious ceremony,[141] because he, among his many attributes, is the one who removes obstacles from new undertakings, protects worshippers, and provides access to other gods and goddesses. Consequently, Gaṇēśa looms large in Hindu worship.[142]

Gaṇēśa images may be seen almost everywhere in India, not only in temples and houses, but also located near the boundaries of villages, at crossroads and river crossings, on tank bunds, under holy trees, atop doorways, in fact in all sorts of odd corners and inaccessible places.[143] However, relatively few Hindus regard Gaṇēśa as their primary deity of devotion.

This pan-Indian god was an ubiquitous deity in Vijayanagara times. Iconographic representations of Gaṇēśa are found from the pre-Vijayanagara times onwards (for example in some of the pre-empire period temples on Hēmakūṭa hill) and from the Vijayanagara period there are numerous representations of him at the site.

There are a few Gaṇēśa shrines extant in the city. On the north bank of the river, near the ferry-landing is a small, probably, pre-Vijayanagara temple (ND u/1). The *mūrti* of Gaṇēśa within is carved on a natural boulder against which the shrine is built. On the southern slope of Hēmakūṭa hill, outside the fort wall, are two shrines with large monolithic Gaṇēśa statues. The larger of the two monoliths is locally known as the Kaḍalekāḷu ("gram") Gaṇēśa. This 4.5 metres high *mūrti* is in a temple comprising a sanctum, antechamber and a fine, open pillared *maṇḍapa* (NL c/2). The smaller one, 2.4 metres high, called the Sāsivekāḷu ("mustard seed") Gaṇēśa (Plate 6), is in an open pavilion (NL g/2).[144] On the north ridge is another temple, with Gaṇēśa carved on a boulder in the back wall of its sanctuary (NN m/2). As already seen, in the Virūpāksha temple complex, too, there are some subsidiary shrines dedicated to Gaṇēśa. However, some of these may be post-1565.

A number of Gaṇēśa *mūrtis* are to be found at the site, placed in *maṇḍapas,* temples or even in the open.[145] Some of these may not have belonged to their present spots. There are Gaṇēśa scultpures also in the Haṁpi Museum.[146]

Reliefs of this god, either alone or with other deities, carved on boulders, walls, etc., are numerous.[147] Pillar reliefs of Gaṇēśa (standing, seated or dancing) occur in Śaivite temples and in many Vaishṇavite temples also. Occasionally Gaṇēśa appears on the lintels of temple doors (e.g., NF w/6, NN x/3, NN y/3). Gaṇēśa sculptures are found even in some pre-Vijayanagara temples (e.g., NF w/9 and NL b/3).

Inscriptional references to Gaṇēśa at the site are few. The earliest available one is, probably, the undated record of land grant to the god Vināyaka of Hodeya Bāgilu by king Harihara[148] (Harihara II). This refers to the Gaṇēśa sculpture near Hodeya Bāgilu (gate NR b).[149] Another of A.D.1410, during Dēvarāya I's rule, states that the minister Lakshmīdhāra Daṇḍanāyaka set up an image of Gaṇapati in a natural cavern on the southern side of Mālyavanta hill and granted land to this deity.[150] Unfortuantely, this shrine cannot be located. A third, of A.D. 1513, records Kṛishṇadēvarāya's grant of a village to Kōṭa-

Vināyaka situated on the "eastern side of the Deveri road in Vijayanagari."[151] This temple, too, cannot be traced. These three inscriptions prove that the worship of Gaṇēśa received court patronage. While the large number of sculptures of the deity found all over the site indicates that great popular patronage was also extended to this cult.

In contrast to Gaṇēśa, Kārtikēya (also called Kumāra, Subrāhmaṇya, etc) the second son of Śiva, is also a popular deity in south India, though without much following in the city. There is no evidence of independent shrines or temples dedicated to him. He might have been placed as a *parivāradēvata* in subsidiary shrines or niches in Śaivite temples. For example, there is the Kumārasvāmi shrine in the Virūpāksha complex. One of the sub-shrines, to the south of the main shrine, in the Kṛishṇa temple complex (NL m/4) has many stucco figures of this deity, seated on a peacock, on its superstructure. Possibly, this might have been a shrine dedicated to Kārtikēya. But, if so, it is strange to find a shrine of a Śaivite deity in a Vaishṇava temple. Perhaps, since the Kṛishṇa temple was built after the victorious Udayagiri campaign, the dedication of a sub-shrine to Kārtikēya, the god of war, might have been a token of gratitude for the military success.

Sculptures of Kārtikēya are also rare. Among the few extant ones is a well-executed relief in the Haṁpi Museum (no. 4 of the Museum collection) and the fine statue of this deity found, during the recent excavations conducted by the A.S.I., in a small Śiva temple (NR p/2) within the "royal centre". In Śaivite temples reliefs of Kārtikēya appear occasionally on pillars. They are not common in the Vaishṇava temples.

6. Other Śaivite deities and forms of Śiva

A number of grants issued in the capital were made in the presence of god Chandramauḷi[152]—"the one holding the moon in his hand"—evidently a form of Śiva. This deity is said to be situated "on the bank of the Tuṅgabhadrā, in Bhāskara-kshētra, at the foot Hēmkūṭa-giri" (Appendix A, no. 43). Since this is the manner in which Virūpāksha is also often described, Chandramauḷi must have been situated in the proximity of the Virūpāksha-liṅga. Besides, certain records mention grants made in the presence of both these deities (nos. 48 and 49). It is significant that the epigraphs referring to Chandramauḷi range from A.D. 1403 to 1474, i.e. from the rule of Harihara II to that of Virūpāksha II.

There are no epigraphical references at the site to help locate the shrine of Chandramauḷi, but oral tradition comes to our aid. The Vidyāraṇya-svāmi *maṭha* (NF v/3), just west of the Virūpāksha temple, has a *mūrti* of Śiva known as Chandramauḷi. It is claimed that this *mūrti,* along with that of goddess Chandramauḷēśvari, was worshipped by the original Vidyāraṇya-svāmi. These *mūrtis* play a prominent part in the annual *Rathōtsava* of the Virūpāksha temple. Chandramauḷi is four-armed; in his upper right hand he holds the moon and in his upper left hand a deer. The lower right and left hands are in the *abhaya* and *varada mudrās,* respectively.[153] Whether or not this image of Chandramauḷi belonged to the great Vidyāraṇya, it is probable that the deity referred to in the above inscriptions is the one from the Vidyāraṇya-svāmi *maṭha.* Since this *maṭha* was a branch of the Śṛīṅgēri *maṭha,* which was particularly favoured by the Saṅgamas, it is not surprising that the references to Chandramauḷi are all in the Saṅgama period inscriptions.

There are a large number of Śaiva temples and shrines at the site (Chapter 11, note 1), many of which are dilapidated and deserted today. While some of these (especially many on Hēmakūṭa hill and to the north of the Virūpāksha complex) are pre-Vijayanagara shrines, the majority belong to the empire period. Since Śiva is primarily worshipped in the aniconic form, these must have originally had *Śiva-liṅgas* in their *garbha-gṛihas.* Apart from these, many *liṅgas* are also found carved on the basal rock, in caverns or rock-shelters, especially along the river bank. Inscriptional and literary references provide the names of some of the *liṅgas.*

One of the greatest Śaivite temples within the Vijayanagara empire was the one at Śrīśailam, enshrining the Mallikārjuna-liṅga (in Kurnool district, Āndhra Pradesh). This is one of the twelve famous *Jyoti-liṅgas*[154] and hence a very important pilgrimage spot. This temple received extensive patronage from the Vijayanagara state. In this temple there are inscriptions recording the benefactions of Harihara II,[155] prince Rāmachandra, the son of Dēvarāya I,[156] Virūpāksha II,[157] Vīra Narasiṁha,[158] Kṛishṇa-dēvarāya[159] etc., besides grants of chiefs and others.[160]

Just as the importance of Virūpāksha is reflected in the setting up of temples to him in other parts of the empire, similarly Śiva was worshipped as Mallikārjuna in a number of temples in the capital.

An undated inscription on a pillar in the dilapidated temple (NQ s/2) in the Kōṭiśaṅkaradēvara Bāgilu identifies it as a temple of god Mallikārjuna.[161] Inscriptions in a rock-shelter (outside the limits of the map) to the west of the Raghunātha temple (NL q/1) refers to Cheñchara-Mallikārjuna[162] and the Śrīśaila-liṅga.[163] In the cave is a *liṅga* on a *piṭha,* the Śrīśaila-liṅga of the inscription. The Cheñchus are tribals living around Śrīśailam and are associated with god Mallikārjuna.

Inscriptions mention other Mallikārjuna temples which cannot be located. An inscription of A.D. 1529-30 records a grant made for god Mallikārjuna near Haṁpeya Virūpāksha.[164] A damaged record of A.D. 1535 mentions god Mallikārjuna of Tirumaladēvī-paṭṭaṇa.[165] An inscription of A.D. 1560 records the erection of a temple on the banks of the lake of Vijayanagaram, the consecration of Mallikārjuna therein and the grant of a garden to the deity.[166] A much-flaked epigraph on a rock to the west of the Kāmalāpuram-Haṁpi road (NQ f or g) reveals a land grant to god Mallikārjuna.[167] An undated, defaced inscription south of Mataṅga hill also records a donation to Mallikārjuna.[168]

In the village of Malpannaguḍi (on the Hospēṭ-Haṁpi road) is a Mallikārjuna temple which is still used for worship. While a major portion of the extant structures here appear to date from the Vijayanagara period, the temple itself may perhaps have existed from earlier times as may be judged from a number of images in archaic style in the temple.[169] A Kannaḍa inscription on a slab in front of the temple, of the reign of Dēvarāya I, dated A.D. 1412, records the construction of a well and watershed (the so-called "Soolai Bāvi" nearby) by Heggaḍe Sōvaṇṇa Aṇṇa. The family deity of the donor is said to be Mailāraśaṅkara.[170] Since this epigraph does not directly refer to the temple near which it is located, it is not clear whether or not the deity mentioned in it is the *mūla-mūrti* of this temple. If the epigraph does refer to this temple, then in the early fifteenth century this temple was dedicated to god Mailāra and not to Mallikārjuna, who is worshipped here at present. The *liṅga* within is not *svayaṁbhū,* hence there is no way of knowing whether it is the original icon or a later replacement. Yet, since all that is stated in the record is that Mailāraśaṅkara was "the family deity of the donor," and there is no other evidence available, the question as to the early cult affiliation of this temple must be left open.

The above inscription indicates the prevalence of the worship of another Śaivite deity, Mailāra, at the site. He is a folk deity,[171] hardly worshipped in the north, but with a great following in the south from the brāhmaṇas to the depressed classes.[172] The worship of the deity dates back to the ninth or tenth centuries of the Śaka era,[173] the cult becoming very popular in Mahārāshṭra, Karṇāṭaka, Āndhra and parts of Tamil Nāḍu between the twelfth and fourteenth centuries.[174]

This deity is known by a variety of names. In Mahārāshṭra Khaṇḍobā is the most popular, while in Karṇāṭaka he is more commonly known as Mailāra or Mallaiah. He is also called Mārtaṇḍa-Bhairava.[175] His principal consort is known as Mhāḷsā in Mahārāshṭra and as Māḷavva in the Dravida country.[176] She is also referred to as Bhairavī.

The names of the deity point to the interesting fact that he is a composite deity, a combination of Śiva, Bhairava and Sūrya.[177] He is worshipped as an immoveable *Svayaṁbhū liṅga,* a man-made moveable *liṅga* and as a *mūrti* . In the latter case his attributes are the *khaḍga, triśūla, ḍamaru* and *kapāla,* the same as those of Bhairava. His *vāhanas* are Nandi as well as the horse.[178] Being Bhairava, he is often accompanied by a dog.[179] The *mūrtis* of Mailāra can be seated, standing or riding on a horse. He is depicted either alone or accompanied by one or two consorts.[180]

Besides the early fifteenth century inscription from Malpannaguḍi, there is only one other record at the site mentioning this deity. This one specifically refers to a temple dedicated to him. Dated A.D. 1380 , it refers to the consecration of god Oreteya Mailāradēva and to the construction of a pond around a natural spring (*orate*).[181] This inscription is located to the east of the Bēṭekārara Hebbāgilu. Near the epigraph is a small temple (NY e/2), consisting of only a sanctum. This is obviously the temple of Oreteya Mailāradēva. The pond referred to in the record is situated adjacent to it.

It is interesting that both these inscriptions referring to Mailāra are of the early Vijayanagara period, when Śaivism was predominant in the city. It was evidently a popular cult in that period.

Regarding sculptures of this god, there are a few that can be identified as his. There are two at the site which might be those of Mailāra. The first is near a temple (NN x/5). Here on a panel carved onto a boulder are depicted Śiva and Pārvatī on Nandi, as well as another couple riding on a horse.[182] The carving is crude and the attributes the latter hold are hence rather indistinct. The second (NT p/1)[183] is a slab on which is carved a couple on a horse, again holding attributes that cannot be clearly ascertained owing to the rough nature of the carving.

There are two other sculptures, now in the Hampi Museum, of a male deity riding on a horse. The first[184] is a relief of a male deity, accompanied by his consort, seated on a horseback. The second[185] is fairly similar to the first one, except that here the deities on horseback are present in a panel along with some other figures. These figures do not have all the iconographical traits of Mailāra.

Mailāra in the *mūrti* form has the same characteristics as Bhairava. Hence, it is possible that some of the Bhairava images referred to earlier in this chapter[186] could be those of Mailāra. But in the absence of any epigraphical or literary evidence it is not feasible to establish whether any of these are meant to be Mailāra.

Kāḷahasti is another celebrated Śaivite centre of pilgrimage in Āndhra. This shrine, too, received many benefactions from the Vijayanagara state, especially from Kṛishṇadēvarāya[187] and Achyutarāya.[188] At the site, a label inscription on a boulder of a rock-shelter (near H.P.C power house) mentions the Kāḷahasti-liṅga. The *liṅga* referred to in the inscription is the one cut on the basal rock in this shelter.[189] Kāḷahasti is linked with Kaṇṇappa, one of the sixty-three *nayanārs* (Śaivite saints), who had manifested his intense devotion to Śiva by offering his eyes to the god. Reliefs of Kaṇṇappa occur frequently on Śaivite temple pillars in Vijayanagara city and also on the exterior walls of the Virūpāksha temple *vimāna.* Kaṇṇappa is the only *nayanār* to be often represented at the site. The stories of the spider, the snake and the elephant devotees from Kāḷahasti[190] are also popular on pillar reliefs, as well as the theme of the cow from the *sthaḷa-purāṇa* of Śrīśailam, which gave its milk as an offering to the Lord.[191]

Of the five important *liṅgas* of the holy Pampā-kshētra, mentioned in the *sthaḷa-purāṇas* of the site, the one that is definitely identifiable is Jambunātha (also known as Jambavatēśvara or Jambukēśvara) of the southern gate. The Jambunātha temple is on a hill side just a few kilometres south of Hospēṭ, along the Bellary road. It is a fairly large Vijayanagara period structure. Epigraphs point to the importance of this Śiva temple. An inscription, dated A.D. 1540, of Achyutarāya records the gift of a village to Jambunātha.[192] Another of A.D. 1543, of Salaka Rāja-Chikka-Tirumala (Achyutarāya's brother-in-law) is of a gift made to the Vīraśaiva ascetic Emmēbasavēndra, who had his head-quarters at Jambunātha.[193] Hanumantadēva of Jambukēśvara hill was the recipient of a grant made by Sadāśiva.[194]

Inscriptions reveal the consecration of other Śaivite temples or *liṅgas* at the site. The earliest of these is from an early fourteenth-century A.D. triple-shrine temple on Hēmakūṭa with Deccan style superstructures (NF w/9). The inscription, engraved on a pillar within, states that Vīra Kampiladēva, son of Mummadi-Singeya (a local ruler of Kampili in the first half of the fourteenth century), constructed the Śivālaya and installed three *liṅgas* in the memory of his parents and of a certain Perumeya-Nāyaka.[195] This was thus a memorial temple and perhaps others on the hill might also have been of the same nature. Another temple on the same hill was dedicated to Jeḍeya-Śaṅkaradēva. This is revealed by an inscription on the bed-rock to the north-east of the double-storeyed gateway (NL b/21). This epigraph, dated A.D. 1397, records the construction of a lamp-pillar in the temple of Jeḍeya-Śaṅkara by Bukkāyave, queen of Harihara II, for the merit of her preceptor Bhāskaradēvayya.[196] The lamp-pillar may be the broken one lying near the inscription and the Jeḍeya-Śaṅkaradēva temple may be one of the temples in the vicinity of the pillar.

On the south bank of the river, on the route from the Virūpāksha to the Viṭhala temple, is an inscription on the bedrock, dated January A.D 1386, that refers to the construction of a temple of Śiva to the west of the god Narasiṁha in Paṁpā-kshētra.[197] This Śiva temple (NG t/3) is the earliest clearly dated Hindu temple of the Vijayanagara period at the site. It consists of a *cella*, with a stone superstructure and a porch. A colonnade was added around these later.

Throughout the Vijayanagara period Śaivite shrines or temples continued to be constructed at the capital and its environs. However, epigraphical references are available of only a few of these. A record from Niṁbāpuram (east of Viṭhalāpura) refers to the construction by king Mallikārjuna in A.D. 1450 of a temple for god Saumya-Sōmēśvara.[198] An inscription from Ānegoṅdi mentions a land grant by Narasa-Nāyaka for the worship of god Siddha.[199] An epigraph from Nāgēnahaḷḷi of A.D. 1516, refers to the construction of the Śaiva temple of Nagēśvara in Nāgladēvī-pura.[200] An inscription from a dilapidated temple on the river bank, north-west of the Virūpāksha complex (outside the limits of the map) records the construction, in A.D.1522, of the temple of god Rāmaliṅga.[201] A record of Achyutarāya's reign, of A.D. 1531, refers to the temple of Gaurēśvara at Tirumaladēvī-ammana-paṭṭaṇa.[202] In A.D. 1534 Achyutarāya, in honour of his grandparents, erected the *siṁhāsana* of god Bukkēśvara to the west of the Virūpāksha temple and gifted a village to it. [203] From the same reign is an inscription at Ānegoṅdi about a land grant to god Mahēśa.[204] At the foot of Mataṅga hill, south of the Nandi *maṇḍapa* (NM b/1), is an inscription referring to the consecration of god Gaṅgādhara.[205] Most of these temples cannot be identified.

Liṅgas cut into the basal rock are to be frequently seen, especially along the south bank of the Tuṅgabhadrā. Around some of them are sockets for pillars, to form a *maṇḍapa*. The presence of many *liṅgas* on the river bank is mentioned in the *Hemakutakhanda*.[206] There are epigraphical or literary references to some of these *liṅgas*. The largest number are at Kōṭi-tīrtha (NG m and n). According to the *Pampamahatmya* it is so called because of the ten million *Śiva-liṅgas* in this place where god Indra did penance and propitiated Śiva.[207] This is, of course, poetic exaggeration, but there are a large number of *liṅgas* here, some with Nandis carved in relief close by. One comprises a large *liṅga* surrounded by innumerable smaller ones (Plate 7) another is of one large *liṅga* and 108 small ones. Other *liṅgas* are scattered over the area.[208] Near the largest group of *liṅgas* is an inscription recording obeisance to the thousand *liṅgas* of Kōṭiśaṅkara.[209] Near the group of 108 liṅgas is a similar record mentioning 108 *liṅgas* of Kōṭiśaṅkara.[210] Other epigraphs in this place refer to Kōṭiśaṅkara[211] and a donation to the god.[212]

Close to Kōṭi-tīrtha is Sītā-kuṇḍa (NG o/2). Near this pool of water are a few small *liṅgas*. According to the *Pampamahatmya*, at this spot Sītā did penance to propitiate the goddess Gaurī.[213] Further west, on the river bank is the holy Chakra-tīrtha (NG r). At this spot three small, separate *liṅgas* are carved. According to tradition it was here that Vishṇu performed severe penances to please Śiva, who was so moved by Vishṇu's devotion that he gave the Sudarśana-chakra (discus) to him. It is said that "even today the Sudarśana discus still resides in this holy shrine."[214] It is of interest that at Chakra-tīrtha is a small temple, still under worship, which has the fairly large and fine statue of the sixteen armed Sudarśana, wrongly called Sūrya-Nārāyaṇa.[215]

Around the bathing *ghāṭ* north of the Virūpāksha temple there are some *liṅgas*. There are inscriptions here naming *liṅgas* such as the Chamuṇḍēśvara-liṅga,[216] the Gaṅgādhara-liṅga,[217] the Vīrabhadra-liṅga[218] and the Nāgabhushana-liṅga.[219] Apart from the *liṅgas* along the south bank there are also others to be found all over the site.[220]

Nandi or Nandikēśvara, Śiva's *vāhana* and a great Śaivite devotee, is a popular minor deity. Although Nandikēśvara is at times represented as a bull faced human being or as a divine being, he is most often represented as bull.[221]

The Nandi cult assumed great importance in south India with the rise of Vīraśaivism, because the great Vīraśaiva reformer, Basava, is considered to be an incarnation of Nandi. The great popularity of Nandi in Vijayanagara must be due to the influence of this sect. A number of monolithic images of Nandi are thus to be found all over the site[222] and also in the Haṁpi Museum.[223] At times he is carved on the *pīṭha* in some Śiva temples (e.g. NN x/3). Reliefs of Nandi, usually facing a *liṅga* are also common.[224] Pillar reliefs of this divinity are also frequent.

Thus the site was an important Śaivite centre from early times. The cult of Paṁpā, the indigenous goddess, and that of Virūpāksha, the prinicipal Śaivite deity, date back to well before the foundation of the empire. Gaṇēśa was also present in pre-Vijayanagara times. Along with these, Bhairava, Vīrabhadra and other Śaivite deities gained a following in the Saṅgama period. Some of these cults have survived to this day, the great Virūpāksha temple enduring as the main cult centre in Haṁpi.

Notes

[1]*SII* IV, no. 260 and *VPR '83-84*, No. 5.

[2]*Pampamahatmya*, first part, chapter 70.

[3]C.T. M. Kotraiah, "The Metropolis of the Vijayanagara Empire," in *The Vijayanagara Urbanity*, ed. K.R. Basavaraja, p.15.

[4]*ARSIE* of 1916, no. 172 and *ARSIE* of 1922, no. 163.

[5]*Pampamahatmya*, first part chapter 7.

[6]*EC* VIII, Sb. 375 and *VPR '83-84*, no. 12.

[7]B. Stein, "Devi Shrines and Folk Hinduism in Medieval Tamilnad," in *Studies in Language and Culture of South Asia*, ed. G. Gerow and M.D. Lang, p. 79.

[8]*IA*. VI, pp. 85-88 and *JBBRAS* XII, p. 337.

[9]R. Shama Sastry, "A few Inscriptions of the Ancient Kings of Anegudi," *QJMS*, VII, p. 290.

[10]*SII* IX, pt. I, no. 80.

[11] Sugandha, *History and Archeology of Anegondi* (Ph.D. diss.), p. 21.

[12]H. Krishna Sastri, *Munirabad Stone Inscription of the 13th Year of Tribhuvanamala - (Vikramaditya VI)*, p. 12.

[13]*EC* VIII, Sb. 375.

[14]B. Venkoba Rao, Introduction to *Sri Vyasayogicaritam*, p. cv.

[15]W.T. Elmore, *Dravidian Gods in Hinduism*, p. 83 and H. Whitehead, *The Village Gods of South India*, p. 126.

[16]*Pampamahatmya*, first part, chapters 6, 61, etc.

[17]D.D. Shulman, *Tamil Temple Myths*, p. 139

[18]Ibid., p. 144.

[19]At present a lake near Ānegoṁdi is pointed out as Paṁpā-saras but, there is some difference of opinion as to the original location of this lake; see chapter IV, p. 46.

[20]*Pampamahatmya*, first part, chapters 4-7.

[21]Ibid. first part, chapters 87 and 88.

[22]Ibid., first part, chapter 90. In this chapter the story of the burning of Kāma is given.

[23]V. Filliozat, "Iconography : Religious and Civil Monuments," in *Vij. City & Emp.*, vol. 1, p. 312.

[24]*SII* IV, no. 260.

[25]*EC* V, Bl. 148.

[26]*VPR '83-84*, no. 5.

[27]*SII* IV, no. 252.

[28]T.A. Gopinatha Rao, *Elements of Hindu Iconography*, vol. 2, part I, p. 66.

[29]J. Dowson, *A Classical Dictionary of Hindu Mythology*, p. 300.

[30]T. A. Gopinatha Rao, op. cit., vol. 2, part. I, pp. 82-85.

[31]See Appendix A., nos. 27, 67, 77, 80, etc.

[32]*Pampamahatmya*, first part, chapters 9, 92 and first half of the middle part, chapters 4-5, etc.; *Hemakutakhanda of the Skanda Purana*, synopsis in English of the Sanskrit manuscript by Allan A. Shapiro (henceforth cited as *Hemakutakhanda*), chapter 4.

[33]*FE*, p. 261.

[34]Dr. A.A. Shapiro, personal communication.

[35]C.T.M. Kotraiah "Vijayanagara paintings at the Virupaksha temple, Haṁpi," *QJMS*, XLIX, p. 231.

[36]The masked Virūpāksha-liṅga and Nandi are shown in separate shrines, above the *śikharas* of which are leaping monkeys, birds, etc. At present monkeys seem to have the free run of the temple complex. Evidently, the same was true in the past. This is not surprising since the site is identified with Kishkindhā, the home of the *vānaras*!

[37]*Pampamahatmya*, first part, chapters 1 and 2 and first half of the middle part, chapters 5, 6, 7, 11, etc; *Hemkutakhanda*, chapters1, 5, 6, 15.

[38]*Sources*, p. 142.

[39]*Pampamahātmya*, last part, chapter 18.

[40]Ibid., first half of the middle part, chapter 9.

[41]Ibid., first part, chapter 8.

[42]*Hemakutakhanda*, chapters 1, 5, 6, 28.

[43]For details of the eight gates of the holy Paṁpā region see *Pampamahatmya*, first part, chapter 8f; and first half of the middle part, chapters 9-15; *Hemakutakhanda*, chapters 9-17.

[44]*SII* IV, no. 267.

[45]R. Narasimhacharya, *Karnataka Kavi Charite*, part. I, pp. 257-277.

[46]*SII* IV, no. 260.

[47]*ARSIE* of 1934-35, No. 355; *Annual Report of the ASI*, 1925-26 p. 140.

[48]D. Devakunjari, *Hampi*, p. 59.

[49]*EC* V, Cn. 256.

[50]*EC* IV, Yd. 46.

[51]*EC* VIII, Tl. 11, 23, 126, 148; *EC* VII. Sh. 70.

[52]H. Heras, *The Aravidu Dynasty of Vijayanagara*, vol. I, pp. 546 - 547.

[53]*EC* XII, Tm. II.

[54]*EI* I, pp. 361-371; *IA* V, 73-76; *SII* IV, no. 258.

[55]K.A. Nilakanta Sastri and N. Venkataramanayya, *Further Sources of Vijayanagara History* (henceforth cited as *Further Sources*), Vol. III, pp. 46-47.

[56]The granite portion of the *gōpura*, appears to be a 16th century structure. The repair work must have been more in the nature of a major renovation, obliterating

much of its earlier features.

[57]R. Narasimhacharya, op. cit., pt. II, pp. 40-41.

[58] *FE*, p. 260.

[59]Unfortunately neither the *Pampamahatmya* nor the *Hemakutakhanda* can be accurately dated. Besides, there may even be some recent interpolations within these texts.

[60]*Pampamahatmya*, fist part, chapter 92.

[61]Ibid. first part, Chapters 94-99.

[62]Ibid., Latter half of the middle part, chapter 4.

[63]Ibid., first part, chapter 98, etc. and *Hemakutakhanda* chapter 19.

[64]*Hemakutakhanda*, chapters 21-24 and *Pampamahatmya*, latter half of the middle part, chapters 3-4.

[65]*Hemakutakhanda,* chapter 25.

[66] *ARSIE* of 1934-35, no. 356.

[67]*ARIE* of 1964-65, no. 398.

[68]*SII* IX, pt. II, no. 493.

[69]*VPR '84-87*, no. 23.

[70]Ibid., no. 125.

[71]*MAR* of 1927, no. 139.

[72]*VPR '83-84*, no. 89.

[73]*ARSIE* of 1922, no. 700.

[74]*VPR '83-84*, no. 14.

[75]*MAR* of 1921, pp. 29-30.

[76]*VPR '84-87*, no. 2.

[77]*ARIE* of 1977-78., no. 89.

[78]*EC* XI, Cl. 54.

[79]*ARIE* of 1975-76, no. 108.

[80]*VPR '84-87*, nos. 5 and 126.

[81]*VPR '83-84*, nos. 47, 48, 49, 50, 52.

[82]*SII* IV, no. 271.

[83]VPR '84-87, no. 20.

[84]*SII* IV, nos. 273 and 278.

[85]N. Venkataramanayya, "A note on Śrī Virūpāksha," *JOR*, 5, 245.

[86]R. Narasimhacharya, op. cit., pt. II, p. 260.

[87]*Sources*, pp. 310-311.

[88]N. Venkataramanayya, op. cit., pp. 242-245.

[89]J.M. Fritz, G. Michell and M.S. Nagaraja Rao, *The Royal Centre at Vijayanagara : Preliminary Report*, p. 58

[90]Ibid., pp. 58-61.

[91]*SII* IX, pt. II, no. 491.

[92]*VPR '84-87*, no. 152.

[93]*ARSIE* of 1934-35, no. 351 (the intact epigraph) and no. 352 (the damaged one).

[94]*ARIE* of 1962-63, no. 11.

[95]*ARSIE* of 1940-41, nos. 96, 97, etc.

[96]*EC* X, Mb. 2 and 96.

[97]*ARIE* of 1978-79, no. 173.

[98]*EC* VI, Kp. 17.

[99]*ARSIE* of 1919, no. 703; *ARSIE* of 1913, no. 196; *ARSIE* of 1904, no. 27.

[100]T.A. Gopinatha Rao, *Elements of Hindu Iconography*, vol. 2, pt. I, p. 176.

[101]Ibid.

[102]Ibid., p. 177.

[103]J.N. Banerjee, *Religion in Art and Archaeology*, p. 73.

[104]W.D.O'Flaherty, *Asceticism and Eroticism in the Mythology of Siva*, p. 124.

[105]G.W. Briggs, *Gorakhnāth and the Kānphaṭa Yogis*, pp. 159-160 and 171.

[106]See chapter 9, p. 113.

[107]e.g. a *mūrti* of Bhairava is prominently displayed in the courtyard of the Vīraśaiva temple of Mudu Vīraṇṇa (NL w/3).

[108]A. Sundara, "New Lights on Religious Trends in Anegondi Region during Vijayanagara Period," *QJMS*, LXVIII, p. 15.

[109]Bhairava reliefs occur on pillars in the east and north gateways of the early 15th century Rāmachandra temple (NR w/1). Indeed, one of the finest Bhairava sculptures in the city is the one on a pillar in the passageway of the east gate of this temple. In the Virūpāksha complex a shrine of Kālabhairava is positioned just outside the north *gōpura.*

[110]*Pampamahatmya*, first half of the middle part, chapters 9-15.

[111]Sculptures of Bhairava have been found:

- in front of NG s/3
- near NGm/1
- in NG m/2 - Bhairava and Bhairavī reliefs are found facing each other, in the entrance of this temple set in the rocks
- in the courtyard of temple NL w/3
- NM m/3 among the Śaivite and Śākta sculptures at NM x/2
- NM y/2 - Bhairava and Bhairavī;
- NM z/2 - here Bhairava is flanked by a large scorpion and a seven-headed cobra, thus, his fearsome nature is highlighted (Plate 4)
- in NN v/1
- NQ o/2 - seated Bhairava and Bhairavī
- near NS z/1
- NU f/6
- NU g/1
- in gate NV k.

[112]Sugandha, op. cit., pp. 301-313.

[113]Nos. 83. 217, 244, 305, 347, 518, 668, 671, 679, 706, 748, 754, 1623, 1698, 2112, 2146, 7142, etc. of the Haṁpi Museum collection.

[114]R. Shama Sastry, "A few Inscriptions of the Ancient Kings of Anegundi," *QJMS*, VII, p. 290.

[115]*ARIE* of 1958-59, No. 681.

[116] *SII* XVI, no. 216 and *ARSIE* of 1922, no. 694.

[117]*SII* IV, No. 260.

[118]A. Sundara, "A Unique Vīrabhadra Image from Mulgund," in *Śrīnidhih : Perspectives in Art, Archaeology & Culture, Sri K.R. Srinivasan Festschrift*, p. 154.

[119]T.A. Gopinatha Rao, op. cit., vol. 2, pt. I, p. 182.

[120]Ibid., p. 183 and p. 186.

[121]A. Sundara, loc. cit.

[122]K. Sarojini Devi, "Religion in Vijayanagara" (Ph.D. diss.), p. 374.

[123]K. Sarojini Devi, "The Cult of Vīrabhadra in Vijayanagara," *QJMS*, LXXVIII, p. 3.

[124]A. Sundara, "New Light on Religious Trends in Anegondi Region during Vijayanagara Period," *QJMS*, LXVIII, p. 15.

[125]K. Sarojini Devi, loc. cit.

[126]Ibid., p. 6.
[127]Ibid., p. 8.
[128]*ARSIE* of 1912, nos. 572, 575, 579.
[129]*VPR '83-84*, no. 44.
[130]Ibid., nos. 50, 51, 53.
[131]Ibid., no. 20.
[132]Ibid., no. 45.
[133]Cited by V. Filliozat, *L'Épigraphie de Vijayanagara du début à 1377*, p. 135.
[134]*SII* IV, no. 266.
[135]C.T.M. Kotraiah, personal communication; also see chapter 9, p. 112.
[136]For details see D. Dēvakunjari, *Hampi*, p. 46.
[137]These are:
1. NM y/3 - a double-shrine complex dedicated to Vīrabhadra and Bhadrakāḷī
2. NN a/1
3. NN v/4
4. NP s/1
5. NQ d/2 - Vīrabhadra shrine attached to the Guha-guhēśvara āśrama
6. NQ u/1
7. NS s/1
8. NT k/3
9. NT z/5 - one of the two shrines here is of Vīrabhadra
10. NX k/1 - one of the two shrines here is dedicated to Vīrabhadra.

[138]They can be seen:
-on gateway NF w/8
-in NG n/5
-in NG m/2
-NL h/5
-NM m/1
-in NM s/2
-near NN n/1
-NQ j/4
-in NS a/3.

[139]Nos. 87, 202, 261, 419, 509, 614, 628, 631, 684, 749, 750, 1614, 02114, etc. of the Hampi Museum collection.
[140]Balasubrahmanya, "Vīrabhadra Sculptures in Hampi," in *VPR '83-84*, pp. 133-135 & Plates LXXIV-LXXX.
[141]R.N. Saletore, *Vijayanagara Art*, p. 108.
[142]P. Courtright, *Gaṇēśa: Lord of Obstacles, Lord of Beginnings*, pp. 162-163.
[143]Ibid., p. 163; see also T.M.P. Mahadēvan, *Outlines of Hinduism*, p. 181.
[144]D. Devakunjari, op. cit., p. 49.
[145]These are:
-in a shrine at NF v/1
-in NL w/2
-in NM g/6
-NR d/1
-near NV j/1
-near NY f/2
-in NG w/2
-NP x/1
-in NR g/3
-in a shrine in gate NX o
-NY m/3.

[146]Nos. 179, 209, 233, 380, 405, 484, 624, 646, 667, 697, 702, 723, 725, 1000, 1005, 1062, 1100, 1721, 1722, 1731 of the Hampi Museum collection.
[147]They are found :
1. in NG n/5
2. NG y/1
3. near NL h/4
4. in NM m/1
5. in NM s/2
6. in NM x/2 group of sculptures
7. in NM y/3 - in a panel along with other deities
8. near NN h/1
9. NN t/4
10. in NN z/1
11. NQ d/1
12. NQ j/3
13. NQ q/2
14. near gate NR b
15. NR h/3
16. in NR o/1
17. in NS a/3
18. NT o/1.

[148]*VPR '84-87*, no. 124.
[149]This inscription is interesting because it mentions a gate in the fortification wall of the "urban core". If the king is taken to be Harihara II, this record, together with the one (*VPR '84-87*, no. 105) referring to the Bēṭekārara Hebbāgilu (NY e), of A.D., 1380 prove that the circuit wall around the "urban core" or at least a part of it, was extant during the rule of Harihara II.
[150]*SII* IV, no. 267.
[151]*EI* IV, pp. 266-267.
[152]Appendix A, nos. 21, 30, 32, 43, 46, 48, 49 and 52.
[153]A.A. Shapiro, "The Kalyanotsava of Paṁpādēvī and Paṁpāpati." Mimeographed.
[154]A.P. Karmarkar, *The Religions of India Vol. I: The Vratya or the Dravidian Systems*, p. 88.
[155]*ARSIE* of 1915, no. 11.
[156]*ARIE* of 1965-66, A.1.
[157]*EI* XV, pp. 24-25.
[158]*ARSIE* of 1915, no. 54.
[159]Ibid., nos. 18 and 19.
[160]M. Rama Rao, *The Temples of Srisailam*, pp. 16-17.
[161]*VPR '84-87*, no. 82.
[162]Ibid., nos. 147 and 148.
[163]Ibid., no. 147.
[164]*SII* IX, pt. II, no. 530.
[165]*EC* IX, Nl. 2.
[166]*Top. List.*, vol. I, Bellary dist., no. 368.
[167]*VPR '83-84*, no. 22.
[168]Ibid., no. 43.
[169]D. Devakunjari, op. cit., p. 71.
[170]*SII* IX, pt. II, no. 436.
[171]G.H. Khare, *Mahārāshṭrācī Cār Daivete*, p. 146.
[172]Ibid., Summary in English.
[173]Ibid., p. 146.
[174]Ibid., pp. 138-140.
[175]Ibid., pp. 126 and 145.
[176]Ibid., p. 152.
[177]Ibid. Summary in English.

[178]Ibid.

[179]G.D. Sontheimer, *Birobā, Mhaskobā und Khaṇḍobā*, p. 250.

[180]G.H. Khare, op. cit., p. 158.

[181]*VPR '84-87*, no. 105.

[182]G. Michell, *Vijayanagara : Architectural Inventory of the Urban Core*. vol. 1, p. 57 and vol. 2, Plate 109.

[183]Ibid., vol. 1, p. 182 and vol. 2. Plate 380.

[184]Haṁpi Museum, no. 124.

[185]Haṁpi Museum, no. 834.

[186]Chapter 2, notes 111, 112 and 113.

[187]*ARSIE* of 1924, nos. 150, 151, 161, 166; *SII* VIII, no. 495.

[188]*SII* IX, pt. II, no. 550

[189]*VPR '84-87*, no. 142.

[190]The spider worshipped the *liṅga* by spinning a web over it, the snake protected the *liṅga* by spreading its hood over it, while the elephant did *abhishēka* to the *liṅga* with water it brought in its trunk. A similar story of a spider and an elephant are also related of the temple at Jaṁbukēśvara near Śrīraṅgam.

[191]Besides Śrīśailam, the legend of the devout cow is associated with other Śaivite temples too. See N. Ramesan, *Temples and Legends of Andhra Pradesh*, pp. 47 and 52-53.

[192]*ARSIE* of 1944-45, no. 80.

[193]*MAR* of 1944, no. 25.

[194]*SII* IX, pt. II, nos. 635 and 637.

[195]*ARSIE* of 1934-35, no. 353; *VPR '83-84*, no. 1.

[196]*ARSIE* of 1934-35, no. 350; *SII* XXIII, no. 501.

[197]*VPR '83-84*, no. 11; *ARIE* of 1975-76, no. 99.

[198]*SII* IX, pt. II, no. 453.

[199]R. Shama Sastry, op. cit., p. 291.

[200]*SII* IX, pt. II, no. 504.

[201]*VPR '84-87*, no. 3.

[202]*SII* IX, pt. II, no. 539.

[203]Ibid., no. 565.

[204]R. Shama Sastry, op. cit., p. 291.

[205]*VPR. '84-87*, no. 37.

[206]*Hemakutakhanda*, chapter 2.

[207]*Pampamahatmya*, first part, chapter 75.

[208]C.S. Patil, "Sculptures at Kōṭiliṅga," in *VPR '83-84*, p. 138.

[209]*VPR '84-87*, no. 49.

[210] Ibid., no. 48

[211] Ibid., no. 50.

[212]*VPR '83-84*, no. 60.

[213]*Pampamahatmya*, first part, chapter 73.

[214]Ibid. first part, chapter 76.

[215]W.E. Begley, *Viṣṇu's Flaming Wheel*, pp. 71-72.

[216]*VPR '84-87*, no. 11.

[217]Ibid., no. 14.

[218]Ibid., nos. 15 and 16.

[219]Ibid., no. 18.

[220]. They are found:
- near NL b/17 - 3 separate liṅgas
- north-east of NL b/21 - a group of 5 liṅgas and another of 3
- in rock-shelter NG n/5
- NL m/2 - giant liṅga, about 3 metres high, in a shrine, near the Lakshmī-Narasiṁha monolith
- in a cave on Matanga hill (NM g/4)
- outside NM g/6
- near NM z/2
- in NN v/2
- in NT c/1
- in the colonnade around NT d/4
- NT d/7—20 liṅgas and Nandis
- in NU h/1
- in NY f/1
- near NY f/2.

There are a few liṅgas (nos. 157, 164, 508, 527 and 1710) in the Haṁpi Museum collection also.

[221]T.A. Gopinath Rao, op. cit., vol. 2, pt. II, pp. 459-460.

[222]These are:
- near NL b/20
- near NF r/1 - about 3 images
- in NJ x/1
- in NJ x/2
- in NL h/7
- in NM b/1 - a large Nandi at the end of the Virupaksha carstreet
- in NM d/4
- in NM h/3
- in NM g/4
- in NM j/1
- in NN n/1
- in NN r/1
- near NN y/2
- in NN c/1
- in NP o/1
- in NP r/2
- in NP s/1
- in NQ y/1
- in NS z/2
- in NT c/1
- NU s/1
- in NU t/2
- in NV c/2
- in gate NV k
- near NW r/1
- NY q/4
- in gate NY x
- NX q/1.

[223]Nos. 7, 36, 74, 75, 145, 146, 163, 216, 262, 316, 394, 604, 634, 643, 650, 757, 821, 832, 838, 857, 887, 951, 1023, 1077, 1642, 1643, 1896, in the Haṁpi Museum.

[224]For example:

near entrance of NM g/4
- in NM s/2
- in NQ j/2
- in NS a/3
- NT d/7
- near NT k/3
- NT k/5.

CHAPTER 3

The Narasiṁha Cult

The earliest non-Śaivite cult in the city of Vijayanagara was probably that of Narasiṁha, the man-lion deity, one of the *avatāras* of Vishṇu. Although the Narasiṁha worship at the site is not as ancient as that of the local *Śaktī* Paṁpā and the Śaivite tradition of Virūpāksha, there is evidence to prove that it had gained ground at least by the early fourteenth century. This cult, which already existed in the city before the founding of the empire, continued to be popular and to enjoy much patronage right through the period under survey.

It is not surprising that this cult pre-dates other non-Śaivite traditions in the city, for Narasiṁha was a very popular deity in south India well before the Vijayanagara empire. In Karṇāṭaka in the period from the fourth to the sixth century A.D. when the *avatāra* aspect of Vishṇu attained popularity, the bias appears to have been towards the devotion to the Narasiṁha *avatāra* and it retained its eminence in the succeeding times.[1] In the period between the rise of the Chālukyas of Kalyāṇi and the fall of the Sēuṇas and the Hoysaḷas, Narasiṁha was the most popular among the *avatāras*.[2]

In the Āndhra region, already by the fourth century A.D., Narasiṁha had been included in the Vaishṇavite pantheon.[3] In the medieval age Ahōbalam in the Kurnool district and Siṁhāchalam near modern Visakhapatnam were important pilgrimage centres of Narasiṁha worship. In Tamil Nāḍu, by the period of the *āḷvārs*, this deity was an extremely popular one as is evidenced by their hymns and there are Pallava and Pāṇḍya cave temples of the seventh and eighth centuries A.D. dedicated to Narasiṁha.[4] The Chōḷa inscriptions bear ample evidence to the building of many shrines for this god. The wide proliferation of this *avatāra* in south India is proved by the development of a variety of Narasiṁha images under the Vijayanagara rulers and the extensive patronage enjoyed by this cult.[5] In north India, too, from the Gupta period onwards Narasiṁha exerted a great influence on the lives of the people.[6] Thus, before and during the Vijayanagara period Narasiṁha occupied the position of a cult deity rather than remaining merely as one of the incarnations of Vishṇu; the only other *avatāras* to enjoy such a position of prominence are Rāma and Kṛishṇa.

Being a popular deity, Narasiṁha would naturally have a following in the city. Besides, this cult was greatly favoured by the Mādhvas who have a high reverence for Narasiṁha and Kṛishṇa[7] (and also for Viṭhala, another form of Kṛishṇa). Mādhva ascetics were active at this site, especially around Ānegoṅdi, from the beginning of the fourteenth century till the early seventeenth century A.D.[8] The Śrī-Vaishṇavas also venerate Narasiṁha. Ahōbalam, which from the mid-fifteenth century became the seat of an important Vaḍagalai *maṭha,* is a notable centre of Śrī-Vaishṇavism.

The Sāḷuva and Tuḷuva monarchs were deeply devoted to Narasiṁha. In inscriptions it is mentioned that Sāḷuva Narasiṁha was born by the grace of god Narasiṁha of Ahōbalam.[9] He was a great devotee of Narasiṁha of Ahōbalam and Veṅkaṭēśvara of Tirumalai-Tirupati and the Vaḍagalai Vān Śathakōpa *maṭha* at Ahōbalam and its branch at Tirumalai-Tirupati enjoyed the patronage of this king.[10]

Kṛishṇadēvarāya patronised many temples including the Narasiṁhasvāmi temple at Ahōbalam. In A.D. 1515 he presented the god with valuable jewellery, a golden plate, a thousand gold coins and granted a village to the temple, while one of his queen gifted a precious pendant to the deity.[11] The Lakshmīnarasiṁhasvāmi temple at Siṁhāchalam was also the recipient of expensive jewels from the king and his two queens[12] and of several villages from the king.[13]

The large number of the records of Sadāśiva's reign found at Ahōbalam and the mention made of numerous gifts of *maṇḍapas*, lands, tanks, gardens and groves made by him or by chiefs subordinate to him, fully indicate the influence of this cult on the members of the royal family and their relatives.[14] Two important donors were the powerful Āravīḍu brothers, Aubhalarāja[15] and Koṇḍarāja,[16] sons of *Mahāmaṇḍalēśvara* Rāmarāja Kōnēṭirāja, the first cousin of Aḷiya Rāmarāja.

There are Narasiṁha temples in the city dating from pre-Vijayanagara times till the sixteenth century A.D. The two earliest ones are located one on each bank of the Tuṅgabhadrā. The one on the south bank (NG t/4) is within the "sacred centre", about half way between the Virūpāksha and Viṭhala temples, while the one on the north bank (NE m/1) is in Ānegoṅdi, near the Chintāmaṇi *āśrama* (NE g/1).

The north-east facing Narasiṁha temple on the south bank (NG t/4) has been wrongly identified by some scholars as a Jaina temple[17] and by others as a Rāma temple.[18] The reason for the former view is its Deccan style superstructure, for early art historians erroneously associated this exclusively with Jaina temple architecture and therefore labelled most of the pre-Vijayanagara temples in the city as belonging to that religion.[19] But, careful survey of the monuments reveals that there is no pre-Vijayanagara Jaina temple extant in the entire city. The genesis of the mistaken associations of this temple with Rāma is not known; perhaps its proximity to "Sugrīva's Cave" and the "Sītā Sarōvar" gave rise to this supposition.

There is no iconographic evidence in this temple to indicate its cultic affiliation. The only reliefs here are of two elephants on the outer walls of the antechamber, Hanumān and Garuḍa on either side of the two doors of the *maṇḍapa*, Vaishṇava *dvārapālas* on the jambs and Gajalakshmī on the lintels of these doors. The correct name was revealed only in some recently discovered inscriptions which are situated near this monument.

This temple (Plate 8) stands within a *prākāra*, which has a four-pillared gateway on the north-west side and a double storey gate on the south-east side. The temple, comprising a *vimāna* (*cella* and antechamber) and an enclosed *maṇḍapa*, was not constructed at one time, the difference in the plinth mouldings of these two parts and the slight disjointing of the architectural elements where they meet indicate this. The close similarity of the *vimāna*, with its stepped pyramidal stone superstructure and *śukanāsa* projection over the antechamber, with the early fourteenth century pre-Vijayanagara temple on Hēmākuṭa (NF w/9) hints at its being a pre-Vijayanagara structure. The arrangement of the interior of its *maṇḍapa* compares with that of the small "Kṛishṇa" temple (NM z/2) in the "urban core" which belongs to the formative stage in the development of the Vijayanagara temple architecture, the last quarter of the fourteenth century A.D.[20] An inscription on a rock within the *prākāra*, dated A.D. 1379, records the construction of a *maṇḍapa* for god Narasiṁha by Nalānuchakravarti-ayya during the reign of Harihara II.[21] It is likely that the enclosed *maṇḍapa* is the one referred to in the above inscription. Another, undated inscription besides the first one records obeisance to god Narasiṁha on the bank of the Paṁpā by Sīregāri, father of Nalānuchakravarti-ayya.[22]

An inscription, engraved on the bed-rock at a little distance away to the north-west of the temple, dated January 30th A.D. 1386, refers to the construction of a Śiva temple (NG t/3) to the west of the god Narasiṁha in Paṁpā-kshētra.[23] Another record from the vicinity of the temple, of A.D. 1400, records the donation of a water pond to the god Narasiṁha situated in Bhāskara-kshētra on the bank of the Tuṅgabhadrā.[24]

A record engraved on a fallen lamp-pillar within the *prākāra* of the Narasiṁha temple, dated A.D. 1406, notes the construction of a temple for god Gōpinātha by Nāgeyanāyaka.[25] Perhaps this refers to the shrine, comprising a *cella*, ante-chamber and porch, that is within the courtyard behind the main temple. That the same donor in A.D. 1410, constructed a *maṇḍapa* for god Gōpinātha and goddess Mahālakshmī is revealed in another epigraph from the temple.[26] It is possible that this refers to the structure within the *prākāra* to the south-east of the main temple. Another, partly defaced, inscription mentions the same two deities.[27] Yet another undated record from the temple refers to the celebration of the divine marriage of the goddess Kaliyuga Mahālakshmi with god Narasiṁha.[28] Thus, the consort of this deity was Mahālakshmī and the *Kalyāṇōtasava* was, probably, celebrated in this temple. Still another undated inscription mentions the services of an individual to god Narasiṁha.[29] These epigraphs and the various additions made to the temple complex point to the importance of this temple, especially in the early Vijayanagara times.

It is clear that this Narasiṁha temple was in existence prior to A.D. 1379 and that already by A.D. 1386 it was an important one and a landmark in Paṁpā-kshētra, so much so that the location of a new construction is cited in reference to this temple.

This monument is particularly significant because it is, as far as archaeological and epigraphical evidence reveal, the only non-Śaivite temple of the pre- or very early Vijayanagara period in the "sacred centre".[30] It is situated within the holy Bhāskara-kshētra, but at a distance from the Śaivite group of early temples on or around the Hēmakūṭa hill. It stands on a low hillock with a commanding view of the entire *tīrtha*—the river that takes a northerly turn near it, the Mataṅga hill to the south-west, the Virūpāksha and the Hēmakūṭa group of temples further east and the great sixteenth century Vaishṇavite complex around the Viṭhala to the north-east. It is located almost midway on the route along the river bank between the two great sixteenth century temple complexes—the Śaivite Virūpāksha and the Vaishṇavite Viṭhala, that rivalled each other in importance in the last phase of the city's history.

The Narasiṁha temple in Ānegoṅdi (NE m/1), commonly called the "Mukti-Narasiṁha" temple, is a living one where worship continues to this day. The *mūrti* in this temple is probably original.[31] It is of Lakshmī-Narasiṁha and hence this should rightly be termed as the Lakshmī-Narasiṁha temple. This east-facing temple consists of a *cella*, a small ante-chamber, an enclosed *maṇḍapa* and a verandah in front. No superstructure is extant over the *vimāna*. The verandah stylistically is of a later date than the other parts. It is of the Vijayanagara period, while the rest of the temple can be, on the basis of architectural style, deemed as pre-Vijayanagara.[32] But there is no inscription to indicate the exact date of construction.

Thus, at the site, there are two early Narasiṁha temples, placed in strategically important locations on either bank of the Tuṅgabhadrā. They manifest the importance of this cult from the pre-Vijayanagara period onwards.

From the intermediate phase, between the above mentioned early temples and the sixteenth century constructions, is the medium-sized Narasiṁha temple (NL h/1) just north of the great Kṛishṇa temple in Kṛishṇāpura. This interesting temple unfortunately has been generally ignored or unnoticed by scholars writing about the city and its monuments, perhaps it has been overshadowed by its magnificent sixteenth century neighbour. Even the fact that it is a temple of Narasiṁha, the only one at the site south of the river, with an intact image of this deity in its sanctum, has not been noted. This may be partly due to the fact that it is very dark in the *cella* and a powerful torchlight is needed to see the icon.[33]

This south-facing temple, standing within its own *prākāra* with gateways on the south, east and west, consists of a main shrine, a subsidiary shrine, both facing south, and a smaller shrine facing east in the south-west corner of the enclosure (in which there is a large image of Hanumān or Āñjanēya). The main shrine comprises a *cella*, two antechambers and an enclosed *maṇḍapa* which has doors on the south and east sides and a sub-shrine on the west side. The *cella* is built against a rock on which is carved the image of Narasiṁha standing within an elaborate *makara-tōraṇa*. He has in his upper right and left hands the *chakra* and *śaṅkha* and the lower right and left hands are with the *abhaya-mudrā* and *gadā* respectively. On the four central pillars of the *maṇḍapa* also there are reliefs of Narasiṁha in a variety of poses.

There is no inscription to help accurately date this temple. On the basis of its architectural style it can be grouped with the "intermediate" Vijayanagara monuments (e.g., the temples of Tiruveṅgaḷanātha— NX f/1, Mādhava—NR t/2, and Chandraśēkhara—NX 1/1 within the "royal centre").[34] Perhaps it belongs to the second half of the fifteenth century. Its alignment proves that it is earlier than the Kṛishṇa temple (NL m/4). Since it faces south, the main gate of the Narasiṁha temple fronts the blank wall of the outer *prākāra* of the Kṛishṇa temple. Thus, the sixteenth century construction has blocked the main approach-way to this monument. It is possible that the east gate, which is more elaborate than the main south gate, was added after the building of the Kṛishṇa temple.

The gigantic and magnificent, 6.7 metres high, Lakshmī-Narasiṁha monolith (NL m/1) within a single-celled shrine in Kṛishṇāpura was the contribution of Kṛishṇadēvarāya. An inscription in front of the shrine[35] reveals that this monolithic statue was called Lakshmī-Narasiṁhadēva (and not Ugra-Narasiṁha as it is popularly known today) and it was consecrated on April 2, A.D. 1528 on the orders of Kṛishṇadēvarāya by Ārya Kṛishṇa Bhaṭṭa who appears to have been his domestic priest. In the following year, on the occasion of a lunar eclipse, the king gifted two villages for daily food offerings to this deity.

This shrine of Lakshmī-Narasiṁha is one of three temples in the city built entirely by Kṛishṇadēvarāya (besides the additions he made to the Virūpāksha and Viṭhala complexes). The other two royal constructions of his reign are the Kṛishṇa temple in Kṛishṇāpura in A.D. 1515[36] and the Anantapadmanābha in Sāle-Tirumale-Mahārāya-pura in A.D. 1524.[37] The Lakshmī-Narasiṁha monolith, the last construction of this monarch, shows his special attachment to this deity.

An inscription on a rock east of the P.W.D. inspection bungalow, dated April 1, A.D. 1531, records a gift of land for burning a perpetual lamp before the god Lakshmī-Narasiṁha in Koṇḍamarasayana-Pāḷya in Kāmalāpuram.[38] The inspection bungalow, a converted Vaishṇava temple, is the one referred to in this epigraph.[39] This was originally a fairly small structure with only a *cella*, an antechamber and a *maṇḍapa*. The door-frame of the *cella*, with Vaishṇava *dvārapālas* on the jambs and Gajalakshmī on the lintel, points to the Vaishṇava nature of this monument. The verandah of the inspection bungalow has one pillar with three fine Narasiṁha reliefs. These, and two others on the pillars of the *maṇḍapa*, are the only iconographic clues of this having been a Narasiṁha temple. That this was a Śrī-Vaishṇava temple is indicated by the carvings of the *nāmams* and of Rāmānuja and *āḷvārs* on the pillars. Since the above-mentioned inscription is a donational and not a foundational one there is no epigraphical data available regarding the date of this temple. Due to the reconstruction, many architectural details have been obliterated; therefore it is virtually impossible to date it on stylistic grounds.

Another inscription mentions a donation by Konamarasayya to god Narasiṁha located near the elephant stables.[40] This inscription cannot be dated since the Śaka year is not given, but only cyclic year Śubhakṛit.[41] This temple is, probably, the Vaishṇava temple NR n/1 near which the inscription slab was found. The elephant stables mentioned in this epigraph is not the famous monument that is popularly known as the "Elephant Stables" (NR p/3), but it is, possibly, some structure within the large enclosure near this temple (in NR s and x) in which the present-day tourist canteen is located. For, during the recent excavation carried out here by the Directorate of Archaeology and Museums, Karṇāṭaka, the skeleton of an elephant was discovered.

Besides these six temples, inscriptions reveal that there were a few more Narasiṁha temples in the city, that, unfortunately, cannot be located. A record of Vīra Narasiṁha, of A.D. 1505 states that the king set up the god Lakshmī-Narasiṁha on the bank of the Tuṅgabhadrā.[42] There are two inscriptions carved on rock-surfaces to the north of the gate called Siṅghārada Hebbāgilu. The first of these records a grant of land to god Narasiṁha for the merit of king Sadāśiva.[43] The second refers to the garden of god Narasiṁha.[44] Whether both these records refer to the same Narasiṁha temple cannot be determined. An undated record engraved on a boulder to the east of the Lakshmī-Narasiṁha monolith (NL m/1) mentions the flower garden for the god Varada Narasiṁha of Hēmakūṭa.[45] The land in which the inscription is located appears to be the garden referred to in this record. However, on Hēmakūṭa there is no trace of a Narasiṁha temple. Yet this record is of special interest, since it is the only one available that mentions the presence of any Vaishṇava structure on Hēmakūṭa.

Side by side with the temples and shrines dedicated to this deity, there were also sub-shrines enshrining Narasiṁha within larger temple complexes. In the year A.D. 1532 the great Mādhva teacher Vyāsatīrtha set up the god Yōga-Varada-Narasiṁha in the courtyard of the Viṭhala temple,[46] to the north-west of the main shrine. Within the Virūpāksha complex there is a small shrine of Narasiṁhasvāmi. However this might be a post-A.D. 1565 addition. In the Rāmachandra temple (NR w/1) the subsidiary shrine has some striking Narasiṁha reliefs on both the inner and outer walls. This shrine has two *cellas*, one of which might have been dedicated to Narasiṁha.

Besides the architectural evidence of the existence of the Narasiṁha cult in the city in pre-Vijayanagara times there is also sculptural proof of this. On the superstructure of the triple-shrine temple (NF w/9) on Hēmakūṭa, built by Kaṁpilarāya in the first quarter of the fourteenth century,[47] reliefs of Narasiṁha occur at least twice along with those of Śiva, Gaṇēśa, Brahmā, Sūrya and Vishṇu.

The survey of the Narasiṁha temples and shrines reveals that none of them are large temples like the Virūpāksha, Viṭhala, Kṛishṇa and Tiruveṅgaḷanātha. Despite this, the importance of this cult is demonstrated by the number of temples consecrated to this deity, ranging chronologically from the pre-Vijayanagara period to almost the mid-sixteenth century and their wide geographical spread from Ānegoṅdi in the north to Kāmalāpuram in the south.

The coalescing of the two streams of religious traditions is visible in the Narasiṁha cult at Vijayanagara, namely, the "greater" tradition of canonical Hinduism and the "lesser" tradition of folk and tribal religions. While the "greater" tradition had its source in the *Purāṇas* and other Sanskṛit texts, the roots of the "lesser" lay in the fervent and exuberant religiosity of the masses who worshipped a lion divinity which in the course of time came to be known as Narasiṁha, the man-lion.

The canonical Narasiṁha story dates mainly from the Purāṇic age. Vēdic literature contains no reference to a half man, half lion deity, the sole exception being the last book of the *Taittiriya Āraṇyaka* written in the early centuries of the Christian era. Although the *Mahābhārata* refers to this incarnation in several places, the full development of the Narasiṁha legend is to found only in the *Harivaṁsa Purāṇa* (ca. A.D. 400) and in the *Matsya*, *Padma*, *Kurma*, *Bhāgavata* and *Vishṇu Purāṇas*.[48] There are variations in the myth in the different sacred texts. In brief, the story of this *avatāra* is centred around the destruction of the demon Hiraṇyakaśipu, who by severe austerities had received the boon from Brahmā that he would not meet death at the hands of men, beasts, gods or *asuras*; that he would not die inside or outside the house, by day or by night, nor by any weapon. In his extreme arrogance, Hiraṇyakaśipu forbade the worship of Vishṇu in his kingdom, but, his son Prahlāda, an ardent devotee of the god, remained unshaken in his fervour despite all the threats and punishments inflicted by his irate father. Finally, Hiraṇyakaśipu challenged the omnipotence of Vishṇu by his mocking query whether the deity resided in the pillar of the palace hall, which he thereupon kicked. Immediately, the pillar burst open and the fearsome Narasiṁha appeared and after a fight killed Hiraṇyakaśipu at dusk by tearing open his abdomen with his claws.

According to the iconographic rules, this man-lion incarnation of Vishṇu is depicted in a variety of forms—Kēvala or Yōga, Sthauṇa, Ugra and with the consort.[49] The term Kēvala-Narasiṁha may be used to denote the single Narasiṁha figure, either standing or seated. The most common form of the solitary Narasiṁha image is of Yōga-Narasiṁha, seated in the *utkuṭikāsana* or *yōgāsana* with the *yōgapaṭṭa* around his knees. This image may have either two or four arms, in the latter case the upper right and left hands carry the *chakra* and *śaṅkha* respectively, while the lower hands rest on the knees.[50] The depiction of the god emerging from the pillar and fighting the demon is termed Sthauṇa-Narasiṁha, while Ugra-Narasiṁha is in the process of killing Hiraṇyakaśipu. In the Lakshmī-Narasiṁha image the divinity is usually shown in *lalitāsana*, the right leg hanging down and the left on the seat, holding the *chakra* and *śaṅkha* in the upper hands, with the lower right in *abhaya mudra* and the lower left hand around the waist of the goddess, who is seated on Narasiṁha's left knee.[51]

Narasiṁha icons, based on the iconographic texts, are numerous from the Gupta period onwards in north India. In the Deccan and south India they appear in Bādāmi and at Ellora in the Chālukya and Rāshṭrakūṭa periods and thereafter they enter the mainstream of south Indian iconography.

The earliest representation, dating back to the fourth century A.D., of the god as a purely lion deity is from Kondamotu in coastal Āndhra.[52] Narasiṁha is here depicted as a squatting lion, with the only difference that two hands, in which he holds the *gadā* and *chakra*, are added to the figure at the neck level. The addition of extra hands is merely an indication of the figure's divinity and need not be assumed to reflect the composite nature of the deity.[53]

The tradition of the deity as a complete lion seems to have been current in Karṇāṭaka too. One such zoomorphic example of the Rāshṭrakūṭa period survives in the Vyāghra-Narasiṁha temple at Megharavaḷḷi (Shimoga district).[54] The early two-armed Narasiṁha icons of Karṇāṭaka are only derivatives of the type. Examples from the fifth to eighth centuries A.D. have survived in which Narasiṁha, with a lion's head and human body, is seated in *maharājalīlāsana* (one leg bent at the knee with the foot resting on the pedestal and the other leg bent and fully resting on the pedestal), with only two hands, both resting on the knees. He has no *kirīṭa* and is little ornamented. These sculptures do not follow the iconographic rules of the *Purāṇas* or *Āgamas*.[55] Such icons were common in the Tuḷuva region around the eighth century A.D.[56]

The lion deity was also worshipped by some tribes. The Cheñchūs who live in the Nallamalai forests flanking the river Kṛishṇā in the heart of Āndhra Pradesh in the Mahbūbnagar, Kurnool and Prakasam districts[57] still worship such a deity. The Cheñchūs traditionally clothed themselves with leaves and carried bows and arrows.[58] They claim the god Narasiṁha of Ahōbalam, whom they call Ōbalēsudu, as their brother-in-law for they believe that he married a beautiful Cheñchū girl[59], who came to be called Cheñchū-Lakshmī. According to local legend, Narasiṁha, while wandering in the Nallamalai forests, met the Cheñchū beauty and wanted to marry her, thereupon her father, the Cheñchū chieftain, put the stranger to a series of tests like climbing precipices and tall trees, collecting wild honey, digging termite mounds, hunting, etc. Having successfully achieved these tasks, Narasiṁha secured the chieftain's consent to the marriage.[60] There are excellent sculptural representations at the Ahōbalam temple of Cheñchū-Lakshmī, wearing a leaf skirt, aiming her bow and arrow and also of the episode of Narasiṁha removing the thorn from her foot. In the latter relief, the size of tribal goddess is much larger compared to Narasiṁha; she supports herself on a tall bow while the diminutive Narasiṁha extracts the thorn from the sole of her foot.[61]

In the sculptures and reliefs in the city of Vijayanagara both the canonical and folk themes of the Narasiṁha tradition are to be seen. The Cheñchū-Lakshmī and Narasiṁha story was extremely popular with the Vijayanagara sculptors from the fourteenth century onwards. This is not surprising because the Cheñchū was the nearest tribe to the imperial capital[62] and Ahōbalam was an important pilgrimage centre. The most common sculptural themes at the site from this legend are of Narasiṁha removing the thorn from the foot of his beloved and of Cheñchū-Lakshmī leaning on her tall bow. Narrative reliefs of the story are also present, for example on the "Mahānavamī Dibba" (NW d/1) and on the east gate of the Rāmachandra temple (NRw/1). On the former these occur on the east and south facing outer walls of the south side steps, on both the walls, where there are bands of reliefs, the Cheñchū-Lakshmī-Narasiṁha story is carved at the lowest level (Plate 10). In both the friezes Cheñchū-Lakshmī and Narasiṁha, both wearing leaf skirts, are shown hunting in a forest full of wild animals, Narasiṁha is seen carrying across his shoulder a deer that has been killed in hunt while the Cheñchū girl leads him by the hand, elsewhere she is leaning against her bow and in the middle of each panel is the sculptor's favourite episode of the removal of the thorn from Cheñchū-Lakshmī's foot (Plate 11). These carvings belong to the first building phase of this great platform and hence can be dated to the fourteenth century.[63] On the plinth of the early fifteenth century eastern gateway of the Rāmachandra temple there are stray reliefs of the goddess leaning on her bow, hunting deer and wild boars, Cheñchū- Lakshmī leading Narasiṁha who is carrying the animal killed in the hunt, etc.

The representations of Narasiṁha removing the thorn and of the tribal goddess with her bow are to be found on temple pillars right through the site, from the early Vijayanagara period to the mid-sixteenth century. They cut across sectarian lines, recurring not only in Vaishṇava temples of diverse deities but also in Śaiva temples, such as in the double-shrine Śaiva temple on Hēmakūṭa (NF w/5) of the pre- or early Vijayanagara times (Plate 12), in the early fifteenth century *raṅga-maṇḍapa* of the Viṭhala temple, in the *mahā-raṅga-maṇḍapa* of the Virūpāksha temple built in 1509-10,[64] on the superstructure of the east *gōpura* of the Viṭhala of A.D. 1513,[65] in the *mahā-maṇḍapa* of the great temple in Sāle-Tirumale-Mahārāya-pura of A.D. 1524, in the *raṅga-maṇḍapa* built for music and dance in A.D. 1545[66] in the Mādhava temple (NR t/2), and in the Tiruveṅgaḷanātha temple, locally known as the "Chaṇḍikēśvara" temple (NL w/6), in Kṛishṇāpura, also of A.D. 1545.[67]

The popularity of the tribal Cheñchū-Lakshmī and Narasiṁha (Ōbalēsudu of the Cheñchūs) of Ahōbalam was indeed extensive. However, the reliefs of this divine couple occur only on plinths, temple pillars and *gōpuras*. There are no large sculptures nor, as far as evidence is available, shrines dedicated to them. Therefore, we conclude that despite this popularity the Cheñchū-Lakshmī-Narasiṁha tradition was in terms of worship relegated to a minor position.

Other non-canonical forms of Narasiṁha to be seen in the Vijayanagara sculptures include the two-armed standing or dancing Narasiṁha, shown sometimes with and at other times without the *kirīṭa* or crown, and the two-armed standing or dancing Narasiṁha holding a snake in one hand. These folk themes are seen in temples of all the phases of the city's history as a capital, including the last years before its destruction, such as a fine relief of the two-armed dancing Narasiṁha holding a snake on a pillar in the *maṇḍapa* of the Tirumaṅgai-āḷvār temple (NC v/3) built in A.D. 1556.[68] The folk type of the seated two-armed man-lion deity, without any divine attributes, prevalent in Karṇāṭaka during the fifth to eighth centuries A.D., is also to be found. A very fine example of this is the statue in the Narasiṁhasvāmi shrine within the Virūpāksha temple complex (Plate 13).

In the temples, canonically recognised sculptures— especially of Yōga-Narasiṁha, Sthauṇa-Narasiṁha and Lakshmī-Narasiṁha— were not only very common, but were even more frequent than the folk representations of the deity. The best narrative reliefs of the traditional story of Narasiṁha and Prahlāda are in the subsidiary shrine of the Rāmchandra temple. On the west wall of the *maṇḍapa* of this shrine are the following: Hiraṇyakaśipu ordering Prahlāda to be trampled to death by an elephant, Prahlāda standing before the animal which refuses to crush him, Hiraṇyakaśipu in rage taunting his son and kicking the pillar from which the awesome Narasiṁha emerges, the fierce fight between the god and the demon and the death of the latter. The narrative is continued on the outer north side wall of this shrine where Lakshmī-Narasiṁha are seated in divine splendour with Prahlāda in adoration before them.

A careful survey of the Narasiṁha reliefs in the Vijayanagara temples reveals that the canonical and folk varieties of sculptures are to be found side by side in the temples; there was no exclusive preference for only one or the other type. To give just one example, in the great Kṛishṇa temple complex in Kṛishṇāpura reliefs of the folk themes of Cheñchū-Lakshmī and Narasiṁha, the two-armed standing and dancing Narasiṁha, the man-lion deity holding a snake and also the representation of the classical themes such as Kēvala-Narasiṁha, Yōga-Narasiṁha and Ugra-Narasiṁha are present. This proves that both varieties were accepted in the repertoire of Narasiṁha sculptures and reliefs; the Vijayanagara sculptors had freed themselves from the rigid adherence to rules as laid down in Sanskṛit texts.

Besides the reliefs and sculptures in the temples, there are also some interesting rock carvings of this deity. Some of the these are located on the south bank of the river around Kōṭi-tīrtha, not far from the early Narasiṁha temple on the south bank. Near NG m/1 is a fine relief of Lakshmī-Narasiṁha. Another very unusual one of Lakshmī-Narasiṁha is located near NG n/3. Here Narasiṁha holds a *chakra* in his upper right hand and a bow and arrow in the upper left, while the lower hands are in *abhaya* and *varada mudrās* (Plate 14). The deity is seated on the coils of the cosmic serpent Śēsha, who shelters the deities under his multiple hoods.

In the rock shelter, NG n/6, there is a group of sculptures including reliefs of the standing Kevala-Narasiṁha and Ugra-Narasiṁha. In another rock shelter, NG n/5, there is a relief of the seated Narasiṁha in one niche, while in another niche there is one of Ramā-Sītā-Lakshmaṇa. The presence of these Narasiṁha reliefs and their proximity to the Narasiṁha temple indicates the importance of the deity in this part of the "sacred centre".

Within the "royal centre" are some other Narasiṁha reliefs, for instance near NR k/1 & 2 there is a boulder on which there are exquisite carvings of Ugra-Narasiṁha and Yōga-Narasiṁha, besides one of the god Veṅkaṭēśa. Not far away, to the north-east of this group, is a rock shelter, NS a/1, in which there is a magnificent series of Vaishṇavite reliefs. Among these, is the representation of the Narasiṁha story—Prahlāda standing before a pillar, which Hiraṇyakaśipu kicks, it splits open and Narasiṁha emerges, a vigorous fight between the man-lion deity and the demon ensues and finally Narasiṁha triumphs and is shown garlanding himself with the intestines of the dead demon king lying on his lap. This panel portrays power, movement and ferocity.[69]

Besides these rock carvings there are also a couple of Lakshmī-Narasiṁha icons and a few broken Narasiṁha sculptures in the Archaeological Museum at the site. Probably these were from some of the temples of the site.

The greatest Narasiṁha sculpture in the city and the best example of the Vijayanagara sculptor's skill is the giant Lakshmī-Narasiṁha monolith (Plate 15) of Kṛishṇadēvarāya in Kṛishṇāpura which, despite its sadly mutilated condition, remains one of the most impressive monuments in the city. Inconographically this statue is unusual. Narasiṁha is seated under a large *makara-tōraṇa* on the three coils of the cosmic serpent which raises its seven hoods over his head. Narasiṁha originally held the *chakra* in the upper right hand and the *dhanus* and *bāṇa* in his upper left hand while the lower hands were in *abhaya* and *varada.*[70] Although the *Skanda Purāṇa* describes Lakshmī-Narasiṁha as holding a discus and bow,[71] this type of image is most atypical. Were the sculptors of the monolith following the *Skanda Purāṇa*? Or were they influenced by the folk tradition of Narasiṁha as a *kirāta* hunter wandering with his Cheñchū consort in the Nallamalai forests? It is possible that the "lesser" tradition blended with "greater" in the making of this icon. The absorption and synthesis of a variety of influences, both classical and folk, distinguishes this cult in the city.

The survey of the Narasiṁha cult at the site reveals its popularity and significance. Nevertheless, it is true that Narasiṁha could in no way rival Paṁpā-Virūpāksha in importance. Besides, in the fifteenth century the cult of Rāma and in the early sixteenth century those of Kṛishṇa, Viṭhala and Veṅkaṭēśvara gained ground and these, especially the last two, came to overshadow that of Narasiṁha in prestige and public patronage. However, the Narasiṁha cult, unlike other non-Śaivite ones, had following from the pre-Vijayanagara times up to the destruction of the city. To this day, this deity is worshipped in the Narasiṁha temple at Ānegoṅdi. The prominence of this *avatāra* before the fourteenth century A.D. explains the presence of Narasiṁha in the city in pre-Vijayanagara times. His continued popularity during the period of the empire was perhaps due to the fact that he suited well the temper of the times. Narasiṁha symbolises the wrathful aspect of Vishṇu, famous for destroying those opposed to him. In an empire constantly at war, it was natural that his protection and blessing would be eagerly sought.

Notes

[1]S.V. Padigar, "The Cult of Vishṇu in Karnataka" (Ph.D. diss), pp. 435-436.

[2]Ibid., pp. 442-443.

[3]Md. Abdul Waheed Khan, *An Early Sculpture of Narasiṁha.*

[4]R. Champakalakshmi, *Vaiṣṇava Iconography in the Tamil Country,* p. 93.

[5]Ibid., p. 102.

[6]K. Desai, *Iconography of Viṣṇu,* p. 94.

[7]V. Filliozat, "The history, social and economic conditions of the Viṭhala temple at Hampi," *South Asian Archaeology,* 1981, pp. 305-306.

[8]S. Hanumantha Rao, "The influence of the religious school of Sri Madhwa on the history of Vijayanagara," *QJMS,* XX, pp. 284-287.

[9]*MAR* of 1932, no. 45.

[10]S.R. Reddy, "History of Religious Institutions in Andhra" (Ph.D. diss.), p. 191.

[11]*ARSIE* of 1915, no. 64.

[12]*ARSIE* of 1900, nos. 243 and 245.

[13]Ibid., 244.

[14]*ARSIE* of 1915, p. 110.

[15]Ibid., nos. 65, 66 and 72.

[16]Ibid., no. 61.

[17]A.H. Longhurst, *Hampi Ruins,* p. 118.

[18]D. Devakunjari, *Hampi,* p. 61.

[19]Even though the epigraphical and iconographic study of these monuments has clearly proved that none of them are Jaina temples, the monument attendants of the A.S.I. and the local tourist guides still persist in calling the Hēmakūṭa hill temples the "Jaina group of temples."

[20]C.S. Patil, "Krishna Temple," in *VPR '79-83*, pp. 61-63.

[21]*VPR '84-87,* no. 58.

[22]Ibid., no. 59.

[23]*VPR '83-84,* no. 11.

[24]Ibid., no. 12.

[25]*VPR '84-87,* no. 62.

[26]Ibid., no. 60.

[27]Ibid., no. 61.

[28]Ibid., no. 63.

[29]*VPR '83-84,* no. 59.

[30]There is a Vaishṇava shrine within the Virūpāksha temple complex, known locally as the Gulaguñji Mādhava shrine. Originally this might have been a detached structure of the 11th-12th centuries A.D., which got absorbed into the Virūpāksha temple complex during the 16th century expansion of the temple and got partly buried due to the rise of the working ground level in the Vijayanagara times. However, there is no proof that this was a Vaishṇava shrine in the pre-Vijayanagara period. The earliest mention of the *mūrti* of Guñja Mādhava is in the *Virūpāksha Vasantōtsava Champū* of Ahōbala (V. Raghavan, "The Virūpāksha Vasantōtsava Champū of Ahobala," *JOR,* XIV, p. 22), a Vijayanagara period *kāvya.* Besides, even if the shrine of this Vaishṇavite deity is an early one, it does not appear to have enjoyed a significance independent of the Virūpāksha temple complex.

[31]The base of the *mūrti* fits well into the *pīṭha* on which it rests, the angles and indentations of the two are identical. The *pīṭha* is half buried since the floor level of the *cella* has risen due to the centuries of repair and renewal of the flooring. Thus, it is a very early image.

[32]Sugandha, "History and Archeology of Anegondi" (Ph.D. diss.), p. 144.

[33]It must be mentioned that in a book published at the end of 1988, *Hampi-Vijayanagara: The Temple of Viṭhala* by P. and V. Filliozat, p. 10, this has been rightly identified as a Narasiṁha temple. However, my identification was made independently of this publication during the course of my field trip to Haṁpi in October 1985.

[34]G. Michell, "Architectural Traditions at Vijayanagara: Temple Styles," in *Vij. City & Emp.,* vol. 1, pp. 277-278.

[35]*EI* I, pp. 398-402.

[36]*SII* IV, nos. 254 and 255.

[37]*ARSIE* of 1922, no. 683.

[38]*SII* IX, pt. II, no. 533; also *ARSIE* of 1904, no. 22.

[39]V. Filliozat "Les Quartiers et Marchés de Hampi," *Bulletin de l'Ecole Française d'Extrême Orient,* 64, p. 40.

[40]*VPR '83-84,* no. 29.

[41]During the Vijayanagara period the year Śubhakrit coincides with A.D. 1362-63, 1422-23, 1482-83 and 1542-43.

[42]*EC* X, Gd. 77.

[43]*VPR '84-87,* no. 92.

[44]Ibid., no. 95.

[45]Ibid., no. 81.

[46]*ARSIE* of 1922, no. 710.

[47]*ARSIE* of 1934-35, no. 353; also *VPR '83-84,* no. 1, p. 21.

[48]Suvira Jaiswal, "Evolution of the Narasiṁha legend and its possible sources," *PIHC,* 34, 1973, pp. 140-142.

[49]V.N. Hari Rao, *The Śrīraṅgam Temple: Art and Architecture,* p. 86.

[50]T.A. Gopinatha Rao, *Elements of Hindu Iconography,* vol. 1, pt. I, p. 150.

[51]R. Champakalakshmi, op.cit., p. 103.

[52]Md. Abdul Waheed Khan, op.cit.

[53]Suvira Jaiswal, op.cit., p. 143.

[54]S.V. Padigar, op.cit., p. 362; also p. Gururaja Bhatt, *Studies in Tuḷuva History and Culture,* Plate 380b.

[55]A. Sundara, "Narasiṁha Sculptures from Hosa Mahākuṭa and Kuppaṭūru: Some early types and significance," *Karnatak Historical Review,* XIII, pp. 10-11.

[56]P. Gururaja Bhatt, op.cit., p. 325.

[57]D. Rabinandan Pratap, *Tribes of Andhra Pradesh,* pp. 39-43.

[58]E. Thurston, *Castes and Tribes of Southern India,* vol. II, p. 28.

[59]Ibid., p. 42.

[60]M.L.K. Murthy, "Ethnoarchaeology of the Kurnool Cave Areas," *World Archaeology,* 1985, p. 202; also G.D. Sontheimer, "Folk Deities in the Vijayanagara Empire—Mallaṇṇa/Mailār," in *Vij. City & Emp.,* vol. 1, p. 146.

[61]M.L.K. Murthy, op.cit., pp. 202-203.

[62]D. Rabinandan Pratap, op.cit., p. 6.

[63]J.M. Fritz, G. Michell and M.S. Nagaraja Rao, *The Royal Centre at Vijayanagara,* p. 100.

[64]*EI* I, pp. 361-371.

[65]*SII* IV, no. 273.

[66]Ibid., no. 248.

[67]Ibid., no. 265.

[68]Ibid., no. 280.

[69]*VPR '79-83,* p. 38.

[70]Since the statue is mutilated the attributes cannot be seen, but some broken pieces of these lie in the vicinity of the monolith. Conservation work on the statue was taken up by the ASI in 1985. According to the conservation officer, T.N. Padmanaban, this giant sculpture was modelled on a smaller relief of Lakshmī-Narasiṁha—the one near NG n/3—close to Koṭi-tīrtha. Unfortunately, the work has been stopped before completion due to public controversy over the type of conservation being effected. It is regrettable that the present state of the monolith is worse than its condition before 1985.

[71]D. Desai, loc.cit.

CHAPTER 4

The *Rāmāyaṇa* Tradition

Vijayanagara city and its environs have been closely associated with the *Rāmāyaṇa*; certain incidents related in the epic are said to have taken place in this locality. From the early fifteenth century A.D. onwards the cult of Rāma gained in popularity and enjoyed the patronage of both the court and the populace. The survey of this cult in the city also reveals that a homology was established between Rāma and the king. In this chapter an attempt is made to trace the antiquity of the association of this site with episodes of the *Rāmāyaṇa* and to study the evolution, extent and patronage of the Rāma cult in the city and of the parallel drawn between the universal king, Rāma, and the earthly monarch.

Many places in Karṇāṭaka are associated with the incidents and heroes of the *Rāmāyaṇa*. Vāli and Sugrīva are said to have lived near Haṁpi; places like Sitimani in the Bijāpur district, Chaya Bhagavati near Muddebihala and Birakabbi in Bāgalkoṭe *taluka* still retain the memory of Rāma and Hanumān who are said to have camped there.[1] The Jatinga Ramēśvara hill in the Chitradurga district is believed to be the place where Jaṭāyu fought with Rāvaṇa and lost his life.[2] Many place names in Karṇāṭaka are based on the stories from the *Rāmāyaṇa*. In some of these places, Rāma is stated to have lived with Sītā and Lakshmaṇa, while in others, he is said to have left the mark of his feet. At many riverside places where Sītā is believed to have dwelt and bathed, the water is said to be still yellow because of the turmeric she used![3] Of all the *Rāmāyaṇa* sites in the state, none perhaps is as important as that of Haṁpi and its surroundings which is claimed to be locale of many of the events narrated in the Kishkindhā Kāṇḍa, one of the seven *kāṇḍas* of the epic.

It must be noted that there is considerable academic controversy over the *Rāmāyaṇa*–about when and even whether Rāma existed, about the route that Rāma took in his southern wanderings, about the location of Daṇḍakāraṇya, Kishkindhā, Laṅkā, etc. To cite just a few examples: Daṇḍakāraṇya has been located both in Mahārāshṭra and in Orissa;[4] while the people of Karṇāṭaka assert that Hanumān was born near Ānegoṅdi, the tribals of Madhya Pradesh believe that he was born in Anjan village in Gumla-Paramandal in the Rānchi district and countless legends related to his life are woven around the old temples scattered all over this region; still others hold that Hanumān was a descendant of the monkey clan that inhabited central India.[5] Regarding Kishkindhā, besides Ānegoṅdi, Vādhya Kishkindhā on the Vindhyas and Kekind near Jodhpur in Rajasthān are some of the places that claim to be the city of Vāli and Sugrīva.[6] Besides the most common assumption of Śrī Laṅkā being the Laṅkā of Rāvaṇa, places as far apart as the Amarakanṭaka peak in central India,[7] the Maldives[8] and the northern part of the Āndhra country on the shores of the Bay of Bengal[9] have been identified as Laṅkā. Different views are held regarding the route that Rāma took in his southern journey. While the most commonly accepted view is that Pañchavaṭī, the place of Sītā's abduction, was near Nāsik on the Godāvari, in Mahārāshṭra, and that from here Rāma followed a southerly route through Karṇāṭaka in his search for Sītā, another theory locates Pañchavaṭī in Āndhra and the route of Rāma's southward progress along the east coast.

Such controversies are outside the scope of this study. From our point of view what is important is that for centuries countless numbers of people have venerated certain spots in and around Haṁpi as places hallowed by Rāma's presence. The genesis of this tradition dates back to the pre-Vijayanagara times and gained in popularity during the empire period. To this day thousands of devout pilgrims visit these places with the greatest reverence.

The events of the *Rāmāyaṇa* related to this site centre around the meeting of Rāma with Hanumān and Sugrīva and the alliance entered into with them. When Sītā was abducted by

Rāvaṇa, Rāma and Lakshmaṇa began their famous search for her. In their journey through the Daṇḍaka forest they encountered the giant *rākshasa* Kabandha,[10] who advised them to ally themselves with Sugrīva, the exiled prince of the *vānaras* or monkeys, and directed them to go to lake Paṁpā and Ṛishyamūka hill.[11] Rāma and Lakshmaṇa reached the west bank of the Paṁpā[12] and near it they visited the *āśrama* of the old female ascetic Śabarī, the disciple of *ṛishi* Mataṅga. Sugrīva, the exiled prince, with Hanumān and his three other faithful companions, is said to have been dwelling at Ṛishyamūka;[13] from here they saw Sītā being carried away southwards by Rāvaṇa in his aerial chariot. Seeing them, the desperate Sītā dropped her ornaments and a garment,[14] hoping that these would guide her husband in his quest for her.

When Rāma approached with Lakshmaṇa, Sugrīva fled, suspecting them to be emissaries of his rival Vāli. Hanumān, who was sent by Sugrīva, at first accosted the two strangers in the guise of a mendicant but soon realised his mistake, whereupon both sides offered friendly explanations.[15] This meeting occurred at Ṛishyamūka hill.[16] Hanumān now fetched Sugrīva to meet the illustrious brothers; Rāma and Sugrīva made a pact of friendship and the latter brought out Sītā's garment and the jewels from the cave in which he had hidden them.[17] Rāma and Sugrīva went to Kishkindhā, where Rāma killed Vāli, the reigning king, and enthroned Sugrīva in his place. Then, as the rainy season had begun and no operations could be undertaken, Rāma and Lakshmaṇa took shelter for four months on Mālayavat hill,[18] also called Prasravaṇa.[19] When the rains passed, Lakshmaṇa asked for Sugrīva's help in finding Sītā and Sugrīva repaired to Rāma at Mālayavat hill.[20] Summoning his vassal *vānaras*, Sugrīva despatched them in four bands east, south, west and north, to discover within one month where Rāvaṇa kept Sītā in captivity. Hanumān and his band who went south, found Sītā in Laṅkā city and returned with the good news to Kishkindhā.[21] Before reaching Rāma with the happy tidings, the *vānara* band celebrated their triumph by alighting at Madhuvana, the protected park of the *vānara* king, where they indulged in unrestrained revelry. Regardless of the warnings of the guards, they drank the honey, ate the fruits, uprooted trees and ruined the beautiful park. Rāma and Lakshmaṇa along with *vānara* army then proceeded south towards Laṅkā.

The places mentioned in the above account from the *Rāmāyaṇa* are all located in and around Haṁpi. Kishkindhā is said to be in the hills that surround Ānegoṁdi. Āñjanadri hill, to the northwest of Ānegoṁdi, is reputed to be the birthplace of Hanumān or Āñjanēya. Paṁpā Sarōvar (also called Paṁpā Saras) is near the foot of this hill. Close to this lake is a small cavern in the rock that is identified as Śabarī's hermitage. The Ṛishyamūka hill is on a large island in the Tuṅgabhadrā, to the north of Mataṅga. A small cave amidst boulders on the south bank of the river (NG o/1), known as Sugrīva's Cave, is identified as the place where Sugrīva hid Sītā's jewellery. Certain streaks on the sheet rock near the cave are pointed out as the marks made by Sītā's garment. At Chintāmaṇi, in Ānegoṁdi, Rāma is said to have given the garland for Sugrīva to wear, in order to distinguish him from his brother Vāli in their deadly combat, which took place on a nearby rocky island in the river. A huge mound of scoriaceous ash in the village of Niṁbāpuram on the south bank of the river is claimed to be the cremated remains of Vāli. Lakshmaṇa is said to have crowned Sugrīva king at the site of the Kōdaṇḍarāma temple (NG w/1), also located on the south bank. During the rainy season Rāma and Lakshmaṇa waited on Mālyavanta hill. Madhuvana, where Hanumān and his cohorts descended to celebrate their success in discovering Sītā, is said to be located on the Hospēṭ-Kāmalāpuram-Kaṁpili road, about one-and-a-half kilometres beyond the circuit wall of the "urban core". A small lake near Sugrīva's Cave is locally known as Sītā Sarōvar or Sītā-kuṇḍa.[22] The *Rāmāyaṇa* makes no mention of such a spot. Perhaps, it came to be so called because Sītā's jewels are believed to have fallen nearby. The *Pampamahatmya* gives an interesting account of this lake. According to it, Sītā, after her abandonment by Rāma, was advised by Vālmīki to bathe in that lake, pray to the goddess Gaurī and do penance. Sītā did so and the goddess Paṁpā appeared to her and reassured her; thereupon Sītā returned to the hermitage of Vālmīki.[23] The *Hemakutakhanda* and the *Pampamahatmya*, the local *sthaḷa-*

purāṇas, corroborate the oral tradition by mentioning Kishkindhā, lake Paṁpā, Ṛishyamūka, Madhuvana, Āñjanadri hill etc., as being at the site.[24]

A careful survey of the monuments and remains at these spots reveals no traces of any pre-Vijayanagara structures. If there is no archaeological proof that the *Rāmāyaṇa* association with this site pre-dates the empire, there are a few epigraphical and literary sources that indicate this link at least from the eleventh century A.D. onwards. A Kannaḍa inscription dated A.D. 1069 from Dēvīghaṭ about 10 kilometres away from Ānegoṅdi refers to Kishkindhā.[25] A later Chālukyan record, dated A.D. 1088, in a Śiva temple of Sōmanātha at Munirābad, a village about 6.5 kilometres north-west of Hospēṭ, mentions Kishkindhā as being to the north and Ṛishyamūka to the east of this temple.[26] The Jaina version of the Rāma story, *Rāmachandra-Charita-Purāṇa* of the eleventh or twelfth century A.D. by Nāgachandra or Abhinava Paṁpā, claims that the residents of this area were not monkeys but a tribe who had the monkey insignia on their flag.[27]

From the Vijayanagara period, we have many proofs of the firm belief that Kishkindhā was located in this area. In Ānegoṅdi, across the village from south to north, there are about seven or eight stone temples of Hanumān now in ruins. The pillars of these and other temples are scattered about the village. On these pillars there are numerous representations of Hanumān and his heroic exploits. What is noteworthy is the exclusive representation of Hanumān in these and not of the main events of the entire epic. Obviously this is due to the attempt to commemorate the tradition that this is the place of Kishkindhā.[28]

In the *Virūpāksha Vasantōtsava Chaṁpū* of Ahōbala, Kishkindhā and Vāli Bhaṇḍāra (the treasury of Vāli) are mentioned as being on the northern side of the Tuṅgabhadrā,[29] the Ṛishyamūka hill is also referred to.[30] This is a work of the Vijayanagara period, but the exact dating of it remains a problem.[31]

By the early fifteenth century, when the Rāmachandra temple (NR w/1) was built in the heart of the "royal centre", the *Rāmāyaṇa* association with the site seems to have been widely accepted. The Rāmachandra temple is axially and visually aligned with hills to the north and north-east that are connected with this epic. The "route of Rāma" and the sculptural panels on the temple walls circumambulate the temple.[32] The north-south axis of this temple, if extended northward, passes through the Mataṅga hill, the Kōdaṇḍarāma temple, close by the Ṛishyamūka hill and through the Āñjanadri hill; while a north-east axis converges on the Mālyavanta hill. The "route of Rāma" at the site is a complete half circle of clockwise movement around this temple–from the Ṛishyamūka hill to the north, the Mālyavanta to the north-east and finally the departure for Laṅkā southward. The *Rāmāyaṇa* panels on the exterior wall of the *raṅga-maṇḍapa* of the Rāmachandra temple also encircle the temple in a clockwise direction three times.[33]

In the Rāmachandra temple there are two series of *Rāmāyaṇa* panels, the first, as mentioned above, around the *raṅga-maṇḍapa* and the second on the inner face of the *prākāra* walls between the northern and eastern gateways. In both, the Kishkindhā episodes are well depicted. A third complete *Rāmāyaṇa* series is found on the walls of the sixteenth century *gōpura* of the south-facing temple (NC w/3), north-east of the Viṭhala temple, locally known as the 'Old Śiva Temple'. Here 32 panels, out of a total of 131, are related to the Kishkindhā Kāṇḍa.[34] Thus, it is clear that by the sixteenth century it was widely accepted that the city and its surroundings was the locale of these incidents. Even the foreign visitors to the city seemed to be well aware of this, for Nuniz reports, "they say that in the former times this land belonged all to the monkeys and that in those days they could speak".[35]

Āñjanadri hill, the supposed birthplace of Āñjanēya, is crowned by a temple dedicated to this deity, where worship still continues. The large relief of Āñjanēya, in heroic pose, in the *garbha-gṛiha* is most probably a Vijayanagara period carving. An inscription on a rock in a field close to the hill records a land grant to Hanumantadēva of the hill by Nāgaṇṇadēva of Ānegoṅdi[36] who appears to be a minister of a Vijayanagara king.[37] Unfortunately this record cannot be dated since the Śaka year is not given in it, but only the cyclic year Svabhānu.

There seems to be some confusion regarding the location of Paṁpā Saras during the

Vijayanagara period. An inscription of A.D. 1400[38] identifies what is now called Sītā-kuṇḍa (NG o/2) as the Paṁpā Saras. However, in another inscription of A.D. 1534[39] this lake is clearly named as Sītā-kuṇḍa, it being mentioned as the northern boundary of Achyutarāya-pēṭe. Evidently a change in identification occurred during the 134 years between these two epigraphs. Perhaps, with the growing popularity of the Rāma cult in the city and due to the proximity of this lake to the small cavern, that is called Sugrīva's Cave, this lake came to be associated with Sītā, while the lake to the north of the river became known as Paṁpā Saras. That the latter was considered a sacred spot at least by the late Vijayanagara period is indicated by the presence of a *dēvī* temple and a Śiva shrine, of the late sixteenth or early seventeenth century A.D on its banks.[40] Besides its association with the *Rāmāyaṇa*, this lake is more famous as the site of Paṁpā-dēvī's austerities, hence the *dēvī* and Śiva shrines near it are appropriate.

The site of Sugrīva's coronation is marked by the temple of Kōdaṇḍarāma (NG w/1). In its sanctum is a large relief, carved on a rock, of Rāmā-Sītā-Lakshmaṇa, with a small figure of Sugrīva to one side. The temple, with its composite pillars, appears to be a sixteenth century construction. At Madhuvana is a modern temple, enshrining a very large relief of Āñjanēya in the striding, heroic pose. That this place was known as Kaḷasāpura in the Vijayanagara times is revealed in an undated inscription.[41] An inscription of A.D. 1434, near this temple, records the gift of Dēvarāya II to god Hanumantadēva.[42] Thus, evidently, there was a temple here in the fifteenth century and this spot must have been of special significance. It is likely that the modern temple is built on the site of the Vijayanagara temple and that the *mūrti* is the original one.

Mālyavanta, where Rāma is said to have stayed for four months and from where he started on his campaign against Laṅkā, is graced by a large Raghunātha temple. However, the Mālyavanta hill appears to have also been a Śaivite sacred spot. According to the *Pampamahatmya*, sage Mālyavanta, a great devotee of Śiva, did severe penances on this hill.[43] Around A.D. 1410 Lakshmīdhāra, a minister of Dēvarāya I, consecrated Gaṇēśa in a cave temple on the southern slope of this hill;[44] no mention is made of Raghunātha in this record. On this hill there is also a group of twenty *liṅgas* and Nandis carved on the bedrock (NT d/7), flanking a crevice filled with water. Surprisingly, this crevice is locally known as Lakshmaṇa-bāṇa, for it is believed that Lakshmaṇa shot his arrow into the ground here to get water. Perhaps, this may indicate a conflation of the earlier Śaivite cult with the cult of Rāma at this spot. Much of the Raghunātha temple complex dates from the sixteenth century. It is possible that the nucleus of this temple is of an earlier date, since in the *Narasiṁhapurāṇam* of Haribhaṭṭa it is written that one Prōlugaṅti Tippa, a contemporary of Dēvarāya II, gifted a valuable crown to god Raghunātha of Mālyavanta hill.[45] However, since this work was composed only about the year A.D. 1580[46] its reliability as a source of information may be questioned. While there are sixteenth century epigraphical references to this temple,[47] there does not seem to be any inscriptional evidence of its existence in the fourteenth or fifteenth centuries.

Thus, although the association of Haṁpi *tīrtha* and its immediate environs with the Kishkindhā section of the *Rāmāyaṇa* cannot be dated exactly, it definitely pre-dates the Vijayanagara empire. It is likely that, besides the association of the site with Paṁpā and Virūpāksha, the *Rāmāyaṇa* tradition at the site was a reason for its choice as the capital city. Yet the first Saṅgama rulers made no reference to Rāma or to the *Rāmāyaṇa* at this site in their inscriptions and there are no pre-fifteenth century temples dedicated to Rāma in the city. It was in the fifteenth and sixteenth centuries that the various pilgrimage spots linked with Rāma's exploits here were clearly identified and reliefs, shrines or temples were set up to highlight their importance.

It is not surprising that, despite the *Rāmāyaṇa* association at this site, the worship of Rāma in the city is not very ancient. For although the belief in Rāma as an *avatāra* of Vishṇu existed from the early centuries of the Christian era, the cult of Rāma came into existence only about the eleventh century A.D.[48] So far no shrine dedicated to Rāma and no cult image of this deity has come to light before the medieval period.[49] In Karṇāṭaka, although there are representations of the *Rāmāyaṇa* themes and of Rāma on temple walls from the early

Chālukya and Rāshṭrakūṭa periods, there are no temples dedicated to him till the Hoysaḷa period.[50] In the state, Rāma gained importance from the latter half of the Hoysaḷa period and became a popular deity during the Vijayanagara times.[51] Thus, the strong prevalence of the Rāma cult is a relatively later phenomenon, for the incarnation of Rāma definitely remained a minor one till the late medieval period.[52] Undoubtedly, in south India the Rāma cult became widely popular only during the Vijayanagara period.[53]

Within the empire, the royal patronage of the cult of Rāma dates from the early fifteenth century. In A.D. 1406, on the occasion of his coronation, Dēvarāya I gifted a village as an *agrahāra* to several brāhmaṇas after granting one share of it to the gods Rāmachandra and Śaṁbhu (Śiva).[54] An inscription of A.D. 1433 of Dēvarāya II, records a gift of a village to a temple of Rāmachandra.[55] Both Dēvarāya II[56] and Mallikārjuna[57] patronised the Raghūttama *maṭha* at Gōkarṇa and the temple of Rāma in it. Among the later rulers, Kṛishṇadēvarāya was the most generous in the lavish endowment of temples of various deities, including the temples of Rāma,[58] in different parts of his empire.

Within the capital, probably the earliest and certainly the most important Rāma temple is the one popularly known as Hazāra-Rāma (NR w/1), the real name of which, inscriptions reveal, was Rāmachandra temple.[59] It is located in the heart of the "royal centre", in the middle of the royal enclosures. As already seen, a north-south axis and a north-east axis link it with prominent natural features in the city. To the west of the Rāmachandra temple and aligned with it on an east-west axis, is the temple of Prasanna Virūpāksha, the royal chapel dedicated to the tutelary deity of the empire and the earliest temple within the "royal centre".

The Rāmachandra temple (Plate 16) was the first major construction in the capital in the imported Tamil style; it was worked on by the most skilled artisans and sculptors of the day, for the quality of its architecture and sculpture is truly outstanding. The temple complex is a fairly small one (see Fig. 15). It consists of a rectangular courtyard, with gateways in the east (A) and north (B) walls and a small doorway in the south wall (C), which was probably a private entrance for the ruler. The principal, east-facing shrine (D) has a square sanctum, a rectangular antechamber, a transitional rectangular bay and a square hall (*raṅga-maṇḍapa*) with porches on the east, north and south sides. In the sanctuary is a rectangular *pīṭha* (pedestal) with three socket holes, probably for statues of Rāma, Sītā and Lakshmaṇa. The open pillared *maṇḍapa* (E) to the east of the *raṅga-maṇḍapa* is a later addition. The subsidiary shrine (F) has two sanctuaries, an antechamber and a pillared hall. The enclosed *utsava-maṇḍapa* (G) in the north-east corner of the courtyard is probably a sixteenth century structure. This temple complex is fairly small. The limited space suggests a restricted use—possibly only for the king and his family, his priests and high officials. In all likelihood it was a state chapel.

The high enclosure wall of this temple complex is unique, for this is the only example in the city where there are continuous reliefs along the outer face of the wall. These reliefs, arranged in five sculptured friezes, run in a clockwise direction around three sides of the temple. The friezes display a procession of elephants, horses, soldiers, dancing girls and mythological scenes; occasionally seated royal figures are also present, leaning on cushions inside pavilions, sometimes with attendants. More than eighty metres east of the Rāmachandra temple and aligned with its east gateway are the remains of a lofty stone pillar and a shrine, which was probably intended to house Garuḍa or Hanumān.

The strategic location of the temple, the remarkable quality of its architecture and sculpture and the royal imagery on its enclosure walls—all indicate that it was a royal construction. But, there is no foundational inscription to reveal clearly who the royal founder was. The earlier writers[60] on Vijayanagara have erroneously attributed the temple construction to Kṛishṇadēvarāya. This temple is definitely of the early fifteenth century. A Sanskṛit inscription mentions king Dēvarāya and the goddess Paṁpā.[61] According to N. Venkataramanayya, the temple was built by the last Saṅgama ruler, Virūpāksha II, who following his conversion to Śrī-Vaishṇavism transformed an earlier Paṁpā temple into a temple of Rāma.[62] However, as seen in Chapter 1, the story of the conversion of Virūpāksha is based only on the

Prapannāmṛitam, a late piece of Śrī-Vaishṇava hagiography and is not supported by any other evidence. Besides, throughout the period under survey, Paṁpā-Virūpāksha remained the tutelary deity of the empire and it is highly unlikely that any ruler, whatever be his personal affiliation, would have replaced an extant temple dedicated to Paṁpā-dēvī by a temple to another deity.

This inscription carved on the east porch of the *raṅga-maṇḍapa* (Fig. 15: 1) has puzzled historians, for no mention is made in it of god Rāmachandra. It reads "Just as Vāṇi was gracious to Bhōja Rāja, Tripurāmba to Vatsa Rāja and Kāḷī to Vikramārka, just so is Paṁpā now gracious to king Dēvarāya." Michell has proposed an interesting explanation for this invocation by the king of the blessing of the goddess. Paṁpā, as seen in Chapter 2, was the local goddess of the site selected by the early Saṅgamas for their capital, the *śaktī* of Virūpāksha the tutelary deity of the kings. Therefore, some need must have been felt to integrate the older Śaiva cult with the rising importance of Rāma, a god who came to be worshipped in a splendidly appointed new temple in the heart of the king's own capital. Through this Sanskṛit *śloka*, Dēvarāya asserts that despite his patronage of Rāma, and his incorporation of the cult of this god into his "royal centre", he is still concerned about benefiting from the blessing of the goddess. "Dēvarāya has no intention of relinquishing his links with Paṁpā despite the dedication of his new royal shrine to Rama. This, we believe, is the basic intention of the epigraph and it provides us with an insight into the conflicts that must have arisen as the Vijayanagara kings broadened the scope of their religious beliefs."[63]

The above inscription indicates that one of the Dēvarāyas built the temple. This inscription, when read together with a second one (2), also on the basement of the east porch, reveals that the king was probably Dēvarāya I. It is likely that these two epigraphs, engraved one above the other and prominently displayed just north of the main entrance of the principal shrine, date from the consecration of the temple. In the second inscription[64] it is stated that Aṇṇala-dēvī presented gold vessels to Śrī Rāmachandra, on the first day of the bright fortnight of *Chaitra* in the year Durmukhi.[65] It is very probable that Durmukhi here represents A.D. 1416 and that Aṇṇala-dēvī may have been a queen of Dēvarāya I.[66] The type of royal figures depicted on the outer faces of the enclosure walls also indicates that this is an early temple.[67]

An inscription (3) dated 12 March A.D. 1513, on the south wall of the *utsava-maṇḍapa*[68] records the gift made by Kṛishṇadēvarāya of six villages to this temple.[69]

Another inscription (4) on the south basement of the *raṅga-maṇḍapa* of the principal shrine,[70] of A.D. 1521, and a damaged, unpublished one on the south basement of the sanctum (5) record the devotion of Timmarāja, son of *Mahāmaṇḍalēśvara* Chikka Timmayyadēva, the ruling king of Yeruva, to this temple deity. He built an *utsava-maṇḍapa* and made an endowment for the celebration of a number of festivals and services in the temple.

On the west wall of the north gateway (6) is the record of the installation of *āḷvārs* in the temple by Āravīṭi Veṅgaḷarāju.[71] The Āravīṭi chiefs, Rāmarāya, his brothers and cousins, rose to prominence during the reign of Sadāśiva. Hence, it is likely that this undated epigraph is of the last phase of the city's history. We do not know of an Āravīṭi prince named Veṅgaḷarāju. But, a younger brother of Aḷiya Rāmarāya is named Veṅkaṭādri. Since Veṅkaṭa and Veṅgaḷa are both names of the deity of Tirumalai-Tirupati it is possible that this prince was the author of the inscription.[72]

These inscriptions reveal the importance of this temple. It enjoyed patronage from the early fifteenth century up to the mid-sixteenth century. The authors of the inscriptions are all distinguished persons, namely, two kings, a queen, the son of a subordinate prince and a highly connected chief. The significance of the Rāmachandra temple is also indicated by its position in the centre of the royal enclosures, at the heart of the "royal centre" and its alignment with salient landmarks and structures. This temple was the key organizing feature of the plan of the "royal centre" and the city, for all the radial roads from outside into the city converged on the plaza adjacent to the temple, while the ring roads of the city pivoted around the royal enclosures at the centre of which is the Rāmachandra temple.[73]

The Rāmachandra temple is the only temple

in the city dedicated to this cult deity that can be definitely assigned to the fifteenth century on the basis of epigraphical evidence. However, as already seen, it is probable that the core of the Mālyavanta Raghunātha temple (Fig. 16) was also constructed during the Saṅgama period. This temple is built around a large boulder, which is completely incorporated into the *vimāna*, only protruding above the roof. In the sanctum (A) is a relief carved on this rock of the Rāma-Sītā-Lakshmaṇa-Hanumān group. Rāma and Sītā are seated, the former has his right hand in the *jñāna-mudrā*, while the left rests against the knee and the goddess holds a lotus flower in one hand; Lakshmaṇa is standing and Hanumān kneeling in adoration. All the figures wear magnificent head-dresses and ornaments. Stylistically these figures appear to have been carved during the period of the Saṅgama rulers.[74]

Many additions were made to the Mālyavanta Raghunātha temple in the sixteenth century A.D., such as the *mahā-maṇḍapa* (B) which has composite pillars and the detached columned hall (C) in the south-west corner of the courtyard. The latter is a typical feature of the sixteenth century temple complexes in Vijayanagara. This temple is one of the largest temples dedicated to Rāma in the city. The frequent occurrence of the *nāmam* and of reliefs of the *ālvārs* and Rāmānuja on pillars indicate that this was a Śrī-Vaishṇava temple. For many years it was deserted, but in fairly recent times worship has been revived in it and an annual car festival is organized by *bairāgis* from Bihār who have occupied it.[75]

On the south bank of the Tuṅgabhadrā, near the sacred Chakra-tīrtha, is the small, north-facing, sixteenth century temple of Kōdaṇḍarāma (NG w/1), the name indicating that Rāma holds the Kodaṇḍa or bow. As at Mālyavanta the images here are carved on a single boulder. Rāma, Sītā and Lakshmaṇa are standing, while Sugrīva bows low at Rāma's feet. These figures are not refined. Stylistically they probably belong to the reign of the last kings of Vijayanagara.[76] The temple belonged, most probably, to the Vaḍagalai Śrī-Vaishṇava sect, for the *nāmam* of the northern school appears on the temple pillars. It is a living temple; even today the *archakas* conducting the rituals are Vaḍagalai Śrī-Vaishṇavas.

That the cult of Rāma was popular in the city in the sixteenth century A.D. is revealed by the number of temples built in honour of this deity. To the north of the Hiriya Kāluve (Turutta canal) is a dilapidated Raghunātha temple (NL q/1) built in A.D. 1524 by Gōpinātha Dīkshita, who also donated some land to the temple. At the same time Kṛishṇadēvarāya laid down a system of offering daily a quantity of supplies from the Kṛishṇa temple for the food offerings to this god; while from the Paṁpā-Virūpāksha temple, too, a stipulated amount of rice and oil was to be supplied daily.[77]

The largest temple in the site dedicated to this deity is the so-called Paṭṭābhirāma temple, east of Kāmalāpuram (Plate 18). Although there is no foundational inscription in this temple, its construction can be assigned to the period of Achyutarāya since it is located in the new suburb built during his reign in honour of the queen. Besides, the inscriptions within the temple also belong to the reign of this king. An epigraph of A.D. 1539[78] reveals that this temple in Varadadēvī-ammana-paṭṭaṇa was of god Raghunātha and it records a gift to the deity of the toll revenue on garden produce, amounting to *varāhas* 1050, by one Achyutarāya-Mallapaṇṇa. This was also one of the temples in the capital on which king Achyutarāya inscribed his gift of *Ānandanidhi* to the brāhmaṇas in A.D. 1539.[79] On the east gōpura there are two Sanskṛit records of this, one in the Telugu script and the other in Nāgarī.[80] This temple, too, was undoubtedly a Śrī-Vaishṇava one.

During the same reign, in A.D. 1540, Timmarāju, son of Hiriya-Abbarāja, installed the god Raghunātha in a temple built by him to the east of Varada-dēvī-ammana-paṭṭaṇa near the Penugoṇḍa gate and made a grant of lands for the services in the temple.[81] This inscription is engraved on a large slab in front of this temple.

A slab erected in front of a small ruined temple (NS x/1) on a hill to the south-east of the Sōmavārada Bāgilu (Monday Gate) records a donation to god Gavikēri Raghunātha during the reign of Sadāśivarāya.[82] Since this is a donative grant, it is not possible to date this temple of Gavikēri Raghunātha. East of this temple is a deserted double-shrine temple (NT z/5). In the lower shrine is a relief of Vīrabhadra, while the upper one is built against a boulder on which is a carving of the *paṭṭābhishēka* (coronation) scene of the seated Rāma and Sītā flanked by the standing Lakshmaṇa, Bharata and Śatrughna.[83] This shrine of Paṭṭābhirāma, too, cannot be dated. An inscription on a double-storeyed *maṇḍapa* (NR y/3) east of the Rāmachandra temple records the construction of the *maṇḍapa* by the mercantile guild as a service to god Raghunātha.[84]

Thus, inscriptions or relief carvings indicate the presence of eight Rāma temples at the site. It is likely that there were other temples or shrines dedicated to Rāma of which we have no evidence. The epigraphs reveal that the patronage of the Rāma cult came not only from kings (Dēvarāya I and Kṛishṇadēvarāya), high dignitaries (Āravīṭi Veṅgaḷarāju) and subordinate chiefs (Timmarāja, son of the ruling king of Yeruva), but also from wealthy citizens (Gōpinātha Dīkshita, Achyutarāya-Mallapaṇṇa and Timmarāja, the son of Hiriya-Abbarāja) and from mercantile groups.

Besides the temples, sculptures also highlight the wide popularity enjoyed by this cult. Throughout the site, reliefs of Rāma are common on the pillars of temples, both Vaishṇava and Śaiva. He is usually depicted, according to the iconographic rules,[85] in the standing pose with the *bāṇa* or arrow in the right hand and the *dhanus* or bow in the left. Lakshmaṇa is also to be seen occasionally on pillar reliefs. To distinguish him from Rāma, Lakshmaṇa's bow is slung over one shoulder and his hands are joined in the *añjali-mudrā.* Carvings of the Rāma theme on rocks and isolated boulders are also extant. In the Yantrōdhāraka Āñjanēya shrine (NG w/3), besides the principal Hanumān relief, there is in a side shrine a fine carving of Rāma seated in *lalitāsana* with Sītā on his knee and Lakshmaṇa standing to one side. In a rock shelter (NG n/5) near Kōṭi-tīrtha, alongside the Narasiṁha relief, there is the representation of the Rāma-Sītā-Lakshmaṇa group. In another rock shelter (NS a/1), along with other Vaishṇava themes, is the relief of the seated Rāma and Sītā and standing Lakshmaṇa, flanked by Garuḍa and Hanumān. On the Hēmakūṭa hill, near temple NL b/14, is a rock-carving of Vira-Āñjanēya and to his left that of the standing Rāma, Sītā and Lakshmaṇa. This relief is unique since it is the only definitely non-Śaiva monument of the pre-Vijayanagara or Vijayanagara times extant on this hill. On a rock within the "royal centre" is a relief (NQ u/4) of Rāma and Sītā in a seated posture and Lakshmaṇa standing guard. Below the panel are carved Hanumān, Garuḍa and Śēsha. A large relief of Rāma and Lakshmaṇa appears on a boulder near temple NM d/3.

The *Rāmāyaṇa* association with the city and its surroundings is commemorated by *Rāmāyaṇa* panels. Besides the three complete series of the *Rāmāyaṇa* mentioned earlier (i.e., two from the Rāmachandra temple and one on the *gōpura* of temple NC w/3), which portray the complete story of Rāma from the Bāla Kāṇḍa to the Yuddha Kāṇḍa of the epic, there are also two series of the Uttara Kāṇḍa, the seventh and additional *kāṇḍa.* The first of these is on the exterior walls of the *vimāna* of the subsidiary shrine within the Rāmachandra temple complex. The main episodes of Uttara Kāṇḍa are to be found here, arranged in two tiers. The second occurs in the *uyyāle-maṇḍapa* of the principal shrine in the Viṭhala complex (NH a/1). This *maṇḍapa* is divided into three parts: in the central portion of the north aisle there are vertical slabs forming an architrave above the pillars. Along these are panels of some of the episodes of the Uttara Kāṇḍa—the *aśvamedha* sacrifice organized by Rāma, the capture of the horse by the twins, Lava and Kusha, etc. A number of *Rāmāyaṇa* reliefs are also seen on the two pillars of the north porch of the principal shrine of the Viṭhala complex and on the east *gōpura* of the Tiruveṅgaḷanātha temple (NM h/1). Stray reliefs of incidents from the epic are to be found on pillars of many temples such as in the Śiva temple NG t/3, in the *raṅga-maṇḍapa* of the principal shrine of the Viṭhala temple and in the south-east corner pavilion in the same complex.

Rāmāyaṇa themes may have also been popular in temple paintings. Unfortunately, very few paintings have survived at the site. The best preserved paintings are on the ceiling of the *mahā-raṅga-maṇḍapa* of the Virūpāksha temple (NF w/1). Here the depiction of the *Sītā-svamyamvara* and the marriage of Rāma and Sītā are prominent.

In the Indian tradition, Rāma is considered to be the ideal king. One reason for the wide prevalence of the Rāma cult and the royal patronage it enjoyed in Vijayanagara was, perhaps, the homology drawn between Rāma, the ideal, universal monarch and the earthly king reigning from his capital. The city was compared to Ayōdhyā, Rāmā's capital. For example an inscription of A.D. 1379 states, "in the same city (Vijaya) did Harihara dwell, as in former times Rāma dwelt in the midst of the city of Ayōdhyā."[86]

Fritz and Michell have highlighted the centrality of the Rāmachandra temple in the urban planning of the city. It is the key to the understanding of the partnership envisaged between the deity and the king. This temple is at the nucleus of the "royal centre", from where the king's authority emanated outwards to the city and the empire; around it are arranged all the enclosures and architectural elements of this zone. The temple is the focus of the radial road system of the city and it also acts as a pivot for the concentric circumambulatory routes. The temple helps to define the "royal centre" into two parts. The north-south axis of the temple, besides axially aligning the temple with important landmarks, also separates the "royal centre" into the zones of royal performance and royal residence. The zone to the east of this axis is connected with the public roles of the king (administrative, military and ritualistic), while in the enclosures to the west of this axis were enacted the private roles of the royal household. Thus, the god is at the centre of the king's public and private life. Such an emphasis on Rāma as the nucleus of the city plan suggests the profound significance of this deity for the Vijayanagara rulers. The king and the god were the focus of the "royal centre" and the city; the monarch was the most powerful terrestrial partner of the god.[87]

It has been suggested that "Ramachandra was conceived as being 'within' the king, 'empowering' or 'generating' his activities."[88] This aspect of the relationship between the god and the king is hinted at in the arrangement of the reliefs on the enclosure walls of the Rāmachandra temple complex. On the inner faces of the walls, between the north and east getaways, are *Rāmāyaṇa* reliefs distributed in panels on six horizontal courses (Plate 17). On the outer faces of the walls are the five courses of reliefs displaying royal pageantry—the celebration of the royal rituals of the *Mahānavamī* and *Vasantōtsava* festivals. While in the interior Rāma is the focus of the friezes, on the exterior the attention is directed to the king and his power and wealth.

If the king in Vijayanagara is identified with Rāma, in turn Rāma is also portrayed as a king. This is to be found in certain reliefs in the temples, which are at variance with the traditionally accepted iconographic representations of this god.[89] In these unusual reliefs, Rāma is shown sitting on a throne-like seat, leaning against a cushion or bolster, with one leg crossed over the other, often with one hand raised in the *tarjanī-mudrā* (one finger pointing upwards) and usually with a shawl draped around one arm (Plate 19). He is depicted exactly as the kings are on the enclosure walls of the Rāmachandra temple complex (Plate 20), on the Mahānavamī Platform and elsewhere. The only difference is in the headdress: while the god wears the *kirīṭa-mukuṭa*, the typical crown worn by Vishṇu in his diverse manifestations, the kings are bareheaded or wear the *kullāyi.* Occasionally in such reliefs, Rāma is accompanied by Lakshmaṇa or Hanumān, either in the same panel or in the adjacent one.[90]

Thus, Vijayanagara and its surroundings are considered to be intimately connected with the earthly adventures of god Rāmachandra. The cult of Rāma from the fifteenth century onwards enjoyed an extensive following in the city and it had a special significance for the kings.

Notes

[1]H.V. Sreenivasa Murthy and R. Ramakrishna, *A History of Karnataka: From the Earliest Times to the Present Day*, p. 23.

[2]Ibid.

[3]Masti Venkatesa Iyengar, *Popular Culture in Karnataka*, p. 136.

[4]D.R. Bhandarkar, "Daṇḍakāraṇya", in *Jha Commemoration Volume*, ed. K. Chattopadhyaya et al., pp. 48-50.

[5]K.C. Aryan and S. Aryan, *Hanuman in Art and Mythology*, p. 72, (a footnote).

[6]D.R. Bhandarkar, op.cit., pp. 51-52.

[7]M.V. Kibe, "Rāvana's Laṅkā located in Central India," *IHQ*, IV, pp. 694-702; G. Ramadas, "Rāvana's Lanka," *IHQ*, IV, pp. 339-346; R.B. Hiralal, "The Situation of Rāvana's Lanka" in *Jha Commemoration Volume*, ed. K. Chattopadhyaya et al., pp. 151-161.

[8]V.H. Vader, "Situation of Ravana's Lanka on the

Equator," *IHQ*, II, pp. 345-350.

[9]D.P. Mishra, "The Search for Laṅkā," *Mahakōśala Historical Society*, vol. I, cited by S.B. Chaudhuri, "Lanka," *IHQ*, XXVII, p. 119.

[10]Araṇya Kāṇḍa lxxiv. 19 (of the Vālmīki *Rāmāyaṇa*), cited by F.E. Pargiter, "The Geography of Rāma's Exile," *JRAS*, 1894, p. 250.

[11]Araṇya Kāṇḍa lxxv. 57-66, Ibid., p. 251.

[12]Araṇya Kāṇḍa lxxvii. 2-5, Ibid., p. 252.

[13]Araṇya Kāṇḍa lxxv. 63, Ibid., p. 254.

[14]Araṇya Kāṇḍa lx. 3-12, Ibid., p. 255.

[15]Kishkindhā Kāṇḍa ii and iii, Ibid.

[16]Kishkindhā Kāṇḍa iv, 1, Ibid.,

[17]Kishkindhā Kāṇḍa iv, v and vii, Ibid.

[18]Kishkindhā Kāṇḍa xxvii, 1., Ibid., p. 256.

[19]Kishkindhā Kāṇḍa xxvi, 1-4, Ibid.

[20]Kishkindhā Kāṇḍa xxxviii, 11, 36, Ibid.

[21]Sundara Kāṇḍa lxvi.1, Ibid.

[22]These spots connected with the Rāmayana that are listed above are as pointed out by the local pilgrim guides and as given in the pilgrim maps. Many of these were also mentioned by H. Daniel Smith in his talk "Rāma Padyātra," delivered on 29 March 1988, at the University Club House, Bombay, under the aegis of the Anantacharya Indological Research Institute and the Museum Society.

[23]*Pampamahatmya*, first part, chapter 73.

[24]*Hemakutakhanda*, chapters 32-34 and *Pampamahatmya*, first part, chapter 67.

[25]A. Sundara, "New Lights on Religious Trends in Anegondi Region during Vijayanagara Period," *QJMS*, LXVIII, p. 9.

[26]H. Krishna Sastri, *Munirabad Stone Inscription of the 13th Year of Tribhuvanamala (Vikramaditya VI)*.

[27]P.B. Desai, ed., *A History of Karnataka*, pp. 40-41.

[28]A. Sundara, op.cit., pp. 10-11.

[29]V. Raghavan, "The Virūpākṣa Vasantotsava Campū of Ahōbala," *JOR*, XIV, p. 23.

[30]Ibid., p. 32.

[31]According to V. Raghavan, this work must have been produced during the time of Harihara I (Ibid., p. 17). According to R.S. Panchamukhi (Introduction to the *Virūpāksha Vasantōtsava Chaṁpū*, p. xvi), it belongs to the second half of the 14th century A.D. However, the internal evidence indicates that it is highly unlikely that this was a 14th century work. In the *Chaṁpū* the city is referred to as Vidyānagara, but this name became current only in the 16th century. Mention is made in it of the great eastern *gōpura* of the temple, but it is unlikely that this could have existed in the 14th century. The reference to the pulling of the temple chariot up to the Nandi statue at the foothill of Mataṅga indicates the existence of the *ratha-vīdhi*, which appears to be part of the late 15th or 16th century expansion of the temple. The main reason for attributing it to the 14th century is that Vidyāraṇya is stated to be present and to play an honoured role in the festival, as did the king. The two learned authors were probably unaware that Vidyāraṇya became the title of the ruling pontiff of the Advaita *maṭha* at Vijayanagara (just as Sankarāchārya is the honorific title assumed by the heads of the *pīṭhas* that trace their origin to the great *advaitin* sage), which was originally a branch of the *Śrīṅgeri maṭha*. This is indicated in an inscription of Kṛishṇadēvarāya of A.D. 1515 (B.R. Gopal, *Vijayanagara Inscriptions*, vol. II, no. 526). Even today, the present head of the Haṁpi *maṭha*, Narasiṁha Bharati, is called Vidyāraṇya *svāmi*. In modern times, too, the spiritual descendant of the original Vidyāraṇya *svāmi* and the descendant of the Vijayanagara rulers, the erstwhile ruler of Ānegoṅdi, played an important role in the annual car-festival of Virūpāksha. Thus, it is possible that this *chaṁpū* was a 16th century literary work.

[32]J.M. Fritz, "Vijayanagara : Authority and Meaning of a South Indian Imperial Capital," *American Anthropologist*, 88 (1), p. 53.

[33]J.M. Fritz, "Was Vijayanagara A 'Cosmic City'?" in *Vij. City & Emp.* vol. 1, pp. 266-269.

[34]Anna L. Dallapiccola and Anila Verghese, "Ramayana Panels on the Gopura of the 'Old Shiva' Temple, Vitthalapura", in *VPR '87-88*, pp. 143-153.

[35]*FE*, p. 390.

[36]R. Shama Sastry, "A Few Inscriptions of the Ancient Kings of Anegondi," *QJMS*, VII, pp. 287 and 291.

[37]Ibid., p. 285.

[38]*VPR '83-84*, no. 12, p. 29.

[39]*SII* IX, pt. II, no. 564.

[40]C.T.M. Kotraiah, "Pampa Sarassu, Kiskindha and Hampi," paper read at the Centenary Celebrations of the Mysore Directorate of Archaeology and Museums, p. 8.

[41]*VPR '84-87*, no. 161.

[42]*SII* IX, pt. II, no. 445.

[43]*Pampamahatmya*, first part, chapter 61.

[44]*SII* IV, no. 267.

[45]*Further Sources*, vol. III, pp. 46-47.

[46]*QJMS*, XXXI, p. 148.

[47]*EC* XI, Hr. 75 and 76; *SII* IX, pt. II, no. 670.

[48]R.G. Bhandarkar, *Vaisṇavism, Śaivism and Minor Religious Systems*, p. 47.

[49]K. Desai, *Iconography of Viṣṇu*, p. 116.

[50]S.V. Padigar, "The Cult of Vishṇu in Karnataka" (Ph.D. diss.), p. 380.

[51]Ibid., p. 336.

[52]K. Desai, op.cit., p. 120.

[53]K.V. Soundara Rajan, *The Art of South India: Tamil Nadu and Kerala*, p. 49.

[54]*EC* V, Hn. 133.

[55]*ARSIE* of 1929-30, B.K. no. 119.

[56]*MAR* of 1933. nos. 26 and 27.

[57]*EC* VIII, Nr. 68 and 69.

[58]*SII* IX, pt. II., no. 496; *EC* V, Ag. 86; *ARSIE* of 1942-43, no. 183; A Butterworth and V. Venugopal Chetty, *A Collection of Inscriptions on Copper-Plates and Stones in the Nellore District* (referred to hereafter as *Nel. Ins.*), pt. III, Udaygiri, no. 37.

[59]*SII* IV, nos. 250, 251, 253; *VPR '83-84*, no. 67.

[60]R. Sewell, *FE*, p. 161; A.H. Longhurst, *Hampi Ruins*, p. 69.

[61]*SII* IV, no. 252.

[62]N. Venkataramanayya, "The Date of the Construction of the Temples of Hazāra-Rāmasvāmi and Viṭṭhala at Vijayanagara," *JOR*, XVI, pp. 84-87.

[63]G. Michell, "Kings and Cults," in *The Ramachandra*

Temple at Vijayangara by A.L. Dallapiccola, J.M. Fritz, and G. Michell, p. 20.

[64]*SII* IV, no. 251.

[65]The cyclic year Durmukhi during the Vijayanagara period coincided with A.D. 1356-57, 1416-17, 1476-77 and 1536-37.

[66]*MAR* of 1920, p. 36.

[67]These figures are very similar to the regal figures depcited on the 14th century first phase of the Mahānavamī Platform. In both cases, the men wear only a short *dhōti*. They have long hair, tied up in a large knot at the back of the head. In the later period there is a definite change in the courtly attire—the kings and other noble personages always wear a high cap, the *kullāyi*, and besides the *dhōti* they often also wear a short jacket and often have a shawl thrown over one arm. This can be seen on the 16th century A.D. third phase of the Mahānavamī Platform, in the statue of Kṛishṇadēvaraya at Tirumalai, on the pillar reliefs in the subsidiary shrine of the Tiruveṅgaḷanātha temple (NM h/1), etc. The earliest example of this type of costume is to be seen in the so-called Āñjanēya temple (NV o/1) of Mallikārjuna's reign where, in the portrait sculptures of the king and his attendant Śiraṅgu, both sport the *kullāyi* (see *VPR '79-83*, plate LIII; and N. Lakshminarayan Rao, "Portrait Sculpture of the Vijayanagara King Mallikarjuna," in *Studies in Indian History and Culture*, ed. S. Ritti and B.R. Gopal, pp. 181-82). Thus, in the 14th and early 15th centuries A.D., the kings were bareheaded and had hair tied in a big knot, while from the mid-15th century onwards the *kullāyi*, which covered the hair, became *de rigueur*.

[68]*SII* IV, no. 253.

[69]At the same time the king made similar grants to three other temples. These grants were all made on the auspicious occasion of a solar eclipse that occurred on the 7th March A.D. 1513 (*SII* IX, pt. II, no. 490). The other temples were the great Virūpāksha (*SII* IX, pt. II, no. 493), the Prasanna Virūpāksha (*SII* IX, pt. II, no. 491) and the Viṭhala (*SII* IV, nos. 273 and 278) temples. The choice of these four temples for rich endowments on the same occasion is significant. They are the temple of the tutelary deity, the royal chapel dedicated to the same deity within the "royal centre", the state chapel of Rāmachandra and the temple which in the 16th century became the most important Vaishṇava centre in the city.

[70]*SII* IV, no. 250.

[71]*VPR '83-84*, no. 67, p. 49.

[72]16th century A.D. inscriptions reveal many variations in the names of Āravīḍu chiefs. For example, Tirumala, the younger brother of Aḷiya Rāmarāya, who became the first king of fourth dynasty, is also referred to as Yera-Timmarāja (*SII* IV, no. 265 and 266). Thus, Tirumala and Timma are used interchangeably. Similarly, Rāmarāya's paternal uncle Peda Koṇḍrāja is mentioned as Koṇḍaiyadēva (*SII* IV, no. 275) and his son Kōnēṭirāja as Kōnetayyadēva (Ibid.) and Kōnēṭi-Timmarāja (*SII* IX pt. II, no. 616). Suffixes such as rāja or rāju, dēva and ayya are often added to the names and are also used interchangeably.

[73]J.M. Fritz, "The Roads of Vijayanagara : A Preliminary Study," in *VPR '79-83*, pp. 55-56.

[74]V. Filliozat, "Iconography," in *Splendours of the Vijayanagara Empire: Hampi*, ed. G. Michell and V. Filliozat, p. 129.

[75]A.H. Longhurst, *Hampi Ruins*, p. 134.

[76]V. Filliozat, loc.cit.

[77]*VPR '83-84*, no. 16, pp. 31-32.

[78]*SII* IX, pt. II, no. 595.

[79]The other temples are the Viṭhala (NH a/1), Tiruveṅgaḷanātha (NM h/1), Kṛishṇa (NL m/4) temples and the Chinnahudiyam temple near Kāmalāpuram.

[80]*SII* XVI, no. 120 and *ARSIE* of 1904, no. 20.

[81]*SII* IV, no. 245.

[82]*VPR '83-84*, no. 65, p. 48.

[83]According to R. Champakalakshmi, *Vaiṣṇava Iconography in the Tamil Country*, p. 125, it is only in the coronation scene that Bharata and Satrughna are shown along with the seated Rāma and Sītā and the standing Lakshmaṇa.

[84]*VPR '83-84*, no. 68, p. 49.

[85]T.A. Gopinatha Rao, *Elements of Hindu Iconography*, vol. 1, pt. I, p. 189.

[86]Cited by B.A. Saletore, *Soc. & Pol. Life*, vol. I, p. 121.

[87]J.M. Fritz and G. Michell "Interpreting the plan of a medieval Hindu capital, Vijayanagara," *World Archaeology*, 19, 1, pp. 123-127.

[88]J.M., Fritz, "Archaeological Documentation at Vijayanagara," in *South Asian Archaeology—1983*, ed. J. Schotsmans, and M. Taddei, p. 883.

[89]According to R. Champakalakshmi, op.cit., pp. 124-125, Rāma is usually depicted in a standing pose, holding the bow and arrow in his two hands; occasionally he is shown with four hands, in which case in the upper hands he holds the *śaṅkha* and *chakra*. At times, Rāma is shown along with Sītā, Lakshmaṇa and Hanumān, all four may be standing or Rāma and Sītā may be seated while Lakshmaṇa and Hanumān are standing. It is only in the *paṭṭābhishēka* scene that the other two brothers are also represented. In this scene the god and goddess are usually represented as seated (in *lalitāsana*). Thus, an icon of Rāma seated by himself does not occur in the iconographic canon.

[90]In my first field trips to Haṁpi, such images of Rāma were wrongly identified by me as that of Vijayanagara kings. It was only the occasional presence of Hanumān or Lakshmaṇa near Rāma or in an adjacent panel and *kirīṭa-mukuṭa* worn by the deity that helped in identifying this unusual type of image as that of Rāma. In a discussion about the nature of such images with Dr. A.L. Dallapiccola, it was suggested that the Vijayanagara sculptors had resorted to "intentional ambiguity" in these reliefs, in order perhaps to draw a parallel between the divine and earthly kings.

CHAPTER 5

Kṛishṇa and Viṭhala Cults

Among the most important Vaishṇava cults in the city were those of Kṛishṇa and of Viṭhala (a form of Kṛishṇa). These gods, especially the latter, were extremely popular in the sixteenth century. While other significant cults in the city had a number of temples or shrines dedicated to their respective cult deities, in the case of the Kṛishṇa and Viṭhala cults there was only one great temple dedicated to each of these divinities, besides some minor shrines. The Kṛishṇa temple (NL m/4) was constructed in the early sixteenth century A.D., while the famous Viṭhala temple (NH a/1), although dating back to the fifteenth century, rose to prominence only in the sixteenth century. These temples, especially the latter, played a key role in the religious life of the city in the sixteenth century. Indeed, not only did the Viṭhala temple during the Tuḷuva period become the most important Vaishṇava temple in Vijayanagara, in the last twenty-five years of the city's history it even overshadowed in importance the great Virūpāksha temple.

The Mādhvas in particular and the Śrī-Vaishṇavas, to a lesser extent, are great adorers of Kṛishṇa. Mādhvas worship Vishṇu and have a high reverence for Kṛishṇa and Narasiṁha, the eighth and fourth *avatāras* of Vishṇu. They worship Kṛishṇa as a baby boy; Viṭhala is considered to be another form of Kṛishṇa.[1] The centre of Madhvāchārya's religion is *bhakti* to Kṛishṇa as taught in the *Bhāgavata Purāṇa*, Rādhā having no place in it.[2] All the other *avatāras* are revered; Śiva is venerated and the 'five gods' (*Pāñchāyatana*) are recognized.[3] According to tradition, Madhvāchārya set up a *maṭha* of Kṛishṇa at Uḍipi. Towards the close of his life he had ordained eight monks for the conduct of worship at this *maṭha*. These established lines of their own and these lines of ascetics became the precursors of the *ashṭamaṭhas* of later times.[4] The *maṭha* of Kṛishṇa at Uḍipi, where Madhvāchārya set up the image of Śrī Kṛishṇa, is the historical and spiritual capital of the Mādhva community as a whole.[5] The immense popularity of Kṛishṇa and Viṭhala among the Mādhvas can be seen at the site in the reliefs on the *bṛindāvanas* or *samādhis* of two Mādhva saints, Vyāsarāya and Raghunandana. On the four faces of the *bṛindāvana* of Vyāsarāya, at Navabṛindāvana near Ānegoṅdi, are carved Bālakṛishṇa, Viṭhala, Narasiṁha and Rāma-Sītā-Lakshmaṇa; on that of Raghunandana (NG n/1) are reliefs of Kṛishṇa as Vēṇugōpāla, Viṭhala, Mādhava (one of the twenty-four forms of Vishṇu, shown holding the *chakra, śaṅkha, gadā* and *padma* in his upper right, upper left, lower right and lower left hands respectively) and Rāma.

1. The Kṛishṇa Cult

In Karṇāṭaka, Kṛishṇa was already recognized as an *avatāra* of Vishṇu during the period of the early western Chālukyas. In the last phase of this period Kṛishṇa is represented prominently and individually in his different feats on the pillars of temples. During the Rāshṭrakūṭa period Kṛishṇa's popularity as Gōpāla is implied in the prominent depictions of this form in the caves at Ellora, as well as by the image of Vēṇugōpāla found in south Kanara. During the tenth to the fourteenth centuries representations of Vēṇugōpāla were common.[6] In the Tamil country the *Bhāgavata* stories of Kṛishṇa appear to have been extremely popular in the seventh to ninth centuries A.D. as evidenced by frequent references to them in the hymns of the *āḻvārs*.[7] *Bhāgavata* scenes begin to appear in sculptures from the seventh century onwards and increase by about the end of the ninth century A.D.[8] The earliest cult images of Kṛishṇa in Tamil Nāḍu date from the tenth century A.D.[9] In north India there are reliefs of Kṛishṇa's exploits dating even from the Kushāna period, i.e., the second century A.D., and from the Gupta period.[10] However, although the acceptance of Kṛishṇa as an *avatāra* of Vishṇu dates back to fairly early times, in general, the images of Kṛishṇa till the medieval period are more illustrative reliefs than static cult images.[11]

Of the reliefs in the Vijayanagara temples, none probably are as recurrent as those of the diverse feats of Bālakṛishṇa. The wide prevalence of the *Kṛishṇa-līlā* scenes cut across sectarian lines–they are found in Vaishṇava and Śaiva temples alike. Some of the favourites themes of the sculptors are of the crawling Bālakṛishṇa, who at times is shown holding a ball of butter in one hand, the child Kṛishṇa stealing butter or dancing with joy at having secured a ball of butter to eat (Navanīta-nṛitta-mūrti), Bālakṛishṇa holding his ears in penitence, the Yamalārjuna-bhañga episode when Kṛishṇa–who had been tied with a rope to a mortar by his foster mother Yaśodā–tried to pass through the Yamala and Arjuna trees and in the process uprooted them, the subjugation of the serpent Kāliya (Kāliya-mardana), Kṛishṇa hiding the clothes of the *gopīs* who were bathing in the river Yamunā and Kṛishṇa delighting the *gopas, gopīs* and the cows with his enchanting flute music (Vēṇugōpāla).

In Vijayanagara, reliefs of Kṛishṇa are to be found not only in temples throughout the city, but also right through the period under survey. A few examples will illustrate the extensive popularity of the Kṛishṇa narrative reliefs. The earliest image of this deity at the site is probably the Navanīta-nṛitta-Kṛishṇa carved on the lintel of the pre-Vijayanagara door-frame[12] of the Gavi Raṅganātha shrine in Ānegoṅdi. In the triple-shrine Śaiva temple on Hēmakūṭa hill (NL b/1) of the early Vijayanagara period, there are some fine reliefs on the exterior walls of the central shrine of Vēṇugōpāla, Bālakṛishṇa stealing butter from a hanging pot and Kṛishṇa stealing butter while Yaśodā is churning. In the fifteenth century *raṅga-maṇḍapa* of the Viṭhala temple there are pillar reliefs of Navanīta-nṛitta-Kṛishṇa, the baby Kṛishṇa killing the demoness Pūtanā, Bālakṛishṇa stealing butter, Yamalārjuna-bhañga, Kāliyamardana, Bālakṛishṇa holding his ears, the destruction of the crane demon Bakāsura, the Govardhana-dhāra episode, when Kṛishṇa protected his cowherd companions by lifting the mountain over them, and the destruction of the elephant Kuvalayāpīḍa. A number of *Kṛishṇa-līlā* scene are seen on the pillars of the *mahā-raṅga-maṇḍapa* of the Virūpāksha temple that was built by Kṛishṇadēvarāya in A.D. 1509-10 and naturally also in the Kṛishṇa temple that was constructed by him a few years later. The most complete series of the adventures of Bālakṛishṇa is in the *uyyāle-maṇḍapa* of the Viṭhala temple, built in A.D. 1554. In the central portion of the south aisle of this *maṇḍapa* the ceiling is raised by vertical slabs, all along which are the reliefs of episodes such as Pūtanā-vadha, Bakāsura-vadha, Kāliya-mardana, Aghāsura-vadha (killing of the monstrous python demon), Śakaṭa-bhañga (over-turning a cart), Bālakṛishṇa stealing butter, Vēṇugōpāla, Govardhana-dhāra, the defeat of the wrestlers Śala, Chāṇūra and Mushṭika, and the destruction of Kuvalayāpīḍa.

Despite the frequent depictions of narrative reliefs of the Kṛishṇa story, we do not have conclusive proof of temples dedicated to this deity before the construction of the great Kṛishṇa temple complex by Kṛishṇadēvarāya in A.D. 1515. There are three temples which, on the basis of iconographic evidence, might have been dedicated to Kṛishṇa. The earliest of these is a small temple in the "urban core" (NN z/2), which probably belongs to the last quarter of the fourteenth century.[13] There are no images in this temple besides the carvings on the lintels of the two doorways. On the lintel of the main (southern) door-frame is seated Lakshmī, whereas on the eastern doorway is a crawling Bālakṛishṇa. Lakshmī is commonly depicted on door-frames of Vaishṇava and even Śaiva temples, but the presence of Bālakṛishṇa is an indicator that this might have been a Kṛishṇa temple.

The second is the so-called "Āñjanēya" temple (NV o/1) of the reign of king Mallikārjuna, in which there are two brief inscriptions on either side of the doorway into the sanctum;[14] while one mentions Mallikārjuna,[15] the other states that the temple was built by Śiraṅgu an attendant of the king.[16] On the lintel of the sanctum door is carved Yamalārjuna-bhañga. That this was probably a Śrī-Vaishṇava temple is indicated by the number of reliefs of *āḻvārs* and of Rāmānuja that are present on the pillars.[17]

The third temple is the one that is now known as the "Sarasvatī" temple (NL s/1) which is not far from the great Kṛishṇa temple. In this small, dilapidated temple there are no images or reliefs to reveal its cultic affiliation. But, in a brick and mortar niche above and directly behind the sanctum is a large stucco image of Yamalārjuna-bhañga. From this we can conjecture that Kṛishṇa was originally enshrined within.

The lintel images of first two temples and the stucco figure above the sanctum of the third indicate that these three might have been dedicated to Kṛishṇa. However, although usually the *lalāṭabiṁba* or the image on the lintel is an indicator of the deity to whom the temple is dedicated, the presence of Bālakṛishṇa as the *lalāṭabiṁba* of the Gavi Raṅganātha temple shows that this cannot be relied on as conclusive evidence as to its affiliation. Similarly, the stucco figure above the sanctum also cannot be taken as conclusive proof that the deity within the sanctum was Kṛishṇa. Therefore, in the absence of *mūrits* in the sanctums and of corroborating epigraphical or literary evidences, we cannot assert definitively that these three were Kṛishṇa temples.

The Kṛishṇa cult in the city was propagated and fostered by the great Kṛishṇadēvarāya, who, following his victorious Udayagiri campaign, brought an icon of the deity from Udayagiri and installed it in a magnificent and spacious temple complex (NL m/4) that he built in his capital in A.D. 1515 (Plate 21). There is iconographic evidence that the king was well aware that he was incorporating and promoting a practically new cult in the city. In the *mahā-maṇḍapa* of the temple there is an unusual porch-like projection in the middle of the front, or eastern, side in which there are pillars with exquisite reliefs. On the south-east pillar of this porch, on the west face (i.e., facing the sanctum) mid-square is the carving of a standing royal devotee with hands joined in adoration before Bālakṛishṇa (Plate 23). On the opposite north-west corner pillar, on the top square of the south face is a similar noble parsonage worshipping a *Śiva-liṅga* (Plate 24). This is the only representation of a *liṅga* in the entire complex. This fact and the prominent location of this relief hints at its special significance. As seen in Chapter 2, Virūpāksha, the tutelary deity of the Vijayanagara rulers, was only represented in the aniconic form of a *liṅga* and even in epigraphs this deity is often known as Virūpāksha-liṅga. It is most likely that the noble person depicted is the king himself and that he is shown rendering homage to both the tutelary deity, whose temple he had richly endowed a few years previously on the occasion of his coronation,[18] and to Bālakṛishṇa the cult deity consecrated in this new, superb temple.

In Chapter 4 it was seen that Dēvarāya I, on the occasion of the consecration of Rāmachandra in the "royal centre", felt it necessary to invoke the blessing of goddess Paṁpā (and through her that of her consort Virūpāksha) and thus to integrate the older Śaiva cult with the rising importance of Rāma. A hundred years later, Kṛishṇadēvarāya experienced a similar compulsion to assert, through these two reliefs, that despite his patronage of Kṛishṇa and the promotion of this cult in the capital, he had no intention of relinquishing his links with Virūpāksha.

The splendid temple built to house the *mūrti* brought as a war-trophy by the king was situated in the new quarter of the city named Kṛishṇāpura.[19] An inscription of A.D. 1543 reveals that Kṛishṇāpura was an *agrahāra*.[20] In it was a market, Kṛishṇāpura-pēṭe, that extended southwards from the Kṛishṇa temple at least till the Mudu-Vīraṇṇa temple (NL w/3).[21] In Kṛishṇāpura-pēte there was a grain market (*davasada-aṅgaḍi*).[22]

The cult icon that was installed in the temple is referred to in the dedicatory inscriptions[23] both as Kṛishṇa and as Śrī-Bālakṛishṇa. In later inscriptions[24] the deity is invariably called by the latter name. Hence the temple should more appropriately be referred to as the Bālakṛishṇa temple; but, since the area is known as Kṛishṇāpura and the deity has also been termed as Kṛishṇa, it can also be called the Kṛishṇa temple. At present the sanctum is empty, but in A.D. 1916, during the clearance work carried out in its precincts, the original *mūrti* was found and can today be seen in the Madras Museum (Plate 22).

It was lying in a corner of the *cella* where it has been thrown either by the Muslim soldiers or by treasure-seekers. Like most idols found in the city, it is severely mutilated. It is a stone statue of Bālakṛishṇa. The deity is represented as chubby boy seated on a pedestal with the right foot resting on a lotus flower which serves as a foot-stool. The arms are missing, but, in all probability, the right hand held a butter ball and the left hand rested on the left thigh. The image including the pedestal is about a metre in height and is carved out of a block of greenish black stone similar to that found at Udayagiri in the Nellore district. The figure is in the nude but is profusely decorated with jewellery. The image originally stood on a large detached *pīṭha* of the same material.[25] A.H. Longhurst, who discovered this image, claims to have seen the original pedestal, now broken, in the Kṛishṇa temple at Udayagiri. According to him this was the image brought by Kṛishṇadēvarāya after his successful campaign.[26]

However, V. Filliozat asserts that this image is not the Udayagiri icon. In Kṛishṇadēvarāya's inscriptions in the temple[27] it is mentioned that the Udayagiri image was placed in a jewelled *maṇḍapa* (*maṇi-maṇḍapa*), in other words, it was not installed in the sanctum. According to her, the Udayagiri statue was the *utsava-mūrti* and not the *mūla-mūrti*. The statue now in the Madras Museum was the *mūla-mūrti* (i.e, the cult image in the sanctum) and it was a Vijayanagara icon.[28]

There is no trace of the *mūrti* of Kṛishṇa's consort from this temple. Epigraphical evidence reveals that she was called Lakshmī-dēvī (and not Rukmiṇī) and that provision was also made for her worship.[29]

The Kṛishṇa temple (Fig. 17) is one of the largest in the city. It has two *prākāras* or courtyards, one within the other, each surrounded by high enclosure walls. Within the inner *prākāra* is the main shrine and subsidiary structures. The main, east-facing shrine (A) consists of *garbha-gṛiha*, two antechambers, an enclosed circumambulatory passage, a *raṅga-maṇḍapa* with porches on the north and south sides and an open *mahā-maṇḍapa* with a four-pillar porch-like projection in front. To the north-west of this principal shrine is the subsidiary shrine (B) comprising an east-facing *cella* and antechamber, a *maṇḍapa* and a small, south-facing *cella* that opens onto the *maṇḍapa*. An unusual feature of this temple complex is the presence of four small shrines, probably for attendant deities, around the principal shrine. There is one each in the north-east (C) and south-east (D) sides and two in the south-west (E).

Along the enclosure wall there is pillared gallery right around the *prākāra*. In the north-east and south-east corners of this gallery there is an enclosed *maṇḍapa* (F). These *maṇḍapas* probably served as storerooms or kitchens. There is a *gōpura* in the middle of the east, north and south walls. The east *gōpura* (G) is a majestic monument; on its super-structure there is an interesting depiction in stucco of a war scene, probably of an actual historical event, such as the Udayagiri campaign.

The outer *prākāra* has simple gateways, without superstructures. In the north-west corner of this *prākāra* is a sixteen-pillared open *maṇḍapa* (H) and a small tank (I). On the south-west side is a unique six-domed structure (J), the only example of an "Islamic style" building within a temple complex in the city. This building has small entrance positioned in the middle of its long, eastern side; steps ascend up to the roof. The lack of openings in the structure and the holes in the domes suggests that this was some sort of storehouse, perhaps even a granary.[30]

On the eastern side of the outer *prākāra* there are some small structures. Adjoining the inner *prākāra* wall, to the south of the eastern *gōpura*, is a pillared *maṇḍapa* (K), which has been recently dismantled by the A.S.I. for conservation purposes. To the north-east of this is a tall four-pillared pavilion (L). Near the eastern gateway of the outer *prākāra*, to its north-west, is a six-pillared open structure (M) in which there is large rectangular hollow granite block with three openings on the top. On the western vertical surface of this is carved the Teṅgalai *nāmam* flanked by the *chakra* and *śaṅkha*. Between this structure and the east gateway there is another, partially collapsed, columned pavilion (N). From the east gateway (O), also dismantled a couple of years ago by the A.S.I., steps lead down to the long *ratha-vīdhi* (P), which is now under cultivation. The Kṛishṇa temple is one of the four temple complexes in the city that has such a chariot street, the others being the Virūpāksha (NF w/1), Viṭhala (NH a/1) and Tiruveṅgaḷanātha (NM h/1) temples. There are the typical pillared galleries on either side of the *ratha-vīdhi*. About half-way down the street on the north side is a small gateway into the large temple tank (not shown in the Figure). The tank, too, is surrounded by pillared galleries; in the centre of the tank is a small pavilion and on the western side a *maṇḍapa*.

Thus, the Kṛishṇa, temple was an immense complex enshrining the principal divinity and subsidiary and attendant deities, with provision for storing grain and other supplies for cooking the daily food offerings, *maṇḍapas* to serve on various festive occasions, a long chariot street for the *Rathōtasava* and a tank for the floating festival.

Inscriptions within the temple highlight the importance of the temple in the life of the city from its consecration in A.D. 1515 till its destruction in A.D. 1565. There are two inscriptions of Kṛishṇadēvarāya, three of Achyutarāya and one of the period of Sadāśiva.

Krishṇadēvarāya's epigraphs are prominently displayed; one (1) is inscribed on a slab positioned in front of the *mahā-maṇḍapa* of the principal shrine.[31] On this stone, above the lines of the inscriptions, is incised a Teṅgalai *nāmam* flanked by the *chakra* and *śaṅkha*. The second (2) is engraved on the outer walls of the small shrine to the north-east of the principal shrine.[32] Both are in Kannaḍa script, however the records are partly in Sanskṛit and partly in the Kannaḍa language. They are dated 16 February 1515. These mention not only the construction of the temple and the installation of the deity by the king, but also his munificent gifts and endowments made on the occasion of the consecration. Kṛishṇadēvarāya offered the deity valuable ornaments set with gems, golden and silver articles for the services, eleven villages to meet the expenses of the different offerings and festivals and additional lands for the maintenance of the temple brāhmaṇas. Thirty-seven brāhmaṇas, named in the epigraphs, were appointed for various services in the temple, such as *archakas*, reciters of the *Vēdas* and the *Purāṇas*, astrologers, accountants, *sthānikas* (managers) etc. These two inscriptions make clear that this was a royal temple—the king not only built it and installed the deity therein, but also made elaborate arrangements for the conduct in perpetuity of the rituals and festivals with full pomp and splendour. To no other temple in the city did Kṛishṇadēvarāya make such an extensive endowment on a single occasion.

In A.D. 1532 Achyutarāya made arrangements for the supply of gold coins for certain food offerings to god Bālakṛishṇa and for the swing (*Uyyāle*) and summer (*Kōḍe*) festivals. At the same time queen Varadāji-dēvī arranged for the supply of nine *chakra-gaḍyāṇas* each day for one food offering daily to the deity. This inscription (3) is engraved on the south wall of the *vimāna* of the principal shrine.[33] Two epigraphs (4) on the east *gōpura*, one in Nāgari and the other in Kannaḍa script, record Achyutarāya's gift of *Ānandanidhi* to the brāhmaṇas in A.D. 1539.[34]

On the north wall of the temple is a damaged inscription (5), dated A.D. 1544-45, of a private endowment made for the daily offering of a sweet dish to Śrī-Bālakṛishṇa.[35] In A.D. 1517 minister Mallarasa made a grant of land to the temple of god Tirumala at Jajūru in the presence of gods Virūpāksha, Viṭhalēśvara and Kṛishṇa (see Appendix A: no. 72). This is the only record made in the presence of god Kṛishṇa and it is a rare instance of a grant made in the presence of three divinities. Evidently, the minister wanted to render homage to the three principal deities of the city during the reign of Kṛishṇadēvarāya.

There is a controversy over whether the Kṛishṇa temple was a Mādhva or Śrī-Vaishṇava one. It is said that the Mādhva sage Vyāsarāya sang in Kannaḍa on the coming of Bālakṛishṇa from Udaygiri to Vijayanagara.[36] It is also claimed that the names of two of the brāhmaṇas appointed by the king to serve in the temple, Rāmaṇṇāchārya and Mulbāgal Timmaṇāchārya,[37] are Mādhva names. Therefore, it is claimed that the temple was under Mādhva control.[38]

The fact that Vyāsarāya sang a special hymn at the time of the installation of Bālakṛishṇa is not conclusive evidence of this being a Mādhva temple. Since Kṛishṇa is the favourite deity of the Mādhvas, it would be natural for the sage to welcome the god with joy, whether the temple in which he was installed was a Mādhva one or not. Also, the Mādhvas do not have the exclusive monopoly over the names Rāmaṇṇāchārya and Timmaṇāchārya, these could as well be Śrī-Vaishṇava names.

A careful survey of the monument and its inscriptions provides concrete evidence of its having been a Śrī-Vaishṇava temple. An important proof of this is the presence of the Śrī-Vaishṇava *nāmam*. Although this sectarian mark does not occur in the principal shrine, within the inner *prākāra* it is found on the inscription slab, in the front part of the *maṇḍapa* of the subsidiary shrine and in a small pavilion (Q). In many of the structures of the outer *prākāra* the *nāmam* is frequently carved. The most conspicuous are the Teṅgalai *nāmam* on the large granite hollow block (in M) and a stucco Teṅgalai one above the entrance of the six-domed structure (J). *Nāmams* also occur on the pillars of the gateway and *maṇḍapa* of the temple tank.

Epigraphical evidence reveals that in Achyuta's reign the temple was a Śrī-Vaishṇava one, for in the inscription of A.D. 1532[39] it is recorded that the *prasāda* from the endowment made by the queen was to be distributed daily to five itinerant Śrī-Vaishṇavas. Archaeological data proves that at the time of its destruction the temple was definitely Śrī-Vaishṇava. During the clearance work carried out in the temple complex in 1986-87 by the A.S.I. a number of broken statues were recovered. Among these are about three broken statues of seated *āḷvārs*, a mutilated standing figure, probably, of Tirumaṅgai-aḷvār and a statue of Vishvaksēna, the chief of Vishṇu's retinue. Since in the Śrī-Vaishṇava tradition the worship of Vishvaksēna and the *āḷvārs* was emphasised, while the Mādhvas do not enshrine images of the the *āḷvārs*, the discovery of these damaged icons indicates that at the time the temple was destroyed and the *mūrtis* mutilated the Śrī-Vaishṇava practices were in force. Thus, there is no doubt that the temple was a Śrī-Vaishṇava one.

2. The Viṭhala Cult

The cult of Viṭhala in the city dates from at least the early fifteenth century or even earlier, but it became highly popular only in the sixteenth. During the fifteenth century the worship of Rāma and of Viṭhala was fostered by the building of an important temple to each of these deities. While the Rāmachandra temple (NR w/1) was a royal foundation, located in the heart of the "royal centre", that of Viṭhala (NH a/1) was situated at a distance in the "sacred centre" and there is no indication as to who its original patron was. The Rāma cult, as noted in Chapter 4, flourished in the sixteenth century when many temples to this deity were built. The Viṭhala cult, too, enjoyed a wide following in the Tuḷuva period, but apart from the great Viṭhala temple, we have evidence of only one other temple (NG w/5) in the entire site dedicated to this god. The Viṭhalasvāmi temple (NH a/1) during the last half-century of the city's existence undoubtedly became the pre-eminent Vaishṇava temple and in the last quarter, before the destruction in A.D. 1565, it was the most outstanding religious centre in the capital.

The main centre of Viṭhala or Viṭhōbā worship is Paṇḍharpūr in the Shōlapur district of modern Mahārāshṭra. An interesting legend explains the presence of Viṭhōbā at Paṇḍharpūr. Nārada, during one of his wanderings on earth, witnessed the extraordinary devotion of Puṇḍalika for his aged parents and he reported it at once to Lord Kṛishṇa. Both of them repaired to the place where Puṇḍalika was performing his duties, but the lad, fully engrossed in his loving service, tossed a brick towards Kṛishṇa and asked him to wait. Thus the god stands on the brick, with his arms akimbo.[40]

It is evident, therefore, that Viṭhōbā or Viṭhala is considered to be a form of Kṛishṇa. However, Viṭhōbā was originally, probably, a tribal cattle-god.[41] The statue of Viṭhōbā seems to be a later development of a primitive hero stone, commemorating a hero who had died while protecting cattle.[42] There is an unnoticed *vīra-kal* (hero stone) near the spot which must have been the original shrine of Viṭhala, close to the *mahā-dvāra* of the modern Viṭhōbā temple at Paṇḍharpūr. The changeover from the worship of the hero stone to that of Viṭhala must have taken place when the hero stone was given a human form in the present image of Viṭhōbā and since Kṛishṇa was the "protector of cows" par excellence, Viṭhala came to be identified with him.[43]

It has been claimed that Viṭhala of Paṇḍharpūr was originally a Kannaḍa deity.[44] A poem of the Mahārāshṭrian poet saint Jñānēśvara of the thirteenth century and another of Ekanātha of the sixteenth refer to Viṭhala as Kannaḍa deity.[45] Paṇḍharpūr was within the empire of Kannaḍa-speaking dynasties such as the early western Chālukyas, the Rāshṭrakuṭas and the later Chālukyas. It was only with the breaking up of the Kalyāṇi Chālukyan empire that Mahārāshṭra and Karṇāṭaka were separated. There were then two centres of culture, Dēvagiri in the Marāṭhī part and Dvārasamudra in the

Kannaḍa part.[46] In the twelfth and thirteenth centuries A.D. Paṇḍharpūr was first under the Marāṭhī speaking Yādavas, later under the Kannaḍa Hoysaḷas, only to become once again a part of the Yādava territory.[47] Marāṭhī must have gained ground in the region in the tenth to eleventh centuries, but Kannaḍa continued to be spoken there till the end of the thirteenth century A.D.[48] From this time onwards Marāthī became the literary language under Yādava patronage and, due to the activities of the Mahārāshṭrian *bhakta* saints of the Vārkari *saṁpradāya*, the Viṭhala cult spread among the Mārāṭhi-speaking people and Paṇḍharpūr became an important place of pilgrimage. At the same time its fame was not limited to the Marāṭhī-speaking area. Kannaḍa people as well went to Paṇḍharpūr and Viṭhala did not cease to be one of their favourite gods.[49]

Thus, Viṭhala was already a popular deity in Karṇāṭaka in pre-Vijayanagara times. The Hoysaḷa king Vishṇuvardhana (A.D. 1108-1142) was called after him and temples dedicated to Viṭhala were built in several places, such as the one mentioned in an inscription from the Shimoga district of A.D. 1216.[50] Sculptural representations of the deity are found on the ornate Hoysaḷa temples and there are numerous references in epigraphs to persons bearing this name.[51]

The continued popularity of this god during the Vijayanagara period is reflected in the occurrence of the name of Viṭhala, in varied forms, in the inscriptions of the time, such as Viṭheya Nāyaka, Viṭhaṇe, Viṭhaparya, Viṭhaladēva, Viṭhala, Viṭhaṇṇa, Viṭhappa, Viṭhalarāya, Viṭhalēśvara, Viṭhalarāju, etc. To cite just a few examples, a late fourteenth century inscription refers to Viṭhalanātha, Bukkarāya's soldier;[52] a copper-plate grant of A.D. 1385 mentions three brāhmaṇas named Viṭhṭhapa;[53] from the early fifteenth century there are a number of inscriptions of Viṭhala or Viṭhaṇṇa Voḍeyar, the governor of Āraga, who was closely connected to the Saṅgama family;[54] during the reign of Virūpāksha II, Viṭṭharasa was ruling Bārakurarājya.[55] An inscription of the fifteenth century refers to Viṭhaladēvī, the queen of Vīra Bukka.[56] In the sixteenth century very many persons named after the deity are mentioned in the epigraphs, the most famous being Aḷiya Rāmarāya's cousin Viṭhalarāju, who led the successful invasion against the ruler of Travancore and who made many religious benefactions.[57] The adoption of the name of Viṭhala is indicative of the devotion of the people to this deity.

The *bhakta* saints of the Mādhva sect, known as the Haridāsas, greatly propagated the Viṭhala cult in the city and the empire, especially in the sixteenth century. These poet saints were first and foremost followers of Viṭhala (of Paṇḍharpūr) and also of Kṛishṇa of Uḍipi and Veṅkaṭēśa of Tirumalai-Tirupati.[58] The earliest of the *dāsas* was Narahari Tīrtha, who spent the last years of his life at Haṁpi and died here in A.D. 1333. The next great saint of this *saṁpradāya* was Śrīpadarāya who assumed the nom de plume Raṅga-Viṭhala. The Haridāsa movement received a tremendous boost from Vyāsarāya and from his greatest disciple Purandaradāsa who adopted the name of Purandara-Viṭhala. Both lived in Vijayanagara in the sixteenth century.[59] Of the eighteen prominent Haridāsas, eleven have Viṭhala appended to their names for their *mudrika* (nom de plume), such as Raṅga-Viṭhala, Purandara-Viṭhala, Vijaya-Viṭhala, Gōpāla-Viṭhala, Jagannātha-Viṭhala and so on.[60]

Hitherto it was generally believed that there was only one temple dedicated to Viṭhala in Vijayanagara city, namely, the great Viṭhala temple (NH a/1) in Viṭhalāpura. However, two recently discovered inscriptions[61] reveal the presence of another temple dedicated to this god in the "sacred centre". It was known as the Prāta (or old) Viṭhala temple; therefore, we may presume that it existed earlier than the famous Viṭhala temple. This temple (NG w/5) is known nowadays as the Hastagiri Raṅganātha-svāmi temple and a *mūrti* of Raṅganātha is enshrined in it at present. The first inscription, which cannot be dated since the Śaka year is not given, is on a rock in the small *maṇḍapa* just behind the temple. It records the construction of this *maṇḍapa* of Viṭhalēśvara. The second is found on a boulder in front of the temple. It mentions the grant of a village to god Prāta Viṭhala by a private donor on 12 January 1560.

The Prāta-Viṭhala temple is small and rather insignificant, comprising only a *vimāna* and a *maṇḍapa*. The *vimāna* (*cella* and antechamber) is in the archaic style—it has a plinth of unadorned courses, a plain wall surface and a stone pyramidal superstructure (Plate 25). The pillared *maṇḍapa* in front appears to be a later addition. The numerous reliefs of the *nāmam* on the *maṇḍapa* pillars probably indicate that this was a Śrī-Vaishṇava temple.

Since there is no foundational inscription, the exact date of the construction of the Prāta-Viṭhala temple cannot be determined. The inscription of A.D. 1560 indicates that worship continued to be conducted here at least till the destruction of the city.

There are two schools of opinion as to the place of origin of the *mūla-mūrti* of the famous Viṭhala temple (NH a/1) of Vijayanagara. N. Venkataramanayya asserts that the image was brought from Tirumalai-Tirupati. He quotes a *saṅkīrtana* by Tāllapākam Annamāchārya (A.D. 1408-1503) in support of this contention: "Viṭṭhala scatters his boons in every quarter of the city of Vijayanagara. Having come from the holy Venkaṭa hill, Viṭṭhala and Rukmini reside in their temple."[62] This view is accepted by other scholars as well.[63] This theory implies that Tirumalai-Tirupati was a centre of the Viṭhala cult and the statue and cult travelled from there to the capital. But, a careful survey of the monuments and inscriptions of that pilgrimage spot reveals that there was not even a shrine dedicated to Viṭhala there before A.D. 1546, when Udayagiri Dēvarāya Bhaṭṭar installed Viṭhalēśvara-svāmi in the shrine of Hanumān at Tirupati.[64] A number of inscriptions of A.D. 1547 mention this newly installed deity and festivals instituted in his honour.[65] By Sadāśiva's reign the Viṭhala cult was extremely popular in Vijayanagara. It is likely that the installation of Viṭhalēśvara at Tirupati reflects this popularity rather than the opposite being true—of the image having been taken from Tirumalai-Tirupati to Vijayanagara. Besides, although the consort of Viṭhōbā in Paṇḍharpūr is Rukmiṇī, in the Vijayanagara temple the goddess consort is clearly named as Lakshmī-dēvī.[66] In other words, the historical accuracy of the *saṅkīrtana* is doubtful. Tāḷḷapākam Annamāchārya had intense devotion to Veṅkaṭēśa of Tirumalai and from A.D. 1424 till 1503 he is said to have sung one or more *saṅkīrtanas* daily in the presence of this deity.[67] The one quoted above is one such song. If such were his devotion, it is not unlikely that even while singing about another cult deity the poet would try to link that divinity to the holy Veṅkaṭa hill.

Another belief is that the Viṭhala image was brought by Rāmarāya or Kṛishṇadēvarāya from Paṇḍharpūr and that Bhānudāsa, the grandfather of the sixteenth century saint Ekanātha, came to the city and took it back to Paṇḍharpūr during the reign of Sadāśiva. But this story, current in Mahārāshṭra, is first found in works of the seventeenth-eighteenth centuries. Besides, Bhānudāsa died before the rule of Rāmarāya and Sadāśiva and hence this traditional account can be dismissed as apocryphal.[68] However, there is kernel of truth in this legend. During the fourteenth to sixteenth centuries A.D. Paṇḍharpūr was under Muslim rule when Viṭhōbā worship suffered a severe setback. During that time Vijayanagara took over from Paṇḍharpūr the privilege of being the centre of the Viṭhala cult and the legend is a symbol of the temporary succession of Vijayanagara to Paṇḍharpūr. It was not the idol but the worship of Viṭhala that travelled from Paṇḍharpūr to Vijayanagara.[69]

The *mūrti* in the Viṭhala-svāmi temple in the city was, in all probability, a Vijayanagara statue. The one C. Narayana Rao claimed to have found[70] was so badly damaged that it cannot be definitely identified as the *mula-mūrti.* There is sculptural evidence of the presence of the Viṭhala cult in the city from at least the early fifteenth century. Possibly the earliest extant representation of the deity is to be found in the Rāmachandra temple complex. There is a relief of Viṭhala on a pillar in each of the three porches of the *raṅga-maṇḍapa.* From this time onwards, especially in the sixteenth century, carvings of Viṭhala appear, mainly on pillars, in Vaishṇava temples, at times even in Śaiva ones. However, despite the extraordinary popularity generally enjoyed by this cult, reliefs of Viṭhala are less frequent than the *Kṛishṇa-līlā* scenes, the representations of *Rāmāyaṇa* themes and the images of the diverse forms of Narasiṁha.[71] This is probably due to the fact that the Viṭhala image is rather static and does not lend itself to much variation.

In the reliefs and sculptures at Vijayanagara, Viṭhala is mostly shown clothed and only rarely in the nude. He wears a tall cylindrical crown and the usual jewellery. He stands in the erect *samabhaṅga* pose, with the feet together, arms akimbo and hands held near the hips. In the Viṭhōbā statue of Paṇḍharpūr, the deity holds a *śaṅkha* in his left hand and a lotus with a stalk in the right and he is standing on a brick. In Vijayanagara, occasionally Viṭhala is shown holding a conch-shell, but never a lotus; the brick, too, is not often to be seen. At times the god has one or both hands, which are placed near the hips, in the *varada-mudrā*; often he is depicted holding by the collar a pot-shaped bag either in one hand or in both, for Viṭhala as Bālakṛishṇa is stated to hold a bag containing round nuts used by children as marbles for playing.[72] Although usually Viṭhala is shown alone, sometimes he is flanked by a consort on each side; very occasionally he is accompanied by only one consort.

Besides the reliefs on pillars, Viṭhala images are not common in the city. A fine relief (Plate 26) is found on the outer west wall beside the small south entrance of the Rāmachandra temple. Viṭhala is present, along with many other Vaishṇava deities, in the rock shelters NG n/6 and NS a/1. Viṭhala also appears on the architrave reliefs of the ceiling of the *uyyāle-maṇḍapa* of the Viṭhala complex and in an unfinished *gōpura* (NH a/6) in Viṭhalāpura. In a niche on the north face of the granite base of the south *gōpura* of the Viṭhala temple there is a fine sculpture of Viṭhala and on the superstructure of this gateway there are at least two stucco images of the deity, though now somewhat decayed.

In many of the early writings[73] on Vijayanagara the commencement of the construction of the Viṭhala temple has been attributed to Kṛishṇadēvarāya and it is also stated that the temple was neither completed nor consecrated. The first inscription in the temple, dated A.D. 1513, is of this ruler and hence the introduction of the cult in the city has been wrongly ascribed to him. But epigraphical, monumental and literary data indicate that the temple had already been in existence prior to this record. There are over thirty inscriptions in and around the Viṭhala complex, the largest number in any one temple in the city, and from these it is abundantly clear that worship was elaborately conducted in the temple for a considerable length of time.

Since the earliest inscription engraved on the monument is only of the sixteenth century and as it does not refer to the construction of the temple, we have to look elsewhere for evidence to help date the temple. There are two significant epigraphs from Tīrthahaḷḷi *tālūka* in Shimoga district. While the first, dated A.D 1406, mentions Prasanna Viṭhalāpura,[74] the second of A.D. 1408[75] refers to a grant made in the presence of god "Vithalēśvara on the bank of the Tuṅgabhadrā" (see Appendix A, no. 25). It is possible that Prasanna Viṭhalāpura refers to the quarter around the Viṭhala temple in Vijayanagara. However, in the sixteenth century inscriptions this area is called Viṭhalāpura and not Prasanna Viṭhalāpura.[76] In records of the grants made in the sixteenth century in the presence of Viṭhala in Vijayanagara (see Appendix A), the deity is usually referred to as "Viṭhalēśvara on the bank of the Tuṅgabhadrā." Hence, it is possible that the same deity is the one referred to in the epigraph of A.D. 1408. Besides, there is no temple of Viṭhala "on the bank of the Tuṅgabhadrā" in the Tīrthahaḷḷi *tālūka*.[77]

Literary, epigraphical and monumental data indicate that the temple existed in the fifteenth century. In the *Narasiṁhapurāṇam* Prōluganti Tippa, a commander of Dēvarāya II, is said to have built a *bhoga-maṇḍapa* for god Viṭhala.[78] If this late sixteenth century literary work is accurate, the temple was already in existence in the fifteenth century. In *Śrī Vyāsayōgicharitam*, the life of the Vyāsarāya, mention is made of the temples of Virūpāksha and Viṭhala when Vyāsarāya first came to Vijayanagara in A.D. 1498.[79] From the reign of Immaḍi Narasiṁha there are two grants, dated A.D. 1493 and 1503, made in the presence of Viṭhalēśvara (see Appendix A, nos. 53 and 54). Thus, it is clear that the temple was not built by Kṛishṇadēvarāya.

On stylistic grounds the *vimāna* (i.e., the sanctum, two antechambers and the circumambulatory passage) and the *raṅga-maṇḍapa* of the Viṭhala temple (Fig. 18: A and B) can be ascribed to the fifteenth century. The sixteen massive, disengaged pillars of the *raṅga-maṇḍapa*, each with a separate moulded base and bevelled corbels and the seating slabs between the engaged columns are typical features of the early Vijayanagara temple architecture. On the south-east corner pillar (mid-square, north face) is the relief of a seated "royal" or noble figure and attendant. The noble personage wears no *kullāyi*, his hair is tied in a large knot. Such type of royal figures, as noted earlier, do not appear in the sixteenth century (see Chapter 4, note 67). The *vimana* and *ranga-maṇḍapa* of the main shrine and the north-west and south-west subsidiary shrines (C & D) belong to the initial building phase,[80] that is, the fifteenth century. The north-west secondary shrine was originally of the same design and size as the south-west one. At later date it was enlarged with the addition of two *maṇḍapas*, one closed and the other open; on the north side of inner *maṇḍapa* there is an extension for a *cella*. An inscription of A.D. 1529, engraved on the older part, mentions the shrine of Ādinārāyaṇa,[81] but we do not know if it refers to the older shrine or to the later one.

In the sixteenth century, that is during the reigns of Kṛishṇadēvarāya, Achyutarāya and Sadāśiva, the Viṭhala cult became extremely popular and many additions were made to the temple complex. In A.D. 1513 the queens of Kṛishṇarāya, Chinnā-dēvī and Tirumaladēvī, constructed the *gōpuras*.[82] That the king himself built the hundred-pillared hall (H), probably for music and dance, in A.D. 1516, is testified by the three inscriptions engraved on the north wall of this hall, in Kannaḍa, Telugu and Tamil, the three principal languages of the empire.[83]

In A.D. 1532 the great Mādhva teacher, Vyāsatīrtha, set up the image of god Yōga-Varada-Narasiṁha (I), to the north-west of the principal shrine.[84] In A.D. 1534 the thirteen *āḷvārs* including Tirukachinambiyāḷvār were installed in a shrine (J) to the north within the enclosure of the temple.[85] An inscription of A.D. 1545 in a deserted shrine to the west (K) of the central shrine records an endowment for the daily worship of Lakshmī-Nārāyaṇa in the temple of Viṭhalēśvara.[86] This is a donative grant, but it proves that the shrine of Lakshmī-Nārāyaṇa was constructed in or before A.D. 1545. In 1554 the magnificent *uyyāle* (swing) *maṇḍapa* (L) was constructed by the Āravīḍu chief Udayagiri Timmarāju, for mounting the deity on a swing on festive occasions.[87] This structure, with its fifty-six composite pillars and especially the famous "musical pillars", marks the zenith of Vijayanagara architecture and sculpture. There are no records to indicate the date of construction of the splendid south-east pavilion (M), popularly known as the *kalyāna-maṇḍapa* and the north-east pavilion (N), locally called the *utsava-maṇḍapa*. The style of these seems to be intermediary between that of the hundred-pillared pavilion and the *uyyāle-maṇḍapa*. Therefore, they were probably built sometime between A.D. 1516 and 1554.[88] Vishṇu's *vāhana*, Garuḍa, is enshrined in the stone *ratha* or chariot (O); this shrine is a very original conception, a jewel of so different a spirit, that it can hardly be compared with any other part of the complex, especially for chronological inferences[89] (Plates 27, 28, 29).

Besides the numerous sixteenth century additions within the temple complex, there was extensive building activity around the temple in Viṭhalāpura. The temple faces east and overlooks a chariot street or *ratha-vīdhi*, about one kilometre long and forty metres wide. This street has a tank (NH d/1) and at the end of it is an exquisite pavilion (Plate 30); probably this is the *Pārāṅkuśa-maṇḍapa*, mentioned in the inscription, dated A.D. 1559, of the rich citizen named Nammāḷvār.[90] The Viṭhala temple was surrounded by four streets, so that the deity could be taken in procession around the temple complex. Along these streets are a number of shrines and structures. To the north-west of Viṭhala temple is the shrine of Tirumaṅgai-āḷvār (NC v/3) built in A.D. 1556, by Aubhaḷarāju,[91] the brother of Udayagiri Timmarāju. On the north-south street that joins the street in front of the Viṭhala temple, are two temples. The triple-shrine temple (NC w/2) was dedicated to the Mudal-āḷvārs or the first three *āḷvārs*; this is stated in an inscription of 1543[92] and another of A.D. 1559.[93] The south-facing temple at the end of this street (NC w/3) is probably the Rāmānuja temple referred to in another inscription of Sadāśiva's reign.[94] The temple of Nammāḷvār, near Viṭhala, to which Aḷiya Rāmarāja made a gift in A.D. 1555,[95] is possibly the superb temple (NH a/10) facing the south *gōpura* of Viṭhala. The temple of Tirumadiśai-āḷvār, situated near the chariot of Viṭhala,[96] cannot be clearly identified; it must be one of the dilapidated structures in Viṭhalāpura.[97] In the Tirumaṅgāi-āḷvār and Mudal-āḷvār temples there were *Rāmānuja-*

kūṭas or free feeding houses for the Śrī-Vaishṇavas.[98]

The remains of numerous shrines and temples, *maṇḍapas, Rāmānuja-kūṭas,* tanks, gateways, streets and the many inscriptions reveal that Viṭhalāpura was the scene of extensive building activity, especially in the sixteenth century.[99] Some of the structures are of the earliest phase of Vijayanagara architecture. The most ancient is, perhaps, a small temple (NC v/6) to the north of the Viṭhala temple, while others are from the most developed phase of Vijayanagara buildings. That new building projects were underway at the time of the turning point of Rakkasa-Taṅgaḍi is evident from two superb but unfinished *gōpuras* (NH a/6 and NC v/5). The extensive and elaborate constructional activity both within and around the Viṭhala temple, the splendour of the architecture and sculpture, especially of the sixteenth century structures and the presence of a number of subsidiary deities surrounding Viṭhala, all reveal the vital importance of this temple and cult in the city.

The rich endowments made to the temple and the list of donors also highlight the extensive patronage enjoyed by this cult. In A.D. 1513 Kṛishṇadēvarāya, on the auspicious occasion of a solar eclipse, granted three villages and some lands to the temple, while his queens, besides building the *gōpuras,* also gifted a golden plate, twenty-five silver lamps, and cows to supply *ghee* for the light offerings.[100] Another record of the king lists various villages and lands given on different occasions, from A.D. 1513 to 1526, and also the taxes on the ferry service on the Tuṅgabhadrā.[101] A record of A.D. 1529 mentions a private donation for offerings and services in the temple of Ādinārāyaṇa.[102]

In A.D. 1531 Achyutarāya gifted a village for the daily offerings to Viṭhaladēva. The same inscription also mentions the donation made by Bōugaṇṇa, a boatman of Ānegoṅdi.[103] The following year Tāḷapāka Tirumalayya, a member of an important Śrī-Vaishṇava family that was prominent at Tirupati and Ahōbalam, gifted three villages, which had been granted to him by Achyutarāya, to the temple.[104] A record of A.D. 1533 mentions the king's gift of Suvarṇameru,[105] or a "mountain of gold".[106] In A.D. 1534 when Gaṇdhada Tippi Setti installed the thirteen *āḻvārs* in a special shrine within the temple complex he also gave 100 *gaḍyānas* to the temple treasury for the daily offering of food, light and flower garlands to these deities.[107] In the same year Varadapa-Nāyaka made a cash gift to the treasury so that daily offerings could be made to god Viṭhala for the merit of the king and Chikkarāya (crown prince).[108] Another officer of the king gave 200 *ghaṭṭi-varāhas* for one food offering daily, also in order that merit might accrue to the king and the prince.[109] During the same period Chikka Timmapa gave 200 *ghaṭṭi-varāhas* for the expenses of perpetual lamps in the presence of Viṭhala.[110] A damaged inscription mentions the gift made by another officer, Tirumala Nāyaka, for the merit of the king.[111] In A.D. 1538 two brothers, Hiriya Timmappa-Nāyaka and Rāghavappa-Nāyaka set up up gold pinnacles on the east and north *gōpuras* of the temple for the merit of the king.[112] On the south *gōpura* Achyutarāya's gift of Ānandanidhi to brāhmaṇas in A.D. 1539 was engraved twice.[113]

In A.D. 1543 the Śrī-Vaishṇava teacher Tirumala-Auku-Tātāchārya gifted to the temple land in Niṭūru village that had been given to him by Sadāśiva, for the daily offerings and for special offerings on specified festivals.[114] In A.D. 1545 Kōnēṭi-Timmarāja, son of Koṇḍarāja, granted to the deity the toll revenue of Ravudūr village.[115] This donor is probably the father of the Āravīḍu chiefs and important donors Aubhaḷarāju, Koṇḍarāja and Udayagiri Timmarāju, their grandfather being (Peda) Koṇḍarāja. In A.D. 1554 Udayagiri Timmarāju granted the village of Tirumalapura, for the merit of his father Kōnēṭaya; it was to cover the cost of offerings to Viṭhala when he was mounted on the swing in the *uyyāle-maṇḍapa* built by Timmarāju, on various festival days, among which were the ten days of the *Tiruvadhyāna* festival or the recitation of the *Divyaprabandham* of the *āḻvārs.*[116] Another temple inscription of the same year lists the grant of lands with an annual revenue of 300 *ghaṭṭi-varāha-gaḍyaṇas* for offerings to Viṭhaladēva and Lakshmī-dēvī.[117]

In A.D. 1556 Āravīḍu Aubhaḷaraju gave lands to Tirumaṅgai-āḻvār's temple for different expenses, including for food offerings when Viṭhala was taken in procession along the temple streets.[118] Nammālvār in A.D. 1559[119] made an exchange of lands to the temple to meet the expenses of Viṭhala when he was taken in procession to the *Pārāṅkuśa-maṇḍapa* on 142 days in a year. Āravīḍu Koṇḍarāja gifted land in Rāmasāgara village in A.D. 1561 for the celebration of an additional two days of the ten-day *Tiruvadhyāna* festival instituted by his brother Udayagiri Timmarāju.[120] In the same year a gift of garden land was made by Kuruchēṭi Śrīraṅgarāju to the Tirumaṅgai-āḻvār shrine and arrangements made for the payment of a stipulated amount annually to the treasury of god Viṭhala.[121] In A.D. 1563 Nammāḻvār gave an endowment to the temple treasury so that daily *prasāda* from the deity's morning meal should be sent to the donor,[122] accompanied by the dancers and musicians of the temple. The last grant is dated November 1564, just a year before the destruction of the city.[123] In it are listed grants of lands and villages made by a number of individuals including Rāja-Rāmarāja.

A survey of these endowments reveals that all of them belong to the period of Kṛishṇadēvarāya, Achyutarāya and Sadāśiva, the greatest number being from the last reign. The endowments of Kṛishṇadēvarāya's period are royal grants, while in the reigns of Achyutarāya and Sadaśiva they were also made by subordinate chiefs, important officials, sectarian leaders and wealthy citizens.

The exceptional significance of the Viṭhala temple, particularly in the last decades of the city's life, is also evident in the number of grants made by the rulers, ministers and others in the presence of this deity (see Appendix A). In the first one and a half centuries of the empire's history most donations registered in Vijayanagara were done in the presence of Virūpāksha, the tutelary deity of the kings and the principal god of the holy *tīrtha* of Paṁpā-kshētra. The first grant recorded in the presence of Viṭhala was in A.D. 1408 (no. 25). However, till the reign of Sāḷuva Immaḍi Narasiṁha (nos. 53 and 54) no other record mentions Viṭhala on the bank of the Tuṅgabhadrā.

In the sixteenth century, during the period of Kṛishṇadēvarāya, although the majority of the grants were made in the presence of Virūpāksha, a sizeable number were registered in Viṭhala's presence, too. The epigraphs of ministers Mallarasa (no. 72) and Sāḷuva Gōvindarāja (no. 78) attempt at reconciling the most important Śaivite and Vaishṇavite cults in the city by registering land grants in the presence of both Virūpāksha and Viṭhala. More than half the records of Achyuta's period were issued in the presence of Viṭhalēśvara, yet a large number were also made with the blessing of Virūpāksha. During the rule of Sadāśiva and Rāmarāya, especially from A.D. 1545 to 1565 (nos. 124 to 139) Virūpāksha seems to have been almost totally eclipsed by the unparalleled popularity enjoyed by the Viṭhala cult.

It has been suggested that during the period of Vyāsarāya's influence at the court and in the city, Mādhva ceremonies and festivals were in force in the Viṭhala temple,[124] and that after his death, during the period of Sadāśiva and Rāmarāya, all the positions of temporal power in the capital were occupied by the Śrī-Vaishṇava āchāryas, who, with the help of their influential disciples such as the Āravīḍu chiefs Udayagiri Timmarāju and his brothers, introduced Śrī-Vaishṇava festivals, rituals and food habits in the temple.[125] It is true that the Viṭhala cult was of great importance for the Mādhvas, in particular for the Haridāsas, and it is but natural that they would have frequented the temple and patronised it. Yet from this it does not automatically follow that the temple was originally under Mādhva control. For the Mādhvas to frequent Śrī-Vaishṇava shrines is not unknown. For example, the Haridāsas also have a great veneration for Veṅkatēśa of Tirumalai; Vyāsarāya himself is reputed to have spent twelve years there before he came to Vijayanagara and he had *maṭhas* in Tirumalai and Tirupati,[126] although Tirumala-Tirupati is one of the most celebrated Śrī-Vaishṇava pilgrimage spots. The only epigraphical evidence of the Vyāsarāya's connection with the Viṭhala temple is that of his installing Narasiṁha in a small shrine there[127] and the assigning of a share of the *prasāda* to him in an inscription of Kṛishṇadēvarāya.[128]

Monumental and epigraphical sources point to the likelihood that the Viṭhala temple was Śrī-Vaishṇava one. The Śrī-Vaishṇava *nāmam* is to be seen in many parts of the temple. It does not occur in the fifteenth century structures. But in the hundred-pillared hall built by Kṛishṇadēvarāya, in the gallery along the enclosure wall, in the outer *maṇḍapa* of the north-west subsidiary shrine and also in the north-east pavilion this sectarian mark is very common on pillar reliefs. If Vyāsarāya is mentioned in two epigraphs, Śrī-Vaishṇava teachers such as Tāḷapāka Tirumalayya,[129] Tirumala-Auku-Tātāchārya[130] and Kaṇḍāla Śrīraṅgāchārya[131] are referred to in a number of inscriptions. During the lifetime of Vyāsarāya itself thirteen *āḷvārs* were installed within the complex in A.D. 1534; also around the temple complex were a number of *āḷvār* shrines. The *āḷvār* and *āchārya* worship and the presence of *Rāmānuja-kūṭas* for the feeding of the Śrī-Vaishṇava brāhmaṇas reveal the influence of these sectarians in Viṭhalāpura. A survey of the inscriptions also shows that, as far as we have evidence, the festivals and ceremonies in the temple were according to Śrī-Vaishṇava practices. We have no inscriptional data of Mādhva festivals and rituals being conducted here. Thus, it can be concluded that, despite its special significance for the Mādhvas, the Viṭhala temple was a Śrī-Vaishṇava one.

So great was the popularity of Viṭhala in the capital in the sixteenth century that the cult spread from Vijayanagara even to distant parts of the empire where there was no previous tradition of Viṭhala worship. In A.D. 1519 a Viṭhalēśvara temple was set up in Chingleput district,[132] in A.D. 1535 an image of the deity was consecrated in the Viṭhalam village in the Chittoor district[133] and a record of 1546 mentions a Viṭhaladēva temple in the South Kanara district.[134] An inscription from the Raṅganāthasvāmi temple, Śrīraṅgam, of A.D. 1546 records the consecration of Viṭhalēśvara by the Āraviḍu prince Viṭhaladēva-mahārāja.[135] Besides Śrīraṅgam, the other great Śrī-Vaishṇava centre, Tirupati, also saw the installation of this deity in the same year.[136]

Kṛishṇa and Viṭhala enjoyed a vast following in Vijayanagara, especially in the Tuḷuva period, both among the Mādhvas and the Śrī-Vaishṇavas. The great Kṛishṇadēvarāya vigorously promoted these cults by building and richly endowing the splendid Kṛishṇa temple and by making extensive additions to the Viṭhala complex and giving valuable grants to it on many occasions. Yet, while the hey day of the Kṛishṇa temple was during his rule, the Viṭhala cult flourished even more extensively during the reigns of his successors. The patronage of these cults came from kings and queens, subordinate chiefs and high officials, sectarian leaders and rich citizens. However, both were, in a sense "imported" cults. Thus, after A.D. 1565, when the temples were desecrated and the patronage ceased, these cults became extinct at the site.

Notes

[1]V. Filliozat, "The history, social and economic conditions of the Vitthala temple at Hampi," *South Asian Archaeology*, 1981, pp. 305-306.

[2]In south India the Rādhā cult is not prevalent; generally Rukmiṇī is represented as the consort of Kṛishṇa.

[3]K.A. Nilakanata Sastri, *A History of South India: From Pre-historic Times to the Fall of Vijayanagara*, p. 420.

[4]B.N.K. Sharma, *A History of the Dvaita School of Vedānta and its Literature*, vol. II, p. 255.

[5]Ibid., p. 261.

[6]S.V. Padigar, "The Cult of Vishṇu in Karnataka" (Ph.D. diss.), pp. 438-444.

[7]R. Champakalakshmi, *Vaiṣṇava Iconography in the Tamil Country*, p. 130.

[8]Ibid., p. 135,.

[9]Ibid., p. 141.

[10]Ibid., p. 135.

[11]K. Desai, *Iconography of Viṣṇu*, p. 132.

[12]Sugandha, "History and Archeology of Anegondi" (Ph.D. diss.), p. 157.

[13]C.S. Patil, "Kṛishṇa Temple," in *VPR '79-83*, p. 63.

[14]See N. Lakshminarayan Rao, "Portrait Sculpture of the Vijayanagara King Mallikarjuna," *Studies in Indian History and Culture*, ed. S. Ritti and B.R. Gopal, pp. 181-2.

[15]*ARIE* of 1957-58, no. 204.

[16]Ibid., no. 205.

[17]According to V. Filliozat, "The Town-Planning of Vijayanagara," *Art and Archaeology Research Papers*, 14, p. 58, this was a Śrī Raṅganātha temple. This surmise is based on the fact that it was built by a person named Śiraṅgu and that the *pīṭha* in the sanctum is oblong. However, in Vijayanagara we have no evidence of patrons building temples only of the deity after whom they are named. The *pīṭha*, although it is rectangular in shape, is not long enough for a reclining statue of Raṅganātha. It is like the *pīthas*, in many dilapidated Vaishṇava shrines, meant for the deity and his consort or consorts. Carved on the centre of the *pīṭha* base, instead of the usual Garuḍa, is a small relief of a seated lion.

[18]*EI*, pp. 361-371.

[19]Ibid., pp. 398-402.

[20]*ARSIE* of 1935-36, no. 337.

[21]*SII* IV, no. 266.

[22]Ibid., no. 262.

[23]Ibid., nos. 254 and 255.

[24]Ibid., nos. 262 and 263.

[25]*Annual Report of the Archaeological Department, Southern Circle, Madras*, 1916-17, p. 29.

[26]Ibid., pp. 28-30.

[27] *SII* IV, nos. 254 and 255.

[28]V. Filliozat, "Iconography: Religious and Civil Monu-

ments," in *Vij. City & Emp.,* vol. 1, p. 312.

[29]*SII* IV, no. 255.

[30]G. Michell, "Architectural Traditions at Vijayanagara : Islamic Styles," in *Vij. City & Emp.*, vol. 1, p. 285.

[31]*SII* IV, no. 254.

[32] Ibid., no. 255.

[33] Ibid., no. 262.

[34] Ibid., nos. 256 and 257.

[35] Ibid., no. 263.

[36] No. 60 of *Vyāsarayāra Kīrtanegalu*, Udipi Edition, cited by B.N.K. Sharma, *A History of the Dvaita School of Vedānta and its Literature*, vol. II, p. 30; B. Venkoba Rao, *Sri Vyasayogicaritam*, Introduction, p. cxxxiii.

[37] *SII* IV, nos. 254 and 255.

[38] B.N.K. Sharma, loc. cit. and B. Venkoba Rao, op.cit., p. cxxxii.

[39] *SII* IV, no. 262.

[40] G.A. Deleury, *The Cult of Viṭhobā*, p. 144.

[41] Ibid., p. 203.

[42] Ibid., p. 198.

[43] G.D. Sontheimer, "Hero and Sati-stones in Maharashtra," in *Memorial Stones*, ed. S. Settar and G.D. Sontheimer, p. 267.

[44]S.G. Tulpule, "Karnatak Origins of the Cult of Vitthala," paper read at the centenary celebrations of the Mysore Directorate of Archaeology and Museums.

[45]Ibid., pp. 8-9.

[46]G.A. Deleury, op.cit, pp. 28-32.

[47]Ibid., p. 193.

[48]Ibid., p. 33.

[49]Ibid., pp. 34-36.

[50]*EC* VII, Sh. 54.

[51]S.V. Padigar, op.cit., p. 223.

[52]*EC* IX, Ma. 20.

[53]*MAR* of 1941, no. 48.

[54]*EC* VI, Kp. 52 and 53; *EC* VIII, Tl. 129 and 130.

[55]*SII* IX, pt. II, nos. 464, 465, 468 and 469.

[56]*ARSIE* of 1939-40, B.K., 105.

[57]*SII* IX, pt. II, no. 642; *SII* XVI, no. 211; *EC* XI, Mk. 4.

[58]A.P. Karmarkar and N.B. Kalamdani, *Mystic Teachings of the Haridasas of Karnatak*, p. 24.

[59]B.N.K. Sharma, op.cit., vol. II, pp. 317-319.

[60]B. Chitgupi, "Nada-Brahma of Pandharpūr," *Studies in Indian History and Culture*, ed. S. Ritti and B.R. Gopal, p. 176.

[61]*VPR '84-87*, nos. 69 and 71.

[62]N.Venkataramanayya, "The Date of the Construction of the Temples of Hazāra-Rāmasvāmi and Viṭṭhala at Vijayanagara," *JOR*, XVI, pp. 88-90.

[63]S. Rajasekhara, *Masterpieces of Vijayanagara Art*, pp. 25-26.

[64]*TTDES* V, no. 66.

[65]Ibid., nos. 87, 88, 89, 100 and 118.

[66]*SII* IX, pt. II, no. 654.

[67]Sadhu Subrahmanya Sastry, *Report on the Inscriptions of the Devasthanam Collection with Illustrations*, p. 280.

[68]G.H. Khare, "Krishnadevaraya of Vijayanagara and the Vitthala Image of Pandharpūr," in *VSCV*, pp. 191-196.

[69]C. Narayana Rao, "An identification of the Idol of Vithala in the Vitthala Temple at Hampi," *Proceedings and Transactions of the Eighth All India Oriental Conference*, 1935, p. 723.

[70]Ibid., pp. 715-728.

[71]There are a few exceptions to this, of course. For example, in the pillared hall of the Mālyavanta Raghunātha complex (Fig. 16: C), reliefs of the Viṭhala appear nearly forty times on the pillars.

[72]K. Sarojini Devi, "The Cult of Vithoba in Vijayanagara," in *Dr. N. Venkataramanayya Commemoration Volume: JAHRS, XXXVIII, pt. IV*, ed. R. Subrahmanyam and V.V. Krishna Sastry, p. 97.

[73]*Annual Report of the ASI*, 1922-23, p. 67; A.H. Longhurst, *Hampi Ruins*, p. 121; Percy Brown, *Indian Architecture (Buddhist and Hindu)*, p. 92.

[74]*EC* VIII, Tl, 221.

[75]Ibid., Tl, 222.

[76]*SII* IV, nos. 272 and 280.

[77]V. Filliozat, "Nouvelles Identifications de Monuments à Hampi," *Journal Asiatique*, 266, p. 126.

[78]*Further Sources*, vol. III, pp. 46-47.

[79]B. Venkoba Rao, op.cit., pp. xii-xiii.

[80]P. Filliozat, "Techniques and Chronology of Construction in the temple of Vitthala at Hampi," in *Vij. City & Emp.*, vol. 1, p. 301.

[81]P. Filliozat and V. Filliozat, *Hampi-Vijayanagara: The Temple of Viṭhala,* Inscription IV, pp. 54-55.

[82]*SII* IV, nos. 273 and 278.

[83]*ARSIE* of 1922, nos. 711, 712 and 713.

[84]Ibid., no. 710.

[85]*SII* IX, pt. II, no. 566.

[86]*SII* XVI, no. 141.

[87]*SII* IX, pt. II, no. 653.

[88]P. Filliozat, op.cit., p. 305.

[89]Ibid.

[90]*SII* IX, pt. II, no. 668.

[91]*SII* IV, no. 280.

[92]*SII* IX, pt. II, no. 607.

[93]*ARIE* of 1975-76, no. 98.

[94]*Top. List* I, Bellary dist., no. 347.

[95]*SII* IX pt. II, no. 657.

[96]*VPR '83-84*, no. 21, pp. 35-36.

[97]The *āḷvār* and *āchārya* worship and their shrines in Viṭhalāpura discussed in greater detail in Chapter 6.

[98]*SII* IV, no. 280 and *SII* IX, pt. II, no. 607.

[99]A list of the monuments in Viṭhalāpura is included in Appendix B.

[100]*SII* IV, nos. 273 and 278.

[101]Ibid., no. 277.

[102]P. Filliozat & V. Filliozat, loc. cit.

[103]*SII* IX, pt. II, no. 534.

[104]Ibid., no. 543.

[105]Ibid., nos. 557 and 558.

[106]C. Hayavadana Rao ed., *Mysore Gazetteer*, vol. II, pt. III, p. 2007.

[107]*SII* IX, pt. II, no. 566.

[108]Ibid., no. 570.

[109]Ibid., no. 574.

[110]*SII* IV, no. 274.

[111]*SII* IX, pt. II, no. 575.

[112]Ibid., nos. 586 and 589.

[113]*SII* XVI, no. 118 and *ARSIE* of 1904, no. 1.

[114]*SII* IX, pt. II, no. 607.

[115]Ibid., no. 616.

[116]Ibid., no. 653.

[117]Ibid., no. 654.

[118]*SII* IV, no. 280.

[119]*SII* IX, pt. II, no. 668.

[120]*SII* IV, no. 275.

[121]*SII* XVI, no. 251.

[122]*SII* IX, pt. II, no. 678.

[123]*SII* IV, no. 272.

[124]According to traditional accounts Vyāsarāya made Vijayanagara his main base from A.D. 1498 till his death in A.D. 1539.

[125]V. Filliozat, "The history, social and economic conditions of the Vitthala temple at Hampi," *South Asian Archaeology*, 1981, p. 306.

[126]*TTDES* III, nos. 157, 158 and 159.

[127]*ARSIE* of 1922, no. 710.

[128]*SII* IV, no. 277.

[129]*SII* IX, pt. II, no. 543.

[130]Ibid., no. 607 and *SII* IV, no. 280.

[131]*SII* XVI, no. 141; *SII* IX, pt. II, no. 653 and *SII* IV, no. 275.

[132]*ARSIE* of 1932-33, no. 117.

[133]*ARSIE* of 1936-37, no. 371.

[134]*ARSIE* of 1927, no. 394.

[135]*ARIE* of 1953-54, no. 375.

[136]*TTDES* V, no. 66.

CHAPTER 6

Śrī-Vaishṇava Traditions from the Tamil Country

During the Sāḷuva and Tuḷuva periods Śrī-Vaishṇavism became the leading sect in Vijayanagara city. Almost all the large sixteenth century Vaishṇava temple complexes, and probably many of the smaller shrines belonged to this sect. The dominance of Śrī-Vaishṇavism in the late fifteenth and sixteenth centuries led to the incorporation of the cults of the deities of the great pilgrimage centres of this sect and of various other Śrī-Vaishṇava practices into the city.

Śrī-Vaishṇavism was already prevalent from the early part of the eleventh century onwards in the south-western precincts of Karṇāṭaka which formed part of the Chōḷa territory. It gained ground in south Karṇāṭaka in the twelfth century A.D., during the reign of Hoysaḷa Vishṇuvardhana, because of Śrī-Rāmānuja's active presence in this area.[1] However, in the northern parts of the state it did not have a following till the Vijayanagara period when Śrī-Vaishṇavism gained importance throughout Karṇāṭaka and in the whole of south India.[2]

The most holy places for Śrī-Vaishṇavites are Śrīraṅgam, Tirumalai and Kāñchi in the Tamil country, which are referred to by them as Kōil, Tirumalai and Perumāḷ-Kōil, respectively.[3] In modern times Tirumalai is within the Āndhra border, but Vēṅgaḍam or Tirumalai-Tirupati was traditionally considered the northern boundary of the Tamil land, passing across which one entered into a region where the Tamil language was not spoken.[4] That it was within the Tamil country in pre-Vijayanagara and Vijayanagara times can be seen from the inscriptions. Except for a few, almost all the epigraphs at Tirumalai and Tirupati are in the Tamil language, with only about fifty (out of a total of approximately 1250 published epigraphs) in Telugu or Kannaḍa; of the period prior of Kṛishṇadēvarāya there is only one in Telugu and two in Kannaḍa.[5]

Although the Śrī-Vaishṇavas also worship Rāma, Kṛishṇa and other forms of Vishṇu and there are Śrī-Vaishṇava temples of Narasiṁha, Rāma, Kṛishṇa, etc. in the capital, Raṅganātha of Śrīraṅgam, Śrīnivāsa or Veṅkaṭēśa of Tirumalai and Varadarāja of Kāñchi are the three greatest deities of this sect. In the Saṅgama period itself Śrī-Vaishṇavism enjoyed a wide following. The special importance of these three sacred spots in the fourteenth century is reflected in the "Jaina-Śrī-Vaishṇava compact" of A.D. 1368 of Bukka I in which "Kōvil, Tirumale and Perumāḷ-Kōvil" are specifically mentioned.[6] The continued importance of these is seen in one of the latest inscriptions in the city, of A.D. 1556, in which provision was made for the feeding of the Śrī-Vaishṇava saints from these three great religious centres.[7]

The immense prestige enjoyed by these gods and their cult centres in the fifteenth and sixteenth centuries is evident in the extensive patronage extended to them, particularly to Veṅkaṭēśvara of Tirumalai, by the rulers and the people. Therefore, in order to assess the impact of these cults in the city, a brief survey of the popularity of these three centres during this period is necessary.

Veṅkaṭēśa acquired a big following in the city in the sixteenth century, followed in popularity by Raṅganātha and, to a lesser extent, Varadarāja. Besides the intense veneration of these deities, the worship of the *āḷvārs* and *āchāryas* considered to be partial incarnations of Vishṇu, was adopted; their statues were consecrated in the temples and even separate shrines erected for them. Images of Vishvaksēna were also installed and the Śrī-Vaishṇava *nāmam* came to be prominently displayed in Śrī-Vaishṇava temples and shrines throughout the site. Provision was also made in many a temple for the free feeding of the Śrī-Vaishṇava brāhmaṇas, including the itinerant ascetics coming from the great centres of the sect.

1. The Tiruveṅgaḷanātha Cult

The Śrī Veṅkaṭēśvara temple on Tirumalai hill

is in the modern Chandragiri *tālūka* of Chittor district in Āndhra Pradesh. The deity of this temple is known by a variety of names: Śrīnivāsa, Veṅkaṭēśa or Veṅkaṭēśvara, Tirumala-dēva or Tirumalēśvara and Tiruveṅgaḷanātha—the last name being the most commonly used in Vijayanagara. North Indians address the god as Bāḷāji.

The origin of the incarnation of Vishṇu as Veṅkaṭēśvara is explained by an interesting legend. Ṛishi Bhṛigu, in order to test whether Brahmā, Śiva or Vishṇu was the greatest of the gods, went to visit each of them in turn. He was treated with disrespect by Brahmā and Śiva, while Vishṇu greeted the sage courteously, even though Bhṛigu had awakened him from his sleep by unceremoniously kicking him on the chest, the sacred place where Lakshmī resided. Bhṛigu was pleased and declared Vishṇu as the greatest. However, Lakshmī enraged because the kick of the sage had fallen on her, picked a quarrel with her Lord and left Vaikunṭha in a huff. Bereft of his consort, Vishṇu went away from his palace and came to Tirumalai. Here he fell in love with and married the princess Padmāvati, the foster daughter of Ākaśa Rāja.[8]

Veṅkaṭēsa is depicted in *samabhaṅga* with the *chakra* and *śaṅkha* in his upper right and left hands respectively, the lower right hand is in the *varada-mudrā*, while the lower left hand rests on the hip. In Vijayanagara, Veṅkaṭēśa is occasionally shown with the lower right hand in *abhaya-mudrā* and he is at times flanked by two consorts. The iconography of the god enshrined in the Tirumalai temple has evoked much controversy. The Vaishṇavas have always contended that the god is Vishṇu, the Śaivas claim that he is Śiva or Subrahmanya. Another view is that he is Harihara; it is even stated that the temple was originally dedicated to Dēvī. Such controversy is outside the scope of this study. However, literary references amply demonstrate that from early times the temple was a Vaishṇava *kshētra* and this is confirmed by the inscriptions in the temple;[9] certainly during the period under survey the divinity was considered to be a manifestation of Vishṇu.

This pilgrimage centre figures in the earliest Tamil secular literature of the Saṅgam age and also in poems of the *āḷvārs*.[10] The great Śrī-Vaishṇava reformer, Rāmānuja, is said to have paid four or more visits to this holy shrine and to have built the temple in Tirupati, at the foot of Tirumalai, for Gōviṅdarāja whose shrine at Chidambaram had been destroyed by the Chōḷa monarch, a fanatical Śaivite.[11] The growth in importance of Tirumalai-Tirupati as a pilgrimage spot was due, in part, to the persecution of Vaishṇavites during the Chōḷa period, especially in the eleventh century when it became a sanctuary for Vaishṇavites. Another factor in the growing importance of the temple prior to the fifteenth century was the occupation and plunder of many Hindu temples in the southern part of the peninsula by the Muslims in the fourteenth century. In this period the temple became the refuge for many Vaishṇavite priests from southern Tamil Nāḍu and even for the major deity Śrī-Raṅganātha of Śrīraṅgam.[12]

After a long history as a sacred pilgrimage place, the Tirumalai temple rose to the status of a great temple in the Vijayanagara period. The Saṅgama rulers were Śaivites and less interested, therefore, in this Vishṇu temple. In the mid-fifteenth century the temple attracted the support of an important ruling family in the Tirupati area. One of the members of this family, Sāḷuva Narasiṁha, while still only a military leader of local renown, became an important patron. When Sāḷuva Narasiṁha became the emperor of Vijayanagara in A.D. 1485, full imperial patronage was bestowed upon the temple by him and later by his successors of the Tuḷuva family.[13] During the sixteenth century the Veṅkaṭēśvara temple was regarded as the greatest temple in south India.

The study of the inscriptions at Tirumalai-Tirupati reveals that this sacred *kshētra* rose to prominence only in the Vijayanagara period, especially under the second and third dynasties. Although the records cover a period of nearly eleven centuries they are not fully representative of all the south Indian dynasties, for there is a disproportionately large number of inscriptions belonging to the Vijayanagara period, while the earlier dynasties are represented very scantily and the post-Vijayanagara times by scarcely any.[14] Out of the 1250-odd epigraphs published by the *Dēvasthanam* there are fewer than 150 records of the pre-Vijayanagara period, while 59 are of the Saṅgama period, 168 of the Sāḷuva period, 229 of the reign of Kṛishṇadēvarāya, 251 of Achyutarāya's period, 176 of Sadāśiva's reign and 192 of Veṅkaṭa II's period. The donors during the Vijayanagara period included state donors (such as kings, queens, viceroys, ministers, generals and royal officers), various types of temple functionaries, local residents, merchants and devotees.

Epigraphs of the pre-Vijayanagara times generally record services of lighting lamps and also of gifts of lands, jewels and money.[15] In the Vijayanagara period the services and charities instituted took the form mainly of food offerings to the deities, festivals with processions and offerings, flower gardens and the construction of *maṇḍapas*, *gōpuras*, shrines and *Rāmānuja-kūṭas.*[16] Provision for the food offerings, and festivals were made by gifts of lands and villages as well as of money and gold. The money and gold deposited was usually invested in the temple villages to excavate fresh irrigation sources or to repair existing ones,[17] resulting in a tremendous increase in agricultural facilities in the region.

Of the first dynasty, an inscription of Harihara II records the institution of a festival for Śrī Veṅkaṭēśvara in the name of the king.[18] Dēvarāya II visited the temple in A.D. 1429 and presented 1,200 gold coins for daily offerings. He also instituted a *Brahmōtsavam* and granted three villages for conducting it.[19] In A.D. 1433 he renewed the *Vēdapārāyaṇam* services in the temple by granting a share of certain receipts of the royal treasury.[20]

Sāḷuva Narasiṁha was a great devotee of Veṅkaṭēśvara. His devotion to this god may be explained to some extent by the fact that he was the great grandson of *Mahāmaṇḍalēśvara* Maṅgidēva who gilded the sanctum of the temple and mounted a golden pinnacle on it.[21] The Sāḷuva family was closely associated with the region of Tirumalai-Tirupati since their headquarters were at Chandragiri, only 12 kilometres south-west of Tirupati town.[22] From A.D. 1457 onwards till the end of the century the inscriptions in this pilgrimage centre seem to refer largely to members of this family and their benefactions.[23] Sāḷuva Narasiṁha greatly enhanced the reputation and prestige of the temple by instituting new services and charities in the form of festivals and processions,[24] flower gardens[25] and *Rāmānuja-kūṭas* both at Tirumalai and Tirupati[26] and extending the temples by building *maṇḍapas*,[27] a tank[28] and a new shrine.[29] For the maintenance of all this he endowed the temple with about a dozen villages.[30] He also exerted himself in regulating the worship in the temple of Gōviṅdarāja on the lines of the practice obtaining in the Śrī Veṅkaṭēśvara temple.[31] Kanḍāḍai Rāmānuja Aiyangar, the spiritual preceptor of the king,[32] was the main agent of Sāḷuva Narasiṁha at Tirumalai-Tirupati. He and his successors were in charge of the *Rāmānuja-kūṭas* at Tirumalai and Tirupati and the king also appointed him as the guardian of the gold treasury of the Tirumalai temple.[33] This teacher was himself a great donor.[34] Sāḷuva Narasiṁha's munificence to the temples of Tirumalai-Tirupati was emulated by his subordinate officials.

When the authority passed from the Sāḷuvas to the Tuḷuva dynasty the religious attachment to the temple continued and reached its zenith under Krishṇadēvarāya and Achyutarāya and was continued by the Āravīḍu dynasty. Vīra Narasiṁha performed the *tulāpurusha-dāna* in gold in the temple.[35] Kṛishṇadēvarāya's patron deity was Veṅkatēśvara of Tirumalai. Thus, the longed-for heir, born in A.D. 1518, was named Tirumala after the god. The king also dedicated his literary masterpiece *Āmuktamālyada* to Veṅkaṭēśvara. According to the *Dēvasthanam* inscriptions the king made seven visits to Tirumalai. On his first visit in A.D. 1513 he presented a jewelled crown, other jewels and twenty-five silver plates[36] and his two queens each presented a gold cup to the deity.[37] The king's second visit was in the same year when he gifted a number of ornaments.[38] During his third visit, also in A.D. 1513, he granted three villages.[39] His fourth visit took place in A.D. 1514 when he presented 30,000 gold coins and a village.[40] During his fifth visit in A.D. 1517 he gifted another 30,000 gold coins for gilding the *vimāna* and a valuable pendant.[41] There is no specific mention of his sixth visit, which is said to have been made on 16 October 1518, with his senior queen Tirumala-dēvī, in gratitude for the birth of their son.[42] On the occasion of his seventh visit, in A.D. 1521, the king granted, among other gifts, 10,000 gold coins and Tirumala-dēvī presented a pendant.[43] To no other temple outside his capital did the king make seven visits. The bronze statues of the king and his two queens in the Tirumalai temple also indicate Krishṇadēvarāya's extraordinary devotion to Veṅkaṭēśvara. Important royal officers such as Sāḷuva Timmarasa,[44] Sāḷuva Gōvindarāja,[45] Koṇḍamarasayya,[46] *guru* Vyāsarāya[47] and many private donors also figure in the epigraphs of his reign.

So great was Achyutarāya's devotion to this deity that he named his son Veṅkaṭādri after the god[48] and crowned himself emperor in the presence of Veṅkaṭēśvara at Tirumalai,[49] following which he was crowned again at Kāḷahasti and at Vijayanagara. On his first visit to the temple as king in A.D. 1533 along with queen Varadājiamman and prince Veṅkaṭādri he presented valuable ornaments[50] and on his second visit in A.D. 1535 he instituted two new festivals.[51] The king appears to have made a third visit in A.D. 1537, from certain gifts made by a number of his officers almost simultaneously. Among other benefactions of the king was the construction of granite steps all around the sacred Kapila-tīrtham in Tirupati,[52] the erection of the temple of Achyuta-Perumāḷ in Tirupati[53] and the sending of dancers to the temple from Vijayanagara.[54] During this reign the donations of officers and private individuals were even more than the royal grants.

The donations of Sadāśiva are fewer than those of his predecessors, the most important was the grant of specified taxes in sixteen provinces of the empire to the Nammāḷvār *Rāmānujakūṭa* at Tirupati built by the Āravīḍu chief Koṇḍarāja.[55] More important than the royal benefactions were those made by members of the influential Āravīḍu family.[56] The large number of private donations made during this period is an indication of the intense devotion of the people to the deity. Among the later rulers the most important patron was Veṅkaṭa II (A.D. 1586-1614). So great was his veneration for this deity that he even replaced the royal sign-manual "Śrī Virūpāksha", that had been in use for 250 years, by "Śrī Veṅkaṭēśa."

The unparalleled importance in the Vijayanagara empire of Śrī Veṅkaṭēśvara of Tirumalai from the mid-fifteenth century onwards was naturally reflected in the capital city in the setting up of temples and sculptures of the god. We have evidence at the site of eight temples and shrines dedicated to this deity, though probably there were more.

The earliest epigraphical mention of this deity in Vijayanagara is found in Krishṇadēvarāya's inscription of A.D. 1515 within the Krishṇa temple, in which, while assigning shares of land to the temple brāhmaṇas, three *koḷagas* of wetlands were granted by the king also to "Tirumaladēva of the four gates of Haṁpe".[57] It is difficult to state what is exactly meant by this sentence; perhaps there were four gates in Haṁpe *tīrtha*, in each of which was a small shrine of this deity. However, neither the gates nor shrines can be located today.

Two inscriptions in the city mention land grants to god Kariya Tiruveṅgaḷanātha of Añjanagiri (another name for Tirumalai) at Chikkarāya tank in Vijayanagara. Both the grants were made in the presence of Viṭhalēśvara on the bank of the Tuṅgabhadrā and in both there is a verse in praise of Rāmānujāchārya. The first of these records, of 30 June 1517, is of Krishṇadēvarāya.[58] The second, of 30 October 1518, is of queen Tirumala-dēvī, this grant was made for the merit of Tirumalarāya.[59] Apparently this was a gift made for the welfare of the prince in the year of his birth. Unfortunately, this temple of Tiruveṅgaḷanātha cannot be traced. An undated inscription on a boulder north of Veṅkaṭapuram village (on the Kāmalāpuram-Kaṁpili road) records a private donation of wetlands to Kariya Tiruveṅgaḷanātha of Komaragiri.[60] Whether this also refers to the above-mentioned temple cannot be determined.

Of the eight Tiruveṅgaḷanātha temples that can be identified on the basis of epigraphical or iconographical data, the earliest one in importance is the small temple in the "royal centre" (NX f/1), which is incorrectly known as the "Sarasvatī" temple. This belongs to the intermediate phase of temple building in the city, between the early fifteenth century temples and the sixteenth century projects.[61] This north-facing monument consists only of a sanctum, an antechamber and an enclosed pillared hall. The Vaishṇava themes of the temple reliefs, the four *nāmams* carved on the pillars, the relief of Garuḍa on the *pīṭha* within the sanctum—all reveal the sectarian affiliation of this temple. That it was a Tiruveṅgaḷanātha temple is only indicated by an inscription, dated 8 November

1543, on the walls of the temple.[62] It registers a gift of lands in Kṛishṇāpuram-agrahāra, founded by Kṛishṇadēvarāya, to the temple of Tiruveṅgaḷanātha by a certain Tippamma Būmakkaṅgāru for the merit of her ancestors. This record gives no clue as to the date of the construction of this structure. Although by itself this small temple is rather unremarkable, its situation within the "royal centre" and its proximity to important monuments within the royal enclosures gives it importance. It is significant that there was a temple of this deity within the "royal centre", probably built before the end of the fifteenth century.

An inscription of A.D. 1535 found in Hospēṭ, refers to the reign of Achyutarāya. It records that Abbarāja Timmapa, the agent of *Pradhāna* (minister) Tirumalarāja, made a gift of the cess with the consent of the merchants of Ayyāvali, Tirmaladēvīyara-paṭṭaṇa, Varadarāja-ammana-paṭṭaṇa and Kṛishṇāpura for the service of god Tiruveṅgaḷanātha at Tirumaladēvīyara-paṭṭaṇa, for the merit of the king.[63] As seen in Chapter 1, the suburb of Tirumala-dēvī paṭṭaṇa was laid out during the reign of Kṛishṇadēvarāya in honour of the senior queen. Each of the sixteenth century suburbs and quarters of Vijayanagara had its own temple. It is likely that the main temple in Tirumala-dēvī-paṭṭaṇa was of the deity after whom the queen was named, namely, Tirumaladēvā or Tiruveṅgaḷanātha, and that this temple, built during the reign of Kṛishṇadēvarāya, is the one mentioned in this donative record. This temple is no longer extant and its exact location cannot be determined.

The great popularity of the cult in the reign of Achyutarāya is hinted at by the fact that the merchants of many suburbs and townships assented to the granting of the cess to Tiruveṅgaḷanātha. Abbarāja Timmapa must have been a high official. Minister Tirumalarāja, mentioned in the epigraph, was probably the king's brother-in-law Salakarāja Tirumalarāja, for in other inscriptions[64] this chief has been referred to as the *pradhāni* of king. A great devotee of god Tiruveṅgaḷanātha, he had built in the previous year the magnificent temple for the deity in the "sacred centre" of the city (NM h/1).

The largest and most important temple of Tiruveṅgaḷanātha in the city was the one built by *Mahāmaṇḍalēśvara* Hiriya Tirumalarāja, son of Salakarāja, the brother-in-law of king Achyutarāya.[65] Queen Varadāṁbika, or Varadājiamman, was the daughter of Salakarāja and sister of Pedda (or Hiriya or Periya, meaning the elder) Tirumala and Pina (or Chikka, meaning the younger) Tirumala, who played a very prominent role in the affairs of the empire during and also shortly after the reign of Achyutarāya. She also had two sisters, Akkāchi-amman and Koṇḍamma.[66] The existence of a third brother Siṅgarāja is revealed in an inscription at Tirumalai.[67] The great devotion of the Salakarāja brothers and their wives to god Tiruveṅgaḷanātha is seen in the notable endowments made to the Tirumalai temple by them.[68]

The north-facing Tiruveṅgaḷanātha temple (NM h/1), known popularly as the "Achyutarāya" temple, is one of the large sixteenth century temple complexes in the "sacred centre" (Fig. 19). It has two enclosures or *prākāras.* Within the inner enclosure is the principal shrine, which has a sanctum, two antechambers, an enclosed circumambulatory passage, a *raṅga-maṇḍapa* with two side-porches, an open *mahā-maṇḍapa* and a small *vāhana-maṇḍapa.* The subsidiary shrine is to the south-west of the main shrine. Along the *prākāra* wall there is pillared gallery, while in the north-east corner is a small enclosed structure. There are three *gōpuras* in this enclosure wall, the northern one being the most imposing. The outer *prākāra* has a large north *gōpura,* two smaller gateways on the western side and a small opening to the south. The most important structure in the outer *prākāra* is the large hall, with outstanding pillar reliefs, in the north-west corner. Like the other great temple complexes, this one, too, has *ratha-vīdhi* and a temple tank (Plate 31).

The foundational inscriptions of Hiriya Tirumalarāja is engraved on the north *gōpura* of the inner *prākāra.* Dated 26 April 1534, it records the consecration of Śrī Tiruveṅgaḷanātha and the gift to the deity of costly ornaments, golden and silver articles and three villages by the founder and the appointment of a number of brāhmaṇas for the various services in the temple. It also mentions that king Achyutadēva-mahārāya gifted the village of Chōramanūrsīme, renamed Achyutarāyapura, for food offerings and festivals. On the same *gōpura* is inscribed twice Achyutarāya's gift of *Ānandanidhi.*[69] There is also another undated epigraph which consists of a Sanskṛit verse in praise of king Achyutēndra and of the usual imprecatory verses.[70]

Overlooking the *ratha-vīdhi* of the Tiruveṅgaḷanātha temple is a small, west-facing Vaishṇava temple (NG x/2), comprising only a sanctum, an antechamber and a *maṇḍapa*. During clearance work conducted here by the A.S.I. in 1987 a mutilated, but finely carved, *mūrti* was discovered in the sanctum. Even though the upper arms are broken, the *mudrās* of the lower ones prove that this was a statue of Tiruveṅgaḷanātha. Since this was in all likelihood the *mūla-mūrti* this temple can be classified as one dedicated to this divinity. The location of the temple suggests that its construction is not anterior to that of the *ratha-vīdhi.*

Situated near the Chakra-tīrtha is another temple of this god (NG x/1). It is an east-facing triple-shrine temple, with a rectangular antechamber and a fairly large *maṇḍapa.* The central sanctum is built against a rock carving of Vishṇu, flanked by consorts. The sculpture is badly mutilated, but could possibly be of Tiruveṅgaḷanātha; the side shrines are empty. An inscription of A.D. 1556 reveals the cultic affiliation of this temple, for it records the obeisance of the merchant Tirumalaśeṭṭi to god Veṅkaṭēśa residing at the Chakra-tīrtha.[71] It is not possible to date the temple. It is likely that the entire temple was not constructed at one time, for the front part of the *maṇḍapa* appears to be a later addition.

Two small shrines (NM r/2 and NQ m/1) of the deity are built against boulders on which are well-executed reliefs of Veṅkaṭēśa. Their size, location and the simplicity of their architecture indicate that these were not foundations of the king or court; they represent the popular devotion to this god.

Among the temples of this deity at the site, after the great Tiruveṅgaḷanātha temple (NM h/1), the next in importance is the one in Kṛishṇāpura (NL w/6) which is incorrectly called the "Chaṇḍikēśvara" temple. This medium-sized east-facing temple was constructed by *Daḷavāyi* (General) Jaṅgamaya, the agent of *Pradhāni* (minister) Yera-Timmarāja, the younger brother of Rāmarāja, for the merit of the king, Ramarāja and Yera-Timmarāja.[72] The donor also provided gold ornaments and silver articles and made provisions for food offerings to the god and the maintenance of the temple brāhmaṇas. Jaṅgamaya was obviously an influential officer serving under Tirumala.[73] The very name of this officer indicates that he was a Vīraśaiva. He also consecrated the Mudu Vīraṇṇa temple (NL w/3) on the same date (22 May 1545) as the Tiruveṅgaḷanātha temple. As seen in Chapter 2, this temple of Vīrabhadra was probably attached to the Vīraśaiva *maṭha* of the Hiriya Chattra. Such was the religious climate in Sadāśiva's reign that this Vīraśaiva general while constructing a temple to the deity of his sect, considered it expedient and politic to also build one for the favourite god of his patrons, the Āravīḍu brothers Tirumala and Aḷiya Rāmarāya.[74]

Besides these eight temples dedicated to Tiruveṅgaḷanātha that are identified on the basis of iconographic or epigraphic data, the existence of others during the empire-period is attested to by the number of statues of the deity found in the Hampi Museum.[75]

Sculptures of Veṅkaṭēśa are found on temple pillars, mainly in Vaishṇava shrines, from the early fifteenth century onwards, but they are not as recurrent as those of the *Kṛishṇa-līlā* scenes, *Rāmāyaṇa* themes and the Narasiṁha episodes. There are also at least three rock carvings of the deity. In the rock shelter NG n/6, Veṅkaṭēśa is present along with other Vaishṇava deities. On a boulder near NR k/1 & 2, besides the two reliefs of Narasiṁha, there is an extremely well executed one of Veṅkaṭēśa with two consorts. Another relief is on a rock behind and slightly above temple NG w/3, near the holy Chakra-tīrtha (Plate 33).

This brief survey discloses the great popularity of Tiruveṅgaḷanātha in the city, especially in the sixteenth century. The construction of temples for the deity and/or the endowments made by state donors such as the powerful Salakarāja Tirumala, General Jaṅgamaya and Abbarāja Timmapa, and the benefactions of Kṛishṇadēvarāya, Tirumala-dēvī and Achyutarāya highlight the court patronage of the cult. The records of the devout merchants, the pious woman and the miscellaneous small shrines of this god testify to the extensive popular support enjoyed by this cult.

2. The Raṅganātha Cult

Of the three Śrī-Vaishṇava temples, that of Raṅganātha at Śrīraṅgam is the most sacred and is known to Śrī-Vaishṇavas by the distinguished name of Kōil, meaning 'the temple.' This temple has come to occupy this foremost position on account of its great antiquity and historical association with the *āḻvārs* and *āchāryas.*[76] A survey of the over 300 inscriptions published from this temple[77] reveals its long history for they span the Chōḷa, Pāṇḍya, Hoysaḷa, Vijayanagara and Nāyaka periods. This is the one Vaishṇava temple that enjoyed state patronage throughout the Vijayanagara period, from early Saṅgama times onwards. The importance of this temple is reflected in the existence of the Raṅganātha cult in Vijayanagara city and its environs.

This spiritual centre of immense sanctity was sacked and destroyed during the early fourteenth century Muslim invasions. After prolonged suffering, the survivors carried the *utsavamūrti* of the deity to Tirupati from where it was brought back and reconsecrated by the Vijayanagara general Gōpaṇārya, who had ably assisted Kumāra Kampaṇa in liberating the far south from Muslim rule, in A.D. 1371-1372[78] Gōpaṇārya is said to have granted fifty-two villages to the temple.[79] Sāḷuva Maṅgu (Maṅgidēva) helped in the reconsecration and also made a sizeable donation to god Rāṅganātha.[80]

During the Saṅgama period the members of the Uttamanaṁbi family were the wardens of the temple and various donations and grants by princes, officers and private persons were entrusted to them. The Uttamanaṁbi family claims descent from Periyāḻvār and their rise to power began in the lifetime of Periya Kṛishṇa Uttamanaṁbi. During the reigns of Dēvarāya I and Dēvarāya II, two brothers of the family became all powerful in the Śrīraṅgam temple.[81] Periya Kṛishṇa Uttamanaṁbi visited Vijayanagara several times and obtained land grants from Harihara II and a number of highly placed chiefs.[82] Among the Saṅgama kings and princes who made noteworthy benefactions to the Raṅganātha temple either directly or through the Uttamanaṁbis were Virūpāksha, son of Harihara II,[83] Bukka II,[84] Vīra-Bhūpati, the son of Bukka II,[85] Dēvarāya I,[86] Vijaya-Bhūpati, the son of Dēvarāya I,[87] Dēvarāya II[88] and Mallikārjuna.[89] Dēvarāya I and Dēvarāya II greatly honoured Uttamanaṁbi by granting him a number of royal emblems.[90]

In the transition period following the breakdown of the first dynasty and the rise of the Sāḷuva dynasty, the Uttamanaṁbis appear to have retained much of their power. But they did have to make one major accommodation to the new rulers of Vijayanagara, conceding considerable status to a foreign sectarian leader, Kanḍāḍai Rāmānuja Aiyangar, who arrived at Śrīraṅgam after having established his credentials as the agent of Sāḷuva Narasiṁha at Tirumalai-Tirupati.[91] He filled up a long trench that had been formed by an overflowing of the Kāvēri, constructed a tank, two *gōpuras* and made a number of other grants.[92]

The Tuḷuvas were also devotees of Raṅganātha. Kṛishṇadēvarāya visited the temple and gave an endowment of five villages in A.D. 1516.[93] He visited it again in 1517 and gifted jewels and precious stones.[94] He granted a village in 1524[95] and gold-plated the doors of the *mukhamaṇḍapa* in 1526.[96] Officers of the king such as Timmappa-Nāyaka,[97] Sāḷuva Timma,[98] Koṇḍamarasa,[99] etc. also made grants. Achyutarāya visited the temple in 1533 and granted three villages and 1,200 gold coins;[100] in May 1538 he gifted a village[101] and in July of the same year a pearl cuirass to the god and a jewelled crown to the goddess.[102] In 1539 he gifted more ornaments.[103] and later in the year performed the *tulāpurusha-dāna.*[104] The gifts of queen Varadājiamman's mother, brother, sister and sisters-in-law are also recorded in the temple.[105] Among the inscriptions of Sadāśiva's reign is the record of the Āravīḍu chief Viṭhaladēva-mahārāja who granted a village and some lands and consecrated the god Viṭhalēśvara at Śrīraṅgam.[106]

In the statue of Raṅganātha of the *śayana* or reclining type, Vishṇu is on Ananta, the cosmic serpent, afloat on the cosmic ocean; often Brahmā is depicted seated on a lotus that emerges from the navel of Vishṇu. Each form of Vishṇu, whether standing, seated or reclining, has four varieties—*yōga, bhōga, vīra* and *abhichārika.* In the *yōga* variety of the *śayana* images, the god appears alone, while in the *bhōga* variety Śrī is at his head and Bhū at his feet. In the *vīra* type both the goddesses are at Vishṇu's feet. In the fourth form Vishṇu is shown lying in deep slumber, with scanty clothing and thin limbs, his head to the north.[107] The Śrīraṅgam statue is a *yōgaśayanamūrti*.[108]

Śrī-Raṅganātha came to be frequently represented during the Vijayanagara period. Raṅganātha is more or less the same as Anantaśayana of the preceding period, but the style is different. The canopy over Vishṇu's head formed by Ananta's seven hoods is shown in profile, and the god, lying on his right side on the coiled body of the snake, is shown actually holding the *śaṅkha* and *chakra* in his upper hands. His head is kept on the lower right palm and his left hand is stretched along the upper, that is his left, side. In the preceding periods, the hood-canopy of the serpent is shown frontally, the lower right hand of the deity in *yōga-mudrā* and his attributes are shown by his side.[109]

The most ancient temple of Raṅganātha at the site is the Gavi (cave) Raṅganātha temple in Ānegoṅdi, located in the hill range about a kilometre westwards of the village. Here there was some pre-Vijayanagara period construction which has been added to and repaired in later days, including the post-Vijayanagara period.[110] It consists of a very small cave, a cave sanctuary and a hall. In the *Virūpāksha Vasantōtsava Champū* it is mentioned that the car festival of this temple followed immediately that of the great Virūpāksha temple.[111] Although small, it must have been an important temple as this god was the family deity of the rulers of Ānegoṅdi. Worship was carried on here till fairly recent times. At present, the *mūla-mūrti* and other statues from the Gavi Raṅganātha temple are housed in the Raṅganātha temple in Ānegoṅdi. The *mūrti* is of the *vīra* variety.

The Raṅganātha temple in the village of Ānegoṅdi is a fairly large one, with two courtyards. The presence of a number of pre-Vijayanagara style chlorite pillars and other architectural pieces lying around the premises indicate the existence of some pre-Vijayanagara temple at or near the site of the Raṅganātha temple, but whether the earlier structure was a temple dedicated to the same deity is not known. The temple as it stands today is a Vijayanagara period construction, possibly with some post-1565 additions. According to a Telugu work, *Rāmarājiyamu*, by Venkayya, Timma or Tirumala, a nephew of Śrīraṅga III (the last Āravīḍu king), "made an extensive and cool garden by the side of Tuṅgabhadra in Kishkindha, and there built the temple of Sriranganatha resembling Srirangam on the banks of the Kaveri."[112] Since the description fits no temple in Ānegoṅdi village (Kishkindhā) except the Raṅganātha temple, it must be the one referred to. However, this is not a seventeenth century structure. Probably, with poetic exaggeration the author is referring to some additions or embellishments done to this temple by prince Timma. Worship is still carried on in this temple.

In the "sacred centre" are two Vijayanagara period Raṅganātha temples. The first (NG s/2) consisting of a sanctum, an antechamber and *maṇḍapa*, is built against a rock on which is a fine relief of the four-armed Vīra-Raṅganātha (Plate 32). It is not possible to date it accurately. The second (NL h/9) is on the original Vijayanagara road from the Kṛishṇa temple complex to the Virūpāksha temple. In the sanctum of this small temple is a rough rock carving of Vīra-Raṅganātha. No worship is conducted in these two deserted shrines. Although at present in the so-called "Hastagiri Raṅganātha-svāmi" temple (NG w/5) at Chakra-tīrtha there is a *mūrti* of this deity, this was not originally a Raṅganātha temple, as already seen in Chapter 5, but was a shrine dedicated to Viṭhala.

In Nāgēnahaḷḷi (the sixteenth century suburb of Nāgalāpura) is a Raṅganātha temple. That this medium-sized temple was constructed in A.D. 1516 is indicated by an inscription found here. It records that Raṅganātha Dīkshita, the *purōhita* of king Kṛishṇadēvarāya, received the village from the king and constructed therein a tank called Nāgasamudra after Nāgaladēvī, the mother of the king, and the temples Nāgēśvara and Nāgendraśayana. He made the village an *agrahāra*.[113] The Śiva temple of Nāgēśvara is also still extant; the Vishṇu temple is this Raṅganātha temple. The deity, called Nāgendraśayana in honour of the queen mother, was a form of Raṅganātha.

The largest temple dedicated to the reclining form of Vishṇu at the site is the enormous and unusual temple in modern Anantaśayana-guḍi. The deity of this temple was called Ananta-padmanābha (the name of the god of the famous Vaishṇava temple in Trivandrum) or

Anantasayana. Since this is also a reclining *mūrti* of Vishṇu we can include this temple within the group of Raṅganātha shrines. The temple stands within a courtyard with three *gōpuras*. The principal shrine consists of a large rectangular sanctum and antechamber and a large pillared *mahā-maṇḍapa*. The sanctum is about twenty-four metres high and has a vaulted dome. Besides the main shrine there is also subsidiary shrine and other small structures within the *prākāra*. The inscription of Kṛishṇadēvarāya of A.D. 1524[114] records the construction of the temple for god Anantapadmanābha in Sāle-Tirumala-Mahārāya-pura, the gift of several villages to it and the appointment of three priests of the Vaikhānasa sect for conducting the worship of the god.[115] The temple must have been constructed in commemoration of the coronation of Prince Tirumala.[116] If so, it is highly significant that on the occasion of the birth of Tirumalarāya in A.D. 1518 an endowment was made to a Tiruveṅgaḷanātha temple and six years later, when he was crowned as the heir apparent, the construction and endowing of an Anantapadmanābha temple took place, both deities being important Śrī-Vaishṇava gods. An inscription of Sadāśiva of A.D. 1549 in this temple refers to the divinity as Anantaśayana.[117] It is likely that there were other temples in the city dedicated to Raṅganātha, for at least two fine sculptures of this deity are found in the Hampi Museum.[118]

Apart from the *mūrtis* in the shrines, there are not many sculptures of this deity at the site. Raṅganātha almost never appears on temple pillars, probably because it was difficult to carve such a relief in the restricted space on pillars. The finest relief of Raṅganātha is on a natural rock on the river bank near NG m/1, of the *vīra* variety. Another is found on a rock south-east of temple NG x/1; within this temple is fairly large stucco statue of this divinity on an architrave above the pillars of the front part of the *maṇḍapa*. A relief is also carved on the wall of the verandah of temple NQ n/1. There are a couple of other small reliefs elsewhere in the city.

Thus, the temple at Śrīraṅgam was a highly important religious centre during Vijayanagara times and in the city Raṅganātha was a fairly popular deity. The cult was probably present even before the founding of the empire at the site, from where it has not completely disappeared even today.

3. The Varadarāja Cult

The Varadarājasvāmi temple in Kāñchipuram is the third great Śrī-Vaishṇava pilgrimage centre in Tamil Nāḍu. Owing to Rāmānuja's connection with this temple and with Kāñchi, it rose to importance during the eleventh and twelfth centuries. Nearly 350 inscriptions from the temple have been published (mainly in *ARSIE* of 1919), belonging to the Chōḷa, Pāṇḍya, Hoysaḷa, Kākaṭiya, Telugu-Chōḍa, Kāḍavarāya, Śaṁbuvarāya, Vijayanagara and post-Vijayanagara periods. Less than one-fourth of the records are of Vijayanagara times.

The fifteenth century onwards was a prosperous period for the Varadarājasvāmi temple when it received enormous gifts by way of land, money, jewels, vehicles and structural additions of a *gōpura*, many *maṇḍapas* and separate shrines for the *āḷvārs* and *āchāryas*. A notable development was the enormous increase in the celebration of festivals, not only for the main deity but also for the *āḷvārs* and *āchāryas*.[119] However, a careful perusal of the records shows that the patronage was mostly from kings Kṛishṇadēvarāya, Achyutarāya, Veṅkaṭa II and the Āraviḍu chiefs. The temple did not receive the patronage from the Vijayanagara court throughout the period under survey, nor did it enjoy wide popular support in the form of numerous gifts and grants from nobles, officials and private citizens.

The greatest donors were Kṛishṇadēvarāya and Achyutarāya. The former in A.D. 1514 gilted with gold the *vimāna* of the temple,[120] in 1516 gifted five villages[121] and the year after regulated the processional routes of the Śaiva Ēkāmranātha and Vaishṇava Varadarāja temples and presented a vehicle to each.[122] Guru Vyāsatīrtha also granted a village, which he had received from the king, and presented a serpent vehicle.[123]

The most munificent benefactions of Achyutarāya were to the Varadarājasvāmi temple. At the time of his coronation he presented a number of villages to be divided equally between Ēkāmranātha and Varadarāja.[124] He gifted fourteen villages to the temple of Varadarāja on another occasion[125] and in A.D. 1533, in the company of queen Varada-dēvī and prince Veṅkaṭādri, he performed the *tulābhāra* in pearls and assigned it the income of seventeen villages, gave 1,000 cows and other valuable gifts.[126] Of the next reign, there is a record of Rāmarāya's repair of the stone steps of a tank and of gifts to the temple.[127] A number of subordinate chiefs also made endowments.[128]

Varadarāja means 'king among boon-givers.' The story of the Varadarāja (also called Karivarada or Gajēndramōksha) form of Vishṇu is that of the god saving the king of elephants who was caught in the clutches of a deadly crocodile. Gajēndra prayed intensely to Vishṇu for help and the deity rushed to the spot on his mount, Garuḍa, and rescued his devotee.[129] According to Gopinatha Rao, the iconography of Varadarāja is of the deity seated on Garuḍa.[130] But this is only true of representations of the Gajēndramōksha episode. The *mūla-mūrti* and the *utsava-mūrti* in the Varadarājasvāmi temple are depicted in *samabhaṅga*, with the *chakra* and *śaṅkha* in the upper right and left hands and the lower right and left in *abhaya-mudrā* and holding a *gadā*, respectively. He is flanked by a consort on each side. Sometimes in place of the *gadā* the lower left hand of the deity is in the *varada-mudrā*.[131]

That the cult of Varadarāja or Allāḷaperumāḷ was already prevalent in south-east Karṇāṭaka from the thirteenth century onwards is indicated by epigraphs.[132] However, despite the importance of the Varadarājasvāmi temple of Kāñchi during the Vijayanagara period, neither is there epigraphical evidence of temples dedicated to this god in the capital, nor do we have any archaeological proof of this. The only indication of the impact of this cult in Vijayanagara are some reliefs of the deity. The only rock carving of Varadarāja is within the "urban core" on a rock in the north ridge (NM z/3). Here the god is represented along with his two consorts. Reliefs of the deity also occur on temple walls, for example on the exterior walls of the *vimāna* of the Rāmachandra temple and on the architrave of the nave of the *uyyāle-maṇḍapa* of the Viṭhala temple. On temple pillars the narrative reliefs of the Gajēndra-mōksha episode and of the deity in *samabhaṅga* occur here and there. The most complete representation of this is in the east porch of the temple NC w/3 in Viṭhalāpura. Here on the south pillar, arranged in four panels, is the complete story—the elephant in distress, Vishṇu to the rescue seated on Garuḍa, the god blessing his devotee and Varadarāja in divine form in *samabhaṅga* (Plate 34).

Of the three great Śrī-Vaishṇava deities of Tirumala-Tirupati, Śrīraṅgam and Kāñchi, the most popular in the city was undoubtedly Tiruveṅgaḷanātha. Raṅganātha, too, was an important deity. But, the Varadarāja cult never became one of the significant cults in the city. This is not surprising, for the Tirumalai-Tirupati temple became the greatest temple and Veṅkatēśvara the most popular divinity in the empire after the mid-fifteenth century. The Śrīraṅgam temple also enjoyed the patronage of the state and the people from the rule of the first Vijayanagara dynasty onwards. It was also the spiritual centre of the Teṅgalai sub-sect, which was predominant during the Sāḷuva-Tuḷuva periods in the city. The Varadarājasvāmi temple, no doubt, did receive extensive patronage during Vijayanagara times, but the support was mainly restricted to the Tuḷuva period and to state donors. This temple was also the stronghold of the Vaḍagalais and this sub-sect was less important in the city.

4. Worship of the Āḷvārs and Āchāryas

The veneration of the Tamil Śrī-Vaishṇava saints (*āḷvārs*) and preceptors (*āchāryas*) is a peculiar feature of Śrī-Vaishṇavism. The worship of *āḷvārs* was probably already current by the eleventh and twelfth centuries A.D., for Rāmānuja is said to have installed the images of these saints in the Gōvindarāja temple at Tirupati.[133] The deification of the *āchāryas* also followed in course of time. Yet, it was only during the Vijayanagara period that the cult of these minor divinities became popular[134] and separate shrines were even built for them in Śrīraṅgam, Tirupati, Kāñchi and other Śrī-Vaishṇava temples.[135]

At Vijayanagara, there are no reliefs of these saints and teachers in the early fifteenth century parts of the Rāmachandra temple complex, but in the mid-fifteenth century temple of Mallikārjuna's reign (NV o/1) the *āḷvārs* and Rāmānuja appear in the pillar reliefs. Iconographically the *āḷvārs* are usually portrayed seated cross-legged with hands joined in *añjali-mudrā*. Rāmānuja, also called Uḍayavar or Bhāshyakāra, is portrayed like these saints, except for his ascetic's staff, with a cloth tied to the top, resting against one shoulder. Nammāḷvar, the greatest of these saints, has the right hand in the *vyākhyāna* (teaching) *mudrā* and the left in the *dhyāna-mudrā* (meditation pose). Some of the *āḷvārs* are at times shown standing, notably Tirumaṅgai-āḷvār, who holds a sword and shield, because he had been a robber chieftain before his conversion to sainthood. The statues of the *āḷvārs* and of the *āchāryas* are usually made of a greenish coloured chlorite. Some stucco images of these divinities are also available at the site, for example, on the brick and mortar superstructures of temple (NG x/1) and the *Pārāṅkuśa-maṇḍapa* (NJ g/1).

Epigraphical and literary evidence both support the archaeological data pointing to the immense popularity of the *āḷvār-āchārya* cult in the city, especially in the sixteenth century. Kṛishṇadēvarāya's *Āmuktamālyada* is a glowing tribute to these minor deities, for the text is based on the story of Āṇḍāḷ, the only woman *āḷvār*, called Āmuktamālyada in Telugu, and of her foster-father Periyāḷvār. Intertwined with the main theme is the story of one of the most important *āchāryas* of all, Yāmunāchārya.[136]

The inscription of A.D. 1534 from the Viṭhala temple states that the thirteen *āḷvārs*, including Tirukachinaṁbi (one of the preceptors), were installed in a specially constructed shrine.[137] Unfortunately, none of these statues are *in situ*. However, during excavation conducted by the A.S.I. in and around the Viṭhala complex in the mid-1970s and again in the mid-1980s, a number of *āḷvār* statues were unearthed, most of them badly mutilated. The finest of these is the one that has been wrongly identified as the image of Purandaradāsa, the Haridāsa saint, by S.R. Rao and installed in a deserted temple (NH a/10) in Viṭhalāpura. Viṭhalāpura was sacked in A.D. 1565 and worship discontinued. Since Purandaradāsa died only in A.D. 1564, it is not likely that he was already deified and his image worshipped before the destruction. This seated saint is undoubtedly Toṇḍaraḍipoḍi-āḷvār, as the little basket for flowers that hangs on his left arm is characteristic of this saint. This statue is like the bronze statue of this saint in the Madras Museum.[138]

An unfinished *āḷvār* statue, found during the excavations of the 1970s and placed in a sub-shrine of the temple NC w/3, shows that even at the time of the destruction of the city statues of these saints were being prepared.

The installation of the *āḷvārs* in the Rāmachandra temple complex by Ārāvīṭi Velgaḷarāju[139] must have occurred in the sixteenth century. As already discussed in Chapter 4 the donor was probably Veṅkaṭādri, brother of Aḷiya Rāmarāya. These images are no longer in the temple; a broken statue of an *āḷvār* lying in the rubble and debris behind the temple complex is possibly one of these images.

It is likely that *āḷvār* and *āchārya* statues were consecrated in practically all the Śrī-Vaishṇava temples in the city, for wherever clearance work has been undertaken such statues have been recovered. Thus, during the recent work at the Kṛishṇa temple complex at least three statues of seated *āḷvārs* and a broken statue probably of Tirumaṅgai were found. During the excavations carried out by the A.S.I. in the mid-1980s in the "royal centre", a statue of Rāmānuja from the Royal Enclosure, one of Nammāḷvār from the big Vishṇu temple (NS 1/1), and from a small Vishṇu temple (NS 1/3) broken statues of an *āḷvār* and of Rāmānuja were recovered. In the excavations conducted by the Directorate of Archaeology and Museums, Karṇāṭaka, in the "Noblemen's Quarters" area, a statue of Nammāḷvār was found in a small temple (NR q/3). A large number of such statues are also in the Haṁpi Museum. Unfortunately, the exact locations from where these were collected have not been noted. Many of these sculptures have not even been numbered.

Besides the installation of these subsidiary deities within Śrī-Vaishṇava temples, separate temples were also built for them in Viṭhalāpura. We have epigraphical evidence of the consecration of shrines for the Mudal-āḷvārs, (that is the first three *āḷvārs*, Poygai, Bhūtam and Pēy), Tirumaṅgai, Nammāḷvār or Śaṭhakōpa and Tirumadiśai (or Tirumaḷiśai) āḷvār, and of Rāmānuja. It is possible that others were also enshrined of which no inscriptional proof is available.

Two mid-sixteenth century records from

Viṭhalāpura mention the Mudal-āḷvār temple (NC w/2).[140] This north-facing structure has three shrines (facing north, east and west), an antechamber and a *maṇḍapa*. A pillared gallery surrounds the temple on four sides.

Two inscriptions on the outer east wall of the Tirumaṅgai-āḷvār temple (NC v/3) refer to this temple. The first, of A.D. 1556, records the construction of the temple by the Āravīḍu chief Aubhaḷarāju, the son of Kōnēṭirāja, who also made an endowment for the daily offerings to the deity and for offerings to Viṭhala and Nammāḷvār, when these deities were brought in procession to the temple of Tirumaṅgai-āḷvār.[141] The second notes the gift of an orchard to the temple by Kuruchēṭi Śrīraṅgarāju.[142] This temple consists of a sanctum, two antechambers, an enclosed *maṇḍapa* with two side-porches and a *Rāmānuja-kūṭa* (Plate 36). On the south-east pillar in the *maṇḍapa* is a relief of Tirumaṅgai, facing the sanctum.

An inscription of Aḷiya Rāmarāya mentions the gift of a village for the service of Nammāḷvār near Viṭhala.[143] The above inscriptions of Aubhaḷarāju also refers to Nammāḷvār. An inscription found on a rock to the east of Viṭhalāpura refers to the garden of (the temple of) god Nammāḷvār.[144] Hence there must have been a temple dedicated to this deity. It is my hypothesis that the fine, north-facing temple (NH a/10), facing the south *gōpura* of Viṭhala is this shrine. Its location fits the description "Nammāḷvār near Viṭhala". This temple has a sanctum, two antechambers, an enclosed *maṇḍapa* and also side-porches. The reliefs of this temple are extremely fine. The temple is very similar to the Tirumaṅgai-āḷvār temple, but there are sculptures here on the exterior walls of the temple, while the walls of the Tirumaṅgai-āḷvār temple are plain. Such a superb monument would be most fitting for Nammāḷvār, the greatest of the *āḷvārs*. That it is an *āḷvār* shrine is indicated by the large number of reliefs of *āḷvārs* that occur on the temple walls and pillars, including an unusual relief of Tiruppāṇ-āḷvār (who is standing, holding a *vīṇa* in one hand) and of Tirumaṅgai on either side of the east doorway of the temple. The prominence given to the reliefs of Nammāḷvār is another clue that this was a temple dedicated to him. He appears once on the outer walls of the *maṇḍapa* and of the sanctum, on a pillar of the west porch and on the north-east pillar in the *maṇḍapa*, facing the sanctum.[145]

An inscription from Viṭhalāpura mentions a grant made in "in the presence of Tirumadiśe-āḷuvār located near the chariot of god Viṭhala."[146] Therefore, there must have been a temple or shrine of Tirumaḷiśai-āḷvār to the east of the Viṭhala temple near or along the chariot-street, which extended from the east *gōpura* to the *Pārāṅkuśa-maṇḍapa* (NJ g/1) because the chariot of the temple would have been placed on this street. At present only one temple is extant near or along the *ratha-vīdhi*—the sixteenth century temple NH j/1, which faces the car street. Perhaps this was the Tirumaḷiśai-āḷvār shrine, but in the absence of any other corroborating data we cannot make a definitive statement.

Another inscription from Viṭhalāpura, which no longer appears to be extant at the site, stated that Śrīraṅgayya, son of Rāmarāja Kōnēṭayya, measured the streets of the temple of Bhāshyakāra during the reign of Sadāśiva.[147] This indicates the existence of a Rāmānuja temple. It is my suggestion that the temple (NC w/3) to the north of the Viṭhala temple, which is most inappropriately called the "Old Śiva temple", is this shrine. It is the only temple in Viṭhalāpura that has its own street, besides, of course, the great Viṭhala temple. It consists of a sanctum, two antechambers, an enclosed circumambulatory passage, a *raṅga-maṇḍapa* with two side-porches (of which the west porch has been enclosed to form a sub-shrine), a *māha-maṇḍapa,*—all within a *prākāra* with a *gōpura* on the south side and a pillared gallery along the enclosure wall. On the *gōpura* of this temple is the complete series of *Rāmāyaṇa* reliefs. Rāmānuja's favourite and personal deity was Rāma.[148] Hence, it is appropriate that the story of Rāma should be highlighted in a temple of Rāmānjua. Reliefs of this teacher are prominently displayed in this temple. For example, in the *mahā-maṇḍapa* the ceiling is raised in the central part of the hall by vertical slabs above the pillars. Along these slabs are reliefs of *āḷvārs* and *āchāryas*, flanked by deities or devotees. Rāmānuja is shown twice; on the south slab, i.e., facing the sanctum, he is seated in the centre, flanked by Rāma and Sūrya. Thus, just as in the

Tīrumaṅgai-āḷvār temple the saint is shown facing the sanctum, here Rāmānuja is portrayed in a similar manner.[149]

Therefore, along the processional streets and near the Viṭhala temple there were temples of the *āḷvārs* and Rāmānuja. It is likely that, as indicated in the inscription in the Tirumaṅgai-āḷvār temple, the processional deity of Viṭhala would halt at these shrines when he was taken around on festival days.

The greatest patrons of the *āḷvār-āchārya* cult in particular and of Śrī-Vaishṇavism in general were the Āravīḍu princes and chiefs. Aḷiya Rāmāraya and, possibly, his brother Veṅkaṭādri had a special veneration for the *āḷvārs* as seen from their records. The brothers Aubhaḷarāju and Śrīraṅgayya, the sons of Kōnēṭiraja,[150] were also generous donors. One of their two other brothers, Udayagiri Timmarāja, instituted the ten-day *Tiruvadhyāna* festival—the recitation of the *Divyaprabandham* of the *āḷvārs* [151] —and Koṇḍarāja, the other brother, added an additional two days to this festival.[152] Inscriptions from other parts of the empire bear witness to the great promotion of Śrī-Vaishṇavism by these brothers, especially the elder two, Aubhaḷarāja and Koṇḍarāja. For example, Aubhaḷarāja's benefactions at Ahōbalam were so noteworthy that the Śrī-Vaishṇava *āchārya* Pārānkuśa Vaṅ-Śathogōpa accorded him a special honour.[153] Koṇḍarāja built the Nammāḷvār *Rāmānuja-kuṭa* in Tirupati, granted ten villages to it[154] and secured from Sadāśiva certain taxes from sixteen provinces of the empire towards this institution.[155] He was also instrumental in getting the emperor to grant thirty-one villages to Rāmānuja (that is to the shrine of Rāmānuja and to the Śrī-Vaishṇavas of the place) at Śrīperumbudūr.[156] These brothers were the disciples of highly influential Śrī-Vaishṇava *āchāryas*. Aubhaḷarāja was the disciple of Tirumala-Auku-Tātāchārya[157] and Koṇḍarāja[158] and Timmarāja[159] of Kaṅḍāla Śrīraṅgāchārya.

5. Other Śrī-Vaishṇava Practices

Vishvaksēna or Sēnai Mudaliyar holds an honoured place in the Śrī-Vaishṇava pantheon of minor divinities. He is the commander-in-chief of Vishṇu's retinue, door-keeper of Vaikunṭha, custodian of the personal effects of Vishṇu and controller of his finances.[160] His position and role is parallel to that of Gaṇēśa and Chaṇḍēśa in the Śaiva religion.[161] In Śrī-Vaishṇavism he is considered to be *prathamāchārya* (first preceptor).[162] In the temples his shrine is in the north-east corner.[163]

Iconographically Vishvaksēna is portrayed in *lalitāsana* with the right leg hanging down, the left folded and resting on the seat. He holds the *chakra* and *śaṅkha* in the upper right and left hands respectively, while the lower left hand holds the *gadā* and the lower right is in the *abhaya-mudrā* (or in *tarjanī*). Images of Vishvaksēna are distinguishable from seated Vishṇu figures only by the absence of the *yajñopavīta* and the *śrīvatsa* mark.[164] The discovery of two partly broken, chlorite statues of the deity during the recent excavations carried out in the Viṭhala and Kṛishṇa temple complexes, the relief of Vishvaksēna (Plate 39) on the side wall of the antechamber of the Rāṅganātha temple (NG s/2) (on the opposite walls of which is a relief of Rāmānuja and Nammāḷvār-Plate 35), the relief of this minor deity in rock shelter NS a/1 along with Rāmānuja and some *āḷvārs* and the reliefs on pillars reveal that Senai Mudaliyar was venerated in the Śrī-Vaishṇava temples of the city.

In the large Śrī-Vaishṇava temples, such as at Tirumalai-Tirupati, arrangements for the feeding of the Śrī-Vaishṇava pilgrims were made by instituting *Rāmānuja-kūṭas*. This institution was present in the temples at Vijayanagara too. Epigraphical data support the archaeological evidence of the presence of two such feeding places, namely in the Tirumaṅgai-āḷvār temple[165] and in the Mudal-āḷvār temple.[166] In the former it is situated in the south-east corner of the temple enclosure and in the latter in the eastern wing of the pillared gallery. In both cases a part of the ceiling is raised, with a clerestory to serve as an outlet for the smoke. Such type of structures are also found in most of the larger Śrī-Vaishṇava temples. These might have been *Rāmānuja-kūṭas* or kitchens where the food offerings were prepared.

The *nāmam* begins to appear in the Śrī-Vaishṇava temples from the Vijayanagara times onwards.[167] The Vaḍagalai *nāmam* is shaped like a 'U' (Plate 38) while the Teṅgalai one is somewhat like a 'Y' with a distinct *pāda* projection at the bottom (Plate 37).[168] In the early fifteenth century structures of the Rāmāchandra temple this sectarian mark is noticeable by its absence. It makes its appearance in the mid-fifteenth century temple NV o/1 and thenceforth it is a common feature. It is held that only Teṅgalai *nāmam* occurs in the Haṁpi monuments.[169] However, the detailed survey of all the temples and structures reveals that although the Teṅgalai *nāmam* is more common and the Teṅgalai influences were therefore greater in the city, the Vaḍagalai *nāmam* is also seen occasionally. An unusual features is the presence of both Teṅgalai and Vaḍagalai sectarian marks in some of the monuments in Vijayanagara.[170] From this we can conclude that the antagonism between the two sub-sects was not so highly marked prior to A.D. 1565. The Vaḍagalai-Teṅgalai schism in medieval Śrī-Vaishṇavism was then only a scholastic controversy; it became a full-fledged battle for temple control only in the late sixteenth, seventeenth and eighteenth centuries.[171]

The Tamil influence is also noticeable in the names of festivals and food offerings mentioned in the sixteenth century inscriptions. Festivals such as the *Tepa-Tirunāḷ, Tōpu-Tirunāḷ, Koḍa-Tirunāḷ*[172] and *Tiruvadhyāna*[173] were celebrated and food items like *dadheyonam, dōḍaki-prasāda,*[174] *karuchiappa,* and *sukhinappas*[175] were offered to the deities.

Thus, the Vijayanagara state had penetrated into the far south and annexed the Tamil country in the latter half of the fourteenth century. In turn, the Tamil traditions of temple architecture, cults and rituals, worship and festivals made their way to the capital and became dominant, especially in the sixteenth century.

Notes

1. S.V. Padigar, "The Cult of Vishṇu in Karnataka" (Ph. D. diss.), p. 258.
2. B.R. Gopal, "Śrī Āndāḷ in Karnataka," *QJMS*, LXXVI, p. 160 ff.
3. S. Krishnaswami Aiyangar, *A History of Tirupati*, vol. II, p. 140; K.V. Raman, *Śrī Varadarajaswāmi Temple - Kañchi*, p. 7.
4. S. Krishnaswami Aiyangar, op.cit., vol. I, pp. 4-5.
5. Sadhu Subrahmanya Sastry, *Report on the Inscriptions of the Dēvasthanam Collection with Illustrations*, p. 3.
6. *EC* II, SB. 344 (1923 ed.).
7. *SII* IV, no. 280.
8. S. Krishnaswami Aiyangar, op.cit., vol. I, pp. 34-42.
9. R. Champakalakshmi, *Vaiṣṇava Iconography in the Tamil Country*, pp. 181-182.
10. S. Krishnaswami Aiyangar, op.cit., vol. I, p. 377.
11. Ibid., p. 262 ff.
12. Burton Stein, *All the King's Mana: Papers on Medieval South Indian History*, p. 163.
13. Ibid.
14. Sadhu Subrahmanya Sastry, op.cit., pp. 2-3.
15. Ibid.
16. Ibid., p. 33.
17. Ibid., p. 4.
18. *TTDES* I, no. 185.
19. Ibid., no. 192.
20. Ibid., no. 199.
21. Ibid., nos. 179 and 180.
22. V.N. Srinivasa Rao, "Chandragiri," *QJMS*, XXIII, p. 375.
23. S. Krishnaswami Aiyangar, op.cit., vol. I, p. 453.
24. *TTDES* II, no. 50.
25. Ibid., no. 25.
26. Ibid., no. 4.
27. Ibid., nos. 31 and 51.
28. Ibid., no. 51.
29. Ibid., no. 82.
30. Ibid., nos. 4, 30, 31, 34, 50 and 51.
31. *ARSIE* of 1916, no. 762.
32. TTDES II, no. 13.
33. Ibid., no. 133.
34. Ibid., nos. 26, 33, 36, 38, 44, 45, 81, 134, 135, 140, etc.
35. *MAR* of 1920, p. 37.
36. *TTDES* III, nos. 32 to 39.
37. Ibid., nos. 40 to 59.
38. Ibid., nos. 60 to 63.
39. Ibid., nos. 64 and 65.
40. Ibid., nos. 66 to 68.
41. Ibid., no. 80.
42. S. Krishnaswami Aiyangar, op.cit., vol. II, p. 118.
43. *TTDES* III, nos. 83 to 86.
44. Ibid., no. 21.
45. Ibid., no. 154.
46. Ibid., nos. 130 and 131.
47. Ibid., nos. 157, 158, 159, 165 and 175.
48. Tirumalāmbā, *Varadāmbika-pariṇaya-campū*, verse 167.
49. Rājanātha Diṇḍima, *Achyutarāyābhudaya*, Canto III, verse 23.
50. *TTDES* IV, nos. 16 and 17.
51. Ibid., nos. 54 and 58.
52. Ibid., nos. 8 to 10.
53. Ibid., no. 123.
54. Ibid., nos. 11 and 142.
55. *TTDES* V, no. 154.
56. Ibid., nos. 29, 51, 52, 53, 85A, 125, 133, 141, 155, 168.
57. *SII* IV, no. 255, line 47.
58. Ibid., no. 249.
59. *SII* IX, pt. II, no. 510.
60. *VPR '84-87*, no. 160.

[61]G. Michell, "Architectural Traditions at Vijayanagara: Temple Styles," in *Vij. City & Emp.*, vol. 1, pp. 277-278.

[62]*ARSIE* of 1935-36, no. 337.

[63]*SII* IX pt. II, no. 573.

[64]*ARSIE* of 1938-39, no. 334.

[65]*SII* IX, pt. II, no. 564.

[66]*EI* XXXIII, p. 200.

[67]*TTDES* IV, no. 88.

[68]Ibid., nos. 25, 31, 66, 88, 168 and 170.

[69]*SII* IV, nos. 268 and 269.

[70]*SII* IX, pt. II, no. 598.

[71]*SII* XVI, no. 217.

[72]*Top. List* I, Bellary dist. no. 369; *SII* IV, no. 265.

[73]According to C. Hayavadana Rao, ed., *Mysore Gazetteer*, vol. II, pt. III, p. 2108, Yara-Timma is a corruption for Hire Tirumala.

That this variation of the name of Tirumala was commonly used is clear from Ferishta's account of the history of the period, for he always refers to this chief as Yeltumraj (see J. Briggs, *History of the Rise of Mahomedan Power*, vol. III, p. 78, pp. 151, 238 and 252).

[74]There are not many records of Tirumala's benefactions to temples but to the Tirumalai shrine he has made a note-worthy contribution (*TTDES* V, no. 168); Rāmarāya was one of the greatest patrons of that temple during this period (Ibid., nos. 29, 85A 155).

[75]Nos. 48, 65, 144, 535, 612, 1772 of the Haṁpi Museum collection.

[76]T.A. Gopinatha Rao, *Elements of Hindu Iconography*, vol. 1, pt. I, p. 269.

[77]Mainly in *ARSIE* of 1936-37, 1937-38 and 1938-39 and in the *SII* series.

[78]*EI* VI, pp. 322-330; C. Srinivasachari, "A Great Contribution of Vijayanagara to the Tamil Country", *Karnatak Historical Review*, IV, pp. 12-13; A. Krishnaswami, *The Tamil Country Under Vijayanagara*, p. 56.

[79]. Kōil Olugu, p. 135, cited by V.N. Hari Rao, *The Śrīraṅgam Temple : Art and Architecture*, p. 9.

[80]C. Srinivasachari, op.cit., p. 13.

[81]A. Appadurai, "Kings, Sects and Temples in South India, 1350-1700 A.D.", in *South Indian Temples*, ed. Burton Stein, pp. 60-61.

[82]Kōil Oḷugu, pp. 127-128, cited in *Further Sources*, vol. III, p. 41.

[83]*ARSIE* of 1938-39, no.153.

[84]*ARSIE* of 1937-38, no. 417.

[85]*ARSIE* of 1938-39, no. 59.

[86]*EI* XVI, pp. 222-229; *ARIE* of 1953-54, no. 352.

[87]*ARSIE* of 1938-39, no. 53.

[88]*EI* XVII, pp. 110-111; *EI* XVIII, pp. 138-139; *ARSIE* of 1937-38, nos. 119 and 121.

[89]*EI* XVI, pp. 345-353.

[90]*ARSIE* of 1938-39, p. 86.

[91]A. Appadurai, op.cit., pp. 62-63.

[92]V.N. Hari Rao (ed.), *Kōil Oḷugu: The Chronicle of the Srirangam Temple with Historical Notes*, pp. 166-171.

[93]*ARSIE* of 1938-39, no. 98.

[94]*ARIE* of 1950-51, no. 341.

[95]*ARSIE* of 1929-30, no. 258.

[96]*ARSIE* of 1937-38, no. 120.

[97]*ARSIE* of 1938-39, no. 68.

[98]Ibid., no. 30.

[99]Ibid., no. 66.

[100]*ARSIE* of 1938-39, no. 16.

[101]Ibid., no. 114.

[102]Ibid., no. 151.

[103]Ibid., no. 1.

[104]Ibid., no. 15.

[105]Ibid., no. 40; *ARIE* of 1950-51, nos. 318, 323, 324 and 340.

[106]*ARIE* of 1953-54, no. 375.

[107]K.V. Soundara Rajan, "The Typology of Anantaśayi Icon," *Artibus Asiae*, XXIX, pp. 75-76.

[108]V.N. Hari Rao, *The Śrīraṅgam Temple: Art and Architecture*, p. 84.

[109]A. Sundara, "New Light on Religious Trends in Ānegoṅdi Region during the Vijayanagara Period," *QJMS*, LXVIII, pp. 12-13.

[110]Sugandha,"History and Archeology of Anegondi" (Ph.D. diss.), pp. 156-160.

[111]V. Raghavan, "The Virūpākṣa Vasantōtsava Campū of Ahobala,"*JOR*, XIV, p. 23.

[112]*Sources*, p. 311.

[113]*SII* IX, pt. II, no. 504.

[114]*ARSIE* of 1922, no. 683.

[115]It follows from this that the Vaikhānasa *Āgama* was in use in this temple; this is the only example at the site of an epigraph that gives a clue about the *Āgama* used in a temple for the rituals. There are two sets of *Āgamas* used by the Vaishṇavites in south India—the Vaikhānasa and the Pāñcharātra. By the medieval times the latter had become the basis for many, if not most, of the south Indian Vishṇu temples. Yet, in no inscriptions in this site is the Pāñcharātra mentioned. Perhaps, it was so commonly in use that no need was felt to make a specific reference to it.

[116]C. Hayavadana Rao (ed.), op. cit. p. 1962.

[117]*SII* IX, pt. II, no. 637.

[118]Nos. 329 and 1611 of the Haṁpi Museum collection.

[119]K.V. Raman, *Srī Varadarājaswāmi Temple—Kāñchi*, pp. 57, 76.

[120]*ARSIE* of 1919, nos. 478, 513 and 569.

[121]Ibid., nos. 474 and 533.

[122]Ibid., no. 641.

[123]Ibid., no. 370.

[124]Ibid., no. 544, 547 and 584.

[125]Ibid., no. 384.

[126]Ibid., nos. 511, 541, 543, 546 and 549.

[127]Ibid., no. 656.

[128]Ibid., nos. 482, 504, 526, 527, 528, 580, 591 and 592.

[129]T.A. Gopinatha Rao, op.cit., vol. 1, pt. I, p. 267.

[130]Ibid., pp. 268-269.

[131]S.V. Padigar, op.cit., p. 238.

[132]*EC* V, Hn 101 ; *MAR* of 1929, nos. 25 and 47.

[133]S. Krishnaswami Aiyangar, op.cit., vol. I, p. 292.

[134]K.R. Basavaraja, *History and Culture of Karnataka*, p. 524.

[135]. K.V. Raman, "Architecture under Vijayanagara," in *Proceedings of the Seminar on Temple Art and Architecture*, ed. K.K.A. Venkatachari, p. 94.

[136]C. Hayavadana Rao, op.cit., p. 1919 ff.

[137]*SII* IX, pt. II, no. 566.

[138]See J.S.M. Hooper, *Hymns of the Āḷvārs,* Plate opposite page 15. The only difference is that in this statue the saint is standing, while in the one from Viṭhalāpura he is seated.

[139]*VPR '83-84,* no. 67, p. 49.

[140]*SII* IX, pt. II, no. 607; *ARIE* of 1975-76, no. 98.

[141]*SII* IV, no. 280.

[142]*SII* XVI, no. 251 and *SII* IV, no. 279. For the plan and other details of this temple see the booklet *Le Temple de Tirumaṅkaiyāḷvār à Hampi,* by V. Filliozat.

[143]*SII* IX, pt. II, no. 657.

[144] *VPR '84-87,* no. 116.

[145]V. Filliozat, "Nouvelles Identifications de Monuments à Hampi," *Journal Asiatique,* 266, p. 131 and P. and V. Filliozat in *Hampi-Vijayanagara: The Temple of Viṭhala,* p. 24, identify this as the Rāma-Viṭhala temple. This identification is based on copper-plate grants of A.D. 1513 (*EC* III New Series, Naṅjanaguḍu,113 and 114, which is the same as *MAR* of 1944, nos. 23 and 24), of Āravīḍu Rāmarāja, the grandfather of Aḷiya Rāmarāya, in the possession of the Rāghavēndra-svāmi *maṭha* at Naṅjanaguḍu. These record grants made by this chief "in the presence of Rāma-Viṭhala when the *maṭha* was stationed at the southern entrance of Vijaya-Viṭhala" to guru Surēndra, disciple of Raghunandana. However, the authenticity of these copper-plate grants can be questioned, for paramount titles are attributed in them to this chief and they close with the royal signature "Śrī Virūpāksha". During the reign of Kṛishṇadēvarāya, it is unlikely that any subordinate chief would have claimed such titles that were applied to the king himself or used the official "sign-manual." Besides, Surēndra became the spiritual head of the *maṭha* only after the death of Raghunandana in A.D. 1533. Another reason for believing that these two records must be spurious is that the engraver of these two epigraphs of A.D. 1513, Maṅganāchārya, the son of Vīranna, is the same as that of a copper-plate grant of the Āravīḍu king Śrīraṅgarāya I (*MAR* of 1944, no. 22) of A.D. 1576.

Even if the records are genuine they do not necessarily refer to the great Viṭhala temple of Vijayanagara, for in no inscriptions in Hampi, nor in grants made in the presence of Viṭhala in the capital, is the deity referred to as Vijaya-Viṭhala; he is invariably called Viṭhalēśvara, Viṭhaladēva or Viṭhala. The deity enshrined in the Mādhva *maṭha* at Naṅjanagudu was Rāmachandra (see *MAR* of 1944, no. 22). Hence this might be the deity that is mentioned as Rāma-Viṭhala and not the deity of the temple in Viṭhalāpura in Vijayanagara.

Besides, the frequent representation in temple NH a/10 of the Sri-Vaishṇava *nāmam* and the many reliefs of *āḷvārs* and of Rāmānuja prove that this was Śrī-Vaishṇava temple and not a temple attached to a Mādhva *maṭha.*

[146]*VPR '83-84,* no. 21, pp. 35-36.

[147]*Top. List* I, Bellary dist. no. 347.

[148]S. Krishnaswami Aiyangar, op.cit,. vol. II, p. 72. It is also interesting to note that the Śrī Rāmānuja temple at Śrīperumbudūr, the birth place of this saint, has a Vijayanagara period *gōpura* with *Rāmāyaṇa* scenes carved on it.

[149]According to V. Filliozat, "Nouvelles Identifications de Monuments à Hampi," *Journal Asiatique,* 266, p. 131, this is the Brahmā-Viṭhala temple. She makes this identification on the grounds that a swan is carved on the *pīṭha* in the sanctum, an inscription (*SII* IX, pt. II, no. 668) makes a reference to "Brahma-dēvara-guḍi" and in some songs of Purandaradāsa reference is made to "Brahma-Viṭhala-mūruti." It is true that on the *pīṭha* there is relief of a bird; but it is a cross between a swan and a stylised peacock. Possibly, this is just a decorative motif, because the *āḷvārs* and Rāmānuja do not have *vāhanas* that are to be carved on the *pīṭha.* A careful study of the inscription mentioned reveals no reference to a temple of Brahmā; there is only a passing mention of a "Bomma-dēvaraguḍi". Since the exact reference to the poems of Purandaradāsa is not given they cannot be checked to note the context in which the saint makes mention of Brahmā-Viṭhala. Besides, temples to Brahmā are practically non-existent; it is therefore unlikely that a temple to this deity would have been built in Viṭhalāpura. Also there is not a single icon or relief of Brahmā in the temple.

[150]*EI* IV, p. 4, Kōnēṭirāja the son of Peda Koṇḍarāja, the paternal uncle of Aḷiya Rāmarāya, had four sons, Aubhaḷarāja, Koṇḍarāja, Timmarāja and Raṅgarāja.

[151]*SII* IX, pt. II, no. 653.

[152]*SII* IV, no. 275.

[153]*ARSIE* of 1915, no. 65.

[154]*TTDES* V, no. 125.

[155]Ibid., no. 154.

[156]*EI* IV, pp. 1-22.

[157]*SII* IV, no. 280.

[158]Ibid., no. 275.

[159]*SII* IX, pt. II, no. 653.

[160]V. Parthasarthy, "Evolution of Rituals in Viṣṇu Temple Utsavas" (Ph.D. diss.), p. 166.

[161]Ibid., p. 211.

[162]Ibid., p. 191.

[163]Ibid., p. 190.

[164]R. Champakalakshmi, op.cit, p. 236.

[165]*SII* IV, no. 280.

[166]*SII* IX, pt. III, no. 607.

[167]K.V. Raman, *Srī Varadarājaswāmi Temple—Kāñchi,* p. 87.

[168]K. Devanthachariar, "Śrī-Vaiṣṇavism and its Caste Marks," *QJMS,* V, p. 133.

[169]K.V. Raman, loc. cit.

[170]For example, the great Tiruveṅgaḷanātha temple complex, the Anantapadmanābha temple in Anantaśayanagudi, the Paṭṭābhirāma temple complex, the hundred-pillared hall in the Viṭhala complex and the Hastagiri-Raṅganātha-svāmi temple. But in all these, the Teṅgalai sectarian mark is more common.

[171]A. Appadurai, *Worship and Conflict under Colonial Rule: A South Indian Case,* p. 154.

[172]*SII* IX, pt. II, no. 668.

[173]Ibid., no. 653.

[174]Ibid., no. 678.

[175]*SII* IV, no. 250.

CHAPTER 7

Minor Cults and Popular Religion

In the preceding chapters the important Hindu cults in the city, both Śaivite and Vaishṇavite, have been surveyed. In this chapter a number of cults of minor deities and popular religious practices are studied, almost entirely from the monumental data since there are few epigraphical or literary references to them. These include the worship of Harihara, the twenty-four forms of Vishṇu and the *Daśāvatāras*, the goddess cults of both the Sanskṛitic goddesses and the village deities, the intense popularity of Hanumān, the worship of snakes and the installation of snake stones, and the great veneration of *satīs* and heroes.

In Hinduism there is the "great" or "higher" tradition of Śiva, Vishṇu, and Śaktī and the "little" or "lesser" traditions of the popular religion of the village, local or regional deities. The first can also be classified as the Sanskṛitic, brāhmaṇical or canonical religion and the second as the non-Sanskṛitic, non-brāhmaṇical, non-scriptural, folk religion. While some of the cults and practices discussed in this chapter belong to the "great" tradition, others belong to the "little" tradition. In some cases there is an overlapping of the two, such as in the cult of Hanumān or Āñjanēya who, being an associate of the pan-Indian deity Rāmachandra, is a minor deity of supra-regional importance, yet the immense following he enjoyed in the city was characterised by the fervour and exuberance typical of folk culture.

1. Harihara

Harihara or Śaṅkaranārāyaṇa, is a syncretic deity, half Śiva and half Vishṇu. Undoubtedly, the worship of this composite god arose out of the strong desire for a rapprochement between the partisans of the two major and antagonistic sects of Śaivism and Vaishṇavism, by emphasising that Śiva is Vishṇu and Vishṇu is, conversely, Śiva and that they are together essential for the creation, protection and destruction of the Universe.[1] Thus, in the figure of Harihara the right half, from head to toe, is endowed with the aspects and ornaments of Śiva and the left half with those of Vishṇu.

This composite form of the two gods was already known as early as the *Mahābhārata*.[2] It is mentioned in the *Matsya Purāṇa*[3] and also in the *Vāmana* and *Skanda Purāṇas*.[4] In Karṇāṭaka the antiquity of Harihara icons goes back to the Kadaṁba period. Such images are found in great numbers from the early Chālukya period onwards.[5] The cult of Harihara came into vogue in this state after the twelfth century A.D. and various temples of the god were erected.[6]

The great centre of the deity in Karṇāṭaka was the Hariharēśvara temple at Harihara (in Chitradurga district), on the bank of the Tuṅgabhadrā. That this was already an important religious centre of this cult by the mid-twelfth century A.D. is revealed by inscriptions.[7] It continued to be highly popular during the Vijayanagara period.[8]

Harihara was a popular deity during Vijayanagara times. Two kings and a few princes of the first dynasty were named after this god. The popularity of Harihara worship during the period was due to the attempt made by the rulers to defuse the animosity between the votaries of Śiva and Vishṇu.

Naturally, one would expect to find temples and sculptures of this god in Vijayanagara. According to K. Sarojini Devi there is an epigraphical reference (*EC* XI, Dg. 68) to god Hariharēśvara at Haṁpi.[9] This inscription found at Harihara is dated A.D. 1382. It records that in the presence of god Virūpāksha of Paṁpā-kshētra, and in the presence of god Harihar-ēśvara, being ordered by god Hariharēśvara, Harihara II made a grant of a village to Liṅgarasa for the continual recitation of the *Vēdas* and *Śāstras* in the temple of Hariharēśvara. Since only Virūpāksha is mentioned as being in Paṁpā-kshētra and also because this epigraph was found at Harihara and it occurs along with a number of others that refer directly or indirectly to that famous temple,[10] it is more likely that this inscription refers to Hariharēśvara of the temple at Harihara and not to the deity of any temple in Vijayanagara. Obviously, this record was issued in the presence both of the principal deity of the capital and of the deity for whose temple the grant was made. There is another inscription[11] that mentions a grant made on the "bank of the Tuṅgabhadrā, in the presence of Hariharanātha." Although, Virūpāksha, Viṭhala and other deities of Vijayanagara are referred to by the formula "on the bank of the Tuṅgabhadrā" it is my suggestion that this epigraph too refers to the deity of the Harihara temple in the Chitradurga district, who is also referred to in an inscription from that temple as Harihara on the "bank of the Tuṅgabhadrā".[12] Thus, to the best of my knowledge, there is no published inscription referring to a Harihara temple in the capital.

However, archaeological evidence reveals the existence of one Harihara temple (NL c/3) on the eastern slope of the Hēmakūṭa hill. This small, east-facing temple consists only of a sanctum and a pillared hall. Iconographic evidence clearly indicates the affiliation. There is a Śaiva *dvārapāla* on the south side of the door to the sanctum and a Vaishṇava one on the north side. On the wall beside the Vaishṇava gatekeeper is a relief of Sūrya (who is often present in Harihara temples since he is acceptable to both the Śaivas and Vaishṇavas) and beside the Śaiva doorkeeper is a relief of a standing, two-armed *dēvī,* who is holding a lotus in her right hand. On the north wall of the hall is carved Garuḍa and a serpent, while on the south wall are reliefs of Nandi and Hanumān (the attendants of Śiva and Vishṇu). The reliefs of the pillars represent both Śaiva and Vaishṇava themes. Of special interest are the two centre pillars of the front row. The south side pillar has reliefs of the various forms of Śiva (Bhikshātaṇa-mūrti, Kālārmūrti, etc.) On the north side pillar are represented the *avatāras* of Vishṇu.[13]

At present a *liṅga* is enshrined in the sanctum. Whether or not this is the original cult object is not known. Since Harihara is worshipped both in the iconic and aniconic forms,[14] it could be the original *mūrti.* Worship seems to be carried on in the temple even today, hence it is heavily whitewashed. There are many lines of inscription in the Nāgarī script on the two side walls of the hall. These have not been published and unfortunately, due to the heavy coating of lime plaster over the writing, it is not possible to read this epigraph. There are also some devotee figures carved on the walls. Though it is difficult to date this temple accurately, on stylistic grounds it may be assigned to a fairly early phase of Vijayanagara temple building, perhaps it is of the fifteenth century. We have no evidence of any other temple dedicated to Harihara at the site.

There is one rock carving (NQ u/4) of this syncretic deity. On this rock, besides the reliefs of the Rāma-Sītā-Lakshmaṇa group, there is also one of Harihara. He is standing in *samabhaṅga*; in his two left hands he holds the *chakra* and *śaṅkha,* the upper right hand holds the *triśūla* while the lower right one is in the *abhaya-mudrā.* He is encased in a shrine having a triangular canopy.[15] Reliefs of this divinity are almost non-existent in temples or on temple pillars in the city. To the best of my knowledge, there is only one such relief of Harihara (Plate 40). It is found on a pillar in the pillared hall in the outer *prākāra* of the Tiruveṅgaḷanātha temple (NM h/1).

From the data available it appears that Harihara did not have much of a following in the capital. This is surprising when one considers that two emperors bore the name of this deity, that this god was quite popular in the empire and that it was a deliberate policy of the Vijayanagara state to reconcile conflicting sects.

2. Chaturviṁśatimūrtis and Daśāvatāras of Vishṇu

The concept of the twenty-four forms and the *avatāras* is important in the Pāñcharātra system, which conceives of the supreme god Vishṇu in a five-fold aspect—*Para, Vyūha, Vibhava, Antaryāmin* and *Archā.* It appears that the name Pāñcharātra is derived from its central dogma of the five-fold manifestation of the deity.[16] *Para* is the transcendent aspect of god, *Vyūha* means the emanatory forms of the divinity, by *Vibhava* is meant the incarnations or *avatāras,* the *Antaryāmin* is the inner controller who resides in the hearts of all and *Archā* is the image that is worshipped. Since the *Pāñcharātrāgama* is accepted by the Śrī-Vaishṇavas and Mādhvas, both believe in the five-fold manifestations of Vishṇu.

There are four primary *Vyūhas*—Vāsudēva, Saṅkarshaṇa Pradyumna and Aniruddha. Besides these principal four, the Pāñcharātra believed in twenty more secondary *Vyūhas.* The resultant twenty-four form the *Chaturviṁśatimūrtis.* In the Deccan before the eighth century A.D. the concept of the twenty-four forms was either unknown or it had just commenced to be incorporated in the Vaishṇava beliefs.[17] From the tenth to the fourteenth centuries A.D the worship of the *Chaturviṁśatimūrtis* gained popularity in the Upper and Lower Deccan. From the tenth century onwards the best known form of Vishṇu installed in temples was that of Kēśava, the first of the twenty-four.[18] The *Chaturviṁśatimūrtis* are met with more frequently in the Hoysaḷa kingdom than elsewhere. The maximum number of temple dedications were to Kēśava, followed by the worship of Nārāyaṇa, Vāsudēva, Janārdana and Mādhava in that order.[19]

All the twenty-four images are alike. They are all standing figures, with no bends in the body, possessing four arms and adorned with the *kirīṭa* crown and other ornaments. The difference is only in the way in which the *śaṅkha, chakra, gadā* and *padma* are found distributed among the four hands.[20] The number of permutations possible of the four attributes in the four hands is twenty-four. For example, Kēśava holds the *śaṅkha* and *chakra* in the upper right and left hands and the *padma* and *gadā* in the lower right and left respectively.

We have proof of only one temple in Vijayanagara dedicated to one of these twenty-four forms of Vishṇu. This is the Mādhava temple in the "royal centre" (NR t/2), locally known as the Raṅga temple. The original temple building belongs to the "intermediate" phase of the temple architecture in the city, but there are sixteenth century additions within the courtyard. A Telugu inscription, dated A.D. 1545, records the construction of a *raṅga-maṇḍapa* in the temple of god Mādhava by *Mahāmaṇḍalēśvara* Timmarāju.[21] There may have been other shrines or temples of which we have no evidence.

In the city, the whole group of the *Chaturviṁśatimūrtis* is found sculpted twice. The first is in the rock shelter NG n/6 near the river, where there is a long panel of the twenty-four forms, each standing in *samabhaṅga.* There is an inscriptional label in Kannaḍa above each figure and an incised figure of Garuḍa below.[22] The second series occurs on the four highly polished black stone pillars of the *raṅga-maṇḍapa* of the Rāmachandra temple (NR w/1). Here each of the twenty-four figures appears seated in *lalitāsana* under an elaborate arch and is flanked by two consorts. These are iconographically most unusual because the figures of the god are seated and the goddesses are also depicted (Plate 42).

To the best of my knowledge, there are no statues available at the site of the individual *Chaturviṁśatīmūrtis.* Reliefs of the *Chaturviṁśatimūrtis* in temples are also extremely rare. In the Vaishṇava temple NG t/1 there is one pillar relief of Kēśava. In the *maṇḍapa* of the Mudal-āḻvār temple (NC w/2) there is a pillar relief of Janārdana and another possibly of Mādhava. On the *bṛindāvana* of Raghunandana-svāmi (NG n/1) there is another relief of Mādhava.[23]

On the whole, we can conclude that the worship of the *Chaturviṁśatimūrtis* was not very important in Vijayanagara. Considering the great popularity of the twenty-four forms of Vishṇu in Karṇāṭaka in the preceding period this is indeed amazing.

The concept of Vishṇu's *avatāras* (descents or incarnations) is an ancient one. The first explicit mention is in the *Bhagavad Gītā.*[24] The *Rāmāyaṇa* and *Mahābhārata* more or less directly refer to them. The *Purāṇas* such as the *Vishṇu, Matsya, Vāyu* and *Bhāgavata Purāṇas* mention the *avatāras,* but the exact number given of the incarnations varies in these different sources.[25]

Ten *avatāras* are generally recognised as the principal ones. These are Matsya (fish), Kūrma (tortoise), Varāha (boar), Narasiṁha (man-lion), Vāmana (the dwarf) who is also Trivikrama, Paraśurāma, Rāma, Kṛishṇa, Buddha and the future *avatāra* Kalki.[26] Some however do not consider Buddha to be an incarnation of Vishṇu. According to V. Filliozat, the Śrī-Vaishṇavas regard Balarāma, the elder brother of Kṛishṇa, as the eighth and Kṛishṇa and Kalki as the ninth and tenth *avatāras.* The Mādhvas exclude

Balarāma from the list of the ten and include Buddha.[27] The special significance of Balarāma for the Śrī-Vaishṇavas stems from the fact that he is considered to be an incarnation of Śēsha or Ananta, the cosmic serpent, and so also is Rāmānuja, the great preceptor of their sect. Besides the *Daśāvatāras*, there are also a large number of minor incarnations.

Among the ten *avatāras* Narasiṁha, Rāma and Kṛishṇa were especially significant during the Vijayanagara period and were important cult deities, as already seen in earlier chapters. The others enjoyed little importance on their own, but were represented in the *Daśāvatāra* groups of sculptures. There are two rock carvings of the *Daśāvatāras*. In the rock shelter NS a/1 within the "urban core" although there are carvings of other Vaishṇava figures the most important is the *Daśāvatāra* panel, depicting Matsya, Kūrma, Varāha, Narasiṁha, Vāmana, Paraśurāma, Rāma, Balarāma, Jina (instead of Buddha) and Kalki.[28] The second is in the rock shelter in the "sacred centre" NG n/6 in which the *avatāra* group is represented along with the *Chaturviṁśatimūrtis* and other Vaishṇava themes. Here there are eleven incarnations, for besides the ten of the former group of incarnations Kṛishṇa is also shown.[29]

In a number of temples in Vijayanagara there are reliefs of the *Daśāvatāra* group. Examples of these are: on the two engaged pillars at the entrance to the first antechamber of the Rāmachandra temple, a pillar in the Harihara temple (NL c/3), the south-east pillar in the *raṅga-maṇḍapa* of the Kṛishṇa temple (NL m/4), on a pillar in the detached pillared hall in the Paṭṭābhirāma temple, in the Viṭhala complex (NH a/1) on a pillar to the north of the west-side steps in the south-east corner pavilion and along the architrave of the nave and the plinth of the *uyyāle-maṇḍapa*. In most of these Balarāma is represented while Buddha is absent, except in the last example where Jina (not Buddha) in the *kāyotsarga* pose appears. In Vijayanagara Jina seems to be included among the *Daśāvatāras* in place of Buddha.[30]

Besides the *Daśāvatāra* groups, individual *avatāras* are also found on temple pillars. The most common (excluding Kṛishṇa, Rāma and Narasiṁha) are Matsya and Kūrma. These are represented both in the zoomorphic form and also in the their anthropomorphic form. Icons of the less important of these ten *avatāras* are extremely rare. An unusual one is the therianthropomorphic Varāha *mūrti*, about one metre in height, in the collection of the Haṁpi Museum.[31]

Although there are a number of representations of the *avatāras*, as in the case of the *Chaturviṁśatimūrtis*, the *Daśāvatāras* as a group did not enjoy extensive popularity in the city (Fig. 6).

3. Goddesses

The worship of a variety of female divinities was an important element in the religious life of the city. In the goddess or *śaktī* cult we notice two distinct features, the brāhmaṇic (Sanskṛitic) and the non-brāhmaṇic (non-Sanskṛitic). The worship of the goddess probably has deep roots in prehistoric Indian religion, pre-dating the introduction of Āryan forms of worship. In the context of the Āryan religion this ancient mother-goddess element is preserved in the principle of *śaktī*, the active and generative element of the godhead. However, the female deity has been most perfectly preserved in folk religion; village deities worshipped in south India have been mainly goddesses—the *grāma-dēvatās*—to whom animals and, in earlier times, even humans were sacrificed.[32]

The word *śaktī* (which means energy, force or power) is used both to express the energy of the chief gods as manifested in their wives as well as the south Indian female village deities. A third way in which it is used is in reference to *Śāktism*, the object of worship in which is the female principle.[33] According to *Śāktism* God is the Supreme Mother. In her supreme form *śaktī* is identified as Mahādēvī, consort of Śiva, with whose worship *Śāktism* became inextricably bound; yet she herself was conceived as the creator of Śiva and superior to him, just as her lesser emanations, the *śaktīs* of Brahmā and Vishṇu and the rest of gods, were superior to their own male counterparts.[34]

In the city, among the manifestations of *śaktī* of the "greater" traditions, the most popular were Durgā or Mahiśāsurmardinī (the goddess killing the buffalo demon), Kāḷī, Bhadrakāḷī,[35] and Bhairavī.[36] The prominence given to Kāḷī and Bhairavī might be due to the influence of the Kāḷāmukhas who worshipped Bhairava and Kāḷī.[37] Later, when this sect was absorbed by Vīraśaivism, these influences passed into the Vīraśaiva fold.

Independent temples and shrines dedicated to goddesses are few. A very early one is the Durgā-dēvī temple (NF w/25) to the north of the Virūpāksha temple complex. It is in the Rāshṭrakūṭa style of the ninth to tenth centuries A.D. A pre-Vijayanagara inscription of A.D. 1199 in this temple indicates its importance.[38] This small temple consists of only a *cella,* an antechamber and an open *maṇḍapa.*[39] The second is a small shrine of the Vijayanagara period dedicated to Bhadrakāḷī. It is part of a two-temple complex (NM y/3); the other temple is dedicated to Vīrabhadra. The six-armed Bhadrakāḷī icon in the sanctum holds the four usual attributes and also the *ḍamaru* and *triśūla* (trident).

A number of rock carvings reveals the presence of Śāktas in the city.[40] Near the river (near NG m/1) is a fine carving of Mahiśāsuramardinī and another of the two-armed Dēvī, standing in *tribhaṅga,* holding a lotus in one hand; she is flanked by Gaṇēśa and Kārtikēya (this is probably Pārvatī, or Paṁpā-dēvī). In rock shelter NG n/5 there are two reliefs of this same goddess. The same goddess appears again in another panel (NL h/5) near the Kṛishṇa temple complex. In this panel the *liṅga,* Nandi and Vīrabhadra also appear. Not far from the above is a relief of a goddess who is locally identified as Sarasvatī. This goddess is carved on a boulder against which a small shelter has been built (NL s/2). The relief is painted, hence it is difficult to study the details. Probably, this two-armed, seated goddess holds a ladle and a ball of rice. If so, she is Annapūrṇā. To the south of the Tiruveṅgaḷanātha complex is a fine sculpture (NM h/2) of a ten-armed, striding Kāḷī, who is worshipped even today. She is popularly known as Atikayamma or Hathu-Kayi-Amma, the goddess with ten hands. Not far from this is a relief on a south-facing boulder (NM m/2) of two seated goddesses. While one holds the *triśūla, ḍamaru, khaḍga* and *khēṭaka,* the other has the *triśūla, ḍamaru, khaḍga* and *kapāla.* Near the Hiriya Kāluve (Turutta canal) is a rock carving of Mahiśāsuramardinī (NM r/1). Close by is a crudely executed relief of a *dēvī* with a rearing *nāga* hood over her head (NM r/4). The attributes in her four hands are indistinguishable. In a dilapidated *maṇḍapa* (NM s/2) are reliefs on a rock of Bhadrakāḷī and Pārvatī.

The most interesting group of goddess sculptures is on a hillock on the north ridge, south of Mataṅga hill (NM x/2). Here, on one boulder are carved Brahmā and his *śaktī.* Behind, on the same boulder is panel of three forms of *Dēvī*—Bhairavī, Kāḷī (in the centre) and Bhadrakāḷī. Below Kāḷī are seen two human heads and a pot. On another boulder is Mahiśāsuramardinī, flanked by Lakshmī, Bhairavī, Bhairava and Gaṇēśa (Plate 43). On a third rock is a sculpture of Kārtikēya and a panel of five figures—a standing ascetic, a seated ascetic, Matsyēndranātha on a fish, Śiva and Vishṇu.[41] To the west of temple NM y/3 on a vertical boulder is a figure of a goddess. She is depicted standing in *samabhaṅga* holding lotuses in her upper hands and her lower hands in the *vyākhyāna* and *varada mudrās.* There is also a rock sculpture of a seated Bhairavī (NS y/2) in the "urban core". A small shrine has been constructed against this rock and the goddess is worshipped even today.

Among other goddess sculptures is a stone slab with a relief of Bhairavī found in the gate that is locally known as "Bhīma's Gate" (in NX o). A sculpture of Chamuṇḍēśvarī and another of Mahiśāsuramardinī are found in and outside the north *gōpura* of the Virūpāksha temple. Another sculpture of Mahiśāsuramardinī has been placed in the antechamber of a shrine in NF v/1. There are also a few sculptures of goddesses in the Archaeological Museum.[42]

Reliefs of goddesses appear also in the temples and other monuments. The finest reliefs of Mahiśāsuramardinī are perhaps the one on a pillar in the east gateway of the Rāmachandra temple and the one in temple NG m/2. Another relief of the same goddess is found on a *gōpura* (NF w/8) on Hēmakūṭa hill. An exquisite relief of Pārvati (or Paṁpā- dēvī) is found in temple NG m/1 (Fig. 7).[43]

Besides Sanskṛitic goddesses, village deities were also worshipped. The fertility cult and the predominant role of women in an agricultural economy were perhaps responsible for most of these deities being female.[44] Unlike the "greater" gods, the village deities, as a rule, are not served by brāhmaṇa priests; they are worshipped by people living within certain geographical limits or belonging to a particular caste. Their power is often restricted to a locality or to a certain caste function; usually they have small shrines, are sometimes represented only by stones and they usually receive animal sacrifices.[45] In general, these local deities are worshipped by women and persons belonging to the lower castes.[46]

The original local goddess of the Haṁpi area, as seen in Chapter 2, was Paṁpā, who was "Sanskṛitized" by marriage to Virūpāksha, a form of Śiva. In the "royal centre" is the temple of Yellammā (NR y/4), locally known as Paṭṭanada Yellammā (Yellammā of the city). In pre-Vijayanagara times she was probably the local goddess of the area in which the royal citadel was later constructed.[47] The temple faces south and in front of the sanctum is a long *maṇḍapa* with typical Vijayanagara pillars. The goddess is a four-armed seated *Dēvī*, about one metre high, having the *ḍamaru* and *khaḍga* in the right hands and *triśūla* and *kapāla* in the left hands and wearing a skull garland. The sculpturing of the stone idol is in the archaic manner and the temple is now below ground level.[48] Worship continues in this temple even today.[49] Yellammā in Karṇāṭaka is identified with Renukā, the mother of Paraśurāma.[50] Paes has referred to a temple near the king's palace where many sheep were killed every day.[51] Possibly, this is the temple of Paṭṭanada Yellammā, since the village deities are almost universally worshipped with animal sacrifices.[52] In the Ānegoṅdi area there is another Yellammā temple of Vijayanagara times, with a large boulder considered to be the aniconic representation of this folk goddess.[53]

It is likely that another folk-goddess, associated with fertility, who has been identified by different names, such as Aditi-Uttānapad,[54] Lajjā-Gaurī, Nagna Kabandha, etc., was also worshipped in the city. The available specimens of the Lajjā-Gaurī figures show a distribution over north India and the Deccan, the greater concentration being in the Deccan, and they were widely prevalent from the first to the eighth centuries A.D.[55] In the earliest types of the nude goddess only the generative part of the body is depicted, except the head which is replaced by a full-blown lotus. This goddess is in the squatting pose with legs and thighs widely flexed, as if in the act of being delivered of a child; the arms are bent at the elbows and raised upwards, with the palms facing forward.

Such figures of the nude squatting goddess continued to be made until fairly recent times.[56] This goddess is specially prayed to for progeny; butter and vermilion are applied on the vagina and breasts of the Lajjā-Gaurī image.[57] She was also the goddess of vegetative fertility and hence of special significance in the Deccan which is prone to droughts and famine.[58]

While no statues or temples of this nude squatting goddess have been found in the city, she is seen on temple pillars and on the east *gōpura* of the Viṭhala temple where there is a stucco figure of Lajjā-Gaurī. This indicates the probability of her worship in the city. The Lajjā-Gaurī type in Vijayanagara differs from the earlier examples in that here the goddess is always shown with a head. The earliest example of a Lajjā-Gaurī relief is found on the plinth of the east gateway of the Rāmachandra temple. Here the goddess has the arms and legs in the typical pose (Plate 44). Elsewhere, though the lower part of the body is always in the characteristic pose, there are variations in the portrayal of the arms. For examples, in the *mahā-maṇḍapa* of the Tiruveṅgaḷanātha temple (NM h/1) Lajjā-Gaurī appears twice on the pillars, holding a pot (the full pot is another symbol of fertility) in one hand and the other pointing to her vagina. On a relief in the pillared hall of the same temple both the arms of the goddess rest against her knees.[59] A few reliefs of Lajjā-Gaurī are found in the pillared gallery of this temple and she is also seen elsewhere in the city, such as in the pillared halls (for music and dance) that form part of the Viṭhala, Paṭṭābhirāma and Virūpāksha temple complexes.

4. Hanumān

Hanumān or Āñjanēya is the most ubiquitous of all the minor deities in Vijayanagara. Since this site is believed to be his birthplace and the scene of many of his exploits it is but natural that he should be extremely popular. Innumerable shrines, reliefs, and sculptures of Hanumān dot the city.

The Hanumān cult, however, was practically non-existent in the city before the establishment of the empire. There are no pre-Vijayanagara shrines dedicated to this deity nor inscriptions referring to him. Even sculptural representations of the pre-Vijayanagara period are very few. This is not surprising because the popularity of Hanumān is a post-thirteenth century phenomenon in Karṇāṭaka.[60] A few reliefs of the pre- or early Vijayanagara period of Āñjanēya are noted. The first is on the double-storeyed gateway (NF w/3) on the northern slope of the Hēmakūṭa hill, where on a pillar-relief Hanumān appears. The others are on the *maṇḍapa* walls, near the doorways, of the two early Narasiṁha temples, one in the "sacred centre" (NG t/4) and the other in Ānegoṅdi (NE m/1), that have been described in Chapter 3.

During the Vijayanagara period Hanumān rose to great heights of popularity. The following he enjoyed came from all sections of society. There are a few epigraphical references to the patronage of this cult by persons linked with the court. But the vast majority of donors of shrines and sculptures are anonymous. This and the fact that most of the shrines are small and architecturally insignificant indicate that the greater support came from the populace rather than from the court. This was a popular cult that had an extensive support not only during the Vijayanagara period but even in the subsequent ages down to modern times, for Āñjanēya is still a favourite god in Haṁpi and its environs. In modern times almost every village in the Deccan has a temple of Hanumān with non-brāhmaṇic ministrants.[61] In most of the small Āñjanēya shrines in the site where worship is carried on, the service is also conducted by non-brāhmaṇas. An important exception is the Yantrōddhāraka Āñjanēya temple (NG w/3) where the rituals are performed by brāhmaṇas of the Mādhva sect. The present practice of both the brāhmaṇical and non-brāhmaṇical ministrations to Hanumān was possibly the case in Vijayanagara times also.

Hanumān is worshipped by votaries of Vishṇu, Śiva and Śaktī.[62] This is due to the stories connected with his origins and exploits. In the Vālmīki *Rāmāyaṇa* he is only considered as the *aṁśa* (partial incarnation) of Vāyu, the wind god. But in the Tamil *Kamban Rāmāyaṇa* he is considered the *aṁśa* of both Vāyu and Rudra or Śiva.[63] His association with both these deities is widely accepted in Indian mythology, for it is believed that he was fathered by the gods to assist Vishṇu in his incarnation as Rāma.[64]

The Mādhvas in particular have a great reverence for Hanumān. According to them there are three incarnations of Vāyu—Hanumān of the *Rāmāyaṇa*, Bhīma of the *Mahābhārata* and their own great preceptor, Madhvāchārya.[65] The Mādhva sage Vyāsarāya greatly popularised Hanumān worship at the Vijayanagara capital. In Sōmnātha's life of the saint, *Śrī Vyāsayōgicharitam*, it is claimed that Vyāsarāya installed 732 Hanumān idols, including the Yantrōddhāraka Hanumān.[66]

The presence of many shrines of Hanumān in the city in the sixteenth century is revealed by Nuniz who refers to "pagodas in which are (images of?) monkeys..."[67] There are still extant a large number of shrines in the city proper, that is in the "sacred centre" and "urban core", with Hanumān *mūrtis*.[68] These comprise only a *cella* or a *cella* and verandah or a *cella*, antechamber and a small *maṇḍapa*. Many of these were originally Āñjanēya shrines.[69] In many worship is still carried on regularly or sporadically.[70] Originally some of these shrines were definitely not Āñjanēya shrines; the *mūrtis* have been brought and placed there later.[71] Some of the original shrines have Vaishṇava *dvārapālas* (e.g., NR q/2 and NT d/6). It is, therefore, possible that some of the empty Vaishṇava temples in the city were originally Āñjanēya shrines. An undated inscription in a *maṇḍapa* in the gallery of the Tiruveṅgaḷanātha temple (NM h/1) records the offerings of rice on Saturday to god Hanumān of the car street of Tiruveṅgaḷanātha.[72] This shrine cannot be located.

Besides these shrines in the "sacred centre" and the "urban core", there were many Hanumān temples also in "Metropolitan Vijayanagara". On the Āñjanadri hill, the reputed birthplace of Āñjanēya near Ānegoṅdi, is a temple enshrining this deity. There is an empire-period inscription, possibly of a Vijayanagara minister, referring to it.[73] In Ānegoṅdi village from north to south there are about seven or eight stone temples of Hanumanta now in ruins.[74] At Kaḷasāpura on the Kāmalāpuram-Kaṁpili road is the Madhuvana temple, a modern structure, which is probably built on the site of a Vijayanagara period temple. In it is a large *mūrti* of Hanumān, probably of the Vijayanagara period. An inscription near this temple,[75] dated A.D. 1434, records a gift of Dēvarāya II to god Hanumantadēva. At Jaṁbunātha hill, on the way up to the Śiva temple, is a *maṇḍapa* or gateway in which is installed an image of this deity. An inscription of Sadāśiva granting this god four *paḍis* of rice a day out of the provision made for god Anantaśayana is recorded both here[76] and in the Anantaśayanaguḍi temple.[77]

There are numerous reliefs of the god carved on boulders and rock surfaces all over the city.[78] There are also a very large number of stone slabs with reliefs of Āñjanēya. These vary in height from about one metre or less to three-and-a-half metres. Many of these are no longer in their original places.[79]

Thus, Hanumān shrines and sculptures are found all over the city. He is present in the most unexpected and even remote places. The protection of Hanumān is invoked by placing him at especially vulnerable spots such as gateways or crossroads. In an inscription found in front of a gateway in the fortification wall, in which the treasurer of Kōnēṭi Koṇḍarājayya, the agent of affairs of (Aḷiya) Rāmarāja, makes a grant to a shrine of this god, the deity is even referred to as Bāgila (i.e., of the gate) Hanumantarāya.[80]

Most of the reliefs shows the deity in the heroic striding pose, his tail rising over his head, face in profile, his right hand lifted up and the left, which is placed near the hip, often holding a long-stemmed flower or a branch. Often a demon is shown between the wide-spread legs of Hanumān (Plate 41). Besides these carvings of the "Vīra-Āñjanēya" in a few sculptures the deity has his hands joined in *añjali* in the pose of a *bhakta*.

There are two rare reliefs of the deity which are of special sanctity for the Mādhvas. In the Yantrōddhāraka Āñjanēya temple (NG w/3), Hanumān is carved on a rock, in the meditation pose, with a rosary in his hand and seated in *padmāsana*. He is in the centre of two intersecting equilateral triangles inscribed within a circle, the circumference of which is covered by a string of twelve jumping monkeys[81] (Plate 46). The second is on a rock facing the *bṛīndāvana* of Raghunandana-svāmi (in NG n/1). This is an unusual image of Chaturbhuja Hanumān (i.e., with four arms). The two upper hands hold the *chakra* and *śaṅkha*, the two lower ones hold a book (palm leaf manuscript), the symbol of Madhvāchārya, and the *gadā*, the symbol of Bhīma[82] (Plate 45). Thus, it is a composite image representing all the three incarnations of Vāyu.

Another interesting sculpture is located on Hēmakūṭa hill (near temple NL b/14). In the centre of the panel is Hanumān in the typical heroic pose. He is flanked by Rāma, Lakshmaṇa and Sītā on his left and a male and two female devotees on his right.

Besides these large sculptures, Hanumān very often appears on the temple reliefs throughout the site. After the Vīra-Āñjanēya and Bhakta-Āñjanēya carvings, the favourite themes of the temple sculptors are of Hanumān flying through the air carrying rocks in either hand, or bringing the Sañjīvini mountain, or of him before Rāma, or giving Rāma's signet ring to Sītā, or seated on his tail before Rāvaṇa.

5. Nāgas

Throughout India, but particularly in the Deccan, southern India, and on the west coast, there is an extraordinary veneration of the *Nāga*. In southern India carved stone images of the *Nāga* are set up to this day at the entrance of a town or village and ceremonial offering are made to the living cobra. The existing monuments at Vijayanagara supply abundant evidence of extensive *Nāga* worship.[83]

The nature of offerings made to the cobra vary in certain districts and among different castes. The usual form of serpent worship is the vow taken by childless women, to install a snake stone (*Nāgapratishṭai*) if they are blessed with offspring. The ceremony consists in having a figure of a cobra carved on a stone slab, placing it in water for a period of time, "giving it life" (*Prāṇapratishṭai*) by reciting *mantras* and performing other ceremonies over it and then setting it up under a pipal (Ficus Religiosa) or a margosa i.e., a nīm (Melia Azadirachta) tree. Preferably the snake stone (*nāga-kal*) is placed under the shade of a pipal tree that has been "married" to a margosa tree. In "marrying" the trees, two young trees are planted close to each other and tied with ropes so that they will grow interlaced together.[84] The pipal represents a female and the margosa a male.[85] The connection of the *Nāgas* with the pipal and margosa trees is evidently a relic of the ancient tree and serpent worship.[86]

The fifth day of the bright half of the month of *Śrāvaṇa* (July-August) is celebrated as *Nāgapañchamī.*[87] On that day women fast and pour milk over the snake stones or over anthills in which the cobra is believed to reside, or make other types of food offerings. The *Nāga* cult is a part of popular religion. The worship of the snake stones is not conducted by brāhmaṇa ritualists; in general, the worship is confined to women.[88]

In Vijayanagara city *Nāga* worship was definitely popular during the period of our study. Since it was essentially a popular cult there are no epigraphical references to it, but innumerable *nāga-kals* (snake stones) point to its great popularity. In Vijayanagara times, as in the modern period, the installation of snake stones was linked with the desire for progeny. This is indicated by a very interesting snake stone now in the Haṁpi Museum.[89] On this slab is carved a three-hooded snake and a single-hooded snake. To the right of the former is carved a small cradle! The practice of installing such stones has continued down to modern times at the site, in and near temples where worship continues, such as the great Virūpāksha temple (NF w/1), the Kōdaṇḍarāma temple (NG w/1) and the Yantrōddāraka Āñjanēya shrine (NG w/3).[90]

It is most likely that in the city the snake stones were set up under trees, for *nāga-kals* found near temples where worship continues are usually under trees. For example, in front of the Kōdaṇḍarāma and Yantrōddāraka Hanumān (Plate 47) temples they are under pipal trees, while near the Paṭṭanada Yellammā temple (NR y/4) they are under a margosa tree.

The *nāga-kals* show a considerable variety of patterns.[91] All these patterns are to be found at the site. The simplest and commonest type exhibits a single cobra standing on the tip of its tail and curling upwards with expanded hood. In the simplest type of these the cobra has only one hood.[92] Often, presumably to emphasize its divine character, the serpent is polycephalous, with three,[93] five,[94] or seven[95] hoods (the number of heads is always an uneven number). A more elaborate type of *nāga-kal* shows a pair of intertwined cobras, usually both the snakes are monocephalous.[96] In another and still more elaborate type of snake stone, the serpent deity appears as a hybrid being, its upper half being human and the lower half serpentine. The hybrid is female and in all probability represents the serpent goddess Mudama. Over her head she wears the usual hood of three, five or seven heads. She has both hands joined in the *añjali-mudrā* and in the crook of each elbow she has a baby snake.[97]

The large number of snake stones found throughout the site[98] and in the Haṁpi Museum attest to the immense popularity of serpent worship. They are found even in inaccessible and remote spots. They vary in size from a few centimetres to almost two metres in height. On some, the carving is very rough, while others are beautifully sculpted. Although some of the snake stones, especially those found near living temples, are post-1565, the vast majority belong to the period under survey.

6. Satīs and Heroes

Great veneration was accorded to those who had died in a heroic manner and memorial stones were erected in their honour, such as the *satī-kal* or *māsti-kal* (i.e., *mahā-satī-kal*), the *satī-vīra-kal* (a composite tablet, in which the wife or wives took to *satī* after the heroic death of the husband) and the *vīra-kal* or hero stone. A hero may or may not become a god, but a *māsti* is invariably considered as a goddess.[99] Whether the dead hero is deified or not, the hero stone, too, is perceived as the abode of a sacred presence.[100]

Satī or *sahagamana* is an ancient Indian custom by which the wife perished with the body of her dead husband, thereby, it is believed, winning merit for her family as well as wiping out all its sins. A *satī* stone is a memorial slab set up at the place where a faithful wife committed *satī*. *Satī* is not sanctioned by Vēdic ritual, although certain hints in the symbolism connected with funerals come very near it and, in a manner, foreshadow it.[101] Early *Smṛiti* literature allows it, but in general does not strongly emphasize it.[102] *Satī* is nevertheless of great antiquity. At the time of Alexander's invasion the Greeks found it observed in the Punjab.[103] The custom of *satī* gained popularity in the medieval period and was widely prevalent in Karṇāṭaka in the pre-Vijayanagara and Vijayanagara times.

A large number of *satī* stones are found in different parts of the Vijayanagara empire, from the fourteenth to the sixteenth centuries A.D.[104] Quite a few are extant in Vijayanagara city also. The sculpture on a satī stone is very simple. The *satī* is shown with a raised right hand while her husband is shown with the hands in *añjali*. In the top portion of the slab is carved the sun and moon or the man alone or in the company of his wife/wives worshipping a Śiva-liṅga. The sun and moon found on *satī* memorials and also on hero stones are indicative of the lasting nature of the fame of the *satī* or hero. Sometimes in a *satī* stone only the right hand of the *satī*, stretched upwards, attached to a pillar is shown.[105] The raised arm is the most important element in *māsti* sculptures. This posture is *abhaya* by which the *satī* blessed the people with her right hand before entering the fire and continues to bless her devotees.[106] The left hand of the *satī* is stretched downwards, sometimes holding a lemon,[107] a lotus or a hollow container.

Most of the foreign travellers to the empire have left detailed accounts of the practice of *satī*. These include visitors to the capital such as Nicolo Conti in the early fifteenth century,[108] Duarte Barbosa during the reign of Kṛishṇadēvarāya,[109] Fernão Nuniz during Achyutarāya's reign[110] and Caesar Frederick in A.D. 1567.[111] Pietro della Valle, who stayed briefly in the Nāyaka capital of Ikkeri in the early seventeenth century, has also given a graphic description of *satī*.[112] While the common method of performing *sahagamana* was by fire, among the Vīraśaivas, who buried their dead, *satī* was by burying alive.[113] These travel accounts reveal that although the practice of *satī* was greatly revered, it was not obligatory. There are some differences in details in the accounts of these visitors. Probably, there were differences in the customs of different economic or social groups and also from one period to the next.

There are a number of *māsti-kals* in the city; only one (NP q/1) is still extant in the "urban core" (Plate 48). In the Mudu Vīraṇṇa temple (NL w/3) there is one stone and outside it a couple more. On the south bank of the river is an extremely fine one (NG o/3). In the lower panel it depicts two *satīs* with raised hands and the husband with hands in *añjali*, standing in front of an elephant. In the top portion of the slab the man and his two wives are shown in the heaven of Vishṇu, symbolically represented by the *chakra* and *śaṅkha* flanked by Garuḍa and Hanumān (Plate 49). This is the only Vaishṇava memorial stone in the city. In the others, if any sectarian symbol is depicted, it is always the *liṅga* and Nandi. Most of the *satī-kals* found at the site have been placed in the Haṁpi Museum.[114] In these are shown one, two and even three women who have committed *satī*. These stones also reveal that not all the wives of a deceased hero necessarily committed *satī*. In one slab three women are shown, of whom only one has her hand in the typical *satī* pose[115] and in another slab only one out of the two wives is a *satī*.[116] The other women in these two memorial stones have their hands in the *añjali-mudrā*. There are also two *satī*-stones in Ānegoṅdi.[117] To the north-west of the Virūpāksha complex (outside the limits of the map) is a *satī* stone. A label inscription on it gives the name of the *satī* as Vīrayamma, daughter of Vīraṇṇa.[118]

On the whole, only thirty-odd *satī-kals* are available at the site. This is not a large number for such an extensive city that served as the capital for around 200 years. We can conclude that although the practice of *sahagamana* was encouraged and the *satīs* were venerated and worshipped, the custom was not as widespread in the city as the accounts of the foreigners would have us believe. For them this practice of *satī* was so extraordinary and bizarre that they have highlighted and, possibly, even exaggerated its prevalence in their travelogues. For example, it is stated that at the death of a king all the wives and concubines committed *satī*.[119] Yet, we know that Kṛishṇadēvarāya's two principal queens were alive long after the demise of the emperor.[120] Achyutarāya's queen, Varada-dēvī, was not only living but even played an active part in the power struggle that ensued after his death.[121]

In *satī* stones the husband is usually portrayed with hands in *añjali*. He may or may not have died in heroic action, but, the *satī*-cum-hero stones commemorate the death due to some praiseworthy exploit of the man and the *sahagamana* performed by his wife or wives. In such stones the heroic action is depicted. In the empire a sizeable number of such stones were set up.[122] In the city, too, a number of such stones were found.[123] In Ānegoṅdi there are about forty memorial stones, a few of which are of the post-empire period. The majority of these commemorate heroes and their *satī* wives. One of these is unique in its execution and has a man killing a tiger with his dagger. Standing next to him is wife holding the traditional *satī* attributes—a mirror and a lemon in her hands.[124]

The *vīra-kals* were erected to honour a deceased hero. Innumerable hero stones were set up all over the Vijayanagara empire, during the rule of all the dynasties.[125] These stones commend the heroic action that resulted in death, such as retrieving cattle from raiders, defending the honour of women, service to the lord in war, defence of the town or village, fight against outlaws and wild animals, etc.[126] The commonest variety of *vīra-kal* consists of a flat slab of stone divided into three rectangular panels. The lowest shows the scene of the heroic action. In the middle panel, the hero is seen being carried to heaven by two *apsarās*. In the uppermost panel, he is shown worshipping a Śiva-liṅga. In very rare cases representation of either Vishṇu or Dēvī or Jina is found in place of the Śiva-liṅga.[127]

In the Mudu Vīraṇṇa temple (NL w/3) there are two *vīra-kals*. On the southern slope of the Hēmakūṭa hill is a small shrine (NL g/3) built against a boulder on which is carved the scene of a man vanquishing an elephant. Possibly this is a memorial stone, commemorating an historical event. If so, it is the only extant temple in the city enshrining a memorial stone. In the Archaeological Museum, too, there are a number of hero stones.[128]

Another rite that was prevalent was that of self-immolation, in fulfilment of a vow to a deity or as an expression of gratitude for some great favour bestowed. This practice was particularly in vogue among Śaivites and Śāktas and during this period separate shrines dedicated to Bhairava and Vīrabhadra or Kāḷī were built to be used by devotees desiring to sacrifice their lives.[129] Usually this was done by severing one's own head. The existence of this custom in the city is evidenced by some memorial stones. One is located to the north of temple NN z/2. This slab has three registers (Plate 50). The lowest panel depicts the hero ready to sever his head with a sword. There is a mechanical contraption, like a lever, to which the hero's head is tied. The hero has pulled the lever down with his left hand, a sword is held in his right hand. When he releases his left hand the lever would jump up and the sword would sever his head from his body. The head would then be hanging onto the lever. The hero's two wives have already committed *satī* and are shown in the usual *satī* pose. In the middle panel the hero and his wives are journeying to heaven. In the top panel are the *liṅga*, Nandi and a Śaiva priest; the sun and moon are also carved.[130] A memorial stone in the Museum also portrays the severing of the head by heroes,[131] another shows a hero disemboweling himself with a sword.[132] Another method of self-immolation was by throwing oneself in front of the temple chariot during the *ratha* festival.[133]

The custom of self-torture by 'hook swinging,' in thanksgiving to god for a favour received, was also practised in the city. Although no archaeological evidences of this custom are available the accounts of foreign travellers to the city refer to it[134] (Fig. 8).

These minor and popular cults and the religious practices that were prevalent reveal the vibrancy of religious life in Vijayanagara. The patronage for most of these came not from the king and court, but from the populace of this vast metropolis.

Notes

[1]T.A. Gopinatha Rao, *Elements of Hindu Iconography*, vol. 2, pt. II, p. 333.

[2]K. Desai, *Iconography of Viṣṇu*, p. 51.

[3]Ibid., p. 52.

[4] K.S. Ramachandran, "Some Harihara Figures from Nepal," in *Śrīnidhih: Perspectives in Art, Archaeology and Culture*, ed. K.V. Raman et al., p. 163.

[5]S.V. Padigar, "The Cult of Vishṇu in Karnataka," (Ph.D. diss), p. 415.

[6]A.P. Karmarkar, *Cultural History of Karnataka: Ancient and Medieval*, p. 176.

[7]*EC* IX, Dg. 32, 33, 35, 42.

[8]Ibid., nos. 24, 27, 28, 29, 30, 31.

[9]K. Sarojini Devi, "Religion in Vijayanagara" (Ph.D. diss.), p. 271.

[10]*EC* XI, Dg. 22 to 68.

[11]*ARSIE* of 1918, no. 288.

[12]*EC* XI, Dg. 27.

[13]This Harihara temple is not noted in any of the authoritative works on Hampi and its monuments. However, the local people seem to know its identity. After doing the iconographic study of this shrine, and in order to check out my conclusion, I asked a local who was resting nearby as to whose temple it was. Ready came the answer: "Of god Harihara."

[14]S.V. Padigar, op.cit., p. 250.

[15]*VPR '79-83*, p. 36 and Plate XLIII b.

[16]O.F. Schrader, *Introduction to the Pāñcarātra and the Ahirbudhnya Saṃhitā*, p. 25.

[17]S.V. Padigar, op.cit., p. 217.

[18]Ibid.,

[19]Ibid., pp. 240-241.

[20]T.A. Gopinatha Rao, op.cit., vol. 1, pt. I, pp. 227-228.

[21]*SII* IV, no. 248.

[22]*VPR '83-84*, pp. 138-139 and Plates LXXXVII-LXXXIX.

[23]In both cases the deity, standing in *samabhaṅga*, holds the *chakra* and *śaṅkha* in the upper right and left hands and the *gadā* and *padma* in lower right and left hands respectively. According to the *Rūpamandana* and *Padma-Purāṇa* this is Mādhava (T.A. Gopinatha Rao, op.cit., vol. 1, pt. I, pp. 229-231). But according to other texts (*VPR '83-84*, p. 139) the attributes of Mādhava are arranged differently.

[24]*Bhagavad Gītā*, chapter IV, verses 7-8.

[25]S.V. Padigar, op.cit., pp. 334-335.

[26]T.A. Gopinatha Rao, op.cit., vol. 1, pt. I, p. 120.

[27]V. Filliozat, "Iconography : Religious and Civil Monuments", in *Vij. City & Emp.*, vol. 1, p. 310.

[28]For details, see *VPR '79-83*, p. 38 and Plates XLVI & XLVII.

[29]See *VPR '83-84*, p. 138 and Plate LXXXVI.

[30]*VPR '79-83*, p. 38.

[31]No. 1078 of the Hampi Museum collection. For details see D.K. Sinha, "A Rare Varāha Image of the Archaeological Museum, Hampi", *JIH*, LIII, pp. 353-359.

[32]. Burton Stein, "Devi Shrines and Folk Hinduism in Medieval Tamilnad", in *Studies in the Language and Culture of South Asia*, ed. E. Garrow and M.D. Lang, p. 79.

[33]W.T. Elmore, *Dravidian Gods in Hinduism*, pp. 34-35.

[34]A.P. Karmarkar, *The Religions of India: The Vrātya or Dravidian System*, p. 94.

[35]Bhadrakāḷi is the *śaktī* of Vīrabhadra, hence she holds the attributes typical of the god, namely, the bow and arrow, the sword and the shield.

[36]Bhairavī is the *śaktī* of Bhairava, who, along with Vīrabhadra, was a popular Śaivite deity in the city. This goddess holds the attributes peculiar to her god, namely, the *triśūla* and *ḍamaru* (small drum), *khaḍga* (sword) and *kapāla* (skull-bowl). Twice Bhairava and Bhairavī are represented together, both holding the same attributes. The first is in NM y/2, where they are depicted standing. The second is in NQ o/2, where they are both seated. In the temple NG m/2 Bhairava and Bhairavī, facing each other, are carved on opposite walls of the entrance *maṇḍapa*.

[37]A. Sundara, "New Lights on Religious Trends in Anegondi Region during Vijayanagara Period," *QJMS*, LXVIII, p. 15.

[38]*SII* IV, no. 260.

[39]D. Devakunjari, *Hampi*, pp. 57-59.

[40]A large number of these are located in or near square 'NM' of the map (see Fig. 7). That area seems to have been a centre of *śaktī* worship.

[41]See *VPR '83-84*, pp. 136-137 and plates LXXXI-LXXXIV.

[42]Nos. 08, 129, 539, 627, 669, 724, 755, 758, 763, 839 and 1613 in the Hampi Museum.

[43]See *VPR '83-84*, Plate XCIII.

[44]S.R. Balasubrahmanyam, *Early Chola Art.*, pt. 1, p. 1.

[45]C.G. Diehl, *Instrument and Purpose: Studies in Rites and Rituals in South India*, pp. 173-178.

[46]L.E. Gatwood, *Devi and the Spouse Goddess*, p. 158.

[47]D. Devakunjari, *Hampi*, p. 39.

[48]Ibid.

[49]The weekly *pūjā* here is performed by a non-brāhmaṇa woman. The temple is frequented mainly by women and those belonging to the lower castes.

[50]R. Champakalakshmi, *Vaiṣṇava Iconography in the Tamil Country*, p. 114.

[51]*FE*, pp. 254-255.

[52]H. Whitehead, *The Village Gods of South India*, p. 18.

[53]Sugandha, "History and Archeology of Anegondi," (Ph.D. diss.), pp. 220-222.

[54]Stella Kramrisch, "An Image of Aditi-Uttānapad," in *Exploring India's Sacred Art*, ed. B.S. Miller, pp. 148-158.

[55]J.N. Tiwari, *Goddess Cults in Ancient India*, p. 192.

[56]H.D. Sankalia, "The Nude Goddess or 'Shameless Women' in Western Asia, India and South-Eastern Asia," *Artibus Asiae*, XXIII, p. 121.

[57]Ibid.

[58]M.K. Dhavalikar, "The Goddess of Mahakut," a paper read at the centenary celebration of the Mysore Directorate of Archaeology and Museums.

[59]It was during a field trip to Hampi in October 1985 that I first noticed the Lajjā-Gaurī reliefs in this temple because of the vermilion smeared on the breasts and vagina of these nude goddess figures. Elsewhere white powder is often applied on Lajjā-Gaurī reliefs. This fertility goddess is venerated to this day.

[60]S.V. Padigar, op. cit., p. 252.

[61]L.S.S. O'Malley, *Popular Hinduism*, p. 7.

[62]K.C. Aryan and S. Aryan, *Hanuman in Art and Mythology*, p. 19.

[63]R. Champakalakshmi, op.cit., p. 123.

[64]V. Ions, *Indian Mythology*, pp. 102-104.

[65]A.P. Karmarkar, *The Religions of India, Vol. I: The Vrātya or Dravidian Systems*, p. 187; S. Hanumantha Rao, "Śrī Madhwachārya A.D. 1238-1318", *JIH*, XXVII, p. 25.

[66]B. Venkoba Rao, *Introduction to Sri Vyasayogicaritam: The Life of Sri Vyasaraja*, pp. xiv-xv.

[67]*FE*, p. 390.

[68]1. NC v/2 2. ND y/2 3. ND y/4 4. ND y/6 5. NG n/1 6. NG p/3 7. NG w/3 8. NJ s/2 9. NJ x/2 10. NL b/16 11. NM b/8 12. NL h/1 (a sub-shrine) 13. NN s/2 14. NN y/1 15. NO j/4 16. NQ n/1 17. NQ y/2 18. NR b/2 19. NR g/2 20. NR g/3 21. NR o/1 22. NR q/2 23. NS b/1 24. NS d/1 25. NS o/1 26. NS p/4 27. NS y/1 28. NS z/3 (one of the 2 shrines) 29. NT d/6 30. NT j/1 31. NT o/2 32. NT o/4 33. NT q/2 34. NT w/1 35. NV o/1 36. NX k/1 (one of the 2 shrines) 37. NX q/1 38. NY e/1 39. NY j/1

[69]Nos. 1, 2, 4, 5, 6, 7, 8, 9, 11, 19, 22, 23, 25, 26, 27, 28, 29, 31, 34, 36 of the above list.

[70]Nos 2, 3, 5, 6, 7, 8, 9, 10, 11, 17, 21, 29, 30, 31, 32, 33, 35, 39, of the list.

[71]See nos. 3, 10, 14, 35 and 37 of the list. Of these no. 10 (NL b/16) on Hēmakūṭa hill was not even a shrine; it was a four-pillared open structure that has been enclosed with roughly constructed walls. It is now known as the "Mūla Āñjanēya" temple. No. 35 (NV o/1) is the temple of Mallikārjuna's reign. The Hanumān image in this temple is definitely not the original cult image here.

So great is the devotion to Āñjanēya at the site that sometimes stray icons lying around are taken and placed in empty shrines and worshipped. To cite one example, in 1987 the icon from the dilapidated Āñjanēya shrine NC v/2, near a gateway in Viṭhalāpura, was removed and placed in a four-pillared structure in the Viṭhala complex near the north-east corner pavilion by an official of the A.S.I., who felt that the crowds visiting the Viṭhala temple should be provided with an object of devotion! The A.S.I, attendants have even begun referring to this icon as the "Ghanṭai Hanumanthappa" because of a bell suspended from his tail. Researchers studying the Viṭhala temple in the years to come will be hard-pressed to explain any connection between the Viṭhala cult and Hanumān worship in this complex. If such tampering with historical evidence is done by the guardians of our archaeological heritage, how much more must have been done inadvertently by the simple local folk.

[72]*VPR '84-87*, no. 72.

[73]R. Shama Sastry, "A few Inscriptions of the Ancient Kings of Anegundi," *QJMS*, VII, pp. 287 and 291.

[74]A. Sundara, op.cit., p. 10.

[75]*SII* IX, pt. II, no. 445.

[76]Ibid., no. 635.

[77]Ibid., no. 637.

[78]A few are listed below:

1. near ND y/5	2. behind NG x/1
3. near NH f/5	4. near NL b/14
5. NM z/4	6. near NN x/2
7. near NN z/1	8. near NN z/2
9. NP x/2	10. in NQ m/1
11. NQ u/2	12. NQ u/4
13. near NR e/4	14. NS o/2
15. NS p/6	16. NU g/2
17. NY p/1.	

[79]. 1. In the "Āñjanēya-Svāmi" shrine within the Virūpāksha complex NF w/1.

2. in front of NG k/2
3. in front of NG w/1
4. In the antechamber of NG w/5
5. near NG w/7
6. in a side shrine in NL h/1
7. two slabs with Āñjanēya reliefs behind NL w/5
8. NO w/1
9. NP t/1
10. In NQ e/1
11. in front of NR w/1
12. behind NR w/1
13. in the *maṇḍapa* of NR t/2
14. near NY j/1
15. NYm/1
16. NY m/2
17. NY m/5
18. in gateway in NY x
19. near gateway in NY v.

There are also a large number of slabs in the Haṁpi Museum, e.g, nos. 5, 6, 33, 40, 44, 64, 150, 167, 254, 483, 502, 605, 617, 619, 620, 621, 630, 633, 674, 701, 791, 817, 934, 1053, 1065 and 02113.

[80]*ARIE* of 1957-58, no. 206.

[81]S. Hanumantha Rao, op.cit., p. 40; *ARSIE* of 1919, p. 7.

[82]S. Hanumantha Rao, "The Influence of the Religious School of Sri Madhwa on the History of Vijayanagara," *QJMS*, XX, p. 285.

[83]*Annual Report of the Archaeological Department, Southern Circle, Madras*, of 1914-15, pp. 34-38.

[84]Ibid.

[85]A.P. Karmarkar, op.cit., p. 170.

[86]H. Krishna Sastri, *South Indian Images of Gods and Goddesses*, p. 248.

[87]Swami Sivananda, *Hindu Fasts and Festivals and their Philosophy*, p. 41.

[88]J.S.F. Mackenzie, "Tree and Serpent Worship," *IA* IV, p. 5.

[89]No. 147 of the Haṁpi Museum collection.

[90]This information was supplied by the *archakas* of the Yantrōddhāraka Āñjanēya shrine. Some of the snake stones near this shrine and in front of the Kōdaṇḍarāma temple are evidently recent ones. On one of the *nāga-kals* in front of the latter temple is engraved in roman script the name, "G.S. Ramaprasad." According to the same informants, this stone was installed over ten years ago by one G.S. Ramaprasad and his wife from Gaṅgāvati, Rāichur district, who were childless. Later, when they were blessed with a son, they named the child Ramachandra.

[91]J.Ph. Vogel, *Indian Serpent-Lore or the Nāgas in the Hindu Legend and Art*, pp. 271-272.

[92]Nos. 1061, 1070 and many small unnumbered *nāga-kals* in the Haṁpi Museum.

[93]Nos. 147 and 1679 of the Haṁpi Museum collection.

[94]Nos. 54 and 277 of the Haṁpi Museum collection.

[95]Nos. 161, 655, 1680, 1681, 1682 and 1686 of the Haṁpi Museum collection.

[96]Nos. 160, 1060, 1068 and many small unnumbered snake stones in the Haṁpi Museum.

[97]Nos. 224, 307, 378, 656, 689, 816, 981, 983, 984, 985, 1036, 1672, 1673, 1675, 1676 of the Haṁpi Museum

collection.

[98]Snake stones are found in the following places:

1. In front of temple NF w/27 (about 34 small snake stones)
2. in and around NF w/29 (about 90 stones)
3. In front of NG w/1 (4 stones, some are modern)
4. in front of NG w/3 (about 24, some are modern)
5. in front of NG w/5 (several)
6. in NL w/3 (about 10, some may be modern)
7. in NM s/1 (1 stone)
8. in NM s/2 (2 stones)
9. near NN h/1 (3 stones)
10. near NN s/1 (6 large snake stones)
11. near NN s/3 (5)
12. near NN x/5 (about 8)
13. near NN z/1 (about 60 small snake stones)
14. near NQ d/1 (several small ones)
15. in NQ e/1 (1)
16. in NQ q/1 (1)
17. near NQ t/3 (1)
18. In NQ u/1 (2)
19. in and near NQ u/3 (2)
20. in NR e/3 (10)
21. in and near NR e/5 (3)
22. in NR j/1 (about 7)
23. NR j/2 (the shrine is built against a boulder with 2 *nāgas* carved in relief)
24. in front of NR y/4 (2)
25. in NS d/1 (1)
26. in NS h/1 (1)
27. NT p/1 (several)
28. in NT v/2 (about 10)
29. In NV c/2 (3)
30. near NX q/1 (3)
31. in NY e/1 (several)
32. in gateway in NY x (4)
33. near NZ g/1 (1).

[99]M. Chidanandamurti, "Two Māsti Temples in Karnataka," in *Memorial Stones*, ed. S. Settar and G.D. Sontheimer, p. 129.

[100]D.D. Shulman, *The King and the Clown in South Indian Myth and Poetry*, p. 351.

[101]A. Barth, *The Religions of India*, p. 59.

[102]A.L. Basham, *The Wonder that was India*, p. 187.

[103]A. Barth, loc.cit.

[104]*EC* VIII, Sb. 104; *MAR* of 1941, no. 35; *MAR* of 1930, no. 57, *ARIE* of 1977-78, no. 81; *EC* VII, Sk. 239; *EC* VII, Sb. 165, etc.

[105]No. 831 of the Hampi Museum collection.

[106]M. Chidanandamurti, loc.cit.

[107]Nos. 168 of the Hampi Museum collection and *VPR '84-87*, no. 176.

[108]See Nicolo Conti in *India in the Fifteenth Century*, p. 6.

[109]Duarte Barbosa, *The Book of Duarte Barbosa*, ed. M. Longworth Dames, pp. 213-216.

[110]*FE*, pp. 391-393.

[111]Caesar Frederick, in *Purchas: His Pilgrims*, by Samuel Purchas, vol. X, pp. 94-96.

[112]Pietro della Valle, *The Travels of Pietro Della Valle in India*, vol. II, pp. 273-277.

[113]Duarte Barbosa, op.cit., pp. 217-218; Nuniz in *FE*, p. 393.

[114]Nos. 41, 168, 203, 212, 213, 257, 261, 335, 382, 384, 402, 404, 407, 409, 421, 438, 513, 606, 608, 733, 739, 747, 833, 835, 1063 of the Hampi Museum collection.

[115]No. 212 of the Hampi Museum collection.

[116]Nos. 733 of the Hampi Museum collection.

[117]Sugandha, op.cit., p. 283.

[118]*VPR '84-87*, no. 7.

[119]Nicolo Conti, loc. cit.; Duarte Barbosa, op.cit., p. 216; Nuniz, loc.cit.

[120]N. Venkataramanayya, *Studies in the Third Dynasty of Vijayanagara*, pp. 60 and 90.

[121]Ibid., p. 77.

[122]*MAR* of 1928, no. 88; *SII* XVIII, no. 276; *EC* VIII, Sb. 484; *ARIE* of 1950-51, no. 88; *MAR* of 1923, no. 80.

[123]Nos. 250, 406, 463, 830, 831, 832 of the Hampi Museum collection.

[124]Sugandha, op.cit., pp. 282-283.

The carrying of a mirror by a woman about to commit *sahagamana* is mentioned by Nuniz, op.cit., p. 391 and Caesar Frederick, op.cit., p. 95.

[125]*ARIE* of 1951-52, no. 67; *EC* XII, Si. 102; *EC* XI, Dg. 117; *ARSIE* of 1940-41, B.K. 11: *EC* VIII, Sb. 167; *ARIE* of 1947-48, no. 205; *MAR* of 1930, no. 52; *MAR* of 1927, no. 41, etc.

[126]S. Settar, "Memorial Stones in South India," in *Memorial Stones*, eds. S. Settar and G.D. Sontheimer, pp. 194-195.

[127]M.S. Mate, "Hero-Stones: The 'Folk' and the 'Classic'," in *Memorial Stones* eds. S. Settar and G.D. Sontheimer, p. 80.

[128]Nos. 35, 165, 256, 278, 742, 744, 820, 834, 836, 1700 of the Hampi Museum collection.

[129]M.S. Sarma, *History of the Reddi Kingdoms : circa 1325 to circa 1448 A.D.*, p. 342.

[130]*VPR '79-83*, pp. 38-39 & Plate L a.

[131]No. 219 of the Hampi Museum collection.

[132]No. 251 of the Hampi Museum collection.

[133]Nicolo Conti, op.cit., p. 28.

[134]Nicolo Conti, loc.cit.; Duarte Barbosa, op.cit., pp. 220-222.

CHAPTER 8

Temples and Festivals

As seen in the preceding chapters, the numerous temples and shrines, ranging from large complexes to small shrines of only a *cella*, were centres of religious activity in the city, promoting the various Śaivite and Vaishṇavite cults. A survey of the cycle of ceremonies and *utsavas* in the temples is, therefore, essential. Some of the festivals commemorated in the temples were also celebrated with great pomp in the court, the most famous being the annual public ritual of the *Mahānavamī*. Of course, rituals and festivals were not restricted to the temples and the court. However, no archaeological evidence is available to suggest the nature of private or domestic ceremonies and celebrations.

Although only limited archaeological data about temple rituals and festivals is extant, the available inscriptional and monumental sources do give a glimpse into the intensity and elaborateness of temple activities. Epigraphical information is available mainly from the Vaishṇava temples, principally from the large sixteenth century Śrī-Vaishṇava temple complexes. Hence the inscriptions do not give a comprehensive or complete picture of life in the Vijayanagara temple and shrines in general.

For the organisation and conduct of rituals there were a host of temple functionaries. Their number would naturally have varied from temple to temple. Probably, the numerous small shrines were served by just one *pūjāri*. In the larger temples there were administrative officials, ritual specialists and others performing accessory and menial duties.

The *sthānika* was the manager or trustee of a temple. There are inscriptional references to such an officer from the Viṭhala complex,[1] the Rāmachandra temple[2] and the Raghunātha temple near the Penugoṇḍa gate.[3] Kṛishṇadēvarāya appointed two *sthānikas* in the Kṛishṇa temple.[4] Some epigraphs referring to grants made to the Virūpāksha temple mention the *sthānika* or the *sthānikas*[5] and the *sthānadhipati*.[6] Evidently, there was more than one trustee in this temple and the *sthānadhipati* must have been the head of the Board of Trustees. These three records of grants to Virūpāksha make it clear that the *sthānikas* administered the temple, its lands and properties and received grants and gifts made to the deity. Besides the *sthānikas,* no other officer or ritualist of the Virūpāksha, or of any other Śaiva temple in the city, is mentioned in inscriptions. Records from important Vaishṇava temples refer to the *sēnabōva* or the accounts officer.[7] An inscription from the Rāmachandra temple indicates the existence of the *karaṇika*[8] or accountant; the differences between the duties of these two types of officials is not clear. Large temples such as the Viṭhala, had a treasury or *bhaṇḍāra*, under the supervision of the *bhaṇḍāri*.[9]

A number of brāhmaṇas were engaged in temple services, such as performing the *pūjās* and chanting hymns. For example, Kṛishṇadēvarāya appointed thirty-seven brāhmaṇas to a variety of duties in the Kṛishṇa temple.[10] These included in the *āchāryas* (or *archakas* or *bhaṭṭācharyas*, priests who conducted the worship in the inner shrine), *paurānikas* (reciters of the Purāṇas), *jōtishas* (astrologers), a *sadasya* (or the superintending priest in the performance of rituals and sacrifices), a *brahmā* (chief priest for festivals), those appointed for *vēdapārāyaṇa* (recitation of the *Vēdas*), for *mantra-pushpa* (ceremony of offering flowers while reciting *mantras*), for *pavamānābhishēka* and for *nāmatreya.* The foundational inscription of A.D. 1534 from the Tiruveṅgaḷanātha temple[11] refers to some of the above services, but adds a few more: the *parichārakas* (attendants who render assistance to the officiating priests), brāhmanas for *itihāsa* (recitation of the epics) and *bhāgavata* (recitation of the *Bhāgavata*), the *ghaḷiyāra* (the watchman of the temple, who strikes the hours) and the *kaṭigeya* (a temple servant who also joins the processions of the deity).[12] *Svayampākis*[13] or cooks prepared the food offerings for the deity or for distribution in the *Rāmānuja-kūṭas* or temple *chattras*. The wages of those involved in menial services in the temple kitchen, such as the grinding of wheat, pounding of rice, bringing oil, etc. are also specified.[14] An inscription from the Viṭhala complex refers to those engaged for decorating the temple chariot and erecting and decorating the *paṇḍals* on festive occasions.[15] It is possible that these labourers were not regular temple employees. Inscriptions from this temple also indicate the presence of temple dancers[16] and musicians.[17] In the large temples there must also have been other employees, such as those who carried the processional deities mounted on the *vāhanas*, the parasol-bearers, gardeners, garland makers, artisans and many others of whom, however, we have no contemporary description.

In the city, as elsewhere in south India, at the time of the installation of the deity in a temple provision was usually made by the patron or devotees for the worship. Additional donations were also given from time to time. Unfortunately, we do not have much information about the elaborate rituals in the temples. Perhaps, since many of these must have been based on tradition and hence were commonly known, no need was felt for specifying the details. Besides, there would have been variations in the rituals, depending on the *Āgama* in use in the particular temple. But with one exception there is no mention of the *Āgamic* texts employed (see Chapter 6, note 115). Yet from the limited data available we can draw some general conclusions about temple rituals and festivals.

The inscriptions of A.D. 1513,[18] recording the benefactions made by Kṛishṇadēvarāya to the Virūpāksha, Prasanna Virūpāksha, Rāmachandra and Viṭhala temples on the occasion of the solar eclipse mention also the *nitya* (daily), *naimittika* (special), *paksha* (fortnightly), *māsa* (monthly) and *saṁvatsara* (yearly) rituals or festivals. Religious texts enjoin the performance of daily worship in temples ranging from one to sixteen times a day, three, four, six or eight times being the more common, the number varying from temple to temple. No evidence is available from Vijayanagara as to the specific number of times *pūjās* were performed in individual temples. However, inscriptions from the Viṭhala temple referring to the dawn service[19] and another from the Tirumaṅgai-āḻvār temple mentioning the noon and evening rituals[20] prove that services were held at definite times of the day. In general, in Hindu temples, the daily worship or *nitya-pūjā* consists of the sixteen services or *upachāras* such as meditation (*dhyāna*), invitation (*āvāhana*), offering a seat (*āsana*), offering of water for the feet (*pādya*), giving of water for sipping (*āchamana*), offering of water for drinking (*arghya*), bath (*snāna*), offering of clothes (*vastra*), flowers (*pushpa*), incense (*dhūpa*), light (*dīpa*), cooked food (*naivedya*), etc. These *upachāras* are not described in any of the inscriptions at the site. But the term *aṅga-raṅga-bhōga*, found in most of the donative grants, pertains to these *upachāras*. By *aṅga-bhōga* is meant the *upachāras* performed by the *pūjāris* in the sanctum, while the *raṅga-bhōga* appears to imply the services offered by the remaining temple staff, outside the *garbha-gṛiha* in the *raṅga-maṇḍapa*.[21]

Terms such as *amṛitapaḍi*, *naivedya* or *amṛitapaḍi-naivedya* found in almost all the grants, refer to the sacred food offerings to the deities. The specific items required for the preparation of the *naivedya* are listed in a number of epigraphs, at times with details of the exact weights or measures of each ingredient to be supplied. The most frequently included are rice, green-gram, oil, clarified butter, curds, salt and pepper, *sambhār* powder, curry-powder, jaggery and sugar for the cooked food and also betel leaves and areca nuts.[22] An inscription from the Tiruveṅgaḷanātha temple in Kṛishṇāpura (NL w/6) even specifies the precise quantities of spices and condiments, such as cardamom, turmeric, ginger, cummin-seed, fenugreek and mustard, that were to be provided daily.[23] Apart from the regular *naivedya*, certain other items such as sweetmeats of various types are also listed, either to be prepared on special festive days or for particular offerings of the day, such as *sukhi-paḍi*,[24] *appa-paḍi*,[25] *karuchi-appa*, *attirasa*, *yennehōrige*, *vaḍai*,[26] *dōsai*,[27] *khajāya*,[28] *doḍaki-prasāda*,[29] *paramāna*[30] and curd-rice.[31] The persons among whom the food-offerings are to be distributed are also named in a number of inscriptions.

Apart from cooked food, fruit offerings were made to the deities, for which tender coconuts, coconuts, bananas, and sugarcane had to be supplied.[32] Donative grants ensured the supply of oil, *ghee* and other requirements for the light-offerings to the gods.[33] In A.D. 1513 the two queens of Kṛishṇadēvarāya, Chinnā-dēvī and Tirumala-dēvī, even donated cows to the Viṭhala temple to provide an uninterrupted supply of *ghee* for the sacred lamps.[34] The regular supply of sandalwood[35] for the sacred fires and garlands[36] was also arranged for.

Apart from the elaborate *nitya* (daily) celebrations, there were the *māsa* (monthly) festivals. The *Pañcha-Parva* days were commemorated every month in Śaivite (Virūpāksha,[37] Prasanna Virūpāksha[38] and Mudu Vīraṇṇa[39]) and in Vaishṇavite (Rāmachandra,[40] Viṭhala,[41] and Tiruveṅgaḷanātha[42]) temples alike. An epigraph from the Viṭhala complex notes that in a year there are sixty days of the five *Parvas*.[43] The five *Parva* days every month are the new moon day, full moon day, *saṅkramaṇa* or *saṅkrānti* day[44] and the eighth and fourteenth lunar days of the dark half of every lunar month.[45]

The sixteenth century expansion of temples (Virūpāksha and Viṭhala) and the construction of new temple complexes (Kṛishṇa, Tiruveṅgaḷanātha and Paṭṭābirāma) corresponded to the expansion of temple rituals and festivals. The main deity (*mūla-mūrti*) of the temple was considered to have a spiritual as well as a temporal capacity and the increase in the temple structures was in proportion to the increase in the temporal powers associated with the divinity. In his spiritual capacity the god reigned supreme in the darkened sanctum where he passively received the worship of his devotees. The temporal capacity of the god was manifest on *utsavas*, when he issued forth from his retreat and went out in procession in the form of the *utsava-mūrti*. Thus, the temple had an inner, closed and ritually sacrosanct part and an outer, open, public and less sanctified part, consisting of courtyards with halls, pavilions and other structures.[46]

Important architectural features, built for a variety of festivals that filled the temple calendars, included the *ratha-vīdhi* (of the Virūpāksha, Viṭhala, Kṛishṇa and Tiruveṅgaḷanātha temple complexes), the *kalyāṇa-maṇḍapa* or the pavilion with an elevated platform in the centre for the exhibition of the deity and his consort during the annual marriage-festival and other ceremonial occasions, the *uyyāle-maṇḍapa* (for the swing-festival), the *saṅgīta-maṇḍapa* (where the deity could listen to music), the *maḍapaḷḷi* (kitchen), and the temple tank, usually with a *nīrāḷi-maṇḍapa* in the centre, for the float festival (in the Virūpāksha, Kṛishṇa, Viṭhala, Tiruveṅgaḷanātha and Paṭṭābhirāma temples).

Inscriptions reveal some of the important festivals that were celebrated in the principal temples in the city. However, this can in no way be considered as an exhaustive list of festivals in the Vijayanagara temples, for not all the *utsavas* are necessarily mentioned in inscriptions. Besides, from the vast majority of temples and shrines at the site no epigraphical data regarding *utsavas* is available.

Although there are many inscriptions both within the Virūpāksha temple and elsewhere that refer to it, only one epigraph mentions some of the *utsavas* of the temple–that of Kṛishṇadēvarāya, dated A.D. 1513.[47] The two annual festivals specified in it are the *Rathōtsava* (car festival) in *Chaitra* (March-April) and the *Makara-saṅkrānti*[48] *Rathōtsava*. In modern times the car festival in *Chaitra* is the most important festival in this temple, but the car festival at *Makara-saṅkrānti* is no longer celebrated. The importance of this latter festival in the Virūpāksha temple during the Vijayanagara period is revealed by two grants of Kṛishṇadēvarāya, of A.D. 1510[49] and 1522[50] which were registered in the presence of Virūpāksha on the holy occasion of *Makara-saṅkrānti*.

The *Chaitra Rathōtsava* has survived as the principal festival or *Brahmōtsava* in the Virūpāksha temple. South Indian temples of any size usually have one or more annual festivals of about ten days, called the *Brahmōtsava* or *Mahōtsava*, which generally ends in the car festival or *Rathōtsava*. Although we have no further epigraphical data of the details of this celebration in the Virūpāksha temple, a literary source comes to our aid. The *Virūpāksha Vasantōtsava Champū*, by Ahōbala, deals with this festival.[51] This festival, known as the *Vasantōtsava* (spring festival), is said to have lasted for nine days commencing with the *dhvajārohaṇa* (ceremonial of hoisting the flag) on *Chaitra śuddha navamī*, (the ninth day of the bright fortnight of *Chaitra*,) and ending with the *avabhṛithā*,[52] or the ablution of the idols in the Tuṅgabhadrā. Between these two ceremonies were the important celebrations of the *Rathōtsava*, which took place on the full moon day, the *Mṛgayōtsava* when god Virūpāksha was taken out hunting, the festival of estrangement between Virūpāksha and Paṁpā-dēvī and then the reconciliation and marriage festival (*Kalyāṇōtsava*).[53] Other details provided in this text is that on the car pulling day the temple *ratha* was dragged up to the end of the *ratha-vīdhi* to the *Nandi-maṇḍapa*,[54] the *utsava-mūrtis* were placed in the *yajñaśālā* during the festival days,[55] "Vidyāraṅya-svāmi" mounted the *ratha* and the king (accompanied by many subordinate rulers) also played an active role in the festival, even giving the first pull to the temple chariot.[56] Immediately following the festival in the Virūpāksha temple was the one of god Gavi Raṅganātha in Ānegoṅdi.[57]

It is likely that the *Chaitra Rathōtsava* has been celebrated in the Virūpāksha temple more or less continuously till modern times. A nineteenth century account of this festival in honour of Virūpāksha-svāmi, held around April 15, describes crowds as large as a hundred thousand people, sixty thousand and forty thousand being present in different years.[58] The continuity in its celebration is indicated by the similarity in the festival in modern times when compared with the account given in the *Virūpāksha Vasantōtsava Chaṁpū*. These days it is a nine-day festival commencing on *Chaitra śuddha navamī*, the *Rathōtsava* coinciding with the full moon. During these days the ceremonies of *Kalyāṇōtsava*, *Mṛgayōtsava* and *avabhṛithā* still take place and the *utsava-mūrtis* are kept in the *yajñaśālā*. The lineal descendant of the kings of Vijayanagara (the erstwhile ruler of Ānegoṅdi) and the head of the Vidyāraṇya-svāmi *maṭha* play a significant role in the rituals.[59]

However, there are some differences, too. For example, the *ratha* is no longer dragged up to the *Nandi-maṇḍapa*. The most important difference is the modern celebration of the *Kalyāṇōtsava/Brahmōtsava* of the Kōdaṇḍarāma temple (NG w/1) on the last day of the Virūpāksha temple festival. On this occasion the articles needed for the *pūjā* in the Kōdaṇḍarāma temple are taken in procession there from the Virūpāksha temple. Thus, there is a deliberate conflation of the Śaivite Paṁpā-Virūpāksha cult and the Vaishṇavite cult of Rāma, who is locally considered to be the brother of Paṁpā. (In the south Indian tradition Vishṇu is considered to be the brother of Durgā; therefore in the painting of the marriage of Śiva and Pārvatī or Virūpāksha and Paṁpā, on the ceiling of the *mahā-raṅga-maṇḍapa* of the Virūpāksha temple, Vishṇu performs the *kanyādāna*). Perhaps, this was aimed at mitigating the sectarian rivalries between the temples and devotees of Śiva and Vishṇu. It is not known when this conflation took place and whether it is a pre-or a post-1565 phenomenon; but it must have occurred after the *Virūpāksha Vasantōtsava Chaṁpū* was written. Such a conscious bringing together of Śaivite and Vaishṇavite temples (the Śaivite Minakshi-Sundarēśvara temple and the Vaishṇavite Alagar temple) took place in Madurai, when Tirumala Nāyaka changed the *Kalyāṇōtsava/Rathōtsava* of the Śaivite temple to the month of *Chaitra* to coincide with the annual *yātra* (journey) of Alagar, who came to be regarded as the brother of Mīnakshī.[60] Thus, in Madurai the wedding festival became the "chief ritual through which popular mythology creates and expresses the basic unity of society and of the gods."[61]

Another important festival in the Virūpāksha temple in modern times is the *Phalapūjā* or the betrothal festival of Virūpāksha and Paṁpā-dēvī.[62] Nowadays during the *Phalapūjā* festival, the fixing of the marriage of Paṁpā and Virūpāksha takes place in the Kōdaṇḍarāma temple; on this occasion the *utsava-mūrtis* of the Virūpāksha temple are taken in procession to the Kōdaṇḍarāma temple. No data is available from the Vijayanagara period, to judge whether this was an annual ritual prior to A.D. 1565.

The only other Śaivite temple in the city of which we have information regarding an *utsava* is that of Mudu Vīraṇṇa. Its foundational inscription of A.D. 1545[63] included the provision for the *ratha-mahā-utsava* (car festival). Unfortunately, no further details of the festival are given. This temple has no *ratha-vīdhi*. Thus, car festivals were not restricted to the large temple complexes which had their own car streets. That smaller temples also had *rathas* and car festivals and that such *rathas* were dragged along the public streets is mentioned in the travel narrative of Paes.[64]

Of the Vaishṇava temples, in the inscription of A.D. 1521 from the Rāmachandra temple,[65] the donor, Timmarāja, made arrangements for festivals such as the *Rathōtsava* in the month of *Chaitra*, *Ratha-saptamī*, the *Ūti* festival, the elephant hunt at *Saṅkrānti* and the sacrificial fire in the month of *Pushya*. On these occasions the deity was to be brought to the *utsava-maṇḍapa*; probably it is the one in the north-east corner of the courtyard. In the centre of this *maṇḍapa* is a raised platform, the ceiling above which has a clerestory type of arrangement to let out smoke. This must have served for "the sacrificial fire in the month of *Pushya*." Different types of *vāhanas* (carrier vehicles) to be used on these auspicious days are also mentioned.

In the foundational inscriptions of the Kṛishṇa temple, Kṛishṇadēvarāya gifted a number of villages to the temple for the maintenance of the temple brāhmaṇas and for the various services and offerings, including the *Ratha-mahōtsava*.[66] But, it is not specified when this festival was to be held, nor are other annual rituals mentioned. Another inscription from this temple, dated A.D. 1532, records the grant made by Achyutarāya for two festivals, the *Uyyāle-tirunāḷu* (swing festival) and the *Kōḍe-tirunāḷu* (summer festival).[67]

The inscription of A.D. 1534 that notes the construction of the Tiruveṅgaḷanātha temple by Hiriya Tirumalarāja and his grants to the temple also records the gift by Achyutarāya of a village for different offerings in the temple and for the *Rathōtsava* and the *Koḍe-tirunāḷu*.[68]

The maximum number of references to temple festivals is found in the Viṭhala temple. This is not surprising, since of all the temples in the city this one was the beneficiary of the largest number of grants and has the largest number of inscriptions. In Kṛishṇadēvarāya's grant of A.D. 1513, reference is made to two car festivals, one in *Phālguṇa* (February-March) and the other in *Vaiśākha* (April-May).[69] In an inscription of A.D. 1543 the *Ūṭi* festival is mentioned.[70] Two years later a grant was made for offerings to god Viṭhala "on the day of *Ratha-saptamī*."[71] In A.D. 1554 the Āravīḍu chief Udayagiri Timmarāju constructed the *uyyāle-maṇḍapa* in which the deity was to be mounted on the swing on a number of auspicious occasions—*Prathama-ēkādaśi* and *Dvadaśi*, five days of *Uyyāle* festival, five days of the *Kōḍe* festival, ten days of the *Tiruvadhyāna*, three days of the *dhvajārohaṇa* of the car festivals, three days of *Śrī-Pushya*, one day of *Rāma-jayantī*, one day of *Narasiṁha-jayantī*, three days of *Kṛishṇa-jayantī*, one day of *Vāmana-jayantī*, etc.[72] His brother, Koṇḍarāja gave an endowment in A.D. 1561 for an additional two days to be added to the ten-day *Tiruvadhyāna* festival instituted by Udayagiri Timmarāju.[73] In A.D. 1559 a rich patron, Nammāḷvār, made provision for taking the deity in procession to the Pārāṅkuśa *maṇḍapa* at the end of the Viṭhala *ratha-vīdhī* on 142 days of the year. In this list of festival days are some festivals or details of celebrations not mentioned in previous records, such as three car-festivals, the *Pavitra* festival, ten days of *Mahānavamī-Vijaya-daśamī, Ugādi, Dīpāvaḷi, Teppa-tirunāḷu Makara-saṅkrānti* and *Tōpu-tirunāḷu*.[74] The inscription of A.D. 1556 from the Tirumaṅgai-āḷvār temple in Viṭhalāpura reveals that the practice of celebrating the birth stars of the *āḷvārs* was in vogue and that on such days the *Prabandham* was recited.[75]

A survey of the inscriptions in the city shows that no temple festivals are mentioned in the pre-sixteenth century epigraphs. During the Tuḷuva period, however, grants were made for the celebration of specific festivals. Consequently, there was an increase in the number of temple festivals. In the Viṭhala temple alone we can trace the tremendous growth in festivals from A.D. 1513 to 1559. In A.D. 1513 there were only two car festivals, while by A.D. 1559 there are three. The impact of the Tamil Śrī-Vaishṇava rituals is evident in the introduction of festivals such as the *Tiruvadhyāna*. Since Śrī-Vaishṇavas received extensive patronage in the city under the Tuḷuvas, it is natural that the majority of references to temple *utsavas* are found in Śrī-Vaishṇava temples.

Following the calendar will make clear how elaborate was the cycle of festivals celebrated in the large temples, especially the Vaishṇava ones. The year began in *Chaitra* (March-April) with *Ugādi*, the New Year of the *Śālivāhana Śaka* era. *Rāmanavamī* fell on the ninth day of the bright fortnight and *Vasantōtsava* on the full moon day of *Chaitra*. In *Vaiśākha* (April-May) was *Narasiṁha-jayantī* on the evening prior to the full moon day. The *Kōḍe-tirunāḷu*, the summer or parasol festival, was possibly celebrated in Jyēshṭa (May-June). The *ēkādaśi* (eleventh day of the bright fortnight) of *Āśāḍha* (June-July) was especially auspicious as the *Śayanōtsava* of Vishṇu. It is known as *Prathama-ēkādaśi* and with it started the *Chatur-māsa* (four months) of Vishṇu's rest.[76] On the eighth day of the dark fortnight of *Śrāvana* (July-August) was *Kṛishṇa-jayantī* or *Gokul-ashṭami*. In the great Śrī-Vaishṇava temples of Tamil Nāḍu, the festival of *Uṛikkaṭṭi* or *Uṛiyaṭi* is on the day after *Kṛishṇa-jayantī*. On this day outside the *gōpura* a four-pillared structure is prepared for keeping the pots of curds and milk, which are to be broken during the rituals.[77] Although *Uṛiyaṭi* or *Uṛikkaṭṭi* is not mentioned in the Vijayanagara inscriptions, it is to be noted that outside the *gōpuras* of the Kṛishṇa and Viṭhala temples there are such four-pillared pavilions; they were possibly used for this ritual.

Vāmana-jayantī fell on the twelfth day of the bright fortnight of *Bhādrapada* (August-September).[78] *Navarātrī* or *Mahānavamī* was celebrated from the first to the ninth day of the bright fortnight of *Āśvina* (September-October), the tenth day being *Vijaya-daśamī*. Dīpāvaḷi, according to the *amānta* system[79] falls on *Āśvina amāvāsya* (the new moon). *Kārtika* (October-November) *ēkādaśi* is also an auspicious day. A fast and vigil is observed on this day and on the next day, the twelfth day of the bright fortnight, the image of Vishṇu is bathed, dressed and taken out in procession. This marks the end of *Chatur-māsa*. The *Dvadaśi* festival mentioned in the inscription, probably, refers to this auspicious twelfth day (also known as *Uthāna-dvadaśi*).

The *Tiruvadhyāna* (or *Adhyayanōtsava*) was in the month of *Mārgaśīrsha* (November-December).[80] The main feature of this festival is the chanting of all the four thousand verses of the *āḷvārs*, the *Divyaprabandham*. The *Śrī-Pushya* festival of the Viṭhala temple and the "sacrificial fire in *Pushya*" of the Rāmachandra temple inscription were obviously celebrated in the month of *Pushya* (December-January). The exact nature of these celebrations is not known. The festival of *Makara-saṅkrānti* fell in the month of *Māgha* (January-February). It must have been celebrated in both the Śaivite and Vaishṇavite temples. *Mahāśivaratrī* fell on the fourteenth day of the dark half of *Māgha*. Although we have no epigraphical references to it, this must have been an important festival in Śaivite temples. *Ratha-saptamī* was celebrated on the seventh day of the bright fortnight of this month. In the Viṭhala temple one of the *Rathōtsavas* was celebrated in *Phālguṇa* (February-March), the last month of the year (besides the car festival in *Vaiśākha* and a third of which the month is not specified). With this the liturgical cycle came to an end.

The exact months in which certain festivals took place are not known. The swing festival can be performed during the *Brahmōtsava* and it is also an independent *utsava* celebrated for three, five, seven or nine days. This is common for Vishṇu and Śiva shrines.[81] The *Tōpu-tirunāḷu* was a garden festival when the deity was taken to a grove or garden and placed in a *maṇḍapa* covered with leaves, flowers, etc. It is not known whether it was a part of any other *utsava* or a separate festival. This *utsava* gained importance from the fourteenth century A.D. onwards.[82] The *Teppa-tirunāḷu* was the float festival when the deity was taken around the temple tank on a raft (*teppa*). This may have been a part of the *Brahmōtsava*, as it is today in the Virūpāksha temple *Rathōtsava*, when it marks the finale of the nine-day rituals, or an independent celebration. *Pavitra* was one of the important festivals in the liturgical cycle of both Vaishṇava and Śaiva temples. It was performed as a penitential *utsava* for all the lapses in worship during the previous year. *Ūṭi* festival, probably, refers to the *dhvajārohaṇa* (auspicious hoisting of the flag) day which marked the commencement of the *Brahmōtsava*. On this day the *dhvaja-staṁbha* was decorated with a new white cloth, *uṭi* (or *uḍi* or *uḍai*) meaning covering with a cloth or dress.[83]

With its elaborated round of rituals and festivals it can be claimed that the "temple was not merely a place of worship; it filled a large place in the cultural and economic life of the people."[84] For "its construction and maintenance offered employment to numbers of architects and craftsmen.... The making of icons in stone and metal gave scope to the talents of the best sculptors.... The daily routine, especially of the larger temples, gave constant employment to numbers of priests, choristers, musicians, dancing-girls, florists, cooks and many other classes of servants. The periodical festivals were occasions marked by fairs... and every other form of popular entertainment. The large endowments in land and cash...tended to make it at once a generous landlord and a banker.... The practice of decorating images, particularly those used during processions, with numerous jewels set with precious stones, encouraged the jeweller's art to a considerable extent...."[85]

Besides the celebration of festivals in the temples, a number of festivals were also celebrated in the city at large. Some of these are noted in the accounts of foreign visitors. Nicolo Conti mentions four festivals—the first when men and women, having bathed, "clad themselves in new garments, and spend three entire days in singing, dancing and feasting," the second when inside and outside the temples "innumerable number of lamps of oil" were fixed, the third "which lasts nine days" and the fourth "during which they sprinkle all passers-by, even the king and queen themselves with saffron-water.... This is received by all with much laughter."[86] Sewell has identified these four as the New Year, *Dīpāvaḷi*, *Mahānavamī* and *Hōḷi*.[87] Sewell cites Paes in supporting that New Year was celebrated in October, probably on the first day of *Kārtika*.[88]

The first of the four festivals mentioned by Nicolo Conti could well have been the New Year festival, which was a three-day celebration.[89] However, it is likely that Paes made a mistake in associating the festival he witnessed in the month of October (*Kārtika*) with New Year. For those following the *Vikrāma* era the New Year falls in *Kārtika*,[90] while the New Year of the *Śaka* year, current in Vijayanagara as seen in inscriptions, is the first day of *Chaitra*,[91] called *Ugādi*. The second festival, which Sewell and even B.A. Saletore[92] have claimed was *Dīpāvaḷi*, should more accurately be called *Kārtikōtsava*,[93] which is performed on the full moon day in the month of *Kārtika*. For on this day the temple precincts and other places are illumined with a large number of lamps. This festival, which is celebrated a fortnight after *Dīvāḷi*, is common to both Vaishṇava and Śaiva shrines.[94]

Of the above two festivals there is no archaeological evidence, except for the one reference to *Ugādi* in an inscription from the Viṭhala temple.[95] But of the next two festivals described by Nicolo Conti there is sufficient archaeological data to back the literary citations.

Mahānavamī-Vijayadaśamī was definitely the most popular festival in the city and the court. This festival is associated with Durgā and her victory over Mahiśāsura. According to one tradition, Rāma won his final victory over Rāvaṇa on *Vijaya-daśamī* day. While another tradition connects the *Mahābhārata* war and the victory of the Pāṇḍavas with this day.[96] *Vijaya-daśamī* was essentially a kshatriya festival and the kings considered it very auspicious to review their armies on that day and keep them ready for battle. The month of *Āśvina* was the best time of the year for military operations—there was plenty of water around for the army, rivers maintained a moderate flow and the roads were dry.[97]

The pomp, pageantry and splendour that characterised the annual court celebration of *Mahānavamī* or *Navarātrī* so overawed foreign visitors to the city that many of them, including Paes[98] and Nuniz,[99] have left vivid descriptions of the festivities. 'Abdur Razzāk has also described a court festival that in some points fits with the accounts of the *Mahānavamī*,[100] but it is doubtful if it was the *Navarātrī* celebration, because the duration (three days) and the date of the celebration described by this Persian ambassador do not tally with those of *Mahānavamī*.[101]

Primarily a religious festival, the *Mahānavamī* celebration in the city was a grand public ritual that had political as well as socio-economic and military overtones. Detailed studies of this festival and its significance, based mainly on the foreign travel accounts, have been given elsewhere,[102] hence it is not undertaken here. So important was the *Mahānavamī* ritual that following the break-up of the Vijayanagara empire the court celebration of this festival was adopted in the states that arose on the ruins of Vijayanagara like Mysore[103] and even minor principalities such as Rāmnaḍ.[104]

There is only one epigraphical mention of *Mahānavamī-Vijayadaśamī*, from the Viṭhala temple,[105] but architectural and sculptural evidence of this festival is available at the site. In the "royal centre" there are a number of platforms. The most magnificent is the so-called

Mahānavamī Dibba or platform (NW d/1), a unique monument constructed in at least three phases (the earliest contemporary with the early history of the city, and the third, probably, of the sixteenth century), with vivid carvings (Plate 9). The sculptures on this platform are of courtly scenes such as hunting, wrestling, dancers, musicians and soldiers. According to Paes, the king watched the brilliant *Mahānavamī* festivities from the top of a platform "served by a kind of staircase of stone beautifully wrought," with "two platforms one above the other, beautifully sculptured, with their sides well made and worked."[106] This description fits well with the *Mahānavamī* Dibba. This platform dominates the "royal centre" by its height and commanding location and is clearly a royal monument and a place of public display which "provided a setting for royal rituals of the greatest importance."[107] It is most likely that it was used for the court celebrations of the *Mahānavamī* festival.

An important sculptural source of information is provided by the friezes of animals and human figures that move in a clockwise direction around three sides of the outer-face of the Rāmachandra temple enclosure wall (Plate 51). At the bottom is a long procession of elephants. Next comes a display of horses, mostly led by grooms, but occasionally with riders. The third is of a military parade of foot-soldiers, others on horseback and some on camels and elephants; here and there wrestlers are also to be seen. The fourth is a display of female dancers and musicians. The topmost or fifth row is of female musicians playing on large drums; occasionally reliefs of Bālakṛishṇa and the *Vasantōtsava* scenes are also found. Here and there, watching these endless processions, is a noble figure seated within a pavilion, evidently the king himself. These fifteenth century sculptures, especially of the first four rows, tally very well with Paes' description of the *Mahānavamī* processions. Hence, we can conclude that this is a sculptural representation of that great yearly celebration. Or course, these carvings pre-date Paes' account by about a century. There must have been, therefore, much continuity in the rituals of the *Mahānavamī*.

The fourth festival described by Nicolo Conti has been identified as *Hōḷi* by Sewell, B.A. Saletore,[108] A.H. Longhurst[109] and others. It is my suggestion that this festival could be more accurately described as *Vasantōtsava*, that fell on the full moon of *Chaitra* (March-April), rather than *Hōḷi*, which is celebrated on the full moon of *Phālguṇa* (February-March). There are no epigraphical references to *Hōḷi*, while literary and archaeological data is available of the celebration of *Vasantōtsava* (spring festival) in the city.[110]

Vasantōtsava centres around the worship of *Kāma* (or Madana or Manmatha), the god of love. After Śiva reduced *Kāma* to ashes, seeing the grief of Ratī, Madana's consort, Śiva relented and agreed that on one day in the year Kāma would reassume his bodily form; *Vasantōtsava* commemorates this day.[111] Kāma-dēva is called Vasanta, the demi-god of the spring season[112] and the commander of his forces is Chaitra.[113] The spring festival connected with Madana was very popular in India from at least the third to the twelfth century A.D.,[114] while *Hōḷi* was celebrated mainly from the fourteenth century onwards.[115] *Vasantōtsava* continued to be celebrated even till the end of the sixteenth century, when *Hōḷi* had already become popular. In course of time, the worship of Madana died out and the great festivity connected with it was transferred to the *Hōḷi* festival.[116]

Jāmbavatīkalyāṇam, a Sanskṛit drama said to be written by Kṛishṇadēvarāya, was enacted before the people assembled to witness the spring-festival (*Vasantōtsava*) of god Virūpāksha.[117] The *Rathōtsava* of Virūpāksha, celebrated on *Chaitra pūrṇima,* coincided with *Vasantōtsava*, therefore the *Chaṁpū* (play) about this car festival is titled *Virūpāksha Vasantōtsava Chaṁpū*. According to this work plays were enacted during the festival.[118] The text provides interesting information concerning the placing of the figures of Kāma and his retinue in the front row of the Virūpāksha temple *ratha*[119] and the throwing of saffron water on the people.[120] Some traces of the *Vasantōtsava* celebration survive to this day in the *Chaitra Rathōtsava* in Haṁpi, such as the throwing of coloured powders.[121]

Sculptural evidences of this festival are also extant. Reliefs of Kāma-dēva, often accompanied by his retinue (Plate 52), are occasionally found: for example on pillars in the south-east corner *maṇḍapa* (Fig.18: M), on the plinths of the north-east corner *maṇḍapa* (Fig. 18: N), the stone chariot (Fig. 18: O) and on the pillars of the *raṅga-maṇḍapa* (Fig. 18 : B) in the Viṭhala complex and also on a pillar in the *maha-raṅga-maṇḍapa* of the Virūpāksha temple (Fig. 12: I). Kāma is shown with his usual sugar-cane bow and is often in a chariot drawn by his *vāhana*, the parrot. That the representations of Kāma are linked with *Vasantōtsava* is proved by a study of the reliefs on the outer-face of the Rāmachandra temple enclosure wall. On the topmost frieze there is a depiction of Kāma and his retinue on the east side and close by, on the north side, are shown a man and some women throwing (coloured) water on each other; tubes for squirting are clearly discernible in the hands of some of these women. Such scenes are found elsewhere, too. On the Mahānavamī Platform there are reliefs showing figures playing with water, associated with *Vasantōtsava*, such as on the south side steps (third frieze from the top), belonging to the earliest phase of this monument (Plate 10). A fine depiction of such a scene on a chlorite slab of the third phase of this platform is included in some of the early writings on Vijayanagara history.[122] This slab is, unfortunately, no longer *in situ*. These sculptures on the *Mahānavamī* Dibba prove that the festival was popular in the city throughout the Vijayanagara period.

The finest representation of the *Vasantōtsava* celebration is in the Vishṇu temple within the "royal centre" (NS 1/1), near the Siṅghārada Hebbāgilu. In the central part of its *raṅga-maṇḍapa* the ceiling is raised with horizontal slabs resting on the pillars. On these are carved eight panels of *Vasantōtsava* reliefs of women, occasionally with a man in the centre, engaged in playing with water; a water-squirt is shown in the hands of one woman, while the others are taking water out of big containers with small cups or with their cupped hands. Twice a figure standing or seated in a tub is shown. The presence of a male musician, a female dancer and of a hunchbacked clown holding a water-squirt highlight the lighthearted fun and merriment that marked this festival.

The *Mahānavamī* celebration was a dazzling yet solemn religious spectacle, with political and military overtones with the king at the centre as a dignified ritualist. *Vasantōtsava*, on the other hand, was a boisterous celebration, the king and commoner rubbing shoulders in the free-for-all play with coloured water, the enjoyment of dramas and the pulling of the Virūpāksha temple *ratha*.

Dance and music were essential elements both of the celebrations in temples and of the public rituals and festivals. Foreign visitors to Vijayanagara have left lengthy descriptions of the female dancers and their role in temple services and processions (Paes[123]) and also in the city and court festivals ('Abdur Razzāk,[124] Paes[125] and Nuniz[126]). Paes, the Portuguese visitor to the court of Kṛishṇadēvarāya, even describes in detail the hall where women of the royal household were taught dancing.[127] From these accounts it appears that there were two groups of dancers, those attached to the temples and those attached to the court. However, these groups were not mutually exclusive. Temple dancers were probably also required to participate in the *Mahānavamī* ceremonies at court. This was the practice in some south Indian princely states even in more recent times.[128]

Since extensive accounts of dance and the *dēvadāsi* system in Vijayanagara, based mainly on the accounts of the foreign travellers, are on record,[129] there is no need here to go into those details. This account, hence, deals primarily with the additional information available from the archaeological sources. Inscriptional references to dancers in the city are few (see note 16). However, some epigraphs from Tirumalai-Tirupati provide evidence of the existence of proficient dancers in the capital, for Achyutarāya sent a number of dancers from his capital to serve god Veṅkaṭēśa. Among these was Muddu-kuppāyi, deputed by the king to Tirupati in A.D. 1531.[130] A record registering a gift of money by Hanumasāni for offerings to Veṅkaṭēśa in A.D. 1540, states that she was one among the temple dancers who had been sent by the king.[131]

Apart from the dances performed before the *mūla* and *utsava-mūrtis* during the rituals and festivals, there were also halls especially constructed for music and dance performances within the temples. A Telugu inscription of A.D. 1545 from the Mādhava temple (NR t/2) proves this. It records the construction of the *raṅga-maṇḍapa* for holding dance and both vocal and instrumental music recitals in this temple.[132] The large sixteenth century pillared halls in the Virūpāksha (Fig. 12: D), Viṭhala (Fig. 18: H), Mālyavanta Raghunātha (Fig. 16: C), Tiruveṅgaḷanātha (Fig. 19: A) and Paṭṭābhirāma temples were probably also meant for dance and music. These halls are built at three levels. The topmost level, enclosed on three sides, is a stage with an open area in the centre. The central portion, at a lower level, also has an open space in the middle. The front part is at a still lower level. In these halls, especially in the hundred-pillared hall in the Viṭhala temple and the hall in the Virūpāksha complex, there are many reliefs of dancers.

The numerous sculptural depictions of dancers in the temples and elsewhere reveal that two types of dances were in vogue in the city: the *mārga,* or the complex and strictly codified classical dance, and the *dēśi* or folk dances that reflect the regional and local variations. Some of the sculptures of dancers show them in the elaborate *karaṇas* of the first mode. Of the second variety is the *kolāṭam* or stick-dance. Nicolo Conti has described the stick-dance in the city in the early fifteenth century.[133] The early seventeenth century Italian traveller Pietro della Valle's graphic description of this form of dance in Ikkeri[134] proves that it was widely popular. Some of the finest friezes of the *kōlaṭam* are on the outer-face of the enclosure wall of the Rāmachandra temple and on the earliest phase of the Mahānavamī Platform. The reliefs show pairs of dancers beating their sticks in *karihasta* and *svastikahasta,* the staffs meeting at the head and knee levels (Plates 10 and 51). The pattern is repeated by other pairs. All these couples are self-sufficient in themselves and yet form a group composition.[135] Alongside the *kōlaṭam* dancers there are also reliefs of classical dancers. This is true not only of these sculptures of the early Vijayanagara period, but also of representations of dance in the sixteenth century monuments. Thus, the *mārga* and *dēśi* coexisted and were mutually complementary.[136]

A study of the sculptures also reveals the variations in costumes of the dancing girls. In the early phase (e.g. the Rāmachandra temple frieze and the reliefs on the first phase of the Mahānavamī Platform) the female dancers wear long, loose skirts reaching the ankles. The skirts of the dancing girls depicted in the carvings of the third phase of the Mahānavamī Platform and the sixteenth century temples are shorter, ending just below the knees and are pleated or extremely flared. The coiffures of the sixteenth century dancers are heavy and their jewellery elaborate.

Apart from the female dancers, the presence of male dancers is attested by the sculptures. Among the most common representations are those of male folk dancers who hold either fly-whisks or small frame-drums in their hands.

The dancers are often accompanied by instrumentalists, some of whom are also shown in dancing attitudes. Both male and female instrumentalists are to be seen in sculptures playing a variety of musical instruments. An inscription from the Viṭhala temple[137] supports the sculptural evidence of the employment of both female and male dancers and musicians.

Sculptures reveal that a wide variety of musical instruments were in use. The drums are of different types, broad in the centre and tapering towards the sides and narrow in the centre and wide at the ends. Both these are bifacial and are slung around the neck (Fig. 21: 1 & 3). There is also the large monofacial drum, narrow at the base and wide at the top (Fig. 21: 2). Usually this drum was played with hands, although sticks were also used at times. There was also a small round, portable frame-drum, that looks like a tambourine (Fig. 21: 4). It was beaten by hand. Among the string instrument, the most common was the single-string lute with a cup-shaped resonator (Fig. 21: 12) or a disc-shaped resonator. Among the wind instruments were the flute (Fig. 21: 5), the horn (Fig. 21: 8), a large trumpet-like instrument (Fig. 21: 7), the conch (Fig. 21: 6) and a narrow, wooden wind instrument (Fig. 21: 9). Percussion instruments such as cymbals (Fig. 21: 11) and wooden clappers (Fig. 21: 10) are also represented.

Vocal music was greatly encouraged and developed in the city from the time of the great Vidyāraṇya onwards. The Haridāsas have made a special contribution to the development of Karṇāṭak music. Lakshmī-nārāyana, the author of *Saṅgīta-sūryōdaya,* who served at the court of Kṛishṇadēvarāya, helped towards systematising Karṇāṭak music. Aḷiya Rāmarāya is also said to have been a great patron of music. The development of vocal music in Vijayanagara has been discussed elsewhere.[138] Since little archaeological evidence is available about vocal music it is outside the scope of this book.

The incessant round of festivals and rituals in the temples, the exuberant celebration of public festivals and the lively accompaniment of dance and music that added colour to both were integral aspects of life in the city. These demonstrate the vigour and vitality of religious life in Vijayanagara.

Notes

[1] *SII* IX, pt. II, no. 607.

[2] *SII* IV, no. 250.

[3] Ibid., no. 245.

[4] Ibid., no. 255.

[5] The *sthānika* is referred to in *ARIE* of 1975-76, no. 108. *Sthānikas* are also mentioned in *ARSIE* of 1977-78, no. 89 and B.R. Gopal, *Vijayanagara Inscriptions*, vol. I, no. 413.

[6] *EC* XI, Cl. 54.

[7] *SII* IV, nos. 245, 250, 255; *SII* IX, pt. II, nos. 564 and 607.

[8] *SII* IV, no. 250.

[9] *SII* IX, pt. II, no. 607.

[10] *SII* IV, nos. 254 and 255.

[11] *SII* IX, pt. II, no. 564.

[12] The information regarding the nature of the services peformed by some of these ritual specialists was provided by Drs. B.R. Gopal and K.K.A. Venkatachari by personal communication.

[13] *SII* IV, no. 280; *SII* IX, pt. II, no. 564 and 607.

[14] *SII* IX, pt. II, nos. 653 and 678.

[15] Ibid., no. 668.

[16] Ibid., nos. 607 and 668.

[17] Ibid., nos. 668 and 678.

[18] *SII* IX, pt. II, nos. 490, 491, 493; *SII* IV, nos. 253, 273 and 278.

[19] *SII* IX, pt. II, nos. 654 and 678.

[20] *SII* IV, no. 280.

[21] S.V. Padigar, "The Cult of Vishṇu in Karnataka", (Ph.D. diss.), p. 269.

[22] *SII* IX, pt. II, nos. 616, 653, 668, etc.

[23] *SII* IV, no. 265.

[24] *SII* IX, pt. II, no. 607; *SII* IV, no. 250.

[25] *SII* IX, pt. II, no. 668.

[26] *SII* IV, no. 250.

[27] *SII* IX, pt. II, no. 678; *SII* IV, no. 280.

[28] *SII* IV, no. 275.

[29] *SII* IX, pt. II, no. 678.

[30] *SII* IV, no. 263.

[31] *SII* IX, pt. II, no. 678 and *SII* IV, no. 280.

[32] *SII* IX, pt. II, no. 653; *SII* IV, no. 250.

[33] e.g. *SII* IX, pt. II, no. 653.

[34] *SII* IV, nos. 273 and 278. However, in these two records of the same grant there seems to be some discrepancy. While the first notes that 300 cows were given, the second refers to only 200 cows.

[35] *SII* IX pt. II, no. 654; *SII* IV, no. 250.

[36] *SII* IX, pt. II, nos. 566, 654; *SII* IV, no. 250.

[37] *SII* IX, pt. II, no. 493.

[38] Ibid., no. 491.

[39] *SII* IV, no. 266.

[40] Ibid., no. 253.

[41] *SII* IX, pt. II, no. 607; *SII* IV, no. 277.

[42] *SII* IX, pt. II, no. 564.

[43] Ibid., no. 668.

[44] *Saṅkramaṇa* or *saṅkrānti* is the day on which the sun enters a fresh zodiacal sign. There are twelve of these *saṅkrāntis*. Four of them correspond with the equinoxes and the *solstices*.

[45] *MAR* of 1933, p. 181.

[46] F.H. Gravely and T.N. Ramachandran, *The Three Main Styles of Temple Architecture Recognised by the Silpa Sāstras*, Preface, pp. vi-vii.

[47] *SII* IX, pt. II, no. 493.

[48] *Makara-saṅkrānti* is the first day of the solar month '*makara*.' On this day, according to the Hindu calendar, the sun heads north, heralding longer days and shorter nights. For details see P.V. Kane, *History of Dharma-śāstras*, vol. V, pt. I, pp. 221-224.

[49] P. Sreenivasachar, "Polipadu grant of Kṛishṇa-dēvaraya," *JAHRS*, 10, pp. 121-142.

[50] *EC* IV, Gu. 1.

[51] For the dating of this Sanskṛit work see chapter IV, note 31.

[52] R.S. Panchamukhi, Introduction to *Virūpāksha Vasantōtsava Champū*, p.i.

[53] V. Raghavan, "The Virūpākṣa Vasantōtsava Campū of Ahobala," *JOR*, XIV, p. 27.

[54] Ibid., p. 31.

[55] Ibid., p. 32.

[56] Ibid., p. 18, p. 30, etc.

[57] Ibid., p. 23.

[58] "Archaeology of Belāri District," *IA*, II, p. 179.

[59] A.A. Shapiro, "The Kalyanotsava of Pampadevi and Pampapati." Mimeographed.

[60] D.D. Hudson, "Two Citrā Festivals in Madurai," in *Religious Festivals in South India and Sri Lanka*, ed. G.R. Welbon and G.E. Yocum, pp. 101-156; W.T. Elmore, *Dravidian Gods in Hinduism*, pp. 84-85.

[61] D.D. Hudson, op.cit., p. 140.

[62] D. Kotecha, "Hindu Ritual Movement: Study of Sri Virupaksha Temple, Humpi", (Diss.), pp. 77-79.

[63] *SII* IV, no. 266.

[64] *FE*, p. 255 and p. 262.

[65] *SII* IV, no. 250.

[66] *SII* IV, nos. 254 and 255.

[67] Ibid., no. 262.

[68] *SII* IX, pt. II, no. 564.

[69] *SII* IV, nos. 273 and 278.

[70] *SII* IX, pt. II, no. 607.

[71] Ibid., no. 616.

[72] Ibid., no. 653.

[73] *SII* IV, no. 275.

[74]*SII* IX, pt. II, no. 668.

[75]*SII* IV, no. 280.

[76]H. Daniel Smith, "Festivals in Pāñcarātra Literature," in *Religious Festivals in South India and Sri Lanka*, eds. G.R. Welbon and G.E. Yocum, pp. 32-33; see also P.V. Kane, op.cit., vol. V, pt. I, p. 109.

[77]V. Parthasarathy, "Evolution of Rituals in Viṣṇu Temple Utsavas (with special reference to Śrīraṅgam, Tirumala and Kāñci)", (Ph.D. Diss.), pp. 568-570.

[78]P.V. Kane, op.cit., vol. V, pt. I, p. 404.

[79]According to the *amānta* system, which prevails in south India, the lunar month is reckoned between successive new moons. According to the *pūrṇimānta* system, prevalent in north India, the month ends with the full moon. The two systems share the same month's name only during the bright fortnights. Thus, according to the *pūrṇimānta* system, *Dīvalī* is said to fall on *Kārtika amāvāsya*. It must be emphasised that the actual observances take place on the same new moon throughout India, regardless of the fact that the fortnight falls in different months according to the two systems. For details of the *amānta/pūrṇimānta* systems see Karen L. Merrey, "The Hindu Festival Calendar"," in *Religious Festivals in South India and Sri Lanka*, eds. G.R. Welbon and G.E. Yocum, pp. 1-8.

[80]V. Parthasarathy, op.cit., p. 355.

[81]Ibid., p. 585.

[82]Ibid., pp. 536-538.

[83]Dr. B.R. Gopal, personal communication.

[84]K.A. Nilakanta Sastri, *A History of South India: From Prehistoric Times to the Fall of Vijayanagara*, p. 314.

[85]Ibid.

[86]Nicolo Conti, *India in the Fifteenth Century*, ed. R.H. Major, p. 28.

[87]FE, pp. 85-86.

[88]Ibid., pp. 281-282 and p. 141.

[89]Abbé Dubois, *Hindu Manners, Customs and Ceremonies*, p. 567.

[90]P. Thomas, *Epics, Myths and Legends of India*, p. 93.

[91]P.B. Desai (ed.), *A History of Karnataka*, pp. 87-88.

[92]*Soc. & Pol. Life*, vol. II, p. 387.

[93]T.V. Mahalingam, *Administration and Social Life in Vijayanagar*, pt. II, p. 242.

[94]V. Parthasarathy, op.cit., p. 579.

[95]*SII* IX, pt. II, no. 668.

[96]K. Sarojini Devi, "Religion in Vijayanagara", (Ph.D. Diss.), pp. 401-405.

[97]Ibid., p. 405.

[98]FE, pp. 262-275.

[99]Ibid., pp. 376-379.

[100]ʿAbdur Razzāk, *India in the Fifteenth Century*, ed. R.H. Major, pp. 35-38.

[101]Sewell, *FE*, pp. 93-94; T.V. Mahalingam, op.cit., pt. II, p. 240.

[102]To cite just a few: *Soc. & Pol. Life*, vol. II, pp. 372-386; T.V. Mahalingam, op.cit., pt. II, pp. 48-49, 238-241; Burton Stein, "Mahānavamī: Medieval and Modern Kingly Ritual in South India," in *All the King's Mana: Papers on Medieval History*, pp. 302-326; Burton Stein, *Peasant State and Society in Medieval South India*, pp. 384-392.

[103]See B. Ramakrishna Rao, "The Dasara Celebrations in Mysore," *QJMS*, IX, pp. 301-309; C. Hayavadana Rao, *The Dasara in Mysore : Its Origin and Significance*.

[104]Carol Appadurai Breckenridge, "From Protector to Litigant: Changing Relations between Hindu Temples and the Raja of Ramnad," in *South Indian Temples*, ed. Burton Stein, pp. 75-105.

[105]*SII* IX, pt. II, no. 668.

[106]*FE*, p. 264.

[107]G. Michell, "The 'Royal Centre' and the Great Platform at Vijayanagara," in *Rupa Pratirupa : Alice Boner Commemoration Volume*, ed. B. Baumer, p. 113.

[108]*Soc. & Pol. Life*, vol. II, pp. 396-397.

[109]A.H. Longhurst, *Hampi Ruins*, pp. 65-66.

[110]However, it must be noted that in *Jaiminīya-nyayamālā-vistara*, a commentary by Madhavāchārya, the two festivals seem to be considered as one ("*Vasantōtsavo holāka*"); quoted in P.V. Kane, *History of Dharmaśāstra*, vol. V, pt. 1, p. 237, footnote 610.

This, to the best of my knowledge, is the only reference to Hōḷi in Vijayanagara literature. Besides, even here Hōḷi is stated to be identical with *Vasantōtsava*. Thus, it is the latter that is emphasised.

[111]M.S. Sarma, *History of the Reddi Kingdoms: circa 1325 A.D. to circa 1448 A.D.*, pp. 354-355.

[112]*Pampamahatmya*, first part, chapter 90.

[113]Ibid.

[114]N.K. Basu, "The Spring Festival in India," *Man in India*, VII, p. 145.

115. S.S. Mehta, "Holika Celebration," *Journal of the Anthropological Society of Bombay*, X, p. 31.

[116]N.K. Basu, loc.cit.

[117]*Sources*, p. 142.

[118]V. Raghavan, op.cit., p. 32.

[119]R.S. Panchamukhi, op.cit., p. xii,

[120]V. Raghavan, op.cit., p. 35.

[121]A.A. Shapiro, op.cit.

[122]A.H. Longhurst, op.cit., p. 65, Fig. 24; *Soc. & Pol. Life*, vol. II, p. 396; H. Heras, "Seven Days at Vijayanagara," *JIH*, IX, Plate IV- 2, opposite p. 109.

[123]*FE*, pp. 241-242 and p. 262.

[124]ʿAbdur Razzāk, op.cit., pp. 36-37.

[125]*FE*, p. 270.

[126]Ibid., p. 379.

[127]Ibid., pp. 288-289.

[128]K.K. Pillay, *The Śucīndram Temple*, p. 285.

[129] e.g.*Soc. & Pol. Life*, vol. II, pp. 408-412; T.V. Mahalingam, op.cit., pt. II, pp. 43-47 and pp. 72-78.

[130]*TTDES* IV, no. 11.

[131]Ibid., no. 142.

[132]*SII* IV, no. 248.

[133]Nicolo Conti, op.cit., p. 29.

[134]Pietro della Valle, *The Travels of Pietro Della Valle in India*, vol. II, p. 257.

[135]K. Vatsyayan, *Classical Indian Dance in Literature and the Arts*, p. 360.

[136]K. Vatsyayan, *Dance in Indian Painting*, p. 48.

[137]*SII* IX, pt. II, no. 668.

[138]*Soc. & Pol. Life*, vol. II, pp. 412-415; P.S. Sundaram Iyer, "Sri Vidyaranya and Music," in *VSCV*, pp. 333-342; H. Krishnacharya, "Music under the Vijayanagara Empire," in *VSCV*, pp. 367-375; K.R. Basavaraja, *History and Culture of Karnataka*, pp. 649-652 etc.

CHAPTER 9

Ascetics, Maṭhas and Agrahāras

Religion in Vijayanagara was propagated by *gurus* and other ascetics, large numbers of whom either resided in the city or visited it. Religious institutions such as *maṭhas* and *agrahāras* also promoted the cause of religion and served as centres of religious activity and learning.

1. Gurus and Ascetics

In Hinduism *gurus* and ascetics play a prominent role in the lives of the devout of the different sects and sub-sects. All the religious schools are agreed that the one who has the authority to initiate others is the *guru*, as a rule a brāhmaṇa (but among the Śaivas and in some Vaishṇava communities also members of other castes), who is often regarded as representing God himself. The Śrī-Vaishṇavas even believe him to be a visible, partial incarnation of God. The importance of *dīkshā* (initiation) of the devotee into the sect by a qualified *guru* is emphasised in both Vaishṇavism and Śaivism.[1]

In the city there were *gurus* and ascetics belonging to the Advaita or Smārta sect, and to different Śaivite sects such as the Kāḷāmukhas (in the fourteenth and early fifteenth centuries) and the Vīraśaivas, as also to Vaishṇavite sects such as the Mādhvas and Śrī-Vaishṇavas. On the reliefs of the pillars throughout the temples a vast variety of ascetic figures appear. They are depicted in different poses (including some complicated *yōgic* ones), at times holding a staff or a pot or a rosary, with varied headdresses and costumes. However, since they are represented in a stereotyped manner, it is almost impossible to group them according to sects and sub-sects. Unfortunately, apart from these reliefs, the monuments provide little evidence of the presence and activities of the ascetics in the capital. Therefore, we have to rely mainly on epigraphical data and corroborating literary references.

Advaita (Smārta) monks were definitely an important group in the city. There was a close relationship between the Vijayanagara rulers and the Śṛiṅgēri Advaita *maṭha*. As seen in Chapter 1, the sage Vidyāraṇya (the head of this *maṭha* from A.D. 1375 to 1386) according to one tradition was associated with the founding of the city and the empire. However, this is based on late texts and spurious records; epigraphical evidence shows that Vidyāraṇya became highly influential only during the reign of Harihara II.[2] Although there are many Vijayanagara inscriptions revealing the strong links between the Vijayanagara rulers, especially the Saṅgamas, and the Śṛiṅgēri *maṭha*[3] there are few that refer to the presence of any monk of that *maṭha* in the city. One epigraph in the possession of the Śṛiṅgēri *maṭha* dated A.D. 1380-81 states that Bukka I got a *Śrīmukha* (letter from a *guru*) from the head of the *maṭha* to Vidyāraṇya, who was at the time in Vāraṇāsi, asking him to come to the capital. Bukka despatched the letter along with a request of his own. Accordingly, Vidyāraṇya came back to Vijayanagara and after a short stay returned to Śṛiṅgēri.[4] One of the panels of paintings on the ceiling of the *mahā-raṅga-maṇḍapa* of the Virūpāksha temple is of a *guru* being carried in procession in a palanquin, attended by many followers. Popular tradition identifies this ascetic as the great sage Vidyāraṇya.[5] In the so-called Vidyāraṇya-svāmi *maṭha* behind Virūpāksha temple, is an image of Vidyāraṇya seated cross-legged with one hand in the *vyākhyāna-mudrā* and with a book in the other hand. This, however, is a modern statue.[6] In the city there are no Vijayanagara sculptures that can be conclusively identified as that of Vidyāraṇya.

An inscription of A.D. 1515 records that Vidyāraṇya-voḍeya (a disciple of Purushōttma Bhāratī II) from the Śrīṅgēri *maṭha* came to Vijayanagara "to give audience to the king" and that he "camped in the *maṭha* at Hampe"[7] (i.e., the Vidyāraṇya-svāmi *maṭha*, a branch of the Śṛiṅgēri *maṭha*). According to tradition there was an unbroken succession of *āchāryas* in this *maṭha* throughout the Vijayanagara period, from the late fourteenth onwards.[8] However, in the absence of corroborating archaeological data we cannot accept this tradition as definitive.

In Vijayanagara, besides the Smārta monks associated with the Śṛiṅgēri *maṭha*, there must have been other Advaita ascetics. Besides the Vidyāraṇya-svāmi *maṭha*, the Chintāmaṇi *maṭha* in Ānegoṅdi was another centre of Advaitism.

The Kāḷāmukha Kriyāśakti *gurus* were very influential in the court during the rule of the early Saṅgamas, that is from mid-fourteenth to early fifteenth century A.D. During the reign of Bukka I, in the Sanskṛit work *Madhurāvijayam* the royal poetess Gaṅgā-dēvī pays obeisance to *guru* Kriyāśakti, who is evidently the family preceptor.[9] A copper-plate grant of A.D. 1378 indicates that Kriyāśakti was the *kula-guru* of king Harihara II.[10] Another record of the same king of A.D. 1379 refers to Kriyāśakti as the *rāja-guru*.[11] Two epigraphs, dated A.D. 1398 and 1399, mention *rāja-rāja-guru-pitāmaha* Kriyāśaktidēva.[12] In records of A.D. 1410 Kriyāśakti is referred to as the *guru* of both Dēvarāya I[13] and of his son Vijaya-Bhūpati.[14] In the fourteenth century inscriptions the names of two Kriyāśakti preceptors, Kāśivilāsa[15] and Vāṇivilāsa[16], appear. A third Kriyāśakti *guru*, Chandrabhūshana, was present in the court of Dēvarāya II.[17] No more is heard of these Kāḷāmukha *gurus* after the reign of Dēvarāya II.

Thus, for approximately a hundred years the Kāḷāmukha ascetics were prominent in the court as *rāja-gurus* and therefore must have been generally resident in the capital. However, the data supplied by the epigraphical and literary sources of the influential role played by the Kriyāśaktis is not backed by any evidences from the monuments. For neither are there traces of *maṭhas* or hermitages of these ascetics nor of any sculptural representation of them in Vijayanagara. There is only one inscription found in the city itself referring to the Kāḷāmukha *gurus*. It is engraved on a boulder west of Hēmakūṭa and south-west of the Virūpāksha temple. Dated A.D. 1390, it records the construction of a well by Bhaktara Nāgappa, a disciple of Kriyāśakti-vōḍeya.[18]

The Kāḷāmukha sect was absorbed by the reformist Vīraśaiva religion. The Vīraśaivas or Liṅgāyats became influential in the city in the later Saṅgama period. According to one school of thought, Dēvarāya II and his successors belonged to this sect. Dēvarāya II is said to have patronised Liṅgāyat *gurus* and during this period some Vīraśaivas, such as general Lakkaṇṇa and Chamarasa, rose high in state service.[19] The Vīraśaivas greatly revere the *gurus* and ascetics of their sect. Every Liṅgāyat must have a *guru* who initiates him into the faith and guides him and he must be attached to a *maṭha*.[20] Besides the *gurus*, the itinerant Vīraśaiva ascetics called *jaṅgamas* are also venerated. For the Vīraśaiva the triad comprising the *guru*, the *liṅga* and the *jaṅgama* are extremely important.[21]

In Vijayanagara there must have been both the Vīraśaiva *gurus*, settled in *maṭhas*, and the *jaṅgamas* who visited the city from time to time. Virūpāksha Paṇḍita, the author of the *Chennabasava Purāṇa*, the famous late sixteenth century Vīraśaiva hagiographical work, was the disciple of a *guru* who resided in the Hiriya-maṭha in Vijayanagara (NL w/4).[22] An undated inscription from the city mentions a great ascetic named Sadāśiva and his disciple Kāmayya Peddiga, son of Kariya Basavaṇṇoḍeya.[23] Probably, he was a Vīraśaiva *guru*. Another undated inscription records a gift of land to Somiyadēva-ayya, a *jaṅgama*.[24] A well known Viraśaiva teacher was Emmēbasavēndra who had his headquarters at Jaṁbunātha hill (south of Hospēṭ) and a *maṭha* at Kuṁbhakōṇam. He was the author of a well known *Kālajñāna* (prophetic work). It would seem that he lived during the reign of Kṛishṇadēvarāya, who unsuccessfully endeavoured to put him down.[25] This *guru* was the recipient of the grant of a village made in A.D.1543 by Salakarāja-Chikka-Tirumala, the brother-in-law of Achyutarāya.[26] A copper-plate grant recording the gift of a village by Veṅkaṭa II in A.D. 1612 to the Vīraśaiva ascetic of the Haṁpe-maṭha at Bukkasāgara (a place near Vijayanagara),[27] reveals that the Vīrśaivas continued to be active in the area even after A.D.1565. Except for these few epigraphical and literary references we have little information about the numerous Vīraśaiva ascetics who must have been active in Vijayanagara.

Among the temple pillar-reliefs, sculptures of a type of ascetic in strange garb recur frequently. The garment is a sort of slipover that covers the body, including the arms, from the neck down the knees. One scholar has suggested that these reliefs might by representations of Vīraśaiva *jaṅgamas.*[28]

In the *Pampamahatmya,* the *sthaḷa-purāṇa* of Pampā-kshētra, different Śaivite sects and ascetics belonging to them are described, such as the Śaivas, Pāśupatas, Kāḷāmukhas and Mahāvratas. In the last category are included the Kāpāḷikas and the Jaṅgamas.[29] The extreme penances performed by the Śaiva ascetics are vividly described in this text. Some *yōgis* stood on one leg, others had both arms raised, others stood on their toes, some sat naked in the midst of five fires. While some survived only on water, others lived on air! Some of these ascetics covered themselves with sacred ash, while others applied it only on their foreheads. Some had their hair tied together to form one great knot, others had three, five or several braids of hair, while still others had their hair left untied and free.[30] This description fits well with the sculptural representations of Śaivite ascetics in the city.

Among the Śaivite ascetics in Vijayanagara there may have been some *yōgis* belonging to the Nātha *sampradāya,* who were proficient in *Hatha-yōga.* During this period the *nāthas* were to be found in coastal Karṇāṭaka and in the Āndhra country.[31] Although there are neither epigraphical references to them in the city, nor is it possible to specifically identify any of the *yōgis* depicted in the reliefs as *nāthas,* the numerous sculptural representations of one of the founders of this sect, Matsyēndranātha or Mīnanātha—occasionally shown with the slit ear-lobes and large earrings typical of the *kānphaṭas* or *nāthas,* in both the Śaivite and Vaishṇavite temples—indicate that the *nāthas* were probably to be found in the city (Plate 53).[32]

In addition to the Śaivite ascetics, Vaishṇavite *gurus* and sages also came to Vijayanagara in large numbers, including many Mādhva ascetics. In those days, as now, great spiritual teachers appear to have arranged that their last resting places or *samādhis* should be where they had the most support.[33] At the site there are *samādhis* or *bṛindāvanas* of eleven Mādhva saints, whose activities cover a span of three centuries from approximately A.D. 1324 to 1623,[34] that is from pre-Vijayanagara to the post-Vijayanagara times. Even in the present day, the followers of these saints observe their memorial days, when they gather in large numbers at their *samādhis.* Nine of these saints are buried at Nava-bṛindāvana, an island in the Tuṅgabhadrā near Ānegoṇdi; two are buried within the limits of the city proper.

It is traditionally believed that Madhvāchārya, near the end of his life, had appointed eight monks for the conduct of the worship of Kṛishṇa at the *maṭha* founded by him at Uḍipi. These became the precursors of the *Ashṭamaṭhas* (of Uḍipi) of later times. It is, however, the *maṭhas* represented by another group of four disciples of Mādhva—Padmanābha, Narahari, Mādhava and Akshobhya—and continued by Jayatīrtha and his successors that made the greatest contribution to the propagation of Mādhvaism.[35] In about A.D. 1412 the main ascetic line, descended from Jayatīrtha, branched off into two, the younger of which was subjected to a further split in about A.D. 1435. These three branches are now known as the Vyāsarāya *maṭha,* the Rāghavēndra-svāmi *maṭha* and the Uttarādi *maṭha.*[36] Thus, during the Vijayanagara period there were three important lines of Mādhva ascetics. Some of the spiritual heads of these *maṭhas* lived and died in the capital, the most famous of them being Vyāsarāya.

One of the foremost disciples of Madhvāchārya, Padmanābha Tīrtha, came to Ānegoṇdi, where he died in A.D. 1324 and was buried in Nava-bṛindāvana. Narahari Tīrtha followed Padmanābha as the head of this spiritual line. To him is attributed the origin of the Haridāsa movement. He died in A.D.1333 and was buried on a small island in the Tuṅgabhadrā, north of Viṭhalāpura (NC m/3). Besides Padmanābha, the other Mādhva *gurus* whose *samādhis* are at Nava-bṛindāvana are Kavindra (d., A.D. 1399), Vāgisa (d., A.D. 1404), Vyāsarāya (d., A.D. 1539), Śrīnivāsa and Rāmatīrtha who followed Vyāsarāya as heads of his *maṭha,* Raghuvarya of the Uttarādi *maṭha* (d., A.D. 1557) and Sudhīndra of the Rāghavēndra-svāmi *maṭha* (d., A.D. 1623). The ninth is Gōvinda, who did not hold any pontifical office but was a devoted disciple of Vyāsarāya.[37]

During the time when Vyāsarāya was at the height of his spiritual influence in Vijayanagara, a number of Mādhva ascetics made their way to the city. Among them, besides Raghuvarya of the Uttarādi *maṭha*, was Raghunandana of the Rāghavēndra-svāmi *maṭha*. He died in A.D.1533 in Vijayanagara and his *bṛindāvana* (NG n/1) is in the "sacred centre" (Plate 55). Opposite this *bṛindāvana* is the unique four-armed image of Hanumān.

Undoubtedly the greatest Mādhva sage to reside in Vijayanagara was Vyāsarāya or Vyāsatīrtha, a contemporary of Sāḷuva Narasiṁha and the Tuḷuva rulers down to Achyutarāya. He attended their courts and was, in a sense, the guardian saint of the empire. Vijayanagara was his main base from about A.D. 1499 till his death in A.D. 1539.[38] There are numerous inscriptions from different parts of the empire that attest to Krishnadēvarāya's special devotion to this *guru*.[39] *Śrī Vyāsayōgicharitam* by Sōmanātha provides, possibly with some exaggeration, a picture of Vyāsarāya's influence at the court. Archaeological data of his presence in the city, besides his *bṛindāvana*, is supplied by two inscriptions in the Viṭhala temple. In the first, of Kṛishṇadēvarāya dated A.D.1513, three shares of the food offerings are assigned to *guru* Vyāsarāya.[40] The second,[41] of Achyutarāya's reign dated A.D. 1532, records the installation of Yōga-Varada-Narasiṁha in the courtyard of the Viṭhala temple by Vyāsatīrtha. These prove that Vyāsarāya was actively engaged in his spiritual ministry in Vijayanagara during the reigns of Kṛishṇadēvarāya and Achyutarāya.

Another Mādhva sage who might have lived for some time in the capital was Vijayīndra, who belonged to the Rāghavēndra-svāmi *maṭha*. According to tradition, he was a disciple of Vyāsarāya.[42] The *Rāghavēndravijaya* by Nārāyaṇa mentions that Vijayīndra was honoured by Rāmarāya with *ratnābishekam* (bathing with jewels) for his scholarship.[43] But, there is no archaeological data available at the site about this *guru*.

Among the Mādhva ascetics, a special place of honour belongs to the *bhakta* poet saints known as the Haridāsas. Since these Haridāsas were particularly devoted to Viṭhala, Vijayanagara was frequented by them and some even lived here. The first of the Haridāsas was Narahari Tīrtha, who lived and died in the city. The next important saint of this line was Śrīpadarāja, who was followed by Vyāsarāya. Vyāsarāya greatly popularised this movement and some of the greatest of the Haridāsas—Purandaradāsa, Kanakadāsa and Vadirāja—were his disciples.[44] Hence, these poet saints must have spent some time in Vijayanagara. Of Purandaradāsa, it is claimed that in his old age he returned to Vijayanagara and lived there,[45] till a few months before his death in A.D. 1564. Purandaradāsa is said to have composed 4,75,000 songs; his contribution to music is invaluable.[46] Although the Haridāsas are believed to have been very active in Vijayanagara till its destruction and many of Purandaradāsa's *kīrtanas* are said to have been composed here, yet there is practically no archaeological data available about them at the site. It is true that local tradition identifies a *maṇḍapa* (NG e/1) near the river, not far from the Viṭhala temple, as the *maṇḍapa* of Purandaradāsa. However, there is no archaeological evidence to back this assumption. On one pillar in this *maṇḍapa* there is sculpture of the saint; but this is obviously a modern carving.

During the Sāḷuva and Tuḷuva periods, Śrī-Vaishṇavism gained ground in Vijayanagara and a number of Śrī-Vaishṇava *gurus* became influential at court. This was especially the case during the reign of Sadāśiva. Some of the illustrious Śrī-Vaishṇava families in the empire during this time were the Tātāchāryas, the Tāḷḷapākam family of poet saints and the Kanḍāḍai and Bhaṭṭar families.[47] The Tātāchāryas, descended from Śrīśailapūrṇa, the maternal uncle of Rāmānujachārya, are found among the Vaḍagalais and Teṅgalais alike, but the majority belong to the Vaḍagalai sect. The *Jīyars* of the Ahōbalam *maṭha* in Kurnool district were also influential Vaḍagalai *gurus*.

A Śrī-Vaishṇava ascetic named Gōvindarāja is named in one inscription as the *guru* of Kṛishṇa-dēvarāya.[48] This king also bestowed great honours on Veṅkaṭa Tātāchārya.[49] The most influential Śrī-Vaishṇava *gurus* in Vijayanagara during Sadāśiva's reign were Tirumala-Auku-Tiruveṅgaḷāchārya and Kanḍāḷa Śrīraṅgāchārya. The former was the *guru* of Rāmarāya. He is also known as Śrīśailapurṇa Tātāchārya.[50] He granted a village to the Viṭhala temple in A.D. 1543.[51] This *āchārya* was also the *guru* of the powerful Āravīḍu chief Aubhaḷarāju.[52] According to inscriptions in the Viṭhaḷa temple the younger brothers of Aubhalarāju, Koṇḍarāja[53] and Udayagiri Timmarāja[54], were the disciples of Kaṅḍāḷa Śrīraṅgāchārya. *Mahāmaṇḍalēśvara* Chikkarāju was another disciple of this *guru* from Kandanavōlu (modern Kurnool).[55] However, these *gurus* do not appear to have resided permanently in Vijayanagara.

Thus, although we have some data regarding the activities of Śrī-Vaishṇava ascetics, we do not know of any famous *āchārya* of this sect who was permanently based in Vijayanagara. The presence of *Rāmānuja-kūṭas* in some of the Śrī-Vaishṇava temples in the city indicates that Śrī-Vaishṇava ascetics from elsewhere visited the city. There are also some sculptural representations of Śrī-Vaishṇava ascetics, the finest being some on the exterior walls of the Nammāḷvār temple (NH a/10).

An unusual type of mendicant figure occurs frequently in the temple reliefs. The figures represents a shepherd or a cow-herd; his head and body are covered with a hood or a cape and he leans on a staff (Plate 54). Such hoods, made of rough woollen blankets, were used by shepherds and cowherds to protect themselves from the rain and the cold.[56] In Vijayanagara such figures are at times prominently displayed, as for instance on either side of the door of the Garuḍa shrine of the Tiruveṅgaḷanātha temple (NM h/1). Probably these represent the Golla-dāsas or mendicants, usually Vaishṇavite, belonging to the Golla or cowherd community, that traces its descent from Lord Kṛishṇa.[57]

2. Maṭhas and Āśramas

A *maṭha* is the official seat of an ascetic, not always a brāhmaṇa, who is the *guru* or spiritual teacher of a sect whose number may be large or small.[58] The *maṭha* roughly corresponds to the Buddhist *vihāra*.[59] *Maṭhas* were established by the protagonists of the different schools of Hinduism and they propagated their particular schools of thought. Generally attached to temples, these *maṭhas* or monasteries afforded shelter to resident as well as itinerant monks and played a significant part in the religious life of the times.[60] Besides being the homes of ascetics and halting places of mendicants, the *maṭhas* also functioned as centres of learning and education, catering to the spiritual and intellectual needs of society;[61] often, they even served as charitable centres.

In a *maṭha*, the *maṭhādhipati* (the head of the *maṭha*), occupied a pivotal position. He was the absolute master of the *maṭha* and had superior authority in matters, both spiritual and secular, pertaining to the institution. He would nominate his successor. Around the *maṭhādhipati* usually gathered a band of monks, who were his spiritual disciples. They received instructions from him in the scriptures of the sect to which the *maṭha* belonged and they rendered him personal service. When a particular *maṭha* had a number of branches at different places, the head of the central or parent *maṭha* appears to have acted as the supreme head of all the branches.[62]

The Hindu *maṭha* helped the spiritual enlightenment of society. The spiritual heads and other occupants of the *maṭhas* engaged in meditation, spiritual discussion, the study and interpretation of the scriptures, the writing of commentaries on the sacred texts, etc. Various methods were adopted by them to propagate and popularize their religious persuasions such as undertaking religious tours and the conduct of discourses.[63] Also, *mūrtis* of gods and goddesses were installed in the *maṭhas* and regular worship was offered to them, as in the case of the famous Śṛiṅgēri *maṭha*, where goddess Śāradā-dēvī and god Vidyāśaṅkara were worshipped. Thus, the *maṭhas*, greatly fostered religion.

The *maṭha* also served as a teaching institution. It was one of the most important agencies for diffusing knowledge, not only for the benefit of their occupants but also for students who came for that purpose from outside. Students were normally provided with free boarding and lodging. The curriculum included both religious and secular subjects, with a stress on the former.[64] Many *maṭhas* maintained regular and full-fledged libraries or *pustaka bhaṇḍārams*.[65]

The *maṭhas* were also charitable institutions. They provided lodging facilities to itinerant ascetics, pilgrims and poor travellers. Many also maintained *chattrams* or free feeding houses. Some *maṭhas* even provided medical facilities.[66] Therefore, like the Christian monastery of medieval Europe, the Hindu *maṭha* was a religious and charitable centre, a school and a library.

In the Vijayanagara empire, there were Advaita or Smārta *maṭhas*, Śaiva *maṭhas* of the different Śaivite schools, including the Vīraśaivas, and also Vaishṇava *maṭhas* of both the Śrī-Vaishṇavas and the Mādhvas. The Śrī-Vaishṇava *maṭhas* can be divided into two groups, Vaḍagalai and Teṅgalai. In the capital there must have been many *maṭhas*. There were also *āśramas* (hermitages or dwellings) of ascetics, which may or may not have carried out all the manifold functions of a *maṭha*. Unfortunately, the monumental data regarding *maṭhas* and *āśramas* is rather scanty. This is probably due to the fact that many of them, like the private dwellings and even palaces, were built of perishable materials. Therefore, the majority of the *maṭhas* and *āśramas* have disappeared. The epigraphical references, too, to these religious institutions are few.

Maṭhas were in existence at the site even before the founding of the empire. An inscription on a broken slab, found during the excavations conducted in the mid-1970s near the Mahānavamī Platform, dated A.D. 1076 is of the Kalyāni-Chālukya period. This damaged and incomplete epigraph records a gift made by a minister, of eighty *lokki-gaḍyāṇas* every year, to the teachers who expounded the *Purāṇas* in a *maṭha* (name not given).[67] This indicates that the site was already a significant religious centre well before the founding of the Vijayanagara empire. Since the inscription slab has been re-used in a later construction and is not in its original place this *maṭha* cannot be located.

There are at least two *maṭhas* of the Advaita (Smārta) sect at the site. The first is the well known Vīdyāraṇya-svāmi *maṭha* (NF v/3) that is situated to the west of the Virūpāksha temple and is connected with it. This *maṭha*, which during the Vijayanagara times was affiliated to the Śṛiṅgēri *maṭha*, as already mentioned, is referred to in a A.D. 1515 inscription of Kṛishṇadēvarāya.[68] The date of the foundation of this *maṭha* is a matter of dispute. While one scholar asserts that it was organised by Vidyāraṇya-voḍeya, a disciple of Purshōttama Bhāratī II, the pontiff of the Śṛiṅgēri *maṭha*, who is mentioned in the above inscription,[69] other works trace an unbroken succession of the *āchāryas* of this *maṭha* from the great Vidyāraṇya, from the fourteenth to the late sixteenth centuries A.D.[70] In the absence of more data it is difficult to determine definitively to which century the institution belonged. However, the inscription itself indicates that the *maṭha* was already in the existence at the time of Vidyāraṇya-voḍeya's visit in A.D.1515, as it is not claimed in it that he founded the *maṭha*. According to local traditions this *maṭha* was founded by the great sage Vidyāraṇya of the fourteenth century A.D. The present head of the *maṭha*, Narasiṁha Bhāratī, traces his spiritual lineage from this famous saint.

The second Smārta *maṭha* is the Chintāmaṇi *maṭha* in Ānegoṅdi (NE g/1). It is believed that this *maṭha* was established in the early fourteenth century A.D. and it continued to be in existence not only during the Vijayanagara period but also in post-Vijayanagara times.[71] This *maṭha* building is an early Vijayanagara structure with many later additions.[72]

Another *maṭha* of the Vijayanagara period in Ānegoṅdi is the so-called Hucchayappa *maṭha* (ND p/1). There are traces of Vijayanagara paintings in it. The exact affiliation of this *maṭha* cannot be determined.

An inscription of the reign of Dēvarāya II, dated A.D. 1430, refers to the Kallu-maṭha of Hampe and to the ascetic Viśvēśvarāraṇya.[73] The Viraśaivas claim that this was a Vīraśaiva *maṭha* and they identify the present Viraśaiva *maṭha* (NF r/4) near the Virūpāksha temple as the Kallu-maṭha.[74] This Vīraśaiva institution is now known as the Koṭur-svāmi *maṭha*. It consists of a big hall, a verandah, a few rooms and a kitchen. According to a local informant it was a deserted structure that was taken over by the Vīraśaivas in the present century. Possibly, it was a *maṭha* during the Vijayanagara times. However, whether or not it was the Kallu-maṭha and also whether it was originally a Vīraśaiva institution cannot be determined.

A Vīraśaiva *maṭha* that can be identifed is the very large, many-pillared structure (NL w/4) in Kṛishṇāpura, near the Hiriya Kāluve. This is referred to as the Hiriya Chattra in two mid-sixteenth century inscripitons.[75] The Vīraśaiva poet, Virūpāksha Paṇḍita, who composed the *Chennabasava Purāṇa* in A.D.1584, was the disciple of a Vīraśaiva ascetic who was the head of the Hiriya-*maṭha* in Vidyānagara.[76] This is probably the same institution as the one mentioned in the two inscriptions. The Mudu Vīraṇṇa temple (NL w/3) was a temple attached to this *maṭha*.[77] An unusual prismatic *liṅga* found in this temple, with diagrammatic carvings on the three faces and thirty-six small *liṅga*-like protuberances on its hemispherical vertex, is a *Sarvāṅga-liṅga*. It symbolically represents the doctrine in Vīrśaivism known as the *Shaṭsthaḷa Siddhānta*.[78]

On a boulder on one of the highest points of the north ridge is a small label inscription mentioning the Paramēśvara *maṭha*.[79] Near the inscription is a large structure (NN v/2) with an open courtyard in the centre, which has a pillared cloister on three sides, and a spacious natural cave on the west. Its entrance, situated on the south-east, has Śaivite *dvārapālas* on the door jambs. An entrance in front of the cave separates it from the courtyard. Inside the cave is a *pañcha-liṅga* carved on a single stone, lying in a pit. Another Śaivite establishment, the Guha-guhēśvara *āśrama* (NQ d/2), is also identified by an inscription.[80] The small Vīrabhadra shrine attached to the *āśrama* is extant, but the *āśrama* structure is no longer in evidence. The presence of the Vīrabhadra *mūrti* indicates that this must have in all likelihood been the *āśrama* of a Vīraśaiva ascetic.

Another Śaivite *maṭha* complex is located to the west of the Mataṅga hill (NM f/1, 2, 3, 4). The complex includes an elaborate entrance or gateway, a couple of wells or small tanks and a large structure comprising an 'L' shaped verandah, a hall and shrine. An inscription carved on a boulder nearby identifies this as the Kariya Siddappa *maṭha*.[81]

Another smaller complex (NM b/7) nearby, that consists of a cavern, a spring, an open courtyard and two small *maṇḍapas*, was possibly a hermitage of the Vijayanagara times. Even today it serves as an *āśrama*. A small Śaiva eremitical dwelling is situated to the north-east of the "Gāṇigitti" temple. Here, on a rock-shelter (in NX k) is a label inscription identifying it as the cave of Śivayōgidēva.[82] A record carved on another rock-shelter against which a structure has been built (in NT r) identifies it as a *maṭha*.[83] Another inscription from the site refers to the Nirāsimaṭha of Nanjedēva.[84] This *maṭha* cannot be traced. At the junction of the Virūpāksha *ratha-vidhi* and the Kāmalāpuram-Hospēṭ road (in NF y) is a *maṭha* that is identified by an epigraph as the Mahamamtina *maṭha*.[85] Nowadays it is called the Mahāntasvāmi *maṭha*.

Another interesting structure (NL o/3) is located on a rock to the north of the *ratha-vīdhi* of the Kṛishṇa temple. It comprises a natural cave and a *maṇḍapa*. Steps lead up to the structure and a small gate permits entrance into the complex. The view from this complex is superb. It would have been an ideal dwelling for ascetics. There are no sectarian marks to indicate the affiliation of this hermitage.

To the north of Viṭhalāpura is an unusual structure (NC n/1) that might have served as a Vaishṇava temple-cum-hermitage. The temple consists of a *maṇḍapa* and a *garbha-gṛiha*, both with Vaishṇava *dvārapālas* on the door jambs. Adjacent to the temple is a fairly large rectangular room. Both the temple and the room open on to a common, open-pillared verandah.

What is surprising is that while some Smārta and Śaiva *maṭhas* or *āśramas* are to be found at the site, except for the last structure, there are no traces of any Vaishṇava *maṭhas* or *āśramas*. The site, as seen earlier, was an important centre of Mādhva activity from the pre-Vijayanagara times onwards. A number of important Mādhva *gurus*, the most famous being Vyāsarāya, took up residence here; therefore, there definitely must have been one or more Mādhva *maṭhas* in the city, of which, unfortunately, no trace has survived.

Under the Sāḷuvas and Tuḷuvas Śrī-Vaishṇavism gained popularity in the city, especially under Sadāśiva and Rāmarāya. Many Śrī-Vaishṇava *gurus* are mentioned in the sixteenth century inscriptions. But again, there is no evidence of any Śrī-Vaishṇava *maṭha* at the site. It is possible that, unlike the Mādhva sages, most of the Śrī-Vaishṇava *gurus* did not reside in the city. When they visited Vijayanagara periodically, they might have taken up residence either in the *Rāmānuja-kūṭas* attached to the Śrī-Vaishṇava temples or elsewhere.

3. Agrahāras

The *agrahāra* was another important institution that promoted religious pursuits and learning. An *agrahāra* is a settlement of scholarly brāhmaṇas endowed with lands, houses and other facilities with a view to help them to engage themselves fully in religious and scholarly undertakings. *Agrahāras* were founded by kings, queens, generals and also by other rich persons. A specified number of brāhmaṇas were invited to an existing village where agriculture was in a flourishing condition and those lands were purchased by the donor and distributed among these brāhmaṇas.[86] The community of brāhmanas in such a settlement formed a corporate body, having control of all the property of the *agrahāra* and administering all its affairs.

In general, an *agrahāra* in medieval times formed a village or a unit of a village and was located in the country.[87] A similar brāhmaṇa settlement in a city or town was called a *brahmapūri*[88] or *brahmādāya*. However, in Vijayanagara city such brāhmaṇa settlements, in the city proper and in the suburban centres, were known as *agrahāras.*

The establishment of *agrahāras* was considered a meritorious act like the construction of a temple or a tank. Although the securing of merit by the donor was an important object, the chief reason for establishing an *agrahāra* was the promotion of religious and secular learning and education. The innumerable *agrahāras* during the Vijayanagara period were great centres of learning. In some cases, provision was made for the maintenance of a school at the time of the foundation of an *agrahāra* and even food and lodging were provided for the brāhmaṇa students. In the *agrahāras* the *Vēdas, Vēdānta, Purāṇas, Āgamas* and other schools of philosophy were taught, as also different disciplines of learning such as astrology, grammar, mathematics, languages, and polity.[89]

During the Vijayanagara period numerous grants of lands in villages or even of whole villages were made to brāhmaṇas.[90] In the capital, also, *agrahāras* were established, of which we have proof of three. Kṛishṇāpura, the area around the Kṛishṇa temple, the new quarter created by Kṛishṇadēvarāya in A.D. 1515, was an *agrahāra.* This is noted in an inscription of A.D.1543.[91] Kṛishṇadēvarāya assigned a large number of brāhmaṇas to various services in the Kṛishṇa temple. To them he allotted specified shares of land, including land in Kṛishṇāpura.[92]

During the reign of the same ruler, another *agrahāra* was established in the new suburban centre named after the queen mother (modern Nāgēnhaḷḷi). According to an inscription dated A.D. 1516 the king granted this as a *mānya* village to his *purōhita*, Raṅganātha Dīkshita. The latter made the village into an *agrahāra*, giving it the name Nāgalādēvī-pura, and gave *vṛittis* (shares) in it to brāhmaṇas. He also constructed therein a tank called Nāgasamudra and the temples of Nāgēśvara and Nāgendraśayana.[93]

The third was the Neḷalahuṇiseya *agrahāra*. This *agrahāra* was in the quarter of the city called Niṁbāpuram[94] (to the east of Viṭhalāpura). In Neḷalahuṇiseya also, Kṛishṇadēvarāya granted some lands to brāhmaṇas engaged in serving god Bālakṛishṇa of the great Kṛishṇa temple.[95] That Neḷalahuṇiseya was an *agrahāra* is specifically mentioned in an inscription of Achyutarāya's reign dated A.D. 1540.[96]

Thus, epigraphs indicate the existence of three *agrahāras* in the city (Kṛishṇāpura, Nāgalādēvī-pura and Neḷalahuṇiseya). Considering the size of the city and the vibrancy of religious life in it, it is possible that there were other *agrahāras* of which, unfortunately, no trace has survived. The brāhmaṇa residents of these *agrahāras* were engaged in temple service and, possibly, in other religious and scholarly activities.

Although the archaeological data is rather limited regarding ascetics, *maṭhas* and *agrahāras*, yet, available evidence proves that a large number of *gurus* and ascetics of different sects and sub-sects lived in the city and there were also a number of religious institutions such as *maṭhas, āśramas* and *agrahāras.* All these promoted the cause of religion in Vijayanagara. (Fig. 11).

Notes

[1]J. Gonda, *Viṣṇuism and Śivaism: A Comparison*, p. 64.

[2]Cf. Chapter 1.

[3]Cf. Chapter 1.

[4]*MAR* of 1933, pp. 226-227.

[5]C.T.M. Kotraiah, "Vijayanagara Paintings at the Virupaksha Temple, Hampi," *QJMS*, XLIX, p. 236.

[6]S. Srikantaya, "An Image at Hampi," *QJMS*, XXVI, p. 232.

[7]B.R. Gopal, *Vijayanagara Inscriptions*, vol. II, no. 526.

[8]*TTDES* VI, pt. II, p. 69.

[9]Gaṅgādēvī, *Madhurāvijayam*, Canto, I, verse 4.

[10]*EC* V, Cn. 256.

[11]*ARSIE* of 1924-25, A. 15.

[12]*MAR* of 1912, pp. 47-48.

[13]*EC* XI, Dg. 23.

[14]*ARSIE* of 1912-13, A.6 and *EI* XIV, pp. 68-83.

[15]*EC* VII, Sk. 281.

[16]*ARSIE* of 1924-25, A.15.

[17]*Sources*, p. 61.

[18]*VPR '84-87*, no. 26.

[19]Cf. Chapter I.

[20]K.A. Nilakanta Sastri, *Development of Religion in South India*, p. 64.

[21]S.C. Nandimath, *A Handbook of Vīraśaivism*, pp. 33-34.

[22]R. Narasimhacharya *Karnataka Kavi Charite*, pt. II, pp. 258-259.

[23]*VPR '83-84*, no. 55, p. 46.

[24]*VPR '84-87*, no. 138.

[25]C. Hayavadana Rao, *Mysore Gazetteer*, vol. II, pt. III, p. 2096.

[26]*MAR* of 1944, no. 25.

[27]*ARIE* of 1959-60, A. 61.

[28]Y. Nirmala Kumari, "Social Life as Reflected in Sculptures and Painting of Later Vijayanagara Period" (Ph.D. diss.), p. 83.

[29]*Pampamahatmya*, first half of the middle part, chapter 19.

[30]Ibid., middle part, Chapter 2.

[31]Cf. Chapter 1.

[32]Matsyēndranātha, one of the Nava-nāthas, is shown seated on a fish. Just as the many reliefs of *āḻvārs* and *āchāryas* in Vijayanagara are an indication of the popularity of Śrī-Vaishṇavism, similarly, the frequent depictions of Matsyēndranātha could be due to the fact that the Nātha *saṁpradāya* was prevalent.

[33]B. Venkoba Rao, Introduction to *Sri Vyasayōgicaritam*, p. cxxvi.

[34]S. Hanumantha Rao, "The Influence of the Religious School of Sri Madhwa on the History of Vijayanagara," *QJMS*, XX, p. 286.

[35]B.N.K. Sharma, *A History of the Dvaita School of Vēdānta and its Literature*, vol. I, pp. 255-256.

[36]Ibid., p. 265.

[37]S. Hanumantha Rao, "Sri Madhwacharya, A.D. 1238-1318," *JIH*, XXVII, pp. 33-39; see also K.T. Pandurangi, "Dvaita Saints and Scholars of the Vijayanagara Period," in *Early Vijayanagara Studies in its History & Culture*, ed. G.S. Dikshit, pp. 60-62.

[38]B. Venkoba Rao, op.cit., p. xiii and p. cxviii.

[39]Cf. Chapter 1.

[40]*SII* IV, no. 277.

[41]*ARSIE* of 1922, no. 710.

[42]*MAR* of 1941, p. 189.

[43]*Sources*, p. 252.

[44]*MAR* of 1941, pp. 189-190.

[45]A.P. Karmarkar and N.B. Kalamdani, *The Mystic Teachings of the Haridāsas of Karnātak*, p. 51.

[46]Ibid., p. 50.

[47]K. Sarojini Devi, "Religion in Vijayanagara" (Ph.D. diss.) pp. 181-196.

[48]*EC* XIV, Md. 115.

[49]*MAR* of 1918, p. 52.

[50]*EI* XXIX, pp. 71-78.

[51]*SII* IX, pt. II, no. 607.

[52]*SII* IV, no. 280.

[53]Ibid., no. 275.

[54]*SII* IX, pt. II, no. 653.

[55]*SII* XVI, no. 141.

[56]Jyotsna Kamat, *Social Life in Medieval Karṇāṭaka*, p. 46.

[57]S.U. Kamath, ed., *Karnataka State Gazetteer*, pt. I, p. 470.

[58]A. Venkata Subbiah, "A 12th Century University in Mysore," *QJMS*, VII, p. 170.

[59]B.S.L. Hanumantha Rao, "Religion in Andhra" (Ph.D. diss.), p. 416.

[60]K. Sarojini Devi, op.cit., p. 348.

[61]B.S.L. Hanumantha Rao, op.cit., p. 417.

[62]R. Soma Reddy, "History of Religious Institutions in Āndhra Pradesh from A.D. 1300-1600" (Ph.D. diss), pp. 275-276.

[63]Ibid., pp. 398-399.

[64]Ibid., pp. 411-412.

[65]K. Sarojini Devi, loc.cit.

[66]R. Soma Reddy, op.cit., pp. 446-447.

[67]*ARIE* of 1975-76, no. 95; also *Indian Archaeology : A Review of 1975-76*, p. 20.

[68]B.R. Gopal, *Vijayanagara Inscriptions*, vol. II, no. 526.

[69]A.K. Shastry Tonnemane, "A History of Śṛiṅgēri" (Ph.D. diss.), p. 55.

[70]*TTDES*, VI, pt. II, p. 69.

[71]P. Vishnu Thirtha, *A Concise History of Srimadjagadguru Kudali Sringeri Sharada Mahapeetha*, p. 159.

[72]Sugandha, "History and Archeology of Anegondi" (Ph.D. diss), pp. 178-184.

[73]*MAR* of 1934, no. 27.

[74]Dr S. Rajasekhara, personal communication.

[75]*SII* IV, nos. 265 and 266.

[76]R. Narasimhacharya, *Karnataka Kavi Charite*, pt. II, pp. 258-259.

[77]C.T.M. Kotraiah, personal communication.

[78]C.T.M. Kotraiah, "A Cave Linga of Hampi," *JAHRS*, 32, pp. 121-125.

[79]*VPR '83-84*, no. 30, p. 39, Figure 18 and Plate LIV.

[80]Ibid., no. 31, pp. 39-41.

[81]*VPR '84-87*, no. 34.

[82]*VPR '83-84*, no. 54.

[83]*VPR '84-87*, no. 101.

[84]Ibid., no. 98.

[85]Ibid. no. 32.

[86]S.U. Kamath, ed., *Karnataka State Gazetteer*, pt. II, p. 525.

[87]A. Venkata Subbiah, op.cit., p. 163.

[88]Ibid., p. 167.

[89]S.U. Kamath, op.cit., p. 527.
[90]Cf. Chapter 1, note 15.
[91]*ARSIE* of 1935-36, no. 337.
[92]*SII* IV, no. 255.
[93]*SII* IX, pt. II, no. 504.
[94]*SII* IV, no. 255.
[95]Ibid.
[96]Ibid., no. 245.

CHAPTER 10

Non-Hindu Religions

An attempt has been made in the preceding chapters to look at the various Hindu sects, cults and religious practices in Vijayanagara. Although Hinduism was by far the most important religion in the city, non-Hindu religious groups were also present. The Jainas were an important community in the capital, especially in the fourteenth and the first half of the fifteenth centuries A.D. A sizeable number of Muslims also resided and carried out their religious activities in the city in the fifteenth and sixteenth centuries A.D. From the beginning of the sixteenth century a number of Christians made their way to Vijayanagara as traders, diplomats and mercenaries. However, the Christian impact on the religious life of the city was negligible.

1. Jainism

By the time the Vijayanagara empire was founded Jainism had been driven from the premier position it had earlier occupied in south India,[1] including Karṇāṭaka where it had continued to be of significance even after its virtual disappearance from elsewhere in the south. During the Vijayanagara period the rising influence of different Śaiva and Vaishṇava schools (especially of the popular sects established by Basava and Rāmānuja) resulted in the corresponding decline of Jainism.[2] The first dynasty of Vijayanagara gave unstinted protection and patronage to the beleaguered Jaina community. The earliest instance was in A.D. 1363 when state intervention resolved the dispute regarding the boundaries of the Pārśvanātha *basadi* of Tadatāla in favour of the Jaina Suris.[3]

Five years later a graver problem confronted Bukka I, when the Jainas complained in A.D.1368, about the injustice done to them by the Śrī-Vaishṇavas. The king effected the famous "Jaina-Śrī-Vaishṇava accord" by declaring that there was no difference between the Jaina and Vaishṇava *darśanas* and confirming the right of the Jainas to use the five great musical instruments and the *Kalaśa* (holy water pot) on ceremonial occasions. Bukka I also enjoined the Śrī-Vaishṇavas to protect the Jaina *darśana*.[4]

In A.D. 1390 Harihara II gifted a village to a Jaina *basadi* and renewed earlier grants.[5] An inscription of Bukka II records a grant to a *basadi* in Mūḍabidire.[6] Bhīma-dēvī, the queen of Dēvarāya-mahārāya (most probably Dēvarāya I) was a Jaina and a lay disciple of the teacher Paṇḍitāchārya. She installed the image of Śāntinātha in the Māṅgāyi *basadi* at Belgoḷa.[7] Dēvarāya II was a generous patron of Jainism. He made a grant of a village to a *basadi* of Neminātha in A.D. 1424.[8] In A.D. 1426 he built the Pārśvanātha *chaityālaya* in Vijayanagara.[9] In A.D. 1430 he installed the statue of Chandraprabha-tīrthaṅkara in a *chaityālaya* at Bidire and made arrangements for the worship in this temple and in other *basadis*, while his wife Nāgalā-dēvī had a *mānastaṁbha* erected and his daughters Lakshmī and Paṇḍitā-dēvī arranged for feeding in the *chaityālaya* at Bidire.[10]

After the Saṅgama period Jainism did not recieve much royal patronage. A notable exception was the grant to the Trailōkyanātha Jaina temple at Tirupparuttinkuṇṛu by Kṛishṇadēvarāya.[11] By the late fifteenth and sixteenth centuries Jainism was on the decline in most parts of the empire. It came to be concentrated mainly in Śravaṇa Belgoḷa, its original home, and in the Tuḷuva country. In the Tuḷuva region it continued to flourish and local rulers and citizens alike took an active interest in constructing and endowing Jaina temples. Two important centres of Jainism were at Mūḍabidire and Kārkala.[12] In the Tuḷuva area two colossal statues of Gommata were consecrated—the forty-two feet high one at Kārkala in A.D. 1432 and the thirty-five feet high one at Vēnūr in A.D. 1604.[13]

Some Jainas served as ministers, generals and provincial governors, especially during the Saṅgama period. The most illustrious of these were Baichappa, his sons and grandsons. Baichappa or Baichaya-daṇṇāyaka served as a minister under Bukka I[14] and Harihara II.[15] The earliest epigraphical reference to him is in an inscription dated A.D. 1358-59.[16] He had four sons, Gōparasa, Maṅgappa, Irugappa (I) and Immaḍi-Bukka.[17] The two elder sons do not seem to have played an influential role in state affairs and are only mentioned in passing.[18] The most famous member of this family and one of the greatest patrons of Jainism during the Vijayanagara period in the capital and elsewhere was Irugappa (I). The earliest, clearly dated epigraphical record of Irugappa is of A.D. 1367, from Bukka I's reign, which mentions him as ruling over Chelumuttūru.[19] Two records of Irugappa are found in the Jaina temple at Tirupparuttikuṇṛu near Kāñchi.[20] The first, dated A.D. 1382 records the gift of a village to the temple and the second of A.D. 1387-88 records the construction of a *maṇḍapa.* In A.D. 1385 he built the *chaityālaya* of Kunthu Jinanātha in Vijayanagara.[21] He also built the Jaina temple in Ānegoṅdi.[22] In A.D. 1389 he was ruling over Bārakūru-rājya.[23] An inscription of A.D. 1394 records the construction of a sluice by him.[24] He was also a literary luminary who had composed the Sanskṛit lexicon named *Nānārtharatnamālā*.[25] Inscriptions of A.D. 1397[26] and A.D. 1403[27] refer to him as ruling the Penugoṇḍa province. An inscription is available of Mallapa-Oḍeya, son of Irugappa, dated A.D. 1396. He was a minister of Bukka II.[28]

The younger brother of Irugappa (I), Immaḍi-Bukka, was both a distinguished general and a patron of Jainism. In A.D. 1395 he constructed the temple of Kunthu-tīrthaṅkara at Kandanavrōlu (modern Kurnool).[29] Another epigraph of A.D. 1397 records his capture of a hill fortress from the Muslims.[30] The two nephews of Irugappa (I), Baicha-daṇṇāyaka and Irugappa (II), were also high officers. In A.D. 1420 Baicha-daṇṇāyaka, on the order of Dēvarāya I, granted a village to Gommata-svāmi of Beḷgoḷa.[31] This general and minister served under Bukka II,[32] Dēvarāya I[33] and even Dēvarāya II.[34] Irugappa (II) in A.D. 1422 gifted a village to Gommata of Śravaṇa Beḷgoḷa in the presence of the ascetic Paṇḍitārya.[35] Probably, this was the same *guru* who was the preceptor of queen Bhīma-dēvī. Thus, this Jaina family served the Vijayanagara state under a number of kings of the first dynasty Bukka I, Harihara II, Bukka II, Dēvarāya I and Dēvarāya II.

Besides the members of the family of Baichappa (I), other important Jainas in state service during the early Vijayanagara period were *Mahāpradhāna* Gōpa Camūpa, a contemporary of Irugappa (I),[36] and also Masanahaḷḷi Kampaṇa Gauḍa and Vallabharāja-dēva-Mahā-arasu.[37]

In the capital, the Jainas were a very influential community particularly in the fourteenth and early fifteenth centuries. In the "Jaina-Śrī-Vaishṇava accord" of Bukka I of A.D. 1368, the petition to the king was made by the Jainas "of all the nāḍus including Aneyagoṅdi, Hosapaṭṭana, Penuguṇḍe and the city of Kalleha...."[38] Therefore, at this time the Jainas formed an important section of the population both in Ānegoṅdi (the first capital) and in Vijayanagara, the newly built city of Bukka, Hosapaṭṭaṇa being another name for Vijayanagara at that time.[39]

There are seven Jaina temples extant at the site (NR p/1, NS q/1, NS t/2, NS u/3, NS u/5, NX n/1 and one in Ānegoṅdi). There are foundational inscriptions in three of them, namely, the so-called "Gāṇigitti" (oil woman's temple, NX n/1), the Pārśvanātha *chaityālaya* (NS q/1) and the temple in Ānegoṅdi. The dates of the first two are clear. The inscription in the "Gāṇigitti" temple is found on the lamp pillar or *mānastaṁbha* in front of the temple. It records that Irugappa-daṇḍanātha, son of Chaicha or Baicha, the hereditary minister of Harihara II, constructed this *chaityālaya* of Kunthu Jinanātha (the 17th *tīrthaṅkara*) at Vijayanagara in the Śaka year 1307 (i.e., A.D. 1385).[40] The inscription in the Pārśvanātha temple is engraved on both sides of the main entrance. It records that in the Śaka year 1348 (A.D. 1426) Dēvarāya II built the *chaityālaya* of Pārśvanātha (the 23rd *tīrthaṅkara*) in the Pānsupāri bāzār (Kramuka-parnāpaṇa-vīdhi) at Vijayanagara.[41]

The Jaina temple in Ānegoṅdi was also built by Irugappa-daṇḍanāyaka, the son of Baicha-daṇḍanātha, the general of Harihara, in the month of *Vaiśākha* in the year Chitrabhānu.[42] This inscription, engraved on the outer north wall of the temple is rather illegible and is partly damaged. The Śaka year is not given in it. The epigraphist has, by an apparently unwarranted assumption, identified king Harihara of this inscription with the first king of the Saṅgama dynasty and the cyclic year Chitrabhānu with the Śaka year 1264 (A.D. 1342), which occurred in the reign of this king. This date has been accepted by other researchers.[43] However, it is my suggestion that the king was Harihara II (not Harihara I) and the year Chitrabhānu of this record should be the one that coincided with the Śaka year 1324 (A.D. 1402), which fell during the period of Harihara II. As seen earlier, Irugappa was the minister of Harihara II. His father Baichappa served under Bukka I and Harihara II and the earliest epigraphical reference available of Baichappa is of A.D. 1358-59. It is most unlikely, therefore, that Irugappa, the son of Baichappa, could have been a minister of Harihara I. Besides, as already noted, the last epigraphical mention of this general Irugappa was in A.D. 1403 and there are a number of inscriptions from A.D. 1367 to 1403 referring to him. Hence, it is improbable that he could have been a general in A.D. 1342, for if it were so, he would have had an active career as a top general, minister and provincial governor for over sixty years! Therefore, the correct dating of this temple should, I think, be A.D. 1402; it was built during the reign of Harihara II.

Thus, of the three dated Jaina temples in the city, the earliest is the Kunthu Jinanātha temple of A.D. 1385, the second the Ānegoṅdi temple of A.D. 1402 and the third the Pārśvanātha *chaityālaya* of A.D. 1426. The three are very similar in architectural style. The Kunthu Jinanātha (Plate 56) and the Pārśvanātha temples, although separated in time by four decades, share many common features (see Fig. 20). Both have a square sanctum, an ante-chamber and a square inner *maṇḍapa* which has four central columns and also columns against the wall. A doorway leads into an outer *maṇḍapa*. A second doorway on axis with the first opens onto the principal porch. Significantly, the outer *maṇḍapa* has a cross axis linking a secondary sanctum to a smaller porch.[44] The interiors, too, of the two temples are similar, the walls are massive and plain. The doorways are all of the same type; some have bands of foliage and a seated Jina image located in the centre of the lintel (Plate 57). The pillars are massive and are of the Kalyāṇi-Chālukya variety. The exteriors of these temples also present a massive simplicity. In the Kunthu Jinanātha temple there is a stone superstructure in six tiers above the principal sanctum. These monuments hark backwards in time to the earlier style of the Deccan. This suggests that the Jainas were inclined to preserve an older architectural style for their temples, thus promoting a conscious archaism.[45]

During the recent clearance work conducted by the A.S.I. in and around the Pārśvanātha temple six finely executed *tīrthaṅkara* images were recovered, each about a metre in height. One is of a Pārśvanātha, for over his head is a five-headed serpent's hood. Possibly, this was the main *mūrti* of the temple. All the six *tīrthaṅkaras* stand in the *kāyōtsarga* pose and a triple umbrella is over their heads. Flanking each figure is a small relief of a *yaksha* and *yakshī*.

The temple built by Irugappa in Ānegoṅdi in A.D. 1402 is similar to the above two *chaityālayas* except that it has only one *maṇḍapa* and no side porch is extant. Hence, this east-facing temple consists of a main sanctum, an ante-chamber, an enclosed *maṇḍapa* and a pillared porch. A subsidiary sanctum opens directly into the *maṇḍapa* and in line with it is a side door. The *maṇḍapa* has four central pillars and twelve engaged columns. The four columns are of the Kalyāṇi-Chālukya pillar variety. No superstructure is extant over the sanctums. There is no image in this temple, but a *piṭha* is found in the main sanctum. In the centre of the base of this pedestal is carved a small squatting lion. Since the lion is the emblem of Mahāvīra, this temple must have been dedicated to him.

The small Jaina temple (NR p/1) near the Pārśvanātha temple consists of a square sanctum, an antechamber and a *maṇḍapa* only.

The south-facing Jaina temple (NS t/2), just east of the gateway in the east valley (Sōmavārada Bāgilu), now in a very dilapidated condition, is a fairly large and superb temple. It must have comprised a main sanctum, an antechamber, an inner *maṇḍapa*, with four central columns and engaged columns against the walls, and an outer *maṇḍapa*. It is likely that there was a subsidiary sanctum that opened directly into the inner *maṇḍapa*, for on the west wall of this *maṇḍapa* is a doorway with a seated Jina image carved on the centre of its lintel, facing into the *maṇḍapa* (if this was a door leading outside, the lintel image should have been on the outer face of the door-frame). In line with this subsidiary sanctum there must have been a doorway in the opposite wall. The outer *maṇḍapa* is obviously a later addition, for the pillars and the exterior walls of this *maṇḍapa* are very different in style from those of the rest of the temple. On the north wall of the outer *maṇḍapa*, on either side of the doorway into the inner *maṇḍapa*, is a fine relief of a four-armed *yaksha* seated on an elephant. Probably, this outer *maṇḍapa* replaced the front pillared porch. If so, the original plan of this temple would have been very similar to that of the Mahāvīra temple in Ānegoṅdi.

Nearby there are two other Jaina temples. Temple NS u/3 is a small, north-facing ruined temple consisting only of a sanctum and an ante-chamber or porch; over the sanctum traces of the stone superstructure are evident. On the lintel of the sanctum door-frame is a seated Jina figure.

The north-facing Jaina temple (NS u/5) is also very dilapidated. It consists of a main sanctum, an ante-chamber, two side *cellas* flanking the antechamber (all the three sanctums face north), a *maṇḍapa* and a pillared porch. A standing Jina figure is carved in the centre of the lintel of the main sanctum door-frame. Both the interior and the exterior of this temple are plain. Over the main sanctum and one subsidiary *cella* (the other subsidiary *cella* has completely collapsed) there are stepped pyramidal brick and mortar superstructures.

These seven Jaina temples all appear to be of the early phase of Vijayanagara temple architecture (the outer *maṇḍapa* of temple NS t/2 is the only structure that can be stylistically assigned to the intermediate or later phase of Vijayanagara temple architecture). The Kunthu Jinanātha temple is of the late fourteenth century and the Mahāvira temple in Ānegoṅdi and the Pārśvanātha temple in the "royal centre" are of the early fifteenth century A.D. Neither on inscriptional nor on architectural evidence can we assign any Jaina temple to the late fifteenth or sixteenth centuries. There are, however, two Jaina inscriptions of the sixteenth century A.D. The first, dated A.D. 1531 (Śaka 1453), from Ānegoṅdi mentions "victory to Jina *sansana.*"[46] The second,[47] of A.D. 1557 records that *Mahāmaṇḍalēśvara* Śrīraṅgarāja Rāmarāja-ayya granted to Śāntinātha of Chikkadēvarabasti the income from a shop and Chikka Vīranarasaṇṇa constructed a roofed *maṇḍapa* (*māḷige*) of seven bays, the four boundaries of which were the royal road to the north, the Uparige gate to the west and the temple to the south. This inscription is engraved on a slab that was originally lying near the Kunthu Jinanātha temple and is now placed within its courtyard. The temple referred to in this inscription cannot be identified, for we do not know which temple was dedicated to Śāntinātha-tīrthaṅkara.

The location of the temples (see Fig. 9) indicates that the Jainas were a privileged and influential community. Two temples (NR p/1 and the Pārśvanātha temple) are located within the "royal centre", near the principal gate called Siṅghārada Hebbāgilu. They face onto one of the principal radial roads of the city, which extends from near the Rāmachandra temple across the north-east valley to the ferry to Ānegoṅdi. Three (NS t/2, NS u/3 and NS u/5) are situated just outside the "royal centre" on another important radial road, which from the "royal centre" leads through the east valley and proceeds eastwards through the city walls. The Kunthu Jinanātha temple (NX n/1) is situated about midway between two gateways leading into the "royal centre". It is located near another radial road that leads through these gates and then through the fortification wall of the "urban core" at the "Domed Gate" (in NY x). It faces onto the "ring road" that leads around the "royal centre" or the citadel.[48] The Mahāvīra temple in Ānegoṅdi is situated on one of the principal roads of this township, not far from the main "square".

There are very few Jaina sculptures to be seen at the site. In the Haṁpi Archaeological Museum there is one image of Gommatēśvara and a slab with four *tīrthaṅkaras* carved in relief.[49] A series of Jaina *niśidhis* (memorials) of the fourteenth century are on a rock below the Gavi Raṅganātha temple in Ānegoṅdi. Each *niśidhi* consists of a sculpture of a *tīrthaṅkara*, standing in *kāyōtsarga*. On either side of him are the figures of a preceptor reciting from the scripture kept on a stand and a deceased devotee seated with hands in *añjali-mudrā*. There is an inscription below each group. The inscription records the names of the preceptors, their lineage and the names of their deceased disciples.[50] Apart from these, in Ānegondi there are three other groups of Jaina images.[51] In some of the *Daśāvatāra* reliefs in Vijayanagara Jina replaces Buddha.[52]

The number of Jaina temples at the site, their strategic location, the important donors named in inscriptions (King Dēvarāya II, General Irugappa (I) and *Mahāmaṇḍalēśvara* Śrīraṅgarāja Rāmarāja-ayya) reveal the importance of this community in the city. But, the fact, that all the temples are of the early phase of Vijayanagara temple architecture and that there is no evidence of a Jaina temple in the city of the late fifteenth or sixteenth centuries A.D. indicates that the hey-day of the Jainas in the capital was in the fourteenth and early fifteenth centuries. It is possible that already by Dēvarāya II's reign, the Jainas in the city were on the decline politically and numerically, and hence to afford them protection and aid this ruler built a temple for them.[53] Yet, as revealed by two sixteenth century inscriptions and by the addition of a *maṇḍapa* to temple NS t/2, Jaina religious activities continued—though probably on a lower scale—in the city till its destruction in A.D. 1565. This gradual decline in importance of Jainism in the capital reflects what was happening to the community throughout the empire, with the exception of Śravaṇa Beḷgoḷa and the Tuḷuva region.

2. Islam

The conflict between the Vijayanagara kings and the Muslim kingdoms was more political than religious. Within their own jurisdiction they tolerated Islam, employed Muslims in their services and patronised them in several ways. From the early days of the empire, Muslim traders and ambassadors visited the capital and from the fifteenth century onwards there was a large group of Muslims resident in the city, substantial numbers of whom served in the army (particularly in the cavalry); possibly Muslims were also employed as artisans.

From about the middle of the fourteenth century A.D. till the close of the fifteenth, the horse trade was the virtual monopoly of the Arab merchants[54] and the Vijayanagara state greatly depended on them for horses for the army. The presence of these Arab horse traders in the city is attested to by sculptural representations of them. On the outer side of the *prākāra* wall of the early fifteenth century Rāmachandra temple there are five panels of reliefs. The second lowest frieze depicts a procession of horses. Many of these are led by Arabs (traders and grooms), characterised by their long robes, beards and headdresses. Here and there they are shown presenting horses before a seated royal figure (Plates 20 and 51). Such foreign-looking men can be seen on some of the reliefs of phase one and two of the Mahānavamī Platform also, presenting horses or riding on them or as grooms leading horses and camels.

Muslim ambassadors from the Deccan Muslim capitals and also from abroad visited Vijayanagara. The most famous of these was 'Abdur Razzāk, the Persian ambassador, who was received with much favour in the court of Dēvarāya II and who has left an interesting account of the court and the capital.[55] Occasionally in the carvings of phase one (of the late fourteenth century) of the Mahānavamī Platform such Muslim ambassadors or visitors are portrayed, bowing before seated royal personages.

Thus, from the early days of the Vijayanagara empire Muslims visited the capital city. But probably there was little impact of Islam on the religious life of the city till the fifteenth century when Muslims began to be employed in substantial numbers in the state service.

The earliest example of a Muslim employed in the Vijayanagara service is, perhaps, from the period of Dēvarāya I, who, according to the *Kaifiyat of Pāṇem Pāḷaiyapat*, allotted the fort of Pāṇem to Sābat Mulk. This fort was held by Muslim officers right up to the Sāḷuva period.[56] However, it was only from the reign of Dēvarāya II onwards that large numbers of Muslims were recruited in the army. According to Ferishta, Dēvarāya II was advised that the Bahmanīs fared well in their wars against Vijayanagara because of their superior cavalry and archery. Therefore, to improve his army Dēvarāya gave "orders to enlist Mussulmans in his service, allotting to them estates, and erecting a mosque for their use in the city of Beejanuggur. He also commanded that no one should molest them in the exercise of their religion, and moreover he ordered a Koran to be placed before his throne on a rich desk so that faithful might perform the ceremony of obeisance in his presence without sinning against their laws."[57] Since Ferishta wrote more than a century-and-a-half after Dēvarāya II's reign, his testimony by itself would not carry much weight if it were not for corroborating epigraphical and archaeological evidences. A copper-plate grant of this king claims that he had "ten thousand Turushka horsemen in his service."[58] Within the city is a mosque built in A.D. 1439 by Ahmad Khān, an officer of the king.[59] There are also at least three tombs at the site that can be assigned to the early part of the fifteenth century—the tomb near this mosque and two tombs near Kaḍirāṁpuram.[60]

Later rulers continued the policy of employing Muslims. Thus under Sāḷuva Narasiṁha many Muslims enjoyed high positions in the state. He also gave substantial aid to Muhammadan institutions; a village was granted to the *dargāh* of the famous Muslim saint Bābayya in Penugoṇḍa.[61] During the reign of Kṛishṇadēvarāya the Muslims were of immense value in the army. According to Paes they were experts in handling firearms and missiles.[62] Nuniz gives a vivid description of Kṛishṇadēvarāya's conquest of Rāichur and the contribution of the Muslims to his success.[63]

According to Ferishta, Rāmarāya accepted in his service three thousand of the foreign troops dismissed by Ibrāhīm 'Ādil Shāh I of Bijāpur.[64] Among the high-ranking Muslims under him were Dilāvar Khan,[65] Ambur Khān, an Abyssinian,[66] Noor Khān and Bijly Khān[67] and, most important, Ein-ool-mulk Geelany who had on many occasions so distinguised himself by his bravery that Rāmarāya used to address him as brother.[68] Rāmarāya allowed the Muslims in Vijayanagara to build mosques and observe all their religious rites. They were even permitted to sacrifice cows in the *Turkavāḍa* of the city, notwithstanding the protests of the brāhmaṇas and the Hindu nobles. Moreover, to ease the conscience of the Mulims in his service, Rāmarāya is said to have placed a Koran near his seat in the *dūrbar* so that they might avoid the sin of offering salute to an infidel master,[69] as was said to have been done by Dēvarāya II. At the battle of Rakkasa-Taṅgaḍi there was a sizeable Muslim contingent in the Vijayanagara army: the treachery of two of the Muslim generals was one of the reasons for the defeat of the Vijayanagara forces.[70]

Thus from the early fifteenth century onwards the Muslims formed an important segment of the population of Vijayanagara. At the east end of the north ridge and extending across the valley to the base of the Mālyavanta hill is the main Muslim quarter in the city. This is indicated by mosques, tombs and graveyards. Contemporary writings confirms the presence of such an Islamic quarter in the city. The Muslim writer Shirāzi refers to the '*Turkavāḍa*' where the Muslims resided, had a mosque and carried out their worship,[71] while the Portuguese traveller Paes states that "at the end of this street is the Moorish quarter, which is at the very end of the city, and of these Moors there are many who are natives of the country and who are paid by the king and belong to his guard."[72] This description aptly fits this Muslim quarter which is in the eastern end of the "urban core" and through which traverses one of the principal roads of the city, leading from the "royal centre" in a north-eastrely direction to Talarighaṭ (see Fig. 10). A number of sixteenth century inscriptions also refer to the "village downwards of the tombs" (*Gōri-keḷagana-grāma*).[73] This must have been the area inhabited mostly by Muslims.[74] The number of Muslim monuments still extant in this quarter reveal that a large Muslim population resided here.

Another Islamic quarter was immediately south of the "urban core," near Kāmalāpuram. Here a cemetery of the Vijayanagara period is found together with numerous modern graves, a *dargāh* and an *idgāh*. Outside the "urban core", to the west, is the village of Kaḍirāṁpuram, incorporating one of the suburban centres of Vijayanagara. A short distance south-west of this village two tombs still stand, around which are the remains of an extensive cemetery. Here, too, a Muslim community must have lived.[75]

Our main source of information about the presence and religious activity of the Muslims in the city are the religious monuments of this community. To begin with, we must distinguish between two groups of monuments at

Vijayanagara, both with Islamic characteristics. One group of buildings (mostly mosques, tombs and gravestones) was erected under the sponsorship of an influential and wealthy Muslim community. Another group of buildings also reveal the impact of Islamic artistic practice; however, these structures are directly associated with the Hindu court, being mostly located within the "royal centre". Here many Islamic features are incorporated into new and original forms—fountains, baths, watch-towers, stables, treasuries, reception halls, gateways, pavilions, etc.[76] Only the first group of buildings is discussed here, for the second group of court-connected structures had no connection with the religious life of the Muslim community of the city. While the latter group of buildings have imbibed the typical elements of Islamic architecture such as the domes, arches and plaster decoration, the former group portrays elements of Hindu architecture, for many of them are of the flat-roofed variety. Thus, there was a blending of architectural styles in the city.

Two mosques are extant in the city. The first is Ahmad Khān's *dharmaśāla* (NO q/1).[77] Rectangular in plan, this flat-roofed building is open to the east, with solid walls on the other three sides. Within are sixteen columns of the Kalyāṇi-Chālukya pillar variety. Almost all the architectural elements are completely un-Islamic in character (Plate 58). The only feature that is distinctly Islamic is the *mihrāb* niche in the middle of the west wall. The *mihrāb* in the form of a trefoil arch, the presence of a well close by (a water tank is an essential part of a mosque) and the situation of this structure in the Muslim quarter leads to the conclusion that this is a mosque.[78] Though the Kannaḍa inscription found here identifies the building as a '*dharmaśāla*,' this, apparently, is not uncommon for mosque inscriptions in vernacular languages.[79] It is significant that within a century of the foundation of the empire the capital included a sizeable number of Muslims in its population, thereby necessitating the construction of a mosque for their use.

The second mosque (NO y/1) is located about half a kilometre to the south-east of Ahmad Khān's mosque, near the foot of Mālyavanta hill. Surrounded by several graves and also a stone-lined well, this monument is now in ruins. Of interest is the *mihrāb* in the middle of the west wall.[80] This mosque has been overlooked in most of the writings and maps on Vijayanagara. However, it is noted as a mosque in one of the early maps of the site published by the A.S.I.[81] Thus, there were at least two mosques in the city. Perhaps, there were others that have not survived.

A number of Muslim tombs or funerary monuments is also evident at the site;[82] some are very dilapidated. Some of these tombs are domed structures. The most important ones of this variety are the tomb (NO q/2) near the first mosque (probably the tomb of Ahmad Khān himself) and the two near Kaḍirāṁpuram (which are the largest tombs at the site.)[83] Others are of the flat-roofed variety (e.g., NN p/9, NO g/1, NO h/3, NO m/4, NT b/2, NT h/4).[84] Some of the tombs are even currently venerated by the local Muslims (e.g, NN p/6 and NN p/9).

Some inscriptions, most of them undated, referring to the construction of tombs are extant at the site. Thus, in the Islamic quarter within the "urban core" there is one that records the construction of a *gummata* (tomb) by Sakalarajāvuta.[85] Another refers to the building of the tomb of Miyarāhuta (a Muslim soldier).[86] A third notes the construction of a tomb by Sakhalādirāhuta. Further it states that no one should bring bodies for burying in this tomb and ends with imprecations against those who might try to use it for burial.[87] Evidently the tomb referred to is the empty, flat-roofed one close to the epigraph (NO m/4). At Kaḍirāṁpuram there are two inscriptions. One mentions the shrine (tomb?) of Sultān Sayyid Pirige Babaya.[88] The second is of the period of king Sāḷuva Narasiṁha. It notes the construction of a tomb and a well. Some Muslim names such as Saidupiru Ali, Abu and Hasadhasani, are mentioned in it.[89]

Surrounding most of the tombs of the Muslim quarters are extensive cemetery complexes. Here numerous gravestones are found, often damaged and frequently overturned.[90] These gravestones are mostly raised on square or rectangular rubble platforms. In some cases, the gravestones are grouped together on one large rectangular platform. In at least one instance (NN p/13) the platform is provided with a miniature *mihrāb* niche. The gravestones appear to be of two types: with a distinctive angled top or a flat top.[91]

In the south-east part of the Muslim quarter there is an unusual structure (NO w/2), now much dilapidated and overgrown. This appears to have served as a prayer hall and a cemetery.[92]

These mosques, tombs and cemeteries of the Muslims prove that this community was allowed full freedom in the practice of their religion. They enjoyed state protection, so much so that Ahmad Khān dedicated the mosque that he constructed for the merit of his patron, Dēvarāya II.[93] It is to be noted that in close proximity with the Islamic monuments, and also with the Jaina temples, are a number of small Hindu temples and shrines. This suggests the integration of the minority communities into the general population. Therefore, although there were particular areas within the city where mainly the Jainas and the Muslims dwelt and carried out their religious activities, these areas were not exclusively occupied by these religious groups.

3. Christianity

A number of Christians visited Vijayanagara, especially in the sixteenth century A.D. as envoys, travellers, traders, soldiers, and adventurers. However, on the whole, they do not appear to have been a part of the resident population of the capital, nor did they engage in any public religious activities.

The advent of Christians to Vijayanagara really began after the arrival of the Portuguese, the first of the colonial powers on the Indian shores at the end of the fifteenth century A.D. There are, of course, a few earlier instances of Christians in the city. For example, in A.D. 1420 Nicolo Conti, a Venetian of noble birth, passed through Vijayanagara and has left his observations on the life of the city.[94] 'Abdur Razzāk, who came to the city in A.D. 1443 refers to a Christian official in the service of Dēvarāya II named Nimeh-pezir.[95] Unfortunately, the identification of this officer cannot be established for lack of corroboration.

From the early sixteenth century onwards the Vijayanagara rulers and the Portuguese entertained sentiments of cordiality towards each other. Both sides benefited: horses for the Hindu rulers (in the beginning of the sixteenth century A.D. the control of the horse trade had been wrested by the Portuguese from the Arabs) and the maritime trade for the Portuguese. Besides, both the Portuguese and Vijayanagara had a common enemy in the 'Ādil Shāhis of Bijāpur. Because of this friendly relationship between the two powers, several Portuguese visited the Hindu capital and many of them have also written down their impressions of Vijayanagara.

Varthema, the Italian visitor, noted that King Vīra Narasiṁha "is a very great friend of the Christians, and especially of the Portuguese."[96] The second Portuguese Viceroy, Affonso de Albuquerque, sent two envoys to the court of Kṛishṇadēvarāya. The first was the Franciscan Friar Luiz in A.D. 1510,[97] whose embassy ended tragically as he was murdered under mysterious circumstances. The second was Gaspar Chanoca in A.D. 1512.[98] Albuquerque's successors exchanged presents and friendly greetings with the *rāya*. Christovão de Figueiredo appears to have visited Vijayanagara twice or thrice in this connection.[99] In A.D. 1520 he met the *rāya* while the latter was investing the fort of Rāichur and rendered him invaluable aid in its capture.[100] The Govenor of Goa, according to Nuniz, on the request of Kṛishṇadēvarāya for some Portuguese masons to help construct an enormous tank at the capital, sent João della Ponte to the city.[101]

The promise of the exclusive supply of horses to Vijayanagara was one of the cementing factors in the early relations between Vijayanagara and the Portuguese. The good relations between Kṛishṇadēvarāya with the Portuguese was continued by Achyutarāya, who purchased 13,000 horses every year.[102] In A.D. 1547 a treaty was concluded between the Portuguese Governor de Castro and Sadāśivarāya. One of the terms of this treaty was that Vijayanagara should have the monopoly of the horse trade of Goa.[103]

According to *Rāmarāja's Bakhair* there were nearly 3,500 Portuguese (Parangis) among the Vijayanagara troops at the battle of Rakkasa-Taṅgaḍi.[104] So close were the economic and political links between the Portuguese and the Vijayanagara state that the Hindu defeat in A.D. 1565 struck a rude blow at the prosperity of the Portuguese trade and from that time it declined.[105] This is confirmed by the contemporary Portuguese historian, Diego de Couto "... the defeat of the king of Bisnagá had very ill consequences for India and for our state. For this kingdom accounted for the largest share of the trade of all. They used to supply it with horses, velvets, satins and others kinds of merchandise, and this brought them great profits."[106]

Although many Christians visited Vijayanagara, none of them (with the possible exception of the Christian official of Dēvarāya II, mentioned by 'Abdur Razzāk) appear to have been resident in the city for any length of time. Besides, these Christians came to Vijayanagara as diplomats, soldiers, traders, artisans, etc.; we have no evidence of any Christian religious activity, nor of the proselytizing associated with the Portuguese presence elsewhere. Even the Franciscan monk, Friar Luiz, came as an envoy and not as a religious teacher. There is no literary evidence of Christian religious activity in the city, nor is there any epigraphical or archaeological evidence of this. There does not seem to be any trace of a Christian church or tomb, nor even of a single Christian symbol, anywhere on the site.

The only evidence from the monuments of the presence of Christians in the city is on the plinth of the *uyyāle-maṇḍapa* (built in A.D. 1554) of the Viṭhala temple and the plinth of the unfinished *gōpura* (NH a/6) in Viṭhalāpura. In both, on one of the plinth mouldings, is carved an endless procession of horses and men. The "men that lead them (horses) by the reins are faithful portraits of the Portuguese *fidalgoes* of the sixteenth century. Boots, trousers, coat and bonnet all belong to their ancient well-known apparel. But the most characteristic feature of these figures is their beard and moustache. The latter turned upwards and the former, trimmed in triangular shape, pointed downwards are two details that cannot be mistaken"[107] (Plate 59). The horse trade being so vital to the Vijayanagara state and since in the late fourteenth and early fifteenth century monuments we have examples of carvings of Arab horse traders, it is not surprising that in some of the sixteenth century structures the Portuguese, who now controlled this trade, should be portrayed. According to H. Heras, one of the figures shown leading such a procession of men and horses in the Viṭhala temple frieze is a Christian padre, for he is dressed in a long gown, his head is covered with a queer bonnet, showing at least two of its angular points and he holds a long staff in one hand. Heras even identifies this figure as Frey Luiz.[108] Possibly this may represent a padre, but it is rather far-fetched to claim that the brief and tragic visit of Frey Luiz to the city in A.D. 1510 is captured in stone forty-four years later! Even these two examples of sculptural representations of Portuguese do not point to any Christian religious impact. For here the Portuguese are shown purely in their secular capacity as traders and not as engaged in any religious activity. Therefore, it can be concluded that the Christians made little or no impact on the religious life of the city.

This survey of the non-Hindu religions in Vijayanagara reveals that the Vijayanagara state and rulers were tolerant of other faiths. Not only did the kings impose no restrictions on the non-Hindus in the practice of their religion, but there are even some examples of active state protection and patronage extended to them. The comment made by Duarte Barbosa about Kṛishṇadēvarāya can, on the whole, be applied to the Vijayanagara rulers in general: "The king allows such freedom that every man may come and go and live according to his own creed, without suffering any annoyance and without enquiry whether he is a Christian, 'Jew', Moor or Heathen".[109]

Notes

[1]B.A. Saletore, *Mediaeval Jainism with Special Reference to Vijayanagara*, p. 283.

[2]K.A. Nilakanta Sastri, *A History of South India: From Prehistoric Times to the Fall of Vijayanagara*, p. 387.

[3]*EC* VIII, T1. 197.

[4]*EC* II (1923 ed.), SB. 344; *IA* XIV, pp. 234-235; *EC* IX, Ma. 18.

[5]*EC* I (1914 ed.) Cg. 39.

[6]*Top. List* II, South Kanara dist. no. 116.

[7]*EC* II (1923 ed), SB. 337.

[8]*ARSIE* of 1928-29, A. 12.

[9]*SII* I, no. 153.

[10]*ARSIE* of 1901, no. 33; B.R. Gopal, *Vijayanagara Inscriptions*, vol. II, no. 1015.

[11]*ARSIE* of 1901, no. 188,

[12]S.U. Kamath, "Tuluva in Vijayanagar Times" (Ph.D. diss.), p. 241.

[13]Ibid., p. 368.

[14]*EC* II (1923 ed.), SB. 253.

[15]*SII* I, no. 152.

[16]*ARSIE* of 1931-32, no. 284.

[17]*ARSIE* of 1939-40 to 1942-43, p. 261.

[18]Gōparasa is mentioned in the record of his son Anantarasa (*ARSIE* of 1942-43, no. 55). Maṅgappa is referred to in an inscription of his son Irugappa; his two sons, Baichappa (II) and Irugappa (II) were important generals (*EC* II, SB. 253).

[19]*SII* IX, pt. II, no. 412.

[20]*EI* VII, pp. 115-116.

[21]*SII* I, no. 152.

[22]*ARIE* of 1958-59, no. 678.

[23]*ARIE* of 1970-71, no. 210.

[24]*EC* XVI, Kg. 50 and *MAR* of 1919, p. 33.

[25]*SII* I, p. 156.

[26]*SII* XVI, no. 9

[27]*EC* XII, Si. 95.

[28]*ARSIE* of 1912, no. 60; *ARSIE* of 1939-40 to '42-43, p. 261.

[29]*ARSIE* of 1935-36, no. 336.

[30]*ARIE* of 1961-62, no. 35.

[31]*EC* V, Mj. 58.

[32]*ARSIE* of 1901, no. 41.

[33]*EC* V, B1. 14; *ARSIE* of 1901, no. 22; *ARSIE* of 1945-46, no. 156, etc.

[34]*MAR* of 1929, no. 114.

[35]*EC* II (1923 ed.), SB. 253.

[36]B.A. Saletore, op. cit., p. 308.

[37]Ibid., p. 309.

[38]*EC* II (1923 ed.), SB. 344.

[39]S. Krishnaswami Aiyangar, "Foundation of Vijayanagara," *QJMS*, XI, p. 22 and V. Filliozat, "The Town-Planning of Vijayanagara," *Art and Archaeology Research Papers* (aarp), 14, p. 54.

[40]*SII* I, no. 152.

[41]Ibid., no. 153.

[42]*ARIE* of 1958-59, no. 678.

[43]V. Filliozat, *L'Épigraphie de Vijayanagara du début à 1377*, p. 139; Sugandha, "History and Archeology of Anegondi" (Ph.D. diss.), p. 274.

[44]G. Michell, "Two Temples from the Early Vijayanagara Period: Studies in Monumental Archaism," in *C. Sivaramamurti Commemoration Volume*, ed. M.S. Nagaraja Rao, p. 214.

[45]Ibid., p. 216.

[46]Sugandha, op.cit., p. 277.

[47]*SII* IV, no. 247.

[48]See J.M. Fritz, "The Roads of Vijayanagara : A Preliminary Study," in *VPR '79-83*, pp. 51-56, for details of the original roads of the city.

[49]No. 766 and 1424 respectively, of the Hampi Museum collection.

[50]*VPR '84-87*, no. 170, 171, 172 and 174.

[51]See Sugandha, op.cit., pp. 301-313.

[52]*VPR* '79-83, p. 38.

[53]S. Rajasekhara, "Inscriptions at Vijayanagara," in *Vij. City and Emp.*, vol., 1, p. 106.

[54]S.K. Shukla, "Horse Trade in Medieval South : Its Political and Economic Implications," in *PIHC*, 42, p. 311.

[55]See "Narrative of the Journey of Abd-er Razzak", in *India in the Fifteenth Century*, ed R.H. Major, pp. 23-44; see also H.M. Elliot and J. Dowson, *The History of India as told by its own Historians*, vol. IV, pp. 103-126.

[56]*Further Sources*, vol. III, pp. 50-51.

[57]John Briggs, *History of the Rise of Mahomedan Power in India till A.D. 1612*, vol. II, p. 266.

[58]*EC* III, Sr. 15.

[59]*SII* IX, pt. II, no. 447.

[60]G. Michell, "Architecture of the Muslim Quarters at Vijayanagara", in *VPR '83-84*, pp. 109-110.

[61]Sree Rama Sarma, *Sāḷuva Dynasty of Vijayanagara*, p. 259.

[62]*FE*, p. 277.

[63]Ibid., p. 329 ff.

[64]John Briggs, op.cit., vol. III, p. 47.

[65]*MAR* of 1941, no. 16 and *EC* X, K1. 147.

[66]Briggs, op.cit., vol. III, p. 197.

[67]Ibid., p. 238.

[68]Ibid., p. 229.

[69]N. Venkataramanayya, *Studies in the Third Dynasty of the Vijayanagara*, pp. 318-319 and *Further Sources*, vol. I, p. 267.

[70]H. Heras, *The Aravidu Dynasty of Vijayanagara*, vol. I, p. 211.

[71]*Further Sources*, vol. I, p. 267.

[72]*FE*, p. 256.

[73]*SII* IV, nos. 272, 273, 278, 279, etc.

[74]C.T.M. Kotraiah, "The Metropolis of the Vijayanagara Empire," in *The Vijayanagara Urbanity*, ed. K.R. Basavaraja, p. 19.

[75]G. Michell, op.cit., p. 105.

[76]Ibid., p. 101.

[77]See for details M.S. Nagaraja Rao "Ahmadkhān's Dharmaśāla," in *VPR '79-83*, pp. 64-65 and Plates XXXIX-XL; also G. Michell, op.cit., pp. 104-105 and Plates XXXI-XXXIV.

[78]S. Rajasekhara, op.cit., p. 107.

[79]G. Michell, op.cit., p. 105.

[80]Ibid., pp. 106-107, plate LXII.

[81]*Annual Report of the ASI*, of 1903-4, map opposite p. 62.

[82]

1. NN p/3	2. NN p/6
3. NN p/7 (probably)	4. NN p/9
5. NN p/10	6. NN p/12
7. NN u/4 (probably)	8. NO g/1
9. NO h/2	10. NO h/3
11. NO h/4	12. NO j/1 (probably)
13. NO m/4	14. NO q/2
15. NO r/2 (Probably)	
16. NT b/2	17. NT h/4

18 & 19. Two large tombs south-west of Kadirāmpuram.

[83]See G. Michell, op.cit., pp. 107-111 and Plates LXIII-LXV.

[84]Ibid., pp. 111-112 and Plates LXVI-LXVIII.

[85]*VPR '84-87*, no. 119.

[86]Ibid., no. 118.

[87]Ibid., no. 120.

[88]Ibid., no. 150.

[89]Ibid., no. 149.

[90] 1. NN p/1 (1) 2. NN p/5 (1)

3. NN p/8 (1) 4. NN p/11 (3)
5. NN p/13 (8) 6. NN p/14 (7)
7. NN p/15 (1) 8. NN p/16 (1)
9. NN u/1 (5) 10. NN u/2 (2)
11. Near NO h/2 (1) 12. east of NO h/4 (several)
13. north of NO j/1 (1) 14. NO j/2 (1)
15. NO j/3 (1) 16. NO 1/2 (2)
17. South-east of NO m/4 (5)
18. near NO n/5 (1) 19. NO w/2 (several)
20. NO y/2 (11) 21. NO y/3 (4)
22. NT h/3 (several) 23. NX w/2 (several)
24. South-west of Kaḍirāṁpuram (over 50 gravestones)

[91]G. Michell, op.cit., p. 115 and Plates LXIX-LXX.

[92]See *VPR* '83-84, Figure 43 and Plate LXVIII b.

[93]*SII* IX, pt. II, no. 447.

[94]Nicolo Conti, "Travels of Nicolo Conti," in *India in the Fifteenth Century*, ed. R.H. Major, pp. 6-29.

[95]'Abdur Razzāk, "Narrative of the Journey of Abd-er-Razzak," Ibid., p. 41.

[96]Varthema, *The Itinerary of Ludovico di Varthema of Bologna from 1502 to 1508*, trans. J.W. Jones, p. 72.

[97]F.C. Danvers, *The Portuguese in India: Being a History of the Rise and Decline of Their Eastern Empire*, vol. I, p. 185.

[98]Ibid., p. 256.

[99]. Gurti, Venkata Rao, "Krishnadevaraya and the Portuguese," *JAHRS*, X, p. 83.

[100]Nuniz., in *FE*, pp. 343-347.

[101]Ibid., p. 364.

[102]Ibid., p. 381.

[103]F.C. Danvers, op.cit., vol. I, p. 478.

[104]*Further Sources*, vol. III, p. 224.

[105]T.V. Mahalingam, *Economic Life in the Vijayanagara Empire*, p. 123.

[106]A.D.'Costa, "The Last Days of Vijayanagara," *Indica*, 3, p. 128.

[107]H. Heras, "Historical Carvings at Vijayanagara," *QJMS*, XVII, p. 88.

[108]Ibid.

[109]Duarte Barbosa, *The Book of Duarte Barbosa*, trans. and ed. M. Longworth Dames, p. 202.

CHAPTER 11

Conclusion

A survey of religion in the city of Vijayanagara prior to A.D. 1565, as revealed primarily through the archaeological data available at the site, has been undertaken in the preceding chapters of this study. The development of various cults, their patronage and popularity, temple rituals and festivals and the propagation of religion by ascetics and *maṭhas* have been traced. This chapter indicates the general conclusions that can be drawn from this study and certain inferences that complete the analysis of religious traditions in Vijayanagara.

It is clear that in pre-Vijayanagara times the site was a significant Śaivite *kshētra*. The cult of the local goddess Paṁpā is an ancient one, which in course of time was absorbed into Śaivism. Paṁpā-Virūpāksha has undoubtedly been the principal deity at the site from before the founding of the empire onwards, and he was adopted as the guardian deity of the Vijayanagara state. Gaṇēśa and Bhairava were also known in pre-Vijayanagara times, but their worship, together with that of Vīrabhadra and other Śaivite deities such as Mallikārjuna, gained in popularity during the Vijayanagara period. Smārtas, Kāḷāmukhas (up to the early fifteenth century), Vīraśaivas etc., patronised these cults. From the pre-Vijayanagara period till almost the end of the fifteenth century A.D. Śaivism was predominant in the city.

Before the founding of the empire Vaishṇava cults had little following at the site. Among the earliest of these was the cult of Narasiṁha, for two of the Narasiṁha temples (NG t/4 and NE m/1) date back to the pre- or early Vijayanagara period. But, although Narasiṁha worship gained in importance in the fifteenth and sixteenth centuries and Narasiṁha was a popular divinity, this deity was not one of the leading Vaishṇava gods of the city. Apart from this one, the only other Vaishṇava cult that is possibly of the pre-empire period is that of Raṅganātha at Ānegoṅdi. While the Gavi Raṅganātha shrine is of the pre-empire period, the Raṅganātha temple in Ānegoṅdi itself, although built on the site of an earlier temple, is evidently of the Vijayanagara period. However, despite the presence of Raṅganātha worship in Ānegoṅdi, there are no traces of this cult at the site to the south of the Tuṅgabhadrā before the Vijayanagara period. Despite the association of this site with Kishkindhā of the *Rāmāyaṇa* at least from the eleventh century A.D. onwards, it is significant that, to the best of my knowledge, there were no temples dedicated to Rāma at the site prior to the early fifteenth century A.D.

The Saṅgama period saw the introduction of two Vaishṇava cults into the city—those of Rāma and Viṭhala. The Rāmachandra temple, with its magnificent architecture, exquisite sculpture and strategic location, was a royal temple closely connected with the king and court. The *Rāmāyaṇa* tradition in the city was developed during the empire-period and temples or sculptures marked many of the spots linked with Rāma's passage through the spot or with Sugrīva and Hanumān. The Prāta Viṭhala shrine was probably constructed prior to the fifteenth century and the great Viṭhala temple in the fifteenth century.

Vaishṇavism gained ground in the city under the Sāḷuvas and, more particularly, the Tuḷuvas. During the late fifteenth and the sixteenth centuries and up to A.D. 1565 Vijayanagara was the scene of the vigorous Mādhva and Śrī-Vaishṇava activity. Mādhva *gurus*, the most famous being Vyāsarāya, the Haridāsa poet saints and Śrī-Vaishṇava teachers spread their different doctrines and received active patronage from the court. After the death of Vyāsarāya, Śrī-Vaishṇavism became the leading sect in the city.

The Tuḷuva period, thus, saw the importation of a number of Vaishṇava cults. The Viṭhala cult, already present at the site, grew from strength to strength, till during the twenty years prior to the city's destruction the Viṭhala temple was the chief centre of religious activity in the city, overshadowing in importance even the great

Virūpāksha temple. The cults of Tiruveṅgaḷanātha, Raṅganātha and Kṛishṇa also gained a wide following. The numerous temples dedicated to Veṅkaṭēśvara or Tiruveṅgaḷanātha attest to the status of Tirumalai-Tirupati as the foremost place of pilgrimage in the empire during the sixteenth century. The Śrī-Vaishṇava cult of the *āḷvārs* and *āchāryas* also became popular during this period, when statues of these saints were enshrined in temples and even separate shrines were constructed in their honour in Viṭhalāpura.

The sixteenth century also saw the most intense temple building activity in the city. Some of the important temples, already existing, such as the Virūpāksha, Viṭhala and Mālyavanta Raghunātha, were considerably expanded by the addition of pavilions, pillared halls for music and dance and car streets. At the same time many new structures were built, including large temple complexes such as the Kṛishṇa, Anantaśayana, Tiruveṅgaḷanātha and Paṭṭābhirāma and medium-sized temples such as the Mudu Vīraṇṇa and the Tiruveṅgaḷanātha temples in Kṛishṇāpura. The peak period of temple building in the city was under Kṛishṇadēvarāya, who constructed the Kṛishṇa, Anantaśayana and Lakshmī-Narasiṁha temples, besides making extensive additions to the Virūpāksha and Viṭhala complexes. His reign also saw the construction of the Nagēndraśayana and Nāgēśvara temples in Nāgalāpura. Achyutarāya himself did not build any temples in the capital but during his rule the Tiruveṅgaḷanātha and Paṭṭābhirāma temples were constructed. Sadāśiva and Rāmarāya, too, did not venture into temple building, but influential nobles and officials patronised constructional works within the Viṭhala complex and in Viṭhalāpura and also built the two medium-sized temples in Kṛishṇāpura.

It is significant that, with the exception of the Virūpāksha temple, all the large temple complexes in the city are Śrī-Vaishṇava ones. This is hardly surprising since in the sixteenth century Śaivism suffered a setback due to the extensive patronage and support enjoyed by Vaishṇavism.

The expansion of the temple corresponded with the increase in the temple festivals and rituals. The round of *utsavas*—daily, fortnightly, monthly and yearly—added to the exuberance and magnificence of religious life in the city.

Alongside the different brāmaṇical cults there were also those of minor and folk deities, such as the village goddess Yellammā, Hanumān, serpent worship, veneration of *satīs* and heroes. Apart from the various Hindu sects and subsects, Jainism and Islam were also extant in Vijayanagara. The presence of six Jaina temples in the "urban core" and one in Ānegoṅdi indicates the existence of a sizeable Jaina population. The Jainas were influential during the Saṅgama period, while in the late fifteenth and sixteenth centuries they declined in importance in the capital. Muslim horse traders came to the city from the early Saṅgama times onwards, but the resident Muslim population at the site dates from the first half of the fifteenth century. The existence of at least two mosques and extensive cemeteries proves that the Muslims were allowed to practise their religion freely. The visits of Christian Portuguese horse traders and others to the city in the sixteenth century is revealed by some sculptural friezes. However, no Christian religious institutions are extant at the site.

From this survey of cults and divinities in the city it is clear that the Vijayanagara period witnessed the following of an increasing number of cults and religions in the capital. This religious pluralism testifies to the desire of the Vijayanagara rulers to establish a realm that would integrate people of varied beliefs in matters of worship and religious practices. The installation in the capital city of deities from different parts of the empire—even from outside the empire—appears to have been the policy of the Vijayanagara state. Thus, Tiruveṅgaḷanātha of Tirumalai-Tirupati, Raṅganātha of Śrīraṅgam, Viṭhala of Paṇḍharpur, Mallikārjuna of Śrīśailam and, to a lesser extent, Kāḷahastīśvara of Kāḷahasti and Varadarāja of Kāñchi found a place in the city alongside the main deity of the site, Paṁpā-Virūpāksha. Conversely, from the capital the cult of Virūpāksha spread to other parts of the empire and temples to the guardian deity of the empire were consecrated in places far from the capital. The immense popularity of the Vithala cult in the city was also reflected in the setting up of Viṭhala shrines in distant corners of the Vijayanagara empire including Tirupati, the greatest religious centre at that time.

The detailed field survey at the site reveals that nearly three hundred and fifty temples and shrines or their ruins are extant in the city proper (i.e., the "sacred centre" and the "urban core"). There may have been more that have vanished leaving no trace behind. This large number points to the religious fervour and enthusiasm that characterised the city in its heyday.

Some of the temples and shrines can be clearly classified as Śaivite or Vaishṇavite. This identification is done on the basis of the *dvārapālas* carved on the door-jambs, or on inscriptional data, or the presence of either the original *mūrti* or at least the *piṭha* on which *vāhana* of the god is carved, or a Nandi statue facing the sanctum. Ninety-one Śaivite temples and shrines can thus be located.[1] However, it is more than likely that there were many more Śaivite shrines that, unfortunately, cannot be identified, for most of the pre- and early Vijayanagara temples have neither reliefs of *dvārapālas* on the door-jambs nor any other iconographic clue to reveal their sectarian affiliation. Some of these temples, such as the pre-Vijayanagara temple of Kampilarāya (NF w/ 9)[2] and the Siva temple on the south bank of A.D. 1386 (NG t/3)[3], can be classified as Śaiva on the basis of inscriptional data. Despite the lack of clear sectarian indications in many of the temples there, the numerous Śaivite inscriptions on Hemakūṭa[4] and the literary sources such as the *Pampamahatmya* reveal that the Hēmakūṭa hill and the area around the Virūpāksha complex (i.e., NF w and NL b) must have been almost entirely Śaivite. However, only those temples of which there is clear evidence of Śaivite affiliation are included in this list.

The greatest concentration of Śaivite shrines and temples was on Hēmakūṭa hill and around the Virūpāksha temple and there are also quite a few along the river at the sacred Chakra-tīrtha and Kōṭi-tīrtha. As seen in Chapter 2, besides shrines and temples there are also a number of *liṅgas*, cut into the basal rock, in this part of the city. This area was, without doubt, the Śaivite centre of the site. Indeed, except for the Guñja Mādhava shrine (see Chapter 3, note 30) within the Virūpāksha complex, no pre-1565 Vaishṇava shrine is extant on the Hēmakūṭa hill or around the Virūpāksha temple.

Of Vaishṇavite temples and shrines ninety-three can be definitively identified.[5] Among these are included also the original Hanumān shrines, many of which have Vaishṇava *dvārapālas* on their door-jambs. It is of interest that the number of identifiable Śaivite and Vaishṇavite shrines extant at the site are almost equal. Of course, what the exact ratio was of Śaivite and Vaishṇavite shrines and temples cannot be determined since there are over 150 shrines whose sectarian affiliations cannot be determined due to lack of evidence.[6]

If along the south bank the western end of the site near the Virūpāksha complex was primarily Śaivite, the eastern end around the Viṭhala complex was a predominantly Vaishṇavite zone. While most of the Śaivite shrines in the western zone, with the exceptions of the sixteenth century additions to the Virūpāksha complex, are of the pre- and early Vijayanagara period, in the eastern end, but for a few early shrines (e.g, NC v/6), the great majority are of the fifteenth and, even more, of the sixteenth century A.D.

Along the south bank between the western (Śaivite) and eastern (Vaishṇavite) zones is an intermediate area with both Śaivite and Vaishṇavite temples and shrines. Here there are some early Śaivite structures such as the Śiva temple (NG s/1), that is locally known as the Varāha temple because of the boar crest of the Vijayanagara state engraved on its *gōpura* a number of times, and temple NG t/3 of A.D. 1386. The dilapidated Śaivite temple (NM d/1) must be earlier than the Tiruveṅgaḷanātha *ratha-vīdhi*, for it faces away from this car street although at present it is a located on it. At NG n/ 1 there are two early shrines, one of which has Śaivite *dvārapālas*. The direct access to these shrines has been blocked off by the sixteenth century *bṛindāvana* of Raghnunandasvāmi and the Chaturbhuja Hanumān shrine that faces it. This appears to be a case of Vaishṇavite encroachment on Śaivite space. The eastern-most Śaivite structure in this intermediate zone is shrine NG p/1, the stucco Nandis on its superstructure revealing its Śaivite affiliation.

In this intermediate zone there are some early Vaishṇavite temples, the most ancient being the pre- or early Vijayanagara period Narasiṁha temple (NG t/4). The Prāta-Viṭhala (NG w/5) temple is probably of the early Vijayanagara period. Most of the other Vaishṇava shrines and temples here are of the late phase, such as the great Tiruveṅgaḷanātha temple and the smaller one (NG x/2) dedicated to the same deity on its *ratha-vīdhi*, or the Yantrōddhāraka Āñjanēya shrine (NG w/3), which is said to have been consecrated by Vyāsarāya, temple NG t/1 etc.

If along the south bank of the Tuṅgabhadrā there seems to be some polarisation between Śaivism and Vaishṇavism, elsewhere in the city both Śaivite and Vaishṇavite temples and shrines are found all over, at times practically adjacent to each other. In two double-shrine temples there are even Śaivite and Vaishṇavite deities in adjoining *cellas*. The first is temple NT z/5, the two sanctums of which are built against rock carvings of Vīrabhadra and of the scene of Rāma's *paṭṭābhisheka*. The second is temple NX k/1 in which Vīrabhadra and Āñjanēya are enshrined. Apart from the Śaivite and Vaishṇavite temples in the city there are also the Harihara temple (NL c/3) in the "sacred centre" and the temple of Paṭṭanada Yellammā (NR y/4) in the "royal centre".

This overview of the distribution of temples in the city hints at both sectarian conflicts as well as co-existence in the city. That religious tensions did exist in the empire and, therefore, also in the capital city is revealed in the A.D. 1368 inscription in which the Jaina complaint of Śrī-Vaishṇava harassment led to the famous "Jaina-Śrī-Vaishṇava accord" of Bukka I.[7] Similar clahses between Jainas and Śaivas over land and honours occurred in the reigns of Dēvarāya I[8] and Achyutarāya,[9] needing official intervention. During the Vijayanagara period there were marked conflicts at Chidambaram between the protagonists of Śaiva Naṭarāja and Vaishṇava Gōvindarāja. The efforts to revive and promote the worship of Gōvindarāja by Vēdānta Dēśika in the fourteenth century, Achyutarāya and Rāmarāya in the mid-sixteenth century and Krishṇappa Nāyaka of Gingee in A.D. 1597 met with fierce opposition from the Śaivas, the struggle between the two factions continuing even well after the downfall of the Vijayanagara empire.[10]

While such religious tensions did exist, it was also, on the whole, the conscious policy of the Vijayanagara rulers to patronise and reconcile the different religions and sects and thus create a realm where people of all faiths would truly find a home. A few examples from elsewhere in the empire will illustrate this reality which was largely true in the capital city too.

The first dynasty, although Śaiva, set the pattern of tolerance. For while Virūpāksha was adopted as the family deity, the royal crest bore the figure of Varāha (an incarnation of Vishṇu). The Saṅgamas made generous gifts for the renovation and reconstruction of various temples which had suffered damage or destruction during the Muslim invasions such as Śriraṅgam (see Chapter 6) and they patronised Vaishṇava temples and even non-Hindu religions, for example Tirumalai-Tirupati (see Chapter 6) and Jainism (see Chapter 10). The famous inscriptions of Harihara II from Belur symbolises this desire for religious harmony: "He whom the Śaivas worship as Śiva, the Vēdāntins as Brahma, the Bauddhas as Buddha, the Naiyāyikas skilled in proof as Kartta, the followers of the Jaina sasana as Arha, the Mimāṁsakas as Karmma that god Kēśava ever grant your desires".[11]

On the whole, the kings of the later dynasties tried to continue this policy in the empire. For example, Kṛishṇadēvarāya, although a staunch Vaishṇava, showed considerable regard for the Śaiva religion. He visited and made generous benefactions to Vaishṇava temples such as Tirumalai-Tirupati, Kāñchi, Siṁhāchalam and Ahōbalam as well as the Śaiva temples at Tiruvaṇṇamalai, Chidambaram, Kāḷahasti, Śrīśailam and Amarāvati.[12] The royal gifts to Śaiva temples took the form of land, jewels, money and the construction of *gōpuras*, hundred or thousand-pillared halls and *maṇḍapas*. Achyutarāya manifested this policy of tolerance by having himself crowned three times—at the Vaishṇava temple of Veṅkaṭēśvara at Tirumalai-Tirupati, the Śaiva temple of Kāḷahasti and in the capital city.[13] On the auspicious occasion of his coronation, Achyutarāya gifted a number of villages to be assigned equally to gods Varadarāja and Ēkāmbaranātha of Kāñchi.[14] Sadāśiva and his regent Rāmarāya were fervent worshippers of Vishṇu. Hardly any records of benefactions made by them to Śaiva temples are to be found. Nevertheless, Sadāśiva was not so staunch a devotee of Vishṇu as to despise the other gods, or to force people to join his own sect.[15] He even sometimes invokes Śiva and Gaṇēśa in the preamble of his grants.[16]

The religious situation within the capital more or less reflected the general climate throughout the empire. Under the Saṅgamas although Śaivism may have been predominant and Śaiva temples (such as NG t/3, the Prasanna Virūpāksha temple and the Virūpāksha temple of 1398) were built and extensions made to the great Virūpāksha temple, a number of Vaishṇava constructions also proceeded side by side. For example, many additions were made to the Narasiṁha temple (NG t/4) and the Prāta Viṭhala temple, the Rāmachandra temple, the so-called Āñjanēya temple (NV o/1) of Mallikārjuna's reign and, probably, the Viṭhala temple were built. The patronage of Vaishṇava institutions came from the court, as in the case of the Rāmachandra temple and the "Āñjanēya" temple, as well as from the people. The iconography in the Śaiva temples (NG t/3) and the fifteenth century *raṅga-maṇḍapa* of the Virūpāksha temple included both Śaiva and Vaishṇava themes. Similarly Śaiva deities make their appearance in the Vaishṇava temples; Bhairava, Gaṇēśa, Kārtikēya or Durgā are commonly found in the Rāmachandra temple. Apart from Vaishṇavism, the Saṅgamas also promoted Jainism within the capital and allowed the Muslims freedom of religious practice.

There are no identifiable monuments in the city of the the brief periods when the Sāḷuvas or the first Tuḷuva king, Vīra Narasiṁha, reigned. Coming to the reign of Kṛishṇadēvarāya, it is of significance that at the time of his coronation he made sizeable additions to the Virūpāksha complex and also gave it land and jewels. No Vaishṇava temple in the capital did he endow on this occasion. It is also interesting that at the time of the solar eclipse, that occurred on 7 March 1513, he gave generous grants to two each of the most important Śaivite and Vaishṇavite temples (Virūpāksha, Prasanna Virūpāksha, Rāmachandra and Viṭhala) as noted in the inscriptions of A.D. 1513 in each of these four. Again in his Śaivite constructions, such as the *mahā-raṅga-maṇḍapa* of the Virūpāksha temple, many Vaishṇavite reliefs are to be found and conversely in his Vaishṇavite structures, such as the Kṛishṇa temple and the hundred-pillared hall in the Viṭhala complex, Śaivite carvings are present. Thus, this great king definitely did try to encourage both Vaishṇavite and Śaivite sects. However, it is also significant that after his initial constructional activity in the Virūpāksha temple, there are no other examples of such benefactions to Śaivite institutions in the city. Also, after A.D. 1513 there are no records of royal grants to Śaivite temples, while many Vaishṇavite temples and structures—Kṛishṇa, additions to the Viṭhala complex, Anantaśayana in the suburb named after the heir-apparent and the Lakshmī-Narasiṁha monolith—were built and very generous grants were bestowed on these and other Vaishṇava temples (e.g. Kariya Tiruveṅgaḷanātha at Chikkarāya tank, see Chapter 6). There is no data available of royal grants to Jaina or Muslim institutions in the city either. This indicates Vaishṇavism's growing strength in the city after the first decade of the sixteenth century A.D. There is no evidence of any Śaivite constructional activity in the city during the reign of Achyutarāya, while new Vaishṇava temple complexes were built and additions were also made to the Viṭhala complex. Royal grants to temples were few during this period, but they were all to Vaishṇava temples (Viṭhala, Kṛishṇa and Tiruveṅgaḷanātha). In the Vaishṇava temples built during this reign there are a few Śaiva reliefs, but they are less than in the Vaishṇava structures of the previous reign. For example, in the Tiruveṅgaḷanātha temple, built by Achyuta's brother-in-law, Śaiva themes are found only in the large pillared hall in the outer *prākāra*.

During the reign of Sadāśiva, Vaishṇavism (Śrī-Vaishṇavism) seems to have secured complete ascendancy in the capital. The numerous new structures, especially in Viṭhalāpura, are all Vaishṇava ones, with the one exception of the Mudu Vīraṇṇa temple in Kṛishṇāpura. This temple of Vīrabhadra was built by a Vīrasaiva court official, General Jaṅgamaya. But such was the religious atmosphere at court, that this officer seems to have considered it prudent also to build at the same time, in the vicinity of the Mudu Vīraṇṇa temple, a temple to Tiruveṅgaḷanātha which was larger and grander than the Śaiva temple and to make liberal endowments to both! The inscription in the Mudu Vīraṇṇa temple records one of the very few grants to Śaiva institutions made during this reign in the city.

A study of the iconography in the monuments of Sadāsiva's reign also reveals the absence of the earlier spirit of tolerance and accommodation of diverse sects, for in many of the Vaishṇava structures there are no Śaiva reliefs at all. This is true of the Mudal-āḷvār shrine (NC w/2), probably built during this time, the Tirumaṅgai-āḷvār temple (NC v/3) of A.D. 1556, the Lakshmī-Nārāyaṇa shrine of A.D. 1545 and the *uyyāle-maṇḍapa* of A.D. 1554 in the Viṭhala complex, and the A.D. 1545 *raṅga-maṇḍapa* for music and dance in the Mādhava temple (NR t/2). In the entire Tiruveṅgaḷanātha temple in Kṛishṇāpura (NL w/6) there are only two Śaiva reliefs, even though the patron was a Vīraśaiva. This narrow sectarianism was a departure from the policy of religious tolerance of the previous two hundred years.

The grants made in the city (see Appendix A) also reflect the shift that took place from Śaivism to Vaishṇavism and the gradual usurpation by Viṭhala of the place of primacy hitherto enjoyed by Virūpāksha. Thus, the construction of temples in the city, the endowments made to them and the grants issued from the capital city all prove that in the sixteenth century there was a gradual extension of Vaishṇava sway over the capital, which reached its peak during the last years before the destruction of the city in A.D. 1565. On the whole, it had been the deliberate policy of the Vijayanagara rulers to tolerate and even encourage all the sects and thus to avoid sectarianism in the empire and in the capital. However the last reign appears to mark a departure from this policy. Under Sadāśiva, although there is no evidence of persecution of the Śaivas or of any hindrance in the practice of religion by all the sects and religions in the city, the all-out official patronage extended to Vaishṇava cults, naturally, resulted in a serious setback to Śaivism in Vijayanagara. The relegation of Śaivism to a secondary status at the site, which was originally a Śaivite *kshētra*, must have been much resented by the staunch Śaivites.

Superstition has it that the stunning defeat at Rakkasa-Taṅgaḍi was the punishment inflicted on the house of Vijayanagara for the neglect of Virūpāksha, the guardian deity of the empire from early times.[17] In a Śaivite work entitled *Jaṅgama Kālajñāna*, the defeat and death of Rāmarāya are given in a prophetic strain by the Vīraśaiva Sarvajña, a *jaṅgama*, and his son Virūpaṇṇa.[18]

The disastrous defeat of A.D. 1565 marked the end of Vijayanagara as the capital. The city was temporarily occupied, looted and many of its temples were desecrated, the *mūrtis* mutilated and worship came to an end in most of them. This does not mean that the temples were razed to the ground, for a large number of temples and shrines are still standing in fairly good condition. One wonders why the Vaishṇava temples experienced such total destruction, while some Śaiva ones were spared. Thus, while worship ceased in all Vaishṇava temple complexes, the great Virūpāksha temple survived largely unscathed. It is remarkable that in some instances a Śaivite temple escaped havoc while the Vaishṇava temple adjacent to it was badly damaged, such as the unbroken Giant Liṅga (NL m/2) and the mutilated Lakshmī-Narasiṁha monolith (NL m/1); the Mudu Vīraṇṇa temple (NL w/3) which is a living temple, and the adjacent Tiruveṅgaḷanātha temple (NL w/6), which is an empty monument. Different explanations have been offered of this phenomenon, especially as to why the Virūpāksha temple was spared.

According to one view, large sums of money were paid to the invaders to keep their iconoclastic hands off these edifices.[19] But this does not explain why Vaishṇava institutions in the city proper were not spared; for why did the authorities of these not buy off the conquerors as the Virūpāksha temple authorities did? According to local tradition,[20] when the invading armies arrived in the city, after crossing over from Ānegoṅdi at Talārighaṭ, they wrecked havoc in Viṭhalāpura and then proceeded towards the Virūpāksha temple; about half-way along the route at the so-called Varāha temple (the Śiva temple NG s/1) with the reliefs of the boar crest, god Varāha appeared in his zoomorphic form and crossed the path in front of the Muslim army. The Muslims interpreted this sighting of the boar, an unclean animal in their eyes, as an inauspicious omen and hence changed their route and went via the Tiruveṅgaḷanātha temple to the "royal centre"! This interesting aetiological legend tries to explain why the Virūpāksha and some small Vaishṇava temples (such as the

Kōdaṇḍarāma and Yantrōddhāraka Āñjanēya shrines) west of the "Varāha" temple were saved. One wonders why this divine intervention by Vishṇu was aimed at saving only the greatest Śaivite temple of the city and not any of the important temples dedicated to him!

Three other explanations can also be offered. It is known that in the Muslim confederate armies, especially in the army of Bijāpur, there were a number of Marāṭhās.[21] Many of the Marāṭhā families were Śaivites and devotees of Khaṇḍobā, a form of Śiva.[22] Perhaps on their intervention, the offer of money made by the devotees of the Virūpāksha and some other Śaiva temples to escape desecration was accepted by the Sultāns. Another explanation is that Śrī-Vaishṇavism was an imported sect; it was not native to Hampi. Therefore, after the battle of Rakkasa-Taṅgaḍi, when Tirumala fled the city with the court and the treasures, the Śrī-Vaishṇava sectarian leaders and temple authorities also left along with the royal retinue. Hence, when the invaders reached the city of Vijayanagara, there was no one in these Vaishṇava temples to accede to their demands for money. As a result, in frustration, they damaged these temples, while the Śaiva temples whose authorities paid them off were spared. A third possibility is that the Muslim armies looted the city but did not damage all, or even most, of the temples and shrines. However, during the period of turmoil and insecurity resulting from the occupation of the city by the victorious armies and following their withdrawal, in the absence of royal protection to Vaishṇava temples, the Śaivas, especially the militant Vīraśaivas, took their revenge for the setback suffered by them in the preceding decades, by attacking Vaishṇava *mūrtis* and temples. Iconoclasm was not peculiar to the Muslims alone; mutual destruction of temples and idols by Hindus of various sects was not unknown in that age. For example, in the sixteenth century, the bitter rivalry between the Śaivites and Vaishṇavites in the Tuḷuva region even led to the use of force in the struggle by Vaishṇavas against temples and *mūrtis* of the Śaivites.[23] Conversely, in A.D. 1578-79 at Ahōbalam, the sultān of Gōlkoṇḍa, with the assistance of the chiefs of the Haṇḍē family—who were probably Vīraśaivas[24]—invaded and plundered the country and occupied the precincts of that famous Vaishṇava temple.[25] It is possible, therefore, that there was some nexus between the invaders and the Śaivites in Vijayanagara and that the Śaivites also had a hand in the devastation of Vaishṇava institutions. In the absence of further evidence it is not possible to give a definitive answer as to why the Virūpāksha temples and some Śaivite temples were spared while in all the great Vaishṇava temples worship came to a sudden halt.

After the disaster of A.D. 1565 some cults have survived at the site till modern times. The most important of these is that of Paṁpā-Virūpāksha. The great Virūpāksha temple has apparently enjoyed a more or less uninterrupted worship. In the "Mūla" Virūpāksha temple, too, worship is conducted, but whether or not the *liṅga* there is the original icon cannot be determined. Other Śaivite temples under worship include the Mudu Vīraṇṇa temple and the Vīrabhadra temple on Mataṅga; it is possible, however, as seen in Chapter 2 that the original *mūrti* of the latter shrine was carried away or broken in A.D. 1565. Since originally this site was a Śaivite *kshētra* it is significant that primarily the Śaivite cults, especially that of Virūpāksha, have survived. The only Vaishṇava temple at the site, south of the river, where worship seems to have continued in the post-1565 era is that of Kōdaṇḍarāma (NG w/1) . It might have been spared either because of the links with Virūpāksha temple (see Chapter 8), if the conflation of these two cults is a pre-1565 occurrence, or because the cult images here are reliefs carved on a boulder and not stone statues.[26] In more recent times, the worship of Rāma in the Mālyavanta Raghunātha temple has been revived. In Ānegoṅdi, north of the river, the worship of Raṅganātha and of Narasiṁha have also survived. Besides these, the popular cult of Hanumān and those of folk religions such as the worship of Yellammā and snake worship have also endured.

It is significant that those cults or traditions that had some early association with the site such as the Paṁpā-Virūpāksha cult, the Vīrabhadra cult, the Rāmāyaṇa traditions to a certain extent, and those of Raṅganātha and Narasiṁha in a small way, have survived to a greater or lesser extent. Hanumān remains a popular god in his reputed birthplace, while some of the folk traditions that did not depend on official patronage have also partially endured. On the other hand, the great Vaishṇava cults (e.g., those of Viṭhala, Tiruveṅgaḷanātha, and Kṛishṇa) that were, in a sense, imported into the city, disappeared once the court patronage was withdrawn. These apparently had not struck deep roots and hence could not survive the calamities that befell the city after the battle of Rakkasa-Taṅgaḍi.

This survey of religious traditions in the city of Vijayanagara proves that this site was the scene of intense religious activity prior to A.D. 1565, especially during the two hundred years or so when it served as the capital of the greatest medieval Hindu empire. Śaivite and Vaishṇavite cults, popular and folk deities, Jainism and Islam all found their place in the city. The temple rituals, the lively celebration of festivals and the services of ascetics and religious institutions such as *maṭhas*, *āśramas* and *agrahāras* sustained the enthusiasm and vigour of religion in Vijayanagara.

Notes

[1]Śaivite temples and shrines:
1. NB y/1 2. ND u/1 3. ND y/1
4. NF q/1
5. NF r/6 6. To the west of gate NF r/5
7. Two shrines in tank-complex NF v/1
8. NF w/1 (Virūpāksha) 9. NF w/5
10. NF w/6 11. NF w/9 (Kaṁpilarāya's temple),
12. NF w/20 13. NF w/23
14. NF w/25 (Durgā-dēvī) 15. NF w/27
16. NF w/29 17. NF x/1 18. NG m/1
19. NG m/2
20. NG n/1 (one of the two shrines adjacent to the bṛindāvana of Raghunandana-svāmi and Chaturbhuja Hanumān)
21. NG n/4 22. NG p/1 23. NG s/1
24. NG t/3
25. At NG r (a collapsed Śaiva shrine at Chakra-tīrtha)
26. NG y/1 27. NJ x/1 28. NJ x/3
29. NL b/1
30. NL b/19 (Virūpāksha temple of A.D. 1398)
31. NL b/20 32. NL c/2 33. NL e/1
34. NL g/2 35. NL g/7 36. NL h/2
37. NL h/4 38. NL h/6 39. NL h/11
40. NL m/2 (Giant Linga) 41. NL w/2
42. NL w/3 (Mudu Vīraṇṇa) 43. NM b/3
44. NM d/1 45. NM g/1 (Vīrabhadra on Mataṅga)
46. NM r/3 47. NM s/1 48. NM y/3
49. NN a/1 50. NN h/1 51. NN m/2
52. NN n/1 53. NNv/2 (part of *maṭha* complex)
54. NN v/4 55. NN x/3 56. NN y/3
57. NO c/1 58. NP o/1 59. NP r/2
60. NP s/1 61. NQ d/2 (part of an āśrama)
62. NQ g/1 63. NQ j/2 64. NQ q/1
65. NQ s/2 66. NQ u/1
67. NQ y/1 (Prasanna Virūpāksha) 68. NR e/2
69. NR e/5 70. NR h́/2 71. NR j/2
72. NR p/2 73. NR x/1 74. NR y/1
75. NS 1/2 76. NS r/3 77. NS s/1
78. NT c/1 79. NT k/3 80. NT z/5b
81. NU h/1 82. NV j/1 83. NW a/1
84. NW s/1 85. NX k/1a 86. NX 1/1
87. in gate NXo 88. NX n/2
89. NY e/2 90. NY f/1 91. NY y/1.

[2]*ARSIE* of 1934-35, no. 353.

[3]*VPR '83-84*, no. 11.

[4]For example *ARSIE* of 1934-35, nos. 350 and 351; *VPR '83-84*, no. 14; *ARIE* of 1975-76, no. 108, etc.

[5]Vaishṇavite temples and shrines:
1. NC n/1 2. NC r/1 3. NC v/2
4. NC v/3 (Tirumaṅgai-āḷvār)
5. NC w/1
6. NC w/2 (Mudal-āḷvārs)
7. NC w/3 (Rāmānuja)
8. ND y/2 9. ND y/6
10. NE m/1 ("Mukti-Narasiṁha)
11. Guñja-Mādhava shrine in the Virūpāksha complex - NF w/1
12. NG k/1 13. NG k/2
14. NG n/1 (Chaturbhuja-Hanumān)
15. NG p/3 16. NG s/2 17. NG t/1
18. NG t/4 (Narasiṁha)
19. NG w/1 (Kōdaṇḍarāma)
20. NG w/2 21. NG w/3 (Yantrōddhāraka Āñjanēya)
22. NG w/5 (Prāta-Viṭhala) 23. NG x/1
24. NG x/2 25. NH a/1 (Viṭhala)
26. NH a/5 27. NH a/10 (Nammāḷvār)
28. NH f/1 29. NH f/2 30. NH f/4
31. NH b/15 32. NH j/1
33. NJ o/1 34. NJ s/2 35. NJ x/2
36. NL h/1 37. NL h/9 38. NL h/14
39. NL m/1 (Lakshmī-Narasiṁha)
40. NL m/4 (Kṛishṇa)
41. NL q/1 42. NL s/1 43. NL w/6
44. NM b/8 45. NM h/1 (Tiruveṅgaḷnātha)
46. NM r/2 47. NM w/2 48. NN r/1
49. NN s/1 50. NN x/1 51. NN x/5
52. NN z/2 53. NO r/3 54. NQ m/1
55. NQ n/1 56. NQ s/1 57. NQ t/4
58. NR c/1 59. NR c/3 60. NR g/1
61. NR g/2 62. NR g/3 63. NR h/1
64. NR n/1 65. NR o/1 66. NR q/2
67. NR t/4 (Mādhava)
68. NR w/1 (Rāmachandra)
69. NR x/4 70. NS b/1 71. NS b/2
72. NS b/4 73. NS g/1 74. NS 1/1
75. NS o/1 76. NS p/4 77. NS y/1
78. NS z/1 79. NS z/3
80. NT d/1 (Mālyavanta Raghunātha)

81. NT d/4 82. NT d/5 83. NT d/6
84. NT o/2 85. NT o/4 86. NT w/1
87. NT z/5a 88. NU 1/2 89. NV o/1
90. NX f/1 91. NX k/1b 92. NX o/1
93. NY j/1.

[6]Temples and shrines whose sectarian affiliations are not known.

1. NC v/6 2. ND y/4 3. NF w/4
4. NF w/7 5. NF w/11 6. NF w/12
7. NF w/13 8. NF w/14 9. NF w/15
10. NF w/16 11. NF w/17 12. NF w/18
13. NF w/19 14. NF w/21 15. NF w/22
16. NF w/24 17. NF w/26 18. NG k/5
19. NG n/3 20. NG s/3 21. NH d/3
22. NJ c/1 23. NJ m/2 24. NJ s/1
25. NL a/1 26. NL a/2 27. NL b/2
28. NL b/3 29. NL b/4 30. NL b/5
31. NL b/11 32. NL b/12 33. NL b/13 (?)
34. NL b/14 35. NL b/15 36. NL b/17
37. NL b/18 38. NL b/24 39. Nl b/26
40. NL c/5 41. Nl g/1 42. NL g/3
43. NL g/5 44. NL g/6 45. NL h/12
46. NL h/13 47. NL h/15 48. NM b/4
49. NM d/2 50. NM j/1 51. NM w/1
52. NM w/3 53. NN s/2 54. NN s/3
55. NN s/4 56. NN s/5 57. NN s/6
58. NN t/1 59. NN t/2 60. NNv/3
61. NN w/1 62. NN x/4 63. NN y/1
64. NN y/2 65. NN z/1 66. NO c/2
67. NO j/4 68. NO 1/1 69. NO q/3
70. NO q/4 71. NO q/5 72. NO r/1
73. NP c/1 74. NQ e/1 75. NQ h/1
76. NQ j/1 77. NQ t/2 78. NQ t/3
79. NQ u/3 80. NQ x/1 81. NQ y/2
82. NR b/2 83. NR c/2 84. NR c/5
85. NR e/4 86. NR e/6 87. NR g/4
88. NR j/1 89. NR m/1 90. NR m/2
91. NR n/2 92. NR q/1 93. NR q/3
94. NR u/1 95. NR w/2 96. NR w/3
97. NR x/2 98. NR x/6 99. NR z/1
100. NS b/3 101. NS d/1 102. NS h/1
103. NS h/3 104. NS l/3 105. NS m/1
106. NS m/4 107. NS q/2 108. NS q/3
109. NS q/4 110. NS r/1 111. NS r/2
112. NS r/4 113. NS s/2 114. NS s/3
115. NS s/4 116. NS s/6 117. NS s/7
118. NS s/8 119. NS t/1 120. NS u/1
121. NS u/2 122. NS u/4 123. NS x/1
124. NS x/2 125. NS z/2 126. NT j/1
127. NT q/1 128. NT q/2 129. NT v/1
130. NT v/2 131. NT v/4 132. NT v/5
133. NU b/1 134. NU f/3 135. NU f/4
136. NU 1/3 137. NU t/2 138. NU x/1
139. NV c/1 140. NV c/2 141. NW k/1
142. NW r/1 143. NX a/2 144. NX c/2
145. NX d/1 146. NX d/2 147. NX h/2
148. NX h/3 149. NX k/2 150. NX 1/2
151. NX o/5 152. NX p/1 153. NX v/1
154. NY e/1 155. NY f/2 156. NZ g/1

[7]*EC* II (1923 ed), *SB.* no. 344; and *IA* XIV, pp. 234-35.

[8]*SII* XX, no. 232.

[9]*ARSIE* of 1935-36, B.K. 18.

[10]T.B. Balasubramanyan, "Chidambaram in Vijayanagara Days," *Journal of the Bombay Historical Society,* IV, pp. 40-53.

[11]*EC* V, B1.3.

[12]N.Venkataramanyya, *Studies in the Third Dynasty of Vijayanagara,* p. 317.

[13]A.N. Krishna Aiyangar, Introduction to *Achyutarāyābhyudaya* by Rājanātha Diṇḍima, pp. 13-14.

[14]*SII* IX, pt. II, nos. 562 and 563; *SITI,* no. 406.

[15]H. Heras, *The Aravidu Dynasty of Vijayanagara,* vol. I, p. 543.

[16]*EI* IV, p. 12.

[17]H. Heras, op.cit., p. 544 and C.R. Krishnamacharlu, "The Religion of the Vijayanagara House," *IA,* XLIV, p. 224.

[18]H. Heras, loc.cit.

[19]S.B. Kodad, *History of Vijayanagar Empire: The Battle of Talikota,* p. 43.

[20]Related by Mohan Joshi, a young *pūjāri* of the Virūpāksha temple.

[21]H. Heras, op.cit., p. 200; H.K. Sherwani and P.M. Joshi (ed.), *History of Medieval Deccan 1294-1724,* vol. I, p. 399.

[22]D.A. Pai, *Monograph on Religious Sects in India among the Hindus,* p. 65.

[23]B.A. Saletore, "Vaiṣṇavism in Vijayanagara," in *D.R. Bhandarkar Commemoration Volume,* ed. B.C. Law, pp. 190-195.

[24]C. Hayavadana Rao, *Mysore Gazetteer,* vol. II, pt. III, p. 2162.

[25]*Sources,* pp. 233-234; *Top.List* vol. II, Kurnool dist., no. 584 and *ARSIE* of 1915, no. 70.

[26]In general the reliefs of deities carved in the temples or on rocks and boulders in the city have not been damaged at all. The zeal of the iconoclasts seems to have been directed principally against the stone idols in the temples, which were mutilated and thrown about. The numerous broken *mūrtis* found during the excavations or clearance work at the Viṭhala, Kṛishṇa and other temples reveal this.

APPENDIX A

Grants, Gifts, etc, made in Vijayanagara city in the presence of Virūpāksha, Viṭhala and other Deities

	Year	Donor		Deity in whose presence grant made			Nature of the Record	Source
	(A.D.)	Kings	Others	Virūpāksha	Viṭhala	Others		
1.	1354	Bukka I		Virūpāksha			grant of a village to a brāhmaṇa	*EC* XI, Dg. 67 & *JBBRAS* XII, pp. 350-351.
2.	?	Bukka I		Virūpāksha in Paṁpā-kshētra			grant of land to a poet	*EC* X, Gd. 46.
3.	1379	Harihara II		Virūpāksha on the bank of the Tuṅgabhadrā			endowment of 22 villages to the temples of Tryaṁbakēśa and Vīra-nārāyaṇa at Gadag and an equal number of villages to brāhmaṇas	*ARSIE* of 1940-41, A-22; *JBBRAS* XII, pp. 377-378.
4.	1381	Harihara II		Virūpāksha			grant of a village as an *agrahāra* to 39 brāhmaṇas	*MAR* of 1913, p. 43.
5.	1381	Harihara II		Virūpāksha in Paṁpā-kshētra			grant of a village to 10 brāhmaṇas	*EC* V, Hn. 36.
6.	1382	Harihara II		Virūpāksha of Paṁpā-kshētra and god Harihareśvara			grant of a village to Liṅgarasa for the continual recitations of the Vedas and Śāstras in the temple of Harihar-ēśvara (at Harihara)	*EC* XI, Dg.68
7.	1385	Harihara II		Tuṅga, Paṁpā and Virūpāksha			grant of a village as an *agrahāra* to brāhmaṇas	*EC* V, B1. 148.
8.	1386	Harihara II		Virūpāksha of Paṁpā-kshetra			grant of lands to Śṛiṅgēri *maṭha* in memory of Vidyāraṇya	*MAR* of 1933, no. 24.
9.	1388	Harihara II		Virūpāksha on the bank of the Tuṅgabhadrā			grant of a village to a brāhmaṇa	*EC* XII, Tp. 9.

10.	1394	Harihara II		Virūpāksha on the bank of the Tuṅgabhadrā in Bhāskara-kshētra		grant of a village to a brāhmaṇa	*MAR* of 1925, no. 20.
11.	1394	Harihara II		Virūpāksha		grant of a village to brāhmaṇas	*EC* VIII, T1, 201.
12.	1395	Harihara II		Virūpāksha on the bank of the Tuṅgabhadrā adorned by Hēmakūṭa		grant of a village to 2 brāhmaṇas	H.T. Colebrooke, *Miscellaneous Essays*, vol. II, pp. 259-260.
13.	1396	Harihara II		Virūpāksha on the bank of the Tuṅgabhadrā		grant of a village as an *agrahāra* to brāhmaṇas	*EC* V, Hn. 86.
14.	1396	Harihara II		Virūpāksha on the bank of the Tuṅgabhadrā		grant of a village to a brāhmaṇa	*EC* V, HN. 7
15.	1397	Harihara II		Virūpāksha		grant of a village to a brāhmaṇa	*MAR* of 1933, no. 25.
16.	1397	Harihara II		Virūpāksha on the bank of the Tuṅgabhadrā		grant of a village to a brāhmaṇa	*EC* III, TN. 134.
17.	1398	Harihara II		Virūpāksha		grant of a village to a brāhmaṇa	*MAR* of 1912, p. 47.
18.	1399	Harihara II		Virūpāksha		grant of a village to a brāhmaṇa	*MAR* of 1912, p. 48.
19.	1399	Harihara II		Virūpāksha in Bhāskara-kshētra		grant of a village to 2 brāhmaṇas	*EI* III, pp. 113-126.
20.	1402	Dēvarāya I		Virūpāksha on the bank of the Tuṅgabhadrā		grant of a village to a brāhmaṇa	*EC* X, Gd. 56.
21.	1403		Irugappa daṇḍanātha, a minister		Chandramauḷi	grant of lands to brāhmaṇas	*EC* XII, Si. 95.
22.	1404	Bukka II		Virūpāksha on the bank of the Tuṅgabhadrā		grant of a village to brāhmaṇas	*EC* VI, Kp. 25.
23.	1405	Bukka II		Paṁpā-Virūpāksha		grant of land to a brāhmaṇa	*EC* XI, Dg. 108.
24.	1406	Dēvarāya I (on the occasion of his coronation)		Virūpāksha of Paṁpā-khsetra		grant of a village as an *agrahāra* to brāhmaṇas	*EC* V, Hn. 133.

25.	1408		farmers & subjects of Āraga Eighteen Kampaṇa and those of the three cities		Viṭhalēśvara on the bank of the Tuṅgabhadrā		grant of a village as an *agrahāra* to brāhmaṇas	*EC* VIII, Tl. 222.
26.	1408	Dēvarāya I		Paṁpāpati			did *tulāpurusha* in gold and gave gift of *Brahmāṇḍa*	*MAR* of 1925, no. 34.
27.	1415	Dēvarāya I		Virūpāksha-liṅga on the bank of the Tuṅgabhadrā			grant of a village to a brāhmaṇa	*EC* III, Nj. 179.
28.	1415	Dēvarāya I		Virūpāksha on the bank of the Tuṅgabhadrā			grant of a village to a brāhmaṇa	*EC* XII, Mi.83.
29.	1424	Dēvarāya II		Virūpāksha on the bank of the Tuṅgabhadrā			grant of an *agrahāra* to 8 brāhmaṇas	*EI* III, pp. 35-41.
30.	1425	Dēvarāya II				Chandramauḷi in Bhāskara-kshētra on the bank of Tuṅgabhadrā	grant of a village as an *agrahāra* to a brāhmaṇa	*EC* IX, Dv. 81.
31.	1426	Dēvarāya II		Virūpāksha on the bank of the Tuṅgabhadrā			grant of a village to a brāhmaṇa	*EC* XII, Tm. 11.
32.	1426	Dēvarāya II				Chandramauḷi	grant of a village to a brāhmaṇa	*MAR* of 1912, p. 49.
33.	1427	Dēvarāya II		Virūpāksha on the bank of the Tuṅgabhadrā			grant of a village and lands to god Raṅganātha of Śrīraṅgam	*EI* XVII, pp. 110- 111.
34.	1428		Lakkaṇṇa Voḍeyar for the merit Dēvāraya II	Virūpāksha on the bank of the Tuṅgabhadrā			grant of a tank and of lands to Annadātta, son of Singarasa	*EC* X, Kl. 104.
35.	1429	Dēvarāya II		Virūpāksha in Hēmakūṭa in Bhāskara-kshētra			grant of a village to brāhmaṇas	*Nel. Ins.* I, C.P. 18.
36.	1429	Dēvarāya II		Virūpāksha on the bank of the Tuṅgabhadrā			grant of a village to brāhmaṇas	*MAR* of 1941, no. 20
37.	1429	Dēvarāya II		Virūpāksha on the bank of the Tuṅgabhadrā			grant of a village to Annamārādhya	*Nel. Ins.* I, C.P. 3.

38.	1430	Dēvarāya II		Virūpāksha in Pampā-kshētra in the region of Hēmakūṭa		Gift of a golden cow and a village as an *agrahāra* to brāhmaṇas	*EC* III, Sr. 15.
39.	1430-31	Dēvarāya II		Virūpāksha on the banks of the Pampā		grant of a tax to a temple.	*ARSIE* of 1916, no. 172.
40.	1432		Dēvamahārāju for the merit of the king	Virūpāksha on the bank of the Tuṅgabhadrā		grant of a village to a temple	*Nel. Ins.* I, no. 20.
41.	1432	Dēvarāya II		Virūpāksha on the bank of the Tuṅgabhadrā		grant of land to the *guru* Purushōttamāranya of Raghuttama *maṭha* at Gōkarṇa	*MAR* of 1916, p. 61 & *MAR* of 1933, no. 26.
42.	1435	Dēvarāya II		Virūpāksha		grant of a village to brāhmaṇas	*MAR* of 1921, pp. 29-30.
43.	1447	Mallikārjuna			Chandramauḷi on the bank of the Tuṅgabhadrā in Bhāskara-kshētra at the foot of Hēmakūṭa-giri	grant of a village to a brāhmaṇa	*EC* XII, Pg. 69.
44.	1448	Mallikārjuna		Virūpāksha		grant of village to a brāhmaṇa	*EC* III, Sr. 11.
45.	1461	Mallikārjuna		Virūpāksha on the bank of the Tuṅgabhadrā		grant of a village as an *agrahāra* to brāhmaṇas	*ARSIE* of 1938-39, A. 16.
46.	1462	Mallikārjuna			Chandramauḷi	grant of a village to god Raṅga-nātha of Śṛīraṅgam	*EI* XVI, pp. 345-353.
47.	1463	Mallikārjuna		Virūpākshēśvara on the bank of the Tuṅgabhadrā at the foot of Hēmādri		grant of certain privileges to Raghavēśvara Bhārati-śrīpada, *guru* of Raghuttama *maṭha*, Gōkarṇa	*EC* VIII, Nr. 68.
48.	1463	Mallikārjuna		Virūpāksha and Chandramauḷi on the bank of the Tuṅgabhadrā, in Bhāskara-kshētra at the foot of Hēmakūṭa	(and Chandra-mauḷi)	grant of three villages to the *guru* of the above *maṭha*	*EC* VIII, Nr. 69.

49.	1463	Mallikārjuna		Virūpāksha and Chandramauli on the bank of the Tuṅgabhadrā, in Bhāskara-kshētra at the foot of Hēmkūṭa hill		(and Chandra-mauḷi)	grant of a village to minister Dēvappa-daṇḍanātha, who with the king's permission gave it as an *agrahāra* to brāhmaṇas	*EC* VIII, T1. 206.
50.	1465	Virūpāksha II (on the occasion of his coronation)		Virūpāksha on the bank of the Tuṅgabhadrā			grant of a village to god Mallikārjuna of Śrīśailam	*EI* XV, pp. 24-25.
51.	1467	Virūpāksha II		Virūpāksha on the bank of the Tuṅgabhadrā			gift of land to brāhmaṇas	*EI* XVII, pp. 203-204.
52.	1474	Virūpāksha II				Chandramauḷi of Bhāskara-kshētra on the bank of the Tuṅgabhadrā	grant of a village to brāhmaṇas	*EC* III, M1. 121.
53.	1493	Immaḍi Narasiṁha•			Viṭhalēśvara		grant of a village to brāhmaṇas	*ARSIE* of 1940-41, A. 38.
54.	1503		Kāmarasu-Tim-mayaṁgaru, for the merit of king Immaḍi Narasiṁha & Narasa Nāyaka		Viṭhaladēva on the bank of the Tuṅgabhadrā		gift of lands to a temple	*ARSIE* of 1935-36, no. 321.
55.	1505	Vīra Narasiṁha		Virūpāksha on the bank of the Tuṅgabhadrā			gift of land to brāhmaṇas	*EC* X, Gd. 77.
56.	1506	Vīra Narasiṁha		Virūpāksha on the bank of the Tuṅgabhadrā			grant of village to Sarvēśvārādhya	*EC* XVI, M1. 131, & *MAR* of 1918, p. 52.
57.	1506	Vīra Narasiṁha		Paṁpā-Virūpāksha			grant of village to a *guru*	*EC* VIII, Nr. 64.
58.	1509-10	Vīra Narasiṁha		Virūpāksha on the bank of the Tuṅgabhadrā			grant of a village to an ascetic of the Śaṅkara *maṭha* at Kāñchi	*EI* XIV, pp. 231-240.
59.	1510	Kṛishṇadēvarāya		Virūpāksha on the bank of the Tuṅgabhadrā			grant of a village to a brāhmaṇa	*JAHRS*, 10, pp. 121-142.
60.	1510		minister Sāḷuva-Timma	Virūpāksha on the bank of the Tuṅgabhadrā			remission of marriage tax	*EC* XII, Mi. 64

61.	1511	Kṛishṇadēvarāya		Virūpāksha on the bank of the Tuṅgabhadrā	grant of a village to brāhmaṇas	*SII* IX, pt. II, no. 484 & *ARSIE* of 1922, no. 724.
62.	1512	Kṛishṇadēvarāya		Virūpāksha on the bank of the Tuṅgabhadrā	grant of a village as an *agrahāra* to Liṅga-bhaṭṭa, who distributed shares in it to other brāhmaṇas	*EC* XI, Hk. 94.
63.	1512-13	Kṛishṇadēvarāya		Virūpāksha on the bank of the Tuṅgabhadrā	grant of a village to a brāhmaṇa	*JBBRAS*, XII, pp. 381-399.
64.	1513	Kṛishṇadēvarāya		Virūpāksha on the bank of the Tuṅgabhadrā	grant of a village to brāhmaṇas	*EC* III, Nj. 16.
65.	1513	Kṛishṇadēvarāya		Virūpāksha on the bank of the Tuṅgabhadrā	grant of a village to a brāhmaṇa	*EC* VII, Sh. 1.
66.	1513	Kṛishṇadēvarāya		Virūpāksha on the bank of the Tuṅgabhadrā	grant of a village to a brāhmaṇa	*ARSIE* of 1941-42, A.7.
67.	1514		Mahāpradhāna (chief minister) Sāḷuva Timmarasa, on the orders of the king	Virūpāksha-liṅga in Paṁpā-kshētra	grant of a village to a temple	*MAR* of 1930, no. 38.
68.	1514	Kṛishṇadēvarāya		Virūpāksha on the bank of the Tuṅgabhadrā near Hēmakūṭa hill	grant of a village to a brāhmaṇa	*EI* XVIII, pp. 160-161.
69.	1516	Kṛishṇadēvarāya		Viṭhalēśvara on the bank of the Tuṅgabhadrā	grant of the village of Maṇḍya, together with some hamlets, to Gōviṅdarāja	*EC* III, Md. 115.
70.	1516	Krishnadēvarāya		Virūpāksha on the bank of the Tuṅgabhadrā adorned with Hēmakūṭa	grant of 3 villages to Vyāsatīrtha	*MAR* of 1941, no. 28.
71.	1517	Kṛishṇadēvarāya		Virūpāksha on the bank of the Tuṅgabhadrā	grant of a village to Nāganātha, who bestowed it on brāhmaṇas	*EC* XII, Pg. 4

72.	1517		Pradhāna (minister) Mallarasa	gods Virūpāksha,	Viṭhalēśvara and Kṛishṇa	grant of a village to a temple of Tirumala at Jajūru	*EC* XI, Hk. 70.
73.	1517	Kṛishṇadēvarāya			Viṭhalēśvara on the bank of the Tuṅgabhadrā	grant of a village to a brāhmaṇa for service in a temple	*EC* IV, Gu. 30.
74.	1517	Kṛishṇadēvarāya			Viṭhalēśvara on the bank of the Tuṅgabhadrā	grant of lands for services in the temple of Tiruveṅgaḷantha at Vijayanagara	*SII* IV, no. 249.
75.	1518	Kṛishṇadēvarāya			Viṭhalēśvara on the the bank of the Tuṅgabhadrā	grant of a village to a brāhmaṇa	*MAR* of 1928, no. 49.
76.	1518		senior queen Tirumala-dēvī, for the merit of Prince Tirumalarāya		Viṭhalēśvara on the bank of the Tuṅgabhadrā	grant of land for service of Kariya Tiruveṅgaḷanātha at Vijayanagara	*SII* IX, pt. II, no. 510.
77.	1518	Kṛishṇadēvarāya		Virūpāksha-liṅga on the bank of the Tuṅgabhadrā		grant of 5 villages to the temple of Kōṭinātha	*EC* VIII, Sb. 278.
78.	1519		minister Sāḷuva Govindarāja, on the order of the king	Virūpāksha	Viṭhala	grant of a village to a brāhmaṇa	*EC* III, TN. 73.
79.	1519		Nayanappa-Nāyaka	Virūpāksha on the bank of the Tuṅgabhadra		gave land for the benefit of two watersheds	*ARSIE* of 1935-36, B.K. 186 & *SII* XVIII, no. 280.
80.	1519		chief minister Saḷuva Goviṅdarāja on the orders of the king	Virūpāksha-liṅga of Paṁpā-kshētra		grant of land	*MAR* of 1917, p. 49.
81.	1519	Kṛishṇadēvarāya		Virūpāksha on the bank of the Tuṅgabhadrā		grant of a village to *guru* Basava-dīkshita	*EC* V, Cn. 167.

82.	1521		chief minister Sāḷuva Goviṁdarāja, for the merit of the king	Virūpāksha of Paṁpā-kshētra		grant of land to brāhmaṇas	*EC* III, TN.42.
83.	1522		Sāḷuva Goviṁdarāja, by the order of the king	Virūpāksha on the bank of the Tuṅgabhadrā in Bhāskara-kshētra		grant of land to a temple	*EC* IV, Gu. 1.
84.	1523	Kṛishṇadēvarāya			Viṭhala on the bank of the Tuṅgabhadrā	grant of a village and its two hamlets to Vyāsatīrtha	*EC* IX, Cp. 153 & *MAR* of 1919, no. 90.
85.	1524	Kṛishṇadēvarāya		Virūpāksha on the bank of the Tuṅgabhadrā		grant of a village to a brāhmaṇa	*EC* V, Hn. 94.
86.	1525	Kṛishṇadēvarāya		Virūpāksha on the bank of the Tuṅgabhadrā		grant of a village to a brāhmaṇa	*EC* XII, Ck. 10.
87.	1526	Kṛishṇadēvarāya			Viṭhalēśvara on the bank of the Tuṅgabhadrā	grant of a village to Vyāsatīrtha	*EI* XXXI, pp. 139-162.
88.	1527	Kṛishṇadēvarāya			Viṭhalēśvara on the bank of the Tuṅgabhadra	grant of 5 villages to an ascetic of the Kūḍali-Ārya-*maṭha*	*EC* VII, Sh. 84.
89.	1527	Kṛishṇadēvarāya		Virūpāksha at Hēmakūṭa		grant of a village to a brāhmaṇa	*ARSIE* of 1937-38, A. 10.
90.	1527	Kṛishṇadēvarāya		Virūpāksha on the bank of the Tuṅgabhadrā in Paṁpā-kshētra		grant of a village to a temple	*MAR* of 1930, no. 16.
91.	1527		Narasappaya, on the orders of the chief of Ummattūr, for the merit of the king & Narasa Nāyaka	Virūpāksha-liṅga, on the bank of the Tuṅgabhadrā in Paṁpā-kshētra		grant of a village to a brāhmaṇa	*MAR* of 1939, no. 57.

92.	1529		Chenni-seṭṭi, for the merit of the king	Virūpāksha of Pampā-kshētra		grant of a village to a temple deity	EC XVI, Ck. 83, & *MAR* of 1918, p. 52.
93.	1529	Kṛishṇadēvarāya		Virūpāksha on the bank of the Tuṅgabhadrā		grant of a village to an ascetic of the Śaṅkarāchārya *maṭha* at Kāñchi	*EI*, XIV, pp. 168-75.
94.	?	Kṛishṇadēvarāya			Viṭhalēśvara on the bank of the Tuṅgabhadrā	grant of a village to a brāhmaṇa	*ARIE* of 1953-54, A. 18.
95.	1530	Achyutarāya		Virūpāksha on the bank of the Tuṅgabhadrā		grant of a village to a brāhmaṇa	*EI* XIV, pp. 310-323.
96.	1530	Achyutarāya			Viṭhalēśvara on the bank of the Tuṅgabhadrā	grant of a village to a brāhmaṇa	*EC* IX, D.B. 30.
97.	1531		Daḷavāyi (general) Nāgappa Nāyaka	Virūpāksha on the bank of the Tuṅgabhadrā		grant of a village to a temple deity	*EC* IX, D.B. 50.
98.	1531	Achyutarāya		Virūpāksha on the bank of the Tuṅgabhadrā		grant of a village for the services of gods Vīrabhadra, Rāghunātha and Pāpavināśa of Lēpākshi	*SII* IX, pt. II, no. 535 & *ARSIE* of 1912, no. 579.
99.	1532		Mahāmaṇḍalēśvara Tirumala-dēva Mahārāja, for the merit of the king	Viśēśvarā-Virūpāksha on the banks of the Tuṅgabhadrā		grant of lands to brāhmaṇas	*ARSIE* of 1935-36, no. 335.
100.	1532	Achyutarāya		Virūpāksha on the bank of the Tuṅgabhadrā		gift of a village by the king, in the name of his brother-in-law Tirumalarāya, to a brāhmaṇa	*ARSIE* of 1937-38, no. 479.
101.	1533		Bācharusu, the agent of the king		Viṭhalēśvara	gift of various imports to a temple deity	*ARSIE* of 1938-39, no. 337.
102.	1533	Achyutarāya			Viṭhalēśvara on the bank of the Tuṅgabhadrā	grant of a village to brāhmaṇas	*EC* XI, Hk. 132.

103.	1533	Achyutarāya		Viṭhalēśvara on the bank of the Tuṅgabhadrā	gift of Suvarṇamēru	*SII* IX, pt. II, nos. 557 & 558.
104.	1533	Achyutarāya		Viṭhalēśvara on the bank of the Tuṅgabhadrā	grant of a village to a brāhmaṇa	*EC* XII, Pg. 75.
105.	1534	Achyutarāya		Viṭhalēśvara on the bank of the Tuṅgabhadrā	grant of a village to a priest of god Raṅganātha of Śrīraṅgam	*MAR* of 1922, pp. 12-13
106.	1534-35	Achyutarāya		Viṭhalēśvara on the bank of the Tuṅgabhadrā	gift of land and a house to two Vaishṇava brāhmaṇas	*Top.List,* I no. 707.
107.	1535	Achyutarāya		Viṭhalēśa-Vishṇu on the bank of the Tuṅgabhadrā	grant of a village to brāhmaṇas	*EC* V, Ak. 126.
108.	1535		minister Siddar-dapaṇṇa-bhūpati	Virūpāksha on the bank of the Tuṅgabhadrā	grant of *kōragāla* to Nañjinātha	*EC* III, M1. 34.
109.	1535		Rāmappa (a chieftain) for the merit of the king	Virūpāksha and Viṭhala on the bank of the (and Viṭhala) Tuṅgabhadrā	grant of a village to brāhmaṇas	*EC* V, Ak. 167.
110.	1535		Rāmappayya, the king's household treasurer, for the merit of the king	Virūpāksha on the bank of the Tuṅgabhadrā	remission of marriage tax in Būdihāḷa-sīme	*EC* XII, Ck. 5
111.	1535		Rāmappaya, the king's household treasurer, for the merit of the king	Virūpāksha on the bank of the Tuṅgabhadrā	remission of marriage tax in Kandikēre-sīme	*EC* XII, Ck. 44.

112.	1535	Achyutarāya			Viṭhalēśvara on the bank of the Tuṅgabhadrā		grant of land to brāhmaṇas	*MAR* of 1947-56, no. 50.
113.	1535		Venkaṭapati-Rāyamahārāya (son of Achyutarāya?)	Virūpāksha-liṅga			grant of a village to a temple of Mallikārjuna	*EC* IX, N1.2.
114.	1536		Sōmaśila-Dēva-Rāūttarāya mahāpatre, on the order of the king and for the merit of the king		Viṭhalēśvara in Paṁpā-kshētra		grant of a village to a temple deity	*EC* IV, Ch. 196.
115.	1536	Achyutarāya			Viṭhalēśvara on the bank of the Tuṅgabhadrā		grant of a village to a brāhmaṇa	*Nel.Ins.*, I, C.P. 10.
116.	1537	Achyutarāya			Viṭhalēśvara on the bank of the Tuṅgabhadrā		grant of 2 villages to the Vīrabhadra temple at Lēpākshi	*ARSIE* of 1912, no. 572.
117.	1539		Rāmabhaṭṭayya, an officer of the king	Virūpāksha at Paṁpā-kshētra			gift of certain income to a temple	*SII* IX, pt. II, no. 592.
118.	1539	Achyutarāya			Viṭhalēśvara on the bank of the Tuṅgabhadrā		gift of Ānandanidhi to brāhmaṇas	*ARSIE* of 1904, nos. 1, 17, 20; *EC* XI, Hk, 123; etc.
119.	1539	Achyutarāya		Virūpāksha-liṅga on the bank of the Tuṅgabhadrā			renewal of a grant of a village	*EC* IX, Ma. 48.
120.	1539	Achyutarāya		Virūpāksha on the bank of the Tuṅgabhadrā			grant of a village to a brāhmaṇa	*EC* XII, Tm. 50.
121.	1539	Achyutarāya				Vrishabēśvara on the bank of the Tuṅgabhadra	grant of a village as an *agrahāra* to brāhmanas	*EC* V, B1.197.

122.	1539	Achyutarāya			Viṭhalēśvara on the bank of the Tuṅgabhardā	grant of a village to brāhmaṇas	*ARIE* of 1972-73, A. 3.
123.	1541	Achyutarāya		Virūpāksha on the bank of the Tuṅgabhadrā		grant of a village to a brāhmaṇa	*Nel. Ins.* I, C.P. 13.
124.	1542	Sadāśiva			Viṭhalēśvara on the bank of the Tuṅgabhadrā	grant of a village to *guru* Tirumala Tatāchārya	*ARSIE* of 1941-42, no. 58.
125.	1543		Salaka-Rāja Chikka Tirumaladēva (brother-in-law of Achyutarāya)	Virūpāksha on the bank of the Tuṅgabhadrā		grant of a village to *guru* Emmēbasavēndra	*MAR* of 1944, no. 25.
126.	1544		Chikka Mallappa Nāyaka	In front of the Virūpāksha temple on the banks of the Pampā river		gift of his share of *prasāda* to another	*ARIE* of 1922, no. 163.
127.	1545	Sadāśiva			Viṭhalēśvara on the bank of the Tuṅgabhadrā	grant of a village to brāhmaṇas	*EC* IV, Ng. 58.
128.	1547		Mahāmaṇḍa-lēśvara Rāmarāju Veṅkatādria-yyadēva, for the merit of his father Śrīraṅgarāja		Viṭhalēśvara	grant of certain taxes and levies to Kaṇḍāla Śrīraṅgāchārya	*ARIE* of 1964-65, no. 57.
129.	1547		Mahāmaṇḍa-lēśvara Rāmarāju Veṅkatādria-yyadēva Mahārāju, for the merit of his father		Viṭhala	grant of a village to Rāvuladēvuṇi Akirāju	*ARSIE* of 1942-43, no. 26.

130. 1549	Sadāśiva		Viṭhalēśvara on the bank of the Tuṅgabhadrā	grant of a village to Āchārayya, a learned brāhmaṇa	*Nel. Ins.*, I, C.P. 14.
131. 1550		Mahāmaṇḍa-lēśvara Jagannātha Rājayya	Viṭhalēśvara on the bank of the Tuṅgabhadrā	grant of a village to a temple deity	*EC* XII, Tp. 6.
132. 1551	Sadāśiva		Viṭhalēśvara on the bank of the Tuṅgabhadrā	grant of a village to brāhmaṇas	*EI* XIV, pp. 210-231.
133. 1551		Kondarājayya's son (name lost)	Viṭhaladēva	gift of a land	*SII* IX, pt. II, no. 645 & *ARSIE* of 1917, no. 29.
134. 1555		Raṅgarājayya-Dēva-Mahā-arasu	Viṭhalēśvara on the bank of the Tuṅgabhadrā	grant of a village to a temple	*EC* IV, Ch. 202.
135. 1556	Sadāśiva		Viṭhalēśvara on the bank of the Tuṅgabhadrā	grant of 31 villages to the temple of Rāmānuja at Śrīperumbudūr	*EI* IV, pp. 1-22.
136. 1556	Sadāśiva		Viṭhalēśvara on the bank of the Tuṅgabhadrā	grant of 2 villages to a brāhmaṇa	*MAR* of 1932, no. 2.
137. 1561	Sadāśiva		Viṭhalēśvara on the bank of the Tuṅgabhadrā	grant of a village to a brāhmaṇa	*EC* V, Hn. 7.
138. 1564	Sadāśiva		Viṭhalēśvara on the bank of the Tuṅgabhadrā	grant of a village to a brāhmaṇa	*ARSIE* of 1935-36, A.8.
139. -	Sadāśiva		Viṭhalēśvara on the bank of the Tuṅgabhadrā	grant of a village to *guru* Tirumala-Naragiri-Tātācharyulu	*ARSIE* of 1938-39, no. 397.

140. -		Kāmagetti Timmaṇṇa Nāyaka	Hampa-Virūpāksha and god Mālyavanta Raghunātha	(and god Mālyavanta Raghunātha)	grant of a village to a *guru*	*EC* XI, Hr. 75 & 76.
141. 1576	Śrīraṅga I		Virūpāksha of Paṁpa-kshētra		grant of 5 villages to Sudhīndra Yatīndra (of the Rāghavēndra-svāmi maṭha at Nanjangūd) for the worship of god Rāmachandra in the maṭha	*MAR* of 1944, no. 22.

The above list of grants, gifts, etc., made in Vijayanagara city in the presence of Virūpāksha, Viṭhala and other deities was prepared after a careful study of the inscriptions published in epigraphical series such as *Annual Report of Indian Epigraphy, Annual Report of South Indian Epigraphy, Epigraphia Carnatica, Epigraphia India, Annual Report of the Mysore Archaeological Department, South Indian Inscriptions, A Topographical List of the Inscriptions of the Madras Presidency* ed. by V. Rangacharya, *A Collection of the Inscriptions on Copper-Plates and Stones in the Nellore District* ed. by A. Butterworth and V. Venugopal Chetty. However, this list may not be completely exhaustive; it is possible that due to oversight, some epigraphs may have been omitted. Some of the inscriptions are reported in two or more series, in such cases all the references have not been given.

APPENDIX B

Preliminary Inventory of Monuments in the "Sacred Centre" and the "Irrigated Valley"

NC m/1 - Maṇḍapa
NC m/2 - Maṇḍapa
NC m/3 - Bṛindāvana of Narahari tīrtha
NC n/1 - North-facing Vaishṇava temple and adjacent room (for an ascetic?).
NC q/1 - Maṇḍapa
NC r/1 - Small, dilapidated, north-facing Vaishṇava temple
NC r/2 - Maṇḍapa
NC r/3 - Maṇḍapa
NC r/4 - Four-pillared structure
NC v/1 - Gateway
NC v/2 - Small, collapsed Āñjanēya temple (the Vīra-Āñjanēya sculpture from here has been recently moved into the Viṭhala complex).
NC v/3 - Tirumaṅgai-āḻvār temple and Rāmānuja-kūṭa
NC v/4 - Large maṇḍapa
NC v/5 - Unfinished gōpura
NC v/6 - Dilapidated, north-facing temple. The temple appears to be an early one, with later additions.
NC v/7 - Maṇḍapa
NC w/1 - A complex consisting of a north-facing shrine and a maṭha or a yajña-sālā with a pillared gallery around them.
NC w/2 - Mudal-āḻvār temple and Rāmānuja-kūṭa
NC w/3 - South-facing Vaishṇava temple complex, probably dedicated to Rāmānuja.
NC w/4 - Collapsed maṇḍapa
NC x/1 - Maṇḍapa
ND y/1 - Small, east-facing Śaiva temple, comprising a maṇḍapa and *cella*.
ND y/2 - Small, west-facing dilapidated Vaishṇava temple. The sculpture of Āñjanēya within is, probably, the original mūrti.
ND y/3 - Ruin
ND y/4 - Small, north-facing temple, consisting of a pillared porch and a *cella*.
ND y/5 - Two maṇḍapas, adjacent to each other. To the north-west of ND y/5 is a rock carving of Vīra-Āñjanēya.
ND y/6 - Small, east-facing, dilapidated temple, consisting of only a porch and a *cella*. Inside the *cella* there is a half-buried sculpture of Vīra-Āñjanēya.
ND y/7 - Maṇḍapa
ND y/8 - A liṅga, a Ganēśa relief and a small monolithic Nandi.
NF q/1 - East-facing Śaiva temple, consisting of a *cella*, antechamber and two maṇḍapas.
NF q/2 - Maṇḍapa
NF q/3 - Maṇḍapa
NF q/4 - Maṇḍapa
NF q/5 - Mandapa
NF q/6 - Gateway and shrine
NF q/7 - Maṇḍapa
NF r/1 - A Nandi monolith and a liṅga.
NF r/2 - Pillar
NF r/3 - Maṇḍapa
Nearby, on rocks in the river there are some Nandi sculptures and liṅgas.
NF r/4 - Large structure (now a Vīraśaiva maṭha, called Koṭur-svāmi maṭha).
NF r/5 - Gateway and two small temples.
NF r/6 - Pre-Vijayanagara Śaiva temple.
NF r/7 - Gateway
NF v/1 - Lokapāvana tank and two Śaiva shrines.
NF v/2 - Vidyāraṇya-svāmi temple
NF v/3 - Vidyāraṇya-svāmi maṭha
NF w/1 - Virūpāksha temple complex
NF w/2 - Manmatha tank
NF w/3 - Double-storeyed gateway
NF w/4 - North-facing, dilapidated temple
NF w/5 - Double-shrine Śaiva temple, consisting of two *cellas*, two antechambers, two maṇḍapas and three porches.
NF w/6 - Triple-shrine Śaiva temple, consisting of three *cellas* and antechambers, with a common maṇḍapa and porch.
NF w/7 - temple
NF w/8 - Gōpura

NF w/9 - Triple-shrine pre-Vijayanagara temple, built in the early 14th century A.D. by Kampilarāya. It comprises three *cellas* and antechambers, one maṇḍapa and porch.
NF w/10 - Ruin
NF w/11 - North-facing shrine
NF w/12 - East-facing pre-Vijayanagara temple.
NF w/13 - Temple
NF w/14 - North-facing, dilapidated shrine
NF w/15 - North-facing dilapidated temple
NF w/16 - North-facing, dilapidated temple
NF w/17 - Small, east-facing temple
NF w/18 - Small, east-facing temple
NF w/19 - Small, east-facing temple
NF w/20 - Small, east-facing Śaiva temple
NF w/21 - Small west-facing temple
NF w/22 - Small, east-facing temple
NF w/23 - East-facing Śaiva temple (in the Rāshṭrakūṭa style of the 9-10th century A.D.).
NF w/24 - East-facing shrine
NF w/25 - Durgā-dēvī temple (in the Rāshṭrakūṭa style).
NF w/26 - Double-shrine temple
NF w/27 - East-facing Śaiva temple
NF w/28 - Maṇḍapa
NF w/29 - Śaiva temple
NF x/1 - Small, north-facing Śaiva temple (now incorporated into a restaurant).
NG e/1 - Large maṇḍapa (the so-called "Purandaradāsa-maṇḍapa").
NG e/2 - Maṇḍapa
NG h/1 - Maṇḍapa
NG k/1 - Vaishṇava shrine
NG k/2 - East-facing Vaishṇava temple
NG k/3 - Double-storeyed gateway and two adjacent shrines.
NG k/4 - Maṇḍapa
NG k/5 - Shrine
NG k/6 - Gateway
NG m/1 - Śaiva temple
NG m/2 - Śaiva temple
NG m & n - Kōṭi-tīrtha
At Kōṭi-tīrtha there are a number of rock-carvings: groups of liṅgas cut into the basal rock, a fine Raṅganātha relief, two reliefs of Lakshmī-Narasiṁha, one of the Mahiśāsuramardini, one of Sūrya, a relief of Pārvatī flanked by Gaṇēśa and Kārtikēya, two sculptures of Bhairava and sculptures of devotees (see *VPR '83-84*, p. 138 and pp. 142-143 and Plates LXXXV, XCV and XCVI).
NG n/1 - Complex comprising the east-facing shrine of Chaturbhuja-Hanumān, the bṛindāvana of Raghunandana-svāmi, and two north-facing shrines, one of which has Śaiva dvārapālas.
NG n/2 - Maṇḍapa
NG n/3 - Dilapidated shrine
NG n/4 - Śaiva temple
NG n/5 - Maṇḍapa in which there are reliefs of Rāma-Sitā-Lakshmaṇa group and Narasiṁha and an adjacent rock-shelter with a liṅga and a panel of Vīrabhadra, Pārvatī, Gaṇēśa and Kārtikēya and another relief of Pārvatī (see VPR '83-84, p. 140 and Plates XC b and c).
NG n/6 - Rock-shelter with sculptures of the twenty-four forms and the avatāras of Vishṇu and also of Viṭhala, Veṅkatēśa and Narasiṁha (see VPR '83-84, pp. 138-140 and Plates LXXXVI-XCA).
NG o/1 - "Sugrīva's Cave"
NG o/2 - "Sītā-Sarōvar"
NG o/3 - Satī-stone
NG p/1 - Small Śaiva temple
NG p/2 - Maṇḍapa
NG p/3 - Āñjanēya shrine
NG p/4 - Maṇḍapa
NG p/5 - Four-Pillared structure
NG r - Chakra-tīrtha: there are traces here of some structures, Śaiva shrine and some liṅgas.
NG s/1 - East-facing Śaiva temple (locally known as the "Varāha temple").
NG s/2 - Raṅganātha temple
NG s/3 - Dilapidated temple
NG s/4 - Maṇḍapa
NG t/1 - North-facing Vaishṇava temple, within a prākāra with a gōpura. The temple itself consists of a maṇḍapa, an antechamber and a *cella*.
NG t/2 - Ruin
NG t/3 - North-facing Śaiva temple (built in A.D. 1386).
NG t/4 - Narasiṁha temple
NG w/1 - Kōdaṇḍarāma temple
NG w/2 - North-facing temple of Sudarśana-chakra (locally known as the "Sūrya-

nārāyaṇa" temple).
NG w/3 - Yantrōddhāraka Āñjanēya temple
NG w/4 - Three long maṇḍapas
NG w/5 - East-facing Prāta-Viṭhala temple (nowadays called the "Hastagiri Raṅganātha-svāmi" temple).
NG x/1 - Triple-shrine Veṅkateśa temple. On a boulder, south-east of this temple, is a fine relief of Raṅganātha. On a boulder to the north-west of the temple is a rock carving of Vīra-Āñjanēya and a long inscription.
NG x/2 - Small Tiruveṅgaḷanātha temple, facing the ratha-vīdhi of the great temple (NM h/1) dedicated to the same deity.
NG x/3 - Temple-tank (of temple NM h/1)
NG y/1 - Structure, and a large Gaṇēśa sculpture.
NH a/1 - Viṭhala temple complex
NH a/2 - Large enclosed maṇḍapa
NH a/3 - Maṇḍapa
NH a/4 - Maṇḍapa
NH a/5 - Vaishṇava temple, comprising a *cella*, an antechamber, two maṇḍapas with a colonnade around these and a column in front.
NH a/6 - Unfinished gōpura
NH a/7 - Frame, consisting of two lofty carved granite pillars supporting a stone beam provided with three hoops on the underside (for a swing?). It is popularly known as the "King's Balance."
NH a/8 - Plinth
NH a/9 - Four-pillared structure
NH a/10 - Vaishṇava temple, probably dedicated to Nammāḷvār.
NH a/11 - Ruin
NH b/1 - Maṇḍapa
NH b/2 - Maṇḍapa
NH b/3 - Four-pillared structure
NH b/4 - Maṇḍapa
NH b/5 - Stump of a large column
NH b/6 - Maṇḍapa
NH b/7 - Ruin
NH b/8 - Maṇḍapa
NH b/9 - Maṇḍapa
NH b/10 - Maṇḍapa
NH b/11 - Dilapidated maṇḍapa
NH b/12 - Four pillars
NH b/13 - Maṇḍapa
NH b/14 - Maṇḍapa
NH b/15 - North-facing temple
NH c/1 - Plinth
NH d/1 - Temple-tank (of the Viṭhala temple complex).
NH d/2 - Maṇḍapa
NH d/3 - Small, south-facing temple
NH d/4 - Maṇḍapa
NH e/1 - Dilapidated tank
NH f/1 - West-facing Vaishṇava temple
NH f/2 - West-facing Vaishṇava temple
NH f/3 - Maṇḍapa
NH f/4 - East-facing Vaishṇava temple
NH f/5 - Well. To the west of the well is a relief of Āñjanēya, carved on a boulder.
NH j/1 - Vaishṇava temple (the temple of Tirumaliśai-āḷvār ?).
NJ c/1 - East-facing temple, comprising a porch, an antechamber and a sanctum.
NJ f/1 - Plinth
NJ g/1 - Pārāṅkuśa maṇḍapa
NJ g/2 - Plinth
NJ g/3 - Plinth
NJ g/4 - Plinth
NJ g/5 - Plinth
NJ m/1 - Ruined maṇḍapa
NJ m/2 - Dilapidated, west-facing shrine
NJ o/1 - North-west-facing Vaishṇava temple
NJ s - Areśaṅkara Bāgilu (known nowadays as the Talārighaṭ gate).
NJ s/1 - East-facing shrine
NJ s/2 - Āñjanēya temple
NJ t/1 - Maṇḍapa
NJ x/1 - North-facing Śaiva temple
NJ x/2 - Āñjanēya temple
NJ x/3 - Temple
NJ y/1 - Tank
NL a/1 - Small, north-facing temple
NL a/2 - Small, east-facing temple
NL b/1 - Triple-shrine, east-facing Śaiva temple (locally known as the "Gāyatrī pīṭha"). It consists of three shrines and antechambers and one maṇḍapa and porch.
NL b/2 - Three shrines adjacent to each other, with a four-pillared structure in front of each.
NL b/3 - Triple-shrine temple, similar to NF w/9.
NL b/4 - Dilapidated, east-facing temple
NL b/5 - Three collapsed structures
NL b/6 - Four-pillared structure
NL b/7 - Four-pillared structure
NL b/8 - Four-pillared structure

NL b/9 - Two four-pillared adjacent structures.
NL b/10 - Natural tank, with a small shrine on its south-east side.
NL b/11 - North-facing temple
NL b/12 - North-facing temple
NL b/13 - East-facing temple (locally known as the Mūla Virūpāksha temple) and a tank. To the west of this temple there are two small shrines.
NL b/14 - North-facing temple. To the south-west of it there is an inscription engraved on the bedrock. To the south of the inscription is a rock carving of Āñjanēya, Rāma-Sītā-Lakshmaṇa group and a male and two female devotees.
NL b/15 - North-facing temple
NL b/16 - Four-pillared structure, converted into the "Mūla Āñjanēya" shrine.
NL b/17 - Dilapidated, north-facing temple. To the west of this are three liṅgas carved in the basal rock.
NL b/18 - North-facing temple
NL b/19 - East-facing temple (Virūpāksha temple of 1398). To its left is a tank. An inscription is engraved on the vertical face of the tank, to the north-east of the temple.
NL b/20 - Śaiva temple
NL b/21 - Double-storeyed gateway. To the north-east of the gateway is a set of five liṅgas, another of three liṅgas and an inscription engraved on the bedrock.
NL b/22 - Column
NL b/23, 24, 25, 26 - Vijayanagara period structures (a well, two shrines and a maṇḍapa) that have been incorporated into the modern Shivarama Avadhoot Āśrama.
NL c/1 - Gateway
NL c/2 - Kaḍalekāḷu Gaṇēśa temple
NL c/3 - Harihara temple
NL c/4 - Maṇḍapa
NL c/5 - Small, west-facing temple
NL c/6 - Maṇḍapa
NL c/7 - Ruin
NL e/1 - North-facing Śaiva temple
NL f/1 - Maṇḍapa
NL f/2 - Satī-stone
NL g/1 - Small, east-facing temple
NL g/2 - Sāsivēkāḷu Gaṇēśa shrine
NL g/3 - Small, east-facing temple
NL g/4 - Gōpura
NL g/5 - Temple with an enclosed colonnade around it.
NL g/6 - West-facing temple
NL g/7 - East-facing Śaiva temple
NL g/8 - Maṇḍapa
NL h/1 - Narasiṁha temple
NL h/2 - West-facing Śaiva temple
NL h/3 - Gateway
NL h/4 - South-facing Śaiva temple. To the south of it is a relief of Gaṇēśa, carved on a boulder.
NL h/5 - Rock carving of Dēvī, a liṅga, Nandi, a devotee and Vīrabhadra.
NL h/6 - Bhairava shrine
NL h/7 - Maṇḍapa. There is a monolithic Nandi in it.
NL h/8 - Maṇḍapa
NL h/9 - Small Raṅganātha temple
NL h/10 - Maṇḍapa
NL h/11 - Small Śaiva temple
NL h/12 - Shrine
NL h/13 - Small, east-facing temple
NL h/14 - West-facing Vaishṇava temple
NL h/15 - Shrine
NL m/1 - Lakshmī-Narasiṁha monolith
NL m/2 - Giant liṅga
NL m/3 - Gateway
NL m/4 - Kṛishṇa temple complex
NL o/1 - Temple-tank (of the Kṛishṇa temple complex).
NL o/2 - Small gate and well
NL o/3 - Maṇḍapa and rock-shelter, probably the dwelling of an ascetic or ascetics.
NL q/1 - Ranghunātha temple
NL r/1 - Small maṇḍapa
NL s/1 - North-facing temple, possibly dedicated to Kṛishṇa (locally known as the "Sarasvatī" temple).
NL s/2 - Dēvī sculpture, within a shelter.
NL w/1 - Shrine (probably, modern).
NL w/2 - Small Śaiva temple
NL w/3 - Mudu Vīraṇṇa temple (nowadays called the "Uddhāna Vīrabhadra" temple).
NL w/4 - Hiriya Chattra or maṭha
NL w/5 - Column. Near it are two Vīra-Āñjanēya sculptures.
NL w/6 - Tiruveṅgaḷanātha temple (known nowadays as the "Chaṇḍikēśvara" temple).
NM a/1 - Large maṇḍapa
NM a/2 - Double-storeyed maṇḍapa, the lower storey has Kalyāṇi-Chālukyan

lathe turned pillars.
NM a/3 - well
NM b/1 - Nandi maṇḍapa
NM b/2 - Gateway
NM b/3 - Small, south-facing Śaiva temple
NM b/4 - Small, dilapidated, north-facing temple
NM b/5 - Maṇḍapa
NM b/6 - Maṇḍapa
NM b/7 - A complex consisting of a cavern, a spring, an open courtyard and two small maṇḍapas; possibly it is a hermitage.
NM b/8 - Āñjanēya shrine
NM b/9 - Maṇḍapa
NM d/1 - East-facing Śaiva temple
NM d/2 - West-facing ruined temple
NM d/3 - Shrine, near it are some sculptures, including one of Rāma and Lakshmaṇa and one of Gaṇēśa.
NM d/4 - Cave, within is a Nandi; according to local informants there was a liṅga in this cave that was smashed by treasure-seekers recently.
NM f/1, 2, 3 & 4 - Maṭha complex (Kariya Siddappa maṭha).
NM f/5 - Structure (now converted into a house).
NM g/1 - Vīrabhadra temple on Mataṅga
NM g/2 - Maṇḍapa
NM g/3 - Maṇḍapa
NM g/4 - Cave in which there is a liṅga on the basal rock. A Nandi monolith faces the liṅga. A relief of Nandi is carved near the entrance to cave.
NM g/5 - Cave
NM g/6 - Cave, inside is a Gaṇēśa image; outside the cave a liṅga is carved in the sheet rock.
NM h/1 - Tiruveṅgaḷanātha temple complex
NM h/2 - Dēvī sculpture (locally this goddess is called "Śrī Athikayamma").
NM h/3 - Maṇḍapa with a large Nandi monolith
NM h/4 - Two adjacent maṇḍapas
NM h/5 - Maṇḍapa
NM j/1 - Collapsed shrine
NM m/1 - Maṇḍapa in which there is a relief of a liṅga, Nandi, Vīrabhadra and Gaṇēśa.
NM m/2 - Two dēvī sculptures
NM m/3 - Rock carving of a two-armed Bhairava, holding the khaḍga and triśūla. There is a relief of Nandi facing Bhairava.
NM n/1 - Large room.
NM r/1 - Rock carving of Mahisāsura-mardini.
NM r/2 - Tiruveṅgaḷanātha shrine
NM r/3 - Collapsed Bhairava shrine
NM r/4 - Relief of a dēvī, with a nāga hood over her head.
NM r/5 - Relief of a seated male Śaivite deity. In his upper hands he holds the triśūla and ḍamaru. The attributes of the lower hands are not distinguishable.
NM r/6 - Ruin
NM r/7 - Ruin
NM s/1 - Ruined Śaiva temple
NM s/2 - Dilapidated maṇḍapa. In it is a relief of a liṅga flanked by Gaṇēśa and Vīrabhadra and another relief of Bhadrakāḷī and Pārvatī. In the maṇḍapa there are two nāga stones.
NM s/3 - Maṇḍapa
NM w/1 - West-facing temple
NM w/2 - Triple-shrine Vaishṇava temple
NM w/3 - Collapsed temple
NM w/4 - Ruin
NM x/1 - Tank
NM x/2 - Sculptures on three boulders (See *VPR '83-84*, pp. 136-137 and Plates LXXXI-LXXXIIIa).
NM x/3 - Ruin
NM y/1 - Watch tower, called Madana Kotaḷa.
NM y/2 - Unfinished relief of a standing Bhairava and Bhairavī.
NM y/3 - Two temples, dedicated to Vīrabhadra and Bhadrakāḷī. To the south-west of the latter shrine is a relief of a standing four-armed dēvī, with a seven-headed snake's hood over her head.
NM y/4 - Ruin
NM z/1 - Ruin
NM z/2 - Relief of Bhairava, flanked by a scorpion and a snake.
NM z/3 - Sculpture of Varadarāja, flanked by consorts.
NM z/4 - Vīra-Āñjanēya relief
NN a/1 - East-facing Vīrabhadra temple
NN g/1 - Islamic-style pavilion
NN g/2 - Maṇḍapa, shrine and column.
NN h/1 - East-facing Śaiva temple, comprising a sanctum, an antechamber and two maṇḍapas. On a boulder to the east of this temple is a relief of Gaṇēśa. Further

east are three nāga stones.

NN m/1 - Well
NN m/2 - Gaṇēśa temple
NN m/3 - Tank
NN n - Gateway
NN n/1 - North-facing Śaiva temple and a Nandi pavilion. Behind the Nandi pavilion is a relief of Vīrabhadra.
NN n/2 - Tank.

The monuments listed in this inventory may be located in the Map Series. No details are given of those monuments that have already been described elsewhere in this monograph. Only a few of the pre-1565 monuments in Hampi village (i.e. the area around and near the Virūpāksha temple complex) have been listed. An exhaustive study of the pre-Vijayanagara and Vijayanagara period structures was not possible there, because many of them have been incorporated into modern dwellings and other buildings.

Bibliography

A. PRIMARY SOURCES

I. Archaeological Sources

Annual Reports of the Archaeological Department, Southern Circle, Madras, Madras: Government Press, 1902-03 onwards.

Annual Reports of the Archaeological Survey of India. Calcutta/Delhi: Archaeological Survey of India, 1887 onwards.

Annual Reports of the Mysore Archaeological Department. Bangalore/Mysore: Government Press, 1906-1956.

Annual Reports on Indian Epigraphy. New Delhi: Published by the Manager of Publications, 1947 onwards.

Annual Reports on South Indian Epigraphy, Madras/Calcutta: Government Press, 1887 onwards.

Butterworth, A. and Venugopal Chetty, V., eds. *A Collection of the Inscriptions on Copper-Plates and Stones in the Nellore District,* 3 Parts. Madras: Government Press, 1905.

Devaraj, D.V. and Patil, C.S., eds. *Vijayanagara: Progress of Research 1984-1987.* Mysore: Directorate of Archaeology and Museums, 1991.

Epigraphia Indica. Calcutta/New Delhi: Archaeological Survey of India, 1892 onwards.

Gopal, B.R., ed. *Vijayanagara Inscriptions,* 3 vols. Mysore: Directorate of Archaeology and Museums, 1985, 1986, 1990.

Hultzsch, E. et al. eds. *South Indian Inscriptions,* 23 vols. Madras: Government Press (vols. 1-13), New Delhi : Archaeological Survey of India (vols. 14-23), 1890-1979.

Indian Archaeology: A Review. New Delhi: Archaeological Survey of India, 1953-54 onwards.

Krishna Sastri, H., ed. *Hyderabad Archaeological Series no. 5: Munirabad Stone Inscription of the 13th Year of Tribhuvanamala - (Vikramaditya VI).* Hyderabad: The Nizam's Government, 1922.

Nagaraja Rao, M.S., ed. *Vijayanagara: Progress of Research 1983-1984.* Mysore: Directorate of Archaeology and Museums, 1985.

Rangacharya, V., ed. *A Topographical List of the Inscriptions of the Madras Presidency,* 3 vols. Madras: Government Press, 1919.

Rice, Lewis B. et al., eds. *Epigraphia Carnatica,* 16 vols. Madras/Bangalore/Mysore : Government Press, 1886-1958.

Sastry, Sadhu Subrahmanya, Vijayaraghavacharya, V. and Narayan, G.A., eds. *Tirumalai-Tirupati: Devasthanam Epigraphical Series,* 6 vols. Madras: Tirumalai-Tirupati Devasthanam Committee, 1931-1938.

Subramaniam, T.N., ed. *South Indian Temple Inscriptions,* 3 vols. Madras: Government Oriental Series, 1953-1957.

The Indian Antiquary: A Journal of Oriental Research, 62 vols. Bombay, 1872-1933.

II. Literary Sources

1. *Literary works in Sanskrit, Kannada, Telugu, Tamil*

Gangadevi, *Vira-Kamparaya-charitam (also called Madhura-vijayam),* Edited by V. Srinivasa Sastri and G. Harihara Sastri, with an introduction by T.A. Gopinatha Rao. Trivandram: Sridhara Press, 1916.

Gangā Dēvī, *Madhurāvijayam*, Edited with an historical introduction by S. Thiruvenkatachari. Annamalainagar: Annamalai University, 1957.

Hari Rao, V.N., ed. *Kōil Olugu: The Chronicles of the Srirangam Temple with Historical Notes.* Madras: Rochouse and Sons, 1961.

"Hemakutakhanda of the Skanda Purana," Synopsis by A.A. Shapiro in English of the Sanskrit manuscript, not published.

Krishnaswami Aiyangar, S., ed. *Sources of Vijayanagara History.* Madras: University of Madras, 1919.

Narasimhacharya, R., ed. *Karnataka Kavi Charite*, 2 pts. 2nd ed. Bangalore: Kannada Sahitya Parishatu, 1972.

Nilakanta Sastri, K.A and Venkataramanyya, N. eds. *Further Sources of Vijayanagara History*, 3 vols. Madras: University of Madras, 1946.

Panchamukhi, R.S., ed. *Virūpāksha Vasantōtsava Champū.* Dharwar : Kannada Research Institute, 1953.

Rājanātha Diṇḍima, *Achyutarāyābhyudaya*, Edited by A.N. Krishna Aiyangar. Madras: Adyar Library, 1945.

Somanatha, *Sri Vyasayogicaritam: The Life of Sri Vyasaraja, A Champu Kavya in Sanskrit*, with historical introduction in English by B. Venkoba Rao. Bangalore: Murti, n.d.

Sri Pampa Mahatme or the Holy Eminence of the Pampa: as described in the travelogue of the seven sages which is part of the Hemakuta chapter of the Skanda Purana, by Sri Guru Omsiddhalingeshvara Swamiji. Holagundi: Sri Guru Vrishabhashrama, 1983 (translated from Kannada into English by G.S. Kalburgi). This Kannada work is based on the Sanskrit text in Telugu characters entitled *Sri Pampa Mahatme: describing the travelogue of the seven sages which is part of the chapter on Mt. Hemakoota in the Skanda Purana*, Edited by Vedanta Vidvashiromani Koratamaddi Venkataramasastri, no.3 in the Shankarananda Book Series, 1933.

Tirumalāmbā, *Varadāmbikā-parinaya-campū*, Edited with an introduction by Lakshman Sarup. Lahore: Motilal Banarasi Das, 1938.

Tirumalāmbā, *Varadāmbikā-parinaya-campū*, with an English translation, notes and introduction by Suryakanta Sastri. Varanasi: Chowkhamba Sanskrit Series Office, 1970.

2. Chronicles and Travellers' Accounts

Barbosa, Duarte, *The Book of Duarte Barbosa—An Account of the Countries Bordering on the Indian Ocean and Their Inhabitants, written by Duarte Barbosa and completed about the year A.D.1518.* Translated, edited and annotated by M. Longworth Dames. 2 vols. London: Hakluyt Society, 1918.

Briggs, John, *History of the Rise of Mahomedan Power in India, till the year A.D. 1612. Translated from the Original Persian of Mahomed Kasim Ferishta.* 4 vols. 2nd reprint. Calcutta: Editions India, 1966.

Conti, Nicolo, "The Travels of Nicolo Conti, in the East, in the Early Part of the Fifteenth Century", in *India in the Fifteenth Century being a Collection of Narratives of Voyages to India.* Edited by R.H. Major. Reprint. Delhi: Deep Publications, 1974.

Della Valle, Pietro, *The Travels of Pietro della Valle in India.* 2 vols. Edited with a life of the author, an introduction and notes by Edward Grey. London: Hakluyt Society, 1892.

Elliot, H.M., *The History of India as told by its own Historians: The Muhammadan Period.* Edited from the posthumous papers of the late Sir H.M. Elliot by Prof. John Dowson. 8 vols. London: Trübner and Co. 1867-1877.

Frederick, Caesar, in *Hakluytus Posthumus or Purchas His Pilgrimes: Contayning a History of the*

World in Sea Voyages and Lande Travells by Englishmen and Others, by Samuel Purchas. Vol. X, pp. 88-143. Glasgow: James MacLehose and Sons, 1905.

Nikitin, Athanasius, "The Travels of Athanasius Nikitin of Twer," in *India in the Fifteenth Century being a Collection of Narratives of Voyages to India.* Edited by R.H. Major. Reprint. Delhi: Deep Publications, 1974.

Nuniz, Fernão, "Chronicle of Fernão Nuniz," in *A Forgotten Empire,* by R. Sewell. Reprint. New Delhi: Asian Educational Services, 1984, pp. 291-395.

Paes, Domingo, "Narrative of Domingo Paes," in *A Forgotten Empire,* by R. Sewell. Reprint. New Delhi: Asian Educational Services, 1984, pp. 236-290.

Razzak, Abd-er, "Narrative of the Journey of Abd-er Razzak," in *India in the Fifteenth Century being a Collection of Narratives of Voyages to India,* Edited by R.H. Major. Reprint. Delhi: Deep Publications, 1974.

Varthema, Ludovico, *The Travels of Ludovico di Varthema A.D. 1503 to 1508.* Translated by John Winter Jones. London: Hakluyt Society, 1863.

Varthema, Ludovico, *The Itinerary of Ludovico di Varthema of Bologna from 1502 to 1508.* Translated with a discourse on Varthema and his travels in Southern Asia by Sir Richard Temple. London: The Argonaut Press, 1928.

B. SECONDARY SOURCES

I. Books and Monographs

Appadurai, A. *Worship and Conflict under Colonial Rule: A South Indian Case.* Cambridge: Cambridge University Press, 1981.

Aryan, K.C., and Aryan S. *Hanuman in Art and Mythology.* Delhi: Rekha Prakashan, n.d.

Balasubrahmanyam, S.R. *Early Chola Art,* Part I. Bombay: Asia Publishing House, 1966.

Banerjea, J.N. *Development of Hindu Iconography.* Calcutta: University of Calcutta, 1941.

Banerjea, J.N. *Religion in Art and Archaeology: Vaishṇavism and Śaivism.* Lucknow: University of Lucknow, 1968.

Barth, A. *The Religions of India,* Translated by J.Wood. 4th ed. Varanasi: Chowkhmba Sanskrit Studies, vol. XXV, 1963.

Basavaraja, K.R., ed. *The Vijayanagara Urbanity.* Hospet: S.P. Gheverchand and G.T. Hanumanthappa for National Symposium on Urban Development, 1978.

Basavaraja, K.R. *History and Culture of Karnataka (Early times to Unification).* Dharwad: Chalukya Publications, 1984.

Basham, A.L. *The Wonder that was India: A Survey of the Culture of the Subcontinent before the coming of the Muslims.* New York: Grove Press Inc. 1954.

Begley, W.E. *Viṣṇu's Flaming Wheel: The Iconography of the Sudarśana-Cakra.* New York: New York University Press, 1973.

Bhandarkar, R.G. *Vaiṣṇavism, Śaivism and Minor Religious Systems.* Reprint. Varanasi: Indological Book House, 1965.

Briggs, G.W. *Gorakhnāth and the Kānphaṭa Yogīs.* Calcutta: Y.M.C.A. Publishing House, 1938.

Brown, Percy. *Indian Architecture (Buddhist and Hindu Periods).* 7th reprint. Bombay : D.B. Taraporevala Sons & Co., 1976.

Champakalakshmi, R. *Vaiṣṇava Iconography in the Tamil Country.* New Delhi: Orient Longman, 1981.

Courtright, P.B. *Gaṇēśa : Lord of Obstacles, Lord of Beginnings.* New York : Oxford University Press, 1985.

Dallapiccola, A.L., ed. *Vijayanagara City and Empire: New Currents of Research.* Stuttgart: Steiner Verlag Wiesbaden GMBH, 1985.

Dallapiccola, A.L., Fritz, J.M., Michell, G., and Rajasekhara, S. *The Ramachandra Temple at Vijayanagara*. New Delhi: Manohar Publications and American Institute of Indian Studies, 1991.

Danvers, F.C. *The Portuguese in India: Being a History of the Rise and Decline of their Eastern Empire*. 2 vols. 2nd impression. London: Frank Cass & Co., 1966.

Deleury, G.A. *The Cult of Viṭhobā*. Poona: Deccan College, 1960.

Desai, K. *Iconography of Viṣṇu*, New Delhi: Abhinav Publications 1973.

Desai, P.B., *Jainism in South India and some Jaina Epigraphs*. Sholapur: Jaina Saṁskṛit Samrakshaka Sangha, 1957.

Desai, P.B., ed. *A History of Karnataka*. Dharwar: Kannada Research Institute, 1970.

Devakunjari, D. *Hampi*. 2nd ed. New Delhi: Archaeological Survey of India, 1983.

Devaraj, D.V. and Patil, C.S., eds. *Vijayanagara: Progress of Research 1987-88*. Mysore: Directorate of Archaeology and Museums, 1991.

Diehl, C.G. *Instrument and Purpose: Studies in Rites and Rituals in South India*. Lund : C.W.K. Gleerup, 1956.

Dikshit, G.S. *Early Vijayanagara : Studies in its History and Culture (Proceeding of S. Srikantaya Centenary Seminar)*. Bangalore: B.M.S. Memorial Foundation, 1988.

Diwakar, R.R. et al. eds. *Karnataka Through the Ages (from Prehistoric Times to the Day of the Independence of India)*. Bangalore : Government of Mysore, 1968.

Dowson, John. *A Classical Dictionary of Hindu Mythology and Religion, Geography, History and Literature*. 4th ed. London: Trübner's Oriental Series, 1903.

Dubois, Abbé J.A. *Hindu Manners, Customs and Ceremonies*. 3rd ed. Reprint. Translated and edited by H.K. Beauchamp. London: Oxford University Press, 1936.

Elmore, W.T. *Dravidian Gods in Modern Hinduism: A Study of the Local and Village Deities of Southern India*. Madras: C.L.S. Press, 1925.

Filliozat, P. and Filliozat, V. *Hampi-Vijayanagar : The Temple of Viṭhala*. New Delhi : Sitaram Bhartia Institute of Scientific Research, 1988.

Filliozat, V. *L'Epigraphie de Vijayanagar du début à1377*. Paris: Ecole Française d'Extrême-Orient, 1973.

Filliozat, V. *Le Temple de Tirumaṅkaiyāḷvār à Hampi*. Pondicherry: Institute Français de Indologie, 1976.

Fritz, J.M., Michell, G., and Nagaraja Rao, M.S. *The Royal Centre at Vijayanagara—Preliminary Report*. Melbourne: Department of Architecture and Building, University of Melbourne, 1984.

Gatwood, L.E. *Devi and the Spouse Goddess: Women, Sexuality, and Marriage in India*. New Delhi: Manohar Publications, 1985.

Getty, A. *Gaṇeśa: A Monograph on the Elephant-Faced God*. Oxford: Clarendon Press, 1936.

Gollings, J., Fritz, J.M., and Michell, G. *City of Victory*. New York: Aperture Foundation, 1991.

Gonda, J. *Viṣṇuism and Śivaism: A Comparison*. London : University of London, 1970.

Gopinatha Rao, T.A. *Elements of Hindu Iconography*. 2 vols. Madras : Law Printing House, 1914-1916.

Govindacharya, A. *The Holy Lives of the Āzhvārs or the Drāvida Saints*. Mysore : GTA Press, 1902.

Gravely, F.H. and Ramachandran, T.N. *The Three Main Styles of Temple Architecture Recognised by the Silpa Sāstras, Bulletin of the Madras Government*. 2nd rev. ed. Madras: Government of Madras, 1934.

Gururaja Bhatt, P. *Studies in Tuḷuva History and Culture: From Pre-Historic Times up to the Modern*. Manipal: Published by the author, 1975.

Hari Rao, V.N. *The Śrīrangam Temple: Art and Architecture*. Tirupati: The Sri Venkatesvara Unversity, 1967.

Hayavadana Rao, C., ed. *Mysore Gazetteer*, vol. II. pt. III. Bangalore: Government Press, 1930.

Hayavadana Rao, C. *The Dasara in Mysore: Its Origin and Significance*. Bangalore: The Bangalore Printing and Publishing Co., 1936.

Heras, H. *The Aravidu Dynasty of Vijayanagara*, Vol. I. Madras: B.G. Paul and Co., 1927.

Heras, H. *Beginnings of Vijayanagara History*. Bombay: Indian Historical Research Institute, 1929.

Hooper, J.S.M. *Hymns of the Āḷvārs*. Calcutta: Oxford University Press, 1929.

Ions, V. *Indian Mythology*. London: Paul Hamlyn, 1967.

Iyengar, Masti Venkatesa. *Popular Culture in Karṇāṭaka*. Bangalore: 1937.

Jouveau-Dubreuil, G. *Dravidian Architecture*, Edited with notes by S.Krishnaswami Aiyangar. 2nd reprint. Varanasi: Bharat-Bharati, 1972.

Jouveau-Dubreuil, G. *Iconography of Southern India*. Translated by A.C. Martin. Varanasi: Bharat-Bharati, 1978.

Kamat, Jyotsna K. *Social Life in Medieval Karṇāṭaka*. New Delhi: Abhinav Publications, 1980.

Kamath, S.U., ed. *Karnataka State Gazetteer*, pts. I and II. Bangalore: Government of Karnataka, 1982, 1983.

Kane, P.V. *History of Dharmaśāstra: Ancient and Mediaeval Religious and Civil Law in India*. 5 vols. Poona: Bhandarkar Oriental Research Institute, 1930-1962.

Karmarkar, A.P. *Cultural History of Karnataka: Ancient and Medieval*. Dharwar: Karnataka Vidyavardhaka Sangha, 1947.

Karmarkar, A.P. *The Religions of India Vol. I: The Vrātya or Dravidian System*. Lonavla : Mira Publishing House, 1950.

Karmarkar, A.P. and Kalamdani, N.B. *Mystic Teachings of the Haridasa of Karṇāṭak*. Dharwar: Karnataka Vidyavardhak Sangha, 1939.

Khan, Md. Abdul Waheed. *An Early Sculpture of Narasimha (Man-Lion Incarnation of Vishnu with Pañcha Vīras)*. Hyderabad: The Government of Andhra Pradesh (Andhra Pradesh Archaeological Series, no. 16), 1964.

Khare, G.H. *Mahārāshṭrāci cār daivete*. Pune: G.H. Khare, 1958.

Kodad, S.B. *History of Vijayanagar Empire: The Battle of Talikota*. New Delhi: Sri Ramachandra Publications, 1986.

Krishna Sastri, H. *South-Indian Images of Gods and Goddesses*. Madras: Madras Government Press, 1916.

Krishnaswami, A. *The Tamil Country under Vijayanagar*. Annamalainagar: The Annamalai University, 1964.

Krishnaswami Aiyangar, S. *A History of Tirupati*. 2 vols. Madras: Tirumala-Tirupati Devastanam, 1940-41.

Krishnaswami Aiyangar, S. *South India and her Muhammadan Invaders*. Reprint, New Delhi: S. Chand & Co., n.d.

Longhurst, A.H. *Hampi Ruins: Described and Illustrated*. Reprint. New Delhi: Asian Educational Services, 1982.

Lorenzen, D.N. *The Kāpālikas and Kālāmukhas: Two Lost Śaivite Sects*. New Delhi: Thomson Press Ltd., 1972.

Mahadevan, T.M.P. *Outlines of Hinduism*, 2nd ed. Bombay: Chetana, 1960.

Mahalingam, T.V. *Economic Life in the Vijayanagara Empire*. Madras: University of Madras, 1951.

Mahalingam, T.V. *Administration and Social Life under Vijayanagara*. 2 pts. 2nd ed. Madras: University of Madras, 1969 and 1975.

Meadows Taylor, P. and Fergusson, J. *Architecture in Dharwar and Mysore*. London: John Murray, 1866.

Michell, G. *Vijayanagara: Architectural Inventory of the Urban Core*. 2 vols. Mysore : Directorate of Archaeology and Museums, 1990.

Michell, G. and Filliozat, V. eds. *Splendours of the Vijayanagara Empire: Hampi*. Bombay: Marg Publications, 1981.

Moraes, G.M. *The Kadamba Kula : A History of Ancient and Medieval Karnataka*. Bombay: B.X. Furtado & Sons, 1931.

Nagaraja Rao, M.S., ed. *Vijayanagara: Progress of Research 1979-1983.* Mysore: Directorate of Archaeology and Museums, 1983.

Nandimath, S.C. *A Handbook of Viraśaivism.* 2nd ed. Delhi: Motilal Banarsidass, 1979.

Nilakanta Sastri, K.A. *A History of South India: from Prehistoric Times to the Fall of Vijayanagar.* 2nd ed. Oxford University Press, 1958.

Nilakanta Sastri, K.A. *Development of Religion in South India.* Madras: Orient Longmans, 1963.

O'Flaherty, W.D. *Asceticism and Eroticism in the Mythology of Śiva.* London: Oxford University Press, 1973.

O'Malley, L.S.S. *Popular Hinduism: The Religion of the Masses.* London: Cambridge University Press, 1935.

Pai, D.A. *Monograph on the Religious Sects in India among the Hindus.* Bombay : The Times Press. 1928.

Pillay, K.K. *The Śucīndram Temple.* Madras: Kalakshetra Publications, 1953.

Rabinandan Pratap, D. *Tribes of Andhra Pradesh.* Hyderabad: World Telugu Conference Office, 1975.

Rajasekhara, S. *Masterpieces of Vijayanagara Art.* Bombay: D.B. Taraporevala Sons and Co., 1983.

Raman, K.V. *Srī Varadarājaswāmi Temple—Kāñchi : A Study of its History, Art and Architecture.* New Delhi: Abhinav Publications, 1975.

Rama Rao, M. *The Temples of Srisailam.* Hyderabad: Government of Andhra Pradesh, Andhra Pradesh Government Archaeological Series no. 23, 1969.

Rama Sharma, M.H. *The History of the Vijayanagara Empire.* 2 vols. Edited by M.H. Gopal. Bombay: Popular Prakashan, 1978, 1980.

Ramaswami Ayyangar, M.S. and Seshagiri Rao, B. *Studies in South Indian Jainism.* 2nd ed. Delhi: Sri Satguru Publications, 1982.

Ramesan, N. *Temples and Legends of Andhra Pradesh.* Bombay: Bharatiya Vidya Bhavan, 1962.

Saletore, B.A. *Social and Political Life in the Vijayanagara Empire (A.D. 1346-A.D. 1646).* 2 vols. Madras: B.G. Paul and Co., 1934.

Saletore, B.A. *Medieval Jainism with Special Reference to the Vijayanagara Empire.* Bombay: Karnataka Publishing House, 1938.

Saletore, R.N. *Vijayanagara Art.* Delhi: Sundeep Prakashan, 1982.

Sarma, Sree Rama P. *Sāḷuva Dynasty of Vijayanagara.* Hyderabad: Prabhakar Publications, 1979.

Sarma, M.S. *History of the Reddi Kingdoms: circa 1325 A.D. to circa 1448 A.D.* Waltair: Andhra University, 1948.

Sastry, Sadhu Subrahmanya. *Report on the Inscriptions of the Devasthanam Collection with Illustrations.* Introduction by K.A. Nilakanta Sastry. Madras: Tirumalai-Tirupati Devasthanam, 1930.

Schrader, O.F. *Introduction to the Pāñcarātra and the Ahirbudhnya Saṃhitā.* Madras: Adyar Library, 1916.

Settar, S. and Sontheimer, G.D. eds. *Memorial Stones: A Study of their Origin, Significance and Variety.* Dharwad and New Delhi: Institute of Indian Art History, Karnatak University and S. Asia Institute, University of Heidelberg, W. Germany, 1982.

Sewell, R. *A Forgotten Empire.* Reprint. New Delhi: Asian Educational Services, 1984.

Sharma, B.N.K. *A History of Dvaita School of Vedānta and its Literature.* 2 vols. Bombay: Booksellers' Publishing Co., 1960-61.

Sherwani, H.K. and Joshi, P.M., eds. *History of Medieval Deccan (1295-1724).* 2. vols. Hyderabad: The Government of Andhra Pradesh, 1973, 1974.

Shulman, D.D. *Tamil Temple Myths: Sacrifice and Divine Marriage in the South Indian Śaiva Tradition.* Princeton. Princeton University Press, 1980.

Shulman, D.D. *The King and the Clown in South Indian Myth and Poetry.* Princeton: Princeton University Press, 1985.

Sivananda, Swami. *Hindu Fasts and Festivals and their Philosophy.* Rishikesh: The Sivanand Press, 1947.

Sivaramamurti, C. *Vijayanagara Painting.* New Delhi: Publications Division, Ministry of Information and Broadcasting, 1985.

Sontheimer, G.D. *Birobā, Mhaskobā und Khaṇḍobā: Ursprung, Geschichte and Umwelt von Pastoralen Gottheiten in Mahārāṣṭra.* Wiesbaden: Franz Steiner Verlag GMBH, 1976.

Soundara Rajan, K.V. *The Art of South India: Tamil Nadu and Kerala.* Delhi: Sundeep Prakashan, 1978.

Sreenivasa Murthy, H.V. and Ramakrishna, R. *A History of Karnataka : From the Earliest Times to the Present Day.* 2nd ed., New Delhi : S. Chand & Co., 1978.

Srinivasan, K.R. *Temples of South India.* New Delhi: National Book Trust, 1972.

Stein, B. *Peasant State and Society in Medieval South India.* Delhi: Oxford University Press, 1980.

Stein, B. *All the King's Mana: Papers on Medieval South Indian History.* Madras: New Era Publications, 1984.

Thomas, P. *Epics, Myths and Legends of India.* Bombay: Taraporewala & Co., n.d.

Thurston, E. *Castes and Tribes of Southern India.* 7 vols. Madras: Government Press, 1909.

Tiwari, J.N. *Goddess Cults in Ancient India: With special reference to the first seven centuries A.D.* Delhi : Sundeep Prakashan, 1985.

Whitehead, H. *The Village Gods of South India.* 2nd ed. Calcutta: Oxford University Press, 1921.

Vatsyayan, K. *Classical Indian Dance in Literature and the Arts.* New Delhi: Sangeet Natak Akademi, 1968.

Vatsyayan, K. *Dance in Indian Painting.* New Delhi: Abhinav Publications, 1982.

Venkataramanayya, N. *Studies in the Third Dynasty of Vijayanagara.* Madras: University of Madras, 1935.

Venkataramanayya, N. *The Early Muslim Expansion in South India.* Madras: University of Madras, 1942.

Venkata Ratnam, A.V. *Local Government in the Vijayanagara Empire.* Mysore: University of Mysore, 1972.

Vijayanagara Sexcentenary Commemoration Volume. Dharwar: Vijayanagara Empire Sexcentenary Association, 1936.

Viraraghavacharya, T.K.T. *History of Tirupati: The Tiruvengadam Temple.* 2 vols. Tirupati: Tirumalai-Tirupati Devasthanam Press, 1953.

Vishnu Thirtha, P. *A Concise History of Srimadjagadguru Sri Kudali Sringeri Sharada Mahapeetha.* Translated into English (from Kannada) by P. Prahlada Rao, not published.

Vogel, J. Ph. *Indian Serpent-Lore or the Nāgas in the Hindu Legend and Art.* London: Arthur Probsthain, 1926.

II. Theses

Hanumantha Rao, B.S.L. "Religion in Andhra: A Survey of the Religious Development from Early Times up to A.D. 1300." Ph.D. dissertation, Karnatak University, Dharwar, 1969.

Kamath, S.U. "Tuluva in Vijayanagara Times (1336-1646)." Ph.D dissertation, University of Bombay, 1965.

Kotecha, D. "Hindu Ritual Movement: Study of Sri Virupaksha Temple, Humpi". Dissertation, School of Architecture, Ahmedabad, 1982.

Nirmala Kumari, Y. "Social Life as Reflected in Sculptures and Paintings of Later Vijayanagara Period (A.D. 1500-1650) with special reference to Andhra." Ph.D. dissertation, Osmania University, Hyderabad, 1984.

Padigar, S.V. "The Cult of Vishṇu in Karnataka From Earliest Times to A.D. 1336: Based on a Study of Inscriptions and Sculpture." Ph.D. dissertation, Karnatak University, Dharwar, 1983.

Parthasarathy, V. "Evolution of Rituals in Viṣṇu Temple Utsavas (with special reference to Śrīraṅgam Tirumalai and Kāñchi)." Ph.D. dissertation, Bombay University, 1983.

Reddy, S.R. "History of Religious Institutions in Āndhra Dēsa from A.D. 1300 to 1600." Ph.D. dissertation, Osmania University, Hyderabad, 1980.

Sadyojata Swamiji. "Śaiva and Vīraśaiva Maṭhas in Karnataka (from the 10th Century to the Present period." Ph.D dissertation, Karnatak University, Dharwar, 1974.

Sarojini Devi, K. "Religion in Vijayanagara, A.D. 1336 to 1565." Ph.D. dissertation, Delhi University, 1969.

Shastry Tonnemane, A.K. "A History of Śṛiṅgēri." Ph.D. dissertation, Karnatak University, Dharwar, 1976.

Sugandha. "History and Archeology of Anegondi." Ph.D. dissertation, Poona University, 1986.

III. Articles

Appadurai, A. "Kings, Sects and Temples in South India, 1350-1700 A.D." In *South Indian Temples—An Analytical Reconsideration,* edited by B. Stein. New Delhi: Vikas Publishing House, 1978, pp. 47-73.

Balasubramanya. "Vīrabhadra Sculptures in Hampi." In *Vijayanagara: Progress of Research 1983-84,* edited by M.S. Nagaraja Rao, pp. 133-135.

Balasubrahmanya, T.B. "Chidambaram in Vijayanagara days." *Journal of the Bombay Historical Society,* IV, 1931, pp. 40-53.

Basu, N.K. "The Spring-Festival in India." *Man in India,* VII, 1927, pp. 112-185.

Bhandarkar, D.R. "Daṇḍakāraṇya." In *Jha Commemoration Volume: Essays on Oriental Subjects,* edited by K. Chattopadhyaya et al., pp. 47-57. Poona: Oriental Book Agency, 1937.

Breckenridge, C.A. "From Protector to Litigant—Changing Relations Between Hindu Temples and the Raja of Ramnad." In *South Indian Temples: An Analytical Reconsideration,* edited by B. Stein, pp. 75-105. New Delhi: Vikas Publishing House, 1978.

Chaudhuri, S.B. "Laṅka". *The Indian Historical Quarterly,* XXVII, pp. 119-128, 1951.

Chidanandamurti, M. "Two Māsti Temples in Karnataka." In *Memorial Stones: A Study of their Origin, Significance and Variety,* edited by S. Settar and G.D. Sontheimer, pp. 117-131.

Chidananda Murthy, M. "Fresh Light on Bukka's Inscription at Shravanabelgola." In *Early Vijayanagara: Studies in its History and Culture,* edited by G.S. Dikshit, pp. 95-100.

Chitgupi, B. "Nada-Brahma of Pandharpur: An Iconographical Hypothesis." In *Studies in Indian History and Culture,* edited by S. Ritti and B.R. Gopal., pp. 171-180. Dharwar: Karnatak University, 1971,

Dallapiccola, A.L. and Verghese, A. "Ramayana Panels on the Gopura of the 'Old Shiva' Temple,. Vithalapura." In *Vijayanagara: Progress of Research 1987-1988,* edited by D.V. Devaraj and C.S. Patil pp. 143-153. Mysore: Directorate of Archaeology and Museums, 1991.

D'Costa, A. "The Last Days of Vijayanagara : New Light from Portuguese Sources." *Indica,* 3, pp. 125-128. 1965.

Desai, P.B. "The Foundations of Vijayanagara." *Journal of the Karnatak University, Social Sciences,* 6, pp. 175-194, 1970.

Devanathachariar, K. "Śrī Vaiṣṇavism and its Caste-Marks." *The Quarterly Journal of the Mythic Society,* V, pp. 125-139, 1915.

Dhavalikar, M.K. "The Goddess of Mahakut". Paper read at the Centenary Celebrations of the Mysore Archaeology Department, 1985, not yet published.

Filliozat, P. "Techniques and Chronology of Construction in the Temple of Vithala at Hampi." In *Vijayanagara City and Empire: New Currents of Research,* edited by A.L. Dallapiccola, pp. 296-307.

Filliozat, V. "Les Quartiers et Marchés de Hampi." *Bulletin de L'Ecole Française d'Extrême Orient,*

64, pp. 39-42, 1977.

Filliozat, V. "Nouvelles Identifications de Monuments à Hampi". *Journal Asiatique*, 266, pp. 125-132, 1978.

Filliozat, V. "The Town Planning of Vijayanagara." *Art and Archaeology Research Papers* (aarp) 14, pp. 54-64, 1978.

Filliozat, V. "Iconography." In *Splendours of the Vijayanagara Empire: Hampi*, edited by G. Michell and V. Filliozat, pp. 127-132.

Filliozat, V. "The History, Social and Economic Conditions of the Vithala Temple at Hampi." In *South Asian Archaeology, 1981*, edited by B. Allchin, pp. 305-307. Cambridge : Cambridge University Press, 1984.

Filliozat, V. "Iconograpy: Religious and Civil Monuments." In *Vijayanagara City and Empire: New Currents of Research*, ed. by A.L. Dallapiccola, pp. 308-316.

Fritz, J.M. "The Roads of Vijayanagara : A Preliminary Study." In *Vijayanagara : Progress of Research 1979-83*, edited by M.S. Nagaraja Rao, pp. 50-56.

Fritz, J.M. "Archaeological Documentation at Vijayanagara." In *South Asian Archaeology, 1983*, edited by J. Schotsmans and M. Taddei, pp. 863-884. Naples: Institute Universitario Orientale, 1985.

Fritz, J.M. "Was Vijayanagara A 'Cosmic City'?" In *Vijayanagara City and Empire*, edited by A.L. Dallapiccola, pp. 257-273.

Fritz, J.M. "Vijayanagara: Authority and Meaning of a South Indian Imperial Capital." *American Anthropologist*, 88, pp. 44-54, 1986.

Fritz, J.M. "Chaco Canyon and Vijayanagara : Proposing Spatial Meaning in two Societies." In *Mirror and Metaphor: Material and Social Constructions of Reality*, edited by D. Ingersoll and G. Bronitsky, pp. 314-349. Lanham : University Press of America, 1987.

Fritz, J.M. and Michell G. "Interpreting the Plan of a Medieval Hindu Capital, Vijayanagara." *World Archaeology*, 19, no. 1, pp. 105-129, 1987.

Gopal, B.R. "Srī Āndāḷ in Karnataka". *The Quarterly Journal of the Mythic Society*, LXXVI, pp. 161-169, 1985.

Good, A. "Divine Coronation in a South Indian Temple." In *Religion and Society in South India: A Volume in Honour of Prof. N. Subba Rao*, edited by V. Sudarsen et al., pp. 37-71. Delhi: B.R. Publishing Corporation, 1987.

Govindacharya, A. "Tengalai and Vadagalai." *Journal of the Royal Asiatic Society of Great Britain and Ireland*, pp. 714-717, 1912.

Hanumantha Rao, B.S.L. "Inspiration for the Foundation of Vijayanagara and other Hindu Kingdoms in the South." In *Dr. N. Venkataramanayya Commemoration Volume: Journal of the Andhra Historical Research Society, Vol. XXXVIII*, edited by R. Subrahmanyam and V.V. Krishna Sastry, pp. 151-164. Hyderabad: The Government of Andhra Pradesh, 1986.

Hanumantha Rao, S. "The Influence of the Religious School of Sri Madhwa on the History of Vijayanagara." *The Quarterly Journal of the Mythic Society*, XX, pp. 284-287, 1930.

Hanumantha Rao, S. "Sri Madhwāchārya, 1238-1318 A.D." *Journal of Indian History*, pp. 25-41, 1949.

Heras, H. "Historical Carvings at Vijayanagara." *The Quarterly Journal of the Mythic Society*, XVII, pp. 85-88, 1926.

Heras, H. "Seven Days at Vijayanagar." *Journal of Indian History*, IX, pp. 103-118, 1930.

Herás, H. and Bhandarkar, V.K. "Vijayanagara Empire : A Synthesis of South Indian Culture." In *Vijayanagara Sexcentenary Commemoration Volume*, pp. 29-38.

Hiralal, R.B. "The Situation of Rāvaṇa's Laṅkā." In *Jha Commemoration Volume: Essays on Oriental Subjects*, edited by K. Chattopadhyaya et al., pp. 151-161. Poona: Oriental Book Agency, 1937.

Hudson, D.D., "Two Citrā Festivals in Madurai". In *Religious Festivals in South India and Sri Lanka*, edited by G.R. Welbon and Y.E. Yocum, pp. 101-156. New Delhi: Manohar Publications, 1982.

Jaiswal, Suvira. "Evolution of the Narasimha Legend and its Possible Sources." *Proceedings of the*

Indian History Congress, pp. 140-151, 34th Session, held at Chandigarh, 1973.

Jash, P. "The Kapalikas—An Obscure Saiva Sect." *Proceedings of the Indian History Congress,* pp. 152-155. 34th Session, held at Chandigarh, 1973.

Khare, G.H. "Krishnadevaraya of Vijayanagara and the Vitthala Image of Pandharpur." In *Vijayanagara Sexcentenary Commemoration Volume,* pp. 191-196.

Kibe, M.V. "Rāvaṇa's Laṅkā located in Central India." *The Indian Historical Quarterly,* IV, pp. 694-702, 1928.

Kotraiah, C.T.M. "Vijayanagara Paintings at the Virupaksha Temple, Hampi." *The Quarterly Journal of the Mythic Society,* XLIX, pp. 228-237, 1959.

Kotraiah, C.T.M. "A Cave Linga of Hampi." In *Journal of the Andhra Historical Research Society,* 32, pp. 121-125, 1971-72.

Kotraiah, C.T.M. "The Metropolis of the Vijayanagara Empire." In *The Vijayanagara Urbanity,* edited by K.R. Basavaraja, pp. 6-24.

Kotraiah, C.T.M. "Hampi before Founding of Vijayanagara." In *Śrīnidhih : Perspectives in Indian Archaeology, Art and Culture, Shri K.R. Srinivasa Festschrift,* edited by. K.V. Raman et al., pp. 381-387. Madras: New Era Publications, 1983.

Kotraiah, C.T.M. "Pampa Sarassu, Kishkindha and Hampi." Paper read at the Centenary Celebrations of the Mysore Department of Archaeology, 1985, not yet published.

Kramrisch, S. "An Image of Aditi-Uttānapad." In *Exploring India's Sacred Art,* edited with a biographical essay by B.S. Miller, pp. 148-158. Philadelphia: University of Pennsylvania Press, 1983.

Krishnacharya, H. "Music under the Vijayanagara Empire." *Vijayanagara Sexcentenary Commemoration Volume,* pp. 367-375.

Krishnamacharlu, C.R. "The Religion of the Vijayanagara House." *The Indian Antiquary,* XLIV, pp. 219-225, 1915.

Krishnaswami Ayyangar, S. "Foundation of Vijayanagara.." *The Quarterly Journal of the Mythic Society,* XI, pp. 13-32, 1920.

Krishnaswami Aiyangar, S. "The Character and Significance of the Empire of Vijayanagara in Indian History." In *Vijayanagara Sexcentenary Commemoration Volume,* pp. 1-28.

Lakshminarayan Rao, N. "Portrait Sculpture of the Vijayanagara King Mallikarjuna." In *Studies in Indian History and Culture,* edited by S. Ritti and B.R. Gopal, pp.181-182. Dharwar: Karnatak University, 1971.

Mackenize, J.S.F. "Tree and Serpent Worship." *The Indian Antiquary,* IV, pp. 5-6, 1875.

Mate, M.S. "Hero-Stones : The 'Folk' and the 'Classic'" In *Memorial Stones: A Study of their Origin, Significance and Variety,* edited by S. Settar and G.D. Sontheimer, pp. 79-82.

Mehta, S.S. "Holika Celebration." *Journal of Anthropological Society of Bombay,* X, pp. 31-37, 1913.

Merrey, K.L. "The Hindu Festival Calendar." In *Religious Festivals in South India and Sri Lanka,* edited by G.R. Welbon and G.E. Yocum. pp. 1-25. New Delhi: Manohar Publications, 1982.

Michell, G. "The 'Royal Centre' and the Great Platform at Vijayanagara." In *Rupa Pratirupa: Alice Boner Commemoration Volume,* edited by B. Baumer, pp.109-118. New Delhi : Biblia Impex, 1982.

Michell, G. "Architecture of the Muslim Quarters at Vijayanagara." In *Vijayanagara: Progress of Research 1983-84,* edited by M.S. Nagaraja Rao, pp. 101-118.

Michell, G. "Architectural Tradition at Vijayanagara: Islamic Style." In *Vijayanagara City and Empire: New Currents of Research,* edited by A.L. Dallapiccola, pp. 282-286.

Michell, G. "Architectural Traditions at Vijayanagara: Temple Styles." In *Vijayanagara City and Empire: New Currents of Research,* edited by A.L. Dallapiccola, pp. 274-281.

Michell, G. "Two Temples from the Early Vijayanagara Period: Studies in Monumental Archaism." In *Kusumāñjali: New Interpretation of Indian Art and Culture, Sh. C. Sivaramamurti Commemoration Volume,* edited by M.S. Nagaraja Rao, vol. I, pp. 213-216. New Delhi: Agam Kala

Prakashan, 1987.

Murty, M.L.K. "Ethnoarchaeology of the Kurnool Cave Areas." *World Archaeology*, 17, pp. 192-205, 1985.

Nagaraja Rao, M.S. "Ahmad Khan's Dharmśāla." In *Vijayanagara: Progress of Research 1979-83*, edited by M.S. Nagaraja Rao, pp. 64-65.

Nagaraja Rao, M.S and Patil C.S. "Epigraphical References to City Gates and Watch Towers of Vijayanagara." In *Vijayanagara: Progress of Research 1983-84*, edited by M.S. Nagaraja Rao, pp. 96-100.

Narayana Rao, C., "An Identification of the Idol of Vitthala in the Vitthala Temple at Hampi," *Proceedings and Transactions of the Eighth All India Oriental Conference*, Session held at Mysore, pp.715-728, 1935.

Pandurangi, K.T. "Dvaita Saints and Scholars of the Vijayanagara Period." In *Early Vijayanagara: Studies in its History & Culture*, edited by G.S. Dikshit, pp. 59-66.

Pargiter, F.E. "The Geography of Rāma's Exile." *Journal of the Royal Asiatic Society of Great Britain and Ireland*, pp. 231-264, 1894.

Patil, C.S. "Krishna Temple." In *Vijayanagara: Progress of Research 1979-83*, edited by M.S. Nagaraja Rao, pp. 61-63.

Patil, C.S. "Palace Architecture at Vijayanagara : New Excavations." In *Vijayanagara City and Empire: New Currents of Research*, edited by A.L. Dallapiccola, pp. 229-239.

Patil, C.S. "Sculptures at Kōtiliṅga." In *Vijayanagara: Progress of Research 1983-84*, edited by M.S. Nagaraja Rao, pp. 138-143.

Raghavan, V. "The Virūpākṣa Vasantōtsava Campū of Ahobala (A 'Vijayanagara-kavya')". *Journal of Oriental Research*, Madras, XIV, pp. 17-40, 1940.

Rajasekhara, S. "Inscriptions at Vijayanagara" In *Vijayanagara City & Empire: New Currents of Research*, edited by A.L. Dallapiccola, pp. 101-119.

Rajasekhara, S. "Sangamas and Vīraśaivism." In *Early Vijayanagara: Studies in its History & Culture*, edited by G.S. Dikshit, pp. 85-93.

Ramachandran, K.S. "Some Harihara Figures from Nepal." In *Śrinidhiḥ: Perspectives in Indian Archaeology, Art and Culture, Shri K.R. Srinivasan Festschrift*, edited by K.V. Raman et al. Madras: New Era Publications, pp. 163-165, 1983.

Ramadas, G. "Rāvaṇa's Laṅkā." *The Indian Historical Quarterly*, IV, pp. 339-346, 1928.

Ramakrishna Rao, B. "The Dasara Celebrations in Mysore." *The Quarterly Journal of the Mythic Society*, XI, pp. 301-311, 1921.

Raman, K.V. "Hoysala Influence on the Vijayanagara Art." In *Śrikanthikā: Dr. Srikantha Sastri Felicitation Volume*, edited by K.V. Ramesh et al., pp. 55-58. Mysore: Geetha Book House, 1973.

Raman, K.V. "Architecture under the Vijayanagar." *Proceedings of the Seminar on Temple Art and Architecture held in March 1980*, edited by K.K.A. Venkatachari, pp. 87-96. Bombay: Anantacharya Indological Research Institute, 1981.

Rama Ṛao, R. "Hinduism under Vijayanagara Kings." In *Vijayanagara Sexcentenary Commemoration Volume*, pp. 39-51.

Saletore, B.A. "The Rise of Vijayanagara III." *The Indian Historical Quarterly*, IX, pp. 521-566, 1933.

Saletore, B.A. "The Rāja Guru of the Founders of Vijayanagara and the Pontiffs of Sringeri Matha." *Journal of the Andhra Historical Research Society*, 9, pp. 33-42, 1934-35.

Saletore, B.A. "Vaiṣṇavism in Vijayanagara." In *D.R. Bhandarkar Volume*, edited by B.C. Law, pp. 193-195. Calcutta: Indian Research Institute, 1940.

Sankalia, H.D. "The Nude Goddess or 'Shameless Woman' in Western Asia, India, and South-Eastern Asia." *Artibus Asiae*, XXIII, pp. 111-123, 1960.

Sarojini Devi, K. "The Cult of Vithoba in Vijayanagara." In *Dr. N. Venkataramanaya Commemoration Volume: Journal of the Andhra Historical Research Society, Vol. XXXVIII*, edited by R. Subrahmanyam and V.V. Krishna Sastry, pp. 93-99. Hyderabad: Government of Andhra

Pradesh, 1987.

Sarojini Devi, K. "The Cult of Virabhadra in Vijayanagara." *The Quarterly Journal of the Mythic Society,* LXXVIII, pp.1-14, 1988.

Shama Sastry, R. "A Few Inscriptions of the Ancient Kings of Anegundi." *The Quarterly Journal of the Mythic Society,* VII, pp. 285-291, 1917

Settar, S. "Memorial Stones in South India." In *Memorial Stones: A Study of their Origin, Significance and Variety,* edited by S. Settar and G.D. Sontheimer, pp. 183-197.

Shapiro, A.A. "The Kalyanotsava of Pampadevi and Pampapati." not yet published.

Shukla, S.K. "Horse Trade in Medieval South: Its Political and Economic Implications." *Proceedings of the Indian History Congress, 42nd Session, held at Magadh University, Bodhgaya,* pp. 310-317, 1981.

Sinha, D.K. "A Rare Varāha Image of Archaeological Museum, Hampi." *Journal of Indian History,* LIII, pp. 353-359, 1975.

Sinnur, M.H. "The Capitals of the Vijayanagara Empire." In *The Vijayanagara Urbanity,* edited by K.R. Basavaraja, pp. 43-49.

Smith, Daniel H. "Festivals in Pāñcarātra Literature." In *Religious Festivals in South India and Sri Lanka,* edited by G.R. Welbon and G.E. Yocum, pp. 27-49. New Delhi: Manohar Publications, 1982.

Sontheimer, G.D. "Hero and Satī-Stones in Maharashtra." In *Memorial Stones : A Study of their Origin, Significance, and Variety,* edited by S. Settar and G.D. Sontheimer, pp. 261-281.

Sontheimer, G.D. "Folk Deities in the Vijayanagara Empire: Narasiṁha and Mallaṇṇa/Mailār." In *Vijayanagara City and Empire: New Currents of Research,* edited by A.L. Dallapiccola, pp. 144-158.

Soundara Rajan, K.V. "The Typology of the Anantaśayī Icon", *Artibus Asiae,* XXIX, pp. 67-84, 1967.

Sreenivasachar, P. "Polipadu Grant of Krishna-Deva-Raya." *Journal of the Andhra Historical Research Society,* 10, pp. 121-142, 1936-37.

Sreenivasa Rao, B.V. "The Religious Policy of Sangama Rulers." *Journal of the Andhra Historical Research Society,* 29, pp. 35-36, 1964.

Srikantaya, S. "An Image at Hampi." *The Quarterly Journal of the Mythic Society,* XXVI, pp. 232-235, 1936.

Srinivasachari, C.S. "A Great Contribution of Vijayanagara to the Tamil Country. The Conquest of the Madura Sultanate and the Restoration of Hindu Orthodoxy." *Karnatak Historical Review,* IV, pp. 6-14, 1937.

Srinivasa Rao, V.N. "Chandragiri." *The Quarterly Journal of the Mythic Society,* XXIII, pp.375-387, 1932-33.

Stein, B. "Devi Shrines and Folk Hinduism in Medieval Tamilnad." In *Studies in the Language and Culture of South Asia,* edited by E. Gerow and M.D. Lang, pp. 75-90. Seattle & London: University of Washington Press, 1973.

Stein, B. "The Problematical 'Kingdom of Vijayanagara'." In *Vijayanagara City and Empire: New Currents of Research,* edited by A.L. Dallapiccola, pp. 1-4.

Stein, B. "Vijayanagara and the Transition to Patrimonial Systems." In *Vijayanagara City and Empire: New Currents of Research,* edited by A.L. Dallapiccola, pp. 73-87.

Sundara, A. "Narasiṁha Sculptures from Hosa Mahākuṭa and Kuppaṭūru: Some Early Types and Significance." *Karnatak Historical Review,* XIII, pp. 9-12, 1977.

Sundara, A. "New Lights on Religious Trends in Anegondi Region During Vijayanagara Periods." *The Quarterly Journal of the Mythic Soceity,* LXVIII, pp. 9-18, 1977.

Sundara, A. "A Unique Virabhadra Image from Mulgund." In *Śrīnidhih: Perspectives in Indian Archaeology, Art and Culture, Shri K.R. Srinivasan Festschrift,* edited by K.V. Raman, et al. pp. 151-154. Madras: New Era Publications, 1983.

Sundaram Iyer, P.S. "Sri Vidyaranya and Music." In *Vijayanagara Sexcentenary Commemoration*

Volume, pp. 333-342.

Thomas, Job. "Cultural Development in Tamil Nadu during the Vijayanagara Period." In *Vijayanagara City and Empire: New Currents of Research,* edited by A.L. Dallapiccola, pp. 5-40.

Tulpule, S.G. "Karnatak Origins of the Cult of Viṭhala." Paper read at the Centenary Celebrations of the Mysore Department of Archaeology, 1985. not yet published.

Vader, V.H. "Situation of Rāvana's Laṅkā : On the Equator." *The Indian Historical Quarterly,* II, pp. 345-350, 1926.

Venkataramanayya, N. "A Note on Śrī Virūpāksa." *Journal of Oriental Research,* Madras, V, pp. 241-245, 1931.

Venkataramanyya, N. "The Date of the Construction of the Temples of Hazāra-Rāma-svāmi and Viṭṭhala at Vijayanagara." *Journal of Oriental Research,* Madras, XVI, pp. 84-90, 1946-47,

Venkata Subbiah, A. "A Twelfth Century University in Mysore." *The Quarterly Journal of the Mythic Society,* VII, pp.157-196, 1917.

Venket Rao, Gurty. "Krishna Deva Raya and the Portuguese." *Journal of the Andhra Historical Research Society,* 10, pp.73-85, 1936-37.

Venket Rao, Gurty. "Bahmani-Vijayanagara Relations." *Proceedings of the Indian History Congress, 2nd Session held at Allahabad,* pp. 264- 277, 1938.

Index

'Abdur Razzāk, 9, 12, 107, 125, 128, 129
āchārya (s), 6, 66, 69, 77-81, 133
Achyutarāya, 2, 8, 11, 21, 24, 28, 29, 49, 58, 59, 63, 64, 65, 71, 72, 73, 75, 77, 94, 103, 107, 114, 118, 128, 133, 135, 149, 150, 151
Achyutarāya-pēṭhe, 11, 46
Achyutarāyapura, 11, 73
Advaita, 3, 4, 5, 6, 7, 111, 112, 116
Āgama(s), 4, 39, 100, 118
agrahāra(s), 11, 21, 47, 76, 111, 117, 118, 139, 142, 143, 146, 150
Ahmad Khān, 126, 127, 128
Ahōbalam, 8, 34, 38, 64, 81, 135, 138
āḻvār(s), 6, 7, 37, 48, 49, 55, 59, 63, 64, 65, 69, 70, 77, 78-81, 133
Āmuktamālyada, 9, 71, 79
Ānandanidhi, 3, 49, 58, 64, 73, 150
Āñjanadri Hill, 44, 45, 91
Āñjanēya, 36, 44, 46, 85, 90-92, 155, 157, 158, 159
Aṇṇala-dēvī, 48
Anantaśayana, 76, 77, 92, 133, 136
Anantaśayana-guḍi, 76, 92
Ānegoṇdi, 9, 10, 11, 23, 30, 34, 36, 43, 44, 45, 54, 55, 76, 90, 91, 94, 95, 102, 112, 113, 116, 122, 124, 125, 132, 133, 137, 138
Arab(s), 7, 128, 129
Āravīḍu dynasty, 2, 9, 19, 48, 77, 81
Areśaṅkara Bāgilu, 13, 157
āśrama(s), 44, 114, 139

Bahamanī, 1, 2
Bālakṛishṇa, 54, 55, 56, 58, 62, 106
Barbosa, Duarte, 9, 94, 129
Basava, 5, 29
Bēṭekārara Hebbāgilu, 13, 28
Bhadrakāḷī, 88-89, 159
Bhāgavata Pūrāṇa, 6, 38, 54
Bhairava, 5, 16, 22, 23, 27, 28, 30, 89, 95, 129, 136, 156, 159
Bhairavī, 22, 27, 88, 89
Bharata, 50
Bhāratitīrtha, 7, 8
Bhāskara-kshētra, 9, 26, 35, 36, 142, 143, 144, 145
Bhuvanēśvari, 11
Brahmā, 17, 22, 38, 70, 75, 88, 89
bṛindāvana(s), 54, 87, 92, 113, 114, 139, 155, 156
Bukka I, 1, 3, 8, 9, 10, 111, 121, 122, 135, 142
Bukka II, 1, 121, 122
Bukkājī-amma, 20

Bukkāyave, 28

Caesar Frederick, 13, 94
Chakra-tīrtha, 11, 29, 49, 74, 76, 134, 156
chaityālaya, 10, 11, 121, 122, 123
Chamarasa, 8, 112
Chāmuṇḍa, 4
Chandragiri, 1, 2
Chandramauḷi, 19, 26, 142, 143, 144, 145
Chandraśēkhara temple, 12, 36
Chaturviṁśatimūrtis, 87, 88
Cheñchū-Lakshmī, 39, 40
Chennabasava Pūrāṇa, 8, 21, 24, 112, 116
Chinnā-dēvī, 63, 101
Chintāmaṇi, 44, 112, 116
Conti, Nicolo, 9, 94, 105, 106, 108, 128
Christian(s), 7, 121, 128, 129, 133

Daksha, 17, 23
Dance, 107-108
Daśāvatāras, 85, 86-88, 125
Dēvarāya I, 1, 26, 27, 46, 47, 48, 50, 56, 75, 112, 121, 122, 125, 135, 142, 143
Dēvarāya II, 1, 8, 9, 19, 20, 21, 23, 46, 47, 62, 71, 75, 92, 112, 116, 121, 122, 125, 126, 128, 129, 142, 143
Dēvī, 70, 86, 89, 90, 94, 158, 159
dharma, 2
Dvaita, 6, 7
Durgā temple, 19, 23, 89, 156

Elephant Stables, 13, 37

Ferishta, 125, 126
Friar Luiz, 128, 129

Gajalakshmī, 35, 37
Gaṇēśa, 16, 25, 26, 38, 46, 81, 89, 132, 136, 155-160
Garuḍa, 35, 47, 50, 63, 72, 77, 86, 87, 94
Gavi Raṅganātha temple, 55, 56, 76, 102, 124
Gōri-keḷagana-grāma, 11, 126
grāma-dēvatas, 7, 88
guru(s), 6, 8, 9, 23, 111, 112, 113, 114, 115, 132

Haṁpi, 9, 10, 16, 18, 30, 43, 82, 90, 91, 94, 106, 138
Haṁpi Archaeological Museum, 30, 41, 74, 77, 79, 88, 89, 93, 95, 124
Haridāsa(s), 7, 60, 65, 79, 108, 113, 114, 132
Hanumān, 35, 36, 43, 44, 45, 47, 49, 50, 51, 85, 86, 90-92, 94, 114, 132, 133, 134, 138
Harihara, 70, 85, 86, 135, 158
Harihara I, 1, 8, 10, 123
Harihara II, 1, 8, 19, 20, 25, 26, 27, 28, 32, 35, 71, 75, 111, 121, 122, 123, 141, 142
Harihara (poet), 18

Hēmakūṭa Hill, 9, 11, 16, 17, 18, 19, 21, 22, 25, 26, 35, 37, 38, 40, 50, 55, 86, 89, 91, 95, 112, 134, 144, 148
Hemakutakhanda, 29, 44
Hiraṇyakaśipu, 38, 40, 41
Hiriya Kāluve, 11, 49, 89, 116
Hiriya-maṭha (Hiriya-Chattra), 24, 74, 112, 116
Hōḷi, 105, 106, 110
Hospēṭ, 9, 10, 11, 28, 45, 73

Irugappa, 10, 122, 123, 125, 142
Islam, 7, 125-128, 133, 139

Jaina(s), Jainism, 7, 12, 24, 42, 69, 121-125, 128, 133, 135, 136, 139
Jambavatēśvara/Jaṁbunātha, 18, 28, 92, 112
Jaṁbavatikalyāṇam, 18, 106
jaṅgama(s), 5, 112, 113, 137
Jaṅgamaya, 24, 74, 136

Kaḍirāṁpuram, 22, 126, 127
Kāḷahasti, 28, 72, 133, 135
Kāḷāmukha, 4, 5, 7, 8, 22, 24, 112, 113, 132
Kāḷī, 88-89, 95
Kalyāṇōtsava, 17, 35, 102
Kāma, 17, 106, 107
Kāmalāpuram, 9, 10, 11, 37, 38, 126
Kaṁpili, 10
Kāñchi, 3, 6, 77, 78, 133, 135
Kaṇṇappa, 28
Kāpāḷika, 4, 5, 22, 113
Kārtikēya, 25, 89, 136, 156
Khaṇḍobā, 27
King's Audience Hall, 12
Kishkindhā, 10, 30, 43, 45, 132
Kōdaṇḍarāma temple, 44, 46, 49, 93, 102, 138, 139, 156
Koḍe-tirunāḷu, 58, 103, 104
kolāṭam, 108
Kōṭiśaṅkaradēvara Bāgilu, 13, 27
Kōṭi-tīrtha, 11, 29, 50, 134, 156
Kramuka-parnāpaṇa-vīdhi, 11, 122
Kṛishṇa, 34, 41, 54-59, 69, 88, 133, 139, 147
Kṛishṇadēvarāya, 2, 8, 9, 10, 11, 18, 19, 20, 21, 22, 25, 27, 28, 34, 37, 41, 47, 48, 49, 50, 56, 57, 58, 61, 62, 63, 64, 65, 66, 69, 70, 71, 72, 73, 75, 76, 77, 79, 94, 99, 100, 101, 103, 106, 107, 108, 112, 114, 116, 118, 121, 126, 128, 129, 133, 135, 145, 146-149
Kṛishṇa-līlā, 55, 61, 74
Kṛishṇāpura, 36, 37, 40, 41, 56, 73, 74, 100, 116, 118, 133, 136, 137
Kṛishṇāpura-pēṭe, 11, 56
Kṛishṇa temple complex, 11, 12, 36, 37, 38, 54, 55, 57, 58, 66, 76, 79, 81, 88, 89, 99, 101, 103, 104, 117, 118, 136, 139
Kriyāśakti, 7, 8, 112,
Kunthu Jinanātha (Gāṇigitti) temple, 10, 122, 123, 124

Lajjā-Gaurī, 90
Lakkaṇṇa, 8, 112, 143
Lakshmaṇa, 43, 44, 47, 49, 50, 51, 92, 156, 158, 159
Lakshmī, 6, 55, 57, 61, 64, 70, 89
Lakshmī-Narasiṁha, 36, 37, 38, 40, 41, 42, 133, 136, 137, 139, 156
Laṅkā, 43, 44, 45
liṅga(s), 5, 6, 18, 22, 23, 26, 27, 29, 30, 46, 56, 86, 94, 95, 112, 117, 134, 137, 138, 155, 158, 159
Liṅgāyat, 5, 10, 112
Lotus Mahal, 12, 17

Mādhava temple, 11, 12, 36, 87, 107, 137, 139
Madhurāvijayam, 1, 8
Madhuvana, 44, 45, 46, 92
Madhvācharya, 6, 7, 54, 91, 92, 113
Mādhva(s)/Mādhvaism, 3, 7, 8, 34, 37, 54, 58, 60, 65, 87, 91, 92, 113, 114, 117, 132
Mahābhārata, 38, 85, 87, 91, 105
Mahānavamī festival, 3, 51, 99, 103, 104, 105, 106
Mahānavamī Dibba/Platform, 13, 39, 51, 106, 107, 108, 116, 125
Mahisāśuramardinī, 88, 89
Mailāra, 27, 28
Mallikārjuna, 26, 27, 132, 133, 145
Mallikārjuna (king), 1, 8, 23, 47, 55, 75, 78, 144, 145
Malpannaguḍi, 27
Mālyavanta Hill, 9, 45, 46, 126, 127
Mālyavanta Raghunātha temple, 12, 46, 49, 108, 133, 138, 139, 154
Manmatha tank, 11
māsti, 94
māsti-kal, 94
Mataṅga Hill, 9, 21, 24, 27, 29, 36, 44, 45, 117, 138, 159
maṭha (s), 3, 8, 47, 54, 102, 111, 112, 115, 116, 117, 118, 132, 139, 155, 159
Matsyēndranātha, 5, 89, 113, 119
Moorish quarter, 11, 126
mosque (s), 127, 133
Mudal-āḷvār temple, 63, 79, 80, 81, 137, 139, 155
Mudama, 93
Mudu Vīraṇṇa temple, 24, 56, 95, 102, 116, 133, 136, 137, 138, 139, 158
Music, 107-109
Muslims, 1, 3, 7, 121, 122-128, 133, 135, 136, 137, 138

nāga (s), 92, 93
nāga-kal (s), 7, 92-93
Nāgalādēvī-pura, 11, 29, 76, 118, 133
Nammāḷvār, 63, 79, 80, 115
nāmam (s), 6, 37, 57, 58, 59, 61, 65, 69, 73, 81, 82
Nandi, 18, 28, 29, 30, 86, 89, 94, 95, 134, 155, 158, 159, 160
Narahari-tīrtha, 6, 113, 114, 155
Narasa Nāyaka, 2, 29, 144, 148
Narasiṁha, 8, 19, 34-41, 54, 61, 69, 74, 88, 91, 132, 138, 156, 158
Narasiṁhapūrāṇam, 20, 46, 62

Nātha (s), 5, 22, 113
Navarātrī, 105
Nava-bṛindāvana, 54, 113
nayanār (s), 5, 7, 28
Nikitin, Athanasius, 13
Niṁbāpuram, 29, 44, 118
Nuniz, Fernão, 9, 45, 91, 94, 107, 126, 128

Paes, Domingo, 4, 9, 10, 11, 18, 20, 90, 105, 106, 107, 126
Prahlāda, 38, 40, 41
Paṁpā, 16, 17, 18, 30, 34, 44, 46, 47, 48, 56, 89, 90, 102, 132
Paṁpa-kshētra, 9, 11, 16, 18, 29, 35, 36, 65, 85, 113, 141, 142, 144, 146, 147, 149, 151, 154
Pampamahatmya, 16, 17, 29, 44, 46, 113
Paṁpāpati, 17, 143
Paṁpa-pura, 9, 11, 16
Paṁpa-Sarōvar (Paṁpa saras), 44, 45, 46
Pāñcharātra, 86, 87
Paṇḍharpūr, 59, 60, 61, 62, 133
Pārāṅkuśa-maṇḍapa, 63, 64, 79, 80, 103, 157
Parśvanātha temple, 11, 121, 123, 124
Pārvatī, 17, 28, 89, 102, 156, 159
Pāśupata, 4, 22, 113
Paṭṭābhirāma temple, 11, 12, 49, 90, 101, 108, 133
Peḍḍa-aṅgadi-vīdhi, 11
Penugoṇḍa Bāgilu, 13, 49, 99
Phalapūjā, 17, 102
Pietro della Valle, 94, 108
Portuguese, 7, 126, 129, 133
Prabhandam/Divyaprabhandam, 6, 64, 81, 103, 104
Prapannāmṛitam, 8, 48
Prōlugaṅti Tippa, 20, 46, 62
Prasanna Virūpāksha temple, 21, 22, 47, 100, 101, 136, 139
Prāta Viṭhala temple, 60, 61, 132, 134, 139, 157
Pūrāṇa (s), 38, 39, 41, 54, 58, 85, 116, 118
Purandaradāsa, 60, 79, 114

Queen's Bath, 12

Raghunandana-svāmi, 54, 87, 92, 114, 134, 139, 156
Rakkasa-Taṅgaḍi, 2, 12, 128, 137, 138, 139
Rāma, 34, 41, 43-51, 56, 59, 69, 80, 88, 91, 92, 102, 105, 132, 135, 138, 156, 158, 159
Rāmachaṇdra, 47, 48, 51, 56, 85, 89
Rāmachandra temple, 12, 17, 21, 38, 39, 40, 45, 47, 48, 50, 51, 59, 61, 62, 78, 82, 87, 88, 90, 99, 100, 103, 104, 106, 107, 108, 124, 125, 132, 136, 139
Rāmānujāchārya, 6, 37, 49, 55, 63, 69, 70, 72, 77, 78, 81, 88, 114, 121
Rāmānuja-kūṭa (s), 63, 64, 66, 71, 72, 80, 81, 100, 115, 117, 155
Rāmarāya, 2, 9, 24, 48, 60, 61, 74, 78, 79, 80, 81, 92, 108, 114, 117, 126, 133, 135, 137
Rāmarājiyamu, 21, 76
Rāmāyaṇa, 43-46, 50, 61, 74, 80, 87, 91, 132, 138
Raṅganātha, 60, 69, 75-77, 132, 133, 138, 143, 144, 156

Ratha-saptamī, 103, 104
Rathōtsava, 26, 58, 101, 102, 103, 104, 106
Rāvaṇa, 44, 92, 105
Ṛishyamūka, 44, 45

Sadāśivarāya, 2, 9, 21,24, 28, 34, 37, 49, 61, 63, 64, 65, 71, 74, 77, 80, 81, 92, 117, 128, 135, 136, 137, 152, 153
Śakta, 7
Śaiva/Śaivism, 4, 5, 8, 16, 48, 50, 55, 70, 85, 95, 105, 111, 113, 116, 117, 121, 132, 133, 134, 135, 136, 137, 138, 155, 156, 157, 158, 159, 160
Śaiva-Siddhānta, 5
Salaka-Rāja-Chikka-Tirumala, 28, 112, 152
Salaka-Rāja-Hiriya-Tirumala, 11, 73
Sale-Tirumale-Mahārāya-pura, 11, 40, 77
Sāḷuva dynasty, 1, 7, 19, 69, 71, 78, 117, 132
Sāḷuva Narasiṁha, 1, 8, 34, 70, 71, 75, 114, 126, 127
Saṅgama dynasty, 1, 7, 8, 9, 19, 26, 30, 46, 48, 49, 60, 70, 75, 111, 112, 121, 123, 132, 133, 135, 136
Śaṅkarāchārya, 4
satī (s), 93-95, 133
satī-kal (s), 93, 156, 158
satī-vīra-kal, 93
Śatrughna, 50
Śēsha, 40, 50, 88
Siṅghārada Hebbāgilu, 10, 37, 107, 124
Sītā, 43, 44, 47, 49, 50, 156, 158
Sītā-kuṇḍa (Sītā-Sarōvar), 29, 35, 44, 46, 92, 156
Śiva, 17, 22, 23, 24, 27, 28, 38, 47, 54, 70, 85, 86, 89, 90, 91, 102, 106, 136
Śivādvaita, 5
Smārta (s), 4, 21, 111, 112, 117, 132
Sōmavārada Bāgilu, 10, 49, 123
Śrī, 6, 75
Śrīṅgēri, 1, 3, 7, 8, 26, 111, 115, 116
Śrīraṅga I, 19
Śrīraṅga III, 21, 76
Śrīraṅgam, 6, 9, 66, 69, 70, 75, 76, 77, 78, 133, 135, 143, 144
Śrīśailam, 5, 7, 26, 28, 133, 135, 145
Śrī-Vaishṇava (s), Śrī-Vaishṇavism, 6, 7, 8, 9, 25, 37, 47, 48, 49, 54, 58, 59, 61, 64, 65, 69-82, 87, 99, 103, 111, 114, 115, 116, 117, 121, 132, 133, 136, 138
Śrī Vyāsayōgicharitam, 8, 62, 91, 114
sthānika (s)/sthānadhipati, 21, 58, 99
Sugrīva, 43, 44, 49, 132
Sugrīva's Cave, 35, 44, 46, 156
Sūrya, 27, 38, 80, 86, 156

Tāḷikōṭa, see Rakkasa-Taṅgadi
Teṅgalai, 6, 57, 58, 59, 78, 81, 82, 114, 116
Teppa-tirunāḷu, 82, 103, 104
Tirumala-dēvī, 11, 63, 71, 101, 147
Tirumala-dēvī-ammana-paṭṭaṇa, 11, 29, 73
Tirumalai-Tirupati, 8, 9, 48, 60, 61, 65, 69, 70, 71, 78, 107, 133, 135

Tirumalarāya (prince), 11, 77, 147
Tirumaṅgai-āḷvār, 59, 79, 80
Tirumaṅgai-āḷvār temple, 40, 63, 65, 78, 80, 81, 100, 137, 139, 155
Tiruveṅgaḷanātha, 69-74, 133, 139
Tiruveṅgaḷanātha temple complex, 11, 12, 38, 50, 57, 73, 74, 86, 89, 90, 91, 99, 101, 103, 108, 115, 133, 135, 136, 137, 139, 159
Tiruvadhyāna, 64, 65, 81, 82, 103, 104
Tōpu-tirunāḷu, 82, 103, 104
Tulāpurusha-dāna, 3, 71, 75, 143
Tuḷuva dynasty, 1, 2, 7, 8, 17, 19, 20, 21, 54, 59, 66, 69, 70, 71, 78, 103, 114, 117, 132
Tuṅgabhadrā, 9, 10, 16, 26, 35, 36, 37, 45, 49, 64, 76, 85, 86, 102, 113, 132, 141-153

Udayagiri, 11, 26, 56, 57
Udayagiri Bāgilu, 13
Udayagiri Timmarāju, 63, 64, 65, 81, 103, 115
Uḍipi, 6, 54, 60, 113
Ugādi, 103, 105
Ūṭada Kāluve, 11
Utī-tirunāḷu, 103, 104
Uyyāle-tirunāḷu, 58, 103

Vaḍagalai, 6, 49, 78, 81, 82, 114, 116
Vaikhānasa, 77
Vaishṇava/Vaishṇavism, 37, 42, 50, 54, 55, 70, 72, 85, 86, 105, 111, 117, 121, 132, 133, 134, 135, 136, 137, 138, 139, 155, 156, 157
Vāli, 43, 44
vānaras, 44
Varadadēvī/Varadāji-amma, 58, 72, 73, 75, 77, 94
Varadadēvī-ammana-paṭṭaṇa, 11, 49, 73
Varadarāja, 3, 69, 77, 78, 133
Varthema, 13, 128
Vasantōtsava, 51, 101, 103, 106, 107, 110
Vēdas, 4, 58, 118
Veṅkaṭa II, 19, 71, 72, 112, 156
Veṅkaṭēśvara, 8, 9, 19, 34, 40, 41, 60, 61, 69-74, 78, 107, 133, 135, 157
Vēṇugōpāla, 54, 55
Vidyāraṇya, 7, 8, 10, 21, 26, 111, 116, 155
Vidyātīrtha, 7, 8
Vīrabhadra, 16, 23-25, 30, 89, 95, 132, 135, 138, 156, 158, 159, 160
vīra-kal(s), 59, 93, 95
Vīra Narasiṁha, 1, 8, 27, 37, 145
Vīraśaiva (s)/Vīraśaivism, 5, 6, 8, 21, 22, 23, 24, 89, 94, 112, 116, 132, 137, 138, 155
Virūpāksha, 9, 16-22, 26, 27, 34, 46, 48, 56, 58, 65, 85, 102, 106, 132, 133, 135, 137, 138, 141-152, 154
Virūpāksha II, 1, 8, 26, 27, 47, 60, 145
Virūpāksha temple complex, 11, 12, 17-21, 25, 29, 35, 38, 40, 49, 57, 62, 76, 86, 89, 90, 94, 99, 100, 101, 102, 107, 108, 111, 116, 133, 134, 136, 137, 138, 155, 160
Virūpāksha Vasantōtsava Champū, 45, 52, 76, 101, 102, 106
Vishṇu, 7, 29, 34, 38, 46, 51, 54, 59, 69, 70, 74, 75, 78, 81, 85, 86, 87, 88, 89, 91, 94, 95, 104, 135, 156
Vishvaksēna, 59, 69, 81
Viśishṭādvaita, 5, 6

Viṭhala/Viṭhalēśvara, 19, 21, 41, 50, 54, 57, 58, 59, 60, 61-66, 72, 81, 86, 88, 114, 132, 133, 136, 137, 139, 141, 145-154, 156
Viṭhalāpura, 11, 60, 62, 63, 64, 79, 80, 103, 117, 129, 133, 137
Viṭhala temple complex, 11, 12, 17, 21, 29, 35, 38, 40, 54, 62-66, 78, 81, 90, 100, 101, 103, 104, 105, 107, 108, 114, 129, 132, 133, 134, 137, 139, 157
Viṭhōbā, 59, 61, 62
Vyāsarāya/Vyāsatīrtha, 3, 7, 8, 37, 54, 58, 60, 63, 65, 66, 67, 72, 77, 91, 113, 114, 117, 132, 135, 146, 147

Yantrōdhāraka Āñjanēya, 50, 91, 92, 93, 135, 138, 139, 157
Yellammā, 7, 90, 93, 133, 135, 138

FIGURES

Figure 1 Vijayanagara City

Important monuments

1. Virūpāksha temple complex (NF w/1)
2. Viṭhala temple complex (NH a/1)
3. Tiruveṅgalnātha temple complex (NM h/1)
4. Kṛishṇa temple complex (NL m/4)
5. Mudu Vīraṇṇa temple (NL w/3)
6. Prasanna Virūpāksha temple (NQ y/1)
7. Rāmachandra temple (NR w/1)
8. Chaityālaya of Parsvanātha (NS q/1)
9. Paṭṭābhirāma (Raghunātha) temple
10. Chaityālaya of Kunthu Jinanātha (NX n/1)
11. Mālyavanta Raghunātha temple complex (NT d/1)
12. Mahānavamī Dibba (NW d/1)
13. King's Audience Hall (NW c/1)
14. Lotus Mahal (NR t/3)
15. Elephant stables (NR p/3)
16. Queen's Bath (NW p/1)
17. Siṅghārada Hebbāgilu (NS s)
18. Sōmavārada Bāgilu (NJ s)
19. Areśaṅkara Bāgilu (NU d)
20. Udayagiri Bāgilu (NU d)
21. Penugoṇḍa Bāgilu
22. Kōṭiśaṅkaradēvara (NQ s and x) Bāgilu
23. Bēṭekārara Hebbāgilu (NY e)

Landmarks, quarters, tīrthas

A. Mataṅga hill
B. Hēmakūṭa hill
C. Mālyavanta hill
D. Virūpākshapura
E. Viṭhalāpura
F. Kṛishṇāpura
G. Achyutarāyapura
H. Koṇḍamarasayana-Pāḷya
I. Varadadēvī-ammanapaṭṭaṇa
J. Gōrī-keḷagaṇa-grāma
K. Chakra-tīrtha
L. Kōṭi-tīrtha

Markets

a. Achyutarāya-pēṭe
b. Kṛishṇāpura-pēṭe
c. Peḍḍā-aṅgaḍi-vīdhi
d. Kramuka-parnāpaṇa-vīdhi

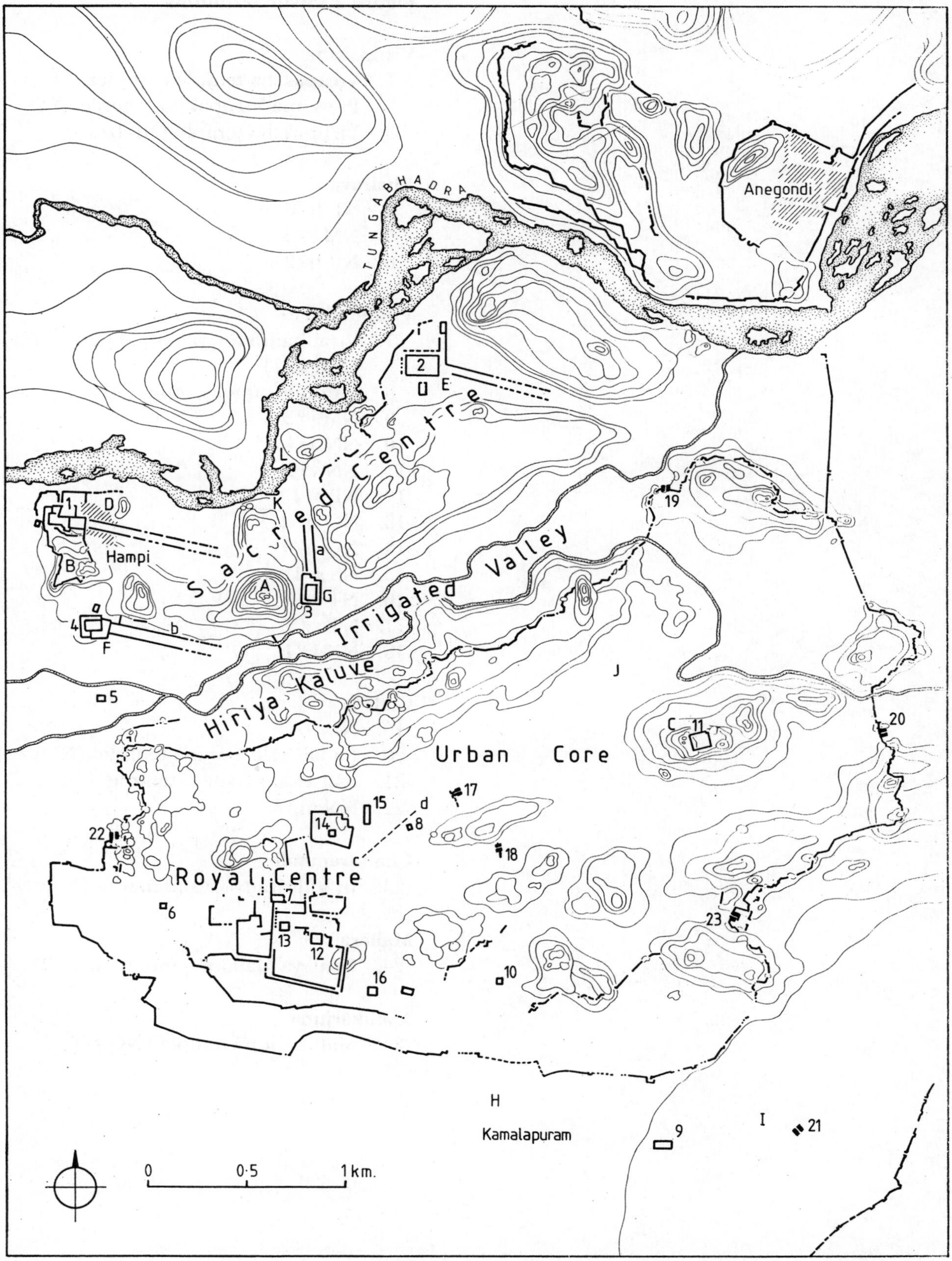

Figure 1 Vijayanagara City

Figure 2 Śaivite traditions

Virūpāksha
1. Virūpāksha temple complex (NF w/1)
2. Prasanna Virūpāksha temple (NQ y/1)
3. Virūpāksha temple (NL b/19)

Bhairava
4. NL h/6
5. NM r/3
6. NR h/2

Vīrabhadra
7. Vīrabhadra temple on Mataṅga hill (NM g/1)
8. Mudu Vīraṇṇa temple (NL w/3)
9. NM y/3
10. NN a/1
11. NN v/4
12. NP s/1
13. NQ d/2
14. NQ u/1
15. NS s/1
16. NT k/3
17. NT z/5
18. NX k/1

Gaṇēśa
19. ND u/1
20. Kaḍalekāḷu Gaṇēśa temple (NL c/2)
21. Sāsivekāḷu Gaṇēśa temple (NL g/2)
22. NN m/2

Chandramauḷi
23. In Vidyāraṇya-svāmi maṭha (NF v/3)

Mailāra
24. Orateya Mailāra temple (NY e/2)

Mallīkārjuna
25. Mallīkārjuna temple (NQ s/2)

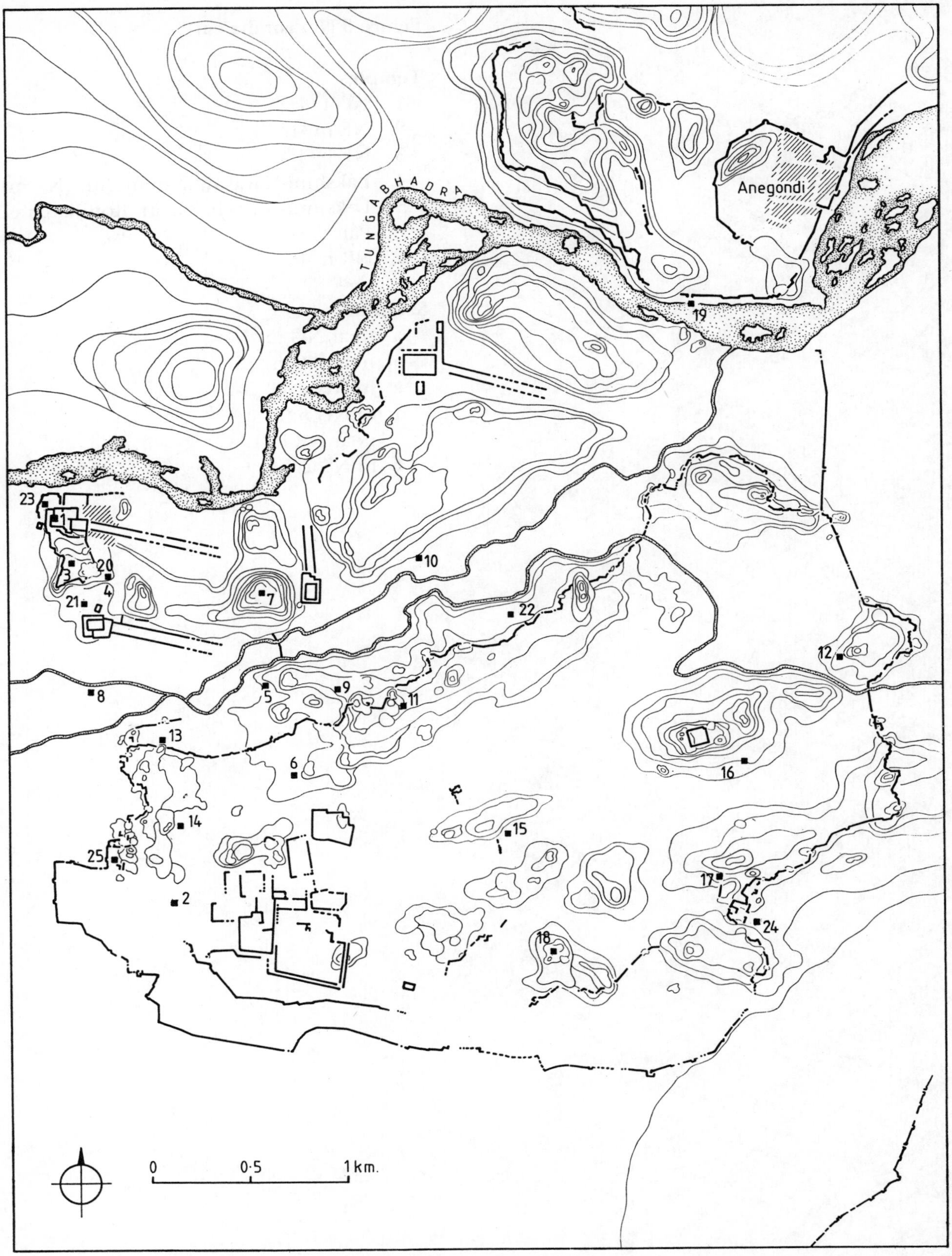

Figure 2 Śaivite traditions

Figure 3 Narasiṁha cult

Temples

1. NG t/4
2. NE m/1
3. NL h/1
4. Lakshmī-Narasiṁha monolith (NL m/1)
5. Lakshmī-Narasiṁha in Koṇḍamarasayana-Pāḷya
6. NR n/1

Sculptures

a near NG m/1
b near NG n/3
c in NG n/6
d in NG n/5
e near NR k/1
f in NS a/1

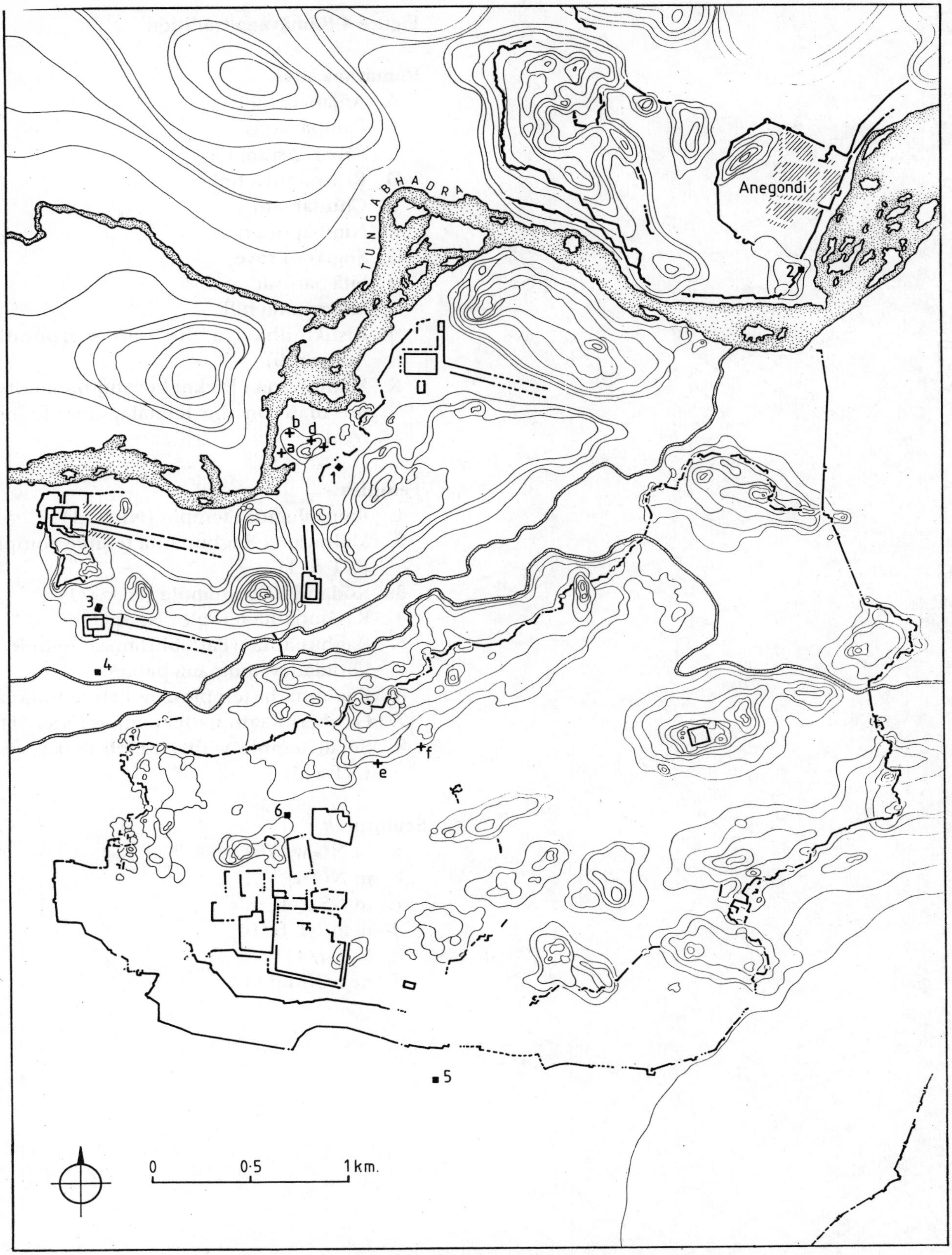

Figure 3 Narasimha cult

Figure 4 Rāmāyaṇa tradition

Rāmāyaṇa sites

A Āñjanadri hill
B Paṁpā Saras
C Śabarī Āśrama
D Ṛishyamūka hill
E Chintāmaṇi
F Niṁbāpuram
G Sugrīva's cave
H Sītā Sarōvar
I Mālyavanta hill
J Kishkindhā (in the hills surrounding Ānegoṅdi)
K Madhuvana (1.5 km beyond the limits of the map, on the Kāmalāpuram-Kaṁpili road)

Temples

1. Rāmachandra temple (NR w/1)
2. Mālyavanta Raghunātha temple complex (NT d/1)
3. Kōdaṇḍarāma temple (NG w/1)
4. Raghunātha temple (NL q/1)
5. Raghunātha (Paṭṭabhirāma) temple in Varadadēvī-ammana-paṭṭaṇa
6. Raghunātha temple near Penugoṇḍa gate
7. Gavikēri Raghunātha temple (NS z/1)
8. Small temple with Paṭṭābhishēka scene (NT z/5)

Sculptures

a in NG w/3
b in NG n/5
c in NS a/1
d near NL b/14
e NQ u/4
f near NM d/3

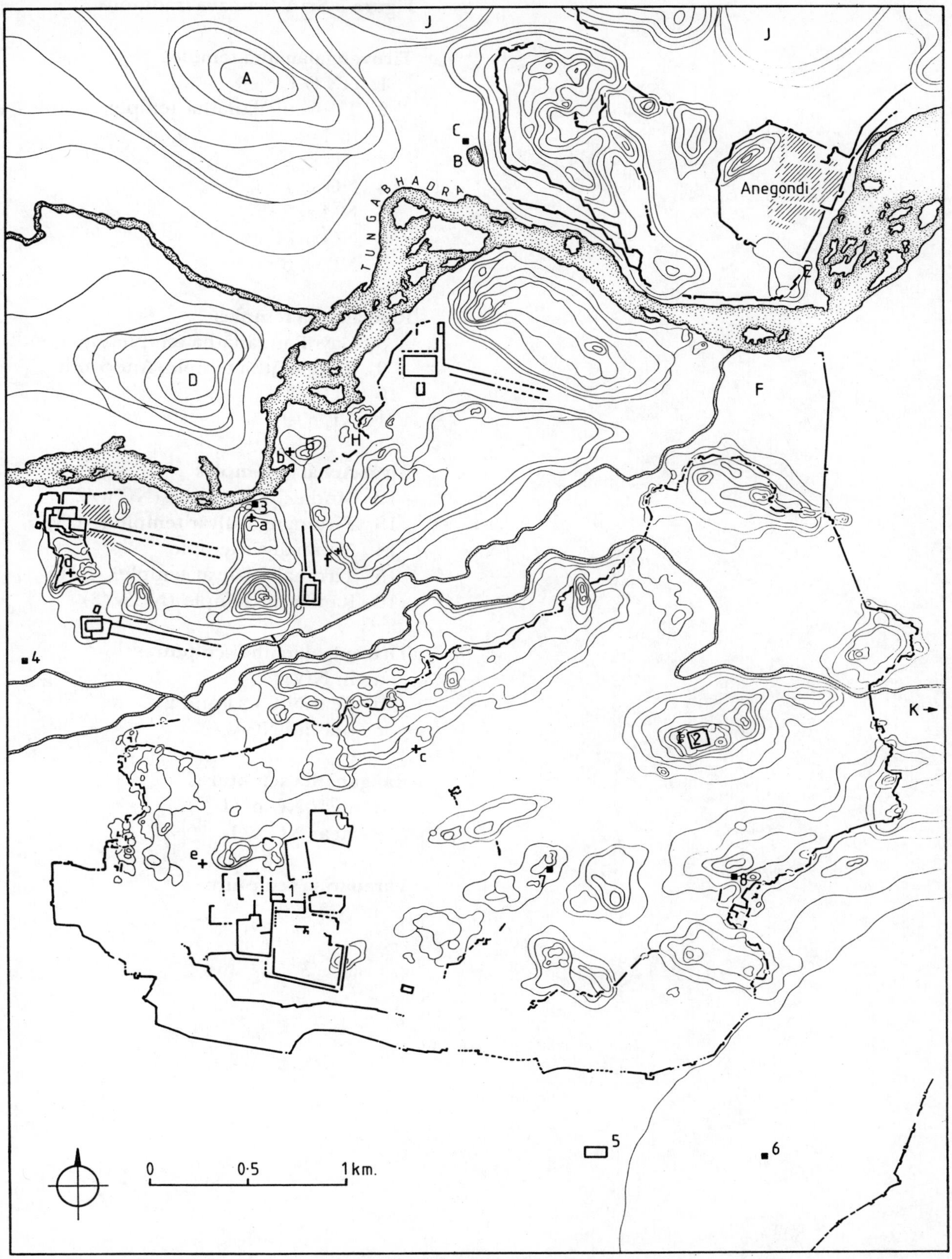

Figure 4 Rāmāyaṇa tradition

Figure 5 Śrī-Vaishnava traditions

Tiruveṅgaḷanātha temples
1 NX f/1
2 Tiruveṅgaḷanātha temple complex (NM h/1)
3 NG x/2
4 NG x/1
5 NM r/2
6 NQ m/1
7 NL w/6

Raṅganātha temples
8 Gavi Raṅganātha temple, Ānegoṇḍi
9 Raṅganātha temple, Ānegoṇḍi
10 NG s/2
11 NL h/9

Āḷvār-Āchārya temples
12 Mudal-āḷvār temple (NC w/2)
13 Tirumaṅgai-āḷvār temple (NC v/3)
14 Nammāḷvār temple
15 Tirumaḷiśai-āḷvār temple? (NH j/1)
16 Rāmānuja temple (NC w/3)

Tiruveṅgaḷanātha sculptures
a in NG n/6
b near NR k/1 and 2
c behind NG w/3

Raṅganātha sculptures
d near NG m/1
e near NG x/1

Varadarāja sculpture
f NM z/3

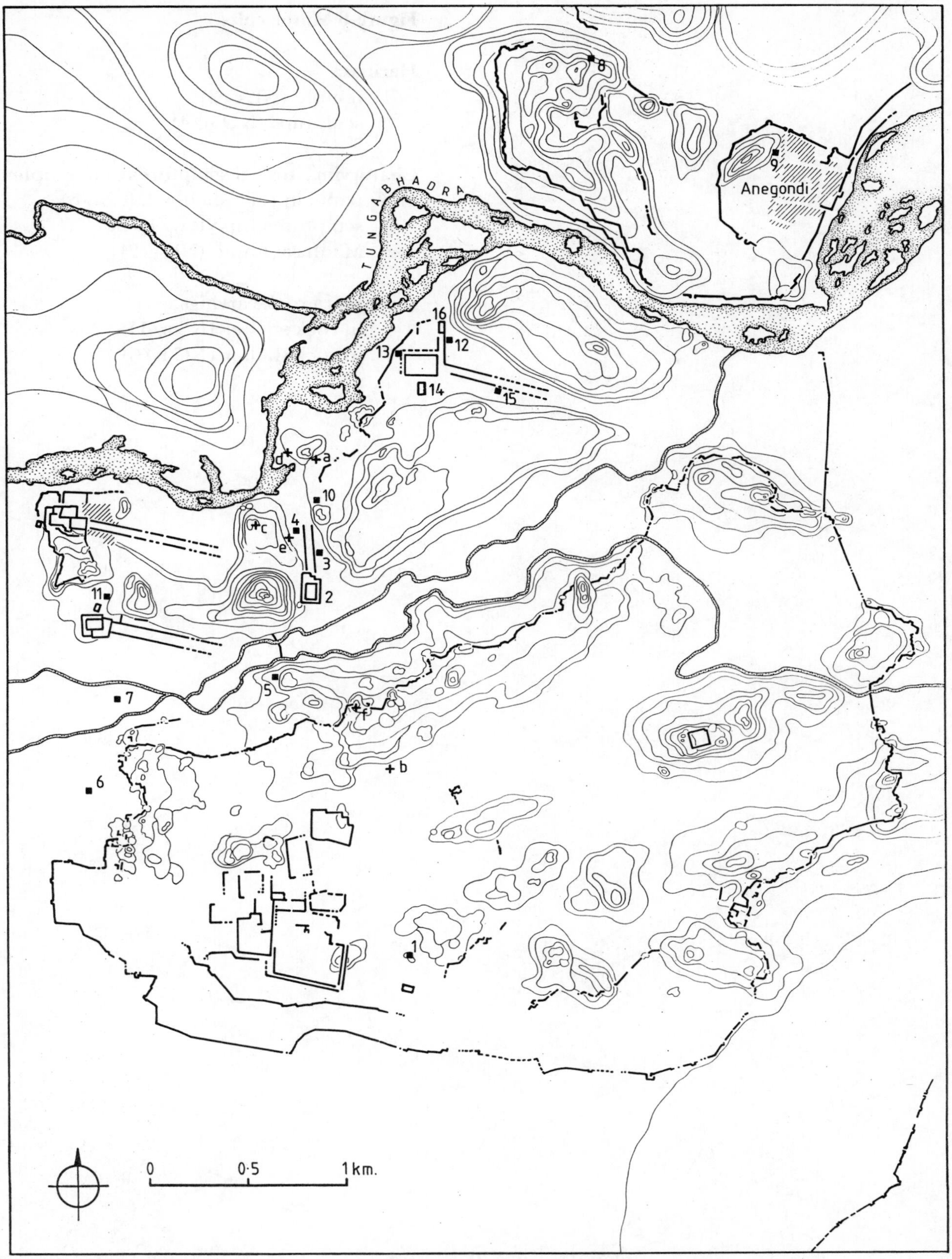

Figure 5 Śrī-Vaishnava traditions

Figure 6 Minor cults

Harihara

1 temple (NL c/3)
2 sculpture (NQ u/4)

Chaturviṁśatmūrti sculptures and temple

3 panel in rock shelter (NG n/6)
4 sculptures (in NR w/1)
5 Mādhava tmple (NR t/2)

Daśāvatāra rock-carvings

6 in rock shelter (NS a/1)
7 in rock shelter (NG n/6)

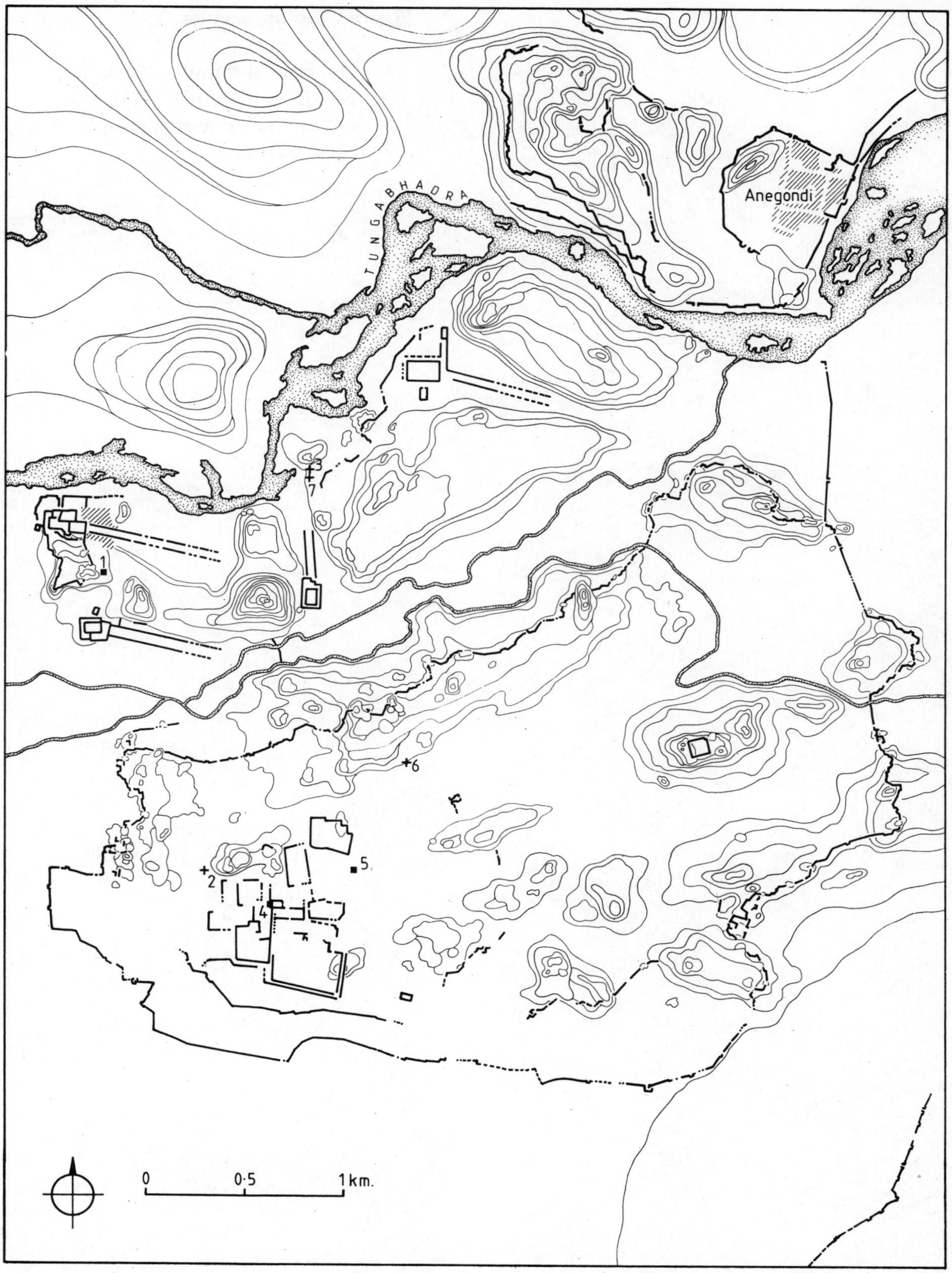

Figure 6 Minor cults

Figure 7 Goddess cults

1. Durgā-dēvī temple (NF w/25)
2. Bhadrakāḷi temple (NM y/3)
3. Paṭṭanada Yellamma temple (NR y/4)

\+ rock carvings

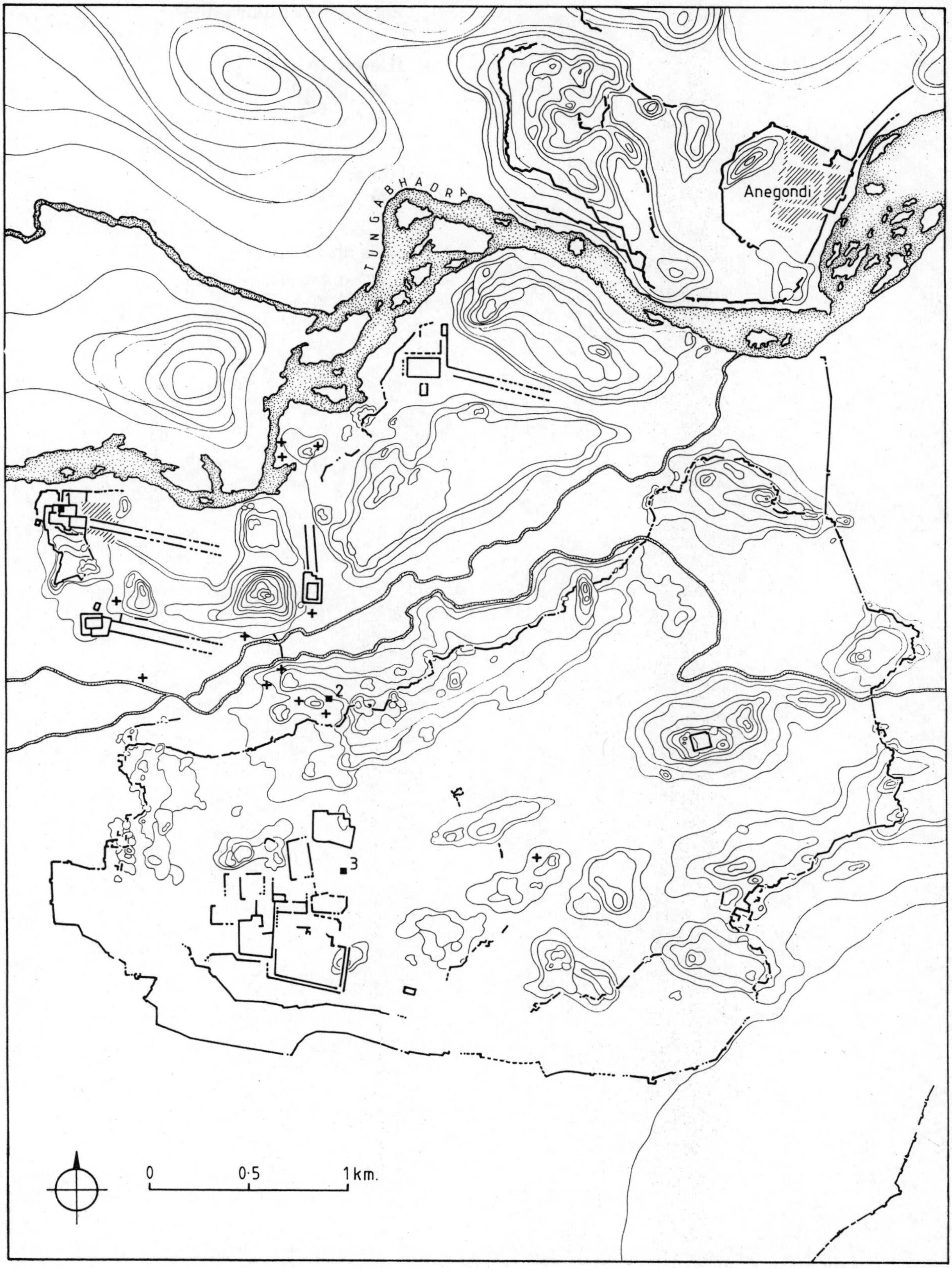

Figure 7 Goddess cults

Figure 8 Popular cults

Hanumān
- ■ temples
- + sculptures on rock and slabs

Nāgas
- ● snake-stones

Satīs and heroes
- x memorial stones

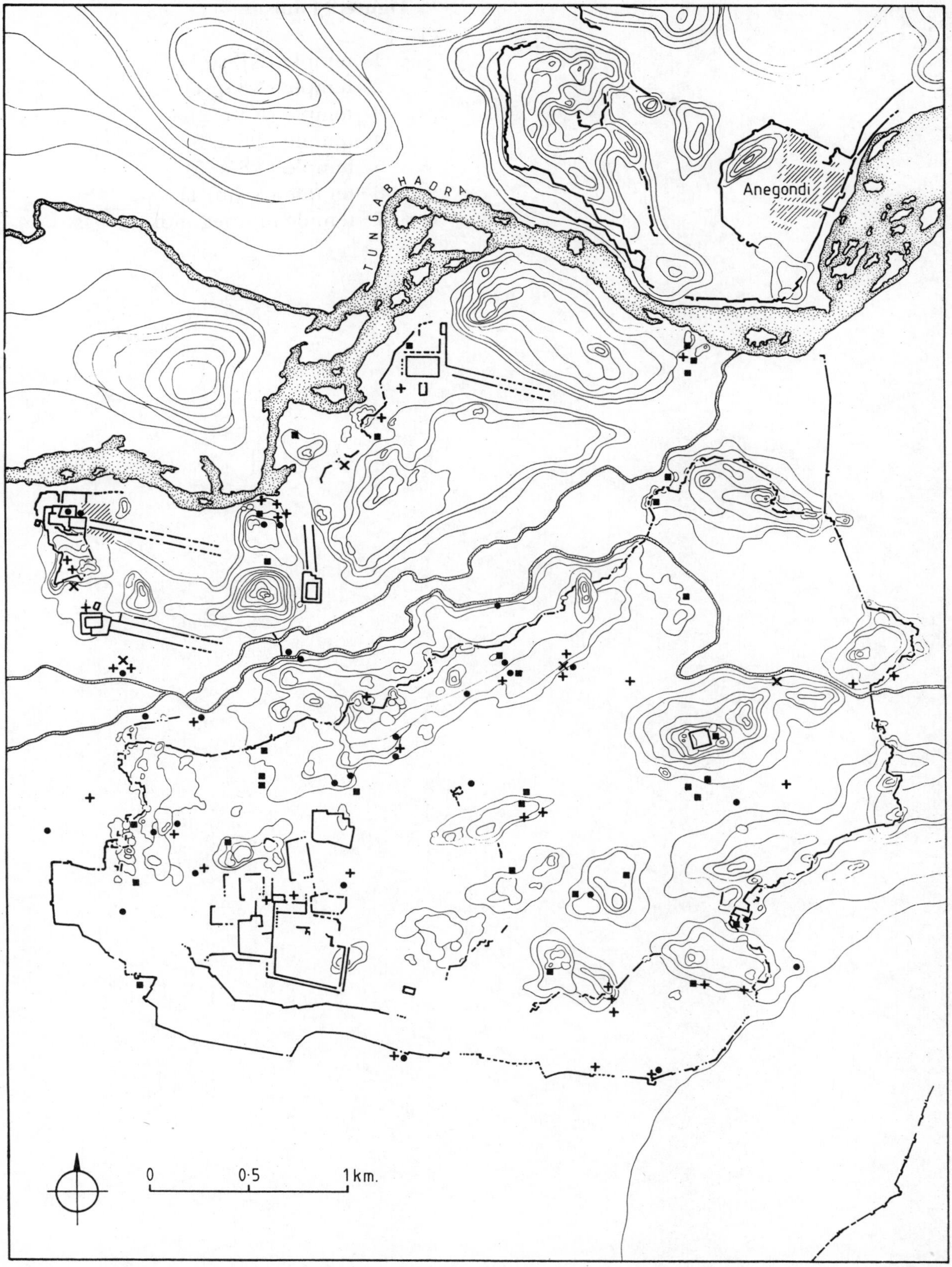

Figure 8 Popular cults

Figure 9 Jainism

1 temple (NR p/1)
2 temple (NS q/1)
3 temple (NS t/2)
4 temple (NS u/3)
5 temple (NS u/5)
6 temple (NX n/1)
7 temple in Ānegoṅdi

Figure 9 Jainism

Figure 10 Islam

1 mosque (NO q/1)
2 mosque (NO y/1)
■ tombs
\+ gravestones

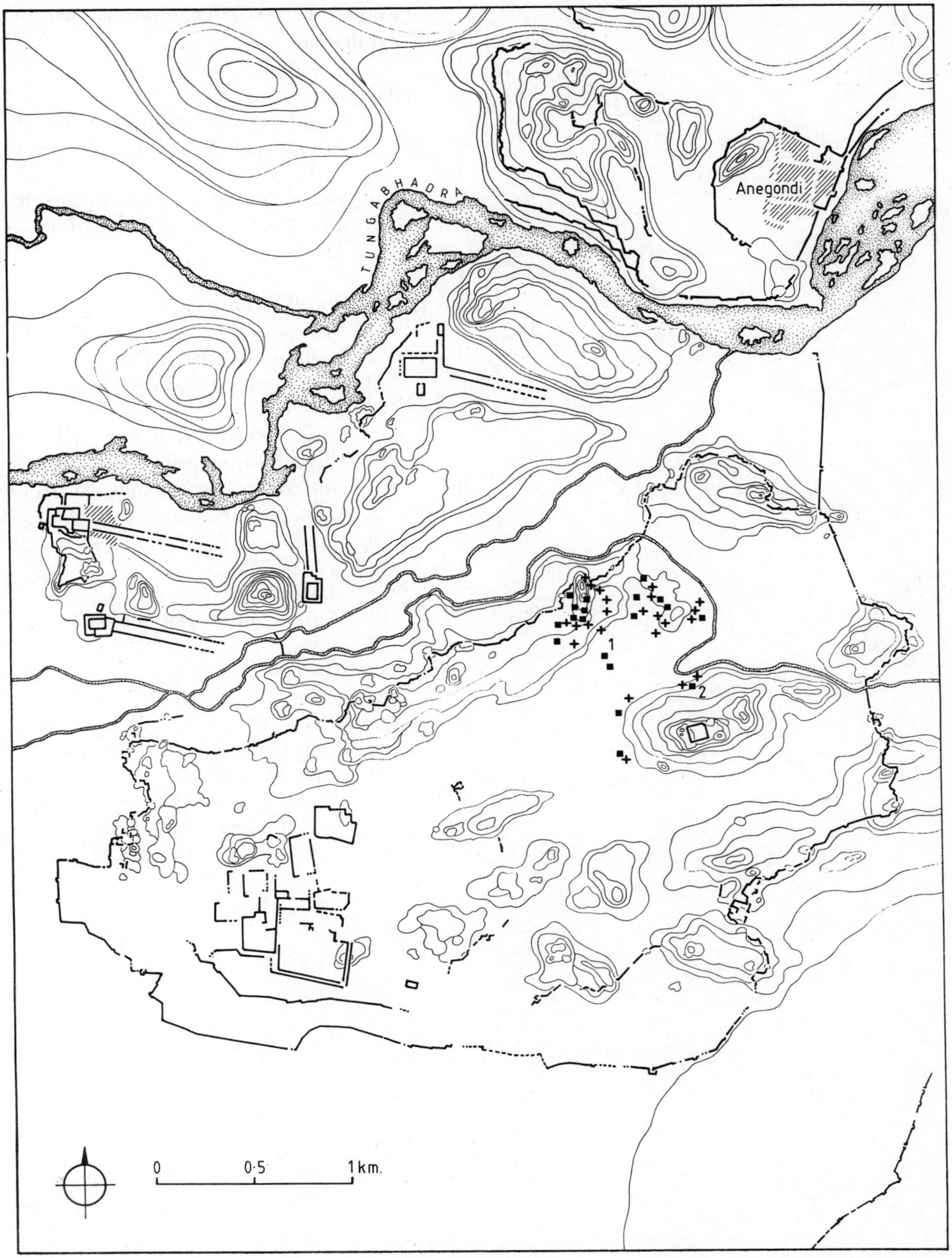

Figure 10 Islam

Figure 11 Ascetics, maṭhas, āśramas and agrahāras

Ascetics
  a bṛindāvana of Narahari Tīrtha (NC m/3)
  b bṛindāvana of Raghunandana-svāmi (NG n/1)
  c Nava-bṛindāvana, near Ānegoṅdi
  d so-called Purandaradāsa-maṇḍapa (NG e/1)

Maṭhas and āśramas
  1 Vidyārāṇya-svāmi maṭha (NF v/3)
  2 Chintāmaṇi maṭha (NE g/1)
  3 Hucchayappa maṭha (ND p/1)
  4 NF r/4
  5 Hiriya maṭha (NL v/4)
  6 Paramēśvara maṭha (NN v/2)
  7 Guha-guhēśvara āśrama (NQ d/2)
  8 Kariya siddapa maṭha (NM f/1, 2, 3 and 4)
  9 NM b/7
 10 in NX k
 11 in NT r
 12 Mahamamtina maṭha (in NF y)
 13 NL o/3
 14 NC n/1

Agrahāras
  A Kṛishṇāpura
  B Neḷahahuṇiseya
  - Nāgaladēvi-pura (modern Nāgēnahaḷḷi, beyond the limit of the map)

Figure 11 Ascetics, maṭhas, āśramas and agrahāras

Figures 12 and 13 Plans, Virūpāksha temple complex (NF w/1)

Parts of the temple

A eastern gōpura
B outer courtyard
C Phalapūjā Maṇḍapa
D Pillared hall
E Rāya Gōpura
F kitchen
G inner courtyard
H Nandi Maṇḍapa, dhvaja-staṁbha
I Mahā-raṅga-maṇḍapa
J Raṅga-maṇḍapa
K Vimāna
L northern gōpura
M Manmatha tank

Subsidiary deities

1 Varadagaṇapati
2 Kumārasvāmi
3 Sūryanārāyaṇa
4 Narasiṁha-svāmi
5 Tarakēśvara
6 Kumbhēśvara
7 Pātalēśvara
8 Bhasmēśvara
9 Navadurgā
10 Sharadā-dēvī
11 Vyomēśvara
12 Gaṇēśa
13 Sudharmēśvara
14 Mahiśāsuramardinī
15 Vidyāraṇya-svāmi
16 Kōṭivināyaka
17 Gaṇēśa
18 Chaṇḍikēśvara
19 Ādiśēshvara
20 Navagraha
21 Paṁpā-dēvī
22 Bhuvanēśvarī
23 Guñja Mādhava
24 Chamuṇḍēśvarī
25 Ratna Gaṇapati
26 Mahiśāsuramardinī
27 Kālabhairava
28 Durgā-dēvī
29 Rudrakēśvara
30 Āñjanēya-svāmi
31 Lakshmī-Veṅkaṭēśvara

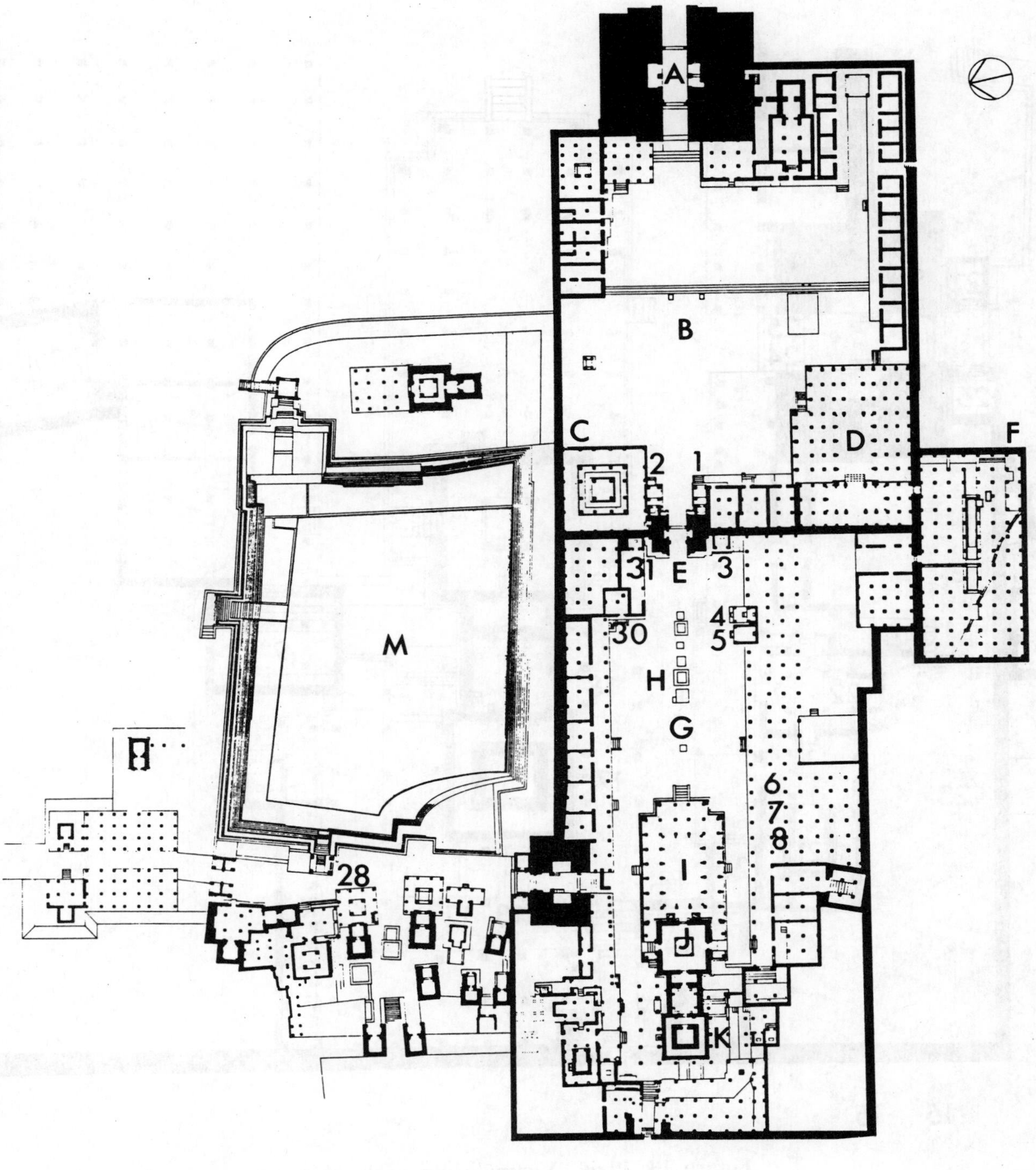

Figure 12 Plan, Virūpāksha temple complex

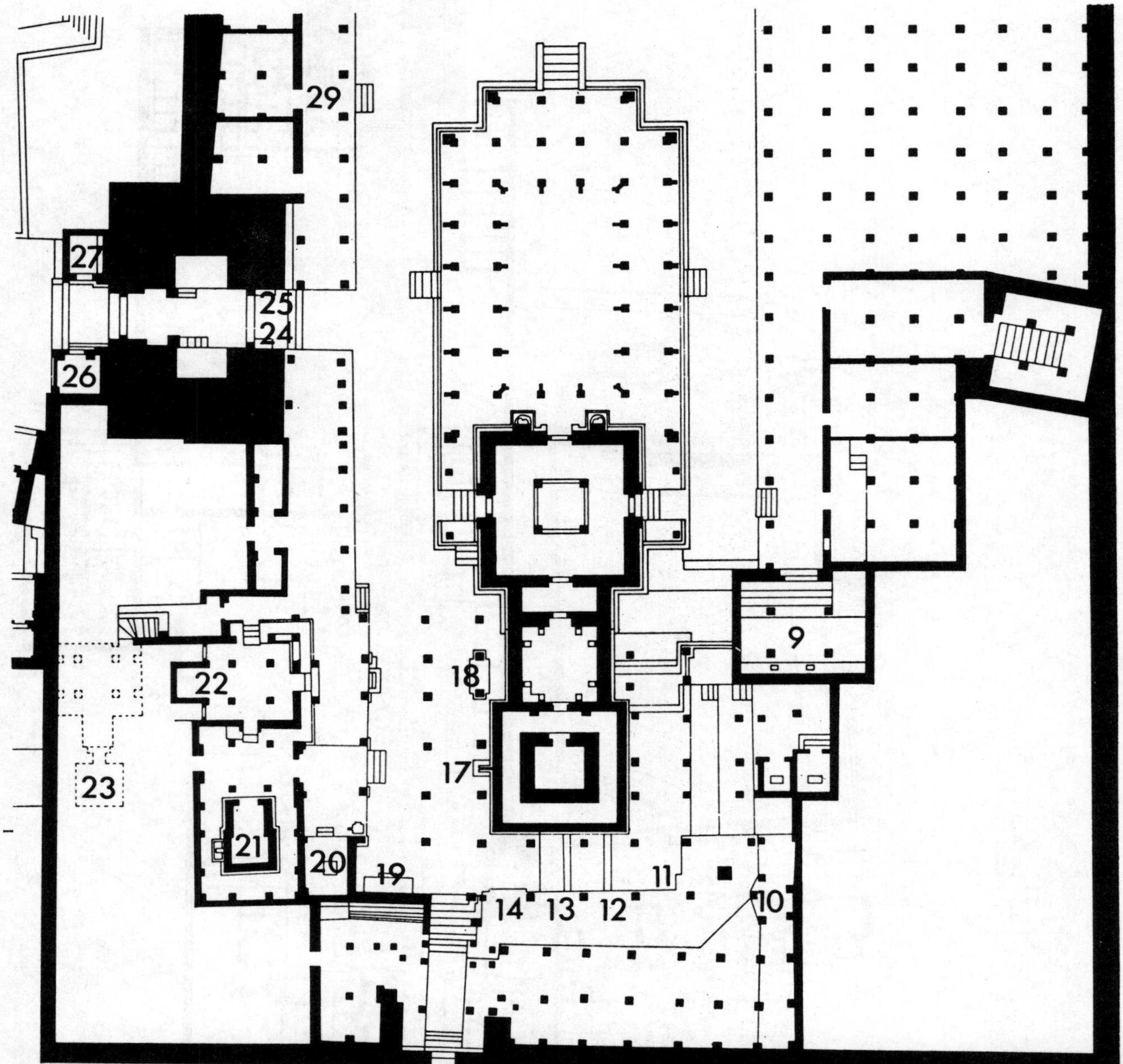

Figure 13 Plan, Virūpāksha temple complex

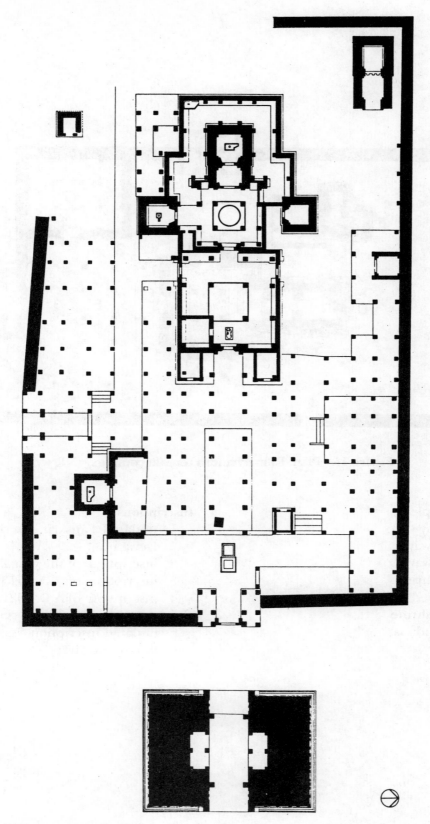

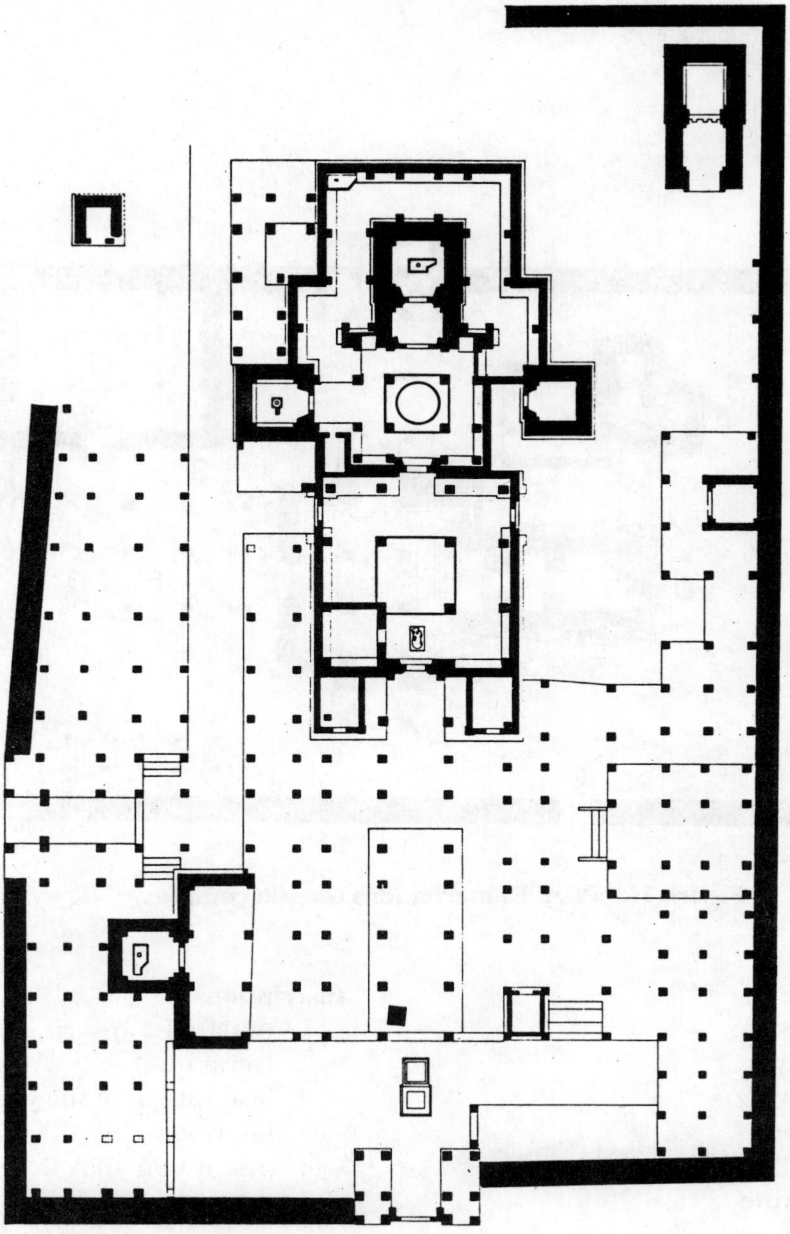

Figure 14   Plan, Prasanna Virūpāksha temple complex (NQ y/1)

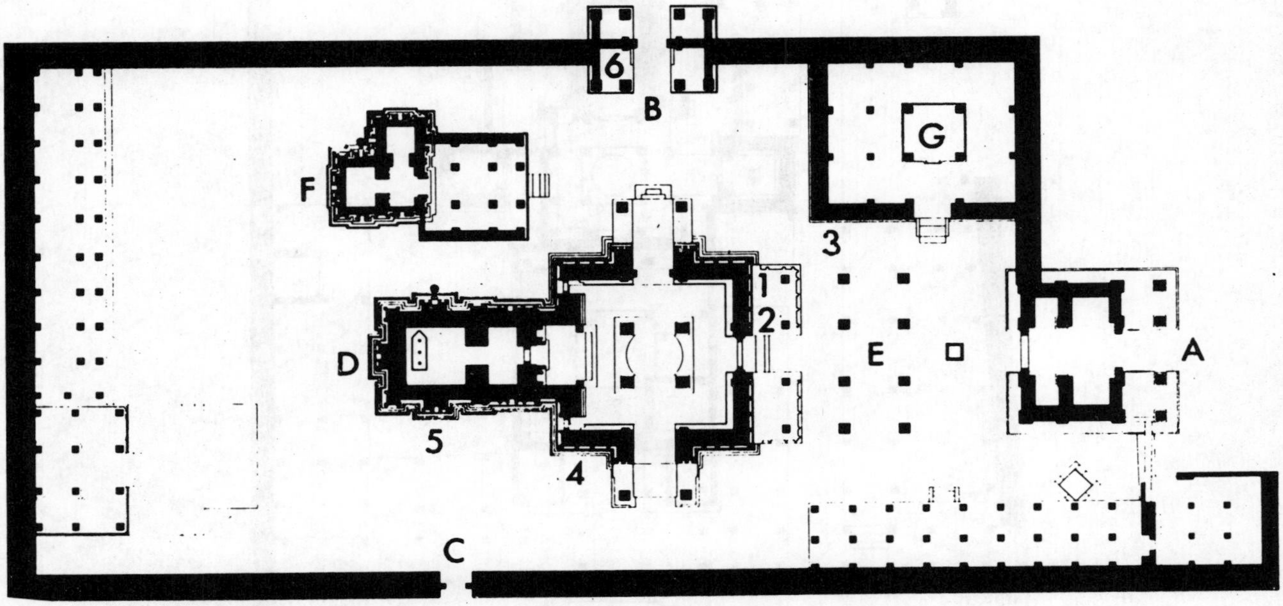

Figure 15 Plan, Rāmachandra temple complex (NR w/1)

Parts of the temple

A east gateway
B north gateway
C south gateway
D principal shrine
E open pillared maṇḍapa
F subsidiary shrine
G Utsava-maṇḍapa

Inscriptions

1 undated Sanskṛit inscription referring to Dēvāraya
2 inscription of the year Durmukhi
3 inscription of A.D. 1513
4 inscription of A.D. 1521
5 damaged inscription (same as 4)
6 undated inscription recording the installation of the āḷvārs

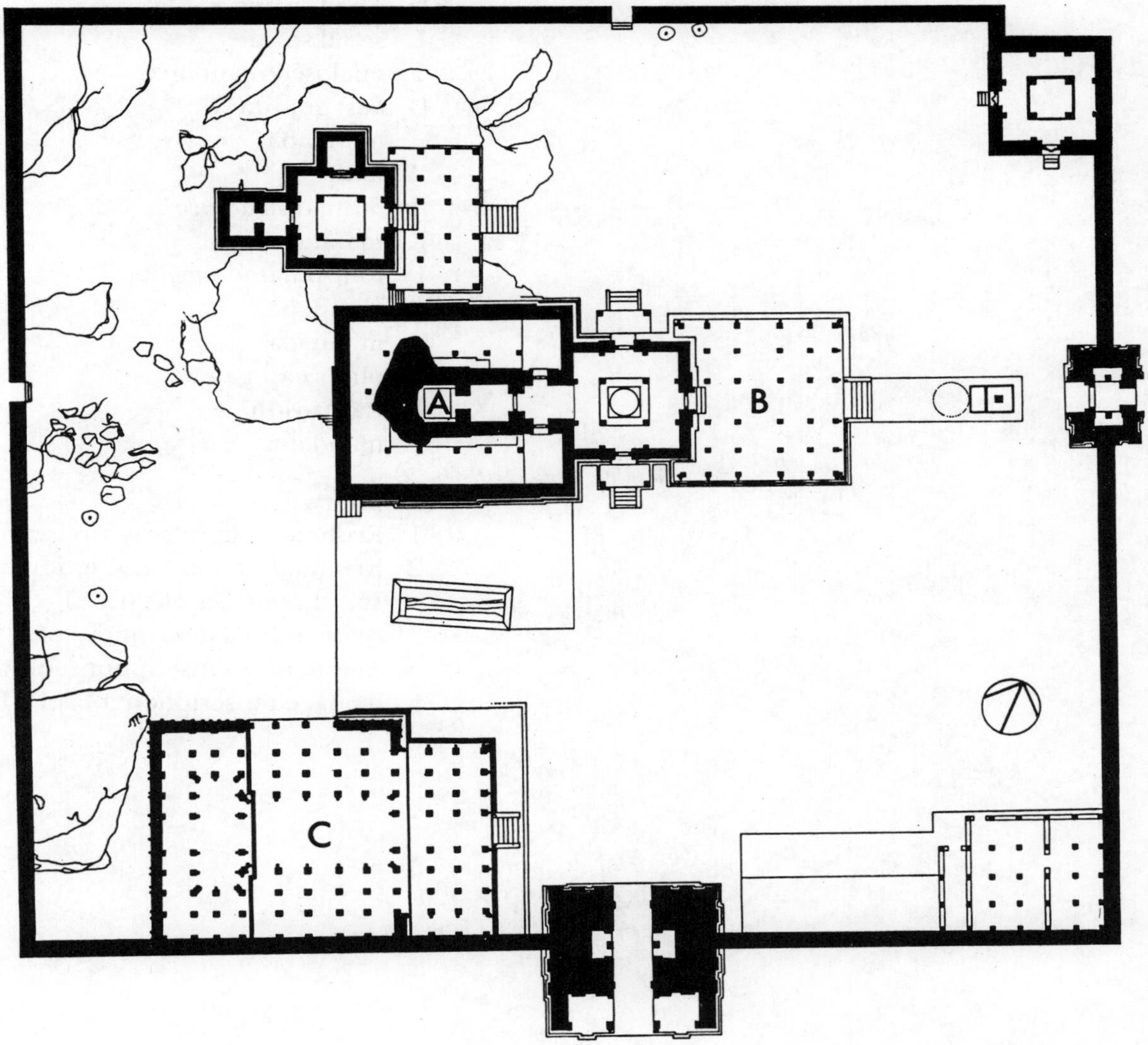

Figure 16 Plan, Mālyavanta Raghunātha temple complex (NT d/1)

Parts of the temple

A garbha-griha

B mahā-maṇḍapa

C detached columned hall

Figure 17 Plan, Kṛishṇa temple complex (NL m/4)

Parts of the temple

A principal shrine
B subsidiary shrine
C small shrine
D small shrine
E small shrine
F enclosed maṇḍapa
G east gōpura
H maṇḍapa
I tank
J domed structure
K maṇḍapa
L four-pillared pavilion
M maṇḍapa
N maṇḍapa
O outer east gateway
P Ratha-vidhī
Q maṇḍapa

Inscriptions

1 Kṛishṇadēvarāya's inscription of A.D. 1515
2 Kṛishṇadēvarāya's inscription of A.D. 1515 (on three sides of shrine)
3 Achutarāya's inscription of A.D. 1532
4 Achutarāya's inscriptions of A.D. 1539
5 damaged inscription of A.D. 1544-45

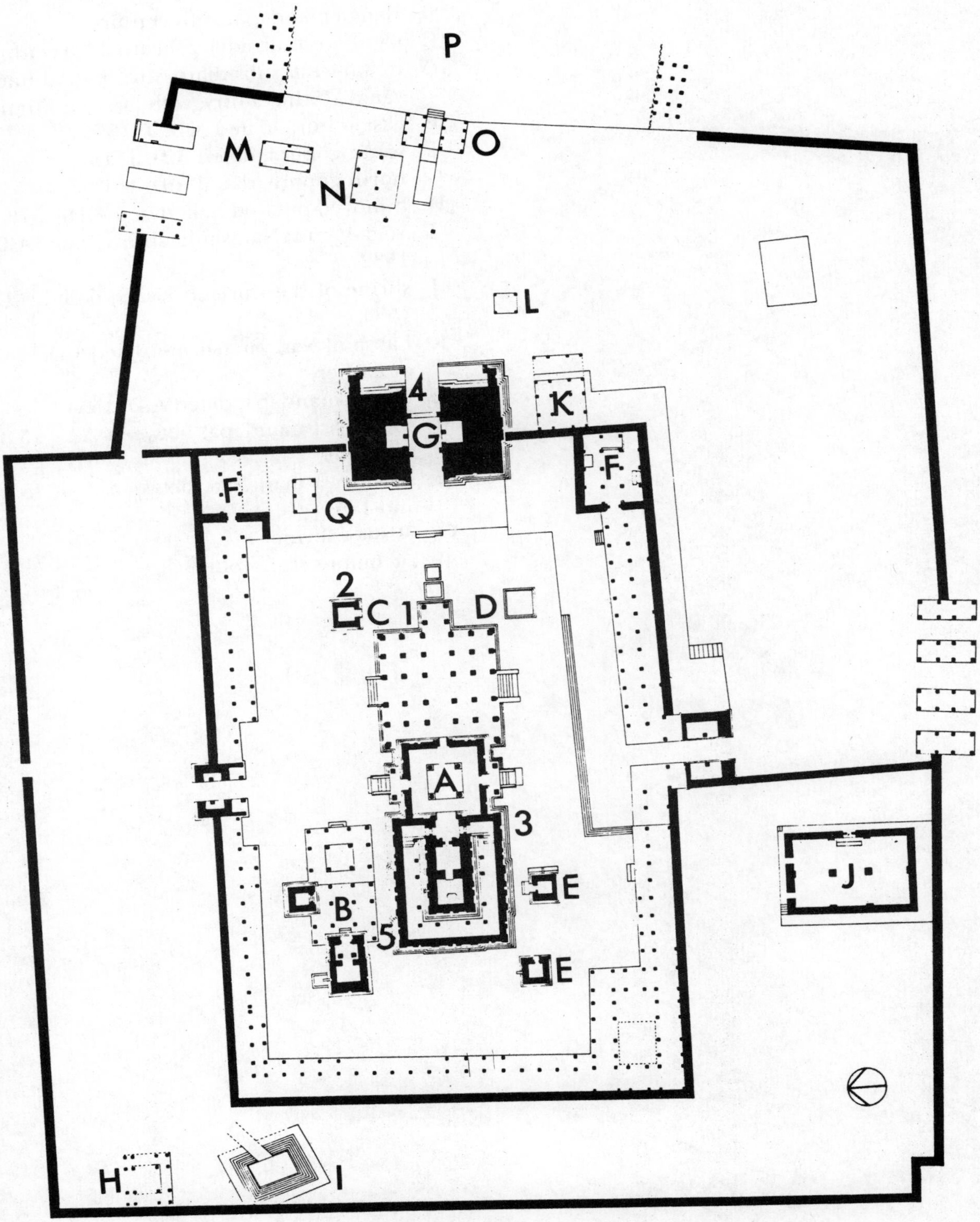

Figure 17 Plan, Krishṇa temple complex (NL m/4)

Figure 18 Plan, Viṭhala temple complex (NH a/1)

Parts of the temple, with dates

A vimāna, 15th century
B Raṅgā-maṇḍapa, 15th century
C south-west subsidiary shrine, 15th century
D north-west subsidiary shrine (Ādinārāyaṇa), 15th century, with later additions
E east gōpura, dated A.D. 1513
F south gōpura, dated A.D. 1513
G north gōpura, dated A.D. 1513
H hundred-pillared hall, dated A.D. 1516
I Yōga-Varada Narasiṁha shrine, dated A.D. 1532
J shrine of the thirteen āḻvārs, dated A.D. 1534
K Lakshmī-Nārāyaṇa shrine, dated A.D. 1545 or earlier
L Uyyāle-maṇḍapa, dated A.D. 1554
M south-east maṇḍapa, between A.D. 1516 and 1554
N north-east maṇḍapa, between A.D. 1516 and 1554
O Garuḍa shrine
P kitchen or store-room

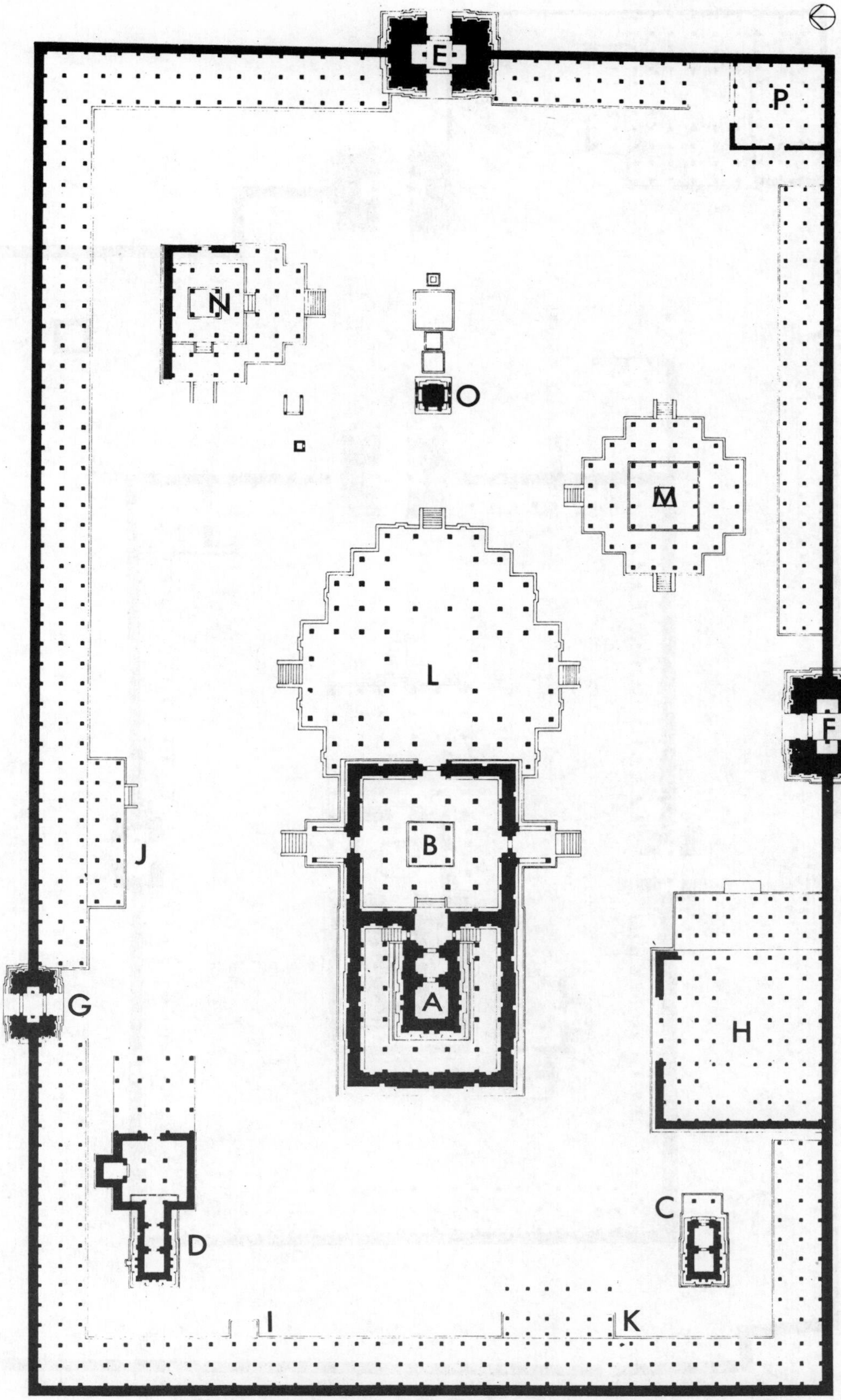

Figure 18 Plan, Viṭhala temple complex (NH a/1)

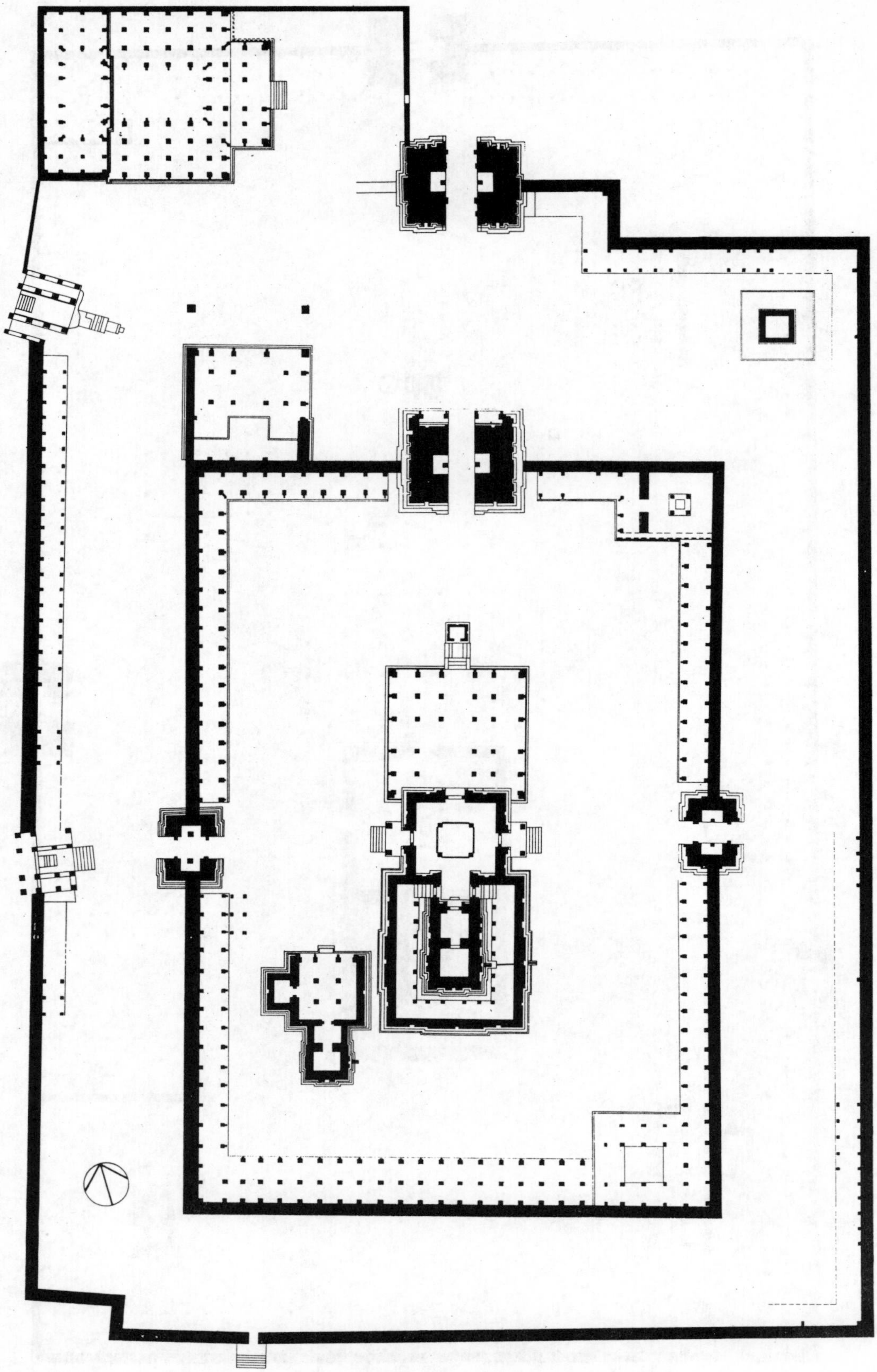

Figure 19 Plan, Tiruveṅgaḷanāthā temple complex (NM h/1)

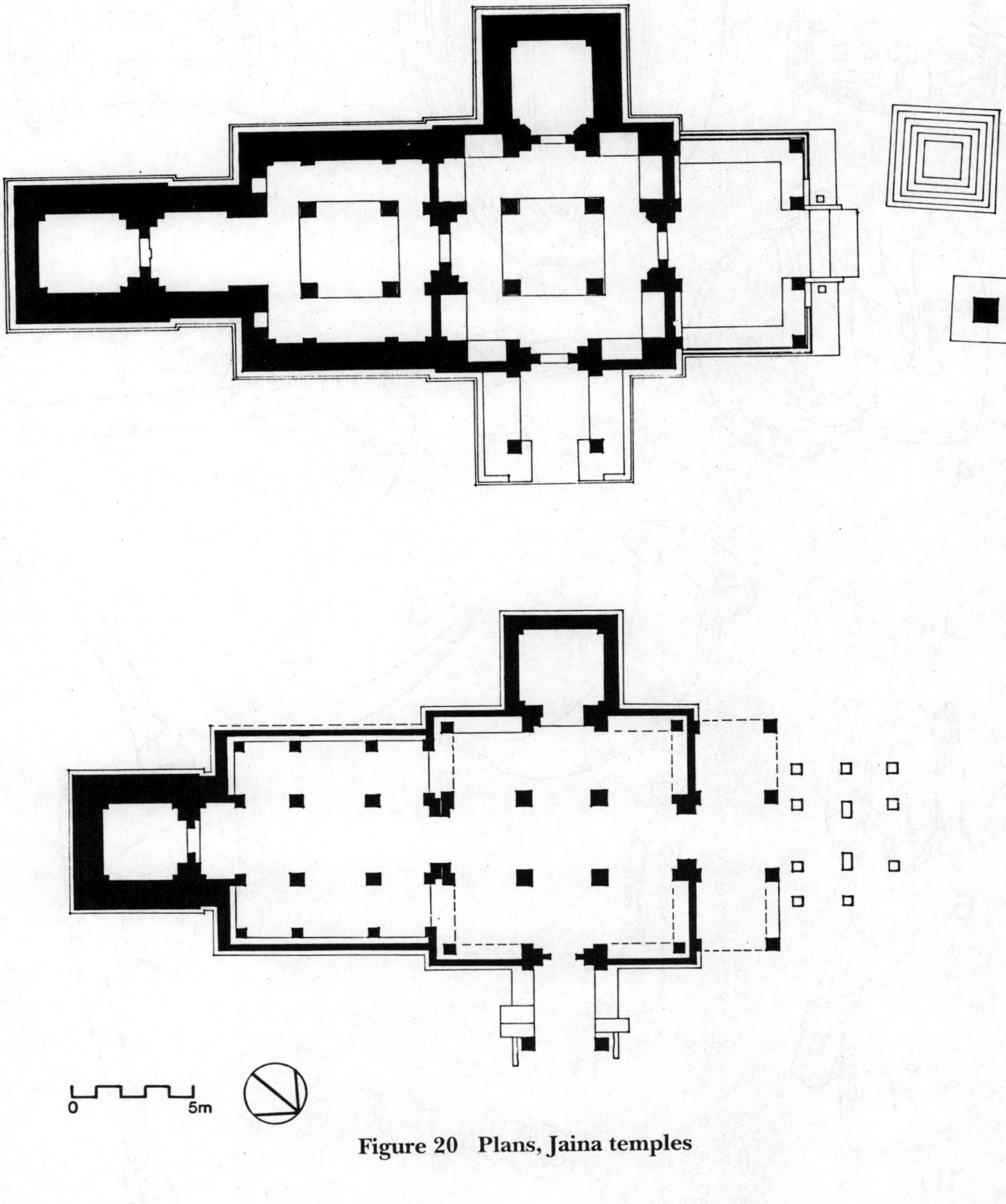

Figure 20 Plans, Jaina temples

above, Kunthu Jinanātha (Gāṇigitti temple (NX n/1) below, Pārśvanātha temple (NS q/1)

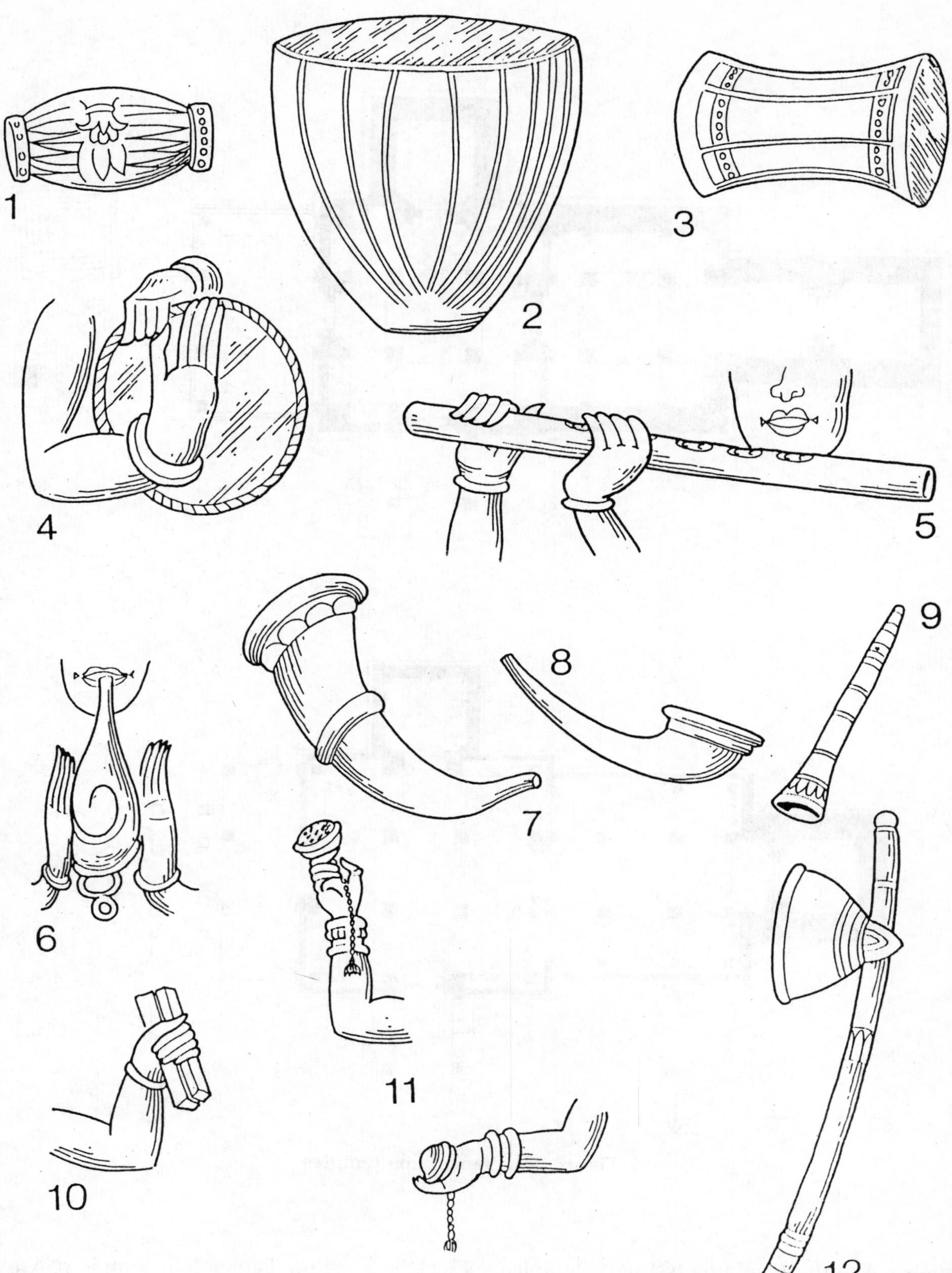

Figure 21 Musical instruments

PLATES

1. View of Virūpāksha temple complex (NF w/1)

2. Virūpāksha temple complex

3. Virūpāksha temple on Hēmakūṭa hill (NL b/19)

4. Bhairava (NM z/2)

5. Vīrabhadra (NQ u/1)

6. Sāsivekāḷu Gaṇēśa monolith (NL g/2)

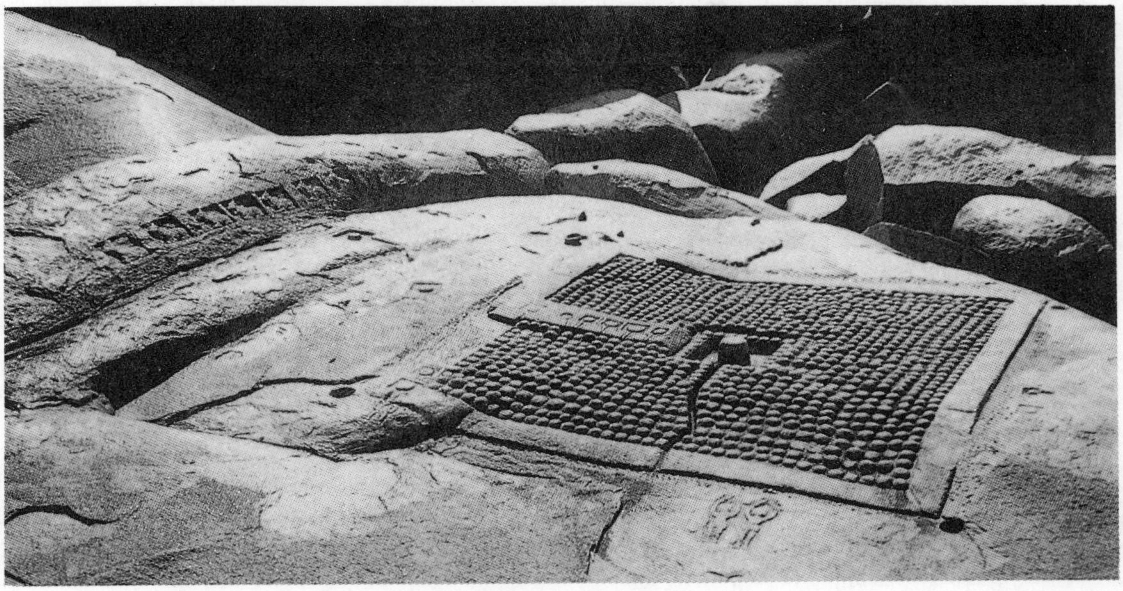

7. Kōṭī-liṅga

8. Narasiṁha temple (NG t/4)

9. Mahānavamī platform (NW d/1)

10. Mahānavamī platform, south steps

11. Mahānavamī platform, Cheñchū-Lakshmī and Narasiṁha

12. Cheñchū-Lakshmī and Narasiṁha (temple NF w/5)

13. Narasiṁha (Virūpāksha temple complex)

14. Lakshmī-Narasiṁha (near NG n/3)

15. Lakshmī-Narasiṁha monolith (NL m/1)

16. Rāmachandra temple (NR w/1)

17. Rāmāyaṇa Panels (Rāmachandra temple, enclosure wall)

18. Paṭṭābhirāma temple complex

19. Seated Rāma (Kṛishṇa temple complex NL m/4)

20. Seated royal figure (Rāmachandra temple, enclosure wall)

21. Kṛishṇa temple complex (NL m/4)

22. Bālakṛishṇa (Kṛishṇa temple complex), now Government Museum, Madras

23. Royal devotee adoring Bālakṛishṇa (Kṛishṇa temple complex)

24. Royal devotee adoring liṅga (Kṛishṇa temple complex)

25. Prāta-Viṭhala temple (NG w/5)

26. Viṭhala (Rāmachandra temple, south entrance)

27. Viṭhala temple complex (NH a/1)

28. Viṭhala temple complex

29. Viṭhala temple complex

30. Pārāṅkuśa maṇḍapa (NJ g/1)

31. View of Tiruveṅgaḷanātha temple complex (NM h/1)

32. Raṅganātha (NG s/2)

33. Tiruveṅgaḷanātha (behind NG w/3)

34. Varadarāja episodes (temple NC w/3)

35. Rāmānuja and Nammāḻvār (temple NG s/2)

36. Tirumaṅgai-āḻvār temple (NC v/3)

37. Teṅgalai nāmam (Viṭhala temple complex, hundred-pillared hall)

38. Vaḍagalai nāmam (Viṭhala temple complex, hundred-pillared hall)

39. Vishvaksēna (temple NG s/2)

40. Harihara (Tiruveṅgaḷanātha temple complex, pillared hall)

41. Vīra-Āñjanēya

42. One of the Chaturviṁśatīmūrtis (Rāmachandra temple)

43. Dēvīs with Gaṇēśa and Bhairava (NM x/2)

44. Lajjā-Gaurī (Rāmachandra temple, east gateway)

45. Chaturbhuja Hanumān (NG n/1)

46. Yantrōddhāraka Āñjanēya (NG w/3)

47. Nāga-stones (Yantrōddhāraka Āñjanēya temple, NG w/3)

48. Satī-stone (NP q/1)

49. Satī-stone (NG o/3)

50. Memorial-stone (near NN z/2)

51. Mahānavamī procession (Rāmachandra temple, enclosure wall)

52. Vasantōtsava, Kāma and retinue (Viṭhala temple complex, north-east pavilion)

53. Matsyēndranātha (temple NF w/5)

54. Ascetic (Viṭhala temple complex, hundred-pillared hall)

55. Bṛindāvana of Raghunandana (NG n/1)

56. Chaityālaya of Kunthu Jinanātha (temple NX n/1)

57. Jina, chaityālaya of Kunthu Jinanātha

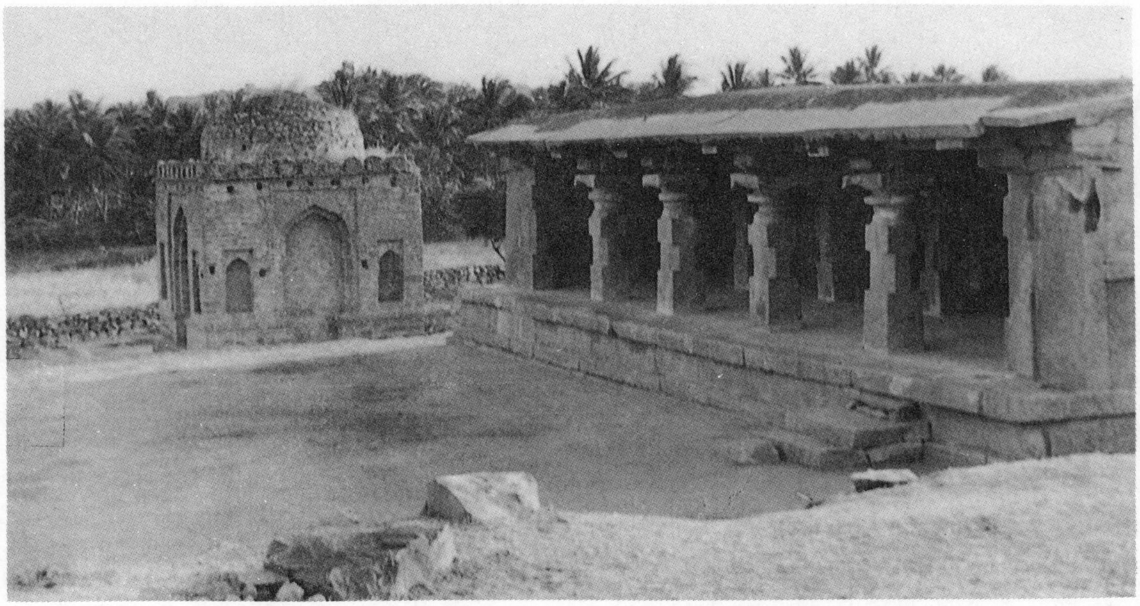

58. Ahmad Khān's mosque and tomb (NO q/1 and 2)

59. Portuguese horse-traders (Viṭhala temple complex)

MAP SERIES

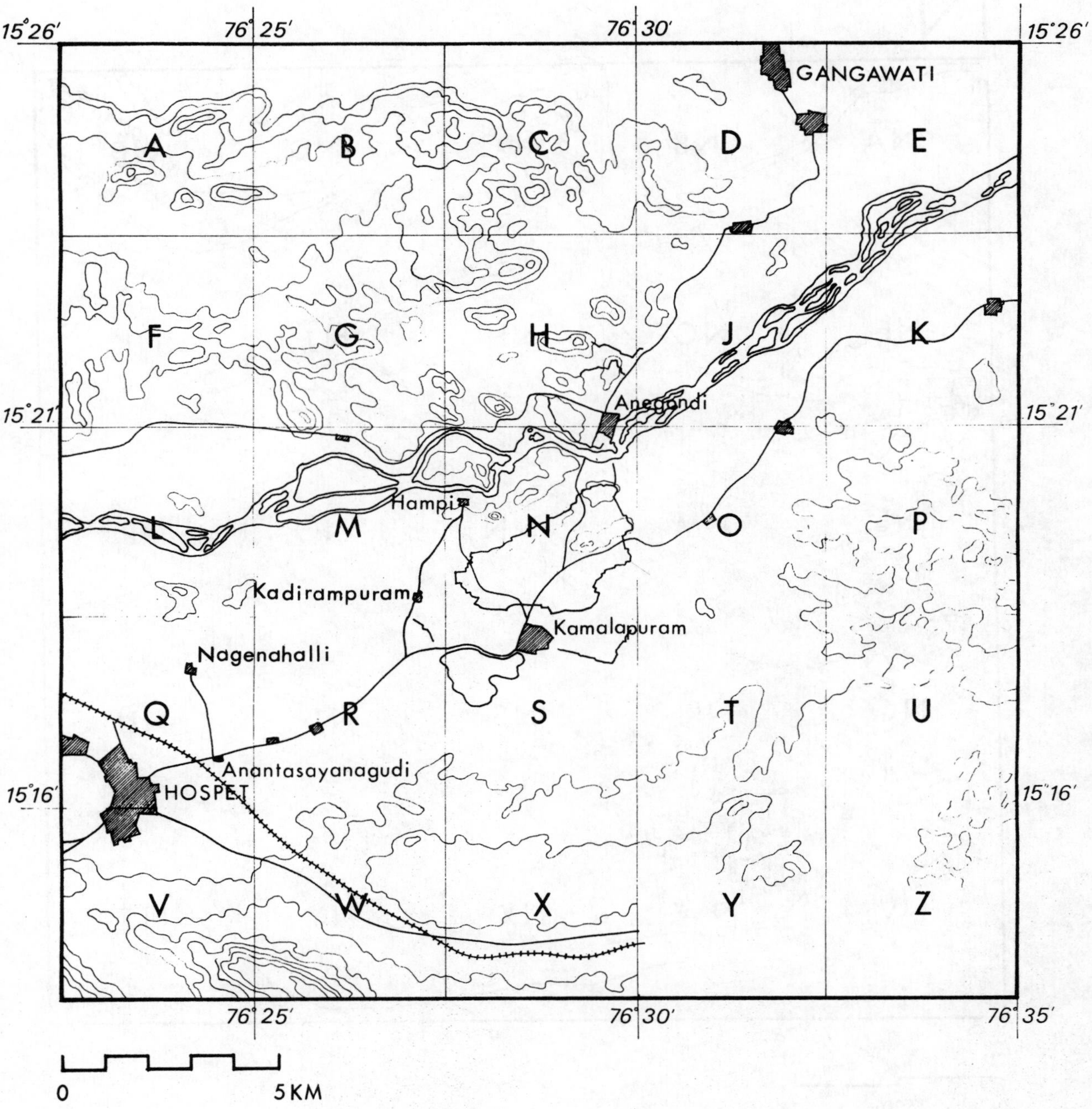
15°26'
76°25'
76°30'
15°26'
GANGAWATI
A
B
C
D
E
F
G
H
J
K
Anegondi
15°21'
15°21'
Hampi
L
M
N
O
P
Kadirampuram
Kamalapuram
Nagenahalli
Q
R
S
T
U
Anantasayanagudi
15°16'
HOSPET
15°16'
V
W
X
Y
Z
76°25'
76°30'
76°35'
0
5 KM

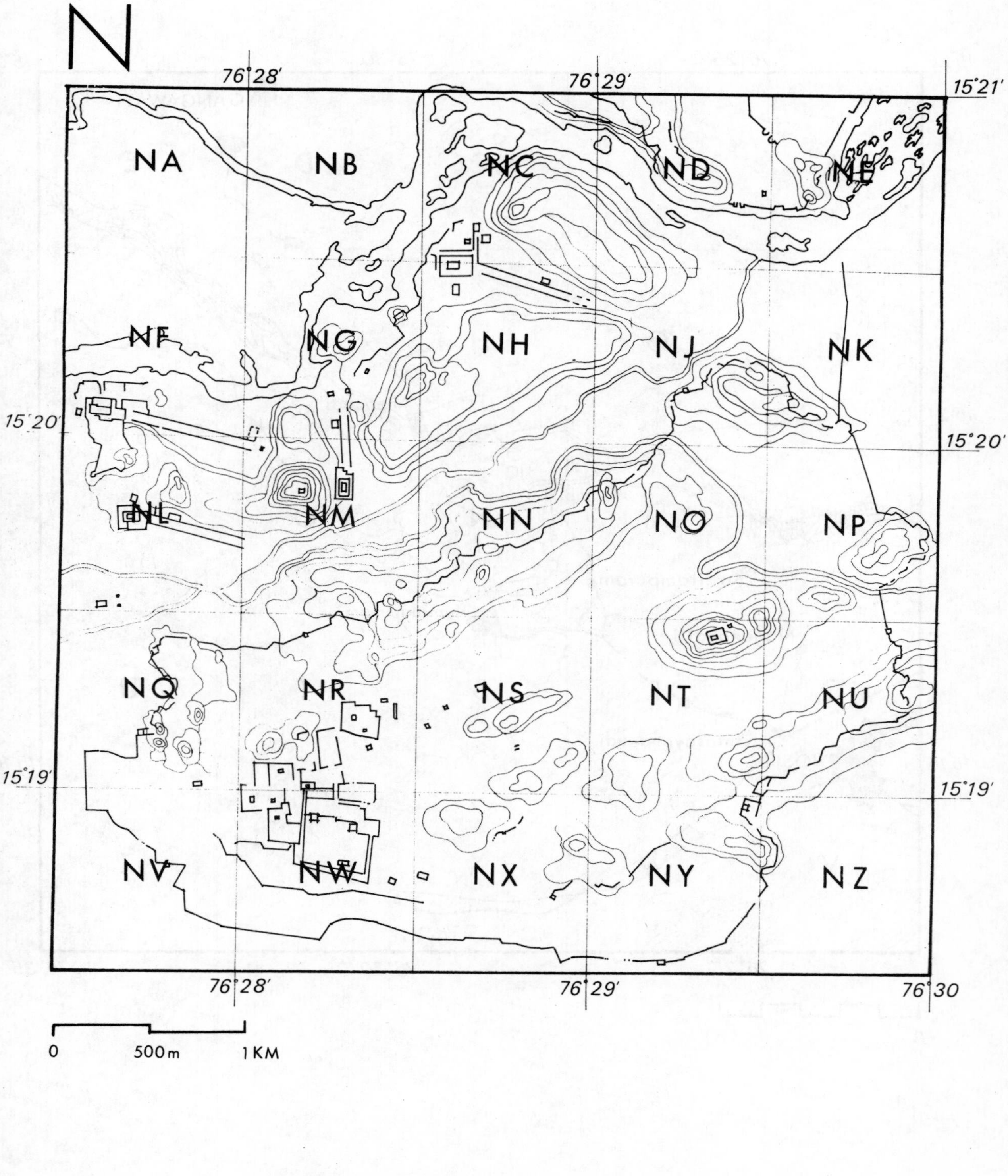
N
76°28'
76°29'
15°21'
NA
NB
NC
ND
NE
NF
NG
NH
NJ
NK
15°20'
15°20'
NL
NM
NN
NO
NP
NQ
NR
NS
NT
NU
15°19'
15°19'
NV
NW
NX
NY
NZ
76°28'
76°29'
76°30
0
500m
1KM

NC

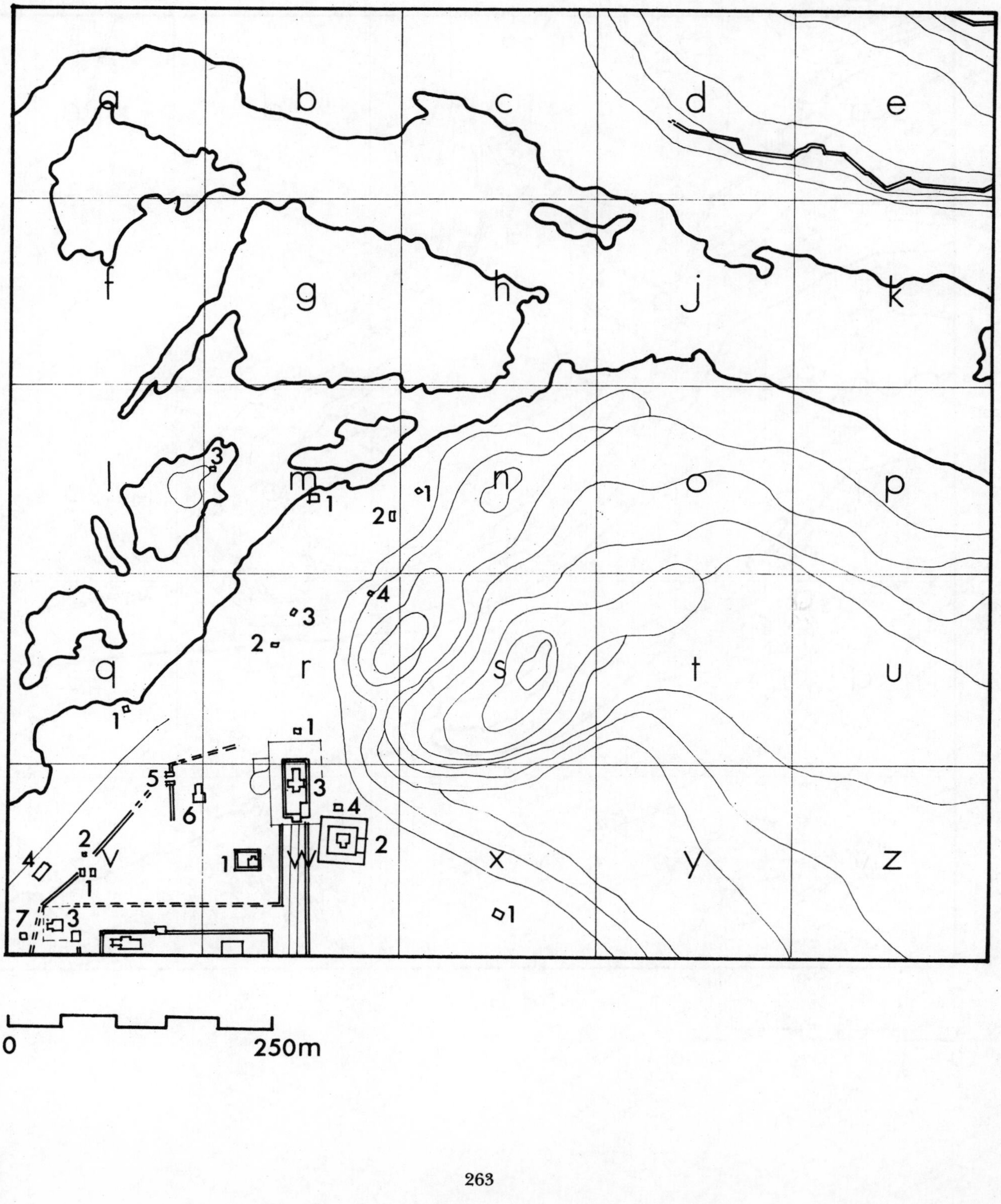

ND

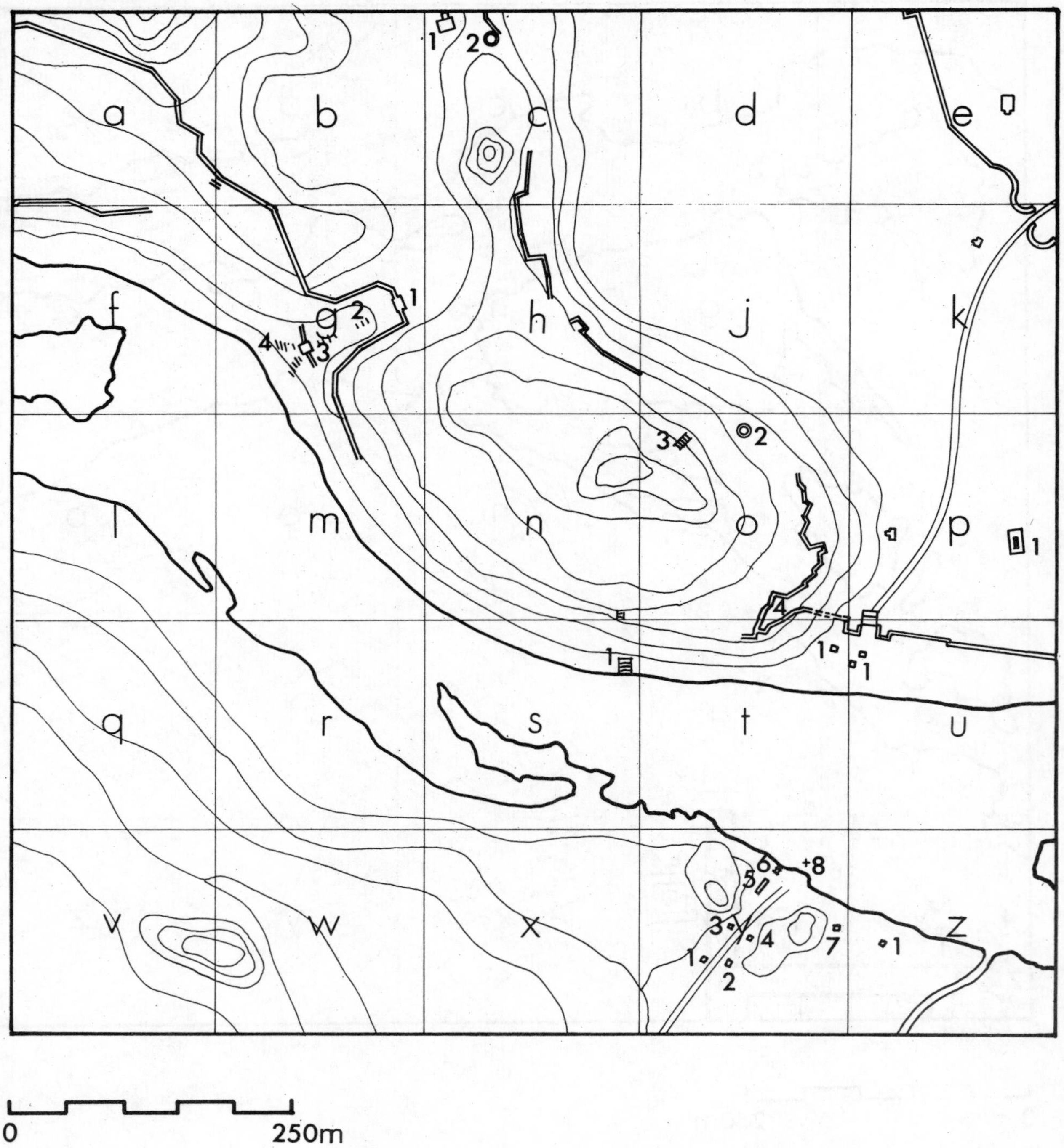

NE

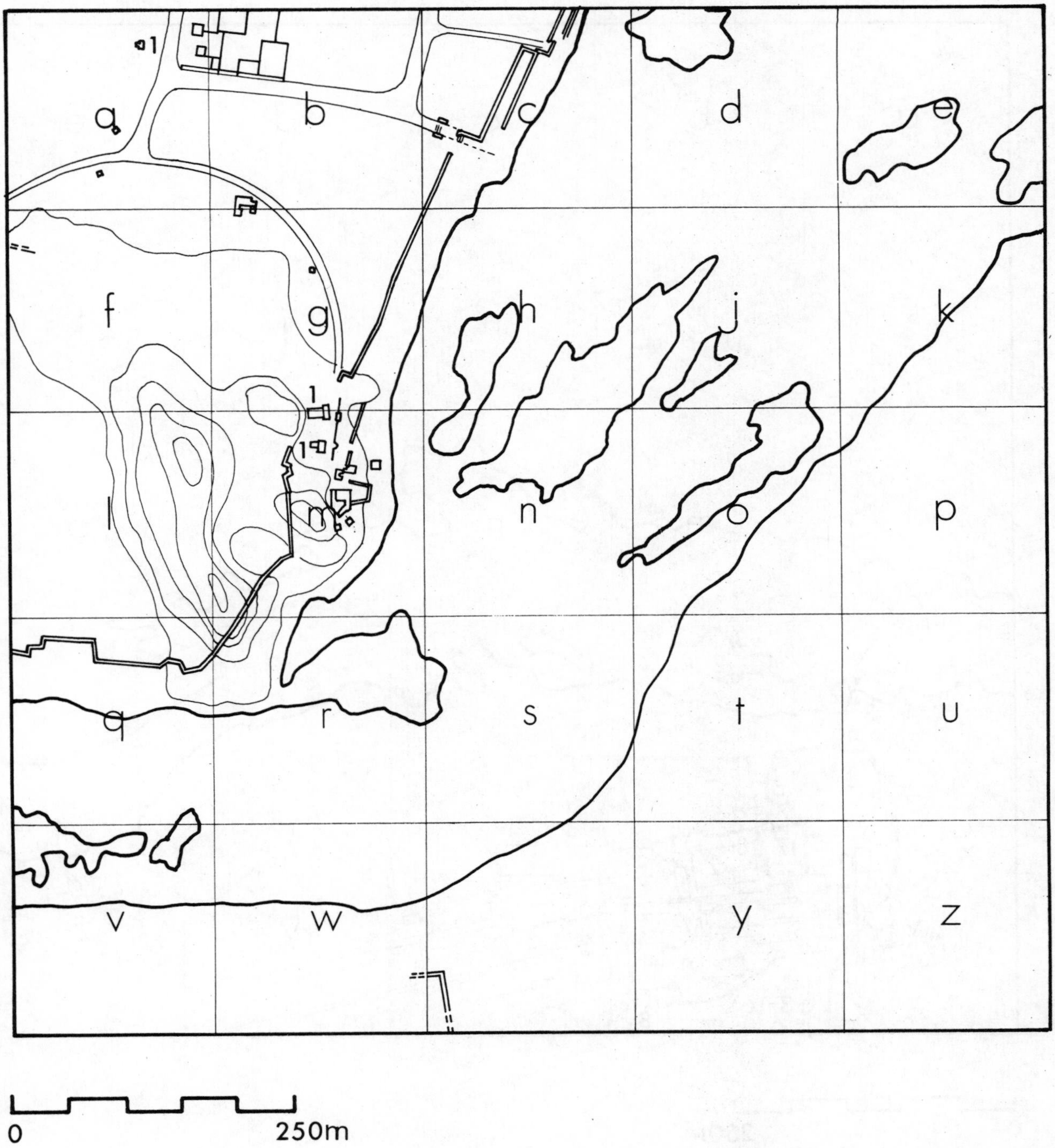

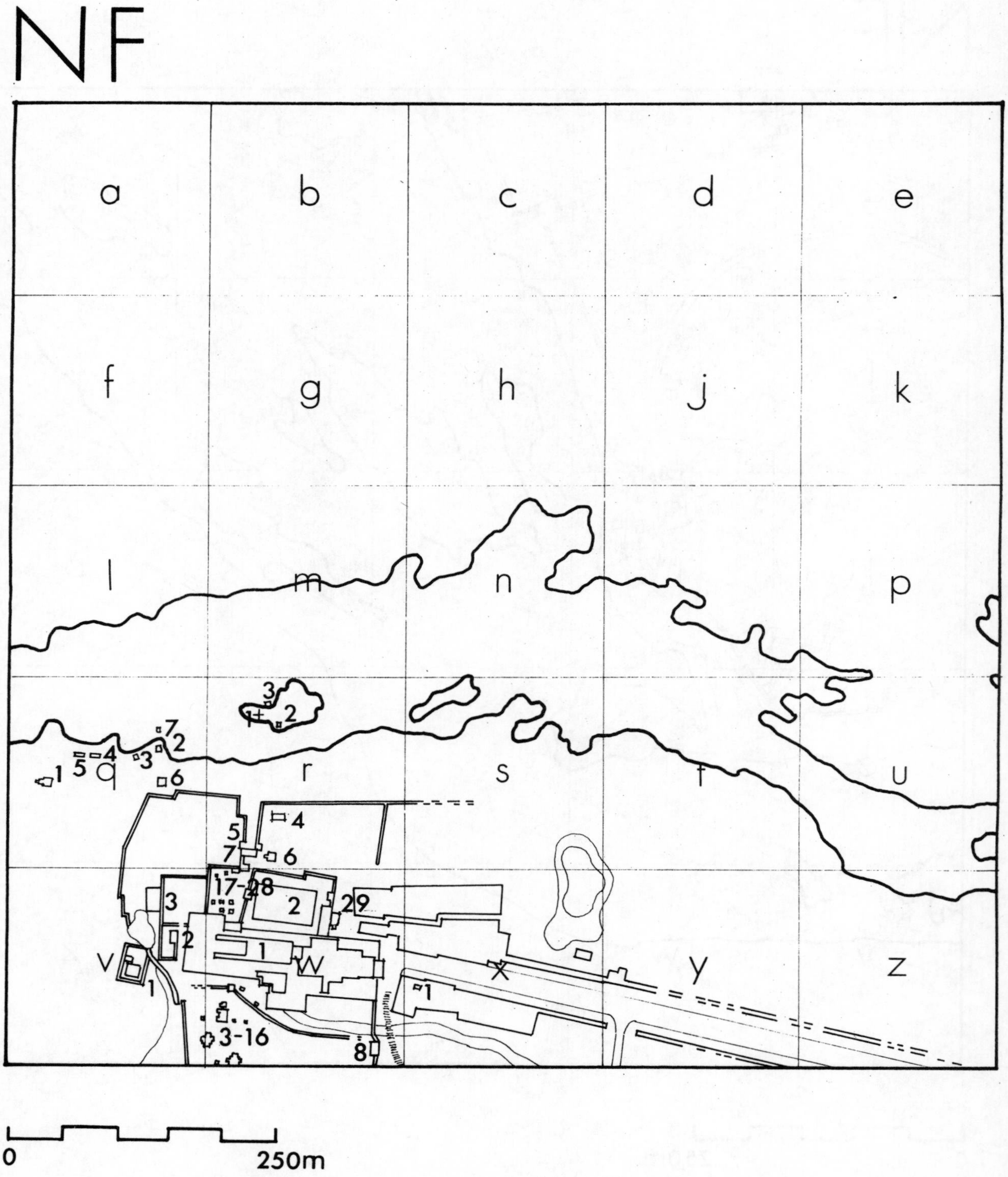
NF
a
b
c
d
e
f
g
h
j
k
l
m
n
p
q
r
s
t
u
v
w
x
y
z
1
2
3
4
5
6
7
17-28
29
3-16
8
0
250m

NG

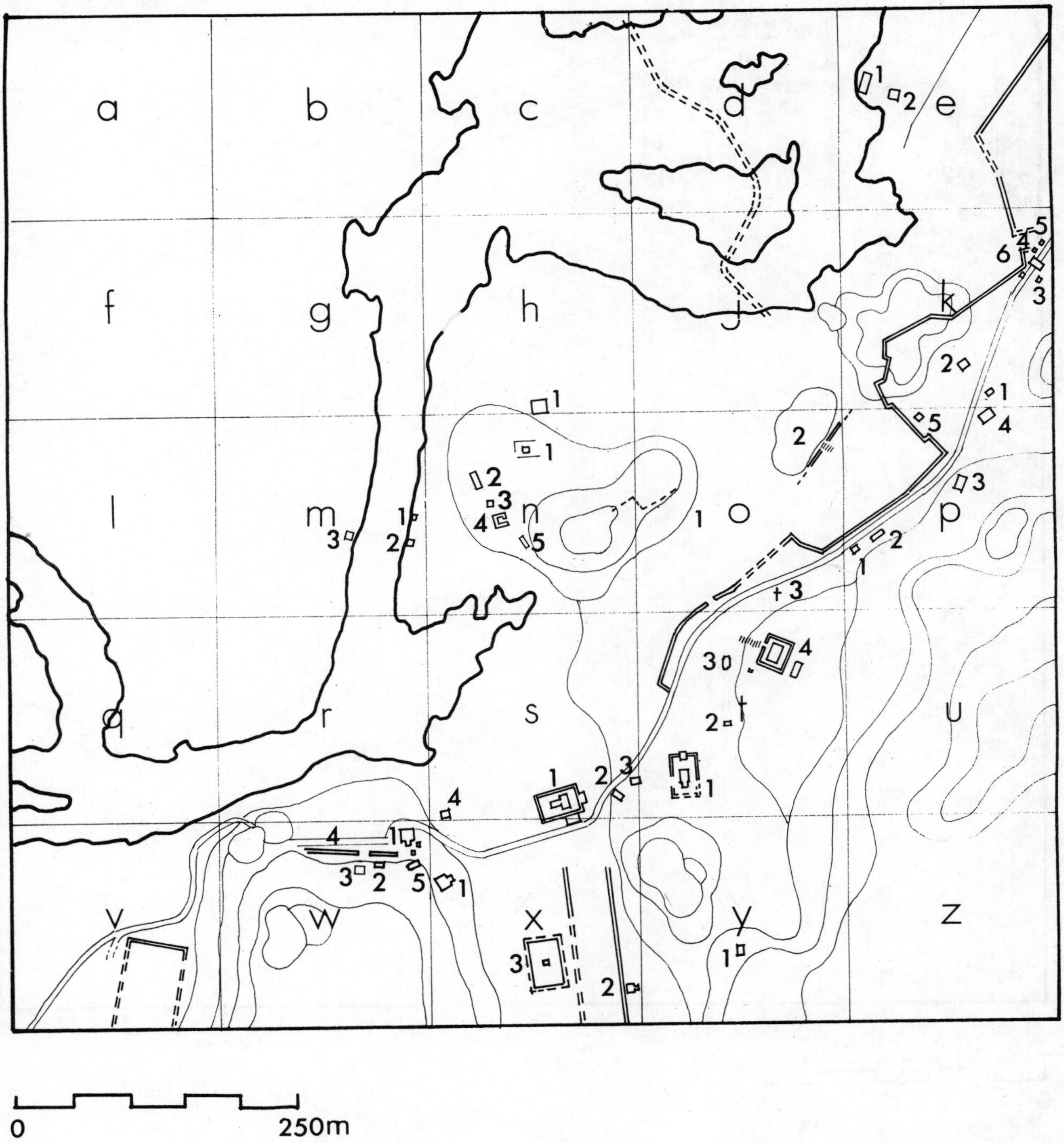

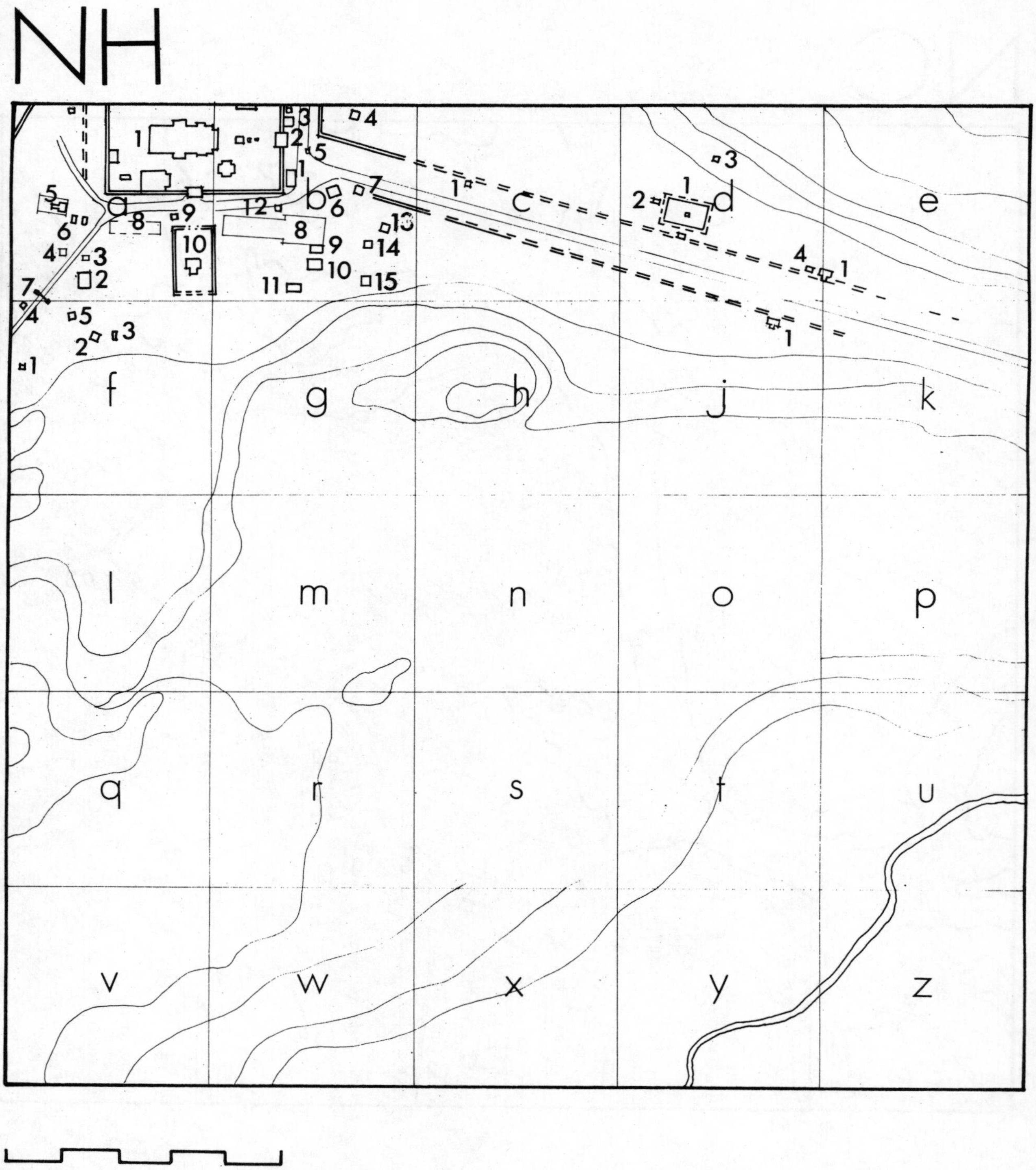
NH
a
b
c
d
e
f
g
h
j
k
l
m
n
o
p
q
r
s
t
u
v
w
x
y
z
0
250m

NJ

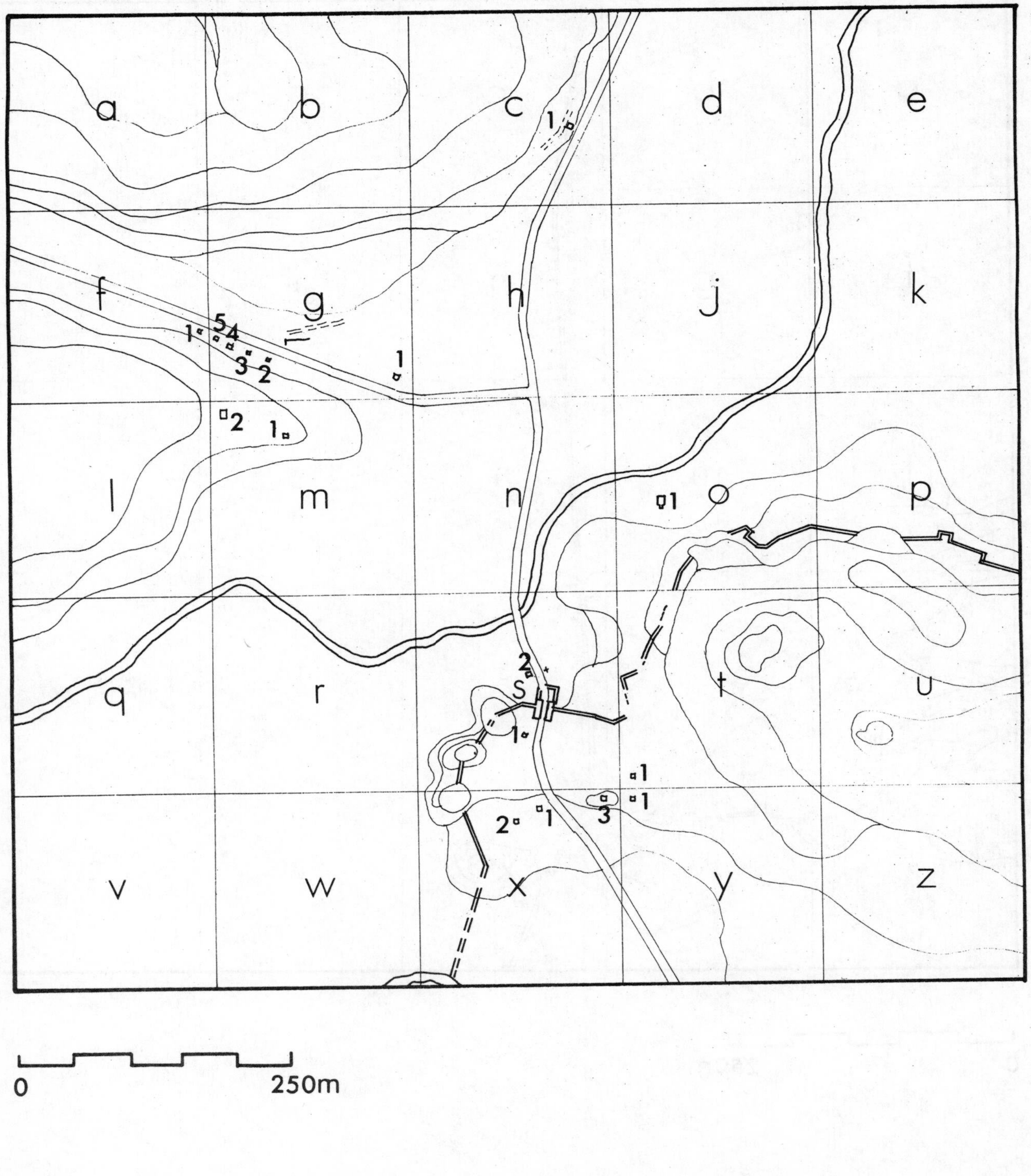

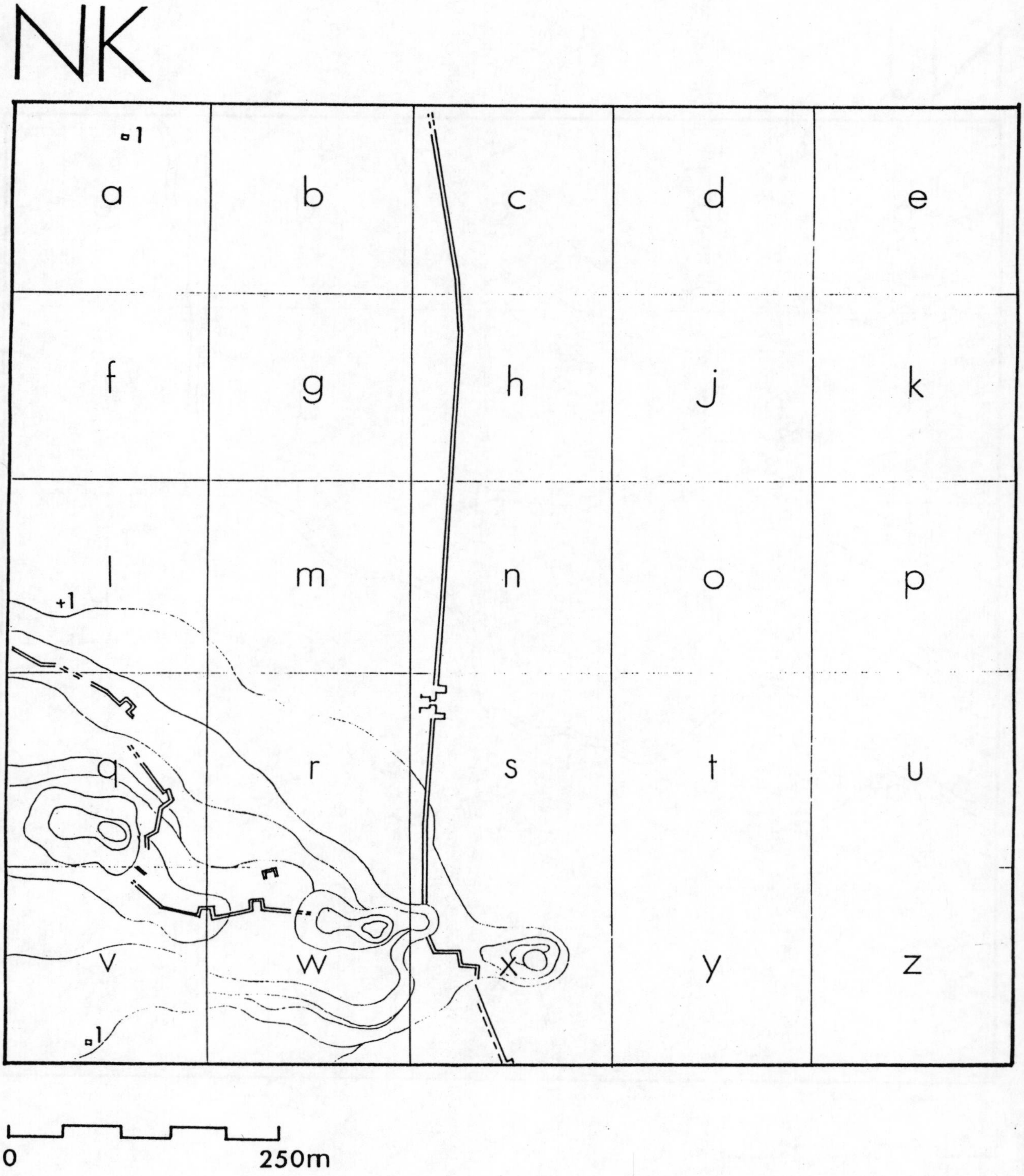
NK
a
b
c
d
e
f
g
h
j
k
l
m
n
o
p
q
r
s
t
u
v
w
x
y
z
0
250m

NL

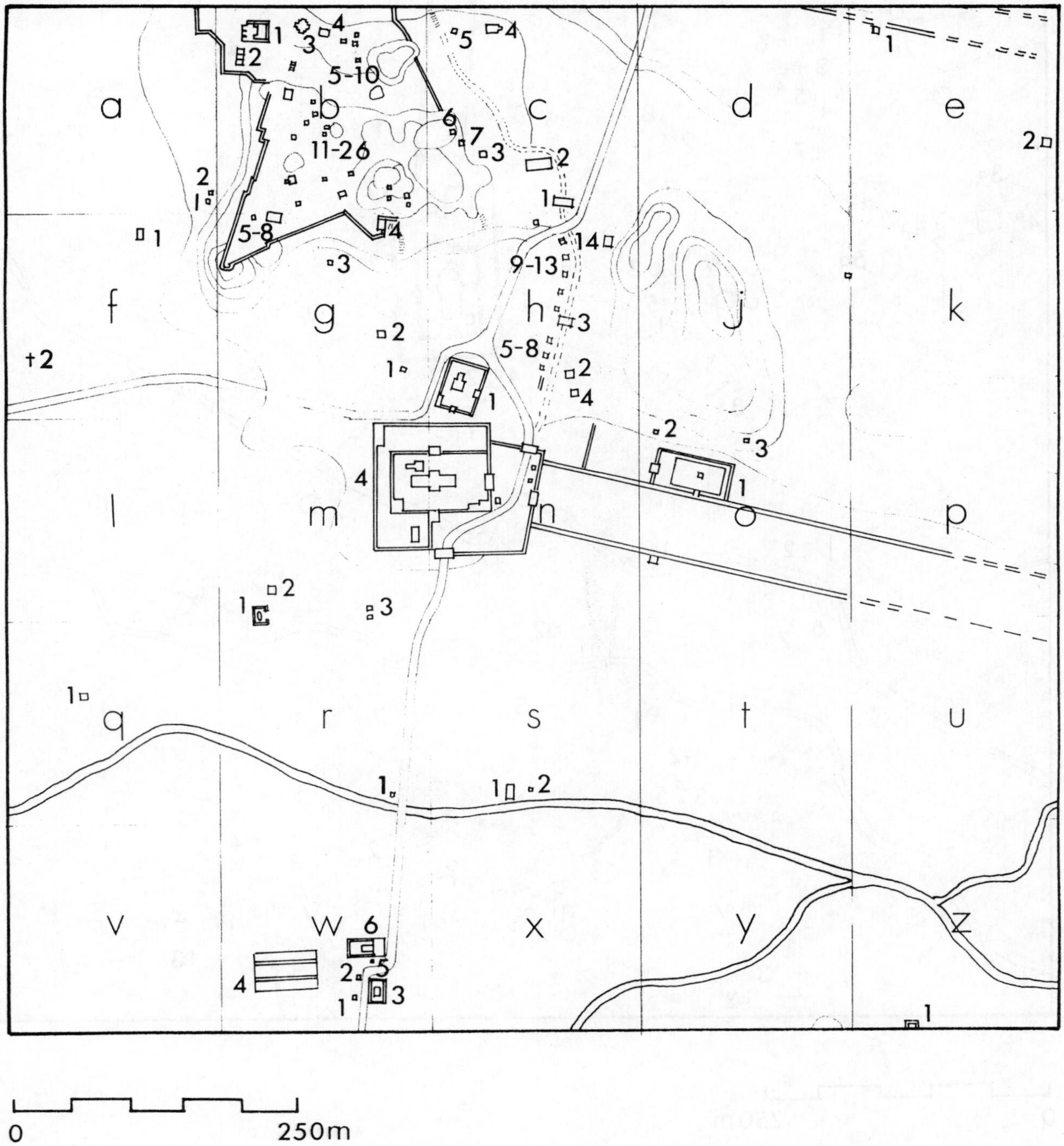

NM

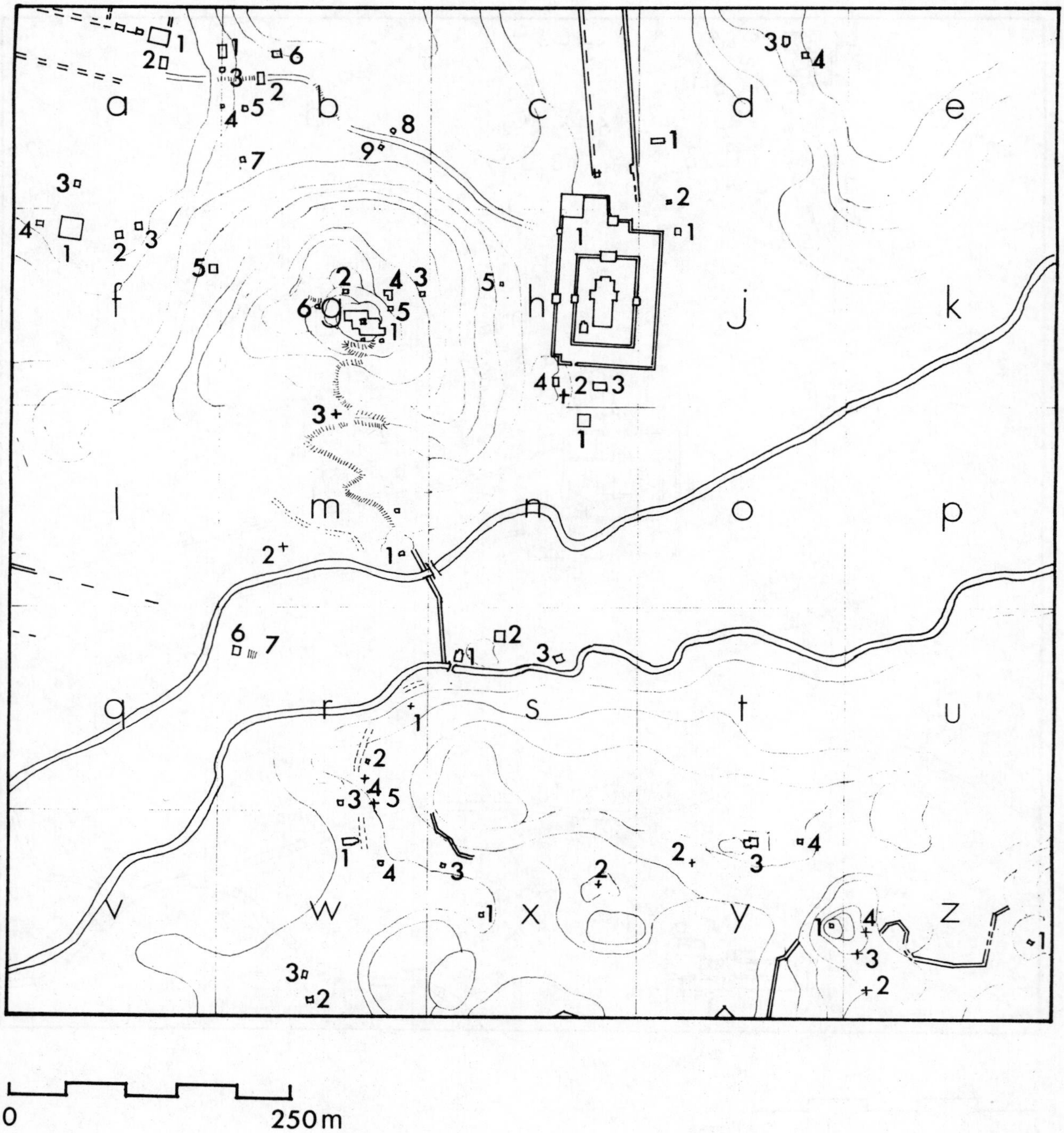

NN

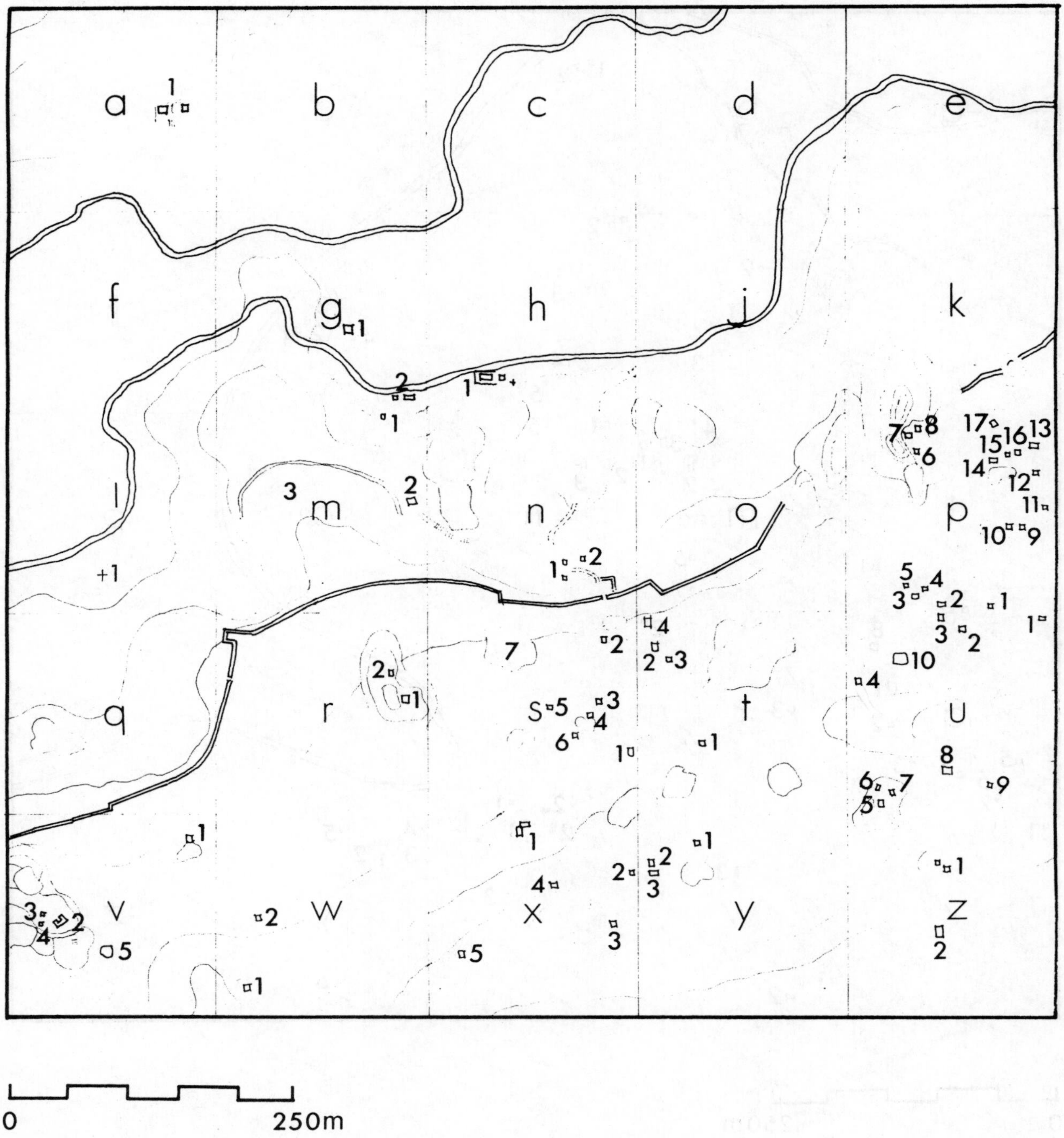

NO

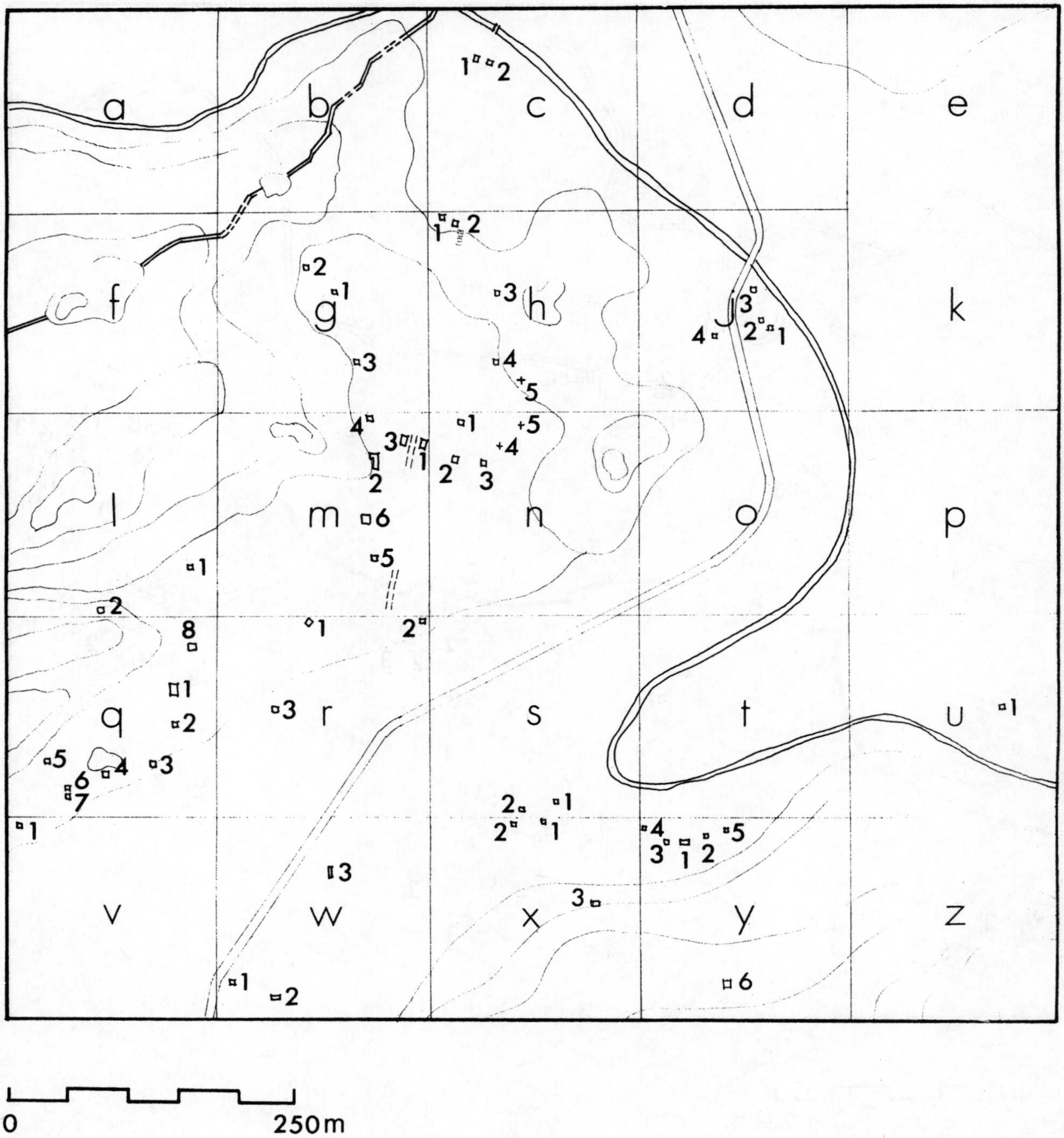

NP

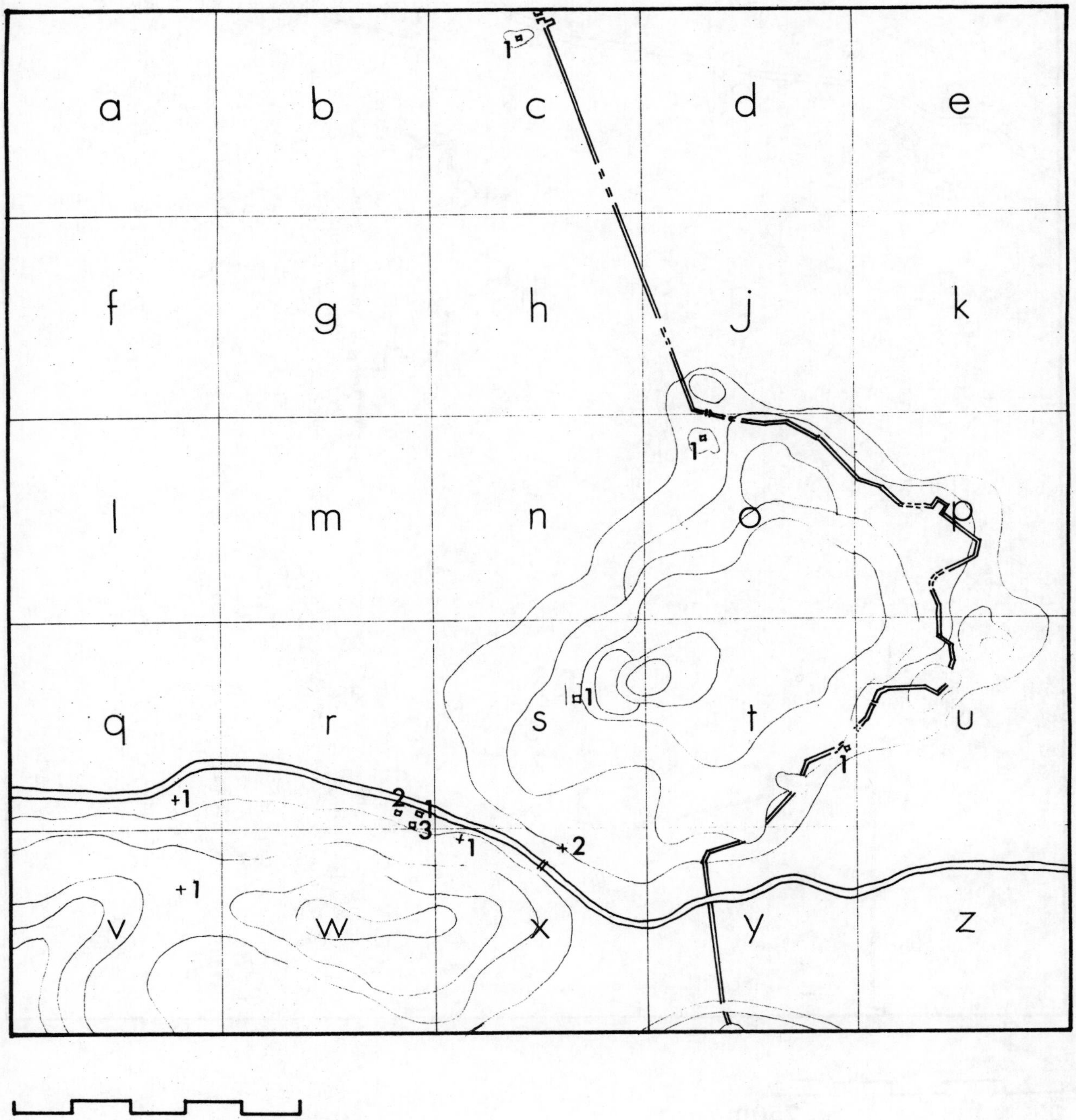

0 250m

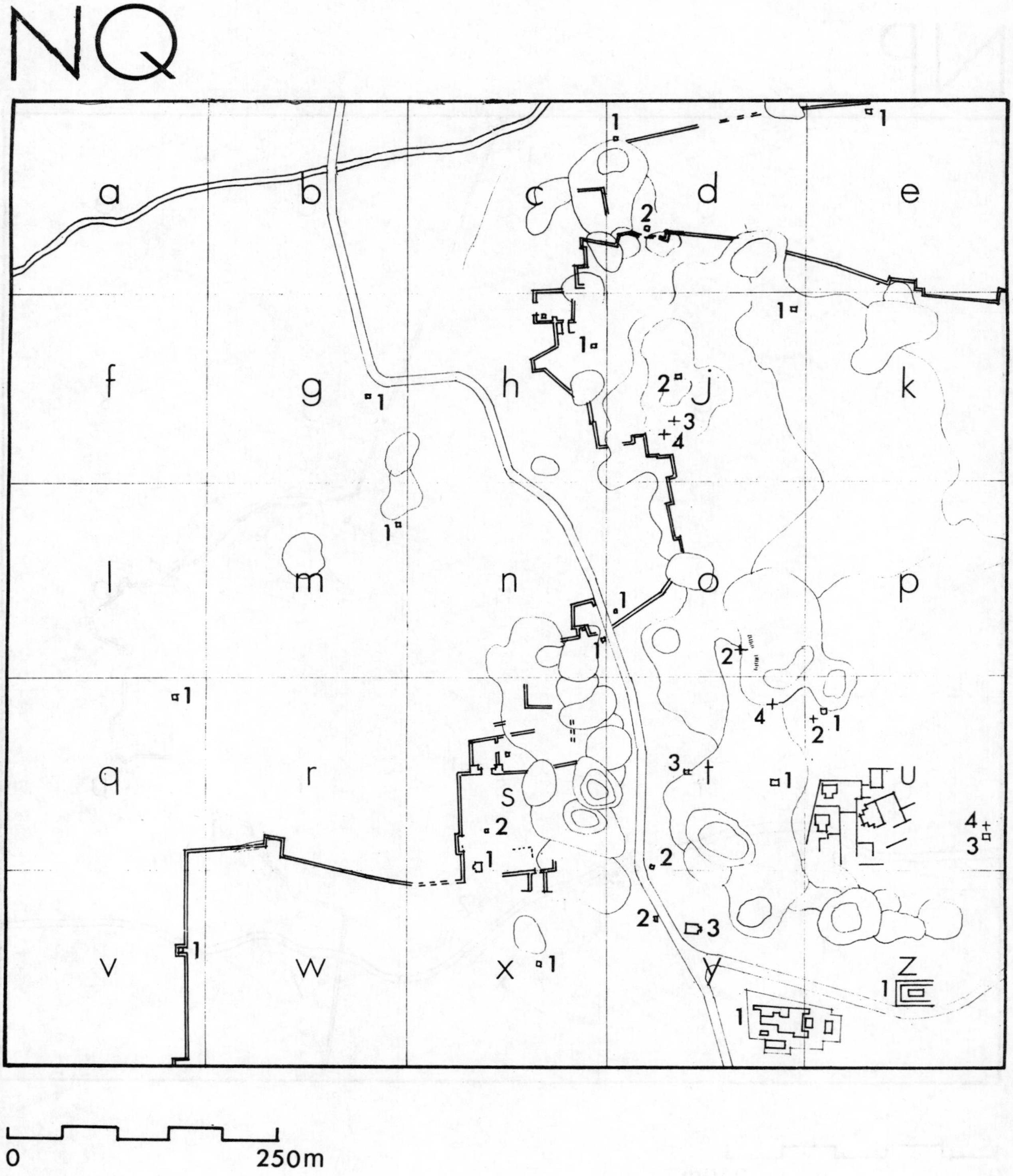
NQ
a
b
c
d
e
f
g
h
j
k
l
m
n
o
p
q
r
s
t
u
v
w
x
y
z
0
250m

NR

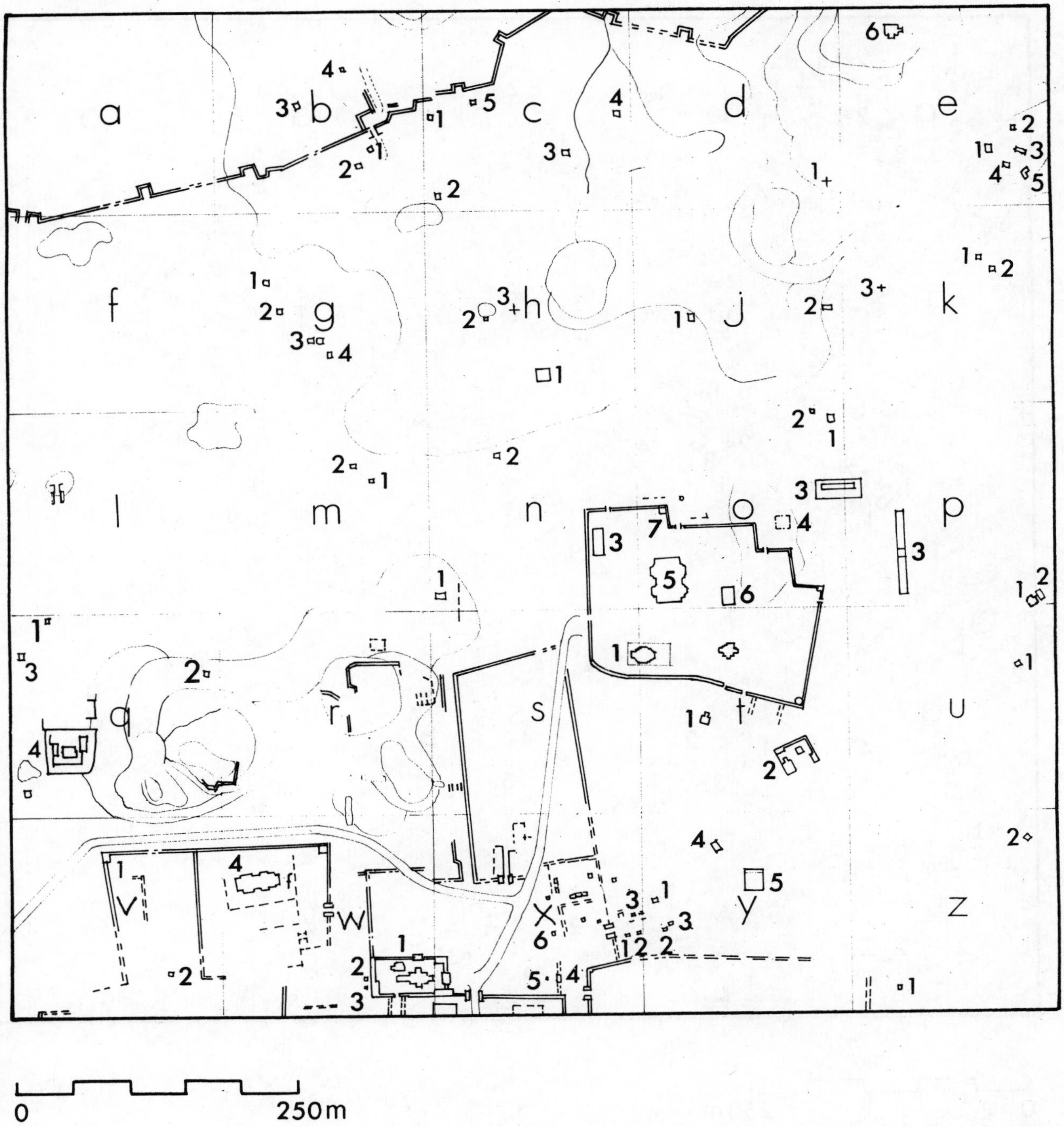

NS

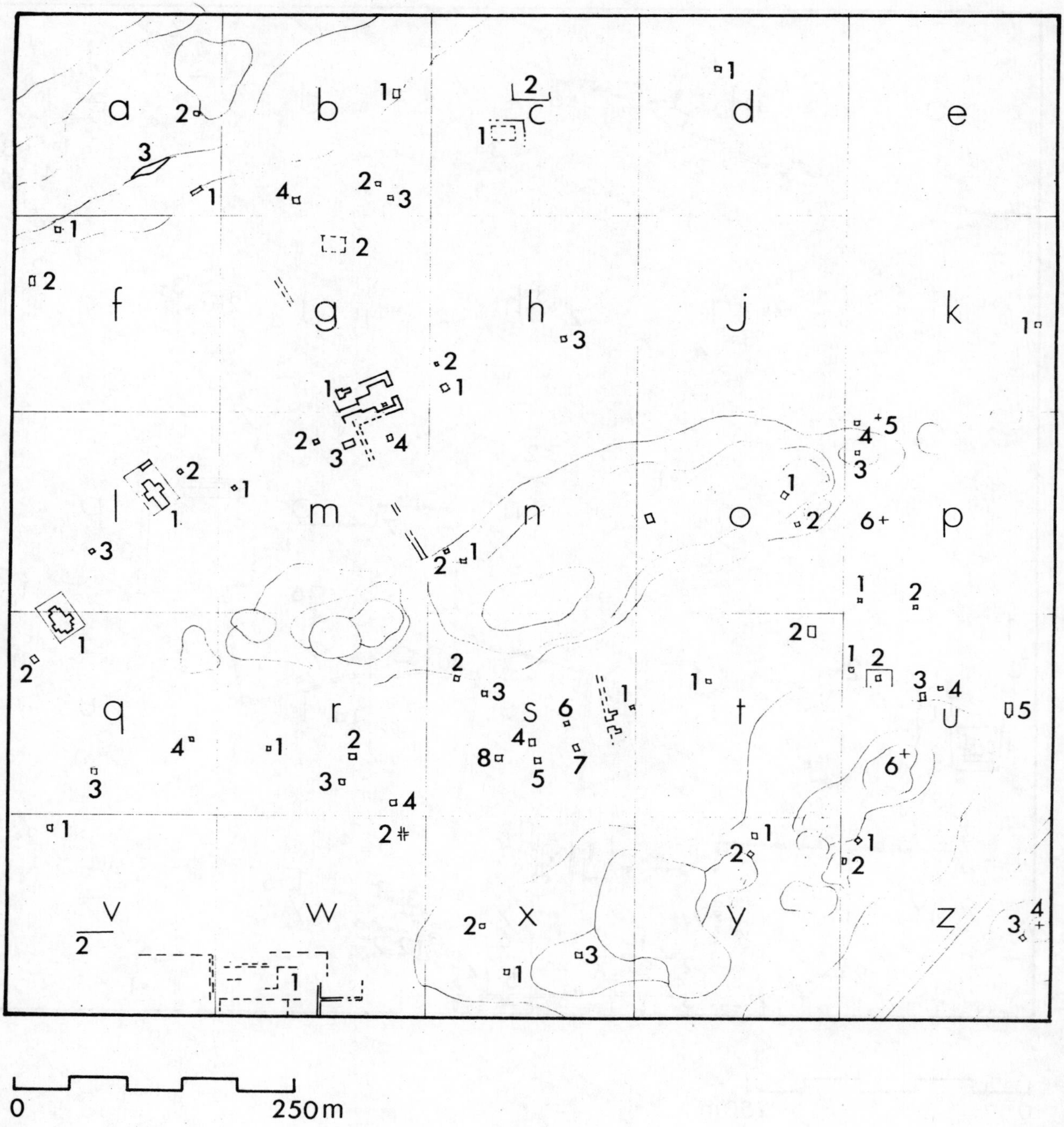

NT

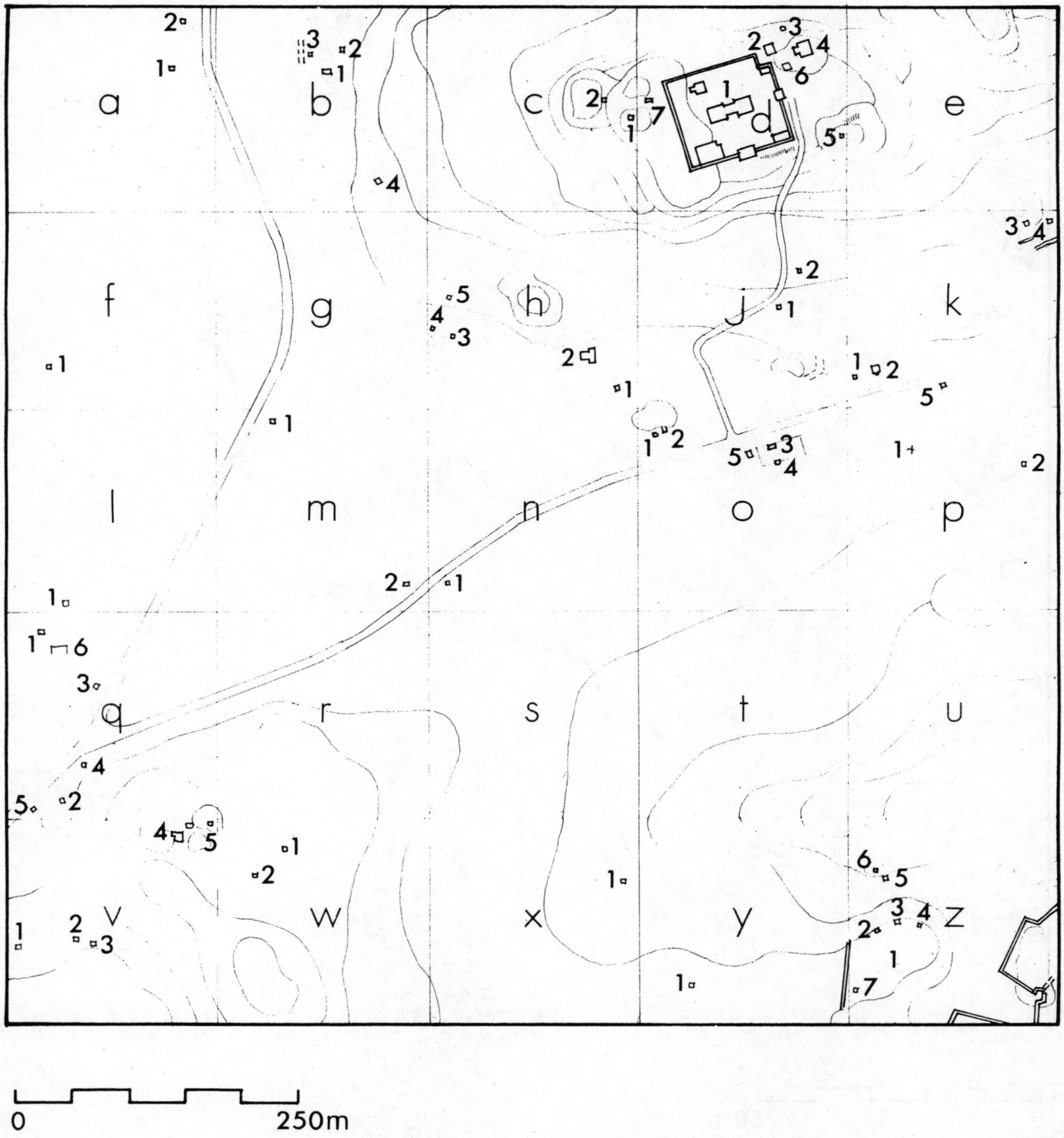

NU

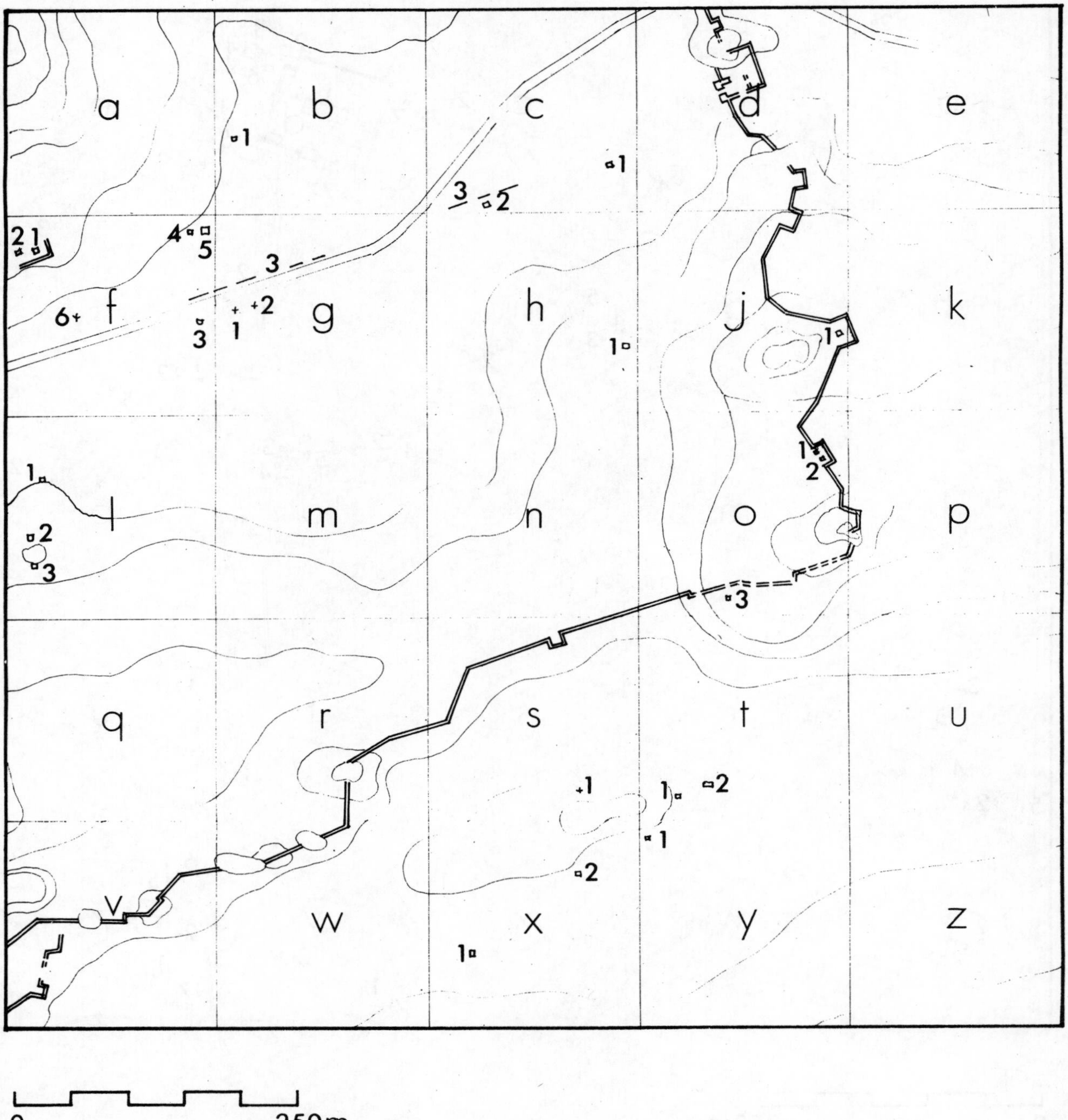

NV

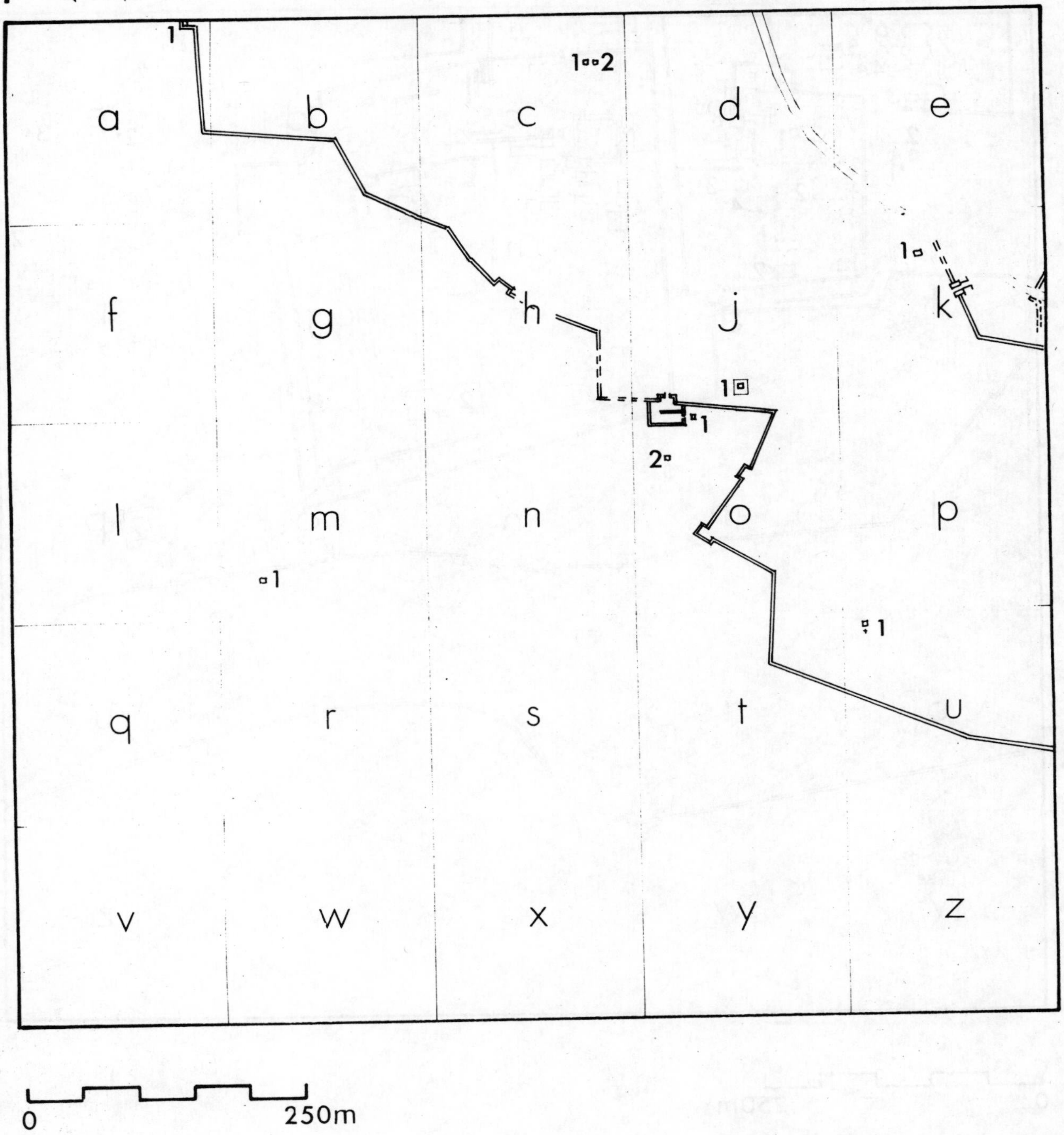

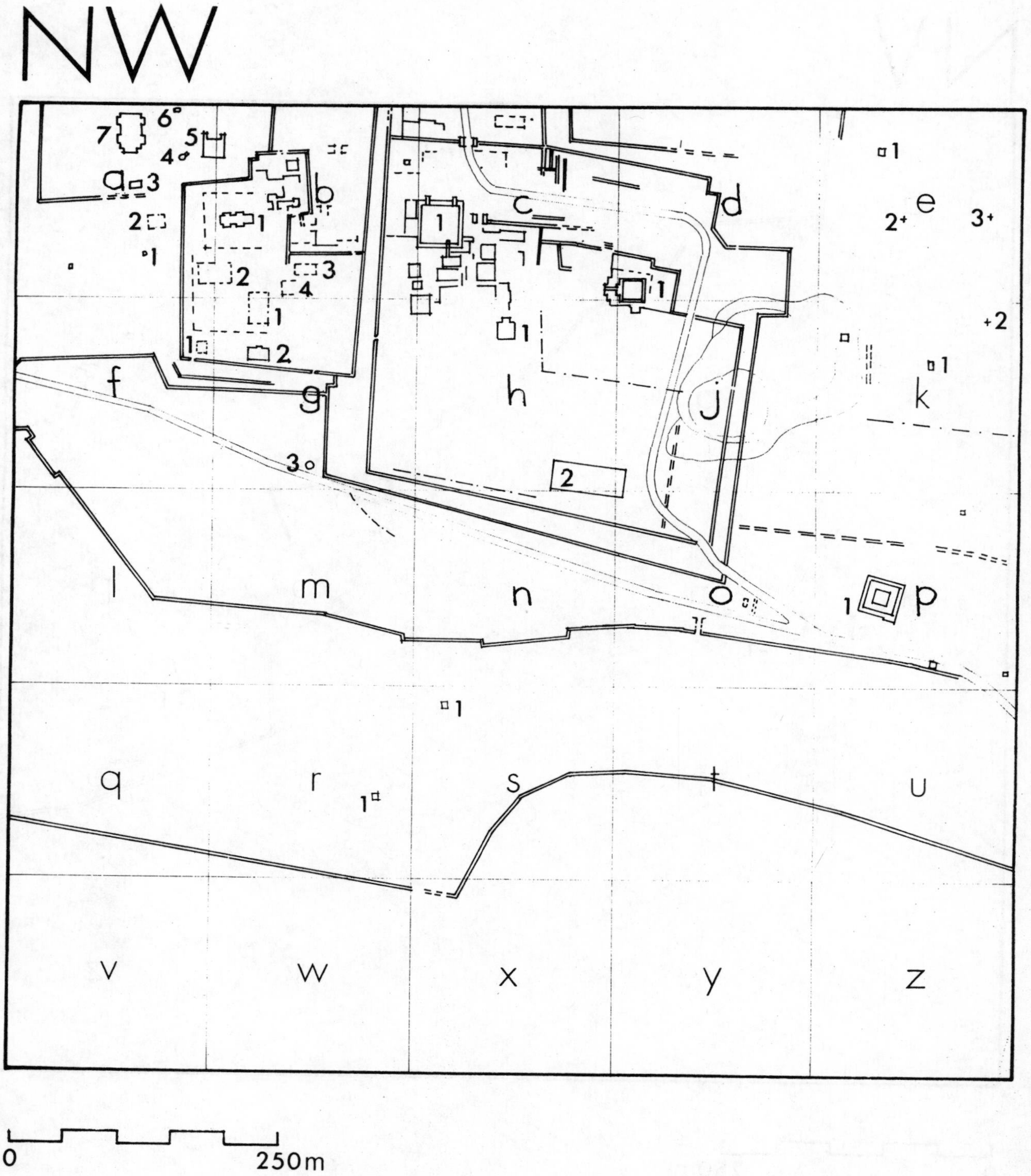
NW
a
b
c
d
e
f
g
h
j
k
l
m
n
o
p
q
r
s
t
u
v
w
x
y
z
0
250m

NX

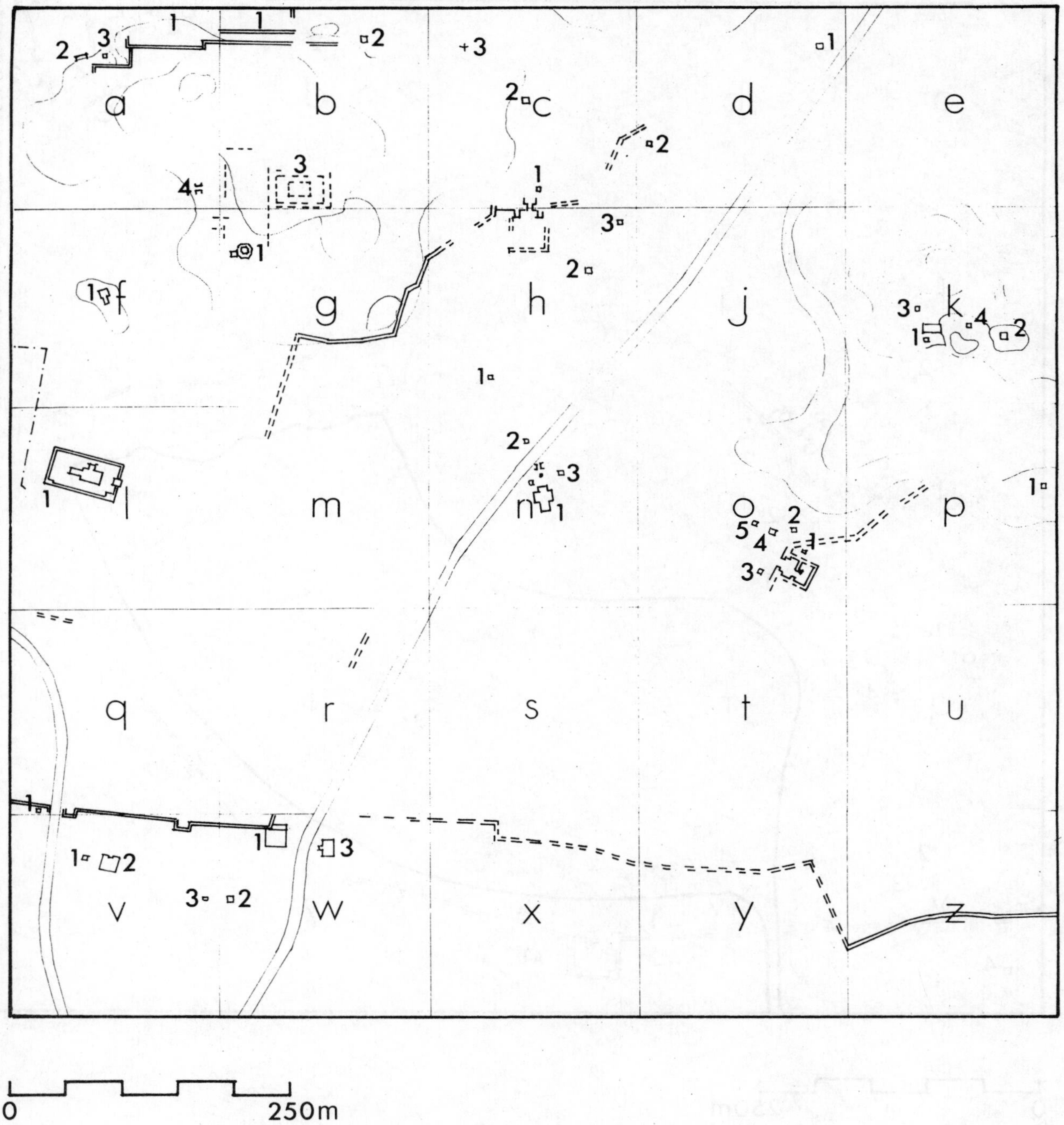

NY

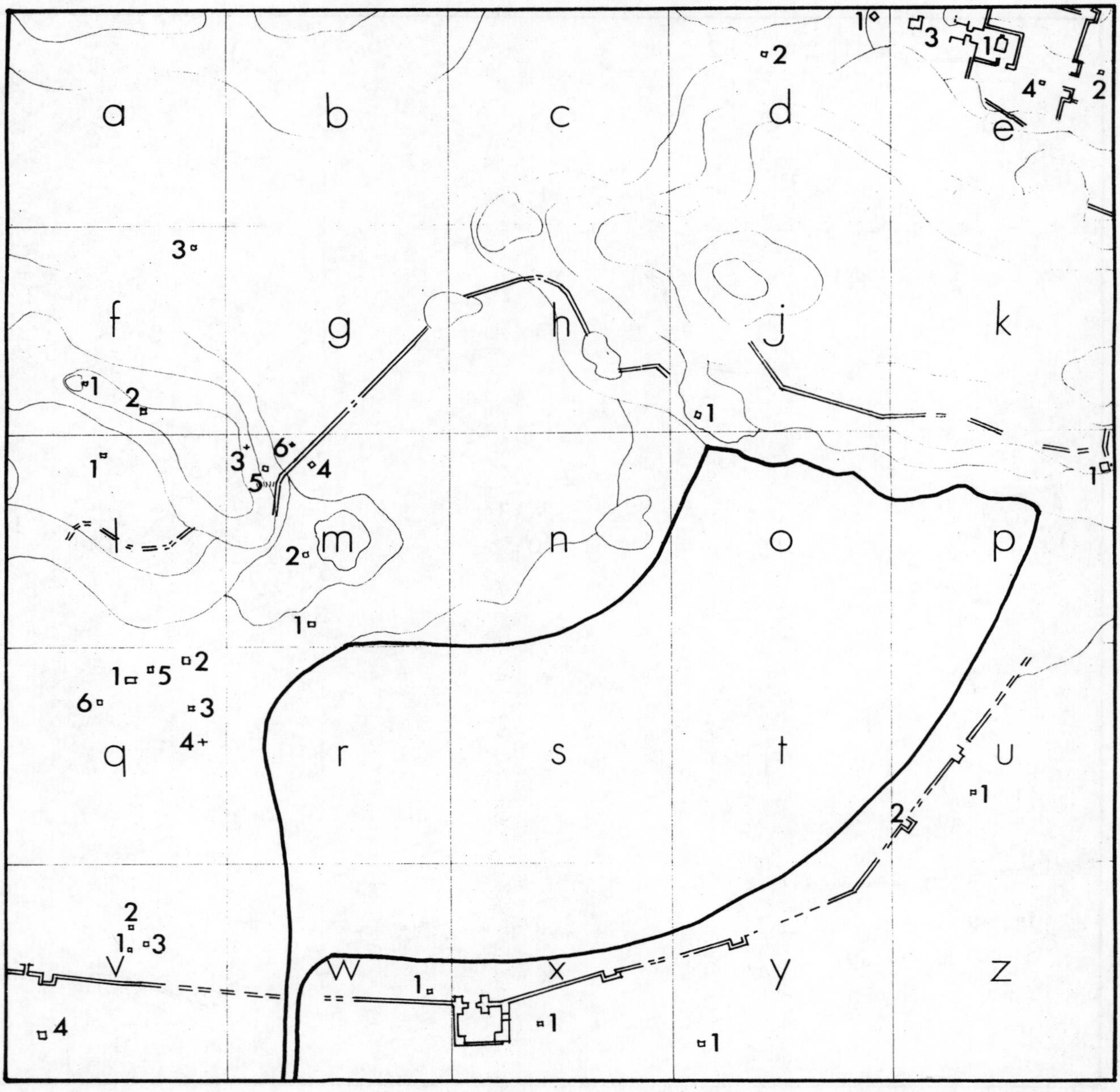

NZ

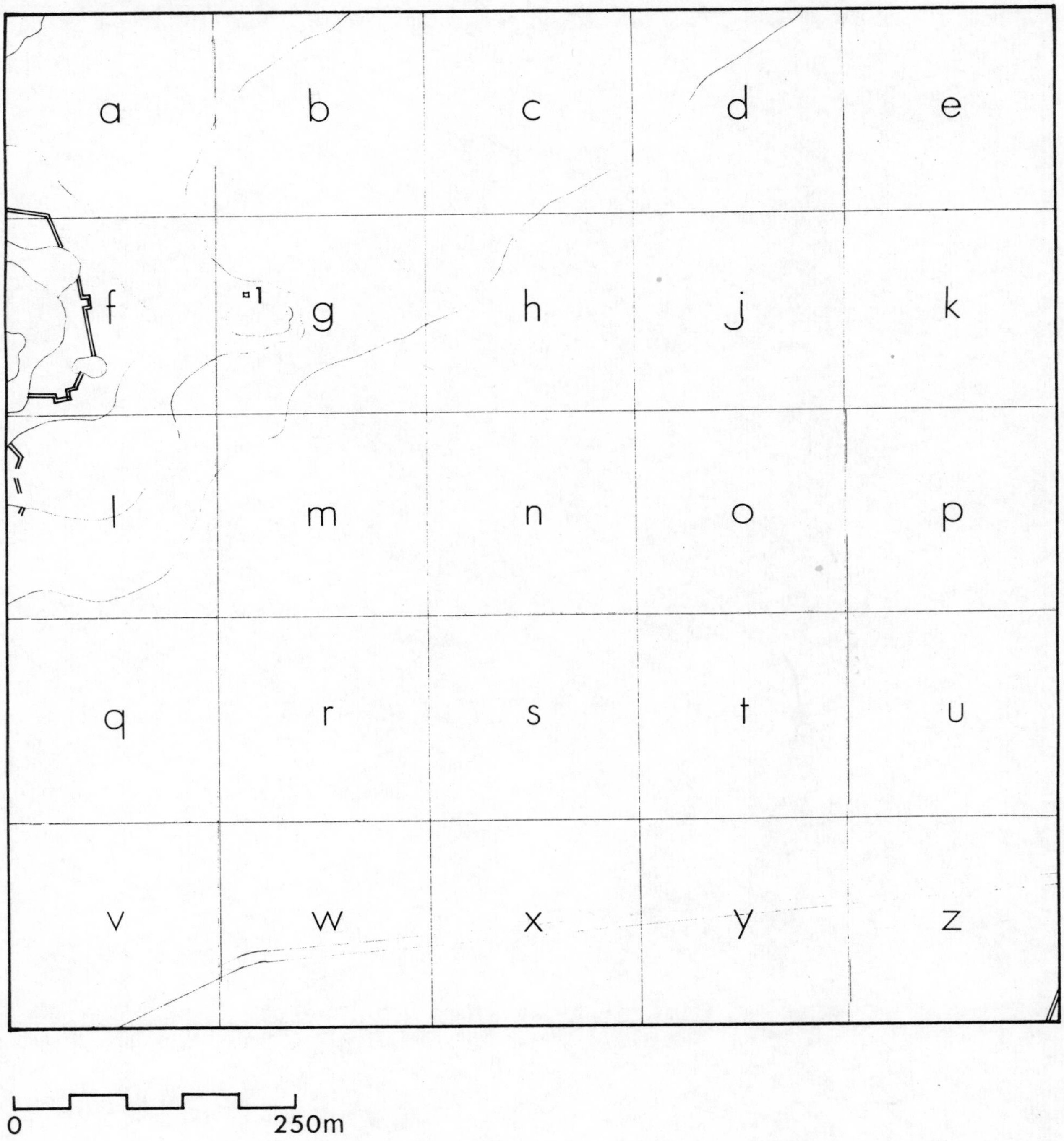